ADONIS
ATTIS
OSIRIS

Studies in the History of Oriental Religion

Two Volumes Bound as One

Statuette of the god Horus in the form of a hawk, wearing the crown of Upper and Lower Egypt. *Bronze. Twenty-sixth Dynasty to Ptolemaic period. Approximately 663-30* B.C.

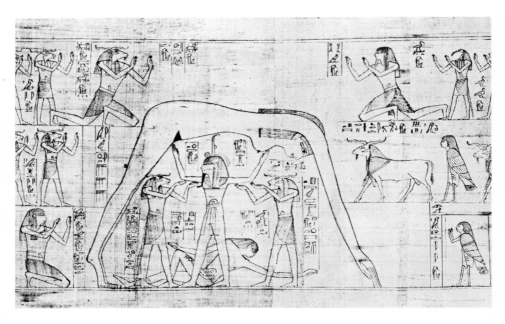

The Sky-goddess Nut supported by the Air-god Shu. *Papyrus from Deir el-Bahri, Tenth century* B.C.

Osiris and Isis

The god Osiris holding the Scepter and Flail. *Bronze figurine, ca. Sixteenth Dynasty*

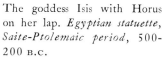

The goddess Isis with Horus on her lap. *Egyptian statuette, Saite-Ptolemaic period, 500-200* B.C.

The goddess Nut holding a tablet on which stands a representation of Horus

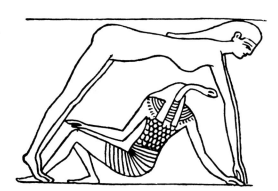

Seb and Nut

Osiris

Osiris wearing the White Crown and Menàt and holding the Scepter, Crook and Flail. Before him are the four children of Horus, and behind him is his wife Isis

The dual god Horus-Set

The Goddess Isis

Goat in a thicket, part of the grave goods in Royal tombs at Ur. *Gold and lapis. ca.* 2250 B.C.

The falcon god Horus with a human body, the form in which he usually appears. *Bronze. Egyptian late Dynastic to Ptolemaic period,* 663-30 B.C.

Goddess with young god. *Bronze, Sardinia, prehistoric*

Isis and the infant Horus

Osiris begetting Horus by Isis, who is in the form of a hawk

Limestone shrine of the scribe Pa-suten-sa (or Pa-sa-nesu), with
figures of Osiris and Horus. *Twelfth Dynasty*

Attis as a Grave Figure

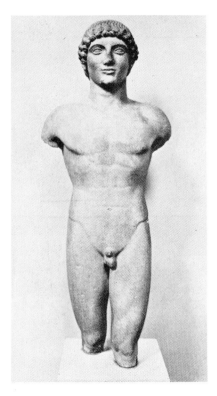

The "Strangford" Apollo. *Life-size marble statue, ca.* 480 B.C.

Sir James George Frazer
January 1, 1854 — May 7, 1941

ADONIS
ATTIS
OSIRIS

Studies in the History of Oriental Religion

By Sir James George Frazer

Hon. D. C. L., Oxford; Hon. L. L. D., Glasgow; Hon. Litt. D., Durham;
Late Fellow of Trinity College, Cambridge.

Third Edition, Revised and Enlarged

In Two Volumes
Bound as One

Part IV of The Golden Bough, *A Study in Magic and Religion*

UNIVERSITY BOOKS *New Hyde Park, New York*

INTRODUCTION
by Sidney Waldron

THE GOLDEN BOUGH is an odd classic. Scholars traditionally present their labors in a conventional three-part form: a thematic beginning is followed by a documentary middle which leads to an ending of irrefutable conclusions. Sir James Frazer's pioneering exploration of magic and religion did not fit this standard structure. Instead it grew organically from its germinal inspiration, an insight into the powers of fertility of the King of the Wood of the sacred grove of Diana at Aricia. Originally published in two volumes in 1890, THE GOLDEN BOUGH had reached thirteen volumes in its third edition in 1914 before Frazer, still unsatisfied, ceased enlarging and adjusting his text.

Anthropology was young in Frazer's day, and its typical descriptions of the religions of non-literate peoples were shallow reports of the physical motions which constituted particular "ceremonies." The essence of religion, what the belief in particular deities meant to the performers of the rituals, was lost. Except for the rudest sort of structural comparisons, analysis of the world's religions thus was impossible if one relied upon clerky erudition. Frazer was dismayed by the surface-level understanding of religion as a universal phenomenon, but was not stopped by the dearth of positivistic data necessary for deeper analysis. Instead of relying on published documents, he relied on his mind. His basic axiom was that every religion, no matter how strange (nor how repulsive it might seem to him), made sense to the participant, was inherently believable. Frazer therefore arranged the various bits and pieces of evidence available into plausible systems of belief, relying on his own sensitivity to decide what was and what was not acceptable.

two difficulties

① Frazer's search for plausibility, his attempt to build believable models, had two major weaknesses. The first was the difficulty in convincing the skeptic, the man of lesser sensibilities, and the man whose mind did not work like Frazer's, that his conclusions were valid. How do you prove plausibility? The second was the necessity to find meaning in the most opaque aspects of religious practises. Besides convincing his critics, Frazer had to convince himself. This internal struggle was the motivating force for ② the development and unending expansion of THE GOLDEN BOUGH. The present unabridged reissue of ADONIS ATTIS OSIRIS (which is Part IV or volumes five and six of the original) contains some of the best examples of Frazer's constant self-criticism and reiterative exemplification, as well as being a permanent contribution to the analysis of religion.

No wonder, then, that THE GOLDEN BOUGH was not conventional in form. It is not a syllogistic statement of hypothesis, data, and conclusions; it is the unfolding of an idea in a mind at work. Stripped to the skeleton, its theme may be presented in a few sentences. The King of the Wood in the grove of Diana was invested with powers which controlled the fertility, and thus the continuity, of living beings. These powers were magical, i.e., capable of coercing the supernatural, as opposed to religious, which are a propitiation of the supernatural forces. A divine king, such as the King of the Wood, possesses a soul which is an incarnation of the supernatural; his body must therefore be a perfect receptacle. When the divine king becomes maimed or debilitated, senile or impotent, the soul's powers are numbed and all life is in danger. Hence the king must now be killed or otherwise removed from the throne and his place taken by a perfect youth, just as spring follows winter, so that seasonal cycles may continue, crops may grow, and the perpetuation of life may be ensured.

The principle of fertility which underlies the concept of the divine king also may be manifested in special deities. There may be, for instance, a particular god upon whose favor the success of the basic subsistence crop depends. These were the spirits of the corn which Frazer found typical of agricultural people. Since such a crop must be harvested, and the harvest could be conceived of as an insult to the god whose essence was the crop, elaborate rituals arose to placate the god. Particular animals were sacrificed at these harvest rituals and, logically enough, these animals also became associated with the god.

Or, instead of having a single vegetative spirit, or a divine king, who alone would be responsible for the perpetuation of life, a hierarchy of powers could emerge in more sophisticated cultures. Attis, Adonis, and Osiris are examples of gods who were the final controllers of fertility in such a hierarchy. The planting of seeds, growing of plants, harvesting of crops, followed by another cycle initiated by another planting symbolized the death and resurrection of these gods, the knowledge of which gave proof of a world after death. These gods were represented on earth by divine kings. In Dynastic Egypt, for instance, the living pharaoh was the god Horus, son of Osiris. Although many signs testified to Osiris' existence, he permanently rested in the afterworld.

Just as harvest must be done in greatest accord with religious strictures, a divine king had to be removed from office with utmost conservatism. The aging body of the king might have polluted the magical powers of the soul. A scapegoat would be sacrificed lest the entire community suffer from this pollution. During the interregnum, society and its ethics are turned upside down. What was good is bad, what was forbidden is approved; this is a time of Mardi-Gras, intense festivity and sexual frenzy. The world's right order returned after the installation of the new divine king. The divine power was transferred from the realm of the supernatural when the king-to-be entered the sacred grove and plucked a golden bough from one of the trees, which was a vegetative manifestation of the powers of fertility.

From this abbreviation of Frazer's thirteen volumes, the progression of the themes may be seen; however, it is, of course, insufficient and even misleading. THE GOLDEN BOUGH is not a unilineal structure of hypothesis, document and proof. It is an intricate system of demonstration where particular examples in their specific sequence must be read and understood before one can sense the plausibility of Frazer's concepts. In structure, THE GOLDEN BOUGH is reminiscent of an ancient mansion which has had rooms and sections added as the inhabitants felt the need for more space. As a result of Frazer's technique, which dictated the unusual form of THE GOLDEN BOUGH. subsequent scholars have been unsure of its correct classification or its proper utility. It has been neglected as subjective and overly repetitive or, as a compromise, it has been flensed and rendered into a one-volume condensation. These one-volume condensations suffer from the same faults as the curt synopsis just presented. If one reassembles a few cornices, gables, and columns from the ancient mansion, one has not captured its essence: one merely has a rather grotesque shack.

Hence it is a pleasant task to introduce to a new generation the unabridged volumes on Adonis, Attis, Osiris. These three were each "a personification of the great yearly vicissitudes of nature," primarily spirits of vegetative fertility, but permeating all aspects of life. These volumes embody the best of Frazer's demonstrative system and show the remarkable scope and originality of his scholarship. Attis in Phrygia, Adonis in Syria and Cyprus, and Osiris in Egypt, controlled the grain crops upon which the very lives of these early Mediterranean agriculturists depend.

Each was part of an elaborate pantheon and, as one would expect, each had his idiosyncracies. Attis and Adonis were rather pathetic figures, murdered painfully each year at harvest time. Attis was believed to be killed either by a wild boar or by self castration; Adonis was killed by a boar.

> Every year, in the belief of his worshippers, Adonis was wounded to death on the mountains, and every year the face of nature itself was dyed with his sacred blood. So year by year the Syrian damsels lamented his untimely fate, while the red anemone, his flower, bloomed among the cedars of Lebanon, and the river ran red to the sea, fringing the winding shores of the blue Mediterranean, whenever the wind set inshore with a sinuous band of crimson.

Although the living representatives of Attis and Adonis were no longer ritually murdered at harvest time, Frazer believed they had been in earlier days. In order to test this supposition, he examined the burned priests of volcanic religions throughout the world. His exposition of the Hanged God is a triumph in his continuing endeavors to find the reasonable explanation he believed to underlie the most atrocious of customs. Ritually murdered men not only gave their lives so that the seasonal cycle might continue uninterrupted but were also assured of resurrection in the world of the gods. As well as solving the problem of life, they solved the dilemma of death.

Attis and Adonis, to Frazer, were preludes to the understanding of Osiris. Osiris was the son of the earth and the sky. He brought his people, the Egyptians, from savagery, replacing their cannibalism with the knowledge of agriculture. (Where grain would not grow, he told them the secrets of wine-making.) He was murdered by his jealous brother, Set, dismembered and scattered throughout the land. His sister-wife, Isis, recovered the parts and Osiris, reassembled, was resurrected.

Dynastic Egypt was a stable world. Egyptian texts are typified by a serenity, a lack of doubt. The Egyptian's concept of success seems to have been the learning and attunement to this stable world order. Manhood was typified, not by aggression and possession of material wealth, but by acceptance and obedience of *Matt*, the essence of existence, a true way of life reminiscent of the Buddhist *dharma* and Islamic *salaam*. The life of Osiris was the charter of *Matt*. The meaning of the name Osiris was "truth," and every man was given this name during his funeral ceremonies as testimony to the gods of his faith and promise of his eternal life.

Egypt is, in reality, dominated by the Nile. The farm-lands extend only a few miles on either side of the river. Although the kingdom of Egypt was hundreds of miles long, it was only a few score miles wide, and in the center was the Nile, which also was Osiris. On both sides was the barren and threatening desert, which was Set, the murderer of Osiris, an evil but visible part of the world. Although the world of Egypt was a stable one, there were crucial unpredictables. When the annual flood of the Nile failed to appear, farmlands were barren and a year of hunger, possibly famine, resulted. Something had gone wrong with the worship of Osiris, and Set was again triumphing. The basis of Egyptian religion, Frazer concluded, rested on this logic: it is better to see famine as a meaningful punishment than as a product of chance; if it is punishment, one can rectify the misdeed and avoid a repetition. If it is mere chance, the world is chaos, there is no *Matt*.

As the principal of fertility, Osiris was also found in the crops themselves. When the Nile flooded, there was rejoicing, for Osiris had returned. The subsequent sowing of the seeds was a time of ceremonial and personal sadness, for these were the pieces of Osiris' dismembered body. The sprouting of the green shoots was celebrated as the resur-rection of Osiris and the promise for all men of everlasting life. Harvest time, which one would expect to be a time of celebration, was instead a period of mourning. Osiris, as manifested in the crops, had been killed so that men might live. The parallel is obvious between this interpretation of harvest and the Christian interpretation of the crucifixion of Christ.

Osiris, although a god, was not merely an abstract power which could not be sensed; he was visible at every crisis time in Egyptian life and promised the perpetuity of *Matt*. He was the connection between man and the other Egyptian gods. His son Horus sat on the throne as pharaoh and supervised the Egyptians in their quest for a proper life.

Despite his undeniable accomplishments, James Frazer was filled with a sense of incompleteness, of interminable toil and insufficiency. As the reader will see, in the preface to the third edition of these volumes, Frazer likened himself to Sisyphus "perpetually rolling his stone up hill only to see it revolve again into the valley." Like Camus, Frazer was trapped by the absurdities of humanity and compelled to face them. But where Camus accepted the inevitability of a final personal chaos, Frazer sought an underlying enlightening order which, however, might be beyond human grasp. This discovery of order and the dispelling of ignorance were Frazer's impossible task, the burden of Sisyphus.

The study of the divine kingship not only astounded Frazer and formed the core of THE GOLDEN BOUGH; it also attracted another of the great students of behavior, Sigmund Freud. The ritual murder of divine kings, which Frazer had interpreted as a necessary part of a system of belief, was interpreted by Freud as an institutionalized expression of father-hatred, a cultural Oedipus complex, resulting in the assassination of a king by his sons and followed by an over-compensatory remorse which eventually resulted in the deification of the dead father king. Frazer, on the other hand, did not conclude that culture is simply analogous to the human mind, or that religion is an enthralling and stifling disciplinary device. Rather he saw religion as belief, as a means of explaining the tragedies and absurdities of life.

Frazer arrived at no simply formulated explanation of ritual murder or of religion itself, but rather stressed the many levels and functions of religion and its interplay with magic. Osiris, Attis, Adonis were not simple Freudian father figures, nor simply equivalent to the vitality of crops, as his oversimplifiers would contend. They were central figures in highly complex religions which controlled and were part of all phases of the right way of life. Frazer's attempt to tie up all loose ends of these religions, to discover the integration of the lives of the believers, satisfied him only partially. In comparing himself with Sisyphus, Frazer despaired at the possibility of success and asked those who followed him to recheck his conclusions as the data and theoretical framework of his field expanded.

His successors, instead, dismembered him. Retrospective criticism is easy, and Frazer's fragile synthesis has been rent by it. Justifiably, his critics have seen the inadequacy of considering all kings of primitive peoples as incarnations of a universal fertility symbol. Expanding ethnography demonstrates that maintenance of royal power depends on the religious requisites but also on all too human political machinations: some old kings die on the throne, impotent but sly; young kings may be slaughtered by challenging cousins, quite out of season and in discordance with the image of the god. Sisyphus' boulder again slips away.

Frazer's methods of inquiry are likewise assailable. To contemporary anthropologists his evolutionary perspective seems naive, confusing, as it does, stages in time with stages in development. "Primitive" may mean the first step in progressive development, or it may mean crudeness and simplicity, lacking in complexity. That man and his inventions — religions, technologies (and neuroses)— evolved is a truism. But that the civilization of Nineteenth Century England was the pinnacle of human accomplishment seems more doubtful to us than it did in Frazer's era. In his search for explanations of the predictable absurdities of his contemporaries, he was too willing to see them as holdovers from a ruder world.

To itemize Frazer's faults and subtract them from his merits is to misunderstand his work. Yet this is exactly what his successors have done. "THE GOLDEN BOUGH is good literature" is the standard quick dismissal afforded it. This is equivalent to calling Sisyphus a nice guy in spite of his difficulties.

However, Frazer did more than analyze Attis, Adonis, and Osiris — he recreated them. Where a contradiction to a previous conclusion threatened his structure, he balanced it with an affirmative from another source. He was not merely a scientific analyst of religion: he was, as his work demonstrates, a formulator of religion as well. Consequently he has been largely ignored or demolished by social scientists who cannot rest with a system which is not totally verifiable regardless of how believable it may be. On the other hand, THE GOLDEN BOUGH continues to attract thousands of readers who find it satisfying in undefinable ways.

This seeming paradox — the satisfying power of THE GOLDEN BOUGH versus its definite lapses as a scientific work — may be approachable, if we accept the possibility that Frazer, in ADONIS ATTIS OSIRIS, was not merely explaining these beliefs, but was also adapting them to his own religious sensibilities. Recently the labyrinthine genius of the French sociologist, Claude Levi-Strauss, has turned to the analysis of myth. Levi-Strauss contends that the essence of myth lies in the arrangement of its parts. All-important but insoluble problems such as creation, the meaning of death, or the explanation of seemingly meaningless acts, are central in myth. Myths are believable, he says, not because they afford any sort of cause-and-effect answers to these problems, but because they balance the believable with the impossible. Myths are delicately balanced systems of truths and falsehoods, affirmables and inaffirmables, compounded and elaborated until all are balanced, one with the other, and the myth has ended. To oversimplify this approach to myth, it could be stated that by confronting impossible situations with the same logic and structure as possible ones, varying and repeating the process, the whole becomes acceptable. Contradictions and dilemmas are preserved through intricate and orderly inter-mixture with everyday experience.

When Sir James Frazer lacked directly pertinent material, he left no gaps, as a positivist should. Instead, he made a believable system out of something unknowable by picking and choosing his source material. When his data failed, his mythopeic understanding triumphed. Thus his version of Osiris should be read in conjunction with that of Plutarch as well as that of Budge.* Together they make an interesting series of variations where each variation has utmost meaning. Frazer's work is all the more valuable for having added dimensions: by following the progression of his analysis, one can see the mind of the maker of myth at work. Like Osiris, Frazer's work has been pulled apart and scattered. As it becomes better understood, and is reissued in its complete form it, like Osiris, will revive as evidence of the underlying order, an order which Sir James Frazer despaired of ever finding.

*There is a comprehensive statement of Plutarch's views in Budge's own OSIRIS: THE EGYPTIAN RELIGION OF RESURRECTION, which has recently been reissued by University Books.

PREFACE TO THE FIRST EDITION

THESE studies are an expansion of the corresponding sections in my book *The Golden Bough*, and they will form part of the third edition of that work, on the preparation of which I have been engaged for some time. By far the greater portion of them is new, and they make by themselves a fairly complete and, I hope, intelligible whole. I shall be glad if criticisms passed on the essays in their present shape should enable me to correct and improve them when I come to incorporate them in my larger work.

In studying afresh these three Oriental worships, akin to each other in character, I have paid more attention than formerly to the natural features of the countries in which they arose, because I am more than ever persuaded that religion, like all other institutions, has been profoundly influenced by physical environment, and cannot be understood without some appreciation of those aspects of external nature which stamp themselves indelibly on the thoughts, the habits, the whole life of a people. It is a matter of great regret to me that I have never visited the East, and so cannot describe from personal knowledge the native lands of Adonis, Attis, and Osiris. But I have sought to remedy the defect by comparing the descriptions of eye-witnesses, and painting from them what may be called composite pictures of some of the scenes on which I have been led to touch in the course of this volume. I shall not have wholly failed if I have caught from my authorities and conveyed to my readers some notion, however dim, of the scenery, the atmosphere, the gorgeous colouring of the East.

J. G. FRAZER.

TRINITY COLLEGE, CAMBRIDGE,
        22nd July 1906.

PREFACE TO THE SECOND EDITION

IN this second edition some minor corrections have been made and some fresh matter added. Where my views appear to have been misunderstood, I have endeavoured to state them more clearly; where they have been disputed, I have carefully reconsidered the evidence and given my reasons for adhering to my former opinions. Most of the additions thus made to the volume are comprised in a new chapter ("Sacred Men and Women"), a new section ("Influence of Mother-kin on Religion"), and three new appendices ("Moloch the King," "The Widowed Flamen," and "Some Customs of the Pelew Islanders"). Among the friends and correspondents who have kindly helped me with information and criticisms of various sorts I wish to thank particularly Mr. W. Crooke, Professor W. M. Flinders Petrie, Mr. G. F. Hill of the British Museum, the Reverend J. Roscoe of the Church Missionary Society, and Mr. W. Wyse. Above all I owe much to my teacher the Reverend Professor R. H. Kennett, who, besides initiating me into the charms of the Hebrew language and giving me a clearer insight into the course of Hebrew history, has contributed several valuable suggestions to the book and enhanced the kindness by reading and criticizing some of the proofs.

J. G. FRAZER.

TRINITY COLLEGE, CAMBRIDGE,
        22nd September 1907.

PREFACE TO THE THIRD EDITION

IN revising the book for this third edition I have made use of several important works which have appeared since the last edition was published. Among these I would name particularly the learned treatises of Count Baudissin on Adonis, of Dr. E. A. Wallis Budge on Osiris, and of my colleague Professor J. Garstang on the civilization of the Hittites, that still mysterious people, who begin to loom a little more distinctly from the mists of the past. Following the example of Dr. Wallis Budge, I have indicated certain analogies which may be traced between the worship of Osiris and the worship of the dead, especially of dead kings, among the modern tribes of Africa. The conclusion to which these analogies appear to point is that under the mythical pall of the glorified Osiris, the god who died and rose again from the dead, there once lay the body of a dead man. Whether that was so or not, I will not venture to say. The longer I occupy myself with questions of ancient mythology the more diffident I become of success in dealing with them, and I am apt to think that we who spend our years in searching for solutions of these insoluble problems are like Sisyphus perpetually rolling his stone up hill only to see it revolve again into the valley, or like the daughters of Danaus doomed for ever to pour water into broken jars that can hold no water. If we are taxed with wasting life in seeking to know what can never be known, and what, if it could be discovered, would not be worth knowing, what can we plead in our defence? I fear, very little. Such pursuits can hardly be defended on the ground of pure reason. We can only say that something, we know not what, drives us to attack the great enemy Ignorance wherever we see him, and that if we fail, as we probably shall, in our attack on his entrenchments, it may be useless but it is not inglorious to fall in leading a Forlorn Hope.

J. G. FRAZER.

CAMBRIDGE,
16*th January* 1914.

CONTENTS

Volume One

BOOK FIRST

CHAPTER IX.—THE RITUAL OF ADONIS . Pp. 223-235

CHAPTER X.—THE GARDENS OF ADONIS . Pp. 236-259

BOOK SECOND

ATTIS . . . Pp. 261-317

CHAPTER I.—THE MYTH AND RITUAL OF ATTIS . . . . . . Pp. 263-276

CHAPTER II.—ATTIS AS A GOD OF VEGETATION . . . . . . Pp. 277-280

CHAPTER III.—ATTIS AS THE FATHER GOD Pp. 281-284

CHAPTER IV.—HUMAN REPRESENTATIVES OF ATTIS . . . . . . Pp. 285-287

CHAPTER V.—THE HANGED GOD . . Pp. 288-297

Volume Two

BOOK THIRD

OSIRIS .   .   . Pp. 1-218

CHAPTER VI.—ISIS . . . . Pp. 115-119

CHAPTER VII.—OSIRIS AND THE SUN . Pp. 120-128

CHAPTER VIII.—OSIRIS AND THE MOON Pp. 129-139

CHAPTER IX.—THE DOCTRINE OF LUNAR
SYMPATHY . . . . . Pp. 140-150

The doctrine of lunar sympathy, 140 *sq.* ; ceremonies at new moon often magical
rather than religious, being intended not so much to propitiate the planet
as to renew sympathetically the life of man, 140 *sq.* ; the moon supposed
to exercise special influence on children, 144 *sqq.* ; Baganda ceremonies
at the new moon, 147 *sq.* ; use of the moon to increase money or decrease
sickness, 148-150.

CHAPTER X.—THE KING AS OSIRIS . Pp. 151-157

Osiris personated by the King of Egypt, 151 ; the Sed festival intended to
renew the king's life, 151 *sqq.* ; identification of the king with the dead
Osiris at the festival, 153 *sq.* ; Professor Flinders Petrie's explanation of
the Sed festival, 154 *sq.* ; similar explanation suggested by M. Alexandre
Moret, 155 *sqq.*

CHAPTER XI.—THE ORIGIN OF OSIRIS . Pp. 158-200

Origin of the conception of Osiris as a god of vegetation and the dead, 158 ;
Osiris distinguished from the kindred deities Adonis and Attis by the
dominant position he occupied in Egyptian religion, 158 ; all great and
lasting religions founded by great men, 159 *sq.* ; the historical reality of
Osiris as an old king of Egypt supported by African analogies, 160 *sq.* ;
dead kings worshipped by the Shilluks of the White Nile, 161-167 ; dead
kings worshipped by the Baganda of Central Africa, 167-173 ; dead kings
worshipped in Kiziba, 173 *sq.* ; ancestral spirits worshipped by the Bantu
tribes of Northern Rhodesia, 174-176 ; the worship of ancestral spirits
apparently the main practical religion of all the Bantu tribes of Africa,
176-191 ; dead chiefs or kings worshipped by the Bantu tribes of Northern
Rhodesia, 191-193 ; dead kings worshipped by the Barotse of the Zambesi,
193-195 ; the worship of dead kings an important element in the religion
of many African tribes, 195 *sq.* ; some African gods, who are now distinguished from ghosts, may have been originally dead men, 196 *sq.* ;
possibility that Osiris and Isis may have been a real king and queen of
Egypt, perhaps identical with King Khent of the first dynasty and his
queen, 197-199 ; suggested parallel between Osiris and Charlemagne,
199 ; the question of the historical reality of Osiris left open, 199 *sq.*

CHAPTER XII.—MOTHER-KIN AND MOTHER
GODDESSES . . . . . Pp. 201-218

§ 1. *Dying Gods and Mourning Goddesses*, pp. 201-202.—Substantial similarity
of Adonis, Attis, and Osiris, 200 ; superiority of the goddesses associated
with Adonis, Attis, and Osiris a mark of the system of mother-kin, 201 *sq.*

ILLUSTRATIONS

Illustrative materials not available in Frazer's time, or then not available for publication, have been culled to provide key symbols to illumine the subject matter. They appear together at the front of the book, each with a caption.

Volume One

BOOK FIRST

ADONIS

CHAPTER I

THE MYTH OF ADONIS

THE spectacle of the great changes which annually pass over the face of the earth has powerfully impressed the minds of men in all ages, and stirred them to meditate on the causes of transformations so vast and wonderful. Their curiosity has not been purely disinterested ; for even the savage cannot fail to perceive how intimately his own life is bound up with the life of nature, and how the same processes which freeze the stream and strip the earth of vegetation menace him with extinction.   At a certain stage of development men seem to have imagined that the means of averting the threatened calamity were in their own hands, and that they could hasten or retard the flight of the seasons by magic art.   Accordingly they performed ceremonies and recited spells to make the rain to fall, the sun to shine, animals to multiply, and the fruits of the earth to grow.   In course of time the slow advance of knowledge, which has dispelled so many cherished illusions, convinced at least the more thoughtful portion of mankind that the alternations of summer and winter, of spring and autumn, were not merely the result of their own magical rites, but that some deeper cause, some mightier power, was at work behind the shifting scenes of nature.   They now pictured to themselves the growth and decay of vegetation, the birth and death of living creatures, as effects of the waxing or waning strength of divine beings, of gods and goddesses, who were born and died, who married and begot children, on the pattern of human life.

The changes of the seasons explained by the life and death of gods.

3

Magical
ceremonies
to revive
the failing
energies of
the gods.

Thus the old magical theory of the seasons was displaced, or rather supplemented, by a religious theory. For although men now attributed the annual cycle of change primarily to corresponding changes in their deities, they still thought that by performing certain magical rites they could aid the god, who was the principle of life, in his struggle with the opposing principle of death. They imagined that they could recruit his failing energies and even raise him from the dead. The ceremonies which they observed for this purpose were in substance a dramatic representation of the natural processes which they wished to facilitate; for it is a familiar tenet of magic that you can produce any desired effect by merely imitating it. And as they now explained the fluctuations of growth and decay, of reproduction and dissolution, by the marriage, the death, and the rebirth or revival of the gods, their religious or rather magical dramas turned in great measure on these themes. They set forth the fruitful union of the powers of fertility, the sad death of one at least of the divine partners, and his joyful resurrection. Thus a religious theory was blended with a magical practice. The combination is familiar in history. Indeed, few religions have ever succeeded in wholly extricating themselves from the old trammels of magic. The inconsistency of acting on two opposite principles, however it may vex the soul of the philosopher, rarely troubles the common man; indeed he is seldom even aware of it. His affair is to act, not to analyse the motives of his action. If mankind had always been logical and wise, history would not be a long chronicle of folly and crime.[1]

---

[1] As in the present volume I am concerned with the beliefs and practices of Orientals I may quote the following passage from one who has lived long in the East and knows it well : "The Oriental mind is free from the trammels of logic. It is a literal fact that the Oriental mind can accept and believe two opposite things at the same time. We find fully qualified and even learned Indian doctors practising Greek medicine, as well as English medicine, and enforcing sanitary restrictions to which their own houses and families are entirely strangers. We find astronomers who can predict eclipses, and yet who believe that eclipses are caused by a dragon swallowing the sun. We find holy men who are credited with miraculous powers and with close communion with the Deity, who live in drunkenness and immorality, and who are capable of elaborate frauds on others. To the Oriental mind, a thing must be incredible to command a ready belief" ("Riots and Unrest in the Punjab, from a corre-

Of the changes which the seasons bring with them, the most striking within the temperate zone are those which affect vegetation. The influence of the seasons on animals, though great, is not nearly so manifest. Hence it is natural that in the magical dramas designed to dispel winter and bring back spring the emphasis should be laid on vegetation, and that trees and plants should figure in them more prominently than beasts and birds. Yet the two sides of life, the vegetable and the animal, were not dissociated in the minds of those who observed the ceremonies. Indeed they commonly believed that the tie between the animal and the vegetable world was even closer than it really is ; hence they often combined the dramatic representation of reviving plants with a real or a dramatic union of the sexes for the purpose of furthering at the same time and by the same act the multiplication of fruits, of animals, and of men. To them the principle of life and fertility, whether animal or vegetable, was one and indivisible. To live and to cause to live, to eat food and to beget children, these were the primary wants of men in the past, and they will be the primary wants of men in the future so long as the world lasts. Other things may be added to enrich and beautify human life, but unless these wants are first satisfied, humanity itself must cease to exist. These two things, therefore, food and children, were what men chiefly sought to procure by the performance of magical rites for the regulation of the seasons.

Nowhere, apparently, have these rites been more widely

---

spondent," *The Times Weekly Edition*, May 24, 1907, p. 326). Again, speaking of the people of the Lower Congo, an experienced missionary describes their religious ideas as " chaotic in the extreme and impossible to reduce to any systematic order. The same person will tell you at different times that the departed spirit goes to the nether regions, or to a dark forest, or to the moon, or to the sun. There is no coherence in their beliefs, and their ideas about cosmogony and the future are very nebulous. Although they believe in punishment after death their faith is so hazy that it has lost all its deterrent force. If in the following pages a lack of logical unity is observed, it must be put to the debit of the native mind, as that lack of logical unity really represents the mistiness of their views." See Rev. John H. Weeks, " Notes on some Customs of the Lower Congo People," *Folk-lore*, xx. (1909) pp. 54 *sq*. Unless we allow for this innate capacity of the human mind to entertain contradictory beliefs at the same time, we shall in vain attempt to understand the history of thought in general and of religion in particular.

Prevalence
of these
rites in
Western
Asia and
Egypt.
and solemnly celebrated than in the lands which border the Eastern Mediterranean. Under the names of Osiris, Tammuz, Adonis, and Attis, the peoples of Egypt and Western Asia represented the yearly decay and revival of life, especially of vegetable life, which they personified as a god who annually died and rose again from the dead. In name and detail the rites varied from place to place : in substance they were the same. The supposed death and resurrection of this oriental deity, a god of many names but of essentially one nature, is the subject of the present inquiry. We begin with Tammuz or Adonis.[1]

The worship of Adonis was practised by the Semitic peoples of Babylonia and Syria, and the Greeks borrowed it from them as early as the seventh century before Christ.[2] The true name of the deity was Tammuz : the appellation of Adonis is merely the Semitic *Adon*, " lord," a title of honour by which his worshippers addressed him.[3] In the Hebrew text of the Old Testament the same name Adonai,

---

[1] The equivalence of Tammuz and Adonis has been doubted or denied by some scholars, as by Renan (*Mission de Phénicie*, Paris, 1864, pp. 216, 235) and by Chwolsohn (*Die Ssabier und der Ssabismus*, St. Petersburg, 1856, ii. 510). But the two gods are identified by Origen (*Selecta in Ezechielem*, Migne's *Patrologia Graeca*, xiii. 797), Jerome (*Epist.* lviii. 3 and *Commentar. in Ezechielem*, viii. *13, 14*, Migne's *Patrologia Latina*, xxii. 581, xxv. 82), Cyril of Alexandria (*In Isaiam*, lib. ii. tomus. iii., and *Comment. on Hosea*, iv. 15, Migne's *Patrologia Graeca*, lxx. 441, lxxi. 136), Theodoretus (*In Ezechielis cap. viii.*, Migne's *Patrologia Graeca*, lxxxi. 885), the author of the Paschal Chronicle (Migne's *Patrologia Graeca*, xcii. 329) and Melito (in W. Cureton's *Spicilegium Syriacum*, London, 1855, p. 44) ; and accordingly we may fairly conclude that, whatever their remote origin may have been, Tammuz and Adonis were in the later period of antiquity practically equivalent to each other. Compare W. W. Graf Baudissin, *Studien zur semitischen Religionsgeschichte* (Leipsic, 1876–1878), i. 299 ; *id.*, in *Realency-*

clopädie für protestantische Theologie und Kirchengeschichte,[3] *s.v.* "Tammuz" ; *id., Adonis und Esmun* (Leipsic, 1911), pp. 94 *sqq.* ; W. Mannhardt, *Antike Wald- und Feldkulte* (Berlin, 1877), pp. 273 *sqq.*; Ch. Vellay, " Le dieu Thammuz," *Revue de l'Histoire des Religions*, xlix. (1904) pp. 154-162. Baudissin holds that Tammuz and Adonis were two different gods sprung from a common root (*Adonis und Esmun*, p. 368). An Assyrian origin of the cult of Adonis was long ago affirmed by Macrobius (*Sat.* i. 21. 1). On Adonis and his worship in general see also F. C. Movers, *Die Phoenizier*, i. (Bonn, 1841) pp. 191 *sqq.*; W. H. Engel, *Kypros* (Berlin, 1841), ii. 536 *sqq.*; Ch. Vellay, *Le culte et les fêtes d'Adonis - Thammouz dans l'Orient antique* (Paris, 1904).

[2] The mourning for Adonis is mentioned by Sappho, who flourished about 600 B.C. See Th. Bergk's *Poetae Lyrici Graeci*,[3] iii. (Leipsic, 1867) p. 897 ; Pausanias, ix. 29. 8.

[3] Ed. Meyer, *Geschichte des Altertums*,[2] i. 2 (Berlin, 1909), pp. 394 *sq.*; W. W. Graf Baudissin, *Adonis und Esmun*, pp. 65 *sqq.*

originally perhaps Adoni, "my lord," is often applied to Jehovah.[1] But the Greeks through a misunderstanding converted the title of honour into a proper name. While Tammuz or his equivalent Adonis enjoyed a wide and lasting popularity among peoples of the Semitic stock, there are grounds for thinking that his worship originated with a race of other blood and other speech, the Sumerians, who in the dawn of history inhabited the flat alluvial plain at the head of the Persian Gulf and created the civilization which was afterwards called Babylonian. The origin and affinities of this people are unknown ; in physical type and language they differed from all their neighbours, and their isolated position, wedged in between alien races, presents to the student of mankind problems of the same sort as the isolation of the Basques and Etruscans among the Aryan peoples of Europe. An ingenious, but unproved, hypothesis would represent them as immigrants driven from central Asia by that gradual desiccation which for ages seems to have been converting once fruitful lands into a waste and burying the seats of ancient civilization under a sea of shifting sand. Whatever their place of origin may have been, it is certain that in Southern Babylonia the Sumerians attained at a very early period to a considerable pitch of civilization ; for they tilled the soil, reared cattle, built cities, dug canals, and even invented a system of writing, which their Semitic neighbours in time borrowed from them.[2] In the pantheon

His worship seems to have originated with the Sumerians.

---

[1] *Encyclopaedia Biblica*, ed. T. K. Cheyne and J. S. Black, iii. 3327. In the Old Testament the title *Adoni*, "my lord," is frequently given to men. See, for example, Genesis xxxiii. 8, 13, 14, 15, xlii. 10, xliii. 20, xliv. 5, 7, 9, 16, 18, 19, 20, 22, 24.

[2] C. P. Tiele, *Geschichte der Religion im Altertum* (Gotha, 1896-1903), i. 134 *sqq.* ; G. Maspero, *Histoire Ancienne des Peuples de l'Orient Classique, les Origines* (Paris, 1895), pp. 550 *sq.* ; L. W. King, *Babylonian Religion and Mythology* (London, 1899), pp. 1 *sqq.* ; *id., A History of Sumer and Akkad* (London, 1910), pp. 1 *sqq.*, 40 *sqq.* ; H. Winckler, in E. Schrader's *Die Keilinschriften und das alte Testament*[3] (Berlin, 1902),

pp. 10 *sq.*, 349 ; Fr. Hommel, *Grundriss der Geographie und Geschichte des alten Orients* (Munich, 1904), pp. 18 *sqq.* ; Ed. Meyer, *Geschichte des Altertums*,[2] i. 2 (Berlin, 1909), pp. 401 *sqq.* As to the hypothesis that the Sumerians were immigrants from Central Asia, see L. W. King, *History of Sumer and Akkad*, pp. 351 *sqq.* The gradual desiccation of Central Asia, which is conjectured to have caused the Sumerian migration, has been similarly invoked to explain the downfall of the Roman empire ; for by rendering great regions uninhabitable it is supposed to have driven hordes of fierce barbarians to find new homes in Europe. See Professor J. W. Gregory's lecture " Is the earth drying up ? "

of this ancient people Tammuz appears to have been one of the oldest, though certainly not one of the most important figures.[1] His name consists of a Sumerian phrase meaning "true son" or, in a fuller form, "true son of the deep water,"[2] and among the inscribed Sumerian texts which have survived the wreck of empires are a number of hymns in his honour, which were written down not later than about two thousand years before our era but were almost certainly composed at a much earlier time.[3]

Tammuz
the lover
of Ishtar.

In the religious literature of Babylonia Tammuz appears as the youthful spouse or lover of Ishtar, the great mother goddess, the embodiment of the reproductive energies of nature. The references to their connexion with each other in myth and ritual are both fragmentary and obscure, but we gather from them that every year Tammuz was believed to die, passing away from the cheerful earth to the gloomy subterranean world, and that every year his divine mistress journeyed in quest of him "to the land from which there is no returning, to the house of darkness, where dust lies on door and bolt." During her absence the passion of love ceased to operate: men and beasts alike forgot to reproduce their kinds: all life was threatened with extinction. So

Descent of
Ishtar to
the nether
world to
recover
Tammuz.

---

delivered before the Royal Geographical Society and reported in *The Times*, December 9th, 1913. It is held by Prof. Hommel (*op. cit.* pp. 19 *sqq.*) that the Sumerian language belongs to the Ural-altaic family, but the better opinion seems to be that its linguistic affinities are unknown. The view, once ardently advocated, that Sumerian was not a language but merely a cabalistic mode of writing Semitic, is now generally exploded.

[1] H. Zimmern, "Der babylonische Gott Tamūz," *Abhandlungen der philologisch-historischen Klasse der Königl. Sächsischen Gesellschaft der Wissenschaften*, xxvii. No. xx. (Leipsic, 1909) pp. 701, 722.

[2] *Dumu-zi*, or in fuller form *Dumu-zi-abzu*. See P. Jensen, *Assyrisch-Babylonische Mythen und Epen* (Berlin, 1900), p. 560; H. Zimmern, *op. cit.* pp. 703 *sqq.*; *id.*, in E. Schrader's

Die Keilinschriften und das Alte Testament[3] (Berlin, 1902), p. 397; P. Dhorme, *La Religion Assyro-Babylonienne* (Paris, 1910), p. 105; W. W. Graf Baudissin, *Adonis und Esmun* (Leipsic, 1911), p. 104.

[3] H. Zimmern, "Der babylonische Gott Tamūz," *Abhandl. d. Kön. Sächs. Gesellschaft der Wissenschaften*, xxvii. No. xx. (Leipsic, 1909) p. 723. For the text and translation of the hymns, see H. Zimmern, "Sumerisch-babylonische Tamūzlieder," *Berichte über die Verhandlungen der Königlich Sächsischen Gesellschaft der Wissenschaften zu Leipzig, Philologisch-historische Klasse*, lix. (1907) pp. 201-252. Compare H. Gressmann, *Altorientalische Texte und Bilder* (Tübingen, 1909), i. 93 *sqq.*; W. W. Graf Baudissin, *Adonis und Esmun* (Leipsic, 1911), pp. 99 *sq.*; R. W. Rogers, *Cuneiform Parallels to the Old Testament* (Oxford, N.D.), pp. 179-185.

intimately bound up with the goddess were the sexual functions of the whole animal kingdom that without her presence they could not be discharged. A messenger of the great god Ea was accordingly despatched to rescue the goddess on whom so much depended. The stern queen of the infernal regions, Allatu or Eresh-Kigal by name, reluctantly allowed Ishtar to be sprinkled with the Water of Life and to depart, in company probably with her lover Tammuz, that the two might return together to the upper world, and that with their return all nature might revive.

Laments for the departed Tammuz are contained in several Babylonian hymns, which liken him to plants that quickly fade. He is

> " *A tamarisk that in the garden has drunk no water,*
>   *Whose crown in the field has brought forth no blossom.*
> *A willow that rejoiced not by the watercourse,*
>   *A willow whose roots were torn up.*
> *A herb that in the garden had drunk no water."*

His death appears to have been annually mourned, to the shrill music of flutes, by men and women about midsummer in the month named after him, the month of Tammuz. The dirges were seemingly chanted over an effigy of the dead god, which was washed with pure water, anointed with oil, and clad in a red robe, while the fumes of incense rose into the air, as if to stir his dormant senses by their pungent fragrance and wake him from the sleep of death. In one of these dirges, inscribed *Lament of the Flutes for Tammuz,* we seem still to hear the voices of the singers chanting the sad refrain and to catch, like far-away music, the wailing notes of the flutes :—

> " *At his vanishing away she lifts up a lament,*
>   *'Oh my child!' at his vanishing away she lifts up a lament;*
>   *'My Damu!' at his vanishing away she lifts up a lament.*
>   *'My enchanter and priest!' at his vanishing away she lifts up a lament,*
>   *At the shining cedar, rooted in a spacious place,*
>   *In Eanna, above and below, she lifts up a lament.*
> *Like the lament that a house lifts up for its master, lifts she up a lament,*
>   *Like the lament that a city lifts up for its lord, lifts she up a lament.*

Her lament is the lament for a herb that grows not in the bed,
   Her lament is the lament for the corn that grows not in the ear.
Her chamber is a possession that brings not forth a possession,
   A weary woman, a weary child, forspent.
Her lament is for a great river, where no willows grow,
   Her lament is for a field, where corn and herbs grow not.
Her lament is for a pool, where fishes grow not.
Her lament is for a thicket of reeds, where no reeds grow.
Her lament is for woods, where tamarisks grow not.
Her lament is for a wilderness where no cypresses (?) grow.
Her lament is for the depth of a garden of trees, where honey and wine
   grow not.
Her lament is for meadows, where no plants grow.
Her lament is for a palace, where length of life grows not." [1]

Adonis
in Greek
mythology
merely a

The tragical story and the melancholy rites of Adonis are better known to us from the descriptions of Greek writers than from the fragments of Babylonian literature or

[1] A. Jeremias, *Die babylonisch-as-syrischen Vorstellungen vom Leben nach dem Tode* (Leipsic, 1887), pp. 4 *sqq.* ; *id.*, in W. H. Roscher's *Lexikon der griech. und röm. Mythologie*, ii. 808, iii. 258 *sqq.* ; M. Jastrow, *The Religion of Babylonia and Assyria* (Boston, 1898), pp. 565-576, 584, 682 *sq.* ; W. L. King, *Babylonian Religion and Mythology*, pp. 178-183 ; P. Jensen, *Assyrisch-babylonische Mythen und Epen*, pp. 81 *sqq.*, 95 *sqq.*, 169 ; R. F. Harper, *Assyrian and Babylonian Literature* (New York, 1901), pp. 316 *sq.*, 338, 408 *sqq.* ; H. Zimmern, in E. Schrader's *Die Keilinschriften und das Alte Testament*, [3] pp. 397 *sqq.*, 561 *sqq.* ; *id.*, "Sumerisch-babylonische Tamūzlieder," *Berichte über die Verhandlungen der Königlich Sächsischen Gesellschaft der Wissenschaften zu Leipzig, Philologisch-historische Klasse*, lix. (1907) pp. 220, 232, 236 *sq.* ; *id.*, "Der babylonische Gott Tamūz," *Abhandlungen der philologisch-historischen Klasse der Königl. Sächsischen Gesellschaft der Wissenschaften*, xxvii. No. xx. (Leipsic, 1909) pp. 725 *sq.*, 729-735 ; H. Gressmann, *Altorientalische Texte und Bilder zum Alten Testamente* (Tübingen, 1909), i. 65-69 ; R. W. Rogers, *Cuneiform Parallels to the Old Testament* (Oxford, N.D.), pp. 121-131 ; W. W. Graf Baudissin, *Adonis und*

Esmun (Leipsic, 1911), pp. 99 *sqq.*, 353 *sqq.* According to Jerome (on Ezekiel viii. 14) the month of Tammuz was June ; but according to modern scholars it corresponded rather to July, or to part of June and part of July. See F. C. Movers, *Die Phoenizier*, i. 210 ; F. Lenormant, "Il mito di Adone-Tammuz nei documenti cuneiformi," *Atti del IV. Congresso Internazionale degli Orientalisti* (Florence, 1880), i. 144 *sq.* ; W. Mannhardt, *Antike Wald- und Feldkulte*, p. 275 ; *Encyclopaedia Biblica, s.v.* "Months," iii. 3194. My friend W. Robertson Smith informed me that owing to the variations of the local Syrian calendars the month of Tammuz fell in different places at different times, from midsummer to autumn, or from June to September. According to Prof. M. Jastrow, the festival of Tammuz was celebrated just before the summer solstice (*The Religion of Babylonia and Assyria*, pp. 547, 682). He observes that "the calendar of the Jewish Church still marks the 17th day of Tammuz as a fast, and Houtsma has shown that the association of the day with the capture of Jerusalem by the Romans represents merely the attempt to give an ancient festival a worthier interpretation."

the brief reference of the prophet Ezekiel, who saw the reflection of the Oriental Tammuz. women of Jerusalem weeping for Tammuz at the north gate of the temple.[1] Mirrored in the glass of Greek mythology, the oriental deity appears as a comely youth beloved by Aphrodite. In his infancy the goddess hid him in a chest, which she gave in charge to Persephone, queen of the nether world. But when Persephone opened the chest and beheld the beauty of the babe, she refused to give him back to Aphrodite, though the goddess of love went down herself to hell to ransom her dear one from the power of the grave. The dispute between the two goddesses of love and death was settled by Zeus, who decreed that Adonis should abide with Persephone in the under world for one part of the year, and with Aphrodite in the upper world for another part. At last the fair youth was killed in hunting by a wild boar, or by the jealous Ares, who turned himself into the likeness of a boar in order to compass the death of his rival. Bitterly did Aphrodite lament her loved and lost Adonis.[2] The strife between the divine rivals for the possession of Adonis appears to be depicted on an Etruscan mirror. The two goddesses, identified by inscriptions, are stationed on either side of Jupiter, who occupies the seat of judgment and lifts an admonitory finger as he looks sternly towards Persephone. Overcome with grief the goddess of love buries her face in her mantle, while her pertinacious rival, grasping a branch in one hand, points with the other at a closed coffer, which probably contains the youthful Adonis.[3] In

---

[1] Ezekiel viii. 14.

[2] Apollodorus, *Bibliotheca*, iii. 14. 4 ; Bion, *Idyl*, i. ; J. Tzetzes, *Schol. on Lycophron*, 831 ; Ovid, *Metam.* x. 503 *sqq.* ; Aristides, *Apology*, edited by J. Rendel Harris (Cambridge, 1891), pp. 44, 106 *sq.* In Babylonian texts relating to Tammuz no reference has yet been found to death by a boar. See H. Zimmern, "Sumerisch-babylonische Tamūzlieder," p. 451 ; *id.*, "Der babylonische Gott Tamūz," p. 731. Baudissin inclines to think that the incident of the boar is a late importation into the myth of Adonis. See his *Adonis und Esmun*, pp. 142 *sqq.* As to the relation of the boar to the

kindred gods Adonis, Attis, and Osiris see *Spirits of the Corn and of the Wild*, ii. 22 *sqq.*, where I have suggested that the idea of the boar as the foe of the god may be based on the terrible ravages which wild pigs notoriously commit in fields of corn.

[3] W. W. Graf Baudissin, *Adonis und Esmun* (Leipsic, 1911), pp. 152 *sq.*, with plate iv. As to the representation of the myth of Adonis on Etruscan mirrors and late works of Roman art, especially sarcophaguses and wall-paintings, see Otto Jahn, *Archäologische Beiträge* (Berlin, 1847), pp. 45-51.

this form of the myth, the contest between Aphrodite and Persephone for the possession of Adonis clearly reflects the struggle between Ishtar and Allatu in the land of the dead, while the decision of Zeus that Adonis is to spend one part of the year under ground and another part above ground is merely a Greek version of the annual disappearance and reappearance of Tammuz.

CHAPTER II

ADONIS IN SYRIA

THE myth of Adonis was localized and his rites celebrated with much solemnity at two places in Western Asia. One of these was Byblus on the coast of Syria, the other was Paphos in Cyprus. Both were great seats of the worship of Aphrodite, or rather of her Semitic counterpart, Astarte ;[1] and of both, if we accept the legends, Cinyras, the father of Adonis, was king.[2] Of the two cities Byblus was the more ancient ; indeed it claimed to be the oldest city in Phoenicia, and to have been founded in the early ages of the world by the great god El, whom Greeks and Romans identified with Cronus and Saturn respectively.[3] However that may have been, in historical times it ranked as a holy place, the religious capital of the country, the Mecca or Jerusalem of the Phoenicians.[4] The city stood on a height beside the sea,[5] and contained a great sanctuary of Astarte,[6] where

[1] The ancients were aware that the Syrian and Cyprian Aphrodite, the mistress of Adonis, was no other than Astarte. See Cicero, De natura deorum, iii. 23. 59 ; Joannes Lydus, De mensibus, iv. 44. On Adonis in Phoenicia see W. W. Graf Baudissin, Adonis und Esmun (Leipsic, 1911), pp. 71 sqq.

[2] As to Cinyras, see F. C. Movers, Die Phoenizier, i. 238 sqq., ii. 2. 226-231 ; W. H. Engel, Kypros (Berlin, 1841), i. 168-173, ii. 94-136 ; Stoll, s.v. "Kinyras," in W. H. Roscher's Lexikon der griech. und röm. Mythologie, ii. 1189 sqq. Melito calls the father of Adonis by the name of Cuthar, and represents him as king of the Phoenicians with his capital at Gebal

(Byblus). See Melito, "Oration to Antoninus Caesar," in W. Cureton's Spicilegium Syriacum (London, 1855), p. 44.

[3] Philo of Byblus, quoted by Eusebius, Praeparatio Evangelii, i. 10 ; Fragmenta Historicorum Graecorum, ed. C. Müller, iii. 568 ; Stephanus Byzantius, s.v. Βύβλος. Byblus is a Greek corruption of the Semitic Gebal (נבל), the name which the place still retains. See E. Renan, Mission de Phénicie (Paris, 1864), p. 155.

[4] R. Pietschmann, Geschichte der Phoenizier (Berlin, 1889), p. 139. On the coins it is designated "Holy Byblus."

[5] Strabo, xvi. 1. 18, p. 755.

[6] Lucian, De dea Syria, 6.

13

in the midst of a spacious open court, surrounded by cloisters and approached from below by staircases, rose a tall cone or obelisk, the holy image of the goddess.[1] In this sanctuary the rites of Adonis were celebrated.[2] Indeed the whole city was sacred to him,[3] and the river Nahr Ibrahim, which falls into the sea a little to the south of Byblus, bore in antiquity the name of Adonis.[4] This was the kingdom of Cinyras.[5] From the earliest to the latest times the city appears to have been ruled by kings, assisted perhaps by a senate or council of elders.[6] The first of the kings of whom we have historical evidence was a certain Zekar-baal. He reigned about a century before Solomon; yet from that dim past his figure stands out strangely fresh and lifelike in the journal of an Egyptian merchant or official named Wen-Ammon, which has fortunately been preserved in a papyrus. This man spent some time with the king at Byblus, and received from him, in return for rich presents, a supply of timber felled in the forests of Lebanon.[7] Another king of Byblus, who bore the name of Sibitti-baal, paid tribute to Tiglath-pileser III., king of Assyria, about the year 739 B.C.[8] Further, from an inscription of the fifth or fourth century before our era we learn that a king of Byblus, by name Yehaw-melech, son of Yehar-baal, and grandson of Adom-melech or Uri-melech, dedicated a pillared portico with a carved work of gold and a bronze altar to the goddess, whom he worshipped under the name of Baalath Gebal, that is, the female Baal of Byblus.[9]

The kings of Byblus.

---

[1] The sanctuary and image are figured on coins of Byblus. See T. L. Donaldson, *Architectura Numismatica* (London, 1859), pp. 105 *sq.*; E. Renan, *Mission de Phénicie*, p. 177; G. Perrot et Ch. Chipiez, *Histoire de l'Art dans l'Antiquité*, iii. (Paris, 1885) p. 60; R. Pietschmann, *Geschichte der Phoenizier*, p. 202; G. Maspero, *Histoire Ancienne des Peuples de l'Orient Classique*, ii. (Paris, 1897) p. 173. Renan excavated a massive square pedestal built of colossal stones, which he thought may have supported the sacred obelisk (*op. cit.* pp. 174-178).

[2] Lucian, *De dea Syria*, 6.

[3] Strabo, xvi. 1. 18, p. 755.

[4] Lucian, *De dea Syria*, 8; Pliny, *Nat. Hist.* v. 78; E. Renan, *Mission de Phénicie*, pp. 282 *sqq.*

[5] Eustathius, *Commentary on Dionysius Periegetes*, 912 (*Geographi Graeci Minores*, ed. C. Müller, ii. 376); Melito, in W. Cureton's *Spicilegium Syriacum*, p. 44.

[6] Ezekiel xxvii. 9. As to the name Gebal see above, p. 13, note [1].

[7] L. B. Paton, *The Early History of Syria and Palestine* (London, 1902), pp. 169-171. See below, pp. 75 *sq.*

[8] L. B. Paton, *op. cit.* p. 235; R. F. Harper, *Assyrian and Babylonian Literature*, p. 57 (the Nimrud inscription of Tiglath-pileser III.).

[9] The inscription was discovered by Renan. See Ch. Vellay, *Le culte et*

The names of these kings suggest that they claimed affinity with their god Baal or Moloch, for Moloch is only a corruption of *melech*, that is, "king." Such a claim at all events appears to have been put forward by many other Semitic kings.[1] The early monarchs of Babylon were worshipped as gods in their lifetime.[2] Mesha, king of Moab, perhaps called himself the son of his god Kemosh.[3] Among the Aramean sovereigns of Damascus, mentioned in the Bible, we find more than one Ben-hadad, that is, "son of the god Hadad," the chief male deity of the Syrians;[4] and Josephus tells us that down to his own time, in the first century of our era, Ben-hadad I., whom he calls simply Adad, and his successor, Hazael, continued to be worshipped as gods by the people of Damascus, who held processions daily in their honour.[5] Some of the kings of Edom seem to have gone a step farther and identified themselves with the god in their lifetime; at all events they bore his name Hadad without any qualification.[6] King Bar-rekub, who

---

les fêtes d'Adonis - Thammouz dans l'Orient antique (Paris, 1904), pp. 38 sq.; G. A. Cooke, *Text-book of North-Semitic Inscriptions* (Oxford 1903), No. 3, pp. 18 sq. In the time of Alexander the Great the king of Byblus was a certain Enylus (Arrian, *Anabasis*, ii. 20), whose name appears on a coin of the city (F. C. Movers, *Die Phoenizier*, ii. 1, p. 103, note 81).

[1] On the divinity of Semitic kings and the kingship of Semitic gods see W. R. Smith, *Religion of the Semites*[2] (London, 1894), pp. 44 sq., 66 sqq.

[2] H. Radau, *Early Babylonian History* (New York and London, 1900), pp. 307-317; P. Dhorme, *La Religion Assyro-Babylonienne* (Paris, 1910), pp. 168 sqq.

[3] The evidence for this is the Moabite stone, but the reading of the inscription is doubtful. See S. R. Driver, in *Encyclopaedia Biblica*, s.v. "Mesha," vol. iii. 3041 sqq.; id., *Notes on the Hebrew Text and the Topography of the Books of Samuel*, Second Edition (Oxford, 1913), pp. lxxxv., lxxxvi., lxxxviii. sq.; G. A. Cooke, *Text-book of North-Semitic Inscriptions*, No. 1, pp. 1 sq., 6.

[4] 2 Kings viii. 7, 9, xiii. 24 sq.; Jeremiah xlix. 27. As to the god Hadad see Macrobius, *Saturn.* i. 23. 17-19 (where, as so often in late writers, the Syrians are called Assyrians); Philo of Byblus, in *Fragmenta Historicorum Graecorum*, ed. C. Müller, iii. 569; F. Baethgen, *Beiträge zur semitischen Religionsgeschichte* (Berlin, 1888), pp. 66-68; G. A. Cooke, *Text-book of North-Semitic Inscriptions*, Nos. 61, 62, pp. 161 sq., 164, 173, 175; M. J. Lagrange, *Études sur les Religions Sémitiques*[2] (Paris, 1905), pp. 93, 493, 496 sq. The prophet Zechariah speaks (xii. 11) of a great mourning of or for Hadadrimmon in the plain of Megiddon. This has been taken to refer to a lament for Hadad - Rimmon, the Syrian god of rain, storm, and thunder, like the lament for Adonis. See S. R. Driver's note on the passage (*The Minor Prophets*, pp. 266 sq., *Century Bible*); W. W. Graf Baudissin, *Adonis und Esmun*, p. 92.

[5] Josephus, *Antiquit. Jud.* ix. 4. 6.

[6] Genesis xxxvi. 35 sq.; 1 Kings xi. 14-22; 1 Chronicles i. 50 sq. Of the eight kings of Edom mentioned in Genesis (xxxvi. 31-39) and in 1 Chron-

reigned over Samal in North-Western Syria in the time of
Tiglath-pileser (745–727 B.C.) appears from his name to
have reckoned himself a son of Rekub-el, the god to whose
favour he deemed himself indebted for the kingdom.[1] The
kings of Tyre traced their descent from Baal,[2] and apparently
professed to be gods in their own person.[3] Several of them
bore names which are partly composed of the names of
Baal and Astarte ; one of them bore the name of Baal pure
and simple.[4] The Baal whom they personated was no
doubt Melcarth, "the king of the city," as his name signifies,
the great god whom the Greeks identified with Hercules ;
for the equivalence of the Baal of Tyre both to Melcarth
and to Hercules is placed beyond the reach of doubt by a
bilingual inscription, in Phoenician and Greek, which was
found in Malta.[5]

In like manner the kings of Byblus may have assumed
the style of Adonis ; for Adonis was simply the divine Adon

---

icles (i. 43-50) not one was the son
of his predecessor. This seems to
indicate that in Edom, as elsewhere, the
blood royal was traced in the female
line, and that the kings were men of
other families, or even foreigners, who
succeeded to the throne by marrying
the hereditary princesses. See *The
Magic Art and the Evolution of Kings*,
ii. 268 *sqq.* The Israelites were forbidden to have a foreigner for a king
(Deuteronomy xvii. 15 with S. R.
Driver's note), which seems to imply
that the custom was known among
their neighbours. It is significant that
some of the names of the kings of Edom
seem to be those of divinities, as Prof.
A. H. Sayce observed long ago (*Lectures on the Religion of the Ancient
Babylonians*, London and Edinburgh,
1887, p. 54).

[1] G. A. Cooke, *op. cit.* Nos. 62, 63,
pp. 163, 165, 173 *sqq.*, 181 *sqq.* ;
M. J. Lagrange, *op. cit.* pp. 496 *sqq.*
The god Rekub-el is mentioned along
with the gods Hadad, El, Reshef, and
Shamash in an inscription of King
Bar-rekub's mortal father, King Pan-
ammu (G. A. Cooke, *op. cit.* No. 61,
p. 161).

[2] Virgil, *Aen.* i. 729 *sq.*, with

Servius's note ; Silius Italicus, *Punica*,
i. 86 *sqq.*

[3] Ezekiel xxviii. 2, 9.

[4] Menander of Ephesus, quoted by
Josephus, *Contra Apionem*, i. 18 and 21 ;
Fragmenta Historicorum Graecorum,
ed. C. Müller, iv. 446 *sq.* According
to the text of Josephus, as edited by
B. Niese, the names of the kings in
question were Abibal, Balbazer, Abd-
astart, Methusastart, son of Leastart,
Ithobal, Balezor, Baal, Balator, Merbal.
The passage of Menander is quoted also
by Eusebius, *Chronic.* i. pp. 118, 120,
ed. A. Schoene.

[5] G. A. Cooke, *Text-book of North-
Semitic Inscriptions*, No. 36, p. 102.
As to Melcarth, the Tyrian Hercules,
see Ed. Meyer, *s.v.* "Melqart," in
W. H. Roscher's *Lexikon d. griech. u.
röm. Mythologie*, ii. 2650 *sqq.* One of
the Tyrian kings seems to have been
called Abi-milk (Abi-melech), that is,
"father of a king" or "father of
Moloch," that is, of Melcarth. A
letter of his to the king of Egypt is
preserved in the Tel-el-Amarna correspondence. See R. F. Harper, *Assyrian
and Babylonian Literature*, p. 237. As
to a title which implies that the bearer
of it was the father of a god, see below,
pp. 51 *sq.*

(handwritten at top: (lord) (master) (king) / Adon, Baal, Melech)

or "lord" of the city, a title which hardly differs in sense from Baal ("master") and Melech ("king"). This conjecture would be confirmed if one of the kings of Byblus actually bore, as Renan believed, the name of Adom-melech, that is, Adonis Melech, the Lord King. But, unfortunately, the reading of the inscription in which the name occurs is doubtful.[1] Some of the old Canaanite kings of Jerusalem appear to have played the part of Adonis in their lifetime, if we may judge from their names, Adoni-bezek and Adoni-zedek,[2] which are divine rather than human titles. Adoni-zedek means "lord of righteousness," and is therefore equivalent to Melchizedek, that is, "king of righteousness," the title of that mysterious king of Salem and priest of God Most High, who seems to have been neither more nor less than one of these same Canaanitish kings of Jerusalem.[3] Thus if the old priestly kings of Jerusalem regularly played the part of Adonis, we need not wonder that in later times the women of Jerusalem used to weep for Tammuz, that is, for Adonis, at the north gate of the temple.[4] In doing so they may only have been continuing a custom which had been observed in the same place by the Canaanites long before the Hebrews invaded the land. Perhaps the "sacred men," as they were called, who lodged within the walls of the temple at Jerusalem down almost to the end of the Jewish kingdom,[5] may have acted the part of the living Adonis to the living Astarte of the women. At all events we know that in the cells of

(marginal notes:) Divinity of the Phoenician kings of Byblus and the Canaanite kings of Jerusalem.

The "sacred men" at Jerusalem.

---

[1] E. Renan, quoted by Ch. Vellay, *Le culte et les fêtes d'Adonis-Thammouz*, p. 39. Mr. Cooke reads ארמלך (Uri-milk) instead of אדמלך (Adon-milk) (G. A. Cooke, *Text-book of North-Semitic Inscriptions*, No. 3, p. 18).

[2] Judges i. 4-7 ; Joshua x. 1 *sqq.*

[3] Genesis xiv. 18-20, with Prof. S. R. Driver's commentary ; *Encyclopaedia Biblica, s.vv.* "Adoni-bezek," "Adoni-zedek," "Melchizedek." It is to be observed that names compounded with Adoni- were occasionally borne by private persons. Such names are Adoni-kam (Ezra ii. 13) and Adoni-ram (1 Kings iv. 6), not to mention Adoni-jah (1 Kings i. 5 *sqq.*), who was a prince and aspired to the throne of his father David. These names are commonly interpreted as sentences expressive of the nature of the god whom the bearer of the name worshipped. See Prof. Th. Nöldeke, in *Encyclopaedia Biblica, s.v.* "Names," iii. 3286. It is quite possible that names which once implied divinity were afterwards degraded by application to common men.

[4] Ezekiel viii. 14.

[5] They were banished from the temple by King Josiah, who came to the throne in 637 B.C. Jerusalem fell just fifty-one years later. See 2 Kings xxiii. 7. As to these "sacred men" (*ḳedēshīm*), see below, pp. 72 *sqq.*

these strange clergy women wove garments for the *asherim*,[1] the sacred poles which stood beside the altar and which appear to have been by some regarded as embodiments of Astarte.[2]   Certainly these "sacred men" must have discharged some function which was deemed religious in the temple at Jerusalem ; and we can hardly doubt that the prohibition to bring the wages of prostitution into the house of God, which was published at the very same time that the men were expelled from the temple,[3] was directed against an existing practice.   In Palestine as in other Semitic lands the hire of sacred prostitutes was probably dedicated to the deity as one of his regular dues : he took tribute of men and women as of flocks and herds, of fields and vineyards and oliveyards.

David as heir of the old sacred kings of Jerusalem.

But if Jerusalem had been from of old the seat of a dynasty of spiritual potentates or Grand Lamas, who held the keys of heaven and were revered far and wide as kings and gods in one, we can easily understand why the upstart David chose it for the capital of the new kingdom which he had won for himself at the point of the sword.   The central position and the natural strength of the virgin fortress need not have been the only or the principal inducements which

---

[1] 2 Kings xxiii. 7, where, following the Septuagint, we must apparently read בָּתִּים for the בָּתֵּי of the Massoretic Text.   So R. Kittel and J. Skinner.

[2] The *ashērah* (singular of *ashērīm*) was certainly of wood (Judges vi. 26) : it seems to have been a tree stripped of its branches and planted in the ground beside an altar, whether of Jehovah or of other gods (Deuteronomy xvi. 21 ; Jeremiah xvii. 2). That the *asherah* was regarded as a goddess, the female partner of Baal, appears from 1 Kings xviii. 19 ; 2 Kings xxi. 3, xxiii. 4 ; and that this goddess was identified with Ashtoreth (Astarte) may be inferred from a comparison of Judges ii. 13 with Judges iii. 7.   Yet on the other hand the pole or tree seems by others to have been viewed as a male power (Jeremiah ii. 27 ; see below, pp. 107 *sqq.*), and the identification of the *asherah* with Astarte has been doubted or disputed by some eminent modern

scholars.   See on this subject W. Robertson Smith, *Religion of the Semites*,[2] pp. 187 *sqq.*; S. R. Driver, on Deuteronomy xvi. 21 ; J. Skinner, on 1 Kings xiv. 23 ; M. J. Lagrange, *Études sur les religions Sémitiques*,[2] pp. 173 *sqq.* ; G. F. Moore, in *Encyclopaedia Biblica*, vol. i. 330 *sqq.*, *s.v.* "Asherah."

[3] Deuteronomy xxiii. 17 *sq.* (in Hebrew 18 *sq.*).   The code of Deuteronomy was published in 621 B.C. in the reign of King Josiah, whose reforms, including the ejection of the *kedeshim* from the temple, were based upon it.   See W. Robertson Smith, *The Old Testament in the Jewish Church*[2] (London and Edinburgh, 1892), pp. 256 *sqq.*, 353 *sqq.* ; S. R. Driver, *Critical and Exegetical Commentary on Deuteronomy*[3] (Edinburgh, 1902), pp. xliv. *sqq.* ; K. Budde, *Geschichte der althebräischen Litteratur* (Leipsic, 1906), pp. 105 *sqq.*

decided the politic monarch to transfer his throne from Hebron to Jerusalem.[1]   By serving himself heir to the ancient kings of the city he might reasonably hope to inherit their ghostly repute along with their broad acres, to wear their nimbus as well as their crown.[2]   So at a later time when he had conquered Ammon and captured the royal city of Rabbah, he took the heavy gold crown of the Ammonite god Milcom and placed it on his own brows, thus posing as the deity in person.[3]   It can hardly, therefore, be unreasonable to suppose that he pursued precisely the same policy at the conquest of Jerusalem.   And on the other side the calm confidence with which the Jebusite inhabitants of that city awaited his attack, jeering at the besiegers from the battlements,[4] may well have been born of a firm trust in the local deity rather than in the height and thickness of their grim old walls.   Certainly the obstinacy

---

[1] He reigned seven years in Hebron and thirty-three in Jerusalem (2 Samuel v. 5; 1 Kings ii. 11; 1 Chronicles xxix. 27).

[2] Professor A. H. Sayce has argued that David's original name was Elhanan (2 Samuel xxi. 19 compared with xxiii. 24), and that the name David, which he took at a later time, should be written Dod or Dodo, "the Beloved One," which according to Prof. Sayce was a name for Tammuz (Adonis) in Southern Canaan, and was in particular bestowed by the Jebusites of Jerusalem on their supreme deity. See A. H. Sayce, *Lectures on the Religion of the Ancient Babylonians* (London and Edinburgh, 1887), pp. 52-57. If he is right, his conclusions would accord perfectly with those which I had reached independently, and it would become probable that David only assumed the name of David (Dod, Dodo) after the conquest of Jerusalem, and for the purpose of identifying himself with the god of the city, who had borne the same title from time immemorial. But on the whole it seems more likely, as Professor Kennett points out to me, that in the original story Elhanah, a totally different person from David, was the slayer of Goliath, and that the part of the giant-killer was thrust

on David at a later time when the brightness of his fame had eclipsed that of many lesser heroes.

[3] 2 Samuel xii. 26-31; 1 Chronicles xx. 1-3. Critics seem generally to agree that in these passages the word מלכם must be pointed *Milcom*, not *malcham* "their king," as the Massoretic text, followed by the English version, has it. The reading *Milcom*, which involves no change of the original Hebrew text, is supported by the reading of the Septuagint Μολχὸμ τοῦ βασιλέως αὐτῶν, where the three last words are probably a gloss on Μολχὸμ. See S. R. Driver, *Notes on the Hebrew Text and the Topography of the Books of Samuel*, Second Edition (Oxford, 1913), p. 294; Dean Kirkpatrick, in his note on 2 Samuel xii. 30 (*Cambridge Bible for Schools and Colleges*); *Encyclopaedia Biblica*, iii. 3085; R. Kittel, *Biblia Hebraica*, i. 433; Brown, Driver, and Briggs, *Hebrew and English Lexicon of the Old Testament* (Oxford, 1906), pp. 575 *sq.* David's son and successor adopted the worship of Milcom and made a high place for him outside Jerusalem. See 1 Kings xi. 5; 2 Kings xxiii. 13.

[4] 2 Samuel v. 6-10; 1 Chronicles xi. 4-9.

with which in after ages the Jews defended the same place against the armies of Assyria and Rome sprang in large measure from a similar faith in the God of Zion.

Traces of the divinity of Hebrew kings.

Be that as it may, the history of the Hebrew kings presents some features which may perhaps, without straining them too far, be interpreted as traces or relics of a time when they or their predecessors · played the part of a divinity, and particularly of Adonis, the divine lord of the land. In life the Hebrew king was regularly addressed as *Adoni-ham-melech*, "My Lord the King,"[1] and after death he was lamented with cries of *Hoi ahi! Hoi Adon!* "Alas my brother! alas Lord!"[2] These exclamations of grief uttered for the death of a king of Judah were, we can hardly doubt, the very same cries which the weeping women of Jerusalem uttered in the north porch of the temple for the dead Tammuz.[3] However, little stress can be laid on such forms of address, since *Adon* in Hebrew, like "lord" in English, was a secular as well as a religious title. But whether identified with Adonis or not, the Hebrew kings certainly seem to have been regarded as in a sense divine, as representing and to

[1] See for example 1 Samuel xxiv. 8; 2 Samuel xiv. 9, 12, 15, 17, 18, 19, 22, xv. 15, 21, xvi. 4, 9, xviii. 28, 31, 32; 1 Kings i. 2, 13, 18, 20, 21, 24, 27; 1 Chronicles xxi. 3, 23.

[2] Jeremiah xxii. 18, xxxiv. 5. In the former passage, according to the Massoretic text, the full formula of mourning was, "Alas my brother! alas sister! alas lord! alas his glory!" Who was the lamented sister? Professor T. K. Cheyne supposes that she was Astarte, and by a very slight change (דדה for הדה) he would read "Dodah" for "his glory," thus restoring the balance between the clauses; for "Dodah" would then answer to "Adon" (lord) as "sister" answers to "brother." I have to thank Professor Cheyne for kindly communicating this conjecture to me by letter. He writes that Dodah "is a title of Ishtar, just as Dôd is a title of Tamûz," and for evidence he refers me to the Dodah of the Moabite Stone, where, however, the reading Dodah is not free from

doubt. See G. A. Cooke, *Text-book of North-Semitic Inscriptions*, No. 1, pp. 1, 3, 11; *Encyclopaedia Biblica*, ii. 3045; S. R. Driver, *Notes on the Hebrew Text and the Topography of the Books of Samuel*, Second Edition (Oxford, 1913), pp. lxxxv., lxxxvi., xc.; F. Baethgen, *Beiträge zur semitischen Religionsgeschichte* (Berlin, 1888), p. 234; H. Winckler, *Geschichte Israels* (Leipsic, 1895–1900), ii. 258. As to Hebrew names formed from the root *dôd* in the sense of "beloved," see Brown, Driver, and Briggs, *Hebrew and English Lexicon of the Old Testament*, pp. 187 sq.; G. B. Gray, *Studies in Hebrew Proper Names* (London, 1896), pp. 60 sqq.

[3] This was perceived by Renan (*Histoire du peuple d'Israel*, iii. 273), and Prof. T. K. Cheyne writes to me: "The formulae of public mourning were derived from the ceremonies of the Adonia; this Lenormant saw long ago."

some extent embodying Jehovah on earth. For the
king's throne was called the throne of Jehovah ;[1] and the
application of the holy oil to his head was believed to
impart to him directly a portion of the divine spirit.[2]
Hence he bore the title of Messiah, which with its Greek
equivalent Christ means no more than "the Anointed One."
Thus when David had cut off the skirt of Saul's robe in the
darkness of a cave where he was in hiding, his heart smote
him for having laid sacrilegious hands upon *Adoni Messiah
Jehovah*, "my Lord the Anointed of Jehovah."[3]

Like other divine or semi-divine rulers the Hebrew kings
were apparently held answerable for famine and pestilence.
When a dearth, caused perhaps by a failure of the winter
rains, had visited the land for three years, King David
inquired of the oracle, which discreetly laid the blame not
on him but on his predecessor Saul. The dead king was
indeed beyond the reach of punishment, but his sons were

The Hebrew kings seem to have been held responsible for drought and famine.

---

[1] 1 Chronicles xxix. 23 ; 2 Chronicles
ix. 8.

[2] 1 Samuel xvi. 13, 14, compare *id.*,
x. 1 and 20. The oil was poured on the
king's head (1 Samuel x. 1 ; 2 Kings
ix. 3, 6). For the conveyance of the
divine spirit by means of oil, see also
Isaiah lx. 1. The kings of Egypt
appear to have consecrated their vassal
Syrian kings by pouring oil on their
heads. See the Tell-el-Amarna letters,
No. 37 (H. Winckler, *Die Thontafeln
von Tell-el-Amarna*, p. 99). Some
West African priests are consecrated
by a similar ceremony. See below,
p. 68. The natives of Buru, an East
Indian island, imagine that they can
keep off demons by smearing their
bodies with coco-nut oil, but the oil
must be prepared by young unmarried
girls. See G. A. Wilken, " Bijdrage
tot de kennis der Alfoeren van het
eiland Boeroe," *Verhandelingen van
het Bataviaasch Genootschap van
Kunsten en Wetenschappen*, xxxviii.
(Batavia, 1875) p. 30 ; *id.*, *Verspreide
Geschriften* (The Hague, 1912), i. 61.
In some tribes of North-West America
hunters habitually anointed their hair
with decoctions of certain plants and
deer's brains before they set out to

hunt. The practice was probably a
charm to secure success in the hunt.
See C. Hill-Tout, *The Home of the
Salish and Déné* (London, 1907), p. 72.

[3] 1 Samuel xxiv. 6. Messiah in
Hebrew is *Mashiah* (מָשִׁיחַ). The English form Messiah is derived from the
Aramaic through the Greek. See
T. K. Cheyne, in *Encyclopaedia
Biblica*, *s.v.* "Messiah," vol. iii.
3057 *sqq.* Why hair oil should be
considered a vehicle of inspiration is
by no means clear. It would have
been intelligible if the olive had been
with the Hebrews, as it was with the
Athenians, a sacred tree under the
immediate protection of a deity ; for
then a portion of the divine essence
might be thought to reside in the oil.
W. Robertson Smith supposed that the
unction was originally performed with
the fat of a sacrificial victim, for which
vegetable oil was a later substitute
(*Religion of the Semites*,[2] pp. 383 *sq.*).
On the whole subject see J. Wellhausen,
" Zwei Rechtsriten bei den Hebräern,"
Archiv für Religionswissenschaft, vii.
(1904) pp. 33-39 ; H. Weinel, " משׁח
und seine Derivate," *Zeitschrift für die
alttestamentliche Wissenschaft*, xviii.
(1898) pp. 1-82.

not. So David had seven of them sought out, and they were hanged before the Lord at the beginning of barley harvest in spring : and all the long summer the mother of two of the dead men sat under the gallows-tree, keeping off the jackals by night and the vultures by day, till with the autumn the blessed rain came at last to wet their dangling bodies and fertilize the barren earth once more. Then the bones of the dead were taken down from the gibbet and buried in the sepulchre of their fathers.[1] The season when these princes were put to death, at the beginning of barley harvest, and the length of time they hung on the gallows, seem to show that their execution was not a mere punishment, but that it partook of the nature of a rain-charm. For it is a common belief that rain can be procured by magical ceremonies performed with dead men's bones,[2] and it would be natural to ascribe a special virtue in this respect to the bones of princes, who are often expected to give rain in their life. When the Israelites demanded of Samuel that he should give them a king, the indignant prophet, loth to be superseded by the upstart Saul, called on the Lord to send thunder and rain, and the Lord did so at once, though the season was early summer and the reapers were at work in the wheat-fields, a time when in common years no rain falls from the cloudless Syrian sky.[3] The pious historian who records the miracle seems to have regarded it as a mere token of the wrath of the deity, whose voice was heard in the roll of thunder ; but we may surmise that in giving this impressive proof of his control of the weather Samuel meant to hint gently at the naughtiness of asking for a king to do for the fertility of the land what could be done quite as well and far more cheaply by a prophet.

In Israel the excess as well as the deficiency of rain seems to have been set down to the wrath of the

---

[1] 2 Samuel xxi. 1-14, with Dean Kirkpatrick's notes on 1 and 10.

[2] *The Magic Art and the Evolution of Kings*, i. 284 *sq.*

[3] 1 Samuel xii. 17 *sq.* Similarly, Moses stretched forth his rod toward heaven and the Lord sent thunder and rain (Exodus ix. 23). The word for thunder in both these passages is "voices" (קֹלֹת). The Hebrews heard in the clap of thunder the voice of Jehovah, just as the Greeks heard in it the voice of Zeus and the Romans the voice of Jupiter.

deity.[1] When the Jews returned to Jerusalem from
the great captivity and assembled for the first time in
the square before the ruined temple, it happened that the
weather was very wet, and as the people sat shelterless
and drenched in the piazza they trembled at their sin and
at the rain.[2] In all ages it has been the strength or
the weakness of Israel to read the hand of God in the
changing aspects of nature, and we need not wonder that
at such a time and in so dismal a scene, with a lowering
sky overhead, the blackened ruins of the temple before their
eyes, and the steady drip of the rain over all, the returned
exiles should have been oppressed with a double sense of
their own guilt and of the divine anger. Perhaps, though
they hardly knew it, memories of the bright sun, fat fields,
and broad willow-fringed rivers of Babylon,[3] which had been
so long their home, lent a deeper shade of sadness to the
austerity of the Judean landscape, with its gaunt grey hills
stretching away, range beyond range, to the horizon, or
dipping eastward to the far line of sombre blue which marks
the sullen waters of the Dead Sea.[4]

Excessive rain set down to the wrath of the deity.

In the days of the Hebrew monarchy the king was
apparently credited with the power of making sick and
making whole. Thus the king of Syria sent a leper to the
king of Israel to be healed by him, just as scrofulous patients

Hebrew kings apparently supposed to heal disease and stop epidemics.

---

[1] Ezekiel xiii. 11, 13, xxxviii. 22 ;
Jeremiah iii. 2 *sq.* The Hebrews
looked to Jehovah for rain (Leviticus
xxvi. 3-5 ; Jeremiah v. 24) just as the
Greeks looked to Zeus and the Romans
to Jupiter.

[2] Ezra x. 9-14. The special sin
which they laid to heart on this occasion was their marriage with Gentile
women. It is implied, though not
expressly said, that they traced the
inclemency of the weather to these
unfortunate alliances. Similarly,
"during the rainy season, when the
sun is hidden behind great masses of
dark clouds, the Indians set up a
wailing for their sins, believing that
the sun is angry and may never shine
on them again." See Francis C.
Nicholas, "The Aborigines of Santa
Maria, Colombia," *American Anthropologist*, N.S., iii. (New York, 1901)

p. 641. The Indians in question are
the Aurohuacas of Colombia, in South
America.

[3] Psalm cxxxvii. The willows beside the rivers of Babylon are mentioned in the laments for Tammuz.
See above, pp. 9, 10.

[4] The line of the Dead Sea, lying
in its deep trough, is visible from the
Mount of Olives ; indeed, so clear is
the atmosphere that the blue water
seems quite near the eye, though in
fact it is more than fifteen miles off
and nearly four thousand feet below
the spectator. See K. Baedeker,
Palestine and Syria[4] (Leipsic, 1906),
p. 77. When the sun shines on it,
the lake is of a brilliant blue (G. A.
Smith, *Historical Geography of the
Holy Land*, London, 1894, pp. 501
sq.) ; but its brilliancy is naturally
dimmed under clouded skies.

used to fancy that they could be cured by the touch of a French or English king. However, the Hebrew monarch, with more sense than has been shown by his royal brothers in modern times, professed himself unable to work any such miracle. "Am I God," he asked, "to kill and to make alive, that this man doth send unto me to recover a man of his leprosy?"[1] On another occasion, when pestilence ravaged the country and the excited fancy of the plague-stricken people saw in the clouds the figure of the Destroying Angel with his sword stretched out over Jerusalem, they laid the blame on King David, who had offended the touchy and irascible deity by taking a census. The prudent monarch bowed to the popular storm, acknowledged his guilt, and appeased the angry god by offering burnt sacrifices on the threshing-floor of Araunah, one of the old Jebusite inhabitants of Jerusalem. Then the angel sheathed his flashing sword, and the shrieks of the dying and the lamentations for the dead no longer resounded in the streets.[2]

The rarity of references to the divinity of Hebrew kings in the historical books may be ex-

To this theory of the sanctity, nay the divinity of the Hebrew kings it may be objected that few traces of it survive in the historical books of the Bible. But the force of the objection is weakened by a consideration of the time and the circumstances in which these books assumed their final shape. The great prophets of the eighth and the

[1] 2 Kings v. 5-7.

[2] 2 Samuel xxiv. ; 1 Chronicles xxi. In this passage, contrary to his usual practice, the Chronicler has enlivened the dull tenor of his history with some picturesque touches which we miss in the corresponding passage of Kings. It is to him that we owe the vision of the Angel of the Plague first stretching out his sword over Jerusalem and then returning it to the scabbard. From him Defoe seems to have taken a hint in his account of the prodigies, real or imaginary, which heralded the outbreak of the Great Plague in London. "One time before the plague was begun, otherwise than as I have said in St. Giles's, I think it was in March, seeing a crowd of people in the street, I joined with them to satisfy my curiosity, and found them all staring up into the air to see what a woman told them appeared plain to her, which was an angel clothed in white with a fiery sword in his hand, waving it or brandishing it over his head. . . . One saw one thing and one another. I looked as earnestly as the rest, but, perhaps, not with so much willingness to be imposed upon ; and I said, indeed, that I could see nothing but a white cloud, bright on one side, by the shining of the sun upon the other part." See Daniel Defoe, *History of the Plague in London* (Edinburgh, 1810, pp. 33 *sq.*). It is the more likely that Defoe had here the Chronicler in mind, because a few pages earlier he introduces the prophet Jonah and a man out of Josephus with very good effect.

seventh centuries by the spiritual ideals and the ethical plained by
fervour of their teaching had wrought a religious and moral the circum-
stances in
reform perhaps unparalleled in history. Under their in- which these
fluence an austere monotheism had replaced the old works were
composed
sensuous worship of the natural powers : a stern Puritanical or edited.
spirit, an unbending rigour of mind, had succeeded to the
old easy supple temper with its weak compliances, its wax-
like impressionability, its proclivities to the sins of the flesh.
And the moral lessons which the prophets inculcated were
driven home by the political events of the time, above all
by the ever-growing pressure of the great Assyrian empire
on the petty states of Palestine. The long agony of the
siege of Samaria [1] must have been followed with trembling
anxiety by the inhabitants of Judea, for the danger was at
their door. They had only to lift up their eyes and look
north to see the blue hills of Ephraim, at whose foot lay the
beleaguered city. Its final fall and the destruction of the
northern kingdom could not fail to fill every thoughtful
mind in the sister realm with sad forebodings. It was as if
the sky had lowered and thunder muttered over Jerusalem.
Thenceforth to the close of the Jewish monarchy, about a
century and a half later, the cloud never passed away,
though once for a little it seemed to lift, when Sennacherib
raised the siege of Jerusalem [2] and the watchers on the walls
beheld the last of the long line of spears and standards
disappearing, the last squadron of the blue-coated Assyrian
cavalry sweeping, in a cloud of dust, out of sight.[3]

It was in this period of national gloom and despondency The
that the two great reformations of Israel's religion were historical
books were
accomplished, the first by king Hezekiah, the second a composed
century later by king Josiah.[4] We need not wonder then or edited
under the

---

[1] 2 Kings xvii. 5 *sq.*, xviii. 9 *sq.*

[2] 2 Kings xix. 32-36.

[3] We owe to Ezekiel (xxiii. 5 *sq.*, 12) the picture of the handsome Assyrian cavalrymen in their blue uniforms and gorgeous trappings. The prophet writes as if in his exile by the waters of Babylon he had seen the blue regiments filing past, in all the pomp of war, on their way to the front.

[4] Samaria fell in 722 B.C., during or just before the reign of Hezekiah : the Book of Deuteronomy, the corner-stone of king Josiah's reformation, was produced in 621 B.C. ; and Jerusalem fell in 586 B.C. The date of Hezekiah's accession is a much-disputed point in the chronology of Judah. See the Introduction to Kings and Isaiah i.-xxxix. by J. Skinner and O. C. Whitehouse respectively, in *The Century Bible.*

influence
of the
prophetic
reforma-
tion.
that the reformers who in that and subsequent ages composed or edited the annals of their nation should have looked
as sourly on the old unreformed paganism of their forefathers as the fierce zealots of the Commonwealth looked
on the far more innocent pastimes of Merry England ; and
that in their zeal for the glory of God they should have
blotted many pages of history lest they should perpetuate
the memory of practices to which they traced the calamities
of their country. All the historical books passed through
the office of the Puritan censor,[1] and we can hardly
doubt that they emerged from it stript of many gay
feathers which they had flaunted when they went in.
Among the shed plumage may well have been the passages
which invested human beings, whether kings or commoners,
with the attributes of deity. Certainly no pages could seem
to the censor more rankly blasphemous ; on none, therefore, was he likely to press more firmly the official sponge.

The Baal
and his
female
Baalath
the sources
of all
fertility.
But if Semitic kings in general and the kings of
Byblus in particular often assumed the style of Baal or
Adonis, it follows that they may have mated with the
goddess, the Baalath or Astarte of the city. Certainly we
hear of kings of Tyre and Sidon who were priests of Astarte.[2]
Now to the agricultural Semites the Baal or god of a land
was the author of all its fertility ; he it was who produced
the corn, the wine, the figs, the oil, and the flax, by means
of his quickening waters, which in the arid parts of the
Semitic world are oftener springs, streams, and underground
flow than the rains of heaven.[3] Further, "the life-giving
power of the god was not limited to vegetative nature, but
to him also was ascribed the increase of animal life, the

[1] Or the Deuteronomic redactor, as
the critics call him. See W. Robertson
Smith, *The Old Testament in the
Jewish Church*[2] (London and Edin-
burgh, 1892), pp. 395 *sq.*, 425 ;
Encyclopaedia Biblica, ii. 2078 *sqq.*,
2633 *sqq.*, iv. 4273 *sqq.* ; K. Budde,
Geschichte der althebräischen Litteratur
(Leipsic, 1906), pp. 99, 121 *sqq.*, 127
sqq., 132 ; Principal J. Skinner, in his
introduction to Kings (in *The Century
Bible*), pp. 10 *sqq.*

[2] Menander of Ephesus, quoted by

Josephus, *Contra Apionem*, i. 18 (*Fragmenta Historicorum Graecorum*, ed.
C. Müller, iv. 446) ; G. A. Cooke,
Text-book of North-Semitic Inscriptions,
No. 4, p. 26. According to Justin,
however, the priest of Hercules, that
is, of Melcarth, at Tyre, was distinct
from the king and second to him in
dignity. See Justin, xviii. 4. 5.

[3] Hosea ii. 5 *sqq.* ; W. Robertson
Smith, *Religion of the Semites*[2] (London, 1894), pp. 95-107.

multiplication of flocks and herds, and, not least, of the human inhabitants of the land. For the increase of animate nature is obviously conditioned, in the last resort, by the fertility of the soil, and primitive races, which have not learned to differentiate the various kinds of life with precision, think of animate as well as vegetable life as rooted in the earth and sprung from it. The earth is the great mother of all things in most mythological philosophies, and the comparison of the life of mankind, or of a stock of men, with the life of a tree, which is so common in Semitic as in other primitive poetry, is not in its origin a mere figure. Thus where the growth of vegetation is ascribed to a particular divine power, the same power receives the thanks and homage of his worshippers for the increase of cattle and of men. Firstlings as well as first-fruits were offered at the shrines of the Baalim, and one of the commonest classes of personal names given by parents to their sons or daughters designates the child as the gift of the god." In short, "the Baal was conceived as the male principle of reproduction, the husband of the land which he fertilised."[1] So far, therefore, as the Semite personified the reproductive energies of nature as male and female, as a Baal and a Baalath, he appears to have identified the male power especially with water and the female especially with earth. On this view plants and trees, animals and men, are the offspring or children of the Baal and Baalath.

If, then, at Byblus and elsewhere, the Semitic king was allowed, or rather required, to personate the god and marry the goddess, the intention of the custom can only have been to ensure the fertility of the land and the increase of men and cattle by means of homoeopathic magic. There is reason to think that a similar custom was observed from a similar motive in other parts of the ancient world, and particularly at Nemi, where both the male and the female powers, the Dianus and Diana, were in one aspect of their nature personifications of the life-giving waters.[2] *Personation of the Baal by the king.*

The last king of Byblus bore the ancient name of Cinyras, and was beheaded by Pompey the Great for his *Cinyras, king of Byblus.*

[1] W. Robertson Smith, *Religion of the Semites*,[2] pp. 107 *sq.*

[2] *The Magic Art and the Evolution of Kings*, ii. 120 *sqq.*, 376 *sqq.*

tyrannous excesses.[1]   His legendary namesake Cinyras is
said to have founded a sanctuary of Aphrodite, that is, of
Astarte, at a place on Mount Lebanon, distant a day's
journey from the capital.[2]   The spot was probably Aphaca,
at the source of the river Adonis, half-way between Byblus
and Baalbec ; for at Aphaca there was a famous grove
and sanctuary of Astarte which Constantine destroyed on

Aphaca
and the
vale of the
Adonis. account of the flagitious character of the worship.[3]   The site
of the temple has been discovered by modern travellers near
the miserable village which still bears the name of Afka at
the head of the wild, romantic, wooded gorge of the Adonis.
The hamlet stands among groves of noble walnut-trees on
the brink of the lyn.   A little way off the river rushes
from a cavern at the foot of a mighty amphitheatre of
towering cliffs to plunge in a series of cascades into the
awful depths of the glen.   The deeper it descends, the
ranker and denser grows the vegetation, which, sprouting
from the crannies and fissures of the rocks, spreads a
green veil over the roaring or murmuring stream in the
tremendous chasm below.   There is something delicious,
almost intoxicating, in the freshness of these tumbling
waters, in the sweetness and purity of the mountain air, in
the vivid green of the vegetation.   The temple, of which
some massive hewn blocks and a fine column of Syenite
granite still mark the site, occupied a terrace facing the
source of the river and commanding a magnificent prospect.
Across the foam and the roar of the waterfalls you look
up to the cavern and away to the top of the sublime
precipices above.   So lofty is the cliff that the goats
which creep along its ledges to browse on the bushes
appear like ants to the spectator hundreds of feet below.
Seaward the view is especially impressive when the sun
floods the profound gorge with golden light, revealing all
the fantastic buttresses and rounded towers of its mountain rampart, and falling softly on the varied green of the
woods which clothe its depths.[4]   It was here that, according

---

[1] Strabo, xvi. 1. 18, p. 755.

[2] Lucian, *De dea Syria*, 9.

[3] Eusebius, *Vita Constantini*, iii. 55 ;
Sozomenus, *Historia Ecclesiastica*, ii. 5 ;
Socrates, *Historia Ecclesiastica*, i. 18 ;

Zosimus, i. 58.

[4] On the valley of the Nahr Ibrahim,
its scenery and monuments, see Edward
Robinson, *Biblical Researches in Palestine*[3] (London, 1867), iii. 603-609 ;

to the legend, Adonis met Aphrodite for the first or the last time,[1] and here his mangled body was buried.[2]   A fairer scene could hardly be imagined for a story of tragic love and death.   Yet, sequestered as the valley is and must always have been, it is not wholly deserted.   A convent or a village may be observed here and there standing out against the sky on the top of some beetling crag, or clinging to the face of a nearly perpendicular cliff high above the foam and the din of the river ; and at evening the lights that twinkle through the gloom betray the presence of human habitations on slopes which might seem inaccessible to man.   In antiquity the whole of the lovely vale appears to have been dedicated to Adonis, and to this day it is haunted by his memory ; for the heights which shut it in Monu-are crested at various points by ruined monuments of his ments of worship, some of them overhanging dreadful abysses, down which it turns the head dizzy to look and see the eagles wheeling about their nests far below.   One such monument exists at Ghineh.   The face of a great rock, above a roughly hewn recess, is here carved with figures of Adonis and Aphrodite.   He is portrayed with spear in rest, awaiting the attack of a bear, while she is seated in an attitude of sorrow.[3]   Her grief-stricken figure may well be the mourning

W. M. Thomson, *The Land and the Book, Lebanon, Damascus, and beyond Jordan* (London, 1886), pp. 239-246 ; E. Renan, *Mission de Phénicie*, pp. 282 *sqq.*; G. Maspero, *Histoire Ancienne des Peuples de l'Orient Classique*, ii. (Paris, 1897) pp. 175-179 ; Sir Charles Wilson, *Picturesque Palestine* (London, N.D.), iii. 16, 17, 27.   Among the trees which line the valley are oak, sycamore, bay, plane, orange, and mulberry (W. M. Thomson, *op. cit.* p. 245).   Travellers are unanimous in testifying to the extraordinary beauty of the vale of the Adonis.   Thus Robinson writes : "There is no spot in all my wanderings on which memory lingers with greater delight than on the sequestered retreat and exceeding love-liness of Afka."   Renan says that the landscape is one of the most beautiful in the world.   My friend the late Sir Francis Galton wrote to me (20th

September 1906) : "I have no good map of Palestine, but strongly suspect that my wanderings there, quite sixty years ago, took me to the place you mention, above the gorge of the river Adonis.   Be that as it may, I have constantly asserted that the view I then had of a deep ravine and blue sea seen through the cliffs that bounded it, was the most beautiful I had ever set eyes on."

[1] *Etymologicum Magnum*, *s.v.* Ἄφακα, p. 175.

[2] Melito, "Oration to Antoninus Caesar," in W. Cureton's *Spicilegium Syriacum* (London, 1855), p. 44.

[3] E. Renan, *Mission de Phénicie*, pp. 292-294.   The writer seems to have no doubt that the beast attacking Adonis is a bear, not a boar.   Views of the monument are given by A. Jeremias, *Das Alte Testament im Lichte des Alten Orients*[2] (Leipsic, 1906), p.

Aphrodite of the Lebanon described by Macrobius,[1] and the recess in the rock is perhaps her lover's tomb. Every year, in the belief of his worshippers, Adonis was wounded to death on the mountains, and every year the face of nature itself was dyed with his sacred blood. So year by year the Syrian damsels lamented his untimely fate,[2] while the red anemone, his flower, bloomed among the cedars of Lebanon, and the river ran red to the sea, fringing the winding shores of the blue Mediterranean, whenever the wind set inshore, with a sinuous band of crimson.

90, and by Baudissin, *Adonis und Esmun*, plates i. and ii., with his discussion, pp. 78 *sqq.*

[1] Macrobius, *Saturn.* i. 21. 5.

[2] Lucian, *De dea Syria*, 8.

CHAPTER III

ADONIS IN CYPRUS

THE island of Cyprus lies but one day's sail from the coast of Syria. Indeed, on fine summer evenings its mountains may be descried looming low and dark against the red fires of sunset.[1] With its rich mines of copper and its forests of firs and stately cedars, the island naturally attracted a commercial and maritime people like the Phoenicians; while the abundance of its corn, its wine, and its oil must have rendered it in their eyes a Land of Promise by comparison with the niggardly nature of their own rugged coast, hemmed in between the mountains and the sea.[2] Accordingly they settled in Cyprus at a very early date and remained there long after the Greeks had also established themselves on its shores; for we know from inscriptions and coins that Phoenician kings reigned at Citium, the Chittim of the Hebrews, down to the time of Alexander the Great.[3]

[1] F. C. Movers, *Die Phoenizier*, ii. 2, p. 224; G. Maspero, *Histoire Ancienne des Peuples de l'Orient Classique*, ii. 199; G. A. Smith, *Historical Geography of the Holy Land* (London, 1894), p. 135.

[2] On the natural wealth of Cyprus see Strabo, xiv. 6. 5; W. H. Engel, *Kypros*, i. 40-71; F. C. Movers, *Die Phoenizier*, ii. 2, pp. 224 *sq.*; G. Maspero, *Histoire Ancienne des Peuples de l'Orient Classique*, ii. 200 *sq.*; E. Oberhummer, *Die Insel Cypern*, i. (Munich, 1903) pp. 175 *sqq.*, 243 *sqq.* As to the firs and cedars of Cyprus see Theophrastus, *Historia Plantarum*, v. 7. 1, v. 9. 1. The Cyprians boasted that they could build

and rig a ship complete, from her keel to her topsails, with the native products of their island (Ammianus Marcellinus, xiv. 8. 14).

[3] G. A. Cooke, *Text-Book of North-Semitic Inscriptions*, Nos. 12-25, pp. 55-76, 347-349; P. Gardner, *New Chapters in Greek History* (London, 1892), pp. 179, 185. It has been held that the name of Citium is etymologically identical with Hittite. If that was so, it would seem that the town was built and inhabited by a non-Semitic people before the arrival of the Phoenicians. See *Encyclopaedia Biblica*, *s.v.* "Kittim." Other traces of this older race, akin to the primitive stock of Asia Minor, have been detected in Cyprus;

Naturally the Semitic colonists brought their gods with them from the mother-land. They worshipped Baal of the Lebanon,[1] who may well have been Adonis, and at Amathus on the south coast they instituted the rites of Adonis and Aphrodite, or rather Astarte.[2] Here, as at Byblus, these rites resembled the Egyptian worship of Osiris so closely that some people even identified the Adonis of Amathus with Osiris.[3] The Tyrian Melcarth or Moloch was also worshipped at Amathus,[4] and the tombs discovered in the neighbourhood prove that the city remained Phoenician to a late period.[5]

Kingdom of Paphos.

But the great seat of the worship of Aphrodite and Adonis in Cyprus was Paphos on the south-western side of the island. Among the petty kingdoms into which Cyprus was divided from the earliest times until the end of the fourth century before our era Paphos must have ranked with the best. It is a land of hills and billowy ridges, diversified by fields and vineyards and intersected by rivers, which in the course of ages have carved for themselves beds of such tremendous depth that travelling in the interior is difficult and tedious. The lofty range of Mount Olympus (the modern Troodos), capped with snow the greater part of the year, screens Paphos from the northerly and easterly winds and cuts it off from the rest of the island. On the slopes of the range the last pine-woods of Cyprus linger, sheltering here and there monasteries

---

amongst them the most obvious is the Cyprian syllabary, the characters of which are neither Phoenician nor Greek in origin. See P. Gardner, *op. cit.* pp. 154, 173-175, 178 *sq.*

[1] G. A. Cooke, *Text-Book of North-Semitic Inscriptions*, No. 11, p. 52.

[2] Stephanus Byzantius, *s.v.* Ἀμαθοῦς; Pausanias, ix. 41. 2 *sq.* According to Pausanias, there was a remarkable necklace of green stones and gold in the sanctuary of Adonis and Aphrodite at Amathus. The Greeks commonly identified it with the necklace of Harmonia or Eriphyle. A terra-cotta statuette of Astarte, found at Amathus (?), represents her wearing a necklace which she touches with one hand. See L. P. di Cesnola,

Cyprus (London, 1877), p. 275. The scanty ruins of Amathus occupy an isolated hill beside the sea. Among them is an enormous stone jar, half buried in the earth, of which the four handles are adorned with figures of bulls. It is probably of Phoenician manufacture. See L. Ross, *Reisen nach Kos, Halikarnassos, Rhodes und der Insel Cypern* (Halle, 1852), pp. 168 *sqq.*

[3] Stephanus Byzantius, *s.v.* Ἀμαθοῦς. For the relation of Adonis to Osiris at Byblus see below, vol. ii. pp. 9 *sq.*, 22 *sq.*, 127.

[4] Hesychius, *s.v.* Μάλικα.

[5] L. P. di Cesnola, *Cyprus*, pp. 254-283; G. Perrot et Ch. Chipiez, *Histoire de l'Art dans l'Antiquité*, iii. (Paris, 1885) pp. 216-222.

in scenery not unworthy of the Apennines. The old city of
Paphos occupied the summit of a hill about a mile from the
sea ; the newer city sprang up at the harbour some ten miles
off.[1] The sanctuary of Aphrodite at Old Paphos (the
modern Kuklia) was one of the most celebrated shrines in
the ancient world. From the earliest to the latest times it
would seem to have preserved its essential features unchanged. For the sanctuary is represented on coins of the
Imperial age,[2] and these representations agree closely with
little golden models of a shrine which were found in two of
the royal graves at Mycenae.[3] Both on the coins and in
the models we see a façade surmounted by a pair of doves
and divided into three compartments or chapels, of which
the central one is crowned by a lofty superstructure. In
the golden models each chapel contains a pillar standing in
a pair of horns : the central superstructure is crowned by
two pairs of horns, one within the other ; and the two side
chapels are in like manner crowned each with a pair of horns
and a single dove perched on the outer horn of each pair.
On the coins each of the side chapels contains a pillar or
candelabra-like object : the central chapel contains a cone
and is flanked by two high columns, each terminating in a
pair of ball-topped pinnacles, with a star and crescent
appearing between the tops of the columns. The doves are
doubtless the sacred doves of Aphrodite or Astarte,[4] and the

Sanctuary of Aphrodite at Paphos.

[1] D. G. Hogarth, *Devia Cypria*
(London, 1889), pp. 1-3 ; *Encyclopaedia Britannica,*[9] vi. 747 ; Élisée
Reclus, *Nouvelle Géographie Universelle* (Paris, 1879–1894), ix. 668.

[2] T. L. Donaldson, *Architectura
Numismatica* (London, 1859), pp. 107-
109, with fig. 31 ; *Journal of Hellenic
Studies,* ix. (1888) pp. 210-213 ; G.
F. Hill, *Catalogue of the Greek Coins
of Cyprus* (London, 1904), pp. cxxvii-
cxxxiv, with plates xiv. 2, 3, 6-8, xv.
1-4, 7, xvi. 2, 4, 6-9, xvii. 4-6, 8, 9,
xxvi. 3, 6-16 ; George Macdonald,
*Catalogue of Greek Coins in the Hun-
terian Collection* (Glasgow, 1899–1905),
ii. 566, with pl. lxi. 19. As to the
existing remains of the temple, which
were excavated by an English expedition in 1887–1888, see " Excavations
in Cyprus, 1887-1888," *Journal of Hel-*

lenic Studies, ix. (1888) pp. 193 *sqq.*
Previous accounts of the temple are in-
accurate and untrustworthy.

[3] C. Schuchhardt, *Schliemann's
Ausgrabungen*[2] (Leipsic, 1891), pp.
231-233 ; G. Perrot et Ch. Chipiez,
Histoire de l'Art dans l'Antiquité, vi.
(Paris, 1894) pp. 336 *sq.,* 652-654 ;
Journal of Hellenic Studies, ix. (1888)
pp. 213 *sq.* ; P. Gardner, *New Chap-
ters in Greek History,* p. 181.

[4] J. Selden, *De dis Syris* (Leipsic,
1668), pp. 274 *sqq.* ; S. Bochart,
Hierozoicon, Editio Tertia (Leyden,
1692), ii. 4 *sqq.* Compare the statue
of a priest with a dove in his hand,
which was found in Cyprus (Perrot et
Chipiez, *Histoire de l'Art dans l'Antiquité,* iii. Paris, 1885, p. 510), with
fig. 349.

horns and pillars remind us of the similar religious emblems which have been found in the great prehistoric palace of Cnossus in Crete, as well as on many monuments of the Mycenaean or Minoan age of Greece.[1] If antiquaries are right in regarding the golden models as copies of the Paphian shrine, that shrine must have suffered little outward change for more than a thousand years ; for the royal graves at Mycenae, in which the models were found, can hardly be of later date than the twelfth century before our era.

The Aphrodite of Paphos a Phoenician or aboriginal deity.Thus the sanctuary of Aphrodite at Paphos was apparently of great antiquity.[2] According to Herodotus, it was founded by Phoenician colonists from Ascalon ;[3] but it is possible that a native goddess of fertility was worshipped on the spot before the arrival of the Phoenicians, and that the newcomers identified her with their own Baalath or Astarte, whom she may have closely resembled. If two deities were thus fused in one, we may suppose that they were both varieties of that great goddess of motherhood and fertility whose worship appears to have been spread all over Her conical image.Western Asia from a very early time. The supposition is confirmed as well by the archaic shape of her image as by the licentious character of her rites ; for both that shape and those rites were shared by her with other Asiatic deities. Her image was simply a white cone or pyramid.[4]

---

[1] A. J. Evans, "Mycenaean Tree and Pillar Cult," *Journal of Hellenic Studies*, xxi. (1901) pp. 99 *sqq.*

[2] Tacitus, *Annals*, iii. 62.

[3] Herodotus, i. 105 ; compare Pausanias, i. 14. 7. Herodotus only speaks of the sanctuary of Aphrodite in Cyprus, but he must refer to the great one at Paphos. At Ascalon a goddess was worshipped in mermaid-shape under the name of Derceto, and fish and doves were sacred to her (Diodorus Siculus, ii. 4 ; compare Lucian, *De dea Syria*, 14). The name Derceto, like the much more correct Atargatis, is a Greek corruption of '*Attâr*, the Aramaic form of *Astarte*, but the two goddesses Atargatis and Astarte, in spite of the affinity of their names, appear to have been historically dis-

tinct. See Ed. Meyer, *Geschichte des Altertums*,[2] i. 2 (Stuttgart and Berlin, 1909), pp. 605, 650 *sq.* ; F. Baethgen, *Beiträge zur Semitischen Religionsgeschichte* (Berlin, 1888), pp. 68 *sqq.* ; F. Cumont, *s.vv.* "Atargatis" and "Dea Syria," in Pauly-Wissowa's *Real-Encyclopädie der classischen Altertumswissenschaft* ; René Dussaud, *Notes de Mythologie Syrienne* (Paris, 1903), pp. 82 *sqq.* ; R. A. Stewart Macalister, *The Philistines, their History and Civilization* (London, 1913), pp. 94 *sqq.*

[4] It is described by ancient writers and figured on coins. See Tacitus, *Hist.* ii. 3 ; Maximus Tyrius, *Dissert.* viii. 8 ; Servius on Virgil, *Aen.* i. 720 ; T. L. Donaldson, *Architectura Numismatica*, p. 107, with fig. 31 ; *Journal of Hellenic Studies*, ix. (1888) pp. 210-

In like manner, a cone was the emblem of Astarte at Byblus,[1] of the native goddess whom the Greeks called Artemis at Perga in Pamphylia,[2] and of the sun-god Heliogabalus at Emesa in Syria.[3] Conical stones, which apparently served as idols, have also been found at Golgi in Cyprus, and in the Phoenician temples of Malta;[4] and cones of sandstone came to light at the shrine of the "Mistress of Torquoise" among the barren hills and frowning precipices of Sinai.[5] The precise significance of such

---

212. According to Maximus Tyrius, the material of the pyramid was unknown. Probably it was a stone. The English archaeologists found several fragments of white cones on the site of the temple at Paphos : one which still remains in its original position in the central chamber was of limestone and of somewhat larger size (*Journal of Hellenic Studies*, ix. (1888) p. 180).

[1] See above, p. 14.

[2] On coins of Perga the sacred cone is represented as richly decorated and standing in a temple between sphinxes. See B. V. Head, *Historia Numorum* (Oxford, 1887), p. 585 ; P. Gardner, *Types of Greek Coins* (Cambridge, 1883), pl. xv. No. 3 ; G. F. Hill, *Catalogue of the Greek Coins of Lycia, Pamphylia, and Pisidia* (London, 1897), pl. xxiv. 12, 15, 16. However, Mr. G. F. Hill writes to me : "Is the stone at Perga really a cone? I have always thought it was a cube or something of that kind. On the coins the upper, sloping portion is apparently an elaborate veil or headdress. The head attached to the stone is seen in the middle of this, surmounted by a tall *kalathos*." The sanctuary stood on a height, and a festival was held there annually (Strabo, xiv. 4. 2, p. 667). The native title of the goddess was *Anassa*, that is, "Queen." See B. V. Head, *l.c.* ; Wernicke, *s.v.* "Artemis," in Pauly-Wissowa, *Real-Encyclopädie der classischen Altertumswissenschaft*, ii. 1, col. 1397. Aphrodite at Paphos bore the same title. See below, p. 42, note [5]. The worship of Pergaean Artemis at Halicarnassus was cared for by a priestess,

who held office for life and had to make intercession for the city at every new moon. See G. Dittenberger, *Sylloge Inscriptionum Graecarum* [2] (Leipsic, 1898–1901), vol. ii. p. 373, No. 601.

[3] Herodian, v. 3. 5. This cone was of black stone, with some small knobs on it, like the stone of Cybele at Pessinus. It is figured on coins of Emesa. See B. V. Head, *Historia Numorum* (Oxford, 1887), p. 659 ; P. Gardner, *Types of Greek Coins*, pl. xv. No. 1. The sacred stone of Cybele, which the Romans brought from Pessinus to Rome during the Second Punic War, was small, black, and rugged, but we are not told that it was of conical shape. See Arnobius, *Adversus Nationes*, vii. 49; Livy, xxix. 11. 7. According to one reading, Servius (on Virgil, *Aen.* vii. 188) speaks of the stone of Cybele as a needle (*acus*), which would point to a conical shape. But the reading appears to be without manuscript authority, and other emendations have been suggested.

[4] G. Perrot et Ch. Chipiez, *Histoire de l'Art dans l'Antiquité*, iii. 273, 298 *sq.*, 304 *sq.* The sanctuary of Aphrodite, or rather Astarte, at Golgi is said to have been even more ancient than her sanctuary at Paphos (Pausanias, viii. 5. 2).

[5] W. M. Flinders Petrie, *Researches in Sinai* (London, 1906), pp. 135 *sq.*, 189. Votive cones made of clay have been found in large numbers in Babylonia, particularly at Lagash and Nippur. See M. Jastrow, *The Religion of Babylonia and Assyria* (Boston, U.S.A., 1898), pp. 672-674.

an emblem remains as obscure as it was in the time of
Tacitus.[1]   It appears to have been customary to anoint the
sacred cone with olive oil at a solemn festival, in which
people from Lycia and Caria participated.[2]   The custom of
anointing a holy stone has been observed in many parts of
the world; for example, in the sanctuary of Apollo at Delphi.[3]
To this day the old custom appears to survive at Paphos, for
" in honour of the Maid of Bethlehem the peasants of Kuklia
anointed lately, and probably still anoint each year, the
great corner-stones of the ruined Temple of the Paphian
Goddess.   As Aphrodite was supplicated once with cryptic
rites, so is Mary entreated still by Moslems as well as
Christians, with incantations and passings through perforated
stones, to remove the curse of barrenness from Cypriote
women, or increase the manhood of Cypriote men."[4]   Thus
the ancient worship of the goddess of fertility is continued
under a different name.   Even the name of the old goddess
is retained in some parts of the island ; for in more than
one chapel the Cypriote peasants adore the mother of Christ
under the title of Panaghia Aphroditessa.[5]

Sacred
prostitu-
tion in the
worship
of the
Paphian
Aphrodite
and of
other
Asiatic
goddesses.

In Cyprus it appears that before marriage all women
were formerly obliged by custom to prostitute themselves to
strangers at the sanctuary of the goddess, whether she went
by the name of Aphrodite, Astarte, or what not.[6]   Similar
customs prevailed in many parts of Western Asia.   Whatever its motive, the practice was clearly regarded, not as an
orgy of lust, but as a solemn religious duty performed in
the service of that great Mother Goddess of Western Asia
whose name varied, while her type remained constant, from
place to place.   Thus at Babylon every woman, whether
rich or poor, had once in her life to submit to the embraces
of a stranger at the temple of Mylitta, that is, of Ishtar or

[1] Tacitus, *Hist.* ii. 3.

[2] We learn this from an inscription
found at Paphos.   See *Journal of
Hellenic Studies*, ix. (1888) pp. 188,
231.

[3] Pausanias, x. 24. 6, with my note.

[4] D. G. Hogarth, *A Wandering
Scholar in the Levant* (London, 1896),
pp. 179 *sq.*   Women used to creep
through a holed stone to obtain children
at a place on the Dee in Aberdeen-

shire.   See *Balder the Beautiful*, ii.
187.

[5] G. Perrot et Ch. Chipiez, *Histoire
de l'Art dans l'Antiquité*, iii. 628.

[6] Herodotus, i. 199 ; Athenaeus,
xii. 11, p. 516 A ; Justin, xviii. 5. 4 ;
Lactantius, *Divin. Inst.* i. 17 ; W. H.
Engel, *Kypros*, ii. 142 *sqq.*   Asiatic
customs of this sort have been rightly
explained by W. Mannhardt (*Antike
Wald- und Feldkulte*, pp. 283 *sqq.*).

Astarte, and to dedicate to the goddess the wages earned by this sanctified harlotry. The sacred precinct was crowded with women waiting to observe the custom. Some of them had to wait there for years.[1] At Heliopolis or Baalbec in Syria, famous for the imposing grandeur of its ruined temples, the custom of the country required that every maiden should prostitute herself to a stranger at the temple of Astarte, and matrons as well as maids testified their devotion to the goddess in the same manner. The emperor Constantine abolished the custom, destroyed the temple, and built a church in its stead.[2] In Phoenician temples women prostituted themselves for hire in the service of religion, believing that by this conduct they propitiated the goddess and won her favour.[3] "It was a law of the Amorites, that

---

[1] Herodotus, i. 199; Strabo, xvi. 1. 20, p. 745. As to the identity of Mylitta with Astarte see H. Zimmern in E. Schrader's *Die Keilinschriften und das alte Testament,*[3] pp. 423, note[7], 428, note[4]. According to him, the name Mylitta comes from *Mu'allidtu,* "she who helps women in travail." In this character Ishtar would answer to the Greek Artemis and the Latin Diana. As to sacred prostitution in the worship of Ishtar see M. Jastrow, *The Religion of Babylonia and Assyria,* pp. 475 *sq.,* 484 *sq.*; P. Dhorme, *La Religion Assyro-Babylonienne* (Paris, 1910), pp. 86, 300 *sq.*

[2] Eusebius, *Vita Constantini,* iii. 58; Socrates, *Historia Ecclesiastica,* i. 18. 7-9; Sozomenus, *Historia Ecclesiastica,* v. 10. 7. Socrates says that at Heliopolis local custom obliged the women to be held in common, so that paternity was unknown, "for there was no distinction of parents and children, and the people prostituted their daughters to the strangers who visited them" (τοῖς παριοῦσι ξένοις). The prostitution of matrons as well as of maids is mentioned by Eusebius. As he was born and spent his life in Syria, and was a contemporary of the practices he describes, the bishop of Caesarea had the best opportunity of informing himself as to them, and we ought not, as Prof. M. P. Nilsson does (*Griechische Feste,* Leipsic, 1906, p. 366 n.[2]), to allow his

positive testimony on this point to be outweighed by the silence of the later historian Sozomenus, who wrote long after the custom had been abolished. Eusebius had good reason to know the heathenish customs which were kept up in his diocese; for he was sharply taken to task by Constantine for allowing sacrifices to be offered on altars under the sacred oak or terebinth at Mamre; and in obedience to the imperial commands he caused the altars to be destroyed and an oratory to be built instead under the tree. So in Ireland the ancient heathen sanctuaries under the sacred oaks were converted by Christian missionaries into churches and monasteries. See Socrates, *Historia Ecclesiastica,* i. 18; *The Magic Art and the Evolution of Kings,* ii. 242 *sq.*

[3] Athanasius, *Oratio contra Gentes,* 26 (Migne's *Patrologia Graeca,* xxv. 52), γυναῖκες γοῦν ἐν εἰδωλείοις τῆς Φοινίκης πάλαι προεκαθέζοντο, ἀπαρχόμεναι τοῖς ἐκεῖ θέοις ἑαυτῶν τὴν τοῦ σώματος αὐτῶν μισθαρνίαν, νομίζουσαι τῇ πορνείᾳ τὴν θέον ἑαυτῶν ἰλάσκεσθαι καὶ εἰς εὐμένειαν ἄγειν αὐτὴν διὰ τούτων. The account of the Phoenician custom which is given by H. Ploss (*Das Weib,*[2] i. 302) and repeated after him by Fr. Schwally (*Semitische Kriegsaltertümer,* Leipsic, 1901, pp. 76 *sq.*) may rest only on a misapprehension of this passage of Athanasius. But if it is correct,

she who was about to marry should sit in fornication seven
days by the gate." [1]   At Byblus the people shaved their
heads in the annual mourning for Adonis.   Women who
refused to sacrifice their hair had to give themselves up to
strangers on a certain day of the festival, and the money
which they thus earned was devoted to the goddess. [2]   This
custom may have been a mitigation of an older rule which
at Byblus as elsewhere formerly compelled every woman
without exception to sacrifice her virtue in the service of
religion.   I have already suggested a reason why the
offering of a woman's hair was accepted as an equivalent
for the surrender of her person. [3]   We are told that in Lydia
all girls were obliged to prostitute themselves in order to
earn a dowry ; [4] but we may suspect that the real motive
of the custom was devotion rather than economy.   The
suspicion is confirmed by a Greek inscription found at
Tralles in Lydia, which proves that the practice of religious
prostitution survived in that country as late as the second
century of our era.   It records of a certain woman, Aurelia
Aemilia by name, not only that she herself served the god
in the capacity of a harlot at his express command, but that
her mother and other female ancestors had done the same
before her ; and the publicity of the record, engraved on a
marble column which supported a votive offering, shows that
no stain attached to such a life and such a parentage. [5]   In
Armenia the noblest families dedicated their daughters to
the service of the goddess Anaitis in her temple at Acilisena,
where the damsels acted as prostitutes for a long time before
they were given in marriage.   Nobody scrupled to take one
of these girls to wife when her period of service was over. [6]

---

we may conjecture that the slaves who
deflowered the virgins were the sacred
slaves of the temples, the *ḳedeshim*, and
that they discharged this office as the
living representatives of the god. As to
these *ḳedeshim*, or "sacred men," see
above, pp. 17 *sq.*, and below, pp. 72 *sqq.*

[1] *The Testaments of the Twelve
Patriarchs*, translated and edited by
R. H. Charles (London, 1908), chapter
xii. p. 81.

[2] Lucian, *De dea Syria*, 6. The
writer is careful to indicate that none

but strangers were allowed to enjoy
the women (ἡ δὲ ἀγορὴ μούνοισι ξείνοισι
παρακέεται).

[3] *The Magic Art and the Evolution
of Kings*, i. 30 *sq.*

[4] Herodotus, i. 93 *sq.* ; Athenaeus,
xii. 11, pp. 515 *sq.*

[5] W. M. Ramsay, "Unedited Inscriptions of Asia Minor," *Bulletin de Corre-
spondance Hellénique*, vii. (1883) p. 276 ;
id., *Cities and Bishoprics of Phrygia*,
i. (Oxford, 1895) pp. 94 *sq.*, 115.

[6] Strabo, xi. 14. 16, p. 532.

Again, the goddess Ma was served by a multitude of sacred harlots at Comana in Pontus, and crowds of men and women flocked to her sanctuary from the neighbouring cities and country to attend the biennial festivals or to pay their vows to the goddess.[1]

If we survey the whole of the evidence on this subject, some of which has still to be laid before the reader, we may conclude that a great Mother Goddess, the personification of all the reproductive energies of nature, was worshipped under different names but with a substantial similarity of myth and ritual by many peoples of Western Asia ; that associated with her was a lover, or rather series of lovers, divine yet mortal, with whom she mated year by year, their commerce being deemed essential to the propagation of animals and plants, each in their several kind ;[2] and further, that the fabulous union of the divine pair was simulated and, as it were, multiplied on earth by the real, though temporary, union of the human sexes at the sanctuary of the goddess for the sake of thereby ensuring the fruitfulness of the ground and the increase of man and beast.[3] And if the

The Asiatic Mother Goddess a personification of all the reproductive energies of nature.

---

[1] Strabo, xii. 3. 32, 34 and 36, pp. 557-559 ; compare xii. 2. 3, p. 535. Other sanctuaries in Pontus, Cappadocia, and Phrygia swarmed with sacred slaves, and we may conjecture, though we are not told, that many of these slaves were prostitutes. See Strabo, xi. 8. 4, xii. 2. 3 and 6, xii. 3. 31 and 37, xii. 8. 14.

[2] On this great Asiatic goddess and her lovers see especially Sir W. M. Ramsay, *Cities and Bishoprics of Phrygia*, i. 87 *sqq.*

[3] Compare W. Mannhardt, *Antike Wald- und Feldkulte*, pp. 284 *sq.* ; W. Robertson Smith, *The Prophets of Israel*, New Edition (London, 1902), pp. 171-174. Similarly in Camul, formerly a province of the Chinese Empire, the men used to place their wives at the disposal of any foreigners who came to lodge with them, and deemed it an honour if the guests made use of their opportunities. The emperor, hearing of the custom, forbade the people to observe it. For three years they obeyed, then, finding that their lands

were no longer fruitful and that many mishaps befell them, they prayed the emperor to allow them to retain the custom, "for it was by reason of this usage that their gods bestowed upon them all the good things that they possessed, and without it they saw not how they could continue to exist." See *The Book of Ser Marco Polo*, translated and edited by Colonel Henry Yule, Second Edition (London, 1875), i. 212 *sq.* Here apparently the fertility of the soil was deemed to depend on the intercourse of the women with strangers, not with their husbands. Similarly, among the Oulad Abdi, an Arab tribe of Morocco, "the women often seek a divorce and engage in prostitution in the intervals between their marriages ; during that time they continue to dwell in their families, and their relations regard their conduct as very natural. The administrative authority having bestirred itself and attempted to regulate this prostitution, the whole population opposed the attempt, alleging that such a measure

Her
worship
perhaps
reflects a
period of
sexual
commun-
ism.

conception of such a Mother Goddess dates, as seems probable, from a time when the institution of marriage was either unknown or at most barely tolerated as an immoral infringement of old communal rights, we can understand both why the goddess herself was regularly supposed to be at once unmarried and unchaste, and why her worshippers were obliged to imitate her more or less completely in these respects.   For had she been a divine wife united to a divine husband, the natural counterpart of their union would have been the lawful marriage of men and women, and there would have been no need to resort to a system of prostitution or promiscuity in order to effect those purposes which, on the principles of homoeopathic magic, might in that case have been as well or better attained by the legitimate intercourse of the sexes in matrimony.   Formerly, perhaps, every woman was obliged to submit at least once in her life to the exercise of those marital rights which at a still earlier period had theoretically belonged in permanence to all the males of the tribe.   But in course of time, as the institution of individual marriage grew in favour, and the old communism fell more and more into discredit, the revival of the ancient practice even for a single occasion in a woman's life became ever more repugnant to the moral sense of the people, and accordingly they resorted to various expedients for evading in practice the obligation which they still acknowledged in theory.   One of these evasions was to let the woman offer her hair instead of her person ; another apparently was to substitute an obscene symbol for the obscene act.[1]   But while the majority of women thus contrived to observe the forms of religion without sacrificing their virtue, it was still thought necessary to the general welfare that a certain number of them should discharge the old obligation in the old way.   These became prostitutes either for life or for a term of years at one of the temples : dedicated to the service of religion, they were invested with

---

would impair the abundance of the crops." See Edmond Doutté, *Magie et Religion dans l'Afrique du Nord* (Algiers, 1908), pp. 560 *sq.*
[1] Clement of Alexandria, *Protrept.*

ii. 14, p. 13, ed. Potter ; Arnobius, *Adversus Nationes*, v. 19 ; compare Firmicus Maternus, *De errore profanarum religionum*, 10.

a sacred character,[1] and their vocation, far from being deemed infamous, was probably long regarded by the laity as an exercise of more than common virtue, and rewarded with a tribute of mixed wonder, reverence, and pity, not unlike that which in some parts of the world is still paid to women who seek to honour their Creator in a different way by renouncing the natural functions of their sex and the tenderest relations of humanity. It is thus that the folly of mankind finds vent in opposite extremes alike harmful and deplorable.

At Paphos the custom of religious prostitution is said to have been instituted by King Cinyras,[2] and to have been practised by his daughters, the sisters of Adonis, who, having incurred the wrath of Aphrodite, mated with strangers and ended their days in Egypt.[3] In this form of the tradition the wrath of Aphrodite is probably a feature added by a later authority, who could only regard conduct which shocked his own moral sense as a punishment inflicted by the goddess instead of as a sacrifice regularly enjoined by her on all her devotees. At all events the story indicates that the princesses of Paphos had to conform to the custom as well as women of humble birth.

The daughters of Cinyras.

The legendary history of the royal and priestly family of the Cinyrads is instructive. We are told that a Syrian man, by name Sandacus, migrated to Cilicia, married Pharnace, daughter of Megassares, king of Hyria, and founded the city of Celenderis. His wife bore him a son, Cinyras, who in time crossed the sea with a company of people to Cyprus, wedded Metharme, daughter of Pygmalion, king of the island, and founded Paphos.[4] These legends

The Paphian dynasty of the Cinyrads.

---

[1] In Hebrew a temple harlot was regularly called " a sacred woman " (*kĕdēsha*). See *Encyclopaedia Biblica*, *s.v.* " Harlot " ; S. R. Driver, on Genesis xxxviii. 21. As to such "sacred women " see below, pp. 70 *sqq.*

[2] Clement of Alexandria, *Protrept.* ii. 13, p. 12, ed. Potter : Arnobius, *Adversus Nationes*, v. 19 ; Firmicus Maternus, *De errore profanarum religionum*, 10.

[3] Apollodorus, *Bibliotheca*, iii. 14. 3.

[4] Apollodorus, *Bibliotheca*, iii. 14. 3. I follow the text of R. Wagner's edition in reading Μεγασσάρου τοῦ

Τριέων βασιλέως. As to Hyria in Isauria see Stephanus Byzantius, *s.v.* Ύρία. The city of Celenderis, on the south coast of Cilicia, possessed a small harbour protected by a fortified peninsula. Many ancient tombs survived till recent times, but have now mostly disappeared. It was the port from which the Turkish couriers from Constantinople used to embark for Cyprus. As to the situation and remains see F. Beaufort, *Karmania* (London, 1817), p. 201 ; W. M. Leake, *Journal of a Tour in Asia Minor* (London, 1824), pp. 114-118 ; R. Heberdey und A.

seem to contain reminiscences of kingdoms in Cilicia and Cyprus which passed in the female line, and were held by men, sometimes foreigners, who married the hereditary princesses. There are some indications that Cinyras was not in fact the founder of the temple at Paphos. An older tradition ascribed the foundation to a certain Aerias, whom some regarded as a king, and others as the goddess herself.[1] Moreover, Cinyras or his descendants at Paphos had to reckon with rivals. These were the Tamirads, a family of diviners who traced their descent from Tamiras, a Cilician augur. At first it was arranged that both families should preside at the ceremonies, but afterwards the Tamirads gave way to the Cinyrads.[2] Many tales were told of Cinyras, the founder of the dynasty. He was a priest of Aphrodite as well as a king,[3] and his riches passed into a proverb.[4] To his descendants, the Cinyrads, he appears to have bequeathed his wealth and his dignities ; at all events, they reigned as kings of Paphos and served the goddess as priests. Their dead bodies, with that of Cinyras himself, were buried in the sanctuary.[5] But by the fourth century before our era the family had declined and become nearly extinct. When Alexander the Great expelled a king of Paphos for injustice and wickedness, his envoys made search for a member of the ancient house to set on the throne of his fathers. At last they found one of

Wilhelm, "Reisen in Kilikien," *Denk-schriften der kais. Akademie der Wissenschaften, Philosoph.-historische Classe,* xliv. (1896) No. vi. p. 94. The statement that the sanctuary of Aphrodite at Paphos was founded by the Arcadian Agapenor, who planted a colony in Cyprus after the Trojan war (Pausanias, viii. 5. 2), may safely be disregarded.

[1] Tacitus, *Hist.* ii. 3 ; *Annals,* iii. 62.

[2] Tacitus, *Hist.* ii. 3 ; Hesychius, *s.v.* Ταμιράδαι.

[3] Pindar, *Pyth.* ii. 13-17.

[4] Tyrtaeus, xii. 6 (*Poetae Lyrici Graeci,* ed. Th. Bergk,[3] Leipsic, 1866–1867, ii. 404) ; Pindar, *Pyth.* viii. 18 ; Plato, *Laws,* ii. 6, p. 660 E ; Clement of Alexandria, *Paedag.* iii. 6, p. 274, ed. Potter ; Dio Chrysostom, *Orat.*

viii. (vol. i. p. 149, ed. L. Dindorf) ; Julian, *Epist.* lix. p. 574, ed. F. C. Hertlein ; Diogenianus, viii. 53 ; Suidas, *s.v.* Καταγηράσαις.

[5] Schol. on Pindar, *Pyth.* ii. 15 (27) ; Hesychius, *s.v.* Κινυράδαι ; Clement of Alexandria, *Protrept.* iii. 45, p. 40, ed. Potter ; Arnobius, *Adversus Nationes,* vi. 6. That the kings of Paphos were also priests of the goddess is proved, apart from the testimony of ancient writers, by inscriptions found on the spot. See H. Collitz, *Sammlung der griechischen Dialektinschriften,* i. (Göttingen, 1884) p. 22, Nos. 38, 39, 40. The title of the goddess in these inscriptions is Queen or Mistress (Ϝαναϭ(σ)ας). It is perhaps a translation of the Semitic Baalath.

them living in obscurity and earning his bread as a market gardener. He was in the very act of watering his beds when the king's messengers carried him off, much to his astonishment, to receive the crown at the hands of their master.[1] Yet if the dynasty decayed, the shrine of the goddess, enriched by the offerings of kings and private persons, maintained its reputation for wealth down to Roman times.[2] When Ptolemy Auletes, king of Egypt, was expelled by his people in 57 B.C., Cato offered him the priesthood of Paphos as a sufficient consolation in money and dignity for the loss of a throne.[3]

Among the stories which were told of Cinyras, the ancestor of these priestly kings and the father of Adonis, there are some that deserve our attention. In the first place, he is said to have begotten his son Adonis in incestuous intercourse with his daughter Myrrha at a festival of the corn-goddess, at which women robed in white were wont to offer corn-wreaths as first-fruits of the harvest and to observe strict chastity for nine days.[4] Similar cases of incest with

Incest of Cinyras with his daughter Myrrha, and birth of Adonis.

[1] Plutarch, *De Alexandri Magni fortuna aut virtute*, ii. 8. The name of the gardener-king was Alynomus. That the Cinyrads existed as a family down to Macedonian times is further proved by a Greek inscription found at Old Paphos, which records that a certain Democrates, son of Ptolemy, head of the Cinyrads, and his wife Eunice, dedicated a statue of their daughter to the Paphian Aphrodite. See L. Ross, "Inschriften von Cypern," *Rheinisches Museum*, N.F. vii. (1850) pp. 520 sq. It seems to have been a common practice of parents to dedicate statues of their sons or daughters to the goddess at Paphos. The inscribed pedestals of many such statues were found by the English archaeologists. See *Journal of Hellenic Studies*, ix. (1888) pp. 228, 235, 236, 237, 241, 244, 246, 255.

[2] Tacitus, *Hist.* ii. 4; Pausanias, viii. 24. 6.

[3] Plutarch, *Cato the Younger*, 35.

[4] Ovid, *Metam.* x. 298 sqq.; Hyginus, *Fab.* 58, 64; Fulgentius, *Mytholog.* iii. 8; Lactantius Placidius, *Narrat. Fabul.* x. 9; Servius on Virgil, *Ecl.* x. 18, and *Aen.* v. 72;

Plutarch, *Parallela*, 22; Schol. on Theocritus, i. 107. It is Ovid who describes (*Metam.* x. 431 sqq.) the festival of Ceres, at which the incest was committed. His source was probably the *Metamorphoses* of the Greek writer Theodorus, which Plutarch (*l.c.*) refers to as his authority for the story. The festival in question was perhaps the Thesmophoria, at which women were bound to remain chaste (Schol. on Theocritus, iv. 25; Schol. on Nicander, *Ther.* 70 sq.; Pliny, *Nat. Hist.* xxiv. 59; Dioscorides, *De Materia Medica*, i. 134 (135); compare Aelian, *De natura animalium*, ix. 26). Compare E. Fehrle, *Die kultische Keuschheit im Altertum* (Giessen, 1910), pp. 103 sqq., 121 sq., 151 sqq. The corn and bread of Cyprus were famous in antiquity. See Aeschylus, *Suppliants*, 549 (555); Hipponax, cited by Strabo, viii. 3. 8, p. 340; Eubulus, cited by Athenaeus, iii. 78, p. 112 F; E. Oberhummer, *Die Insel Cypern*, i. (Munich, 1903) pp. 274 sqq. According to another account, Adonis was the fruit of the incestuous intercourse of Theias, a Syrian

Legends
of royal
incest—a
suggested
explana-
tion.

a daughter are reported of many ancient kings.[1] It seems
unlikely that such reports are without foundation, and perhaps equally improbable that they refer to mere fortuitous
outbursts of unnatural lust. We may suspect that they are
based on a practice actually observed for a definite reason
in certain special circumstances. Now in countries where
the royal blood was traced through women only, and where
consequently the king held office merely in virtue of his
marriage with an hereditary princess, who was the real sovereign, it appears to have often happened that a prince
married his own sister, the princess royal, in order to obtain
with her hand the crown which otherwise would have gone
to another man, perhaps to a stranger.[2] May not the same
rule of descent have furnished a motive for incest with a
daughter? For it seems a natural corollary from such a
rule that the king was bound to vacate the throne on the
death of his wife, the queen, since he occupied it only by
virtue of his marriage with her. When that marriage
terminated, his right to the throne terminated with it and
passed at once to his daughter's husband. Hence if the
king desired to reign after his wife's death, the only way
in which he could legitimately continue to do so was
by marrying his daughter, and thus prolonging through
her the title which had formerly been his through her
mother.

---

king, with his daughter Myrrha.
See Apollodorus, *Bibliotheca*, iii. 14.
4 (who cites Panyasis as his authority) ; J. Tzetzes, *Schol. on Lycophron*, 829 ; Antoninus Liberalis,
Transform. 34 (who lays the scene of
the story on Mount Lebanon). With
the corn-wreaths mentioned in the
text we may compare the wreaths which
the Roman Arval Brethren wore at
their sacred functions, and with which
they seem to have crowned the images
of the goddesses. See G. Henzen, *Acta
Fratrum Arvalium* (Berlin, 1874), pp.
24-27, 33 *sq.* Compare Pausanias, vii.
20. 1. *sq.*

[1] A list of these cases is given by
Hyginus, *Fab.* 253. It includes the
incest of Clymenus, king of Arcadia,
with his daughter Harpalyce (compare

Hyginus, *Fab.* 206) ; that of Oeno-
maus, king of Pisa, with his daughter
Hippodamia (compare J. Tzetzes,
Schol. on Lycophron, 156 ; Lucian,
Charidemus, 19) ; that of Erechtheus,
king of Athens, with his daughter
Procris ; and that of Epopeus, king
of Lesbos, with his daughter Nyctimene
(compare Hyginus, *Fab.* 204).

[2] The custom of brother and sister
marriage seems to have been especially
common in royal families. See my
note on Pausanias, i. 7. 1 (vol. ii. pp.
84 *sq.*) ; as to the case of Egypt see
below, vol. ii. pp. 213 *sqq.* The true
explanation of the custom was first,
so far as I know, indicated by J. F.
McLennan (*The Patriarchal Theory*,
London, 1885, p. 95).

In this connexion it is worth while to remember that at Rome the Flamen Dialis was bound to vacate his priesthood on the death of his wife, the Flaminica.[1] The rule would be intelligible if the Flaminica had originally been the more important functionary of the two, and if the Flamen held office only by virtue of his marriage with her.[2] Elsewhere I have shown reason to suppose that he and his wife represented an old line of priestly kings and queens, who played the parts of Jupiter and Juno, or perhaps rather Dianus and Diana, respectively.[3] If the supposition is correct, the custom which obliged him to resign his priesthood on the death of his wife seems to prove that of the two deities whom they personated, the goddess, whether named Juno or Diana, was indeed the better half. But at Rome the goddess Juno always played an insignificant part; whereas at Nemi her old double, Diana, was all-powerful, casting her mate, Dianus or Virbius, into deep shadow. Thus a rule which points to the superiority of the Flaminica over the Flamen, appears to indicate that the divine originals of the two were Dianus and Diana rather than Jupiter and Juno; and further, that if Jupiter and Juno at Rome stood for the principle of father-kin, or the predominance of the husband over the wife, Dianus and Diana at Nemi stood for the older principle of mother-kin, or the predominance of the wife in matters of inheritance over the husband. If, then, I am right in holding that the kingship at Rome was originally a plebeian institution and descended through women,[4] we must conclude that the people who founded the sanctuary of Diana at Nemi were of the same plebeian stock as the Roman kings, that they traced descent in the female line, and that they worshipped a great Mother Goddess, not a great Father God. That goddess was Diana; her maternal functions are abundantly proved by the votive offerings found at her ancient shrine among the wooded hills.[5] On the other hand, the

---

[1] Aulus Gellius, x. 15. 22; J. Marquardt, *Römische Staatsverwaltung*, iii.[2] (Leipsic, 1885) p. 328.

[2] Priestesses are said to have preceded priests in some Egyptian cities. See W. M. Flinders Petrie, *The Religion of Ancient Egypt* (London, 1906), p. 74.

[3] *The Magic Art and the Evolution of Kings*, ii. 179, 190 *sqq.*

[4] *The Magic Art and the Evolution of Kings*, ii. 268 *sqq.*

[5] *The Magic Art and the Evolution of Kings*, i. 12 note [1].

patricians, who afterwards invaded the country, brought with them father-kin in its strictest form, and consistently enough paid their devotions rather to Father Jove than to Mother Juno.

Priestesses among the Khasis of Assam. A parallel to what I conjecture to have been the original relation of the Flaminica to her husband the Flamen may to a certain extent be found among the Khasis of Assam, who preserve to this day the ancient system of mother-kin in matters of inheritance and religion. For among these people the propitiation of deceased ancestors is deemed essential to the welfare of the community, and of all their ancestors they revere most the primaeval ancestress of the clan. Accordingly in every sacrifice a priest must be assisted by a priestess ; indeed, we are told that he merely acts as her deputy, and that she " is without doubt a survival of the time when, under the matriarchate, the priestess was the agent for the performance of all religious ceremonies." It does not appear that the priest need be the husband of the priestess ; but in the Khyrim State, where each division has its own goddess to whom sacrifices are offered, the priestess is the mother, sister, niece, or other maternal relation of the priest. It is her duty to prepare all the sacrificial articles, and without her assistance the sacrifice cannot take place.[1] Here, then, as among the ancient Romans on my hypothesis, we have the superiority of the priestess over the priest based on a corresponding superiority of the goddess or divine ancestress over the god or divine ancestor ; and here, as at Rome, a priest would clearly have to vacate office if he had no woman of the proper relationship to assist him in the performance of his sacred duties.

Sacred marriage of a priest and priestess as representatives of the Sun-god and the Earth-goddess. Further, I have conjectured that as representatives of Jupiter and Juno respectively the Flamen and Flaminica at Rome may have annually celebrated a Sacred Marriage for the purpose of ensuring the fertility of the powers of nature.[2] This conjecture also may be supported by an analogous custom which is still observed in India. We have seen how among the Oraons, a primitive hill-tribe of Bengal, the

[1] Major P. R. T. Gurdon, *The Khasis* (London, 1907), pp. 109-112, 120 *sq.*

[2] *The Magic Art and the Evolution of Kings*, ii. 191 *sqq.*

marriage of the Sun and the Earth is annually celebrated
by a priest and priestess who personate respectively the god
of the Sun and the goddess of the Earth.[1] The ceremony
of the Sacred Marriage has been described more fully by a
Jesuit missionary, who was intimately acquainted with the
people and their native religion. The rite is celebrated in
the month of May, when the *sal* tree is in bloom, and the
festival takes its native name (*khaddi*) from the flower of the
tree. It is the greatest festival of the year. " The object
of this feast is to celebrate the mystical marriage of the
Sun-god (*Bhagawan*) with the Goddess-earth (*Dharti-mai*),
to induce them to be fruitful and give good crops." At the
same time all the minor deities or demons of the village are
propitiated, in order that they may not hinder the beneficent
activity of the Sun God and the Earth Goddess. On the
eve of the appointed day no man may plough his fields, and
the priest, accompanied by some of the villagers, repairs to
the sacred grove, where he beats a drum and invites all the
invisible guests to the great feast that will await them on
the morrow. Next morning very early, before cock-crow,
an acolyte steals out as quietly as possible to the sacred
spring to fetch water in a new earthen pot. This holy water
is full of all kinds of blessings for the crops. The priest has
prepared a place for it in the middle of his house surrounded
by cotton threads of diverse colours. So sacred is the water
that it would be defiled and lose all its virtue, were any profane eye to fall on it before it entered the priest's house.
During the morning the acolyte and the priest's deputy go
round from house to house collecting victims for the sacrifice.
In the afternoon the people all gather at the sacred grove,
and the priest proceeds to consummate the sacrifice. The
first victims to be immolated are a white cock for the Sun
God and a black hen for the Earth Goddess ; and as the
feast is the marriage of these great deities the marriage
service is performed over the two fowls before they are
hurried into eternity. Amongst other things both birds are
marked with vermilion just as a bride and bridegroom are
marked at a human marriage ; and the earth is also smeared
with vermilion, as if it were a real bride, on the spot where

---

[1] *The Magic Art and the Evolution of Kings*, ii. 148.

the sacrifice is offered.   Sacrifices of fowls or goats to the
minor deities or demons follow.   The bodies of the victims
are collected by the village boys, who cook them on the
spot ; all the heads go to the sacrificers.   The gods take
what they can get and are more or less thankful.   Meantime
the acolyte has collected flowers of the *sal* tree and set them
round the place of sacrifice, and he has also fetched the holy
water from the priest's house.   A procession is now formed
Marriage of
the Sun-
god and
Earth-
goddess
acted by a
priest and
his wife.and the priest is carried in triumph to his own abode.   There
his wife has been watching for him, and on his arrival the
two go through the marriage ceremony, applying vermilion
to each other in the usual way " to symbolise the mystical
marriage of the Sun-god with the Earth-goddess."   Meantime
all the women of the village are standing on the thresholds
of their houses each with a winnowing-fan in her hand.
In the fan are two cups, one empty to receive the holy
water, and the other full of rice-beer for the consumption of
the holy man.   As he arrives at each house, he distributes
flowers and holy water to the happy women, and enriches
them with a shower of blessings, saying, " May your rooms
and granary be filled with rice, that the priest's name may
be great."   The holy water which he leaves at each house
is sprinkled on the seeds that have been kept to sow next
year's crop.   Having thus imparted his benediction to the
household the priest swigs the beer ; and as he repeats his
benediction and his potation at every house he is naturally
dead-drunk by the time he gets to the end of the village.
" By that time every one has taken copious libations of rice-
beer, and all the devils of the village seem to be let loose,
and there follows a scene of debauchery baffling description
—all these to induce the Sun and the Earth to be fruitful." [1]

Thus the people of Cyprus and Western Asia in antiquity
were by no means singular in their belief that the profligacy
of the human sexes served to quicken the fruits of the
earth. [2]

Cinyras is said to have been famed for his exquisite

---

[1] The late Rev. P. Dehon, S.J.,
" Religion and Customs of the Uraons,"
*Memoirs of the Asiatic Society of
Bengal,* vol. i. No. 9 (Calcutta, 1906),
pp. 144-146.

[2] For more evidence see *The Magic
Art and the Evolution of Kings,* ii.
97 *sqq.*

beauty[1] and to have been wooed by Aphrodite herself.[2] Thus it would appear, as scholars have already observed,[3] that Cinyras was in a sense a duplicate of his handsome son Adonis, to whom the inflammable goddess also lost her heart. Further, these stories of the love of Aphrodite for two members of the royal house of Paphos can hardly be dissociated from the corresponding legend told of Pygmalion, the Phoenician king of Cyprus, who is said to have fallen in love with an image of Aphrodite and taken it to his bed.[4] When we consider that Pygmalion was the father-in-law of Cinyras, that the son of Cinyras was Adonis, and that all three, in successive generations, are said to have been concerned in a love-intrigue with Aphrodite, we can hardly help concluding that the early Phoenician kings of Paphos, or their sons, regularly claimed to be not merely the priests of the goddess[5] but also her lovers, in other words, that in their official capacity they personated Adonis. At all events Adonis is said to have reigned in Cyprus,[6] and it appears to be certain that the title of Adonis was regularly borne by the sons of all the Phoenician kings of the island.[7] It is true that the title strictly signified no more than "lord"; yet the legends which connect these Cyprian princes with the goddess of love make it probable that they claimed the

Marginal notes:
Cinyras beloved by Aphrodite.

Pygmalion and Aphrodite.

The Phoenician kings of Cyprus or their sons appear to have been hereditary lovers of the goddess.

---

[1] Lucian, *Rhetorum praeceptor*, 11; Hyginus, *Fab.* 270.

[2] Clement of Alexandria, *Protrept.* ii. 33, p. 29, ed. Potter.

[3] W. H. Engel, *Kypros*, ii. 585, 612; A. Maury, *Histoire des Religions de la Grèce Antique* (Paris, 1857–1859), iii. 197, note [3].

[4] Arnobius, *Adversus Nationes*, vi. 22; Clement of Alexandria, *Protrept.* iv. 57, p. 51, ed. Potter; Ovid, *Metam.* x. 243-297. The authority for the story is the Greek history of Cyprus by Philostephanus, cited both by Arnobius and Clement. In Ovid's poetical version of the legend Pygmalion is a sculptor, and the image with which he falls in love is that of a lovely woman, which at his prayer Venus endows with life. That King Pygmalion was a Phoenician is mentioned by Porphyry (*De abstinentia*, iv. 15) on the authority of Asclepiades,

a Cyprian.

[5] See above, p. 42.

[6] Probus, on Virgil, *Ecl.* x. 18. I owe this reference to my friend Mr. A. B. Cook.

[7] In his treatise on the political institutions of Cyprus, Aristotle reported that the sons and brothers of the kings were called "lords" (ἄνακτες), and their sisters and wives "ladies" (ἄνασσαι). See Harpocration and Suidas, *s.v.* Ἄνακτες. Compare Isocrates, ix. 72; Clearchus of Soli, quoted by Athenaeus, vi. 68, p. 256 A. Now in the bilingual inscription of Idalium, which furnished the clue to the Cypriote syllabary, the Greek version gives the title Fάναξ as the equivalent of the Phoenician *Adon* (אדן). See *Corpus Inscriptionum Semiticarum*, i. No. 89; G. A. Cooke, *Text-book of North-Semitic Inscriptions*, p. 74, note [1].

divine nature as well as the human dignity of Adonis. The
story of Pygmalion points to a ceremony of a sacred
marriage in which the king wedded the image of Aphrodite,
or rather of Astarte. If that was so, the tale was in a sense
true, not of a single man only, but of a whole series of men,
and it would be all the more likely to be told of Pygmalion,
if that was a common name of Semitic kings in general,
and of Cyprian kings in particular. Pygmalion, at all
events, is known as the name of the famous king of Tyre
from whom his sister Dido fled ;[1] and a king of Citium
and Idalium in Cyprus, who reigned in the time of Alexander the Great, was also called Pygmalion, or rather Pumi-
yathon, the Phoenician name which the Greeks corrupted
into Pygmalion.[2] Further, it deserves to be noted that
the names Pygmalion and Astarte occur together in a Punic
inscription on a gold medallion which was found in a grave
at Carthage ; the characters of the inscription are of the
earliest type.[3] As the custom of religious prostitution at
Paphos is said to have been founded by King Cinyras and

Sacred
marriage
of the
kings of
Paphos.

observed by his daughters,[4] we may surmise that the kings
of Paphos played the part of the divine bridegroom in a
less innocent rite than the form of marriage with a statue ;
in fact, that at certain festivals each of them had to mate
with one or more of the sacred harlots of the temple, who
played Astarte to his Adonis. If that was so, there is more
truth than has commonly been supposed in the reproach
cast by the Christian fathers that the Aphrodite worshipped

[1] Josephus, *Contra Apionem*, i. 18,
ed. B. Niese ; Appian, *Punica*, 1 ;
Virgil, *Aen.* i. 346 *sq.* ; Ovid, *Fasti*,
iii. 574 ; Justin, xviii. 4 ; Eustathius
on Dionysius Periegetes, 195 (*Geographi Graeci Minores*, ed. C. Müller
Paris, 1882, ii. 250 *sq.*).

[2] Pumi-yathon, son of Milk-yathon,
is known from Phoenician inscriptions
found at Idalium. See G. A. Cooke,
*Text-book of North-Semitic Inscrip-
tions*, Nos. 12 and 13, pp. 55 *sq.*,
57 *sq.* Coins inscribed with the name
of King Pumi-yathon are also in existence. See G. F. Hill, *Catalogue of
the Greek Coins of Cyprus* (London,
1904), pp. xl. *sq.*, 21 *sq.*, pl. iv. 20-
24. He was deposed by Ptolemy

(Diodorus Siculus, xix. 79. 4). Most
probably he is the Pymaton of Citium
who purchased the kingdom from a
dissolute monarch named Pasicyprus
some time before the conquests of
Alexander (Athenaeus, iv. 63, p. 167).
In this passage of Athenaeus the name
Pymaton, which is found in the MSS.
and agrees closely with the Phoenician
Pumi-yathon, ought not to be changed
into Pygmalion, as the latest editor
(G. Kaibel) has done.

[3] G. A. Cooke, *op. cit.* p. 55, note [1].
Mr. Cooke remarks that the form
of the name (פגמלין instead of פמיית)
must be due to Greek influence.

[4] See above, p. 41.

by Cinyras was a common whore.[1]   The fruit of their union
would rank as sons and daughters of the deity, and would
in time become the parents of gods and goddesses, like
their fathers and mothers before them.   In this manner
Paphos, and perhaps all sanctuaries of the great Asiatic
goddess where sacred prostitution was practised, might be
well stocked with human deities, the offspring of the divine
king by his wives, concubines, and temple harlots.   Any one
of these might probably succeed his father on the throne[2]
or be sacrificed in his stead whenever stress of war or other
grave junctures called, as they sometimes did,[3] for the death
of a royal victim.   Such a tax, levied occasionally on the
king's numerous progeny for the good of the country, would
neither extinguish the divine stock nor break the father's
heart, who divided his paternal affection among so many.
At all events, if, as there seems reason to believe, Semitic
kings were often regarded at the same time as hereditary
deities, it is easy to understand the frequency of Semitic
personal names which imply that the bearers of them were
the sons or daughters, the brothers or sisters, the fathers or
mothers of a god, and we need not resort to the shifts
employed by some scholars to evade the plain sense of the
words.[4]   This interpretation is confirmed by a parallel

*Sons and
daughters,
fathers and
mothers of
a god.*

[1] Clement of Alexandria, *Protrept.*
ii. 13, p. 12; Arnobius, *Adversus
Nationes*, v. 9; Firmicus Maternus,
De errore profanarum religionum, 10.

[2] That the king was not necessarily
succeeded by his eldest son is proved
by the case of Solomon, who on his
accession executed his elder brother
Adoni-jah (1 Kings ii. 22-24).   Similarly, when Abimelech became king
of Shechem, he put his seventy brothers
in ruthless oriental fashion to death.
See Judges viii. 29-31, ix. 5 *sq.*, 18.
So on his accession Jehoram, King
of Judah, put all his brothers to the
sword (2 Chronicles xxi. 4).   King
Rehoboam had eighty-eight children
(2 Chronicles xi. 21) and King Abi-jah
had thirty-eight (2 Chronicles xiii. 21).
These examples illustrate the possible
size of the family of a polygamous king.

[3] *The Dying God*, pp. 160 *sqq.*

[4] The names which imply that a
man was the father of a god have
proved particularly puzzling to some
eminent Semitic scholars.   See W.
Robertson Smith, *Religion of the
Semites*,[2] p. 45, note[2]; Th. Nöldeke,
s.v. "Names," *Encyclopaedia Biblica*,
iii. 3287 *sqq.*; W. W. Graf Baudissin,
Adonis und Esmun, pp. 39 *sq.*, 43
sqq.   Such names are Abi-baal ("father
of Baal"), Abi-el ("father of El"),
Abi-jah ("father of Jehovah"), and
Abi-melech ("father of a king" or
"father of Moloch").   On the hypothesis put forward in the text the
father of a god and the son of a god
stood precisely on the same footing,
and the same person would often be
both one and the other.   Where the
common practice prevailed of naming
a father after his son (*Taboo and the
Perils of the Soul*, pp. 331 *sqq.*), a
divine king in later life might often be
called "father of such-and-such a god."

Egyptian usage; for in Egypt, where the kings were worshipped as divine,[1] the queen was called "the wife of the
god" or "the mother of the god,"[2] and the title "father
of the god" was borne not only by the king's real father
but also by his father-in-law.[3] Similarly, perhaps, among
the Semites any man who sent his daughter to swell the
royal harem may have been allowed to call himself "the
father of the god."

Cinyras,
like King
David, a
harper.
If we may judge by his name, the Semitic king who
bore the name of Cinyras was, like King David, a harper;
for the name of Cinyras is clearly connected with the Greek
cinyra, "a lyre," which in its turn comes from the Semitic
kinnor, "a lyre," the very word applied to the instrument
on which David played before Saul.[4] We shall probably
not err in assuming that at Paphos as at Jerusalem the
music of the lyre or harp was not a mere pastime designed
to while away an idle hour, but formed part of the service
of religion, the moving influence of its melodies being perhaps set down, like the effect of wine, to the direct inspira-
The use of
music as a
means of
prophetic
inspiration
among the
Hebrews.
tion of a deity. Certainly at Jerusalem the regular clergy
of the temple prophesied to the music of harps, of psalteries,
and of cymbals;[5] and it appears that the irregular clergy
also, as we may call the prophets, depended on some such
stimulus for inducing the ecstatic state which they took for
immediate converse with the divinity.[6] Thus we read of a
band of prophets coming down from a high place with a
psaltery, a timbrel, a pipe, and a harp before them, and
prophesying as they went.[7] Again, when the united forces
of Judah and Ephraim were traversing the wilderness of
Moab in pursuit of the enemy, they could find no water for

---

[1] *The Magic Art and the Evolution
of Kings*, i. 418 *sq.*

[2] A. Erman, *Aegypten und aegyptisches Leben im Altertum* (Tübingen,
N.D.), p. 113.

[3] L. Borchardt, "Der ägyptische
Titel 'Vater des Gottes' als Bezeich-
nung für 'Vater oder Schwiegervater
des Königs,'" *Berichte über die Verhandlungen der Königlich Sächsischen
Gesellschaft der Wissenschaften zu
Leipzig, Philolog.-histor. Klasse*, lvii.
(1905) pp. 254-270.

[4] F. C. Movers, *Die Phoenizier*,
i. 243; Stoll, *s.v.* "Kinyras," in
W. H. Roscher's *Lexikon der griech.
und röm. Mythologie*, ii. 1191; I
Samuel xvi. 23.

[5] 1 Chronicles xxv. 1-3; compare
2 Samuel vi. 5.

[6] W. Robertson Smith, *The Prophets
of Israel*[2] (London, 1902), pp. 391
sq.; E. Renan, *Histoire du peuple
d'Israel* (Paris, 1893), ii. 280.

[7] 1 Samuel x. 5.

three days, and were like to die of thirst, they and the beasts
of burden.   In this emergency the prophet Elisha, who was
with the army, called for a minstrel and bade him play.
Under the influence of the music he ordered the soldiers
to dig trenches in the sandy bed of the waterless waddy
through which lay the line of march.   They did so, and
next morning the trenches were full of the water that had
drained down into them underground from the desolate,
forbidding mountains on either hand.   The prophet's success
in striking water in the wilderness resembles the reported
success of modern dowsers, though his mode of procedure
was different.   Incidentally he rendered another service
to his countrymen.   For the skulking Moabites from their
lairs among the rocks saw the red sun of the desert reflected
in the water, and taking it for the blood, or perhaps rather
for an omen of the blood, of their enemies, they plucked up
heart to attack the camp and were defeated with great
slaughter.[1]

Again, just as the cloud of melancholy which from time
to time darkened the moody mind of Saul was viewed as
an evil spirit from the Lord vexing him, so on the other
hand the solemn strains of the harp, which soothed and composed his troubled thoughts,[2] may well have seemed to the
hag-ridden king the very voice of God or of his good angel
whispering peace.   Even in our own day a great religious
writer, himself deeply sensitive to the witchery of music, has
said that musical notes, with all their power to fire the blood
and melt the heart, cannot be mere empty sounds and nothing
more ; no, they have escaped from some higher sphere, they
are outpourings of eternal harmony, the voice of angels, the
Magnificat of saints.[3]   It is thus that the rude imaginings
of primitive man are transfigured and his feeble lispings
echoed with a rolling reverberation in the musical prose of
Newman.   Indeed the influence of music on the develop-

The influence of music on religion.

---

[1] 2 Kings iii. 4-24. And for the
explanation of the supposed miracle,
see W. Robertson Smith, *The Old
Testament in the Jewish Church*[2]
(London and Edinburgh, 1892), pp.
146 *sq.*   I have to thank Professor
Kennett for the suggestion that the
Moabites took the ruddy light on the
water for an omen of blood rather
than for actual gore.

[2] 1 Samuel xvi. 14-23.

[3] J. H. Newman, *Sermons preached
before the University of Oxford*, No.
xv. pp. 346 *sq.* (third edition).

ment of religion is a subject which would repay a sympathetic study. For we cannot doubt that this, the most intimate and affecting of all the arts, has done much to create as well as to express the religious emotions, thus modifying more or less deeply the fabric of belief to which at first sight it seems only to minister. The musician has done his part as well as the prophet and the thinker in the making of religion. Every faith has its appropriate music, and the difference between the creeds might almost be expressed in musical notation. The interval, for example, which divides the wild revels of Cybele from the stately ritual of the Catholic Church is measured by the gulf which severs the dissonant clash of cymbals and tambourines from the grave harmonies of Palestrina and Handel. A different spirit breathes in the difference of the music.[1]

The function of string music in Greek and Semitic ritual.

The legend which made Apollo the friend of Cinyras[2] may be based on a belief in their common devotion to the lyre. But what function, we may ask, did string music perform in the Greek and the Semitic ritual? Did it serve to rouse the human mouthpiece of the god to prophetic ecstasy? or did it merely ban goblins and demons from the holy places and the holy service, drawing as it were around the worshippers a magic circle within which no evil thing might intrude? In short, did it aim at summoning good or banishing evil spirits? was its object inspiration or exorcism? The examples drawn from the lives or legends of Elisha and David prove that with the Hebrews the music of the lyre might be used for either purpose; for while Elisha employed it to tune himself to the prophetic pitch, David resorted to it for the sake of exorcising the foul fiend from Saul. With the Greeks, on the other hand, in historical times, it does not appear that string music served as a means of inducing the condition of trance or ecstasy in the human mouthpieces of Apollo and the other oracular gods; on the contrary, its sobering and composing influence, as contrasted with the exciting influence of flute music, is the aspect which chiefly impressed

---

[1] It would be interesting to pursue a similar line of inquiry in regard to the other arts. What was the influence of Phidias on Greek religion? How much does Catholicism owe to Fra Angelico?

[2] Pindar, *Pyth.* ii. 15 *sq.*

the Greek mind.[1]   The religious or, at all events, the superstitious man might naturally ascribe the mental composure
wrought by grave, sweet music to a riddance of evil spirits,
in short to exorcism ; and in harmony with this view, Pindar,
speaking of the lyre, says that all things hateful to Zeus in
earth and sea tremble at the sound of music.[2]   Yet the
association of the lyre with the legendary prophet Orpheus
as well as with the oracular god Apollo seems to hint that
in early days its strains may have been employed by the
Greeks, as they certainly were by the Hebrews, to bring on
that state of mental exaltation in which the thick·coming
fancies of the visionary are regarded as divine communica-
tions.[3]   Which of these two functions of music, the positive
or the negative, the inspiring or the protective, predominated
in the religion of Adonis we cannot say ; perhaps the
two were not clearly distinguished in the minds of his
worshippers.

A constant feature in the myth of Adonis was his
premature and violent death.   If, then, the kings of Paphos
regularly personated Adonis, we must ask whether they
imitated their divine prototype in death as in life.   Tradition
varied as to the end of Cinyras.   Some thought that he
slew himself on discovering his incest with his daughter ;[4]
others alleged that, like Marsyas, he was defeated by Apollo
in a musical contest and put to death by the victor.[5]   Yet he
cannot strictly be said to have perished in the flower of his
youth if he lived, as Anacreon averred, to the ripe age of one
hundred and sixty.[6]   If we must choose between the two
stories, it is perhaps more likely that he died a violent death
than that he survived to an age which surpassed that of

Traditions as to the death of Cinyras.

[1] On the lyre and the flute in Greek
religion and Greek thought, see L. R.
Farnell, *The Cults of the Greek States*
(Oxford, 1896–1909), iv. 243 *sqq.*

[2] Pindar, *Pyth.* i. 13 *sqq.*

[3] This seems to be the view also of
Dr. Farnell, who rightly connects the
musical with the prophetic side of
Apollo's character (*op. cit.* iv. 245).

[4] Hyginus, *Fab.* 242. So in the
version of the story which made Adonis
the son of Theias, the father is said to
have killed himself when he learned

what he had done (Antoninus Liberalis,
Transform. 34).

[5] Scholiast and Eustathius on
Homer, *Iliad*, xi. 20.   Compare F. C.
Movers, *Die Phoenizier*, i. 243 *sq.* ;
W. H. Engel, *Kypros*, ii. 109-116 ;
Stoll, *s.v.* "Kinyras," in W. H.
Roscher's *Lexikon der griech. und röm.
Mythologie*, ii. 1191.

[6] Anacreon, cited by Pliny, *Nat.
Hist.* vii. 154.   Nonnus also refers to
the long life of Cinyras (*Dionys.* xxxii.
212 *sq.*).

Thomas Parr by eight years,[1] though it fell far short of the antediluvian standard.   The life of eminent men in remote ages is exceedingly elastic and may be lengthened or shortened, in the interests of history, at the taste and fancy of the historian.

[1] *Encyclopaedia Britannica,*[9] xiv. 858.

CHAPTER IV

SACRED MEN AND WOMEN

§ 1. *An Alternative Theory*

IN the preceding chapter we saw that a system of sacred prostitution was regularly carried on all over Western Asia, and that both in Phoenicia and in Cyprus the practice was specially associated with the worship of Adonis. As the explanation which I have adopted of the custom has been rejected in favour of another by writers whose opinions are entitled to be treated with respect, I shall devote the present chapter to a further consideration of the subject, and shall attempt to gather, from a closer scrutiny and a wider survey of the field, such evidence as may set the custom and with it the worship of Adonis in a clearer light. At the outset it will be well to examine the alternative theory which has been put forward to explain the facts.

Sacred prostitution of Western Asia.

It has been proposed to derive the religious prostitution of Western Asia from a purely secular and precautionary practice of destroying a bride's virginity before handing her over to her husband in order that "the bridegroom's intercourse should be safe from a peril that is much dreaded by men in a certain stage of culture." [1] Among

Theory of its secular origin.

---

[1] L. R. Farnell, "Sociological hypotheses concerning the position of women in ancient religion," *Archiv für Religionswissenschaft*, vii. (1904) p. 88; M. P. Nilsson, *Griechische Feste* (Leipsic, 1906), pp. 366 *sq.*; Fr. Cumont, *Les religions orientales dans le paganisme Romain* [2] (Paris, 1909), pp. 361 *sq.* A different and, in my judgment, a truer view of these customs was formerly taken by Prof. Nilsson. See his *Studia de Dionysiis Atticis* (Lund, 1900), pp. 119-121. For a large collection of facts bearing on this subject and a judicious discussion of them, see W. Hertz, "Die Sage vom Giftmädchen," *Gesammelte Abhandlungen* (Stuttgart and Berlin, 1905), pp. 195-219. My attention was drawn to this last work by Prof. G. L. Hamilton of the University of Michigan after my

the objections which may be taken to this view are the following :—

The theory does not account for the religious character of the custom,

(1) The theory fails to account for the deeply religious character of the customs as practised in antiquity all over Western Asia. That religious character appears from the observance of the custom at the sanctuaries of a great goddess, the dedication of the wages of prostitution to her, the belief of the women that they earned her favour by prostituting themselves,[1] and the command of a male deity to serve him in this manner.[2]

nor for the prostitution of married women,

(2) The theory fails to account for the prostitution of married women at Heliopolis[3] and apparently also at Babylon and Byblus ; for in describing the practice at the two latter places our authorities, Herodotus and Lucian, speak only of women, not of virgins.[4] In Israel also we know from Hosea that young married women prostituted themselves at the sanctuaries on the hilltops under the shadow of the sacred oaks, poplars, and terebinths.[5] The prophet makes no mention of virgins participating in these orgies. They may have done so, but his language does not imply it : he speaks only of "your daughters" and "your daughters-in-law." The prostitution of married women is wholly inexplicable on the hypothesis here criticized. Yet it can hardly be separated from the prostitution of virgins, which in some places at least was carried on side by side with it.

nor for the repeated prostitution of the same women,

(3) The theory fails to account for the repeated and professional prostitution of women in Lydia, Pontus, Armenia, and apparently all over Palestine.[6] Yet this habitual prostitution can in its turn hardly be separated

---

manuscript had been sent to the printer. With Hertz's treatment of the subject I am in general agreement, and I have derived from his learned treatise several references to authorities which I had overlooked.

[1] Above, p. 37.

[2] Above, p. 38. Prof. Nilsson is mistaken in affirming (*op. cit.* p. 367) that the Lydian practice was purely secular : the inscription which I have cited proves the contrary. Both he

and Dr. Farnell fully recognize the religious aspect of most of these customs in antiquity, and Prof. Nilsson attempts, as it seems to me, unsuccessfully, to indicate how a practice supposed to be purely secular in origin should have come to contract a religious character.

[3] Above, p. 37.

[4] Above, pp. 36 *sq.*, 38.

[5] Hosea iv. 13 *sq.*

[6] Above, pp. 37 *sqq.*

from the first prostitution in a woman's life. Or are we to suppose that the first act of unchastity is to be explained in one way and all the subsequent acts in quite another? that the first act was purely secular and all the subsequent acts purely religious?

(4) The theory fails to account for the *Kedeshim* ("sacred men") side by side with the *Kedeshoth* ("sacred women") at the sanctuaries;[1] for whatever the religious functions of these "sacred men" may have been, it is highly probable that they were analogous to those of the "sacred women" and are to be explained in the same way.

nor for the "sacred men" beside the "sacred women,"

(5) On the hypothesis which I am considering we should expect to find the man who deflowers the maid remunerated for rendering a dangerous service; and so in fact we commonly find him remunerated in places where the supposed custom is really practised.[2] But in Western Asia it was just the contrary. It was the woman who was paid, not the man; indeed, so well was she paid that in Lydia and Cyprus the girls earned dowries for themselves in this fashion.[3] This clearly shows that it was the woman, and not the man, who was believed to render the service. Or are we to suppose that the man had to pay for rendering a dangerous service?[4]

and is irreconcilable with the payment of the women.

These considerations seem to prove conclusively that whatever the remote origin of these Western Asiatic customs may have been, they cannot have been observed in his-

---

[1] See above, pp. 17 *sq.*

[2] L. di Varthema, *Travels* (Hakluyt Society, 1863), pp. 141, 202-204 (Malabar); J. A. de Mandlesloe, in J. Harris's *Voyages and Travels,* i. (London, 1744), p. 767 (Malabar); Richard, "History of Tonquin," in J. Pinkerton's *Voyages and Travels,* ix. 760 *sq.* (Aracan); A. de Morga, *The Philippine Islands, Moluccas, Siam, Cambodia, Japan, and China* (Hakluyt Society, 1868), pp. 304 *sq.* (the Philippines); J. Mallat, *Les Philippines* (Paris, 1846), i. 61 (the Philippines); L. Moncelon, in *Bulletins de la Société d'Anthropologie de Paris,* 3me Série, ix. (1886) p. 368 (New Caledonia); H. Crawford Angas, in *Verhandlungen der Berliner Gesellschaft für Anthropologie, Ethnologie*

und Urgeschichte, 1898, p. 481 (Azimba, Central Africa); Sir H. H. Johnston, *British Central Africa* (London, 1897), p. 410 (the Wa-Yao of Central Africa). See further, W. Hertz, "Die Sage vom Giftmädchen," *Gesammelte Abhandlungen,* pp. 198-204.

[3] Herodotus, i. 93; Justin, xviii. 5. 4. Part of the wages thus earned was probably paid into the local temple. See above, pp. 37, 38. However, according to Strabo (xi. 14. 16, p. 532) the Armenian girls of rich families often gave their lovers more than they received from them.

[4] This fatal objection to the theory under discussion has been clearly stated by W. Hertz, *op. cit.* p. 217. I am glad to find myself in agreement with so judicious and learned an inquirer.

torical times from any such motive as is assumed by the hypothesis under discussion. At the period when we have to do with them the customs were to all appearance purely religious in character, and a religious motive must accordingly be found for them. Such a motive is supplied by the theory I have adopted, which, so far as I can judge, adequately explains all the known facts.

The practice of destroying virginity has some-times had a religious character. At the same time, in justice to the writers whose views I have criticized, I wish to point out that the practice from which they propose to derive the sacred prostitution of Western Asia has not always been purely secular in character. For, in the first place, the agent employed is sometimes reported to be a priest ;[1] and, in the second place, the sacrifice of virginity has in some places, for example at Rome and in parts of India, been made directly to the image of a male deity.[2] The meaning of these practices is very obscure, and in the present state of our ignorance on the subject it is unsafe to build conclusions on them. It is possible that what seems to be a purely secular precaution may be only a degenerate form of a religious rite ; and on the other hand it is possible that the religious rite may go back to a purely physical preparation for marriage, such as is still observed among the aborigines of Australia.[3] But even if such an

---

[1] L. di Varthema, *Travels* (Hakluyt Society, 1863), p. 141 ; J. A. de Mandlesloe, in J. Harris's *Voyages and Travels*, i. (London, 1744) p. 767 ; A. Hamilton, "New Account of the East Indies," in J. Pinkerton's *Voyages and Travels*, viii. 374 ; Ch. Lassen, *Indische Alterthumskunde*, iv. (Leipsic, 1861), p. 408 ; A. de Herrera, *The General History of the Vast Continent and Islands of America*, translated by Captain J. Stevens (London, 1725–1726), iii. 310, 340 ; Fr. Coreal, *Voyages aux Indes Occidentales* (Amsterdam, 1722), i. 10 *sq.*, 139 *sq.* ; C. F. Ph. v. Martius, *Beiträge zur Ethnographie und Sprachenkunde Amerika's*, i. (Leipsic, 1867) pp. 113 *sq.* The first three of these authorities refer to Malabar ; the fourth refers to Cambodia ; the last three refer to the Indians of Central and South America. See further W. Hertz,

"Die Sage vom Giftmädchen," *Gesammelte Abhandlungen*, pp. 204-207. For a criticism of the Malabar evidence see K. Schmidt, *Jus primae noctis* (Freiburg im Breisgau, 1881), pp. 312-320.

[2] Lactantius, *Divin. Institut.* i. 20 ; Arnobius, *Adversus Nationes*, iv. 7 ; Augustine, *De civitate Dei*, vi. 9, vii. 24 ; D. Barbosa, *Description of the Coasts of East Africa and Malabar* (Hakluyt Society, 1866), p. 96 ; Sonnerat, *Voyage aux Indes Orientales et à la Chine* (Paris, 1782), i. 68 ; F. Liebrecht, *Zur Volkskunde* (Heilbronn, 1879), pp. 396 *sq.*, 511 ; W. Hertz, "Die Sage vom Giftmädchen," *Gesammelte Abhandlungen*, pp. 270-272. According to Arnobius, it was matrons, not maidens, who resorted to the image. This suggests that the custom was a charm to procure offspring.

[3] R. Schomburgk, in *Verhandlungen der Berliner Gesellschaft für Anthro-*

historical origin could be established, it would not explain
the motives from which the customs described in this volume
were practised by the people of Western Asia in historical
times. The true parallel to these customs is the sacred
prostitution which is carried on to this day by dedicated
women in India and Africa. An examination of these
modern practices may throw light on the ancient customs.

§ 2. Sacred Women in India

In India the dancing-girls dedicated to the service of
the Tamil temples take the name of *deva-dasis*, "servants or
slaves of the gods," but in common parlance they are spoken
of simply as harlots. Every Tamil temple of note in
Southern India has its troop of these sacred women. Their
official duties are to dance twice a day, morning and evening,
in the temple, to fan the idol with Tibetan ox-tails, to dance
and sing before it when it is borne in procession, and to
carry the holy light called *Kúmbarti*. Inscriptions show
that in A.D. 1004 the great temple of the Chola king
Rajaraja at Tanjore had attached to it four hundred " women
of the temple," who lived at free quarters in the streets round
about it and were allowed land free of taxes out of its en-
dowment. From infancy they are trained to dance and
sing. In order to obtain a safe delivery expectant mothers
will often vow to dedicate their child, if she should prove to
be a girl, to the service of God. Among the weavers of
Tiru-kalli-kundram, a little town in the Madras Presidency,
the eldest daughter of every family is devoted to the temple.
Girls thus made over to the deity are formally married,
sometimes to the idol, sometimes to a sword, before they
enter on their duties ; from which it appears that they are
often, if not regularly, regarded as the wives of the god.[1]

*Sacred
women in
the Tamil
temples of
Southern
India.*

*Such
women are
sometimes
married to
the god
and pos-
sessed by
him.*

---

pologie, Ethnologie und Urgeschichte,
1879, pp. 235 *sq.* ; Miklucho-Maclay,
ibid. 1880, p. 89 ; W. E. Roth,
*Studies among the North - West-Central
Queensland Aborigines* (Brisbane and
London, 1897), pp. 174 *sq.*, 180 ; B.
Spencer and F. J. Gillen, *Native
Tribes of Central Australia* (London,
1899), pp. 92-95 ; *id.*, *Northern Tribes*

of Central Australia (London, 1904),
pp. 133-136. In Australia the observance of the custom is regularly
followed by the exercise of what seem
to be old communal rights of the men
over the women.

[1] J. A. Dubois, *Mœurs, Institutions et Cérémonies des Peuples de
l'Inde* (Paris, 1825), ii. 353 *sqq.* ;

Among the Kaikolans, a large caste of Tamil weavers who are spread all over Southern India, at least one girl in every family should be dedicated to the temple service. The ritual, as it is observed at the initiation of one of these girls in Coimbatore, includes "a form of nuptial ceremony. The relations are invited for an auspicious day, and the maternal uncle, or his representative, ties a gold band on the girl's forehead, and, carrying her, places her on a plank before the assembled guests. A Brahman priest recites the *mantrams*, and prepares the sacred fire (*hōmam*). The uncle is presented with new cloths by the girl's mother. For the actual nuptials a rich Brahman, if possible, and, if not, a Brahman of more lowly status is invited. A Brahman is called in, as he is next in importance to, and the representative of the idol. It is said that, when the man who is to receive her first favours, joins the girl, a sword must be placed, at least for a few minutes, by her side." When one of these dancing-girls dies, her body is covered with a new cloth which has been taken for the purpose from the idol, and flowers are supplied from the temple to which she belonged. No worship is performed in the temple until the last rites have been performed over her body, because the idol, being deemed her husband, is held to be in that state of ceremonial pollution common to human mourners which debars him from the offices of religion.[1] In Mahratta such a female devotee is called Murli. Common folk believe that from time to time the shadow of the god falls on her and

---

J. Shortt, "The Bayadère or dancing-girls of Southern India," *Memoirs of the Anthropological Society of London*, iii. (1867-69) pp. 182-194; Edward Balfour, *Cyclopaedia of India*[3] (London, 1885), i. 922 *sqq.*; W. Francis, in *Census of India, 1901*, vol. xv., *Madras*, Part I. (Madras, 1902) pp. 151 *sq.*; E. Thurston, *Ethnographic Notes in Southern India* (Madras, 1906), pp. 36 *sq.*, 40 *sq.* The office of these sacred women has in recent years been abolished, on the ground of immorality, by the native Government of Mysore. See *Homeward Mail*, 6th June 1909 (extract kindly sent me by General Begbie).

[1] Edgar Thurston, *Castes and Tribes of Southern India* (Madras, 1909), iii. 37-39. Compare *id.*, *Ethnographic Notes in Southern India* (Madras, 1906), pp. 29 *sq.* In Southern India the maternal uncle often takes a prominent part in the marriage ceremony to the exclusion of the girl's father. See, for example, E. Thurston, *Castes and Tribes of Southern India*, ii. 497, iv. 147. The custom is derived from the old system of mother-kin, under which a man's heirs are not his own children but his sister's children. As to this system see below, Chapter XII., "Mother-kin and Mother Goddesses."

possesses her person.   At such times the possessed woman rocks herself to and fro, and the people occasionally consult her as a soothsayer, laying money at her feet and accepting as an oracle the words of wisdom or folly that drop from her lips.[1]   Nor is the profession of a temple prostitute adopted only by girls.   In Tulava, a district of Southern India, any woman of the four highest castes who wearies of her husband or, as a widow and therefore incapable of marriage, grows tired of celibacy, may go to a temple and eat of the rice offered to the idol.   Thereupon, if she is a Brahman, she has the right to live either in the temple or outside of its precincts, as she pleases.   If she decides to live in it, she gets a daily allowance of rice, and must sweep the temple, fan the idol, and confine her amours to the Brahmans.   The male children of these women form a special class called Moylar, but are fond of assuming the title of Stanikas.   As many of them as can find employment hang about the temple, sweeping the areas, sprinkling them with cow-dung, carrying torches before the gods, and doing other odd jobs.   Some of them, debarred from these holy offices, are reduced to the painful necessity of earning their bread by honest work.   The daughters are either brought up to live like their mothers or are given in marriage to the Stanikas.   Brahman women who do not choose to live in the temples, and all the women of the three lower castes, cohabit with any man of pure descent, but they have to pay a fixed sum annually to the temple.[2]

In Travancore a dancing-girl attached to a temple is known as a *Dâsî*, or *Dêvadâsî*, or *Dêvaratiâl*, "a servant of God."   The following account of her dedication and way of life deserves to be quoted because, while it ignores the baser side of her vocation, it brings clearly out the idea of her marriage to the deity.   "Marriage in the case of a *Dêvaratiâl* in its original import is a renunciation of ordinary family life and a consecration to the service of God.   With a lady-nurse at à Hospital, or a sister at a Convent, a *Dêvadâsî* at a Hindu shrine, such as she probably was in the early ages of Hindu

In Travancore the dancing-girls are regularly married to the god.

[1] E. Balfour, *op. cit.* ii. 1012.
[2] Francis Buchanan, "A Journey from Madras through the countries of Mysore, Canara, and Malabar," in J. Pinkerton's *Voyages and Travels*, viii. (London, 1811) p. 749.

spirituality, would have claimed favourable comparison. In the ceremonial of the dedication-marriage of the *Dâsî*, elements are not wanting which indicate a past quite the reverse of disreputable. The girl to be married is generally from six to eight years in age. The bridegroom is the presiding deity of the local temple. The ceremony is done at his house. The expenses of the celebration are supposed to be partly paid from his funds. To instance the practice at the Suchîndram temple, a *Yôga* or meeting of the chief functionaries of the temple arranges the preliminaries. The girl to be wedded bathes and goes to the temple with two pieces of cloth, a *tâli*, betel, areca-nut, etc. These are placed by the priest at the feet of the image. The girl sits with the face towards the deity. The priest kindles the sacred fire and goes through all the rituals of the *Tirukkalyânam* festival. He then initiates the bride into the *Panchâkshara mantra*, if in a Saiva temple, and the *Ashtâkshara*, if in a Vaishnava temple. On behalf of the divine bridegroom, he presents one of the two cloths she has brought as offering and ties the *Tâli* around her neck. The practice, how old it is not possible to say, is then to take her to her house where the usual marriage festivities are celebrated for four days. As in Brahminical marriages, the *Nalunku* ceremony, *i.e.* the rolling of a cocoanut by the bride to the bridegroom and *vice versa* a number of times to the accompaniment of music, is gone through, the temple priest playing the bridegroom's part. Thenceforth she becomes the wife of the deity in the sense that she formally and solemnly dedicates the rest of her life to his service with the same constancy and devotion that a faithful wife united in holy matrimony shows to her wedded lord. The life of a *Dêvadâsî* bedecked with all the accomplishments that the muses could give was one of spotless purity. Even now she is maintained by the temple. She undertakes fasts in connection with the temple festivals, such as the seven days' fast for the *Apamârgam* ceremony. During the period of this fast, strict continence is enjoined ; she is required to take only one meal, and that within the temple—in fact to live and behave at least for a term, in the manner ordained for her throughout life. Some of the details of her daily work seem interesting ; she attends

the *Dîpâradhana*, the waving of lighted lamps in front of the
deity at sunset every day ; sings hymns in his praise, dances
before his presence, goes round with him in his processions
with lights in hand.   After the procession, she sings a song
or two from Jayadêva's *Gîtagôvinda* and with a few lullaby
hymns, her work for the night is over.   When she grows
physically unfit for these duties, she is formally invalided by
a special ceremony, *i.e. Tôtuvaikkuka*, or the laying down of
the ear-pendants.   It is gone through at the Maha Raja's
palace, whereafter she becomes a *Tâikkizhavi* (old mother),
entitled only to a subsistence-allowance.   When she dies,
the temple contributes to the funeral expenses.   On her
death-bed, the priest attends and after a few ceremonies
immediately after death, gets her bathed with saffron-
powder." [1]

§ 3. *Sacred Men and Women in West Africa*

Still more instructive for our present purpose are the
West African customs.   Among the Ewe-speaking peoples
of the Slave Coast " recruits for the priesthood are obtained
in two ways, viz. by the affiliation of young persons, and by
the direct consecration of adults.   Young people of either
sex dedicated or affiliated to a god are termed *kosio*, from
kono, 'unfruitful,' because a child dedicated to a god passes
into his service and is practically lost to his parents, and *si*,
'to run away.'   As the females become the 'wives' of the
god to whom they are dedicated, the termination *si* in *vŏdu-si*
[another name for these dedicated women], has been translated ' wife ' by some Europeans ; but it is never used in
the general acceptation of that term, being entirely restricted
to persons consecrated to the gods.   The chief business of
the female *kosi* is prostitution, and in every town there is at
least one institution in which the best-looking girls, between
ten and twelve years of age, are received.   Here they remain
for three years, learning the chants and dances peculiar to
the worship of the gods, and prostituting themselves to the

Marginal note: Among the Ewe peoples of West Africa the sacred prostitutes are regarded as the wives of the god.

[1] N. Subramhanya Aiyar, in *Census
of India, 1901*, vol. xxvi., *Travancore*,
Part i. (Trivandrum, 1903), pp. 276
sq.   I have to thank my friend Mr.
W. Crooke for referring me to this and
other passages on the sacred dancing-
girls of India.

priests and the inmates of the male seminaries ; and at the termination of their novitiate they become public prostitutes. This condition, however, is not regarded as one for reproach ; they are considered to be married to the god, and their excesses are supposed to be caused and directed by him. Properly speaking, their libertinage should be confined to the male worshippers at the temple of the god, but practically it is indiscriminate.   Children who are born from such unions belong to the god." [1]   These women are not allowed to marry since they are deemed the wives of a god.[2]

The human wives of the python-god.

Again, in this part of Africa " the female *Kosio* of Dañh-gbi, or *Dañh-sio*, that is, the wives, priestesses, and temple prostitutes of Dañh-gbi, the python-god, have their own organization.   Generally they live together in a group of houses or huts inclosed by a fence, and in these inclosures the novices undergo their three years of initiation.   Most new members are obtained by the affiliation of young girls ; but any woman whatever, married or single, slave or free, by publicly simulating possession, and uttering the conventional cries recognized as indicative of possession by the god, can at once join the body, and be admitted to the habitations of the order.   The person of a woman who has joined in this manner is inviolable, and during the period of her novitiate she is forbidden, if single, to enter the house of her parents, and, if married, that of her husband.   This inviolability, while it gives women opportunities of gratifying an illicit passion, at the same time serves occasionally to save the persecuted slave, or neglected wife, from the ill-treatment of the lord and master ; for she has only to go through the conventional form of possession and an asylum is assured." [3]   The python-god marries these women secretly in his temple, and they father their offspring on him ; but it is the priests who consummate the union.[4]

For our purpose it is important to note that a close

[1] A. B. Ellis, *The Ewe-speaking Peoples of the Slave Coast of West Africa* (London, 1890), pp. 140 *sq.*

[2] A. B. Ellis, *op. cit.* p. 142.

[3] A. B. Ellis, *op. cit.* pp. 148 *sq.* Compare Des Marchais, *Voyage en Guinée et à Cayenne* (Amsterdam, 1731), ii. 144-151 ; P. Bouche, *La Côte des Esclaves* (Paris, 1885), p. 128. The Abbé Bouche calls these women *danwés*.

[4] A. B. Ellis, *op. cit.* p. 60 ; Des Marchais, *op. cit.* ii. 149 *sq.*

connexion is apparently supposed to exist between the fertility of the soil and the marriage of these women to the serpent. For the time when new brides are sought for the reptile-god is the season when the millet is beginning to sprout. Then the old priestesses, armed with clubs, run frantically through the streets shrieking like mad women and carrying off to be brides of the serpent any little girls between the ages of eight and twelve whom they may find outside of the houses. Pious people at such times will sometimes leave their daughters at their doors on purpose that they may have the honour of being dedicated to the god.[1] The marriage of wives to the serpent-god is probably deemed necessary to enable him to discharge the important function of making the crops to grow and the cattle to multiply ; for we read that these people " invoke the snake in excessively wet, dry, or barren seasons ; on all occasions relating to their government and the preservation of their cattle ; or rather, in one word, in all necessities and difficulties, in which they do not apply to their new batch of gods." [2] Once in a bad season the Dutch factor Bosman found the King of Whydah in a great rage. His Majesty explained the reason of his discomposure by saying " that that year he had sent much larger offerings to the snake-house than usual, in order to obtain a good crop ; and that one of his vice-roys (whom he shewed me) had desired him afresh, in the name of the priests, who threatened a barren year, to send yet more. To which he answered that he did not intend to make any further offerings this year ; and if the snake would not bestow a plentiful harvest on them, he might let it alone ; for (said he) I cannot be more damaged thereby, the greatest part of my corn being already rotten in the field." [3]

The Akikuyu of British East Africa "have a custom which reminds one of the West African python-god and his wives. At intervals of, I believe, several years the medicine-men order huts to be built for the purpose of worshipping a river snake. The snake-god requires wives, and women or

Marginal notes:

Supposed connexion between the fertility of the soil and the marriage of women to the serpent.

Human wives of a snake-god among the Akikuyu.

---

[1] Des Marchais, *Voyage en Guinée et à Cayenne* (Amsterdam, 1731), ii. 146 *sq.*

[2] W. Bosman, " Description of the Coast of Guinea," in J. Pinkerton's *Voyages and Travels*, xvi. (London, 1814) p. 494.

[3] W. Bosman, *l.c.* The name of Whydah is spelt by Bosman as Fida, and by Des Marchais as Juda.

more especially girls go to the huts. Here the union is consummated by the medicine-men. If the number of females who go to the huts voluntarily is not sufficient, girls are seized and dragged there. I believe the offspring of such a union is said to be fathered by God (Ngai): at any rate there are children in Kikuyu who are regarded as the children of God." [1]

Among the negroes of the Slave Coast there are, as we have seen, male *kosio* as well as female *kosio* ; that is, there are dedicated men as well as dedicated women, priests as well as priestesses, and the ideas and customs in regard to them seem to be similar. Like the women, the men undergo a three years' novitiate, at the end of which each candidate has to prove that the god accepts him and finds him worthy of inspiration. Escorted by a party of priests he goes to a shrine and seats himself on a stool that belongs to the deity. The priests then anoint his head with a mystic decoction and invoke the god in a long and wild chorus. During the singing the youth, if he is acceptable to the deity, trembles violently, simulates convulsions, foams at the mouth, and dances in a frenzied style, sometimes for more than an hour. This is the proof that the god has taken possession of him. After that he has to remain in a temple without speaking for seven days and nights. At the end of that time, he is brought out, a priest opens his mouth to show that he may now use his tongue, a new name is given him, and he is fully ordained. [2] Henceforth he is regarded as the priest and medium of the deity whom he serves, and the words which he utters in that morbid state of mental excitement which passes for divine inspiration, are accepted by the hearers as the very words of the god spoken by the mouth of the man. [3] Any crime which a priest committed in a state of frenzy used to remain unpunished, no doubt because the act was thought to be the act of the god. But this benefit of clergy was so much abused that under King Gezo the law had to be altered ; and although, while he is still possessed

[1] MS. notes, kindly sent to me by the author, Mr. A. C. Hollis, 21st May, 1908.
[2] A. B. Ellis, *The Ewe-speaking Peoples of the Slave Coast*, pp. 142-144 .

Le R. P. Baudin, "Féticheurs ou ministres religieux des Nègres de la Guinée," *Les Missions Catholiques*, No. 787 (4 juillet 1884), p. 322.
[3] A. B. Ellis, *op. cit.* pp. 150 *sq.*

by the god, the inspired criminal is safe, he is now liable to
punishment as soon as the divine spirit leaves him.   Nevertheless on the whole among these people "the person of a
priest or priestess is sacred.   Not only must a layman not
lay hands on or insult one ; he must be careful not even to
knock one by accident, or jostle against one in the street.
The Abbé Bouche relates [1] that once when he was paying
a visit to the chief of Agweh, one of the wives of the chief
was brought into the house by four priestesses, her face
bloody, and her body covered with stripes.   She had been
savagely flogged for having accidentally trodden upon the
foot of one of them ; and the chief not only dared not give
vent to his anger, but had to give them a bottle of rum as
a peace-offering." [2]

Among the Tshi-speaking peoples of the Gold Coast, Similarly
who border on the Ewe-speaking peoples of the Slave Coast among
to the west, the customs and beliefs in regard to the dedi- peoples of
cated men and dedicated women, the priests and priestesses, Coast there
are very similar.   These persons are believed to be from are sacred
time to time possessed or inspired by the deity whom they women,
serve ; and in that state they are consulted as oracles.   They who are
work themselves up to the necessary pitch of excitement to be in-
by dancing to the music of drums ; each god has his special spired by
hymn, sung to a special beat of the drum, and accompanied
by a special dance.   It is while thus dancing to the drums
that the priest or priestess lets fall the oracular words in a
croaking or guttural voice which the hearers take to be the
voice of the god.   Hence dancing has an important place
in the education of priests and priestesses ; they are trained
in it for months before they may perform in public.   These
mouthpieces of the deity are consulted in almost every concern of life and are handsomely paid for their services. [3]
"Priests marry like any other members of the community,
and purchase wives ; but priestesses are never married, nor
can any 'head money' be paid for a priestess.   The reason
appears to be that a priestess belongs to the god she serves,
and therefore cannot become the property of a man, as would

---

[1] *La Côte des Esclaves*, pp. 127
sq.
[2] A. B. Ellis, *op. cit.* p. 147.

[3] A. B. Ellis, *The Tshi-speaking
Peoples of the Gold Coast of West Africa*
(London, 1887), pp. 120-138.

be the case if she married one. This prohibition extends to marriage only, and a priestess is not debarred from sexual commerce. The children of a priest or priestess are not ordinarily educated for the priestly profession, one generation being usually passed over, and the grandchildren selected. Priestesses are ordinarily most licentious, and custom allows them to gratify their passions with any man who may chance to take their fancy."[1] The ranks of the hereditary priesthood are constantly recruited by persons who devote themselves or who are devoted by their relations or masters to the profession. Men, women, and even children can thus become members of the priesthood. If a mother has lost several of her children by death, she will not uncommonly vow to devote the next born to the service of the gods ; for in this way she hopes to save the child's life. So when the child is born it is set apart for the priesthood, and on arriving at maturity generally fulfils the vow made by the mother and becomes a priest or priestess. At the ceremony of ordination the votary has to prove his or her vocation for the sacred life in the usual way by falling into or simulating convulsions, dancing frantically to the beat of drums, and speaking in a hoarse unnatural voice words which are deemed to be the utterance of the deity temporarily lodged in the body of the man or woman.[2]

§ 4. Sacred Women in Western Asia

In like manner the sacred prostitutes of Western Asia may have been viewed as possessed by the deity and married to the god.

Thus in Africa, and sometimes if not regularly in India, the sacred prostitutes attached to temples are regarded as the wives of the god, and their excesses are excused on the ground that the women are not themselves, but that they act under the influence of divine inspiration. This is in substance the explanation which I have given of the custom of sacred prostitution as it was practised in antiquity by the peoples

[1] A. B. Ellis, op. cit. p. 121.

[2] A. B. Ellis, op. cit. pp. 120 sq., 129-138. The slaves, male and female, dedicated to a god from childhood are often mentioned by the German missionary Mr. J. Spieth in his elaborate work on the Ewe people (Die Ewe-Stämme : Material zur Kunde des Ewe-Volkes in Deutsch-Togo, Berlin, 1906, pp. 228, 229, 309, 450, 474, 792, 797, etc.). But his information does not illustrate the principal points to which I have called attention in the text.

of Western Asia.   In their licentious intercourse at the
temples the women, whether maidens or matrons or professional harlots, imitated the licentious conduct of a great
goddess of fertility for the purpose of ensuring the fruitfulness of fields and trees, of man and beast ; and in discharging
this sacred and important function the women were probably
supposed, like their West African sisters, to be actually
possessed by the goddess.   The hypothesis at least explains
all the facts in a simple and natural manner ; and in assuming that women could be married to gods it assumes a
principle which we know to have been recognized in Babylon,
Assyria, and Egypt.[1]   At Babylon a woman regularly slept
in the great bed of Bel or Marduk, which stood in his temple
on the summit of a lofty pyramid ; and it was believed that
the god chose her from all the women of Babylon and slept
with her in the bed.   However, unlike the Indian and West
African wives of gods, this spouse of the Babylonian deity
is reported by Herodotus to have been chaste.[2]   Yet we may
doubt whether she was so ; for these wives or perhaps para-
mours of Bel are probably to be identified with the wives or
votaries of Marduk mentioned in the code of Hammurabi,
and we know from the code that female votaries of the gods
might be mothers and married to men.[3]   At Babylon the
sun-god Shamash as well as Marduk had human wives
formerly dedicated to his service, and they like the votaries
of Marduk might have children.[4]   It is significant that a
name for these Babylonian votaries was *kadishtu*, which is
the same word as *kedesha*, " consecrated woman," the regular
Hebrew word for a temple harlot.[5]   It is true that the law

[1] *The Magic Art and the Evolution
of Kings*, ii. 129-135.

[2] Herodotus, i. 181 *sq.*   It is not
clear whether the same or a different
woman slept every night in the temple.

[3] H. Winckler, *Die Gesetze Hammurabi*[2] (Leipsic, 1903), p. 31, § 182 ;
C. H. W. Johns, *Babylonian and
Assyrian Laws, Contracts, and Letters*
(Edinburgh, 1904), pp. 54, 55, 59, 60,
61 (§§ 137, 144, 145, 146, 178, 182,
187, 192, 193, of the Code of Hammurabi).   As to these female votaries
see especially C. H. W. Johns, " Notes
on the Code of Hammurabi," *Ameri-*

*can Journal of Semitic Languages and
Literatures*, xix. (January 1903) pp.
98-107.   Compare S. A. Cook, *The
Laws of Moses and the Code of Hammurabi* (London, 1903), pp. 147-150.

[4] C. H. W. Johns, " Notes on the
Code of Hammurabi," *l.c.*, where we
read (p. 104) of a female votary of
Shamash who had a daughter.

[5] *Code of Hammurabi*, § 181 ;
C. H. W. Johns, " Notes on the Code
of Hammurabi," *op. cit.* pp. 100 *sq.*;
S. A. Cook, *op. cit.* p. 148.   Dr.
Johns translates the name by " temple
maid " (*Babylonian and Assyrian Laws,*

severely punished any disrespect shown to these sacred women ;[1] but the example of West Africa warns us that a formal respect shown to such persons, even when it is enforced by severe penalties, need be no proof at all of their virtuous character.[2] In Egypt a woman used to sleep in the temple of Ammon at Thebes, and the god was believed to visit her.[3] Egyptian texts often mention her as " the divine consort," and in old days she seems to have usually been the Queen of Egypt herself.[4] But in the time of Strabo, at the beginning of our era, these consorts or concubines of Ammon, as they were called, were beautiful young girls of noble birth, who held office only till puberty. During their term of office they prostituted themselves freely to any man who took their fancy. After puberty they were given in marriage, and a ceremony of mourning was performed for them as if they were dead.[5] When they died in good earnest, their bodies were laid in special graves.[6]

§ 5. *Sacred Men in Western Asia*

Similarly the sacred men (*kedeshim*) of Western Asia may have been regarded as possessed by the deity and as acting and speaking in his name.

As in West Africa the dedicated women have their counterpart in the dedicated men, so it was in Western Asia ; for there the sacred men (*kedeshim*) clearly corresponded to the sacred women (*kedeshoth*), in other words, the sacred male slaves [7] of the temples were the complement of the sacred female slaves. And as the characteristic feature of the dedicated men in West Africa is their supposed possession or inspiration by the deity, so we may conjecture was it with the sacred male slaves (the *kedeshim*) of Western Asia ; they, too, may have been regarded as temporary or permanent embodiments of the deity, possessed from time to time by

---

Contracts, and Letters, p. 61). He is scrupulously polite to these ladies, but I gather from him that a far less charitable view of their religious vocation is taken by Father Scheil, the first editor and translator of the code.

[1] Any man proved to have pointed the finger of scorn at a votary was liable to be branded on the forehead (*Code of Hammurabi*, § 127).

[2] See above, pp. 66, 69.

[3] Herodotus, i. 182.

[4] A. Wiedemann, *Herodots Zweites Buch* (Leipsic, 1890), pp. 268 *sq.* See further *The Magic Art and the Evolution of Kings*, ii. 130 *sqq.*

[5] Strabo, xvii. 1. 46, p. 816. The title " concubines of Zeus (Ammon) " is mentioned by Diodorus Siculus (i. 47).

[6] Diodorus Siculus, i. 47.

[7] The ἱερόδουλοι, as the Greeks called them.

his divine spirit, acting in his name, and speaking with his voice.[1]   At all events we know that this was so at the sanctuary of the Moon among the Albanians of the Caucasus. The sanctuary owned church lands of great extent peopled by sacred slaves, and it was ruled by a high-priest, who ranked next after the king.   Many of these slaves were inspired by the deity and prophesied ; and when one of them had been for some time in this state of divine frenzy, wandering alone in the forest, the high-priest had him caught, bound with a sacred chain, and maintained in luxury for a year. Then the poor wretch was led out, anointed with unguents, and sacrificed with other victims to the Moon.   The mode of sacrifice was this.   A man took a sacred spear, and thrust it through the victim's side to the heart.   As he staggered and fell, the rest observed him closely and drew omens from the manner of his fall.   Then the body was dragged or carried away to a certain place, where all his fellows stood upon it by way of purification.[2]   In this custom the prophet, or rather the maniac, was plainly supposed to be moon-struck in the most literal sense, that is, possessed or inspired by the deity of the Moon, who was perhaps thought by the Albanians, as by the Phrygians,[3] to be a male god, since his chosen minister and mouthpiece was a man, not a woman.[4]   It can hardly therefore be deemed improbable that at other sanctuaries of Western Asia, where sacred men were kept, these ministers of religion should have discharged a similar prophetic function, even though they did not share the tragic

---

[1] I have to thank the Rev. Professor R. H. Kennett for this important suggestion as to the true nature of the *ḳedeshim*. The passages of the Bible in which mention is made of these men are Deuteronomy xxiii. 17 (in Hebrew 18) ; 1 Kings xiv. 24, xv. 12, xxii. 46 (in Hebrew 47) ; 2 Kings xxiii. 7 ; Job xxxvi. 14 (where *ḳedeshim* is translated "the unclean" in the English version). The usual rendering of *ḳedeshim* in the English Bible is not justified by any of these passages ; but it may perhaps derive support from a reference which Eusebius makes to the profligate rites observed at Aphaca (*Vita Constantini*, iii. 55 ; Migne's *Patrologia Graeca*, xx.

1120) ; Γύνιδες γοῦν τινες ἄνδρες οὐκ ἄνδρες, τὸ σέμνον τῆς φύσεως ἀπαρνησάμενοι, θηλείᾳ νόσῳ τὴν δαίμονα ἱλεοῦντο. But probably Eusebius is here speaking of the men who castrated themselves in honour of the goddess, and thereafter wore female attire. See Lucian, *De dea Syria*, 51 ; and below, pp. 269 *sq.*

[2] Strabo, xi. 4. 7, p. 503.

[3] Drexler, in W. H. Roscher's *Lexikon der griech. und röm. Mythologie, s.v.* "Men," ii. 2687 *sqq.*

[4] It is true that Strabo (*l.c.*) speaks of the Albanian deity as a goddess, but this may be only an accommodation to the usage of the Greek language, in which the moon is feminine.

fate of the moon-struck Albanian prophet. Nor was the influence of these Asiatic prophets confined to Asia. In Sicily the spark which kindled the devastating Servile War was struck by a Syrian slave, who simulated the prophetic ecstasy in order to rouse his fellow-slaves to arms in the name of the Syrian goddess. To inflame still more his inflammatory words this ancient Mahdi ingeniously interlarded them with real fire and smoke, which by a common conjurer's trick he breathed from his lips.[1]

Resemblance of the Hebrew prophets to the sacred men of Western Africa.

In like manner the Hebrew prophets were believed to be temporarily possessed and inspired by a divine spirit who spoke through them, just as a divine spirit is supposed by West African negroes to speak through the mouth of the dedicated men his priests. Indeed the points of resemblance between the prophets of Israel and West Africa are close and curious. Like their black brothers, the Hebrew prophets employed music in order to bring on the prophetic trance;[2] like them, they received the divine spirit through the application of a magic oil to their heads;[3] like them, they were apparently distinguished from common people by certain marks on the face;[4] and like

[1] Florus, *Epitoma*, ii. 7; Diodorus Siculus, Frag. xxxiv. 2 (vol. v. pp. 87 *sq.*, ed. L. Dindorf, in the Teubner series).

[2] Above, pp. 52 *sq.*

[3] 1 Kings xix. 16; Isaiah lx. 1.

[4] 1 Kings xx. 41. So in Africa "priests and priestesses are readily distinguishable from the rest of the community. They wear their hair long and unkempt, while other people, except the women in the towns on the seaboard, have it cut close to the head. . . . Frequently both appear with white circles painted round their eyes, or with various white devices, marks, or lines painted on the face, neck, shoulders, or arms" (A. B. Ellis, *The Tshi-speaking Peoples of the Gold Coast*, p. 123). "Besides the ordinary tribal-tattoo-marks borne by all natives, the priesthood in Dahomi bear a variety of such marks, some very elaborate, and an expert can tell by the marks on a priest to what god he is vowed, and what rank he holds in the order.

These hierarchical marks consist of lines, scrolls, diamonds, and other patterns, with sometimes a figure, such as that of the crocodile or chameleon. The shoulders are frequently seen covered with an infinite number of small marks like dots, set close together. All these marks are considered sacred, and the laity are forbidden to touch them" (A. B. Ellis, *The Ewe-speaking Peoples of the Slave Coast*, p. 146). The reason why the prophet's shoulders are especially marked is perhaps given by the statement of a Zulu that "the sensitive part with a doctor [medicine-man] is his shoulders. Everything he feels is in the situation of his shoulders. That is the place where black men feel the Amatongo" (ancestral spirits). See H. Callaway, *The Religious System of the Amazulu*, part ii. p. 159. These African analogies suggest that the "wounds between the arms" (literally, "between the hands") which the prophet Zechariah mentions (xiii. 6) as the badge of a Hebrew prophet were

them they were consulted not merely in great national emergencies but in the ordinary affairs of everyday life, in which they were expected to give information and advice for a small fee.   For example, Samuel was consulted about lost asses,[1] just as a Zulu diviner is consulted about lost cows ;[2] and we have seen Elisha acting as a dowser when water ran short.[3]   Indeed, we learn that the old name for a prophet was a seer,[4] a word which may be understood to imply that his special function was divination rather than prophecy in the sense of prediction.   Be that as it may, prophecy of the Hebrew type has not been limited to Israel ; it is indeed a phenomenon of almost world-wide occurrence ; in many lands and in many ages the wild, whirling words of frenzied men and women have been accepted as the utterances of an indwelling deity.[5]   What does distinguish Hebrew prophecy from all others is that the genius of a few members of the profession wrested this vulgar but powerful instrument from baser uses, and by wielding it in the interest of a high morality rendered a service of incalculable value to humanity. That is indeed the glory of Israel, but it is not the side of prophecy with which we are here concerned.

More to our purpose is to note that prophecy of the ordinary sort appears to have been in vogue at Byblus, the sacred city of Adonis, centuries before the life-time of the earliest Hebrew prophet whose writings have come down to us.   When the Egyptian traveller, Wen-Ammon, was lingering in the port of Byblus, under the King's orders to quit the place, the spirit of God came on one of the royal

Inspired prophets at Byblus.

---

marks tattooed on his shoulders in token of his holy office.   The suggestion is confirmed by the prophet's own statement (*l.c.*) that he had received the wounds in the house of his lovers (בֵּית מְאַהֲבָי) ; for the same word lovers is repeatedly applied by the prophet Hosea to the Baalim (Hosea, ii. 5, 7, 10, 12, 13, verses 7, 9, 12, 14, 15 in Hebrew).

[1] 1 Samuel ix. 1-20.
[2] H. Callaway, *The Religious System of the Amazulu*, part iii. pp. 300 *sqq.*
[3] See above, pp. 52 *sq.*
[4] 1 Samuel ix. 9.   In the Wiimbaio

tribe of South - Eastern Australia a medicine - man used to be called "*mekigar*, from *meki*, 'eye' or 'to see,' otherwise 'one who sees,' that is, sees the causes of maladies in people, and who could extract them from the sufferer, usually in the form of quartz crystals" (A. W. Howitt, *The Native Tribes of South-East Australia*, London, 1904, p. 380).

[5] That the prophet's office in Canaan was developed out of the widespread respect for insanity is duly recognized by Ed. Meyer, *Geschichte des Altertums*,[2] i. 2. p. 383.

pages or henchmen, and in a prophetic frenzy he announced that the King should receive the Egyptian stranger as a messenger sent from the god Ammon.[1] The god who thus took possession of the page and spoke through him was probably Adonis, the god of the city. With regard to the office of these royal pages we have no information ; but as ministers of a sacred king and liable to be inspired by the deity, they would naturally be themselves sacred ; in fact they may have belonged to the class of sacred slaves or *ḳedeshim*. If that was so it would confirm the conclusion to which the foregoing investigation points, namely, that originally no sharp line of distinction existed between the prophets and the *ḳedeshim* ; both were " men of God," as the prophets were constantly called ;[2] in other words, they were inspired mediums, men in whom the god manifested himself from time to time by word and deed, in short temporary incarnations of the deity. But while the prophets roved freely about the country, the *ḳedeshim* appear to have been regularly attached to a sanctuary ; and among the duties which they performed at the shrines there were clearly some which revolted the conscience of men imbued with a purer morality. What these duties were, we may surmise partly from the behaviour of the sons of Eli to the women who came to the tabernacle,[3] partly from the beliefs and practices

---

[1] W. Max Müller, in *Mitteilungen der Vorderasiatischen Gesellschaft*, 1900, No. 1, p. 17 ; A. Erman, " Eine Reise nach Phönizien im 11 Jahrhundert v. Chr." *Zeitschrift für Ägyptische Sprache und Altertumskunde*, xxxviii. (1900) pp. 6 *sq.* ; G. Maspero, *Les contes populaires de l'Égypte Ancienne*,[3] p. 192 ; A. Wiedemann, *Altägyptische Sagen und Märchen* (Leipsic, 1906), pp. 99 *sq.* ; H. Gressmann, *Altorientalische Texte und Bilder zum Alten Testamente* (Tübingen, 1909), p. 226. Scholars differ as to whether Wen-Ammon's narrative is to be regarded as history or romance ; but even if it were proved to be a fiction, we might safely assume that the incident of the prophetic frenzy at Byblus was based upon familiar facts. Prof. Wiedemann thinks that the god who inspired the page was the Egyptian Ammon, not the Phoenician Adonis, but this view seems to me less probable.

[2] 1 Samuel ix. 6-8, 10 ; 1 Kings xiii. 1, 4-8, 11 etc.

[3] 1 Samuel ii. 22. Totally different from their Asiatic namesakes were the " sacred men " and " sacred women " who were charged with the superintendence of the mysteries at Andania in Messenia. They were chosen by lot and held office for a year. The sacred women might be either married or single ; the married women had to swear that they had been true to their husbands. See G. Dittenberger, *Sylloge Inscriptionum Graecarum*[2] (Leipsic, 1898–1901), vol. ii. pp. 461 *sqq.*, No. 653 ; Ch. Michel, *Recueil d'Inscriptions Grecques* (Brussels, 1900), pp. 596 *sqq.*, No. 694 ; *Leges Graecorum Sacrae*, ed. J. de Prott, L.

as to "holy men" which survive to this day among the Syrian peasantry.

Of these "holy men" we are told that "so far as they are not impostors, they are men whom we would call insane, known among the Syrians as *mejnûn*, possessed by a *jinn* or spirit. They often go in filthy garments, or without clothing. Since they are regarded as intoxicated by deity, the most dignified men, and of the highest standing among the Moslems, submit to utter indecent language at their bidding without rebuke, and ignorant Moslem women do not shrink from their approach, because in their superstitious belief they attribute to them, as men possessed by God, a divine authority which they dare not resist. Such an attitude of compliance may be exceptional, but there are more than rumours of its existence. These 'holy men' differ from the ordinary derwishes whom travellers so often see in Cairo, and from the ordinary madmen who are kept in fetters, so that they may not do injury to themselves and others. But their appearance, and the expressions regarding them, afford some illustrations of the popular estimate of ancient seers, or prophets, in the time of Hosea: 'The prophet is a fool, the man that hath the spirit is mad';[1] and in the time of Jeremiah,[2] the man who made himself a prophet was considered as good as a madman."[3] To complete the parallel these vagabonds "are also believed to be possessed of prophetic power, so that they are able to foretell the future, and warn the people among whom they live of impending danger."[4]

"Holy men" in modern Syria.

Ziehen, Pars Altera, Fasciculus i. (Leipsic, 1906), No. 58, pp. 166 *sqq.*

[1] Hosea ix. 7.

[2] Jeremiah xxix. 26.

[3] S. I. Curtiss, *Primitive Semitic Religion To-day* (Chicago, New York, Toronto, 1902), pp. 150 *sq.*

[4] S. I. Curtiss, *op. cit.* p. 152. As to these "holy men," see further C. R. Conder, *Tent-work in Palestine* (London, 1878), ii. 231 *sq.* : "The most peculiar class of men in the country is that of the Derwîshes, or sacred personages, who wander from

village to village, performing tricks, living on alms, and enjoying certain social and domestic privileges, which very often lead to scandalous scenes. Some of these men are mad, some are fanatics, but the majority are, I imagine, rogues. They are reverenced not only by the peasantry, but also sometimes by the governing class. I have seen the Kady of Nazareth ostentatiously preparing food for a miserable and filthy beggar, who sat in the justice-hall, and was consulted as if he had been inspired. A Derwîsh of peculiar eminence is often dressed in

The licence accorded to such "holy men" may be explained by the desire of women for offspring.

We may conjecture that with women a powerful motive for submitting to the embraces of the "holy men" is a hope of obtaining offspring by them. For in Syria it is still believed that even dead saints can beget children on barren women, who accordingly resort to their shrines in order to obtain the wish of their hearts. For example, at the Baths of Solomon in Northern Palestine, blasts of hot air escape from the ground; and one of them, named Abu Rabah, is a famous resort of childless wives who wish to satisfy their maternal longings. They let the hot air stream up over their bodies and really believe that children born to them after such a visit are begotten by the saint of the shrine.[1] But the saint who enjoys the highest reputation in this respect is St. George. He reveals himself at his shrines which are scattered all over the country; at each of them there is a tomb or the likeness of a tomb. The most celebrated of these sanctuaries is at Kalat el Hosn in Northern Syria. Barren women of all sects, including Moslems, resort to it. "There are many natives who shrug their shoulders when this shrine is mentioned in connection with women. But it is doubtless true that many do not know what seems to be its true character, and who think that the most puissant saint, as they believe, in the world can give them sons." "But the true character of the place is beginning to be recognized, so that many Moslems have forbidden their wives to visit it."[2]

§ 6. *Sons of God*

Belief that men and women may be the offspring of a god.

Customs like the foregoing may serve to explain the belief, which is not confined to Syria, that men and women may be in fact and not merely in metaphor the sons and

good clothes, with a spotless turban, and is preceded by a banner-bearer, and followed by a band, with drum, cymbal, and tambourine. . . . It is natural to reflect whether the social position of the Prophets among the Jews may not have resembled that of the Derwîshes."

[1] S. I. Curtiss, *op. cit.* pp. 116 *sq.*
[2] S. I. Curtiss, *op. cit.* pp. 118, 119.

In India also some Mohammedan saints are noted as givers of children. Thus at Fatepur-Sikri, near Agra, is the grave of Salim Chishti, and childless women tie rags to the delicate tracery of the tomb, "thus bringing them into direct communion with the spirit of the holy man" (W. Crooke, *Natives of Northern India*, London, 1907, p. 203).

daughters of a god; for these modern saints, whether Christian or Moslem, who father the children of Syrian mothers, are nothing but the old gods under a thin disguise. If in antiquity as at the present day Semitic women often repaired to shrines in order to have the reproach of barrenness removed from them—and the prayer of Hannah is a familiar example of the practice,[1] we could easily understand not only the tradition of the sons of God who begat children on the daughters of men,[2] but also the exceedingly common occurrence of the divine titles in Hebrew names of human beings.[3] Multitudes of men and women, in fact, whose mothers had resorted to holy places in order to procure offspring, would be regarded as the actual children of the god and would be named accordingly. Hence Hannah called her infant Samuel, which means "name of God" or "his name is God";[4] and probably she sincerely believed that the child was actually begotten in her womb by the deity.[5] The dedication of such children to the service of God at the sanctuary was merely giving back the divine son to the divine father. Similarly in West Africa, when a woman has got a child at the shrine of Agbasia, the god who alone bestows offspring on women, she dedicates him or her as a sacred slave to the deity.[6]

Thus in the Syrian beliefs and customs of to-day we probably have the clue to the religious prostitution practised in the very same regions in antiquity. Then as now women looked to the local god, the Baal or Adonis of old, the Abu Rabah or St. George of to-day, to satisfy the natural craving of a woman's heart; and then as now, apparently, the part

---

[1] 1 Samuel i.

[2] Genesis vi. 1-3. In this passage "the sons of God (or rather of the gods)" probably means, in accordance with a common Hebrew idiom, no more than "the gods," just as the phrase "sons of the prophets" means the prophets themselves. For more examples of this idiom, see Brown, Driver, and Briggs, *Hebrew and English Lexicon*, p. 121.

[3] For example, all Hebrew names ending in -*el* or -*iah* are compounds of El or Yahwe, two names of the divinity. See G. B. Gray, *Studies in Hebrew Proper Names* (London, 1896), pp. 149 *sqq.*

[4] Brown, Driver, and Briggs, *Hebrew and English Lexicon*, p. 1028. But compare *Encyclopaedia Biblica*, iii. 3285, iv. 4452.

[5] A trace of a similar belief perhaps survives in the narratives of Genesis xxxi. and Judges xiii., where barren women are represented as conceiving children after the visit of God, or of an angel of God, in the likeness of a man.

[6] J. Spieth, *Die Ewe - Stämme* (Berlin, 1906), pp. 446, 448-450.

of the local god was played by sacred men, who in personating him may often have sincerely believed that they were
acting under divine inspiration, and that the functions which
they discharged were necessary for the fertility of the land
as well as for the propagation of the human species.   The
purifying influence of Christianity and Mohammedanism has
restricted such customs within narrow limits ; even under
Turkish rule they are now only carried on in holes and corners.
Yet if the practice has dwindled, the principle which it
embodies appears to be fundamentally the same ; it is a
desire for the continuance of the species, and a belief that
an object so natural and legitimate can be accomplished by
divine power manifesting itself in the bodies of men and
women.

Belief
in the
physical
fatherhood
of God not
confined
to Syria.

Sons of the
serpent-
god.

The belief in the physical fatherhood of God has not
been confined to Syria in ancient and modern times.   Elsewhere many men have been counted the sons of God in
the most literal sense of the word, being supposed to have
been begotten by his holy spirit in the wombs of mortal
women.   Here I shall merely illustrate the creed by a few
examples drawn from classical antiquity.[1]   Thus in order to
obtain offspring women used to resort to the great sanctuary
of Aesculapius, situated in a beautiful upland valley, to
which a path, winding through a long wooded gorge, leads
from the bay of Epidaurus.   Here the women slept in the
holy place and were visited in dreams by a serpent ; and
the children to whom they afterwards gave birth were
believed to have been begotten by the reptile.[2]   That the
serpent was supposed to be the god himself seems certain ;
for Aesculapius repeatedly appeared in the form of a serpent,[3]
and live serpents were kept and fed in his sanctuaries for
the healing of the sick, being no doubt regarded as his
incarnations.[4]   Hence the children born to women who had

---

[1] For more instances see H. Usener,
Das Weihnachtsfest[2] (Bonn, 1911), i. 71
sqq.
[2] G. Dittenberger, *Sylloge Inscriptionum Graecarum*,[2] vol. ii. pp. 662,
663, No. 803, lines 117 *sqq.*, 129
sqq.
[3] Pausanias, ii. 10. 3 (with my
note), iii. 23. 7 ; Livy, xi. Epitome ;

Pliny, *Nat. Hist.* xxix. 72 ; Valerius
Maximus, i. 8. 2 ; Ovid, *Metam.* xv.
626-744 ; Aurelius Victor, *De viris
illustr.* 22 ; Plutarch, *Quaest. Rom.*
94.
[4] Aristophanes, *Plutus*, 733 ; Pausanias, ii. 11. 8 ; Herodas, *Mimiambi*,
iv. 90 *sq.* ; G. Dittenberger, *Sylloge
Inscriptionum Graecarum*,[2] vol. ii. p.

thus visited a sanctuary of Aesculapius were probably fathered on the serpent-god. Many celebrated men in classical antiquity were thus promoted to the heavenly hierarchy by similar legends of a miraculous birth. The famous Aratus of Sicyon was certainly believed by his countrymen to be a son of Aesculapius; his mother is said to have got him in intercourse with a serpent.[1] Probably she slept either in the shrine of Aesculapius at Sicyon, where a figurine of her was shown seated on a serpent,[2] or perhaps in the more secluded sanctuary of the god at Titane, not many miles off, where the sacred serpents crawled among ancient cypresses on the hill-top which overlooks the narrow green valley of the Asopus with the white turbid river rushing in its depths.[3] There, under the shadow of the cypresses, with the murmur of the Asopus in her ears, the mother of Aratus may have conceived, or fancied she conceived, the future deliverer of his country. Again, the mother of Augustus is said to have got him by intercourse with a serpent in a temple of Apollo; hence the emperor was reputed to be the son of that god.[4] Similar tales were told of the Messenian hero Aristomenes, Alexander the Great, and the elder Scipio: all of them were reported to have been begotten by snakes.[5] In the time of Herod a serpent, according to Aelian, in like manner made love to a Judean maid.[6] Can the story be a distorted rumour of the parentage of Christ?

In India even stone serpents are credited with a power of bestowing offspring on women. Thus the Komatis of Mysore "worship *Nága* or the serpent god. This worship is generally confined to women and is carried on on a large

Women fertilized by stone serpents in India.

655, No. 802, lines 116 *sqq.*; Ch. Michel, *Recueil d'Inscriptions Grecques*, p. 826, No. 1069.

[1] Pausanias, ii. 10. 3, iv. 14. 7 *sq.*

[2] Pausanias, ii. 10. 4.

[3] Pausanias, ii. 11. 5-8.

[4] Suetonius, *Divus Augustus*, 94; Dio Cassius, xlv. 1. 2. Tame serpents were kept in a sacred grove of Apollo in Epirus. A virgin priestess fed them, and omens of plenty and

health or the opposites were drawn from the way in which the reptiles took their food from her. See Aelian, *Nat. Hist.* xi. 2.

[5] Pausanias, iv. 14. 7; Livy, xxvi. 19; Aulus Gellius, vi. 1; Plutarch, *Alexander*, 2. All these cases have been already cited in this connexion by L. Deubner, *De incubatione* (Leipsic, 1900), p. 33 note.

[6] Aelian, *De natura animalium*, vi. 17.

scale once a year on the fifth day of the bright fortnight of Srávana (July and August). The representations of serpents are cut in stone slabs and are set up round an *Asvattha* tree on a platform, on which is also generally planted a margosa tree. These snakes in stones are set up in performance of vows and are said to be specially efficacious in curing bad sores and other skin diseases and in giving children. The women go to such places for worship with milk, fruits, and flowers on the prescribed day which is observed as a feast day." They wash the stones, smear them with turmeric, and offer them curds and fruits. Sometimes they search out the dens of serpents and pour milk into the holes for the live reptiles.[1]

§ 7. *Reincarnation of the Dead*

Belief that the dead come to life in the form of serpents. The reason why snakes were so often supposed to be the fathers of human beings is probably to be found in the common belief that the dead come to life and revisit their old homes in the shape of serpents.

This notion is widely spread in Africa, especially among tribes of the Bantu stock. It is held, for example, by the Zulus, the Thonga, and other Caffre tribes of South Africa ; [2] by the Ngoni of British Central Africa ; [3] by the Wabondei,[4] the Masai,[5] the Suk,[6] the Nandi,[7] and the Akikuyu of German and British East Africa ; [8] and by the Dinkas of

---

[1] H. V. Nanjundayya, *The Ethnographical Survey of Mysore*, vi. *Komati Caste* (Bangalore, 1906), p. 29.

[2] T. Arbousset et F. Daumas, *Voyage d'Exploration au Nord-Est de la Colonie du Cap de Bonne-Espérance* (Paris, 1842), p. 277 ; H. Callaway, *Religious System of the Amazulu*, part ii. pp. 140-144, 196-200, 208-212 ; J. Shooter, *The Kafirs of Natal* (London, 1857), p. 162 ; E. Casalis, *The Basutos* (London, 1861), p. 246 ; "Words about Spirits," (*South African*) *Folk-lore Journal*, ii. (1880) pp. 101-103 ; A. Kranz, *Natur- und Kulturleben der Zulus* (Wiesbaden, 1880), p. 112 ; F. Speckmann, *Die Hermannsburger Mission in Afrika* (Hermannsburg, 1876), pp. 165-167 ; Dudley Kidd, *The Essential Kafir* (London, 1904),

pp. 85-87 ; Henri A. Junod, *The Life of a South African Tribe* (Neuchatel, 1912-1913), ii. 358 *sq.*

[3] W. A. Elmslie, *Among the Wild Ngoni* (London, 1899), pp. 71 *sq.*

[4] O. Baumann, *Usambara und seine Nachbargebiete* (Berlin, 1891), pp. 141 *sq.*

[5] S. L. Hinde and H. Hinde, *The Last of the Masai* (London, 1901), pp. 101 *sq.* ; A. C. Hollis, *The Masai* (Oxford, 1905), pp. 307 *sq.*; Sir H. Johnston, *The Uganda Protectorate* (London, 1904), ii. 832.

[6] M. W. H. Beech, *The Suk* (Oxford, 1911), p. 20.

[7] A. C. Hollis, *The Nandi* (Oxford, 1909), p. 90.

[8] H. R. Tate, "The Native Law of the Southern Gikuyu of British East

the Upper Nile.[1]   It prevails also among the Betsileo and other tribes of Madagascar.[2]   Among the Iban or Sea Dyaks of Borneo a man's guardian spirit (*Tua*) "has its external manifestation in a snake, a leopard or some other denizen of the forest.   It is supposed to be the spirit of some ancestor renowned for bravery or some other virtue who at death has taken an animal form.   It is a custom among the Iban when a person of note in the tribe dies, not to bury the body but to place it on a neighbouring hill or in some solitary spot above ground.   A quantity of food is taken to the place every day, and if after a few days the body disappears, the deceased is said to have become a *Tua* or guardian spirit.   People who have been suffering from some chronic complaint often go to such a tomb, taking with them an offering to the soul of the deceased to obtain his help.   To such it is revealed in a dream what animal form the honoured dead has taken.   The most frequent form is that of a snake.   Thus when a snake is found in a Dyak house it is seldom killed or driven away ; food is offered to it, for it is a guardian spirit who has come to inquire after the welfare of its clients and bring them good luck.   Anything that may be found in the mouth of such a snake is taken and kept as a charm." [3]   Similarly in

---

Africa," *Journal of the African Society*, No. xxxv. April 1910, p. 243.

[1] E. de Pruyssenaere, *Reisen und Forschungen im Gebiete des Weissen und Blauen Nil* (Gotha, 1877), p. 27 (*Petermann's Mittheilungen, Ergänzungsheft*, No. 50). Compare G. Schweinfurth, *The Heart of Africa*[3] (London, 1878), i. 55. Among the Bahima of Ankole dead chiefs turn into serpents, but dead kings into lions. See J. Roscoe, " The Bahima, a Cow Tribe of Enkole in the Uganda Protectorate," *Journal of the Anthropological Institute*, xxxvii. (1907), pp. 101 *sq.*; Major J. A. Meldon, " Notes on the Bahima of Ankole," *Journal of the African Society*, No. xxii. (January 1907), p. 151. Major Leonard holds that the pythons worshipped in Southern Nigeria are regarded as reincarnations of the dead ; but this seems very doubtful. See A. G. Leonard, *The*

Lower Niger and its Tribes (London, 1906), pp. 327 *sqq*. Pythons are worshipped by the Ewe - speaking peoples of the Slave Coast, but apparently not from a belief that the souls of the dead are lodged in them. See A. B. Ellis, *The Ewe - speaking Peoples of the Slave Coast of West Africa*, pp. 54 *sqq*.

[2] G. A. Shaw, " The Betsileo," *The Antananarivo Annual and Madagascar Magazine, Reprint of the First Four Numbers* (Antananarivo, 1885), p. 411 ; H. W. Little, *Madagascar, its History and People* (London, 1884), pp. 86 *sq.* ; A. van Gennep, *Tabou et Totémisme à Madagascar* (Paris, 1904), pp. 272 *sqq*.

[3] " Religious Rites and Customs of the Iban or Dyaks of Sarawak," by Leo Nyuak, translated from the Dyak by the Very Rev. Edm. Dunn, *Anthropos*, i. (1906) p. 182. As to

Kiriwina, an island of the Trobriands Group, to the east of New Guinea, "the natives regarded the snake as one of their ancestral chiefs, or rather as the abode of his spirit, and when one was seen in a house it was believed that the chief was paying a visit to his old home. The natives considered this as an ill omen and so always tried to persuade the animal to depart as soon as possible. The honours of a chief were paid to the snake : the natives passed it in a crouching posture, and as they did so, saluted it as a chief of high rank. Native property was presented to it as an appeasing gift, accompanied by prayers that it would not do them any harm, but would go away quickly. They dared not kill the snake, for its death would bring disease and death upon those who did so." [1]

Serpents which are viewed as ancestors come to life are treated with respect and often fed with milk.

Where serpents are thus viewed as ancestors come to life, the people naturally treat them with great respect and often feed them with milk, perhaps because milk is the food of human babes and the reptiles are treated as human beings in embryo, who can be born again from women. Thus " the Zulu-Caffres imagine that their ancestors generally visit them under the form of serpents. As soon, therefore, as one of these reptiles appears near their dwellings, they hasten to salute it by the name of *father*, place bowls of milk in its way, and turn it back gently, and with the greatest respect." [2] Among the Masai of East Africa, "when a medicine-man or a rich person dies and is buried, his soul turns into a snake as soon as his body rots ; and the snake goes to his children's kraal to look after them. The Masai in consequence do not kill their sacred snakes, and if a woman sees one in her hut, she pours some milk on the ground for it to lick, after which it will go away." [3] Among

---

the Sea Dyak reverence for snakes and their belief that spirits (*antus*) are incarnate in the reptiles, see further J. Perham, "Sea Dyak Religion," *Journal of the Straits Branch of the Royal Asiatic Society*, No. 10 (December, 1882), pp. 222-224; H. Ling Roth, *The Natives of Sarawak and British North Borneo* (London, 1896), i. 187 *sq.* But from this latter account it does not appear that the spirits (*antus*) which possess the snakes are supposed to be those of human ancestors.

[1] George Brown, D.D., *Melanesians and Polynesians* (London, 1910), pp. 238 *sq.*

[2] Rev. E. Casalis, *The Basutos* (London, 1861), p. 246. Compare A. Kranz, *Natur- und Kulturleben der Zulus* (Wiesbaden, 1880), p. 112.

[3] A. C. Hollis, *The Masai* (Oxford, 1905), p. 307.

the Nandi of British East Africa, "if a snake goes on to the
woman's bed, it may not be killed, as it is believed that it
personifies the spirit of a deceased ancestor or relation, and
that it has been sent to intimate to the woman that her
next child will be born safely.   Milk is put on the ground
for it to drink, and the man or his wife says : '. . . If thou
wantest the call, come, thou art being called.'   It is then
allowed to leave the house.   If a snake enters the houses of
old people they give it milk, and say : ' If thou wantest the
call, go to the huts of the children,' and they drive it away."[1]
This association of the serpent, regarded as an incarnation
of the dead, both with the marriage bed and with the huts
of young people, points to a belief that the deceased person
who is incarnate in the snake may be born again as a
human child into the world.   Again, among the Suk of
British East Africa " it seems to be generally believed that
a man's spirit passes into a snake at death.   If a snake
enters a house, the spirit of the dead man is believed to be
very hungry.   Milk is poured on to its tracks, and a little
meat and tobacco placed on the ground for it to eat.   It is
believed that if no food is given to the snake one or all of
the members of the household will die.   It, however, may
none the less be killed it encountered outside the house, and
if at the time of its death it is inhabited by the spirit of
a dead man, ' that spirit dies also.' "[2]   The Akikuyu of
British East Africa, who similarly believe that snakes are
ngoma or spirits of the departed, " do not kill a snake but
pour out honey and milk for it to drink, which they say it
licks up and then goes its way   If a man causes the death
of a snake he must without delay summon the senior Elders
in the village and slaughter a sheep, which they eat and cut
a *rukwaru* from the skin of its right shoulder for the
offender to wear on his right wrist ; if this ceremony is
neglected he, his wife and his children will die."[3]   Among

[1] A. C. Hollis, *The Nandi* (Oxford,
1909), p. 90.

[2] Mervyn W. H. Beech, *The Suk,
their Language and Folklore* (Oxford,
1911), p. 20.

[3] H. R. Tate (District Commissioner, East Africa Protectorate), " The
Native Law of the Southern Gikuyu of

British East Africa," *Journal of the
African Society*, No. xxxv., April 1910,
p. 243.   See further C. W. Hobley,
" Further Researches into Kikuyu and
Kamba Religious Beliefs and Customs,"
*Journal of the Royal Anthropological
Institute*, xli. (1911) p. 408.   Accord-
ing to Mr. Hobley it is only one parti-

the Baganda the python god Selwanga had his temple on
the shore of the lake Victoria Nyanza, where he dwelt in
the form of a live python. The temple was a hut of the
ordinary conical shape with a round hole in the wall,
through which the sinuous deity crawled out and in at his
pleasure. A woman lived in the temple, and it was her
duty to feed the python daily with fresh milk from a wooden
bowl, which she held out to the divine reptile while he
drained it. The serpent was thought to be the giver of
children ; hence young couples living in the neighbourhood
always came to the shrine to ensure the blessing of the god
on their union, and childless women repaired from long
distances to be relieved by him from the curse of barrenness.[1] It is not said that this python god embodied the
soul of a dead ancestor, but it may have been so ; his power
of bestowing offspring on women suggests it.

The Greeks and Romans seem to have shared the belief that the souls of the dead can be re-incarnated in serpents. The Romans and Greeks appear to have also believed
that the souls of the dead were incarnate in the bodies of
serpents. Among the Romans the regular symbol of the
genius or guardian spirit of every man was a serpent,[2] and
in Roman houses serpents were lodged and fed in such
numbers that if their swarms had not been sometimes
reduced by conflagrations there would have been no living
for them.[3] In Greek legend Cadmus and his wife Harmonia

---

cular sort of snake, called *nyamuyathi*,
which is thought to be the abode of a
spirit and is treated with ceremonious
respect by the Akikuyu. Compare P.
Cayzac, "La Religion des Kikuyu,"
Anthropos, v. (1910) p. 312 ; and for
more evidence of milk offered to serpents as embodiments of the dead see
E. de Pruyssenaere and H. W. Little,
cited above, p. 83, notes [1] and [2].

[1] Rev. J. Roscoe, *The Baganda*
(London, 1911), pp. 320 *sq*. My
friend Mr. Roscoe tells me that serpents are revered and fed with milk by
the Banyoro to the north of Uganda ;
but he cannot say whether the creatures
are supposed to be incarnations of the
dead. Some of the Gallas also regard serpents as sacred and offer milk
to them, but it is not said that they
believe the reptiles to embody the

souls of the departed. See Rev. J.
L. Krapf, *Travels, Researches and
Missionary Labours in Eastern Africa*
(London, 1860), pp. 77 *sq*. The
negroes of Whydah in Guinea likewise
feed with milk the serpents which they
worship. See Thomas Astley's *New
General Collection of Voyages and
Travels*, iii. (London, 1746) p. 29.

[2] L. Preller, *Römische Mythologie* [3]
(Berlin, 1881-1883), ii. 196 *sq*.; G.
Wissowa, *Religion und Kultus der
Römer* [2] (Munich, 1912), pp. 176 *sq*.
The worship of the *genius* was very
popular in the Roman Empire. See
J. Toutain, *Les Cultes Païens dans
l'Empire Romain*, Première Partie, i.
(Paris, 1907) pp. 439 *sqq*.

[3] Pliny, *Nat. Hist.* xxix. 72.
Compare Seneca, *De Ira*, iv. 31. 6.

were turned at death into snakes.[1] When the Spartan king
Cleomenes was slain and crucified in Egypt, a great serpent
coiled round his head on the cross and kept off the vultures
from his face. The people regarded the prodigy as a proof
that Cleomenes was a son of the gods.[2] Again, when
Plotinus lay dying, a snake crawled from under his bed
and disappeared into a hole in the wall, and at the same
moment the philosopher expired.[3] Apparently superstition
saw in these serpents the souls of the dead men. In Greek
religion the serpent was indeed the regular symbol or
attribute of the worshipful dead,[4] and we can hardly doubt
that the early Greeks, like the Zulus and other African
tribes at the present day, really believed the soul of the
departed to be lodged in the reptile. The sacred serpent
which lived in the Erechtheum at Athens, and was fed with
honey - cakes once a month, may have been supposed to
house the soul of the dead king Erechtheus, who had reigned
in his lifetime on the same spot.[5] Perhaps the libations
of milk which the Greeks poured upon graves [6] were intended to be drunk by serpents as the embodiments of the
deceased ; on two tombstones found at Tegea a man and a
woman are respectively represented holding out to a serpent
a cup which may be supposed to contain milk.[7] We have
seen that various African tribes feed serpents with milk
because they imagine the reptiles to be incarnations of their
dead kinsfolk ; [8] and the Dinkas, who practise the custom,
also pour milk on the graves of their friends for some time
after the burial.[9] It is possible that a common type in
Greek art, which exhibits a woman feeding a serpent out of

[1] Apollodorus, *Bibliotheca*, iii. 5. 4 ;
Hyginus, *Fab.* 6 ; Ovid, *Metam.* iv.
563-603.

[2] Plutarch, *Cleomenes*, 39.

[3] Porphyry, *De vita Plotini*, p. 103,
Didot edition (appended to the lives of
Diogenes Laertius).

[4] Plutarch, *Cleomenes*, 39; Scholiast
on Aristophanes, *Plutus*, 733.

[5] Herodotus, viii. 41 ; Plutarch,
Themistocles, 10 ; Aristophanes, *Ly-
sistra*, 758 *sq.*, with the Scholium ;

Philostratus, *Imag.* ii. 17. 6. See
further my note on Pausanias, i. 18. 2
(vol. ii. pp. 168 *sqq.*).

[6] Sophocles, *Electra*, 893 *sqq.* ;
Euripides, *Orestes*, 112 *sqq.*

[7] *Mittheilungen des Deutsch. Archäo-
log. Institutes in Athen*, iv. (1879)
pl. viii. Compare *ib.* pp. 135 *sq.*,
162 *sq.*

[8] Above, pp. 84 *sq.*

[9] E. de Pruyssenaere, *l.c.* (above,
p. 83, note [1]).

a saucer, may have been borrowed from a practice of thus ministering to the souls of the departed.[1]

The serpents fed at the Thesmophoria may have been deemed incarnations of the dead.

Further, at the sowing festival of the Thesmophoria, held by Greek women in October, it was customary to throw cakes and pigs to serpents, which lived in caverns or vaults sacred to the corn-goddess Demeter.[2] We may guess that the serpents thus propitiated were deemed to be incarnations of dead men and women, who might easily be incommoded in their earthy beds by the operations of husbandry. What indeed could be more disturbing than to have the roof of the narrow house shaken and rent over their heads by clumsy oxen dragging a plough up and down on the top of it? No wonder that at such times it was thought desirable to appease them with offerings. Sometimes, however, it is not the dead but the Earth Goddess herself who is disturbed by the husbandman. An Indian prophet at Priest Rapids, on the Middle Columbia River, dissuaded his many followers from tilling the ground because "it is a sin to wound or cut, tear up or scratch our common mother by agricultural pursuits."[3] "You ask me," said this Indian sage, "to plough the ground. Shall I take a knife and tear my mother's bosom? You ask me to dig for stone. Shall I dig under her skin for her bones? You ask me to cut grass and hay and sell it and be rich like white men. But

Reluctance to disturb the Earth Goddess or the spirits of the earth by the operations of digging and ploughing.

---

[1] See C. O. Müller, *Denkmäler der alten Kunst* [2] (Göttingen, 1854), pl. lxi. with the corresponding text in vol. i. (where the eccentric system of paging adopted renders references to it practically useless). In these groups the female figure is commonly, and perhaps correctly, interpreted as the Goddess of Health (Hygieia). It is to be remembered that Hygieia was deemed a daughter of the serpent-god Aesculapius (Pausanias, i. 23. 4), and was constantly associated with him in ritual and art. See, for example, Pausanias, i. 40. 6, ii. 4. 5, ii. 11. 6, ii. 23. 4, ii. 27. 6, iii. 22. 13, v. 20. 3, v. 26. 2, vii. 23. 7, viii. 28. 1, viii. 31. 1, viii. 32. 4, viii. 47. 1. The snake-entwined goddess whose image was found in a prehistoric shrine at Gournia in Crete may have been a predecessor of the serpent-feeding Hygieia. See R. M. Burrows, *The Discoveries in Crete* (London, 1907), pp. 137 *sq.* The snakes, which were the regular symbol of the Furies, may have been originally nothing but the emblems or rather embodiments of the dead; and the Furies themselves may, like Aesculapius, have been developed out of the reptiles, sloughing off their serpent skins through the anthropomorphic tendency of Greek thought.

[2] Scholia on Lucian, *Dial. Meretr.* ii. (*Scholia in Lucianum*, ed. H. Rabe, Leipsic, 1906, pp. 275 *sq.*). As to the Thesmophoria, see my article, "Thesmophoria," *Encyclopaedia Britannica*,[9] xxiii. 295 *sqq.*; *Spirits of the Corn and of the Wild*, ii. 17 *sqq.*

[3] A. S. Gatschet, *The Klamath Indians of South-Western Oregon* (Washington, 1890), p. xcii.

how dare I cut off my mother's hair ? "[1]   The Baigas, a
primitive Dravidian tribe of the Central Provinces in India,
used to practise a fitful and migratory agriculture, burning
down patches of jungle and sowing seed in the soil fertilized
by the ashes after the breaking of the rains.   " One explanation of their refusal to till the ground is that they consider
it a sin to lacerate the breast of their mother earth with a
ploughshare." [2]   In China the disturbance caused to the
earth-spirits by the operations of digging and ploughing
was so very serious that Chinese philosophy appears to have
contemplated a plan for allowing the perturbed spirits a
close time by forbidding the farmer to put his spade or his
plough into the ground except on certain days, when the
earth-spirits were either not at home or kindly consented to
put up with some temporary inconvenience for the good of
man.   This we may infer from a passage in a Chinese
author who wrote in the first century of our era.   " If it is
true," he says, " that the spirits who inhabit the soil object
to it being disturbed and dug up, then it is proper for us to
select special good days for digging ditches and ploughing
our fields.   (But this is never done) ; it therefore follows
that the spirits of the soil, even though really annoyed when
it is disturbed, pass over such an offence if man commits it
without evil intent.   As he commits it merely to ensure his
rest and comfort, the act cannot possibly excite any anger
against him in the perfect heart of those spirits ; and this
being the case, they will not visit him with misfortune even
if he do not choose auspicious days for it.   But if we believe
that the earth-spirits cannot excuse man on account of the
object he pursues, and detest him for annoying them by disturbing the ground, what advantage then can he derive from
selecting proper days for doing so ? " [3]   What advantage
indeed ?   In that case the only logical conclusion is, with
the Indian prophet, to forbid agriculture altogether, as an
impious encroachment on the spiritual world.   Few peoples,
however, who have once contracted the habit of agri-

[1] Washington Matthews, "Myths of
Gestation and Parturition," *American
Anthropologist*, New Series, iv. (New
York, 1902) p. 738.
    [2] *Central Provinces, Ethnographic*

Survey, iii. *Draft Articles on Forest
Tribes* (Allahabad, 1907), p. 23.
    [3] J. J. M. de Groot, *The Religious
System of China*, v. (Leyden, 1907)
pp. 536 *sq.*

Hence agricultural operations are sometimes forbidden.

culture are willing to renounce it out of a regard for the higher powers; the utmost concession which they are willing to make to religion in the matter is to prohibit agricultural operations at certain times and seasons, when the exercise of them would be more than usually painful to the earth-spirits. Thus in Bengal the chief festival in honour of Mother Earth is held at the end of the hot season, when she is supposed to suffer from the impurity common to women, and during that time all ploughing, sowing, and other work cease.[1] On a certain day of the year, when offerings are made to the Earth, the Ewe farmer of West Africa will not hoe the ground, and the Ewe weaver will not drive a sharp stake into it, "because the hoe and the stake would wound the Earth and cause her pain."[2] When Ratumaimbulu, the god who made fruit-trees to blossom and bear fruit, came once a year to Fiji, the people had to live very quietly for a month lest they should disturb him at his important work. During this time they might not plant nor build nor sail about nor go to war; indeed most kinds of work were forbidden. The priests announced the time of the god's arrival and departure.[3] These periods of rest and quiet would seem to be the Indian and Fijian Lent.

Graves as places of conception for women.

Thus behind the Greek notion that women may conceive by a serpent-god[4] seems to lie the belief that they can conceive by the dead in the form of serpents. If such a belief was ever held, it would be natural that barren women should resort to graves in order to have their wombs quickened, and this may explain why they visited the shrine of the serpent-god Aesculapius for that purpose; the shrine was perhaps at first a grave. It is significant that in Syria the shrines of St. George, to which childless women go to get offspring, always include a tomb or the likeness of one;[5] and further,

---

[1] W. Crooke, *Natives of Northern India* (London, 1907), p. 232.

[2] J. Spieth, *Die Ewe-Stämme* (Berlin, 1906), p. 796.

[3] J. E. Erskine, *Journal of a Cruise among the Islands of the Western Pacific* (London, 1853), pp. 245 *sq.*

[4] Persons initiated into the mysteries of Sabazius had a serpent drawn through the bosom of their robes, and the reptile was identified with the god (ὁ διὰ κόλπου θέος, Clement of Alexandria, *Protrept.* ii. 16, p. 14, ed. Potter). This may be a trace of the belief that women can be impregnated by serpents, though it does not appear that the ceremony was performed only on women.

[5] See above, p. 78. Among the South Slavs women go to graves to get children. See below, p. 96.

that in the opinion of Syrian peasants at the present day women may, without intercourse with a living man, bear children to a dead husband, a dead saint, or a jinnee.[1] In the East Indies also it is still commonly believed that spirits can consort with women and beget children on them. The Olo Ngadjoe of Borneo imagine that albinoes are the off-spring of the spirit of the moon by mortal women, the pallid hue of the human children naturally reflecting the pallor of their heavenly father.[2]

Such beliefs are closely akin to the idea, entertained by many peoples, that the souls of the dead may pass directly into the wombs of women and be born again as infants. Thus the Hurons used to bury little children beside the paths in the hope that their souls might enter the passing squaws and be born again ;[3] and similarly some negroes of West Africa throw the bodies of infants into the bush in order that their souls may choose a new mother from the women who pass by.[4] Among the tribes of the Lower Congo "a baby is always buried near the house of its mother, never in the bush. They think that, if the child is not buried near its mother's house, she will be unlucky and never have any more children." The notion probably is that the dead child, buried near its mother's house, will enter into her womb and be born again, for these people believe in the reincarnation of the dead. They think that "the only new thing about a child is its body. The spirit is old and formerly belonged to some deceased person, or it may have the spirit of some living person." For example, if a child is like its mother, father, or uncle, they imagine that it must

Reincarnation of the dead in America and Africa.

---

[1] S. I. Curtiss, *Primitive Semitic Religion To-day*, pp. 115 *sqq.*

[2] A. C. Kruijt, *Het Animisme in den Indischen Archipel* (The Hague, 1906), p. 398.

[3] *Relations des Jésuites*, 1636, p. 130 (Canadian reprint, Quebec, 1858). A similar custom was practised for a similar reason by the Musquakie Indians. See Miss Mary Alicia Owen, *Folk-lore of the Musquakie Indians of North America* (London, 1904), pp. 22 *sq.*, 86. Some of the instances here given have been already cited by

Mr. J. E. King, who suggests, with much probability, that the special modes of burial adopted for infants in various parts of the world may often have been intended to ensure their re-birth. See J. E. King, "Infant Burial," *Classical Review*, xvii. (1903) pp. 83 *sq.* For a large collection of evidence as to the belief in the re-incarnation of the dead, see E. S. Hartland, *Primitive Paternity* (London, 1909–1910), i. 156 *sqq.*

[4] Mary H. Kingsley, *Travels in West Africa* (London, 1897), p. 478.

have the spirit of the relative whom it resembles, and that therefore the person whose soul has thus been abstracted by the infant will soon die.[1] Among the Bangalas, a tribe of cannibals in Equatorial Africa, to the north of the Congo, a woman was one day seen digging a hole in the public road. Her husband entreated a Belgian officer to let her alone, promising to mend the road afterwards, and explaining that his wife wished to become a mother. The good-natured officer complied with his request and watched the woman. She continued to dig till she had uncovered a little skeleton, the remains of her first-born, which she tenderly cmbraced, humbly entreating the dead child to enter into her and give her again a mother's joy. The officer rightly did not smile.[2] The Bagishu, a Bantu tribe of Mount Elgon, in the Uganda Protectorate, practise the custom of throwing out their dead "except in the case of the youngest child or the old grandfather or grandmother, for whom, like the child, a prolonged life on earth is desired. . . . When it is desired to perpetuate on the earth the life of some old man or woman, or that of some young baby, the corpse is buried inside the house or just under the eaves, until another child is born to the nearest relation of the corpse. This child, male or female, takes the name of the corpse, and the Bagishu firmly believe that the spirit of the dead has passed into this new child and lives again on earth. The remains are then dug up and thrown out into the open."[3]

Measures taken to prevent the rebirth of undesirable spirits.

Again, just as measures are adopted to facilitate the rebirth of good ghosts, so on the other hand precautions are taken to prevent the rebirth of bad ones. Thus, with regard to the Baganda of Central Africa we read that, "while the present generation know the cause of pregnancy, the people in the earlier times were uncertain as to its real cause, and thought that it was possible to conceive without any intercourse with the male sex. Hence their precautions in passing places where

[1] Rev. John H. Weeks, "Notes on some Customs of the Lower Congo People," Folk-lore, xix. (1908) p. 422.

[2] Th. Masui, Guide de la Section de l'État Indépendant du Congo à l'Exposition de Bruxelles - Tervueren en 1897 (Brussels, 1897), pp. 113 sq.

[3] J. B. Purvis, Through Uganda to Mount Elgon (London, 1909), pp. 302 sq. As to the Bagishu or Bageshu and their practice of throwing out the dead, see Rev. J. Roscoe, "Notes on the Bageshu," Journal of the Royal Anthropological Institute, xxxix. (1909) pp. 181 sqq.

either a suicide had been burnt, or a child born feet first had been buried. Women were careful to throw grass or sticks on such a spot, for by so doing they thought that they could prevent the ghost of the dead from entering into them, and being reborn." [1] The fear of being got with child by such ghosts was not confined to married women, it was shared by all women alike, whether young or old, whether married or single ; and all of them sought to avert the danger in the same way.[2] And Baganda women imagined that without the help of the other sex they could be impregnated not only by these unpleasant ghosts but also by the flower of the banana. If while a woman was busy in her garden under the shadow of the banana trees, a great purple bloom chanced to fall from one of the trees on her back or shoulders, it was quite enough, in the opinion of, the Baganda, to get her with child ; and were a wife accused of adultery because she gave birth to a child who could not possibly have been begotten by her husband, she had only to father the infant on a banana flower to be honourably acquitted of the charge. The reason why this remarkable property was ascribed to the bloom of the banana would seem to be that ghosts of ancestors were thought to haunt banana groves, and that the afterbirths of children, which the Baganda regarded as twins of the children, were commonly buried at the root of the trees.[3] What more natural than that a ghost should lurk in each flower, and dropping adroitly in the likeness of a blossom on a woman's back effect a lodgment in her womb?

Again, when a child dies in Northern India it is usually buried under the threshold of the house, " in the belief that as

Belief of the Baganda that a woman can be impregnated by the flower of the banana.

---

[1] Rev. J. Roscoe, *The Baganda* (London, 1911), pp. 46 *sq.* Women adopted a like precaution at the grave of twins to prevent the ghosts of the twins from entering into them and being born again (*id.*, pp. 124 *sq.*). The Baganda always strangled children that were born feet first and buried their bodies at cross-roads. The heaps of sticks or grass thrown on these graves by passing women and girls rose in time into mounds large enough to deflect the path and to attract the notice of travellers. See J. Roscoe, *op. cit.* pp. 126 *sq.*, 289.

[2] Rev. J. Roscoe, *op. cit.* pp. 126 *sq.* In the Senegal and Niger region of Western Africa it is said to be commonly believed by women that they can conceive without any carnal knowledge of a man. See Maurice Delafosse, *Haut - Sénégal - Niger, Le Pays, les Peuples, les Langues, l'Histoire, les Civilisations* (Paris, 1912), iii. 171.

[3] Rev. J. Roscoe, *The Baganda*, pp. 47 *sq.* ; *Totemism and Exogamy*, ii. 506 *sq.* As to the custom of depositing the afterbirths of children at the foot of banana (plantain) trees, see J. Roscoe, *op. cit.* pp. 52, 54 *sq.*

Reincarnation of the dead in India. Means taken to facilitate the rebirth of dead children.

the parents tread daily over its grave, its soul will be reborn in the family. Here, as Mr. Rose suggests, we reach an explanation of the rule that children of Hindus are buried, not cremated. Their souls do not pass into the ether with the smoke of the pyre, but remain on earth to be reincarnated in the household." [1] In the Punjaub this belief in the re-incarnation of dead infants gives rise to some quaint or pathetic customs. Thus, " in the Hissar District, Bishnois bury dead infants at the threshold, in the belief that it would facilitate the return of the soul to the mother. The practice is also in vogue in the Kangra District, where the body is buried in front of the back door. In some places it is believed that, if the child dies in infancy and the mother drops her milk for two or three days on the ground, the soul of the child comes back to be born again. For this purpose milk diluted with water is placed in a small earthen pot and offered to the dead child's spirit for three consecutive evenings. There is also a belief in the Ambala and Gujrat Districts that if jackals and dogs dig out the dead body of the child and bring it towards the town or village, it means that the child will return to its mother, but if they take it to some other side, the soul will reincarnate in some other family. For this purpose, the second day after the infant's death, the mother goes out early in the morning to see whether the dogs have brought the body towards the village. When the child is being taken away for burial the mother cuts off and preserves a piece of its garment with a view to persuade the soul to return to her. Barren women or those who have lost children in infancy tear a piece off the clothing of a dead child and stitch it to their wearing apparel, believing that the soul of the child will return to them instead of its own mother. On this account, people take great care not to lose the clothes of dead children, and some bury them in the house." [2] In Bilaspore " a still-born child, or one who has passed away before the *Chhatti* (the sixth day, the day of purification) is not taken out of the

---

[1] W. Crooke, *Natives of Northern India* (London, 1907), p. 202. As to the Hindoo custom of burying infants but burning older persons, see *The Belief in Immortality and the Worship of the Dead*, i. 162 *sq.*

[2] *Census of India, 1911*, vol. xiv. *Punjab*, Part i., Report, by Pandit Harikishan Kaul (Lahore, 1912), p. 299.

house for burial, but is placed in an earthen vessel and is buried in the doorway or in the yard of the house. Some say that this is done in order that the mother may bear another child." [1] Here in Bilaspore the people have devised a very simple way of identifying a dead person when he or she is born again as an infant. When anybody dies, they mark the body with soot or oil, and the next baby born in the family with a similar mark is hailed as the departed come to life again.[2] Among the Kois of the Godavari district, in Southern India, the dead are usually burnt, but the bodies of children and of young men ·and women are buried. If a child dies within a month of its birth, it is generally buried close to the house " so that the rain, dripping from the eaves, may fall upon the grave, and thereby cause the parents to be blessed with another child." [3] Apparently it is supposed that the soul of the dead child, refreshed and revived by the rain, will pass again into the mother's womb. Indian criminal records contain many cases in which " the ceremonial killing of a male child has been performed as a cure for barrenness, the theory being that the soul of the murdered boy becomes reincarnated in the woman, who performs the rite with a desire to secure offspring. Usually she effects union with the spirit of the child by bathing over its body or in the water in which the corpse has been washed. Cases have recently occurred in which the woman actually bathed in the blood of the child." [4]

On the fifth day after a death the Gonds perform the ceremony of bringing back the soul. They go to the bank of a river, call aloud the name of the deceased, and entering the water catch a fish or an insect. This creature they then take home and place among the sainted dead of the family, supposing that in this manner the spirit of the departed has been brought back to the house. Sometimes the fish or

Bringing back the soul of the dead in a fish or insect.

---

[1] E. M. Gordon, *Indian Folk Tales* (London, 1908), p. 49. Other explanations of the custom are reported by the writer, but the original motive was probably a desire to secure the reincarnation of the dead child in the mother.

[2] E. M. Gordon, *op. cit.* pp. 50 *sq.*

[3] E. Thurston, *Ethnographic Notes in Southern India* (Madras, 1906), p. 155; *id., Castes and Tribes of Southern India* (Madras, 1909), iv. 52.

[4] W. Crooke, *Natives of Northern India*, p. 202; *Census of India, 1901*, vol. xvii. *Punjab*, Part i., Report, by H. A. Rose (Simla, 1902), pp. 213 *sq.*

insect is eaten in the belief that it will be thus reborn as a child.[1] This last custom explains the widely diffused story of virgins who have conceived by eating of a plant or an animal or merely by taking it to their bosom.[2] In all such cases we may surmise that the plant or animal was thought to contain the soul of a dead person, which thus passed into the virgin's womb and was born again as an infant. Among the South Slavs childless women often resort to a grave in which a pregnant woman is buried. There they bite some grass from the grave, invoke the deceased by name, and beg her to give them the fruit of her womb. After that they take a little of the mould from the grave and carry it about with them thenceforth under their girdle.[3] Apparently they imagine that the soul of the unborn infant is in the grass or the mould and will pass from it into their body.

Among the Kai of German New Guinea, "impossible as it may be thought, it is yet a fact that women here and there deny in all seriousness the connexion between sexual intercourse and pregnancy. Of course most people are clear as to the process. The ignorance of some individuals is perhaps based on the consideration that not uncommonly married women remain childless for years or for life. Finally, the animistic faith contributes its share to support the

Marginal notes:

Stories of the Virgin Birth.

Reincarnation of the dead among the South Slavs.

Belief of the Kai that women may be impregnated without sexual intercourse.

---

[1] *Census of India, 1901*, vol. xiii. *Central Provinces*, Part i., Report, by R. V. Russell (Nagpur, 1902), p. 93.

[2] For stories of such virgin births see Comte H. de Charency, *Le folklore dans les deux Mondes* (Paris, 1894), pp. 121-256; E. S. Hartland, *The Legend of Perseus*, vol. i. (London, 1894) pp. 71 *sqq.*; and my note on Pausanias vii. 17. 11 (vol. iv. pp. 138-140). To the instances there cited by me add : A. Thevet, *Cosmographie Universelle* (Paris, 1575), ii. 918 [wrongly numbered 952]; K. von den Steinen, *Unter den Naturvölkern Zentral-Brasiliens* (Berlin, 1884), pp. 370, 373; H. A. Coudreau, *La France Equinoxiale*, ii. (Paris, 1887) pp. 184 *sq.*; *Relations des Jésuites*, 1637, pp. 123 *sq.* (Canadian reprint, Quebec, 1858); Franz Boas, *Indianische Sagen von der Nord-Pacifischen Küste Amerikas* (Berlin, 1895), pp. 311 *sq.*; A.

G. Morice, *Au pays de l'Ours Noir* (Paris and Lyons, 1897, p. 153; A. Raffray, "Voyage à la côte nord de la Nouvelle Guinée," *Bulletin de la Société de Géographie* (Paris), VIe Série, xv. (1878) pp. 392 *sq.*; J. L. van der Toorn, "Het animisme bij den Minangkabauer der Padangsche Bovenlanden," *Bijdragen tot de Taal- Land- en Volkenkunde van Nederlandsch-Indië*, xxxix. (1890) p. 78; E. Aymonier, "Les Tchames et leurs religions," *Revue de l'Histoire des Religions*, xxiv. (1901) pp. 215 *sq.*; Major P. R. T. Gurdon, *The Khasis* (London, 1907), p. 195. In some stories the conception is brought about not by eating food but by drinking water. But the principle is the same.

[3] F. S. Krauss, *Sitte und Brauch der Süd-Slaven* (Vienna, 1885), p. 531.

ignorance." [1]   In some islands of Southern Melanesia the Belief in
natives appear similarly to believe that sexual intercourse is the island of Mota
not necessary to impregnation, and that a woman can con- that a
ceive through the simple passage into her womb of a spirit- woman can conceive
animal or a spirit-fruit without the help of a man.   In the through
island of Mota, one of the Banks' group, " the course of events the entrance
is usually as follows : a woman sitting down in her garden into her of
or in the bush or on the shore finds an animal or fruit in her a spirit animal or
loincloth.   She takes it up and carries it to the village, fruit.
where she asks the meaning of the appearance.   The people
say that she will give birth to a child who will have the
characters of this animal or even, it appeared, would be
himself or herself the animal.   The woman then takes the
creature back to the place where she had found it and places
it in its proper home ; if it is a land animal on the land ; if
a water animal in the pool or stream from which it had
probably come.   She builds up a wall round it and goes to
feed and visit it every day.   After a time the animal will
disappear, and it is believed that that is because the animal
has at the time of its disappearance entered into the woman.
It seemed quite clear that there was no belief in physical
impregnation on the part of the animal, nor of the entry of
a material object in the form of the animal into her womb,
but so far as I could gather, an animal found in this way
was regarded as more or less supernatural, a spirit animal
and not one material, from the beginning.   It has happened
in the memory of an old man now living in Mota that a
woman who has found an animal in her loincloth has carried
it carefully in her closed hands to the village, but that when
she opened her hands to show it to the people, the animal
has gone, and in this case it was believed that the entry had
taken place while the woman was on her way from the bush
to the village. . . .   When the child is born it is regarded as
being in some sense the animal or fruit which had been found
and tended by the mother.   The child may not eat the
animal during the whole of its life, and if it does so, will
suffer serious illness, if not death.   If it is a fruit which has
been found, the child may not eat this fruit or touch the tree

[1] Ch. Keysser, "Aus dem Leben   *Neu - Guinea,* iii. (Berlin, 1911) p.
der Kaileute," in R. Neuhauss's *Deutsch*   26.

on which it grows, the latter restriction remaining in those cases in which the fruit is inedible. . . . I inquired into the idea at the bottom of the prohibition of the animal as food, and it appeared to be that the person would be eating himself. It seemed that the act would be regarded as a kind of cannibalism. It was evident that there is a belief in the most intimate relation between the person and all individuals of the species with which he is identified.

" A further aspect of the belief in the animal nature of a child is that it partakes of the physical and mental characters of the animal with which it is identified. Thus, if the animal found has been a sea-snake, and this is a frequent occurrence, the child would be weak, indolent and slow ; if an eel, there will be a similar disposition ; if a hermit crab, the child will be hot-tempered ; if a flying fox, it will also be hot-tempered and the body will be dark ; if a brush turkey, the disposition will be good ; if a lizard, the child will be soft and gentle ; if a rat, thoughtless, hasty and intemperate. If the object found has been a fruit, here also the child will partake of its nature. In the case of a wild Malay apple (*malmalagaviga*) the child will have a big belly, and a person with this condition will be asked, ' Do you come from the *malmalagaviga* ? ' Again, if the fruit is one called *womarakaraqat*, the child will have a good disposition.

Similar belief in the island of Motlav. " In the island of Motlav not far from Mota they have the same belief that if a mother has found an animal in her dress, the child will be identified with that animal and will not be allowed to eat it. Here again the child is believed to have the characters of the animal, and two instances given were that a child identified with a yellow crab will have a good disposition and be of a light colour, while if a hermit crab has been found, the child will be angry and disagreeable. In this island a woman who desires her child to have certain characters will frequent a place where she will be likely to encounter the animal which causes the appearance of these characters. Thus, if she wants to have a light coloured child, she will go to a place where there are light coloured crabs." [1]

[1] W. H. R. Rivers, "Totemism in Polynesia and Melanesia," *Journal of* *the Royal Anthropological Institute,* xxxix. (1909) pp. 173-175. Compare

Throughout a large part of Australia, particularly in the Centre, the North, and the West, the aborigines hold that the commerce of the human sexes is not necessary to the production of children; indeed many of them go further and deny that sexual intercourse is the real cause of the propagation of the species. Among the Arunta, Kaitish, Luritcha, Ilpirra and other tribes, who roam the barren steppes of Central Australia, it appears to be a universal article of belief that every person is the reincarnation of a deceased ancestor, and that the souls of the dead pass directly into the wombs of women, who give them birth without the need of commerce with the other sex. They think that the spirits of the departed gather and dwell at particular spots, marked by a natural feature such as a rock or a tree, and that from these lurking-places they dart out and enter the bodies of passing women or girls. When a woman feels her womb quickened, she knows that a spirit has made its way into her from the nearest abode of the dead. This is their regular explanation of conception and childbirth. " The natives, one and all in these tribes, believe that the child is the direct result of the entrance into the mother of an ancestral spirit individual. They have no idea of procreation as being associated with sexual intercourse, and firmly believe that children can be born without this taking place." [1] The spots where the souls thus congregate wait-

---

Totemism and Exogamy, ii. 89 *sqq.* As to this Melanesian belief that animals can enter into women and be born from them as human children with animal characteristics, Dr. Rivers observes (p. 174): " It was clear that this belief was not accompanied by any ignorance of the physical *rôle* of the human father, and that the father played the same part in conception as in cases of birth unaccompanied by an animal appearance. We found it impossible to get definitely the belief as to the nature of the influence exerted by the animal on the woman, but it must be remembered that any belief of this kind can hardly have escaped the many years of European influence and Christian teaching which the people of this group have received. It is doubtful

whether even a prolonged investigation of this point could now elicit the original belief of the people about the nature of the influence." To me it seems that the belief described by Dr. Rivers in the text is incompatible with the recognition of human fatherhood as a necessary condition for the birth of children, and that though the people may now recognize that necessity, perhaps as a result of intercourse with Europeans, they certainly cannot have recognized it at the time when the belief in question originated.

[1] Baldwin Spencer and F. J. Gillen, *Northern Tribes of Central Australia* (London, 1904), p. 330, compare *id. ibid.* pp. xi, 145, 147-151, 155 *sq.*, 161 *sq.*, 169 *sq.*, 173 *sq.*, 174-176, 606 ; *id., Native Tribes of Central*

ing to be born again are usually the places where the remote ancestors of the dream-time are said to have passed into the ground ; that is, they are the places where the forefathers of the tribe are supposed to have died or to have been buried.   For example, in the Warramunga tribe the ancestor of the Black-snake clan is said to have left many spirits of Black-snake children in the rocks and trees which border a certain creek.   Hence no woman at the present day dares to strike one of these trees with an axe, being quite convinced that the blow would release one of the spirit-children, who would at once enter her body.   They imagine that the spirit is no larger than a grain of sand, and that it enters the woman through her navel and grows into a child in her womb.[1]   Again, at several places in the wide territory of the Arunta tribe there are certain stones which are in like manner thought to be the abode of souls awaiting re-birth.   Hence the stones are called " child-stones."   In one of them there is a hole through which the spirit-children look out for passing women, and it is firmly believed that a visit to the stone would result in conception.   If a young woman is obliged to pass near the stone and does not wish to have a child, she will carefully disguise her youth, pulling a wry face and hobbling along on a stick.   She will bend herself double like a very old woman, and imitating the cracked voice of age she will say, " Don't come to me, I am an old woman."   Nay, it is thought that women may conceive by the stone without visiting it.   If a man and his wife both wish for a child, the husband will tie his hair-girdle round the stone, rub it, and mutter a direction to the spirits to give heed to his wife.   And it is believed that by performing a similar ceremony a malicious man can cause women and even children at a distance to be pregnant.[2]

Reincarnation of the dead in Northern Australia.
Such beliefs are not confined to the tribes of Central Australia but prevail among all the tribes from Lake Eyre northwards to the sea and the Gulf of Carpentaria.[3]   Thus

---

Australia (London, 1899), pp. 52, 123-125, 126, 132 *sq.*, 265, 335-338.

[1] B. Spencer and F. J. Gillen, *Northern Tribes of Central Australia*, pp. 162, 330 *sq.*

[2] B. Spencer and F. J. Gillen,

Native Tribes of Central Australia, pp. 337 *sq.*

[3] W. Baldwin Spencer, *An Introduction to the Study of Certain Native Tribes of the Northern Territory* (Melbourne, 1912), p. 6: "The two

the Mungarai say that in the far past time their old ancestors walked about the country, making all the natural features of the landscape and leaving spirit-children behind them where they stopped.   These children emanated from the bodies of the ancestors, and they still wait at various spots looking out for women into whom they may go and be born.   For example, near McMinn's bar on the Roper River there is a large gum tree full of spirit-children, who all belong to one particular totem and are always agog to enter into women of that totem.   Again, at Crescent Lagoon an ancestor, who belonged to the thunder totem, deposited numbers of spirit-children ; and if a woman of the Gnaritjbellan subclass so much as dips her foot in the water, one of the spirit-children passes up her leg and into her body and in due time is born as a child, who has thunder for its totem.   Or if the woman stoops and drinks water, one of the sprites will enter her through the mouth.   Again, there are lagoons along the Roper River where red lilies grow ; and the water is full of spirit-children which were deposited there by a kangaroo man. So when women of the Gnaritjbellan subclass wade into the water to gather lilies, little sprites swarm up their legs and are born as kangaroo children.   Again, in the territory of the Nullakun tribe there is a certain spring where a man once deposited spirit-children of the rainbow totem ; and to this day when a woman of the right totem comes to drink at the spring, the spirit of a rainbow child will dart into her and be born.   Once more, in the territory of the Yungman tribe the trees and stones near Elsey Creek are full of spirit-children who belong to the sugar-bag (honeycomb) totem ; and these sugar-bag children are constantly entering into the right women and being born into the world.[1]

---

fundamental beliefs of reincarnation and of children not being of necessity the result of sexual intercourse, are firmly held by the tribes in their normal wild state.   There is no doubt whatever of this, and we now know that these two beliefs extend through all the tribes northwards to Katherine Creek and eastwards to the Gulf of Carpentaria."   In a letter (dated Melbourne, July 27th, 1913) Professor Baldwin

Spencer writes to me that the natives on the Alligator River in the Northern Territory "have detailed traditions—as also have all the tribes—of how great ancestors wandered over the country leaving numbers of spirit children behind them who have been reincarnated time after time.   They know who everyone is a reincarnation of, as the names are perpetuated."

[1] W. Baldwin Spencer, *An Intro-*

Theories
as to the
birth of
children
among the
tribes of
Queens-
land.

The natives of the Tully River in Queensland do not
recognize sexual intercourse as a cause of conception in
women, though curiously enough they do recognize it as the
cause of conception in all animals, and pride themselves on
their superiority to the brutes in that they are not indebted
for the continuance of their species to such low and vulgar
means. The true causes of conception in a woman, according
to them, are four in number. First, she may have received
a particular species of black bream from a man whom the
European in his ignorance would call the father ; this she
may have roasted and sat over the fire inhaling the savoury
smell of the roast fish. That is quite sufficient to get her
with child. Or, secondly, she may have gone out on
purpose to catch a certain kind of bull-frog, and if she
succeeds in capturing it, that again is a full and satisfactory
explanation of her pregnancy. Thirdly, some man may
have told her to conceive a child, and the mere command
produces the desired effect. Or, fourth and lastly, she may
have simply dreamed that the child was put into her, and
the dream necessarily works its own fulfilment. Whatever
white men may think about the matter, these are the real
causes why babies are born among the blacks on the Tully
River.[1] About Cape Bedford in Queensland the natives
believe that babies are sent by certain long-haired spirits,
with two sets of eyes in the front and back of their heads,
who live in the dense scrub and underwood. The children
are made in the far west where the sun goes down, and they
are made not in the form of infants but full grown ; but on
their passage from the sunset land to the wombs they are
changed into the shape of spur-winged plovers, if they are
girls, or of pretty snakes, if they are boys. So when the cry
of a plover is heard by night, the blacks prick up their ears
and say, " Hallo ! there is a baby somewhere about." And
if a woman is out in the bush searching for food and sees
one of the pretty snakes, which are really baby boys on the
look out for mothers, she will call out to her mates, and

---

duction to ⁺he *Study of Certain Native*
Tribes of the Northern Territory (Melbourne, 1912), pp. 41-45.
   [1] Walter E. Roth, *North Queensland*
Ethnography, Bulletin No. 5, *Super-*
stition, Magic, and Medicine (Brisbane,
1903), pp. 22, § 81.

they will come running and turn over stones, and leaves, and logs in the search for the snake ; and if they cannot find it they know that it has gone into the woman and that she will soon give birth to a baby boy.[1]   On the Pennefather River in Queensland the being who puts babies into women is called Anje-a.   He takes a lump of mud out of one of the mangrove swamps, moulds it into the shape of an infant, and insinuates it into a woman's womb.   You can never see him, for he lives in the depths of the woods, among the rocks, and along the mangrove swamps ; but sometimes you can hear him laughing there to himself, and when you hear him you may know that he has got a baby ready for somebody.[2]   Among the tribes of the Cairns district in North Queensland " the acceptance of food from a man by a woman was not merely regarded as a marriage ceremony, but as the actual cause of conception." [3]

Similarly among the Australian tribes of the Northern Territory, about Port Darwin and the Daly River, especially among the Larrekiya and Wogait, " conception is not regarded as a direct result of cohabitation."   The old men of the Wogait say that there is an evil spirit who takes babies from a big fire and puts them in the wombs of women, who must give birth to them.   In the ordinary course of events, when a man is out hunting and kills game or collects other food, he gives it to his wife and she eats it, believing that the game or other food will cause her to conceive and bring forth a child.   When the child is born, it may on no account partake of the food

Theories as to the birth of children in Northern and Western Australia. Belief that conception in women is caused by the food they eat.

---

[1] Walter E. Roth, *op. cit.* p. 23, § 82.

[2] Walter E. Roth, *op. cit.* p. 23, § 83.   Mr. Roth adds, very justly : "When it is remembered that as a rule in all these Northern tribes, a little girl may be given to and will live with her spouse as wife long before she reaches the stage of puberty—the relationship of which to fecundity is not recognised—the idea of conception not being necessarily due to sexual connection becomes partly intelligible."

[3] The Bishop of North Queensland (Dr. Frodsham) in a letter to me, dated Bishop's Lodge, Townsville, Queensland, July 9th, 1909.   The Bishop's authority for the statement is the Rev. C. W. Morrison, M.A., acting head of the Yarrubah Mission. In the same letter Dr. Frodsham, speaking from personal observation, refers to " the belief, practically universal among the northern tribes, that copulation is not the cause of conception."   See J. G. Frazer, " Beliefs and Customs of the Australian Aborigines," *Folk-lore*, xx. (1909) pp. 350-352 ; *Man*, ix. (1909) pp. 145-147 ; *Totemism and Exogamy*, i. 577 *sq.*

which caused conception in the mother until it has got its first teeth.[1]   A similar belief that conception is caused by the food which a woman eats is held by some tribes of Western Australia.   On this subject Mr. A. R. Brown reports as follows : " In the Ingarda tribe at the mouth of the Gascoyne River, I found a belief that a child is the product of some food of which the mother has partaken just before her first sickness in pregnancy.   My principal informant on this subject told me that his father had speared a small animal called *bandaru*, probably a bandicoot, but now extinct in this neighbourhood.   His mother ate the animal, with the result that she gave birth to my informant.   He showed me the mark in his side where, as he said, he had been speared by his father before being eaten by his mother.   A little girl was pointed out to me as being the result of her mother eating a domestic cat, and her brother was said to have been produced from a bustard. . . . The bustard was one of the totems of the father of these two children and, therefore, of the children themselves.   This, however, seems to have been purely accidental.   In most cases the animal to which conception is due is not one of the father's totems.   The species that is thus connected with an individual by birth is not in any way sacred to him.   He may kill or eat it ; he may marry a woman whose conceptional animal is of the same species, and he is not by the accident of his birth entitled to take part in the totemic ceremonies connected with it.

" I found traces of this same belief in a number of tribes north of the Ingarda, but everywhere the belief seemed to be sporadic ; that is to say, some persons believed in it and others did not.   Some individuals could tell the animal or plant from which they or others were descended, while others did not know or in some cases denied that conception was so caused.   There were to be met with, however, some beliefs of the same character.   A woman of the Buduna tribe said that native women nowadays bear half-caste children because they eat bread made of white flour.   Many

[1] Herbert Basedow, *Anthropological Notes on the Western Coastal Tribes of the Northern Territory of South Aus-* *tralia*, pp. 4 *sq.* (separate reprint from the *Transactions of the Royal Society of South Australia*, vol. xxxi. 1907).

of the men believed that conception is due to sexual intercourse, but as these natives have been for many years in
contact with the whites this cannot be regarded as satisfactory evidence of the nature of their original beliefs.

"In some tribes further to the north I found a more
interesting and better organised system of beliefs. In the
Kariera, Ñamal, and Injibandi tribes the conception of a
child is believed to be due to the agency of a particular man,
who is not the father. This man is the *wororu* of the child
when it is born. There were three different accounts of how
the *wororu* produces conception, each of them given to me
on several different occasions. According to the first, the
man gives some food, either animal or vegetable, to the
woman, and she eats this and becomes pregnant. According
to the second, the man when he is out hunting kills an
animal, preferably a kangaroo or an emu, and as it is dying
he tells its spirit or ghost to go to a particular woman. The
spirit of the dead animal goes into the woman and is born
as a child. The third account is very similar to the last.
A hunter, when he has killed a kangaroo or an emu, takes a
portion of the fat of the dead animal which he places on
one side. This fat turns into what we may speak of as a
spirit-baby, and follows the man to his camp. When the
man is asleep at night the spirit-baby comes to him and
he directs it to enter a certain woman who thus becomes
pregnant. When the child is born the man acknowledges
that he sent it, and becomes its *wororu*. In practically
every case that I examined, some forty in all, the *wororu* of
a man or woman was a person standing to him or her in the
relation of father's brother own or tribal. In one case a man
had a *wororu* who was his father's sister. The duties of a
man to his *wororu* are very vaguely defined. I was told
that a man ' looks after ' his *wororu*, that is, performs small
services for him, and, perhaps, gives him food. The conceptional animal or plant is not the totem of either the child or the
wororu. The child has no particular magical connection with
the animal from which he is derived. In a very large number
of cases that animal is either the kangaroo or the emu." [1]

Conception supposed to be caused by a man who is not the father.

[1] A. R. Brown, " Beliefs concerning   *Man*, xii. (1912) pp. 180 *sq.* Com-
Childbirth in some Australian Tribes,"   pare *id.*, " Three Tribes of Western

Some rude races still ignorant as to the cause of procreation.

Thus it appears that a childlike ignorance as to the physical process of procreation still prevails to some extent among certain rude races of mankind, who are accordingly driven to account for it in various fanciful ways such as might content the curiosity of children. We may safely assume that formerly a like ignorance was far more widely spread than it is now ; indeed in the long ages which elapsed before any portion of mankind emerged from savagery, it is probable that the true cause of childbirth was universally unknown, and that people made shift to explain the mystery by some such theories as are still current among the savage or barbarous races of Central Africa, Melanesia, and Australia. A little reflection on the conditions of savage life may satisfy us that the ignorance is by no means so surprising as it may seem at first sight to a civilized observer, or, to put it otherwise, that the true cause of the birth of children is not nearly so obvious as we are apt to think. Among low savages, such as all men were originally, it is customary for boys and girls to cohabit freely with each other under the age of puberty, so that they are familiar with a commerce of the sexes which is not and cannot be attended with the birth of children. It is, therefore, not very wonderful that they should confidently deny the connexion of sexual intercourse with the production of offspring. Again, the long interval of time which divides the act of conception from the first manifest symptoms of pregnancy might easily disguise from the heedless savage the vital relation between the two. These considerations may remove or lessen the hesitation which civilized man naturally feels at admitting that a considerable part or even the whole of his species should ever have doubted or denied what seems to him one of the most obvious and elementary truths of nature.[1]

In the light of the foregoing evidence, stories of the

Australia," *Journal of the Royal Anthropological Institute*, xliii. (1913) p. 168.

[1] Those who desire to pursue this subject further may consult with advantage Mr. E. S. Hartland's learned treatise *Primitive Paternity* (London, 1909–1910), which contains an ample collection of facts and a careful discussion of them. Elsewhere I have argued that the primitive ignorance of paternity furnishes the key to the origin of totemism. See *Totemism and Exogamy*, i. 155 *sqq.*, iv. 40 *sqq.*

miraculous birth of gods and heroes from virgin mothers Legends of virgin mothers. lose much of the glamour that encircled them in days of old, and we view them simply as relics of superstition surviving like fossils to tell us of a bygone age of childlike ignorance and credulity.

§ 8. *Sacred Stocks and Stones among the Semites*

Traces of beliefs and customs like the foregoing may Procreative virtue apparently ascribed to the sacred stocks and stones at Semitic sanctuaries. perhaps be detected among the ancient Semites. When the prophet Jeremiah speaks of the Israelites who said to a stock or to a tree (for in Hebrew the words are the same), " Thou art my father," and to a stone, " Thou hast brought me forth," [1] it is probable that he was not using vague rhetorical language, but denouncing real beliefs current among his contemporaries. Now we know that at all the old Canaanite sanctuaries, including the sanctuaries of Jehovah down to the reformations of Hezekiah and Josiah, the two regular objects of worship were a sacred stock and a sacred stone,[2] and that these sanctuaries were the seats of profligate rites performed by sacred men (*kedeshim*) and sacred women (*kedeshoth*). Is it not natural to suppose that the stock and stone which the superstitious Israelites regarded as their father and mother were the sacred stock (*asherah*) and the sacred stone (*massebah*) of the sanctuary, and that the children born of the loose intercourse of the sexes at these places were believed to be the offspring or emanations of these uncouth but worshipful idols in which, as in the sacred trees and stones of Central Australia, the souls of the dead may have been supposed to await rebirth ? On this view the sacred men and women who actually begot

---

[1] Jeremiah ii. 27. The ancient Greeks seem also to have had a notion that men were sprung from trees or rocks. See Homer, *Od.* xix. 163; F. G. Welcker, *Griechische Götterlehre* (Göttingen, 1857–1862), i. 777 *sqq.*; A. B. Cook, " Oak and Rock," *Classical Review*, xv. (1901) pp. 322 *sqq.*

[2] The *ashera* and the *masseba*. See 1 Kings xiv. 23; 2 Kings xviii. 4, xxiii. 14; Micah v. 13 *sq.* (in Hebrew,

12 *sq.*); Deuteronomy xvi. 21 *sq.*; W. Robertson Smith, *Religion of the Semites*,[2] pp. 187 *sqq.*, 203 *sqq.*; G. F. Moore, in *Encyclopaedia Biblica*, *svv.*, " Asherah " and " Massebah." In the early religion of Crete also the two principal objects of worship seem to have been a sacred tree and a sacred pillar. See A. J. Evans, " Mycenaean Tree and Pillar Cult," *Journal of Hellenic Studies*, xxi. (1901) pp. 99 *sqq.*

or bore the children were deemed the human embodiments of the two divinities, the men perhaps personating the sacred stock, which appears to have been a tree stripped of its branches, and the women personating the sacred stone, which seems to have been in the shape of a cone, an obelisk, or a pillar.[1]

These conclusions confirmed by the excavation of a sanctuary at the Canaanitish city of Gezer.

These conclusions are confirmed by the result of recent researches at Gezer, an ancient Canaanitish city, which occupied a high, isolated point on the southern border of Ephraim, between Jerusalem and the sea. Here the English excavations have laid bare the remains of a sanctuary with the sacred stone pillars or obelisks (*masseboth*) still standing in a row, while between two of them is set a large socketed stone, beautifully squared, which perhaps contained the sacred stock or pole (*asherah*). In the soil which had accumulated over the floor of the temple were found vast numbers of male emblems rudely carved out of soft limestone ; and tablets of terra-cotta, representing in low relief the mother-goddess, were discovered throughout the strata. These objects were no doubt votive-offerings presented by the worshippers to the male and female deities who were represented by the sacred stock and the sacred stones ; and their occurrence in large quantities raises a strong presumption that the divinities of the sanctuary were a god and goddess regarded as above all sources of fertility. The supposition is further strengthened by a very remarkable discovery.

The infants buried in the sanctuary may have been expected to be born again.

Under the floor of the temple were found the bones of many new-born children, none more than a week old, buried in large jars. None of these little bodies showed any trace of mutilation or violence ; and in the light of the customs practised in many other lands [2] we seem to be justified in

---

[1] As to conical images of Semitic goddesses, see above, pp. 34 *sqq.* The sacred pole (*asherah*) appears also to have been by some people regarded as the embodiment of a goddess (Astarte), not of a god. See above, p. 18, note [2]. Among the Khasis of Assam the sacred upright stones, which resemble the Semitic *masseboth*, are regarded as males, and the flat table-stones as female. See P. R. T. Gurdon, *The Khasis* (London, 1907), pp. 112 *sq.*,

150 *sqq.* So in Nikunau, one of the Gilbert Islands in the South Pacific, the natives had sandstone slabs or pillars which represented gods and goddesses. "If the stone slab represented a goddess it was not placed erect, but laid down on the ground. Being a lady they thought it would be cruel to make her stand so long." See G. Turner, LL.D., *Samoa* (London, 1884), p. 296.

[2] See above, pp. 91 *sqq.*

conjecturing that the infants were still-born or died soon
after birth, and that they were buried by their parents in the
sanctuary in the hope that, quickened by the divine power,
they might enter again into the mother's womb and again be
born into the world.[1]   If the souls of these buried babes were
supposed to pass into the sacred stocks and stones and to dart
from them into the bodies of would-be mothers who resorted
to the sanctuary, the analogy with Central. Australia would
be complete.   That the analogy is real and not fanciful is
strongly suggested by the modern practice of Syrian women
who still repair to the shrines of saints to procure offspring,
and who still look on "holy men" as human embodiments
of divinity.   In this, as in many other dark places of
superstition, the present is the best guide to the interpretation of the past ; for while the higher forms of religious faith
pass away like clouds, the lower stand firm and indestructible
like rocks.   The "sacred men" of one age are the dervishes
of the next, the Adonis of yesterday is the St. George of
to-day.

[1] As to the excavations at Gezer, see
R. A. Stewart Macalister, *Reports on the
Excavation of Gezer* (London, N.D.), pp.
76-89 (reprinted from the *Quarterly
Statement of the Palestine Exploration
Fund*) ; id., *Bible Side-lights from the
Mound of Gezer* (London, 1906), pp. 57-
67, 73-75.   Professor Macalister now
inclines to regard the socketed stone as
a laver rather than as the base of the
sacred pole.   He supposes that the
buried infants were first-born children
sacrificed in accordance with the
ancient law of the dedication of the
first-born.   The explanation which I
have adopted in the text agrees better
with the uninjured state of the bodies,
and it is further confirmed by the
result of the Austrian excavations at
Tell Ta'annek (Taanach) in Palestine,
which seem to prove that there children
up to the age of two years were not
buried in the family graves but interred
separately in jars.   Some of these
sepulchral jars were deposited under
or beside the houses, but many were
grouped round a rock-hewn altar in a
different part of the hill.   There is
nothing to indicate that any of the
children were sacrificed : the size of
some of the skeletons precludes the
idea that they were slain at birth.
Probably they all died natural deaths,
and the custom of burying them in or
near the house or beside an altar was
intended to ensure their rebirth in the
family.   See Dr. E. Sellin, "Tell
Ta'annek," *Denkschriften der Kaiser.
Akademie der Wissenschaften, Philosophisch-historische Klasse*, l. (Vienna,
1904), No. iv. pp. 32-37, 96 *sq.*
Compare W. W. Graf Baudissin,
Adonis und Esmun, p. 59 n.[3].   I have
to thank Professor R. A. Stewart
Macalister for kindly directing my
attention to the excavations at Tell
Ta'annek (Taanach).   It deserves to
be mentioned that in an enclosure
close to the standing stones at Gezer,
there was found a bronze model of a
cobra (R. A. Stewart Macalister, *Bible
Side-lights*, p. 76).   Perhaps the reptile
was the deity of the shrine, or an embodiment of an ancestral spirit.

CHAPTER V

THE BURNING OF MELCARTH

Semitic custom of sacrificing a member of the royal family.

IF a custom of putting a king or his son to death in the character of a god has left small traces of itself in Cyprus, an island where the fierce zeal of Semitic religion was early tempered by Greek humanity, the vestiges of that gloomy rite are clearer in Phoenicia itself and in the Phoenician colonies, which lay more remote from the highways of Grecian commerce. We know that the Semites were in the habit of sacrificing some of their children, generally the first-born, either as a tribute regularly due to the deity or to appease his anger in seasons of public danger and calamity.[1] If commoners did so, is it likely that kings, with all their heavy responsibilities, could exempt themselves from this dreadful sacrifice for the fatherland? In point of fact, history informs us that kings steeled themselves to do as others did.[2] It deserves to be noticed that if Mesha, king of Moab, who sacrificed his eldest son by fire, claimed to be a son of his god,[3] he would no doubt transmit his divinity to his offspring; and further, that the same sacrifice is said to have been performed in the same way by the divine founder of Byblus, the great seat of the worship of Adonis.[4] This suggests that the human representatives of Adonis formerly perished in the flames. At all events, a custom of periodically burning the chief god of the city in effigy appears to have prevailed

The burning of Melcarth at Tyre.

---

[1] *The Dying God*, pp. 166 *sqq.* See Note I., "Moloch the King," at the end of this volume.

[2] Philo of Byblus, quoted by Eusebius. *Praepar. Evang.* i. 10. 29 *sq.* ; 2 Kings iii. 27.

[3] See above, p. 15.

[4] Philo of Byblus, in *Fragmenta Historicorum Graecorum*, ed. C. Müller, iii. pp. 569, 570, 571. See above, p. 13.

at Tyre and in the Tyrian colonies down to a late time, and the effigy may well have been a later substitute for a man. For Melcarth, the great god of Tyre, was identified by the Greeks with Hercules,[1] who is said to have burned himself to death on a great pyre, ascending up to heaven in a cloud and a peal of thunder.[2] The common Greek legend, immortalized by Sophocles, laid the scene of the fiery tragedy on the top of Mount Oeta, but another version transferred it significantly to Tyre itself.[3] Combined with the other evidence which I shall adduce, this latter tradition raises a strong presumption that an effigy of Hercules, or rather of Melcarth, was regularly burned at a great festival in Tyre. That festival may have been the one known as "the awakening of Hercules," which was held in the month of Peritius, answering nearly to January.[4] The name of the festival suggests that the dramatic representation of the death of the god on the pyre was followed by a semblance of his resurrection. The mode in which the resurrection was supposed to be effected is perhaps indicated by the statement of a Greek writer that the Phoenicians used to sacrifice quails to Hercules, because Hercules on his journey to Libya had been slain by Typhon and brought to life again by Iolaus, who held a quail under his nose : the dead god snuffed at the bird and revived.[5] According to another account Iolaus burnt a quail alive, and the dead hero, who

Festival of " the awakening of Hercules " at Tyre.

---

[1] See above, p. 16.

[2] Sophocles, *Trachiniae*, 1191 *sqq.* ; Apollodorus, *Bibliotheca*, ii. 7. 7 ; Diodorus Siculus, iv. 38 ; Hyginus, *Fab.* 36.

[3] [S. Clementis Romani,] *Recognitiones*, x. 24, p. 233, ed. E. G. Gersdorf (Migne's *Patrologia Graeca*, i. 1434).

[4] Josephus, *Antiquit. Jud.* viii. 5. 3, *Contra Apionem*, i. 18. Whether the quadriennial festival of Hercules at Tyre (2 Maccabees iv. 18-20) was a different celebration, or only "the awakening of Melcarth," celebrated with unusual pomp once in four years, we do not know.

[5] Eudoxus of Cnidus, quoted by Athenaeus, ix. 47, p. 392 D, E. That the death and resurrection of Melcarth were celebrated in an annual festival at

Tyre has been recognised by scholars. See Raoul-Rochette, " Sur l'Hercule Assyrien et Phénicien," *Mémoires de l'Académie des Inscriptions et Belles-Lettres*, xvii. Deuxième Partie (Paris, 1848), pp. 25 *sqq.* ; H. Hubert et M. Mauss, " Essai sur le sacrifice," *L'Année Sociologique*, ii. (1899) pp. 122, 124 ; M. J. Lagrange, *Études sur les Religions Sémitiques*,[2] pp. 308-311. Iolaus is identified by some modern scholars with Eshmun, a Phoenician and Carthaginian deity about whom little is known. See F. C. Movers, *Die Phoenizier*, i. (Bonn, 1841) pp. 536 *sqq.* ; F. Baethgen, *Beiträge zur semitischen Religionsgeschichte* (Berlin, 1888), pp. 44 *sqq.* ; C. P. Tiele, *Geschichte der Religion im Altertum* (Gotha, 1896-1903), i. 268 : W. W. Graf Baudissin, *Adonis und Esmun*, pp. 282 *sqq.*

loved quails, came to life again through the savoury smell of the roasted bird.[1] This latter tradition seems to point to a custom of burning the quails alive in the Phoenician sacrifices to Melcarth.[2] A festival of the god's resurrection might appropriately be held in spring, when the quails migrate northwards across the Mediterranean in great bands, and immense numbers of them are netted for the market.[3] In the month of March the birds return to Palestine by myriads in a single night, and remain to breed in all the open plains, marshes, and cornfields.[4] Certainly a close connexion seems to have subsisted between quails and Melcarth; for legend ran that Asteria, the mother of the Tyrian Hercules, that is, of Melcarth, was transformed into a quail.[5] It was probably to this annual festival of the death and resurrection of Melcarth that the Carthaginians were wont to send ambassadors every year to Tyre, their mother-city.[6]

Worship of Melcarth at Gades, and trace of a custom of burning him there in effigy.

In Gades, the modern Cadiz, an early colony of Tyre on the Atlantic coast of Spain,[7] there was an ancient, famous, and wealthy sanctuary of Hercules, the Tyrian Melcarth. Indeed the god was said to be buried on the spot. No image stood in his temple, but a perpetual fire burned on the altar, and incense was offered by white-robed priests, with bare feet and shorn heads, who were bound to chastity. Neither women nor pigs might pollute the holy place by their presence. In later times many distinguished Romans went on pilgrimage to this remote shrine on the Atlantic shore when they were about to embark on some perilous

---

[1] Zenobius, *Centur.* v. 56 (*Paroemiographi Graeci*, ed. E. L. Leutsch et F. G. Schneidewin, Göttingen, 1839-1851, vol. i. p. 143).

[2] Quails were perhaps burnt in honour of the Cilician Hercules or Sandan at Tarsus. See below, p. 126, note [2].

[3] Alfred Newton, *Dictionary of Birds* (London, 1893-96), p. 755.

[4] H. B. Tristram, *The Fauna and Flora of Palestine* (London, 1884), p. 124. For more evidence as to the migration of quails see Aug. Dillmann's commentary on Exodus xvi. 13, pp. 169 *sqq.* (Leipsic, 1880).

[5] The Tyrian Hercules was said to be a son of Zeus and Asteria (Eudoxus

of Cnidus, quoted by Athenaeus, ix. 47, p. 392 D; Cicero, *De natura deorum*, iii. 16. 42). As to the transformation of Asteria into a quail see Apollodorus, *Bibliotheca*, i. 4. 1; J. Tzetzes, *Schol. on Lycophron*, 401; Hyginus, *Fab.* 53; Servius on Virgil, *Aen.* iii. 73. The name Asteria may be a Greek form of Astarte. See W. W. Graf Baudissin, *Adonis und Esmun*, p. 307.

[6] Quintus Curtius, iv. 2. 10; Arrian, *Anabasis*, ii. 24. 5.

[7] Strabo, iii. 5. 5, pp. 169 *sq.*; Mela, iii. 46; Scymnus Chius, *Orbis Descriptio*, 159-161 (*Geographi Graeci Minores*, ed. C. Müller, i. 200 *sq.*).

enterprise, and they returned to it to pay their vows when their petitions had been granted.[1] One of the last things Hannibal himself did before he marched on Italy was to repair to Gades and offer up to Melcarth prayers which were never to be answered. Soon after he dreamed an ominous dream.[2] Now it would appear that at Gades, as at Tyre, though no image of Melcarth stood in the temple, an effigy of him was made up and burned at a yearly festival. For a certain Cleon of Magnesia related how, visiting Gades, he was obliged to sail away from the island with the rest of the multitude in obedience to the command of Hercules, that is, of Melcarth, and how on their return they found a monstrous man of the sea stranded on the beach and burning ; for the god, they were told, had struck him with a thunderbolt.[3] We may conjecture that at the annual festival of Melcarth strangers were obliged to quit the city, and that in their absence the mystery of burning the god was consummated. What Cleon and the rest saw on their return to Gades would, on this hypothesis, be the smoulder-ing remains of a gigantic effigy of Melcarth in the likeness of a man riding on a sea-horse, just as he is represented on coins of Tyre.[4] In like manner the Greeks portrayed the sea-god Melicertes, whose name is only a slightly altered form of Melcarth, riding on a dolphin or stretched on the beast's back.[5]

At Carthage, the greatest of the Tyrian colonies, a

[1] Silius Italicus, iii. 14-32 ; Mela, iii. 46 ; Strabo, iii. 5. 3, 5, 7, pp. 169, 170, 172 ; Diodorus Siculus, v. 20. 2 ; Philostratus, *Vita Apollonii*, v. 4 *sq.*; Appian, *Hispanica*, 65. Compare Arrian, *Anabasis*, ii. 16. 4. That the bones of Hercules were buried at Gades is mentioned by Mela (*l.c.*). Compare Arnobius, *Adversus Nationes*, i. 36. In Italy women were not allowed to participate in sacrifices offered to Hercules (Aulus Gellius, xi. 6. 2 ; Macrobius, *Saturn.* i. 12. 28 ; Sextus Aurelius Victor, *De origine gentis Romanae*, vi. 6 ; Plutarch, *Quaestiones Romanae*, 60). Whether the priests of Melcarth at Gades were celibate, or had only to observe con-tinence at certain seasons, does not appear. At Tyre the priest of Mel-carth might be married (Justin, xviii.

4. 5). The worship of Melcarth under the name of Hercules continued to flourish in the south of Spain down to the time of the Roman Empire. See J. Toutain, *Les Cultes païens dans l'Empire Romain*, Première Partie, i. (Paris, 1907) pp. 400 *sqq.*

[2] Livy, xxi. 21. 9, 22. 5-9 ; Cicero, *De Divinatione*, i. 24. 49 ; Silius Italicus, iii. 1 *sqq.*, 158 *sqq.*

[3] Pausanias, x. 4. 5.

[4] B. V. Head, *Historia Numorum* (Oxford, 1887), p. 674 ; G. A. Cooke, *Text-Book of North-Semitic Inscrip-tions*, p. 351.

[5] F. Imhoof-Blumer and P. Gardner, *Numismatic Commentary on Pausanias*, pp. 10-12, with pl. A ; Stoll, *s.v.* "Melikertes," in W. H. Roscher's *Lexikon der griech. und röm. Mytho-logie*, ii. 2634.

Evidence of a custom of burning a god or goddess at Carthage. reminiscence of the custom of burning a deity in effigy seems to linger in the story that Dido or Elissa, the foundress and queen of the city, stabbed herself to death upon a pyre, or leaped from her palace into the blazing pile, to escape the fond importunities of one lover or in despair at the cruel desertion of another.[1] We are told that Dido was worshipped as a goddess at Carthage so long as the country maintained its independence.[2] Her temple stood in the centre of the city shaded by a grove of solemn yews and firs.[3] The two apparently contradictory views of her character as a queen and a goddess may be reconciled if we suppose that she was both the one and the other ; that in fact the queen of Carthage in early days, like the queen of Egypt down to historical times, was regarded as divine, and had, like human deities elsewhere, to die a violent death either at the end of a fixed period or whenever her bodily and mental powers began to fail. In later ages the stern old custom might be softened down into a pretence by substituting an effigy for the queen or by allowing her to

The fire-walk at Tyre. pass through the fire unscathed. A similar modification of the ancient rule appears to have been allowed at Tyre itself, the mother-city of Carthage. We have seen reason to think that the kings of Tyre, from whom Dido was descended, claimed to personate the god Melcarth, and that the deity was burned either in effigy or in the person of a man at an annual festival.[4] Now in the same chapter in which Ezekiel charges the king of Tyre with claiming to be a god, the prophet describes him as walking " up and down amidst the stones of fire." [5] The description becomes at once intelligible

---

[1] Justin, xviii. 6. 1-7 ; Virgil, *Aen.* iv. 473 *sqq.*, v. i. *sqq.* ; Ovid, *Fasti,* iii. 545 *sqq.* ; Timaeus, in *Fragmenta Historicorum Graecorum,* ed. C. Müller, i. 197. Compare W. Robertson Smith, *Religion of the Semites,*[2] pp. 373 *sqq.* The name of Dido has been plausibly derived by Gesenius, Movers, E. Meyer, and A. H. Sayce from the Semitic *dôd,* "beloved." See F. C. Movers, *Die Phoenizier,* i. 616 ; Meltzer, *s.v.* "Dido," in W. H. Roscher's *Lexikon der griech. und röm. Mythologie,* i. 1017 *sq.* ; A. H. Sayce, *Lectures on the Religion of the Ancient Baby-* *lonians* (London and Edinburgh, 1887), pp. 56 *sqq.* If they are right, the divine character of Dido becomes more probable than ever, since " the Beloved " (*Dodah*) seems to have been a title of a Semitic goddess, perhaps Astarte. See above, p. 20, note[2]. According to Varro it was not Dido but her sister Anna who slew herself on a pyre for love of Aeneas (Servius on Virgil, *Aen.* iv. 682).

[2] Justin, xviii. 6. 8.

[3] Silius Italicus, i. 81 *sqq.*

[4] See above, pp. 16, 110 *sqq.*

[5] Ezekiel xxviii. 14, compare 16.

if we suppose that in later times the king of Tyre compounded for being burnt in the fire by walking up and down
on hot stones, thereby saving his life at the expense perhaps
of a few blisters on his feet.   It is possible that when all
went well with the commonwealth, children whom strict law
doomed to the furnace of Moloch may also have been
mercifully allowed to escape on condition of running the
fiery gauntlet.   At all events, a religious rite of this sort has
been and is still practised in many parts of the world : the
performers solemnly pace through a furnace of heated stones
or glowing wood-ashes in the presence of a multitude of
spectators.   Examples of the custom have been adduced
in another part of this work.[1]   Here I will cite only
one.   At Castabala, in Southern Cappadocia, there was   The fire
worshipped an Asiatic goddess whom the Greeks called   walk at
the Perasian Artemis.   Her priestesses used to walk bare-   Castabala.
foot over a fire of charcoal without sustaining any injury.
That this rite was a substitute for burning human beings
alive or dead is suggested by the tradition which placed the
adventure of Orestes and the Tauric Artemis at Castabala ;[2]
for the men or women sacrificed to the Tauric Artemis
were first put to the sword and then burned in a pit of
sacred fire.[3]   Among the Carthaginians another trace of   The Car-
such a practice may perhaps be detected in the story that   thaginian
at the desperate battle of Himera, fought from dawn of day   Hamilcar
till late in the evening, the Carthaginian king Hamilcar   sacrifices
remained in the camp and kept sacrificing holocausts of   the fire.
victims on a huge pyre ; but when he saw his army giving

[1] *Balder the Beautiful*, ii. 1 *sqq.*
But, as I have there pointed out, there
are grounds for thinking that the custom
of walking over fire is not a substitute
for human sacrifice, but merely a stringent form of purification.   On fire as a
purificatory agent see below, pp. 179
sqq., 188 *sq.*

[2] Strabo, xii. 2. 7, p. 537.   In
Greece itself accused persons used to
prove their innocence by walking
through fire (Sophocles, *Antigone*, 264
sq., with Jebb's note).   Possibly the
fire-walk of the priestesses at Castabala was designed to test their chastity.   For this purpose the priests and
priestesses of the Tshi-speaking people

of the Gold Coast submit to an ordeal,
standing one by one in a narrow circle
of fire.   This "is supposed to show
whether they have remained pure, and
refrained from sexual intercourse, during
the period of retirement, and so are
worthy of inspiration by the gods.   If
they are pure they will receive no injury
and suffer no pain from the fire" (A. B.
Ellis, *The Tshi-speaking Peoples of the
Gold Coast*, London, 1887, p. 138).
These cases favour the purificatory
explanation of the fire-walk.

[3] Euripides, *Iphigenia in Tauris*,
621-626.   Compare Diodorus Siculus,
xx. 14. 6.

way before the Greeks, he flung himself into the flames and was burned to death. Afterwards his countrymen sacrificed to him and erected a great monument in his honour at Carthage, while lesser monuments were reared to his memory in all the Punic colonies.[1]   In public emergencies which called for extraordinary measures a king of Carthage may well have felt bound in honour to sacrifice himself in the old way for the good of his country. That the Carthaginians regarded the death of Hamilcar as an act of heroism and not as a mere suicide of despair, is proved by the posthumous honours they paid him.

The death of Hercules a Greek version of the burning of Melcarth.

The foregoing evidence, taken altogether, raises a strong presumption, though it cannot be said to amount to a proof, that a practice of burning a deity, and especially Melcarth, in effigy or in the person of a human representative, was observed at an annual festival in Tyre and its colonies. We can thus understand how Hercules, in so far as he represented the Tyrian god, was believed to have perished by a voluntary death on a pyre. For on many a beach and headland of the Aegean, where the Phoenicians had their trading factories, the Greeks may have watched the bale-fires of Melcarth blazing in the darkness of night, and have learned with wonder that the strange foreign folk were burning their god. In this way the legend of the voyages of Hercules and his death in the flames may be supposed to have originated. Yet with the legend the Greeks borrowed the custom of burning the god ; for at the festivals of Hercules a pyre used to be kindled in memory of the hero's fiery death on Mount Oeta.[2]   We may surmise, though we are not expressly told, that an effigy of Hercules was regularly burned on the pyre.

[1] Herodotus, vii. 167. This was the Carthaginian version of the story. According to another account, Hamilcar was killed by the Greek cavalry (Diodorus Siculus, xi. 22. 1). His worship at Carthage is mentioned by Athenagoras (*Supplicatio pro Christianis*, p. 64, ed. J. C. T. Otto, Jena, 1857.) I have called Hamilcar a king in accordance with the usage of Greek writers (Herodotus, vii. 165 *sq.* ; Aristotle, *Politics*, ii. 11 ; Polybius, vi. 51 ; Diodorus Siculus, xiv. 54. 5). But the *suffetes*, or supreme magistrates, of Carthage were two in number ; whether they were elected for a year or for life seems to be doubtful. Cornelius Nepos, who calls them kings, says that they were elected annually (*Hannibal*, vii. 4), and Livy (xxx. 7. 5) compares them to the consuls ; but Cicero (*De re publica*, ii. 23. 42 *sq.*) seems to imply that they held office for life. See G. A. Cooke, *Text-book of North-Semitic Inscriptions*, pp. 115 *sq.*

[2] Lucian, *Amores*, 1 and 54.

CHAPTER VI

THE BURNING OF SANDAN

§ 1. *The Baal of Tarsus*

IN Cyprus the Tyrian Melcarth was worshipped side by side with Adonis at Amathus,[1] and Phoenician inscriptions prove that he was revered also at Idalium and Larnax Lapethus. At the last of these places he seems to have been regarded by the Greeks as a marine deity and identified with Poseidon.[2] A remarkable statue found at Amathus may represent Melcarth in the character of the lion-slayer, a character which the Greeks bestowed on Hercules. The statue in question is of colossal size, and exhibits a thick-set, muscular, hirsute deity of almost bestial aspect, with goggle eyes, huge ears, and a pair of stumpy horns on the top of his head. His beard is square and curly: his hair falls in three pigtails on his shoulders: his brawny arms appear to be tattooed. A lion's skin, clasped by a buckle, is knotted round his loins; and he holds the skin of a lioness in front of him, grasping a hind paw with each hand, while the head of the beast, which is missing, hung down between his legs. A fountain must have issued from the jaws of the lioness, for a rectangular hole, where the beast's head should be, communicates by a channel with another hole in the back of the statue. Greek artists working on this or a similar barbarous model produced the refined type of the Grecian Hercules with the lion's scalp thrown like a cowl over

The Tyrian Melcarth in Cyprus.

The lion-slaying god.

[1] See above, p. 32.

[2] G. A. Cooke, *Text-book of North-* *Semitic Inscriptions*, Nos. 23 and 29, pp. 73, 83 *sq.*, with the notes on pp. 81, 84.

117

his head. Statues of him have been found in Cyprus, which represent intermediate stages in this artistic evolution.[1] But there is no proof that in Cyprus the Tyrian Melcarth was burned either in effigy or in the person of a human representative.[2]

The Baal of Tarsus, an Oriental god of corn and grapes.

On the other hand, there is clear evidence of the observance of such a custom in Cilicia, the country which lies across the sea from Cyprus, and from which the worship of Adonis, according to tradition, was derived.[3] Whether the Phoenicians ever colonized Cilicia or not is doubtful,[4] but at all events the natives of the country, down to late times, worshipped a male deity who, in spite of a superficial assimilation to a fashionable Greek god, appears to have been an Oriental by birth and character. He had his principal seat at Tarsus, in a plain of luxuriant fertility and almost tropical climate, tempered by breezes from the snowy range of Tarsus on the north and from the sea on the south.[5] Though Tarsus boasted of a school of Greek philosophy which at the beginning of our era surpassed those of Athens and Alexandria,[6] the city apparently remained in manners and spirit essentially Oriental. The women went about the streets muffled up to the eyes in Eastern fashion, and Dio Chrysostom reproaches the natives with resembling the most dissolute of the Phoenicians rather than the Greeks

---

[1] G. Perrot et Ch. Chipiez, *Histoire de l'Art dans l'Antiquité*, iii. 566-578. The colossal statue found at Amathus may be related, directly or indirectly, to the Egyptian god Bes, who is represented as a sturdy misshapen dwarf, wearing round his body the skin of a beast of the panther tribe, with its tail hanging down. See E. A. Wallis Budge, *The Gods of the Egyptians* (London, 1904), ii. 284 *sqq.* ; A. Wiedemann, *Religion of the Ancient Egyptians* (London, 1897), pp. 159 *sqq.* ; A. Furtwängler, *s.v.* "Herakles," in W. H. Roscher's *Lexikon der griech. und röm. Mythologie*, i. 2143 *sq.*

[2] However, human victims were burned at Salamis in Cyprus. See below, p. 145.

[3] See above, p. 41.

[4] For traces of Phoenician influence in Cilicia see F. C. Movers, *Die Phoenizier*, ii. 2, pp. 167-174, 207 *sqq.* Herodotus says (vii. 91) that the Cilicians were named after Cilix, a son of the Phoenician Agenor.

[5] As to the fertility and the climate of the plain of Tarsus, which is now very malarious, see E. J. Davis, *Life in Asiatic Turkey* (London, 1879), chaps. i.-vii. The gardens for miles round the city are very lovely, but wild and neglected, full of magnificent trees, especially fine oak, ash, orange, and lemon-trees. The vines run to the top of the highest branches, and almost every garden resounds with the song of the nightingale (E. J. Davis, *op. cit.* p. 35).

[6] Strabo, xiv. 5. 13, pp. 673 *sq.*

whose civilization they aped.[1] On the coins of the city they assimilated their native deity to Zeus by representing him seated on a throne, the upper part of his body bare, the lower limbs draped in a flowing robe, while in one hand he holds a sceptre, which is topped sometimes with an eagle but often with a lotus flower.   Yet his foreign nature is indicated both by his name and his attributes; for in Aramaic inscriptions on the coins he bears the name of the Baal of Tarsus, and in one hand he grasps an ear of corn and a bunch of grapes.[2]   These attributes clearly mark him out as a god of fertility in general, who conferred on his worshippers the two things which they prized above all other gifts of nature, the corn and the wine. He was probably therefore a Semitic, or at all events an Oriental, rather than a Greek deity.   For while the Semite cast all his gods more or less in the same mould, and expected them all to render him nearly the same services, the Greek, with his keener intelligence and more pictorial imagination, invested his deities with individual characteristics, allotting to each of them his or her separate function in the divine economy of the world.   Thus he assigned the production of the corn to Demeter, and that of the grapes to Dionysus; he was not so unreasonable as to demand both from the same hard-worked deity.

§ 2. *The God of Ibreez*

Now the suspicion that the Baal of Tarsus, for all his posing in the attitude of Zeus, was really an Oriental is confirmed by a remarkable rock-hewn monument which is to be seen at Ibreez in Southern Cappadocia.   Though the

The Baal of Tarsus has his counterpart at Ibreez in Cappadocia.

---

[1] Dio Chrysostom, *Or.* xxxiii. vol. ii. pp. 14 *sq.*, 17, ed. L. Dindorf (Leipsic, 1857).

[2] F. C. Movers, *Die Phoenizier*, ii. 2, pp. 171 *sq.*; P. Gardner, *Types of Greek Coins* (Cambridge, 1883), pl. x. Nos. 29, 30; B. V. Head, *Historia Numorum* (Oxford, 1887), p. 614; G. F. Hill, *Catalogue of Greek Coins of Lycaonia, Isauria, and Cilicia* (London, 1900), pp. 167-176, pl. xxix.-xxxii.; G. Macdonald, *Catalogue of Greek Coins in the Hunterian Collection* (Glasgow, 1899-1905), ii. 547; G. Perrot et Ch. Chipiez, *Histoire de l'Art dans l'Antiquité*, iv. 727.   In later times, from about 175 B.C. onward, the Baal of Tarsus was completely assimilated to Zeus on the coins. See B. V. Head, *op. cit.* p. 617; G. F. Hill, *op. cit.* pp. 177, 181.

place is distant little more than fifty miles from Tarsus as the crow flies, yet the journey on horseback occupies five days ; for the great barrier of the Taurus mountains rises

The pass
of the
Cilician
Gates.

like a wall between. The road runs through the famous pass of the Cilician Gates, and the scenery throughout is of the grandest Alpine character. On all sides the mountains tower skyward, their peaks sheeted in a dazzling pall of snow, their lower slopes veiled in the almost inky blackness of dense pine-forests, torn here and there by impassable ravines, or broken into prodigious precipices of red and grey rock which border the narrow valley for miles. The magnificence of the landscape is enhanced by the exhilarating influence of the brisk mountain air, all the more by contrast with the sultry heat of the plain of Tarsus which the traveller has left behind. When he emerges from the defile on the wide open tableland of Anatolia he feels that in a sense he has passed out of Asia, and that the highroad to Europe lies straight before him. The great mountains on which he now looks back formed for centuries the boundary between the Christian West and the Mohammedan East ; on the southern side lay the domain of the Caliphs, on the northern side the Byzantine Empire. The Taurus was the dam that long repelled the tide of Arab invasion ; and though year by year the waves broke through the pass of the Cilician Gates and carried havoc and devastation through the tableland, the refluent waters always retired to the lower level of the Cilician plains. A line of beacon lights stretching from the Taurus to Constantinople flashed to the Byzantine capital tidings of the approach of the Moslem invaders.[1]

The village of Ibreez is charmingly situated at the northern foot of the Taurus, some six or seven miles south of the town of Eregli, the ancient Cybistra. From the town to the village the path goes through a richly cultivated district of wheat and vines along green lanes more lovely than those of Devonshire, lined by thick hedges and rows of willow, poplar, hazel, hawthorn, and huge old walnut-trees, where in early summer the nightingales warble on

The rock-
sculptures
at Ibreez
represent a
god of corn
and grapes
adored
by his wor-
shipper,
a priest or
king.

[1] Sir W. M. Ramsay, *Luke the Physician, and other Studies in the History of Religion* (London, 1908), pp. 112 *sqq.*

every side. Ibreez itself is embowered in the verdure of orchards, walnuts, and vines. It stands at the mouth of a deep ravine enclosed by great precipices of red rock. From the western of these precipices a river clear as crystal, but of a deep blue tint, bursts in a powerful jet, and being reinforced by a multitude of springs becomes at once a raging impassable torrent foaming and leaping with a roar of waters over the rocks in its bed. A little way from the source a branch of the main stream flows in a deep narrow channel along the foot of a reddish weather-stained rock which rises sheer from the water. On its face, which has been smoothed to receive them, are the sculptures. They consist of two colossal figures, representing a god adored by his worshipper. The deity, some fourteen feet high, is a bearded male figure, wearing on his head a high pointed cap adorned with several pairs of horns, and plainly clad in a short tunic, which does not reach his knees and is drawn in at the waist by a belt. His legs and arms are bare ; the wrists are encircled by bangles or bracelets. His feet are shod in high boots with turned-up toes. In his right hand he holds a vine-branch laden with clusters of grapes, and in his raised left hand he grasps a bunch of bearded wheat, such as is still grown in Cappadocia ; the ears of corn project above his fingers, while the long stalks hang down to his feet. In front of him stands the lesser figure, some eight feet high. He is clearly a priest or king, more probably perhaps both in one. His rich vestments contrast with the simple costume of the god. On his head he wears a round but not pointed cap, encircled by flat bands and ornamented in front with a rosette or bunch of jewels, such as is still worn by Eastern princes. He is draped from the neck to the ankles in a long robe heavily fringed at the bottom, over which is thrown a shawl or mantle secured at the breast by a clasp of precious stones. Both robe and shawl are elaborately carved with patterns in imitation of embroidery. A heavy necklace of rings or beads encircles the neck ; a bracelet or bangle clasps the one wrist that is visible ; the feet are shod in boots like those of the god. One or perhaps both hands are raised in the act of adoration. The large aquiline nose, like the beak of a hawk, is a conspicuous feature in the face both of the god and of his worshipper ; the hair and beard of both are thick and curly.[1]

The situation of this remarkable monument resembles that of Aphaca on the Lebanon ;[2] for in both places we see a noble river issuing abruptly from the rock to spread fertility through the rich vale below. Nowhere, perhaps, could man more appropriately revere those great powers of nature to whose favour he ascribes the fruitfulness of the earth, and through it the life of animate creation. With its cool bracing air, its mass of verdure, its magnificent stream of pure ice-cold water—so grateful in the burning heat of summer—and its wide stretch of fertile land, the valley may well have been the residence of an ancient prince or high-priest, who desired to testify by this monument his devotion and gratitude to the god. The seat of this royal or priestly potentate may have been at Cybistra,[3] the modern Eregli, now a decayed and miserable place straggling amid orchards and gardens full of luxuriant groves of walnut, poplar, willow, mulberry, and oak. The place is a paradise of birds. Here

[1] E. J. Davis, "On a New Hama-thite Inscription at Ibreez," *Trans-actions of the Society of Biblical Archaeology*, iv. (1876) pp. 336-346 ; *id.*, *Life in Asiatic Turkey* (London, 1879), pp. 245-260 ; G. Perrot et Ch. Chipiez, *Histoire de l'Art dans l'Antiquité*, iv. 723-729 ; Ramsay and Hogarth, "Prehellenic Monuments of Cappadocia," *Recueil de Travaux re-latifs à la Philologie et à l'Archéologie Égyptiennes et Assyriennes*, xiv. (1903) pp. 77-81, 85 *sq.*, with plates iii. and iv.; L. Messerschmidt, *Corpus Inscrip-tionum Hettiticarum* (Berlin, 1900), Tafel xxxiv. ; Sir W. M. Ramsay, *Luke the Physician* (London, 1908), pp. 171 *sqq.* ; John Garstang, *The Land of the Hittites* (London, 1910), pp. 191-195, 378 *sq.* Of this sculp-tured group Messrs. W. M. Ramsay and D. G. Hogarth say that "it yields to no rock-relief in the world in im-pressive character" (*American Journal of Archaeology*, vi. (1890) p. 347). Professor Garstang would date the sculptures in the tenth or ninth century B.C. Another inscribed Hittite monu-ment found at Bor, near the site of the ancient Tyana, exhibits a very similar figure of a priest or king in an attitude of adoration. The resemblance ex-tends even to the patterns embroidered on the robe and shawl, which include the well-known *swastika* carved on the lower border of the long robe. The figure is sculptured in high relief on a slab of stone and would seem to have been surrounded by inscriptions, though a portion of them has perished. See J. Garstang, *op. cit.* pp. 185-188, with plate lvi. For the route from Tarsus to Ibreez (Ivriz) see E. J. Davis, *Life in Asiatic Turkey*, pp. 198-244 ; J. Garstang, *op. cit.* pp. 44 *sqq.*

[2] See above, pp. 28 *sq.*

[3] Strabo, xii. 2. 7, p. 537. When Cicero was proconsul of Cilicia (51–50 B.C.) he encamped with his army for some days at Cybistra, from which two of his letters to Atticus are dated. But hearing that the Parthians, who had invaded Syria, were threatening Cilicia, he hurried by forced marches through the pass of the Cilician Gates to Tarsus. See Cicero, *Ad Atticum*, v. 18, 19, 20 ; *Ad Familiares*, xv. 2, 4.

the thrush and the nightingale sing full-throated, the hoopoe
waves his crested top-knot, the bright-hued woodpeckers flit
from bough to bough, and the swifts dart screaming by
hundreds through the air.   Yet a little way off, beyond the
beneficent influence of the springs and streams, all is desolation—in summer an arid waste broken by great marshes and
wide patches of salt, in winter a broad sheet of stagnant
water, which as it dries up with the growing heat of the sun
exhales a poisonous malaria.   To the west, as far as the eye
can see, stretches the endless expanse of the dreary Lycaonian
plain, barren, treeless, and solitary, till it fades into the blue
distance, or is bounded afar off by abrupt ranges of jagged
volcanic mountains, on which in sunshiny weather the shadows
of the clouds rest, purple and soft as velvet.[1]   No wonder that
the smiling luxuriance of the one landscape, sharply contrasting with the bleak sterility of the other, should have rendered
it in the eyes of primitive man a veritable garden of God.

Among the attributes which mark out the deity of The
Ibreez as a power of fertility the horns on his high cap horned
should not be overlooked.   They are probably the horns of god.
a bull; for to primitive cattle-breeders the bull is the most
natural emblem of generative force.   At Carchemish, the
great Hittite capital on the Euphrates, a relief has been
discovered which represents a god or a priest clad in a rich
robe, and wearing on his head a tall horned cap surmounted
by a disc.[2]   Sculptures found at the palace of Euyuk in North-
Western Cappadocia prove that the Hittites worshipped the
bull and sacrificed rams to it.[3]   Similarly the Greeks conceived the vine-god Dionysus in the form of a bull.[4]

[1] E. J. Davis, in *Transactions of the
Society of Biblical Archaeology*, iv.
(1876) pp. 336 *sq.*, 346; *id.*, *Life in
Asiatic Turkey*, pp. 232 *sq.*, 236 *sq.*,
264 *sq.*, 270-272. Compare W. J.
Hamilton, *Researches in Asia Minor,
Pontus, and Armenia* (London, 1842),
ii. 304-307.

[2] L. Messerschmidt, *The Hittites*
(London, 1903), pp. 49 *sq.* On an
Assyrian cylinder, now in the British
Museum, we see a warlike deity with
bow and arrows standing on a lion,
and wearing a similar bonnet decorated
with horns and surmounted by a star

or sun.   See. De Vogüé, *Mélanges
d'Archéologie Orientale* (Paris, 1868),
p. 46, who interprets the deity as the
great Asiatic goddess.   As to the
horned god of Ibreez "it is a plausible
theory that the horns may, in this case,
be analogous to the Assyrian emblem
of divinity.   The sculpture is late and
its style rather suggests Semitic influence" (Professor J. Garstang, in some
MS. notes with which he has kindly
furnished me).

[3] See below, p. 132.

[4] *Spirits of the Corn and of the
Wild*, i. 16 *sq.*, ii. 3 *sqq.*

§ 3. *Sandan of Tarsus*

The god
of Ibreez
a Hittite
deity.

That the god of Ibreez, with the grapes and corn in his hands, is identical with the Baal of Tarsus, who bears the same emblems, may be taken as certain.[1]   But what was his name? and who were his worshippers?   The Greeks apparently called him Hercules; at least in Byzantine times the neighbouring town of Cybistra adopted the name of Heraclea, which seems to show that Hercules was deemed the principal deity of the place.[2]   Yet the style and costume of the figures at Ibreez prove unquestionably that the god was an Oriental.   If any confirmation of this view were needed, it is furnished by the inscriptions carved on the rock beside the sculptures, for these inscriptions are composed in the peculiar system of hieroglyphics now known as Hittite.   It follows, therefore, that the deity worshipped at Tarsus and Ibreez was a god of the Hittites, that ancient and little-known people who occupied the centre of Asia Minor, invented a system of writing, and extended their influence, if not their dominion, at one time from the Euphrates to the Aegean.   From the lofty and arid table-lands of the interior, a prolongation of the great plateau of Central Asia, with a climate ranging from the most burning heat in summer to the most piercing cold in winter,[3] these hardy highlanders seem to have swept down through the mountain-passes and established themselves at a very early date in the rich southern lowlands of Syria and Cilicia.[4]

[1] The identification is accepted by E. Meyer (*Geschichte des Altertums*,[2] i. 2. p. 641), G. Perrot et Ch. Chipiez (*Histoire de l'Art dans l'Antiquité*, iv. 727), and P. Jensen (*Hittiter und Armenier*, Strasburg, 1898, p. 145).

[2] Ramsay and Hogarth, "Pre-Hellenic Monuments of Cappadocia," *Recueil de Travaux relatifs à la Philologie et à l'Archéologie Égyptiennes et Assyriennes*, xiv. (1893) p. 79.

[3] G. Maspero, *Histoire Ancienne des Peuples de l'Orient Classique*, ii. 360-362; G. Perrot et Ch. Chipiez, *Histoire de l'Art dans l'Antiquité*, iv. 572 *sqq.*, 586 *sq.*

[4] That the cradle of the Hittites was in the interior of Asia Minor, particularly in Cappadocia, and that they spread from there south, east, and west, is the view of A. H. Sayce, W. M. Ramsay, D. G. Hogarth, W. Max Müller, F. Hommel, L. B. Paton, and L. Messerschmidt.   See *Palestine Exploration Fund Quarterly Statement for 1884*, p. 49; A. H. Sayce, *The Hittites*[3] (London, 1903), pp. 80 *sqq.*; W. Max Müller, *Asien und Europa* (Leipsic, 1893), pp. 319 *sqq.*; Ramsay and Hogarth, "Pre-Hellenic Monuments of Cappadocia," *Recueil de Travaux relatifs à la Philologie et à l'Archéologie Égyptiennes et Assyriennes*, xv. (1893) p. 94; F. Hommel, *Grund-*

Their language and race are still under discussion, but a great preponderance of opinion appears to declare that neither the one nor the other was Semitic.[1]

In the inscription attached to the colossal figure of the god at Ibreez two scholars have professed to read the name of Sandan or Sanda.[2] Be that as it may, there are independent grounds for thinking that Sandan, Sandon, or Sandes may have been the name of the Cappadocian and Cilician god of fertility. For the god of Ibreez in Cappadocia appears, as we saw, to have been identified by the Greeks with Hercules, and we are told that a Cappadocian and Cilician name of Hercules was Sandan or Sandes.[3]

The burning of Sandan or Hercules at Tarsus.

---

riss der Geographie und Geschichte des alten Orients (Munich, 1904), pp. 42, 48, 54 ; L. B. Paton, *The Early History of Syria and Palestine* (London, 1902), pp. 103 sqq.; L. Messerschmidt, *The Hittites* (London, 1903), pp. 12, 13, 19, 20; D. G. Hogarth, "Recent Hittite Research," *Journal of the Royal Anthropological Institute*, xxxix. (1909) pp. 408 sqq. Compare Ed. Meyer, *Geschichte des Altertums*,[2] i. 2. (Stuttgart and Berlin, 1909) pp. 617 sqq. ; J. Garstang, *The Land of the Hittites*, pp. 315 sqq. The native Hittite writing is a system of hieroglyphics which has not yet been read, but in their intercourse with foreign nations the Hittites used the Babylonian cuneiform script. Clay tablets bearing inscriptions both in the Babylonian and in the Hittite language have been found by Dr. H. Winckler at Boghaz-Keui, the great Hittite capital in Cappadocia ; so that the sounds of the Hittite words, though not their meanings, are now known. According to Professor Ed. Meyer, it seems certain that the Hittite language was neither Semitic nor Indo-European. As to the inscribed tablets of Boghaz-Keui, see H. Winckler, "Vorläufige Nachrichten über die Ausgrabungen in Boghaz-köi im Sommer 1907, I. Die Tontafelfunde," *Mitteilungen der Deutschen Orient-Gesellschaft zu Berlin*, No. 35, December 1907, pp. 1-59 ; "Hittite Archives from Boghaz-Keui," translated from the German transcripts of Dr. Winckler by Meta E. Williams,

Annals of Archaeology and Anthropology, iv. (Liverpool, 1912), pp. 90-98.

[1] G. Maspero, *Histoire Ancienne des Peuples de l'Orient Classique*, ii. 351, note[3], with his references ; L. B. Paton, *op. cit.* p. 109 ; L. Messerschmidt, *The Hittites*, p. 10 ; F. Hommel, *op. cit.* p. 42 ; W. Max Müller, *Asien und Europa*, p. 332. See the preceding note.

[2] A. H. Sayce, "The Hittite Inscriptions," *Recueil de Travaux relatifs à la Philologie et à l'Archéologie Égyptiennes et Assyriennes*, xiv. (1893) pp. 48 sq. ; P. Jensen, *Hittiter und Armenier* (Strasburg, 1898), pp. 42 sq.

[3] Georgius Syncellus, *Chronographia*, vol. i. p. 290, ed. G. Dindorf (Bonn, 1829) : Ἡρακλέα τινές φασιν ἐν Φοινίκῃ γνωρίζεσθαι Σάνδαν ἐπιλεγόμενον, ὡς καὶ μέχρι νῦν ὑπὸ Καππαδόκων καὶ Κιλίκων. In this passage Σάνδαν is a correction of F. C. Movers's (*Die Phoenizier*, i. 460) for the MS. reading Δισανδάν, the ΔΙ having apparently arisen by dittography from the preceding ΑΙ ; and Κιλίκων is a correction of E. Meyer's ("Über einige semitische Götter," *Zeitschrift der Deutschen Morgenländischen Gesellschaft*, xxxi. 737) for the MS. reading Ἰλίων. Compare Jerome (quoted by Movers and Meyer, *ll.cc.*) : "*Hercules cognomento Desanaus in Syria Phoenice clarus habetur. Inde ad nostram usque memoriam a Cappadocibus et Eliensibus* (al. *Deliis*) *Desanaus*

Now this Sandan or Hercules is said to have founded
Tarsus, and the people of the city commemorated him at
an annual or, at all events, periodical festival by erecting
a fine pyre in his honour.[1] Apparently at this festival, as
at the festival of Melcarth, the god was burned in effigy
on his own pyre. For coins of Tarsus often exhibit the
pyre as a conical structure resting on a garlanded altar or
basis, with the figure of Sandan himself in the midst of it,
while an eagle with spread wings perches on the top of the
pyre, as if about to bear the soul of the burning god in the
pillar of smoke and fire to heaven.[2] In like manner when a
Roman emperor died leaving a son to succeed him on the

---

adhuc dicitur." If the text of Jerome
is here sound, he would seem to have
had before him a Greek original which
was corrupt like the text of Syncellus
or of Syncellus's authority. The Cilician
Hercules is called Sandes by Nonnus
(*Dionys.* xxxiv. 183 *sq.*). Compare
Raoul-Rochette in *Mémoires de l'Académie des Inscriptions et Belles-Lettres,*
xvii. Deuxième Partie (Paris, 1848),
pp. 159 *sqq.*

[1] Ammianus Marcellinus, xiv. 8. 3 ;
Dio Chrysostom, *Or.* xxxiii. vol. ii. p. 16,
ed. L. Dindorf (Leipsic, 1857). The pyre
is mentioned only by Dio Chrysostom,
whose words clearly imply that its
erection was a custom observed periodically. On Sandan or Sandon see K.
O. Müller, "Sandon und Sardanapal," *Kunstarchaeologische Werke,* iii.
6 *sqq.* ; F. C. Movers, *Die Phoenizier,*
i. 458 *sqq.* ; Raoul-Rochette, "Sur
l'Hercule Assyrien et Phénicien,"
*Mémoires de l'Académie des Inscriptions
et Belles-Lettres,* xvii. Deuxième Partie
(Paris, 1848), pp. 178 *sqq.* ; E. Meyer,
"Über einige Semitische Götter,"
*Zeitschrift der Deutschen Morgen-
ländischen Gesellschaft,* xxxi. (1877)
pp. 736-740 : *id., Geschichte des Altertums,*[2] i. 2. pp. 641 *sqq.* § 484.

[2] P. Gardner, *Catalogue of Greek
Coins, the Seleucid Kings of Syria*
(London, 1878), pp. 72, 78, 89, 112,
pl. xxi. 6, xxiv. 3, xxviii. 8 ; G. F.
Hill, *Catalogue of the Greek Coins of
Lycaonia, Isauria, and Cilicia* (Lon-
don, 1900), pp. 180, 181, 183, 190,
221, 224, 225, pl. xxxiii. 2, 3, xxxiv.

10, xxxvii. 9 ; F. Imhoof-Blumer,
"Coin-types of some Kilikian Cities,"
Journal of Hellenic Studies, xviii.
(1898) p. 169, pl. xiii. 1, 2. The
structure represented on the coins is
sometimes called not the pyre but the
monument of Sandan or Sardanapalus.
Certainly the cone resting on the square
base reminds us of the similar structure
on the coins of Byblus as well as of the
conical image of Aphrodite at Paphos
(see above, pp. 14, 34) ; but the words
of Dio Chrysostom make it probable
that the design on the coins of Tarsus
represents the pyre. At the same
time, the burning of the god may well
have been sculptured on a permanent
monument of stone. The legend
ΟΡΤΥΓΟΘΗΡΑ, literally "quail-hunt,"
which appears on some coins of Tarsus
(G. F. Hill, *op. cit.* pp. lxxxvi. *sq.*),
may refer to a custom of catching
quails and burning them on the pyre.
We have seen (above, pp. 111 *sq.*)
that quails were apparently burnt in
sacrifice at Byblus. This explanation
of the legend on the coins of Tarsus
was suggested by Raoul-Rochette
(*op. cit.* pp. 201-205). However,
Mr. G. F. Hill writes to me that
"the interpretation of Ὀρτυγοθήρα
as anything but a personal name is
rendered very unlikely by the analogy
of all the other inscriptions on coins of
the same class." Doves were burnt on
a pyre in honour of Adonis (below, p.
147). Similarly birds were burnt on a
pyre in honour of Laphrian Artemis at
Patrae (Pausanias, vii. 18. 12).

throne, a waxen effigy was made in the likeness of the deceased and burned on a huge pyramidal pyre, which was reared upon a square basis of wood ; and from the summit of the blazing pile an eagle was released for the purpose of carrying to heaven the soul of the dead and deified emperor.[1] The Romans may have borrowed from the East a grandiose custom which savours of Oriental adulation rather than of Roman simplicity.[2]

The type of Sandan or Hercules, as he is portrayed on the coins of Tarsus, is that of an Asiatic deity standing on a lion. It is thus that he is represented on the pyre, and it is thus that he appears as a separate figure without the pyre. From these representations we can form a fairly accurate conception of the form and attributes of the god. They exhibit him as a bearded man standing on a horned and often winged lion. Upon his head he wears a high pointed cap or mitre, and he is clad sometimes in a long robe, sometimes in a short tunic. On at least one coin his feet are shod in high boots with flaps. At his side or over his shoulder are slung a sword, a bow-case, and a quiver, sometimes only one or two of them. His right hand is raised and sometimes holds a flower. His left hand grasps a double-headed axe, and sometimes a wreath either in addition to the axe or instead of it ; but the double-headed axe is one of Sandan's most constant attributes.[3]

Sandan of Tarsus an Asiatic god with the symbols of the lion and the double axe.

---

[1] Herodian, iv. 2.

[2] See Franz Cumont, " L'Aigle funéraire des Syriens et l'Apothéose des Empereurs," *Revue de l'Histoire des Religions*, lxii. (1910) pp. 119-163.

[3] F. Imhoof - Blumer, *Monnaies Grecques* (Amsterdam, 1883), pp. 366 *sq.*, 433, 435, with plates F. 24, 25, H. 14 (*Verhandelingen der Konink. Akademie von Wetenschappen*, Afdeeling Letterkunde, xiv.) ; F. Imhoof-Blumer und O. Keller, *Tier- und Pflanzenbilder auf Münzen und Gemmen des klassischen Altertums* (Leipsic,

1889), pp. 70 *sq.*, with pl. xii. 7, 8, 9 ; F. Imhoof-Blumer, " Coin-types of some Kilikian Cities," *Journal of Hellenic Studies*, xviii. (1898) pp. 169-171 ; P. Gardner, *Types of Greek Coins*, pl. xiii. 20 ; G. F. Hill, *Catalogue of the Greek Coins of Lycaonia, Isauria, and Cilicia*, pp. 178, 179, 184, 186, 206, 213, with plates xxxii. 13, 14, 15, 16, xxxiv. 2, xxxvi. 9 ; G. Macdonald, *Catalogue of Greek Coins in the Hunterian Collection*, ii. 548, with pl. lx. 11. The booted Sandan is figured by G. F. Hill, *op. cit.* pl. xxxvi. 9.

§ 4. *The Gods of Boghaz-Keui*

Boghaz-
Keui the
ancient
capital of
a Hittite
kingdom
in Cappa-
docia.

Now a deity of almost precisely the same type figures prominently in the celebrated group of Hittite sculptures which is carved on the rocks at Boghaz-Keui in North-Western Cappadocia. The village of Boghaz-Keui, that is, "the village of the defile," stands at the mouth of a deep, narrow, and picturesque gorge in a wild upland valley, shut in by rugged mountains of grey limestone. The houses are built on the lower slopes of the hills, and a stream issuing from the gorge flows past them to join the Halys, which is distant about ten hours' journey to the west. Immediately above the modern village a great ancient city, enclosed by massive fortification walls, rose on the rough broken ground of the mountain-side, culminating in two citadels perched on the tops of precipitous crags. The walls are still standing in many places to a height of twelve feet or more. They are about fourteen feet thick and consist of an outer and inner facing built of large blocks with a core of rubble between them. On the outer side they are strengthened at intervals of about a hundred feet by projecting towers or buttresses, which seem designed rather as architectural supports than as military defences. The masonry, composed of large stones laid in roughly parallel courses, resembles in style that of the walls of Mycenae, with which it may be contemporary ; and the celebrated Lion-gate at Mycenae has its counterpart in the southern gate of Boghaz-Keui, which is flanked by a pair of colossal stone lions executed in the best style of Hittite art. The eastern gate is adorned on its inner side with the figure of a Hittite warrior or Amazon carved in high relief. A dense undergrowth of stunted oak coppice now covers much of the site. The ruins of a large palace or temple, built of enormous blocks of stone, occupy a terrace in a commanding situation within the circuit of the walls. This vast city, some four or five miles in circumference, appears to have been the ancient Pteria, which Croesus, king of Lydia, captured in his war with Cyrus. It was probably the capital of a powerful Hittite empire before the Phrygians made their way from

Europe into the interior of Asia Minor and established a rival state to the west of the Halys.[1]

From the village of Boghaz-Keui a steep and rugged path leads up hill to a sanctuary, distant about a mile and a half to the east.   Here among the grey limestone cliffs there is a spacious natural chamber or hall of roughly oblong shape, roofed only by the sky, and enclosed on three sides by high rocks.   One of the short sides is open, and through it you look out on the broken slopes beyond and the more distant mountains, which make a graceful picture set in a massy frame.   The length of the chamber is about a hundred feet ; its breadth varies from twenty-five to fifty feet.   A nearly level sward forms the floor.   On the right-hand side, as you face inward, a narrow opening in the rock leads into another but much smaller chamber, or rather corridor, which would seem to have been the inner sanctuary or Holy of Holies.   It is a romantic spot, where the deep shadows of the rocks are relieved by the bright foliage of walnut-trees and by the sight of the sky and clouds overhead.   On the rock-walls of both chamber are carved the famous bas-reliefs.   In the outer sanctuary these reliefs represent two great processions which defile along the two long sides of the chamber and meet face to face on the short wall at the inner end.   The figures on the left-hand wall are for the most part men clad in the characteristic Hittite costume, which consists of a high pointed cap, shoes with turned-up toes, and a tunic drawn in at the waist and

The sanctuary in the rocks.

The rock-sculptures in the outer sanctuary at Boghaz-Keui represent two processions meeting.

---

[1] Herodotus, i. 76 ; Stephanus Byzantius, *s.v.* Πτέριον.   As to the situation of Boghaz-Keui and the ruins of Pteria see W. J. Hamilton, *Researches in Asia Minor, Pontus, and Armenia* (London, 1842), i. 391 *sqq.* ; H. Barth, "Reise von Trapezunt durch die nördliche Hälfte Klein-Asiens," *Ergänzungsheft zu Petermann's Geographischen Mittheilungen*, No. 2 (1860), pp. 44-52 ; H. F. Tozer, *Turkish Armenia and Eastern Asia Minor* (London, 1881), pp. 64, 71 *sqq.* ; W. M. Ramsay, "Historical Relations of Phrygia and Cappadocia," *Journal of the Royal Asiatic Society*, N.S., xv. (1883) p. 103 ; *id.*, *Historical Geography of Asia Minor* (London, 1890), pp. 28 *sq.*, 33 *sq.* ; G. Perrot et Ch. Chipiez, *Histoire de l'Art dans l'Antiquité*, iv. 596 *sqq.* ; K. Humann und O. Puchstein, *Reisen in Kleinasien und Nordsyrien* (Berlin, 1890), pp. 71-80, with Atlas, plates xi.-xiv. ; E. Chantre, *Mission en Cappadoce* (Paris, 1898), pp. 13 *sqq.* ; O. Puchstein, "Die Bauten von Boghaz-Köi," *Mitteilungen der Deutschen Orient - Gesellschaft zu Berlin*, No. 35, December 1907, pp. 62 *sqq.* ; J. Garstang, *The Land of the Hittites* (London, 1910), pp. 196 *sqq.*

falling short of the knees.[1]   The figures on the right-hand
wall are women wearing tall, square, flat-topped bonnets
with ribbed sides ; their long dresses fall in perpendicular
folds to their feet, which are shod in shoes like those of the
men.   On the short wall, where the processions meet, the
greater size of the central figures, as well as their postures
and attributes, mark them out as divine.   At the head of
the male procession marches or is carried a bearded deity
clad in the ordinary Hittite costume of tall pointed cap,
short tunic, and turned-up shoes ; but his feet rest on the
bowed heads of two men, in his right hand he holds on his
shoulder a mace or truncheon topped with a knob, while his
extended left hand grasps a symbol, which apparently
consists of a trident surmounted by an oval with a cross-bar.
Behind him follows a similar, though somewhat smaller,
figure of a man, or perhaps rather of a god, carrying a mace
or truncheon over his shoulder in his right hand, while with
his left he holds aloft a long sword with a flat hilt ; his feet
rest not on two men but on two flat-topped pinnacles, which
perhaps represent mountains.   At the head of the female
procession and facing the great god who is borne on the
two men, stands a goddess on a lioness or panther.   Her
costume does not differ from that of the women : her
hair hangs down in a long plait behind : in her extended
right hand she holds out an emblem to touch that of the
god.   The shape and meaning of her emblem are obscure.
It consists of a stem with two pairs of protuberances,
perhaps leaves or branches, one above the other, the whole
being surmounted, like the emblem of the god, by an oval
with a cross-bar.   Under the outstretched arms of the two
deities appear the front parts of two animals, which have
been usually interpreted as bulls but are rather goats ;
each of them wears on its head the high conical Hittite
cap, and its body is concealed by that of the deity.
Immediately behind the goddess marches a smaller and
apparently youthful male figure, standing like her upon a
lioness or panther.   He is beardless and wears the Hittite

The
central
figures.

[1] This procession of men is broken
(*a*) by two women clad in long plaited
robes like the women on the opposite
wall ; (*b*) by two winged monsters ;
and (*c*) by the figure of a priest or king
as to which see below, pp. 131 *sq.*

dress of high pointed cap, short tunic, and shoes with turned-up toes.   A crescent-hilted sword is girt at his side ; in his left hand he holds a double-headed axe, and in his right a staff topped by an armless doll with the symbol of the cross-barred oval instead of a head.   Behind him follow two women, or rather perhaps goddesses, resembling the goddess at the head of the procession, but with different emblems and standing not on a lioness but on a single two-headed eagle with outspread wings.

The entrance to the smaller chamber is guarded on either side by the figure of a winged monster carved on the rock ; the bodies of both figures are human, but one of them has the head of a dog, the other the head of a lion.   In the inner sanctuary, to which this monster-guarded passage leads, the walls are also carved in relief.   On one side we see a procession of twelve men in Hittite costume marching with curved swords in their right hands.   On the opposite wall is a colossal erect figure of a deity with a human head and a body curiously composed of four lions, two above and two below, the latter standing on their heads.   The god wears the high conical Hittite hat : his face is youthful and beardless like that of the male figure standing on the lioness in the large chamber ; and the ear turned to the spectator is pierced with a ring.   From the knees downwards the legs, curiously enough, are replaced by a device which has been interpreted as the tapering point of a great dagger or dirk with a midrib.   To the right of this deity a square panel cut in the face of the rock exhibits a group of two figures in relief.   The larger of the two figures closely resembles the youth on the lioness in the outer sanctuary. His chin is beardless ; he wears the same high pointed cap, the same short tunic, the same turned-up shoes, the same crescent-hilted sword, and he carries a similar armless doll in his right hand.   But his left arm encircles the neck of the smaller figure, whom he seems to clasp to his side in an attitude of protection.   The smaller figure thus embraced by the god is clearly a priest or priestly king.   His face is beardless ; he wears a skull-cap and a long mantle reaching to his feet with a sort of chasuble thrown over it.   The crescent-shaped hilt of a sword projects from under his

The rock-sculptures in the inner sanctuary at Boghaz-Keui.

The lion-god.

The god protecting his priest.

mantle. The wrist of his right arm is clasped by the god's left hand ; in his left hand the priest holds a crook or pastoral staff which ends below in a curl. Both the priest and his protector are facing towards the lion-god. In an upper corner of the panel behind them is a divine emblem composed of a winged disc resting on what look like two Ionic columns, while between them appear three symbols of doubtful significance. The figure of the priest or king in this costume, though not in this attitude, is a familiar one ; for it occurs twice in the outer sanctuary and is repeated twice at the great Hittite palace of Euyuk, distant about four and a half hours' ride to the north-east of Boghaz-Keui. In the outer sanctuary at Boghaz-Keui we see the priest marching in the procession of the men, and holding in one hand his curled staff, or *lituus*, and in the other a symbol like that of the goddess on the lioness : above his head appears the winged disc without the other attributes. Moreover he occupies a conspicuous place by himself on the right-hand wall of the outer sanctuary, quite apart from the two processions, and carved on a larger scale than any of the other figures in them. Here he stands on two heaps, perhaps intended to represent mountains, and he carries in his right hand the emblem of the winged disc supported on two Ionic columns with the other symbols between them, except that the central symbol is replaced by a masculine figure wearing a pointed cap and a long robe decorated with a dog-tooth pattern. On one of the reliefs at the palace of Euyuk we see the priest with his characteristic dress and staff followed by a priestess, each of them with a hand raised as if in adoration : they are approaching the image of a bull which stands on a high pedestal with an altar before it. Behind them a priest leads a flock of rams to the sacrifice. On another relief at Euyuk the priest, similarly attired and followed by a priestess, is approaching a seated goddess and apparently pouring a libation at her feet. Both these scenes doubtless represent acts of worship paid in the one case to a goddess, in the other to a bull.[1]

Other representations of the priest at Boghaz-Keui and Euyuk.

[1] W. J. Hamilton, *Researches in Asia Minor, Pontus, and Armenia* (London, 1842), i. 393-395 ; H. F. Tozer, *Turkish Armenia and Eastern Asia Minor*, pp. 59 *sq.*, 66-78 ; W. M. Ramsay, " Historical Relations of

We have still to inquire into the meaning of the rock-carvings at Boghaz-Keui. What are these processions which are meeting? Who are the personages represented? and what are they doing? Some have thought that the scene is historical and commemorates a great event, such as a treaty of peace between two peoples or the marriage of a king's son to a king's daughter.[1] But to this view it has

---

Phrygia and Asia Minor," *Journal of the Royal Asiatic Society*, N.S. xv. (1883) pp. 113-120; G. Perrot et Ch. Chipiez, *Histoire de l'Art dans l'Antiquité*, iv. 623-656, 666-672; K. Humann und O. Puchstein, *Reisen in Kleinasien und Nordsyrien*, pp. 55-70, with Atlas, plates vii.-x.; E. Chantre, *Mission en Cappadoce*, pp. 3-5, 16-26; L. Messerschmidt, *The Hittites*, pp. 42-50; Th. Macridy-Bey, *La Porte des Sphinx à Eyuk*, pp. 13 sq. (*Mitteilungen der Vorderasiatischen Gesellschaft*, 1908, No. 3, Berlin); Ed. Meyer, *Geschichte des Altertums*,[2] i. 2. pp. 631 sq.; J. Garstang, *The Land of the Hittites* (London, 1910), pp. 196 sqq. (Boghaz-Keui) 256 sqq. (Eyuk). Compare P. Jensen, *Hittiter und Armenier*, pp. 165 sqq. In some notes with which my colleague Professor J. Garstang has kindly furnished me he tells me that the two animals wearing Hittite hats, which appear between the great god and goddess in the outer sanctuary, are not bulls but certainly goats; and he inclines to think that the two heaps on which the priest stands in the outer sanctuary are fir-cones. Professor Ed. Meyer holds that the costume which the priestly king wears is that of the Sun-goddess, and that the corresponding figure in the procession of males on the left-hand side of the outer sanctuary does not represent the priestly king but the Sun-goddess in person. "The attributes of the King," he says (*op. cit.* p. 632), "are to be explained by the circumstance that he, as the Hittite inscriptions prove, passed for an incarnation of the Sun, who with the Hittites was a female divinity; the temple of the Sun is therefore his emblem." As to the title of "the

Sun" bestowed on Hittite kings in inscriptions, see H. Winckler, "Vorläufige Nachrichten über die Ausgrabungen in Boghaz-köi im Sommer 1907," *Mitteilungen der Deutschen Orient-Gesellschaft zu Berlin*, No. 35, December 1907, pp. 32, 33, 36, 44, 45, 53. The correct form of the national name appears to be Chatti or Hatti rather than Hittites, which is the Hebrew form (חֵת) of the name. Compare M. Jastrow, in *Encyclopaedia Biblica*, ii. coll. 2094 sqq., s.v. "Hittites."

An interesting Hittite symbol which occurs both in the sanctuary at Boghaz-Keui and at the palace of Euyuk is the double-headed eagle. In both places it serves as the support of divine or priestly personages. After being adopted as a badge by the Seljuk Sultans in the Middle Ages, it passed into Europe with the Crusaders and became in time the escutcheon of the Austrian and Russian empires. See W. J. Hamilton, *op. cit.* i. 383; G. Perrot et Ch. Chipiez, *op. cit.* iv. 681-683, with pl. viii. E; L. Messerschmidt, *The Hittites*, p. 50.

[1] W. J. Hamilton, *Researches in Asia Minor, Pontus, and Armenia*, i. 394 sq.; H. Barth, in *Monatsberichte der königl. Preuss. Akademie der Wissenschaften*, 1859, pp. 128 sqq.; *id.*, "Reise von Trapezunt," *Ergänzungsheft zu Petermann's Geograph. Mittheilungen*, No. 2 (Gotha, 1860), pp. 45 sq.; H. F. Tozer, *Turkish Armenia and Eastern Asia Minor*, p. 69; E. Chantre, *Mission en Cappadoce*, pp. 20 sqq. According to Barth, the scene represented is the marriage of Aryenis, daughter of Alyattes, king of Lydia, to Astyages, son of Cyaxares, king of the Medes

been rightly objected that the attributes of the principal figures prove them to be divine or priestly, and that the scene is therefore religious or mythical rather than historical. With regard to the two personages who head the processions and hold out their symbols to each other, the most probable opinion appears to be that they stand for the great Asiatic goddess of fertility and her consort, by whatever names these deities were known ; for under diverse names a similar divine couple appears to have been worshipped with similar rites all over Western Asia.[1]   The bearded god who, grasping a trident in his extended left hand, heads the procession of male figures is probably the Father deity, the great Hittite god of the thundering sky, whose emblems were the thunderbolt and the bull ; for the trident which he carries may reasonably be interpreted as a thunderbolt.   The deity is represented in similar form on two stone monuments of Hittite art which were found at Zenjirli in Northern Syria and at Babylon respectively.   On both we see a bearded male god wearing the usual Hittite costume of tall cap, short tunic, and shoes turned up at the toes : a crescent-hilted sword is girt at his side : his hands are raised : in the right he holds a single-headed axe or hammer, in the left a trident of wavy lines, which is thought to stand for forked lightning or a bundle of thunderbolts.   On the Babylonian slab, which bears a long Hittite inscription, the god's cap is ornamented with a pair of horns.[2]   The horns on the cap are probably

The Hittite god of the thundering sky.

(Herodotus, i. 74).   For a discussion of various interpretations which have been proposed see G. Perrot et Ch. Chipiez, *Histoire de l'Art dans l'Antiquité*, iv. 630 *sqq.*

[1] This is in substance the view of Raoul - Rochette, Lajard, W. M. Ramsay, G. Perrot, C. P. Tiele, Ed. Meyer, and J. Garstang.   See Raoul-Rochette, " Sur l'Hercule Assyrien et Phénicien," *Mémoires de l'Académie des Inscriptions et Belles-Lettres*, xvii. Deuxième Partie (Paris, 1848), p. 180 note[1]; W. M. Ramsay, " On the Early Historical Relations between Phrygia and Cappadocia," *Journal of the Royal Asiatic Society*, N.S. xv. (1883) pp. 113-120;   G. Perrot et Ch.

Chipiez, *Histoire de l'Art dans l'Antiquité*, iv. 630 *sqq.* ; C. P. Tiele, *Geschichte der Religion im Altertum*, i. 255-257 ; Ed. Meyer, *Geschichte des Altertums*,[2] i. 2. pp. 633 *sq.* ; J. Garstang, *The Land of the Hittites*, pp. 235-237 ; *id.*, *The Syrian Goddess* (London, 1913), pp. 5 *sqq.*

[2] K. Humann und O. Puchstein, *Reisen in Kleinasien und Nordsyrien* (Berlin, 1902), Atlas, pl. xlv. 3; *Ausgrabungen zu Sendschirli*, iii. (Berlin, 1902) pl. xli. ; J. Garstang, *The Land of the Hittites*, p. 291, with plate lxxvii. ; R. Koldewey, *Die Hettitische Inschrift gefunden in der Königsburg von Babylon* (Leipsic, 1900), plates 1 and 2 (*Wissenschaft-*

those of a bull ; for on another Hittite monument, found at
Malatia on the Euphrates, there is carved a deity in the
usual Hittite costume standing on a bull and grasping a
trident or thunderbolt in his left hand, while facing him
stands a priest clad in a long robe, holding a crook or curled
staff in one hand and pouring a libation with the other.[1]
The Hittite thunder-god is also known to us from a treaty
of alliance which about the year 1290 B.C. was contracted
between Hattusil, King of the Hittites, and Rameses II.,
King of Egypt.   By a singular piece of good fortune we
possess copies of this treaty both in the Hittite and in the

---

*liche Veröffentlichungen der Deutschen
Orient - Gesellschaft,* Heft 1) ; L.
Messerschmidt, *Corpus Inscriptionum
Hettiticarum,* pl. i. 5 and 6 ; *id.,
The Hittites* (London, 1903), pp. 40-
42, with fig. 6 on p. 41 ; M. J.
Lagrange, *Études sur les Religions
Sémitiques* [2] (Paris, 1905), p. 93.
The name of the god is thought to
have been Teshub or Teshup ; for a
god of that name is known from the
Tel-el-Amarna letters to have been
the chief deity of the Mitani, a people
of Northern Mesopotamia akin in
speech and religion to the Hittites,
but ruled by an Aryan dynasty.   See
Ed. Meyer, *Geschichte des Altertums,*[2]
i. 2. pp. 578, 591 *sq.,* 636 *sq.* ; R. F.
Harper, *Assyrian and Babylonian
Literature,* pp. 222, 223 (where the
god's name is spelt Tishub).   The
god is also mentioned repeatedly in
the Hittite archives which Dr. H.
Winckler found inscribed on clay
tablets at Boghaz - Keui.   See H.
Winckler, "Vorläufige Nachrichten
über die Ausgrabungen in Boghaz-
köi im Sommer 1907," *Mitteilungen
der Deutschen Orient-Gesellschaft zu
Berlin,* No. 35, December 1907, pp.
13 *sq.,* 32, 34, 36, 38, 39, 43, 44, 51
sq., 53 ; "Hittite Archives from
Boghaz - Keui," translated from the
German transcripts of Dr. Winckler,
*Annals of Archaeology and Anthro-
pology,* iv. (Liverpool and London,
1912) pp. 90 *sqq.*   As to the Mitani,
their language and their gods, see
H. Winckler, *op. cit.* pp. 30 *sqq.,*
46 *sqq.*   In thus interpreting the

Hittite god who heads the procession
at Boghaz-Keui I follow my colleague
Prof. J. Garstang (*The Land of the
Hittites,* p. 237 ; *The Syrian Goddess,* pp. 5 *sqq.*), who has kindly
furnished me with some notes on the
subject.   I formerly interpreted the
deity as the Hittite equivalent of
Tammuz, Adonis, and Attis.   But
against that view it may be urged that
(1) the god is bearded and therefore of
mature age, whereas Tammuz and his
fellows were regularly conceived as
youthful ; (2) the thunderbolt which he
seems to carry would be quite inappropriate to Tammuz, who was not a god
of thunder but of vegetation ; and (3)
the Hittite Tammuz is appropriately
represented in the procession of
women immediately behind the Mother
Goddess (see below, pp. 137 *sq.*), and it
is extremely improbable that he should
be represented twice over with different attributes in the same scene.
These considerations seem to me conclusive against the interpretation of
the bearded god as a Tammuz and decisive
in favour of Professor Garstang's view
of him.

[1] J. Garstang, "Notes of a Journey
through Asia Minor," *Annals of Archaeology and Anthropology,* i. (Liverpool
and London, 1908) pp. 3 *sq.,* with
plate iv.; *id., The Land of the Hittites,*
pp. 138, 359, with plate xliv.   In this
sculpture the god on the bull holds in
his right hand what is described as a
triangular bow instead of a mace, an
axe, or a hammer.

Egyptian language. The Hittite copy was found some years ago inscribed in cuneiform characters on a clay tablet at Boghaz-Keui ; two copies of the treaty in the Egyptian language are engraved on the walls of temples at Thebes. From the Egyptian copies, which have been read and translated, we gather that the thunder-god was the principal deity of the Hittites, and that the two Hittite seals which were appended to the treaty exhibited the King embraced by the thunder-god and the Queen embraced by the sun-goddess of Arenna.[1] This Hittite divinity of the thundering sky appears to have long survived at Doliche in Commagene, for in later

Jupiter Dolichenus.

Roman art he reappears under the title of Jupiter Dolichenus, wearing a Phrygian cap, standing on a bull, and wielding a double axe in one hand and a thunderbolt in the other. In this form his worship was transported from his native Syrian home by soldiers and slaves, till it had spread over a large part of the Roman empire, especially on the frontiers, where it flourished in the camps of the legions.[2] The combination of the bull with the thunderbolt as emblems of the deity suggests that the animal may have been chosen to represent the sky-god for the sake not merely of its virility but of its voice ; for in the peal of thunder primitive man may well have heard the bellowing of a celestial bull.

[1] A. Wiedemann, *Ägyptische Geschichte* (Gotha, 1884), ii. 438-440 ; G. Maspero, *Histoire Ancienne des Peuples de l'Orient Classique*, ii. (Paris, 1897) pp. 401 *sq.* ; W. Max Müller, *Der Bündnisvortrag Ramses' II. und des Chetitirkönigs*, pp. 17-19, 21 *sq.*, 38-44 (*Mitteilungen der Vorderasiatischen Gesellschaft*, 1902, No. 5, Berlin) ; L. Messerschmidt, *The Hittites*, pp. 14-19 ; J. H. Breasted, *Ancient Records of Egypt* (Chicago, 1906-1907), iii. 163-174 ; *id.*, *A History of the Ancient Egyptians* (London, 1908), p. 311 ; Ed. Meyer, *Geschichte des Altertums,*[2] i. 2. pp. 631, 635 *sqq.*; J. Garstang, *The Land of the Hittites*, pp. 347-349. The Hittite copy of the treaty was discovered by Dr. H. Winckler at Boghaz-Keui in 1906. The identification of Arenna or Arinna is uncertain. In a forthcoming article, "The Sun God[dess] of Arenna," to be published in the Liverpool *Annals of Archaeology and Anthropology*, Professor J. Garstang argues that Arenna is to be identified with the Cappadocian Comana.

[2] Ed. Meyer, "Dolichenus," in W. H. Roscher's *Lexikon der griech. und röm. Mythologie*, i. 1191-1194 ; A. von Domaszewski, *Die Religion des römischen Heeres* (Treves, 1895), pp. 59 *sq.*, with plate iiii. fig. 1 and 2 ; Franz Cumont, *s.v.* "Dolichenus," in Pauly-Wissowa's *Real-Encyclopädie der classischen Altertumswissenschaft*, v. i. coll. 1276 *sqq.* ; J. Toutain, *Les Cultes païens dans l'Empire Romain*, ii. (Paris, 1911) pp. 35-43. For examples of the inscriptions which relate to his worship see H. Dessau, *Inscriptiones Latinae Selectae*, vol. ii. Pars i. (Berlin, 1902) pp. 167-172, Nos. 4296-4324.

The goddess who at the head of the procession of women The Mother Goddess. confronts the great sky-god in the sanctuary at Boghaz-Keui is generally recognized as the divine Mother, the great Asiatic goddess of life and fertility. The tall flat-topped hat with perpendicular grooves which she wears, and the lioness or panther on which she stands, remind us of the turreted crown and lion-drawn car of Cybele, who was worshipped in the neighbouring land of Phrygia across the Halys.[1] So Atargatis, the great Syrian goddess of Hierapolis-Bambyce, was portrayed sitting on lions and wearing a tower on her head.[2] At Babylon an image of a goddess whom the Greeks called Rhea had the figures of two lions standing on her knees.[3]

But in the rock-hewn sculptures of Boghaz-Keui, who is The youth on the lioness, bearing the double axe, at Boghaz-Keui may be the divine son and lover of the goddess. the youth with the tall pointed cap and double axe who stands on a lioness or panther immediately behind the great goddess? His figure is all the more remarkable because he is the only male who interrupts the long procession of women. Probably he is at once the divine son and the divine lover of the goddess; for we shall find later on that in Phrygian mythology Attis united in himself both these characters.[4]

[1] As to the lions and mural crown of Cybele see Lucretius, ii. 600 *sqq.*; Catullus, lxiii. 76 *sqq.*; Macrobius, *Saturn.* i. 23. 20; Rapp, *s.v.* "Kybele," in W. H. Roscher's *Lexikon der griech. und röm. Mythologie*, ii. 1644 *sqq.*

[2] Lucian, *De dea Syria*, 31; Macrobius, *Saturn.* i. 23. 19. Lucian's description of her image is confirmed by coins of Hierapolis, on which the goddess is represented wearing a high head-dress and seated on a lion. See B. V. Head, *Historia Numorum* (Oxford, 1887), p. 654; G. Macdonald, *Catalogue of Greek Coins in the Hunterian Collection* (Glasgow, 1899–1905), iii. 139 *sq.*; J. Garstang, *The Syrian Goddess*, pp. 21 *sqq.*, 70, with fig. 7. That the name of the Syrian goddess of Hierapolis-Bambyce was Atargatis is mentioned by Strabo (xvi. 1. 27, p. 748). On Egyptian monuments the Semitic goddess Kadesh is represented standing on a lion. See W. Max Müller, *Asien*

und Europa, pp. 314 *sq.* It is to be remembered that Hierapolis-Bambyce was the direct successor of Carchemish, the great Hittite capital on the Euphrates, and may have inherited many features of Hittite religion. See A. H. Sayce, *The Hittites*,[3] pp. 94 *sqq.*, 105 *sqq.*; and as to the Hittite monuments at Carchemish, see J. Garstang, *The Land of the Hittites*, pp. 122 *sqq.*

[3] Diodorus Siculus, ii. 9. 5.

[4] In thus interpreting the youth with the double axe I agree with Sir W. M. Ramsay ("On the Early Historical Relations between Phrygia and Cappadocia," *Journal of the Royal Asiatic Society*, N.S. xv. (1883) pp. 118, 120), C. P. Tiele (*Geschichte der Religion im Altertum*, i. 246, 255), and Prof. J. Garstang (*The Land of the Hittites*, p. 235; *The Syrian Goddess*, p. 8). That the youthful figure on the lioness or panther represents the lover of the great goddess is the view also of Professors Jensen and

The lioness or panther on which he stands marks his affinity with the goddess, who is supported by a similar animal.   It is natural that the lion-goddess should have a lion-son and a lion-lover.   For we may take it as probable that the Oriental deities who are represented standing or sitting in human form on the backs of lions and other animals were originally indistinguishable from the beasts, and that the complete separation of the bestial from the human or divine shape was a consequence of that growth of knowledge and of power which led man in time to respect himself more and the brutes less.   The hybrid gods of Egypt with their human

Hommel.   See P. Jensen, *Hittiter und Armenier*, pp. 173-175, 180 ; F. Hommel, *Grundriss der Geographie und Geschichte des alten Orients*, p. 51. Prof. Perrot holds that the youth in question is a double of the bearded god who stands at the head of the male procession, their costume being the same, though their attributes differ (G. Perrot et Ch. Chipiez, *Histoire de l'Art dans l'Antiquité*, iv. 651).   But, as I have already remarked, it is unlikely that the same god should be represented twice over with different attributes in the same scene.   The resemblance between the two figures is better explained on the supposition that they are Father and Son.   The same two deities, Father and Son, appear to be carved on a rock at Giaour-Kalesi, a place on the road which in antiquity may have led from Ancyra by Gordium to Pessinus. Here on the face of the rock are cut in relief two gigantic figures in the usual Hittite costume of pointed cap, short tunic, and shoes turned up at the toes. Each wears a crescent-hilted sword at his side, each is marching to the spectator's left with raised right hand ; and the resemblance between them is nearly complete except that the figure in front is beardless and the figure behind is bearded.   See G. Perrot et Ch. Chipiez, *Histoire de l'Art dans l'Antiquité*, iv. 714 *sqq.*, with fig. 352 ; J. Garstang, *The Land of the Hittites*, pp. 162-164.   A similar, but solitary, figure is carved in a niche of the rock at Kara-Bel, but there the

deity, or the man, carries a triangular bow over his right shoulder.   See below, p. 185.

With regard to the lionesses or panthers, a bas-relief found at Carchemish, the capital of a Hittite kingdom on the Euphrates, shows two male figures in Hittite costume, with pointed caps and turned-up shoes, standing on a couching lion.   The foremost of the two figures is winged and carries a short curved truncheon in his right hand.   According to Prof. Perrot, the two figures represent a god followed by a priest or a king.   See G. Perrot et Ch. Chipiez, *Histoire de l'Art dans l'Antiquité*, iv. 549 *sq.* ; J. Garstang, *The Land of the Hittites*, pp. 123 *sqq.*   Again, on a sculptured slab found at Amrit in Phoenicia we see a god standing on a lion and holding a lion's whelp in his left hand, while in his right hand he brandishes a club or sword.   See Perrot et Chipiez, *op. cit.* iii. 412-414.   The type of a god or goddess standing or sitting on a lion occurs also in Assyrian art, from which the Phoenicians and Hittites may have borrowed it.   See Perrot et Chipiez, *op. cit.* ii. 642-644.   Much evidence as to the representation of Asiatic deities with lions has been collected by Raoul-Rochette, in his learned dissertation " Sur l'Hercule Assyrien et Phénicien," *Mémoires de l'Académie des Inscriptions et Belles-Lettres*, xvii. Deuxième Partie (Paris, 1848), pp. 106 *sqq.*   Compare De Vogüé, *Mélanges d'Archéologie Orientale*, pp. 44 *sqq.*

bodies and animal heads form an intermediate stage in this evolution of anthropomorphic deities out of beasts.

We may now perhaps hazard a conjecture as to the meaning of that strange colossal figure in the inner shrine at Boghaz-Keui with its human head and its body composed of lions. For it is to be observed that the head of the figure is youthful and beardless, and that it wears a tall pointed cap, thus resembling in both respects the youth with the double-headed axe who stands on a lion in the outer sanctuary. We may suppose that the leonine figure in the inner shrine sets forth the true mystic, that is, the old savage nature of the god who in the outer shrine presented himself to his worshippers in the decent semblance of a man. To the chosen few who were allowed to pass the monster-guarded portal into the Holy of Holies, the awful secret may have been revealed that their god was a lion, or rather a lion-man, a being in whom the bestial and human natures mysteriously co-existed.[1] The reader may remember that on the rock beside this leonine divinity is carved a group which represents a god with his arm twined round the neck of his priest in an attitude of protection, holding one of the priest's hands in his own. Both figures are looking and stepping towards the lion-monster, and the god is holding out his right hand as if pointing to it. The scene may represent the deity revealing the mystery to the priest, or preparing him to act his part in some solemn rite for which all his strength and courage will be needed. He seems to be leading his minister onward, comforting him with an assurance that no harm can come near him while the divine arm is around him and the divine hand clasps his. Whither is he leading him? Perhaps to death. The deep shadows of the rocks which fall on the

The mystery of the lion-god.

[1] Similarly in Yam, one of the Torres Straits Islands, two brothers named Sigai and Maiau were worshipped in a shrine under the form of a hammer-headed shark and a crocodile respectively, and were represented by effigies made of turtle-shell in the likeness of these animals. But "the shrines were so sacred that no uninitiated persons might visit them, nor did they know what they contained; they were aware of Sigai and Maiau, but they did not know that the former was a hammer-headed shark and the latter a crocodile; this mystery was too sacred to be imparted to uninitiates. When the heroes were addressed it was always by their human names, and not by their animal or totem names." See A. C. Haddon, "The Religion of the Torres Straits Islanders," *Anthropological Essays presented to E. B. Tylor* (Oxford, 1907), p. 185.

two figures in the gloomy chasm may be an emblem of darker shadows soon to fall on the priest. Yet still he grasps his pastoral staff and goes forward, as though he said, " Yea, though I walk through the valley of the shadow of death, I will fear no evil ; for thou art with me : thy rod and thy staff they comfort me."

The processions at Boghaz-Keui appear to represent the Sacred Marriage of the god and goddess.

If there is any truth in these guesses—for they are little more—the three principal figures in the processional scene at Boghaz-Keui represent the divine Father, the divine Mother, and the divine Son. But we have still to ask, What are they doing ? That they are engaged in the performance of some religious rite seems certain. But what is it ? We may conjecture that it is the rite of the Sacred Marriage, and that the scene is copied from a ceremony which was periodically performed in this very place by human representatives of the deities.[1] Indeed, the solemn meeting of the male and female figures at the head of their respective processions obviously suggests a marriage, and has been so interpreted by scholars, who, however, regarded it as the historical wedding of a prince and princess instead of the mystic union of a god and goddess, overlooking or explaining away the symbols of divinity which accompany the principal personages.[2] We may suppose that at Boghaz-Keui, as at many other places in the interior of Asia Minor, the government was in the hands of a family who combined royal with priestly functions and personated the gods whose names they bore. Thus at Pessinus in Phrygia, as we shall see later on, the priests of Cybele bore the name of her consort Attis, and doubtless represented him in the ritual.[3]

---

[1] " There can be no doubt that there is here represented a Sacred Marriage, the meeting of two deities worshipped in different places, like the Horus of Edfu and the Hathor of Denderah " (C. P. Tiele, *Geschichte der Religion im Altertum*, i. 255). This view seems to differ from, though it approaches, the one suggested in the text. That the scene represents a Sacred Marriage between a great god and goddess is the opinion also of Prof. Ed. Meyer (*Geschichte des Altertums*,[2] i. 2. pp. 633 *sq.*), and Prof. J. Garstang (*The Land of the*

Hittites, pp. 238 *sq.* ; *The Syrian Goddess*, p. 7).

[2] See above, p. 133.

[3] See below, p. 285. Compare the remarks of Sir W. M. Ramsay ("Pre-Hellenic Monuments of Cappadocia," *Recueil de Travaux relatifs à la Philologie et à l'Archéologie Égyptiennes et Assyriennes*, xiii. (1890) p. 78): " Similar priest-dynasts are a wide-spread feature of the primitive social system of Asia Minor ; their existence is known with certainty or inferred with probability at the two towns Komana ; at Venasa not far north

If this was so at Boghaz-Keui, we may surmise that the chief
pontiff and his family annually celebrated the marriage of
the divine powers of fertility, the Father God and the Mother
Goddess, for the purpose of ensuring the fruitfulness of the
earth and the multiplication of men and beasts. The
principal parts in the ceremony would naturally be played
by the pontiff himself and his wife, unless indeed they
preferred for good reasons to delegate the onerous duty
to others. That such a delegation took place is perhaps
suggested by the appearance of the pontiff himself in a
subordinate place in the procession, as well as by his separate
representation in another place, as if he were in the act of
surveying the ceremony from a distance.[1] The part of the
divine Son at the rite would fitly devolve upon one of the
high-priest's own offspring, who may well have been numerous. For it is probable that here, as elsewhere in Asia
Minor, the Mother Goddess was personated by a crowd of
sacred harlots,[2] with whom the spiritual ruler may have been
required to consort in his character of incarnate deity. But
if the personation of the Son of God at the rites laid a
heavy burden of suffering on the shoulders of the actor, it is
possible that the representative of the deity may have been
drawn, perhaps by lot, from among the numerous progeny
of the consecrated courtesans ; for these women, as incarnations of the Mother Goddess, were probably supposed to
transmit to their offspring some portion of their own divinity.
Be that as it may, if the three principal personages in the
processional scene at Boghaz-Keui are indeed the Father,
the Mother, and the Son, the remarkable position assigned

Traces of
mother-kin
among the
Hittites.

---

of Tyana, at Olba, at Pessinous, at
Aizanoi, and many other places. Now
there are two characteristics which
can be regarded as probable in regard
to most of these priests, and as proved
in regard to some of them : (1) they
wore the dress and represented the
person of the god, whose priests they
were; (2) they were ἱερώνυμοι, losing
their individual name at their succession
to the office, and assuming a sacred
name, often that of the god himself or
some figure connected with the cultus
of the god. The priest of Cybele at
Pessinous was called Attis, the priests
of Sabazios were Saboi, the worshippers of Bacchos Bacchoi." As to the
priestly rulers of Olba, see below,
pp. 144 *sqq.*

[1] See above, p. 132. However,
Prof. Ed. Meyer may be right in
thinking that the priest-like figure in
the procession is not really that of the
priest but that of the god or goddess
whom he personated. See above, p.
133 note.

[2] See above, pp. 36 *sqq.*

to the third of them in the procession, where he walks
behind his Mother alone in the procession of women, appears
to indicate that he was supposed to be more closely akin to
her than to his Father. From this again we may conjecturally infer that mother-kin rather than father-kin was
the rule which regulated descent among the Hittites. The
conjecture derives some support from Hittite archives, for
the names of the Great Queen and the Queen Mother are
mentioned along with that of the King in state documents.[1]
The other personages who figure in the procession may
represent human beings masquerading in the costumes and
with the attributes of deities. Such, for example, are the
two female figures who stand on a double-headed eagle;
the two male figures stepping on what seem to be two
mountains ; and the two winged beings in the procession of
men, one of whom may be the Moon-god, for he wears a
crescent on his head.[2]

§ 5. *Sandan and Baal at Tarsus*

Sandan at
Tarsus
appears to
be a son of
Baal, as
Hercules
was a son
of Zeus.

Whatever may be thought of these speculations, one thing
seems fairly clear and certain. The figure which I have called
the divine Son at Boghaz-Keui is identical with the god Sandan, who appears on the pyre at Tarsus. In both personages
the costume, the attributes, the attitude are the same. Both
represent a man clad in a short tunic with a tall pointed cap
on his head, a sword at his side, a double-headed axe in his
hand, and a lion or panther under his feet.[3] Accordingly, if
we are right in identifying him as the divine Son at Boghaz-

[1] H. Winckler, "Vorläufige Nachrichten über die Ausgrabungen in
Boghaz-köi im Sommer 1907," *Mitteilungen der Deutschen Orient-Gesellschaft*, No. 35, December, 1907, pp.
27 *sq.*, 29 ; J. Garstang, *The Land of
the Hittites*, pp. 352 *sq.*; "Hittite
Archives from Boghaz-Keui," translated from the German transcripts of
Dr. Winckler by Meta E. Williams,
*Annals of Archaeology and Anthro-
pology*, iv. (Liverpool and London,
1912) p. 98. We have seen (above,
p. 136) that in the seals of the
Hittite treaty with Egypt the Queen
appears along with the King. If Dr.

H. Winckler is right in thinking (*op.
cit.* p. 29) that one of the Hittite
queens was at the same time sister to
her husband the King, we should have
in this relationship a further proof that
mother-kin regulated the descent of
the kingship among the Hittites as
well as among the ancient Egyptians.
See above, p. 44, and below, vol. ii.
pp. 213 *sqq.*

[2] Compare Ed. Meyer, *Geschichte
des Altertums*,[2] i. 2. pp. 629-633.

[3] The figure exhibits a few minor
variations on the coins of Tarsus. See
the works cited above, p. 127.

Keui, we may conjecture that under the name of Sandan he bore the same character at Tarsus. The conjecture squares perfectly with the title of Hercules, which the Greeks bestowed on Sandan ; for Hercules was the son of Zeus, the great father-god. Moreover, we have seen that the Baal of Tarsus, with the grapes and the corn in his hand, was assimilated to Zeus.[1] Thus it would appear that at Tarsus as at Boghaz-Keui there was a pair of deities, a divine Father and a divine Son, whom the Greeks identified with Zeus and Hercules respectively. If the Baal of Tarsus was a god of fertility, as his attributes clearly imply, his identification with Zeus would be natural, since it was Zeus who, in the belief of the Greeks, sent the fertilizing rain from heaven.[2] And the identification of Sandan with Hercules would be equally natural, since the lion and the death on the pyre were features common to both. Our conclusion then is that it was the divine Son, the lion-god, who was burned in effigy or in the person of a human representative at Tarsus, and perhaps at Boghaz-Keui. Semitic parallels suggest that the victim who played the part of the Son of God in the fiery furnace ought in strictness to be the king's son.[3] But no doubt in later times an effigy would be substituted for the man.

§ 6. *Priestly Kings of Olba*

Unfortunately we know next to nothing of the kings and priests of Tarsus. In Greek times we hear of an Epicurean philosopher of the city, Lysias by name, who was elected by his fellow-citizens to the office of Crown-wearer, that is, to the priesthood of Hercules. Once raised to that dignity, he would not lay it down again, but played the part of tyrant, wearing a white robe edged with purple, a costly cloak, white shoes, and a golden wreath of laurel. He truckled to the mob by distributing among them the property of the wealthy, while he put to death such as refused to open their money-bags to him.[4] Though we cannot distinguish in this account

Priests of Sandan-Hercules at Tarsus.

---

[1] Above, p. 119.
[2] *The Magic Art and the Evolution of Kings*, ii. 358 *sqq.*
[3] *The Dying God*, pp. 166 *sqq.*

[4] Athenaeus, v. 54, p. 215 B, C. The high-priest of the Syrian goddess at Hierapolis held office for a year, and wore a purple robe and a golden tiara

between the legal and the illegal exercise of authority, yet we may safely infer that the priesthood of Hercules, that is of Sandan, at Tarsus continued down to late times to be an office of great dignity and power, not unworthy to be

Kings of Cilicia related to Sandan.

held in earlier times by the kings themselves. Scanty as is our information as to the kings of Cilicia, we hear of two whose names appear to indicate that they stood in some special relation to the divine Sandan. One of them was Sandu'arri, lord of Kundi and Sizu, which have been identified with Anchiale and Sis in Cilicia.[1] The other was Sanda-sarme, who gave his daughter in marriage to Ashurbanipal, king of Assyria.[2] It would be in accordance with analogy if the kings of Tarsus formerly held the priesthood of Sandan and claimed to represent him in their own person.

Priestly kings of Olba who bore the names of Teucer and Ajax.

We know that the whole of Western or Mountainous Cilicia was ruled by kings who combined the regal office with the priesthood of Zeus, or rather of a native deity whom, like the Baal of Tarsus, the Greeks assimilated to their own Zeus. These priestly potentates had their seat at Olba, and most of them bore the name either of Teucer or of Ajax,[3] but we may suspect that these appellations are merely Greek distortions of native Cilician names. Teucer (*Teukros*) may be a corruption of Tark, Trok, Tarku, or Troko, all of which occur in the names of Cilician priests and kings. At all events, it is worthy of notice that one,

---

(Lucian, *De dea Syria*, 42). We may conjecture that the priesthood of Hercules at Tarsus was in later times at least an annual office.

[1] E. Meyer, *Geschichte des Alterthums*, i. (Stuttgart, 1884) § 389, p. 475; H. Winckler, in E. Schrader's *Keilinschriften und das Alte Testament*,[3] p. 88. Kuinda was the name of a Cilician fortress a little way inland from Anchiale (Strabo, xiv. 5. 10, p. 672).

[2] E. Meyer, *op. cit.* i. § 393, p. 480; C. P. Tiele, *Babylonisch-assyrische Geschichte*, p. 360. Sandon and Sandas occur repeatedly as names of Cilician men. They are probably identical with, or modified forms of, the divine name. See Strabo, xiv. 5. 14, p. 674; Plutarch,

Poplicola, 17; *Corpus Inscriptionum Graecarum*, ed. August Boeckh, etc. (Berlin, 1828-1877) vol. iii. p. 200, No. 4401; Ch. Michel, *Recueil d'Inscriptions Grecques* (Brussels, 1900), p. 718, No. 878; R. Heberdey und A. Wilhelm, "Reisen in Kilikien," *Denkschriften der Kaiser. Akademie der Wissenschaften, Philosoph.-histor. Classe*, xliv. (Vienna, 1896) No. vi. pp. 46, 131 *sq.*, 140 (Inscriptions 115, 218, 232).

[3] Strabo, xiv. 5. 10, p. 672. The name of the high-priest Ajax, son of Teucer, occurs on coins of Olba, dating from about the beginning of our era (B. V. Head, *Historia Numorum*, Oxford, 1887, p. 609); and the name of Teucer is also known from inscriptions. See below, pp. 145, 151, 159.

if not two, of these priestly Teucers had a father called Tarkuaris,[1] and that in a long list of priests who served Zeus at the Corycian cave, not many miles from Olba, the names Tarkuaris, Tarkumbios, Tarkimos, Trokoarbasis, and Trokombigremis, besides many other obviously native names, occur side by side with Teucer and other purely Greek appellations.[2] In like manner the Teucrids, who traced their descent from Zeus and reigned at Salamis in Cyprus,[3] may well have been a native dynasty, who concocted a Greek pedigree for themselves in the days when Greek civilization was fashionable. The legend which attributed the foundation of the Cyprian Salamis to Teucer, son of Telamon, appears to be late and unknown to Homer.[4] Moreover, a cruel form of human sacrifice which was practised in the city down to historical times savours rather of Oriental barbarity than of Greek humanity. Led or driven by the youths, a man ran thrice round the altar ; then the priest stabbed him in the throat with a spear and burned his body whole on a heaped-up pyre. The sacrifice was offered in the month of Aphrodite to Diomede, who along with Agraulus, daughter of Cecrops, had a temple at Salamis. A temple of Athena stood within the same

The Teucrids of Salamis in Cyprus.

Burnt sacrifices of human victims at Salamis and traces of a similar custom elsewhere.

---

[1] E. L. Hicks, "Inscriptions from Western Cilicia," *Journal of Hellenic Studies*, xii. (1891) pp. 226, 263 ; R. Heberdey und A. Wilhelm, "Reisen in Kilikien," *Denkschriften der Kaiser. Akademie der Wissenschaften*, xliv. (1896) No. vi. pp. 53, 88.

[2] Ch. Michel, *Recueil d'Inscriptions Grecques*, pp. 718 *sqq.*, No. 878. Tarkondimotos was the name of two kings of Eastern Cilicia in the first century B.C. One of them corresponded with Cicero and fell at the battle of Actium. See Cicero, *Epist. ad Familiares*, xv. 1. 2 ; Strabo, xiv. 5. 18, p. 676 ; Dio Cassius, xli. 63. 1, xlvii. 26. 2, l. 14. 2, li. 2. 2, li. 7. 4, liv. 9. 2 ; Plutarch, *Antoninus*, 61 ; B. V. Head, *Historia Numorum* (Oxford, 1887), p. 618 ; W. Dittenberger, *Orientis Graeci Inscriptiones Selectae* (Leipsic, 1903–1905), ii. pp. 494 *sq.*, Nos. 752, 753. Moreover, Tarkudimme or Tarkuwassimi occurs as the name of a king of Erme (?) or Urmi (?) in a

bilingual Hittite and cuneiform inscription engraved on a silver seal. See W. Wright, *The Empire of the Hittites*[2] (London, 1886), pp. 163 *sqq.* ; L. Messerschmidt, *Corpus Inscriptionum Hettiticarum*, pp. 42 *sq.*, pl. xlii. 9 ; *id.*, *The Hittites*, pp. 29 *sq.* ; P. Jensen, *Hittiter und Armenier* (Strasburg, 1898), pp. 22, 50 *sq.* In this inscription Prof. Jensen suggests Tarbibi- as an alternative reading for Tarku-. Compare P. Kretschmer, *Einleitung in die Geschichte der griechischen Sprache* (Göttingen, 1896), pp. 362-364.

[3] Isocrates, *Or.* ix. 14 and 18 *sq.* ; Pausanias, ii. 29. 2 and 4 ; W. E. Engel, *Kypros*, i. 212 *sqq.* As to the names Teucer and Teucrian see P. Kretschmer, *op. cit.* pp. 189-191. Prof. Kretschmer believes that the native population of Cyprus belonged to the non-Aryan stock of Asia Minor.

[4] W. E. Engel, *Kypros*, i. 216.

sacred enclosure. It is said that in olden times the sacrifice was offered to Agraulus, and not to Diomede. According to another account it was instituted by Teucer in honour of Zeus. However that may have been, the barbarous custom lasted down to the reign of Hadrian, when Diphilus, king of Cyprus, abolished or rather mitigated it by substituting the sacrifice of an ox for that of a man.[1] On the hypothesis here suggested we must suppose that these Greek names of divine or heroic figures at the Cyprian Salamis covered more or less similar figures of the Asiatic pantheon. And in the Salaminian burnt-sacrifice of a man we may perhaps detect the original form of the ceremony which in historical times appears to have been performed upon an image of Sandan or Hercules at Tarsus. When an ox was sacrificed instead of a man, the old sacrificial rites would naturally continue to be observed in all other respects exactly as before : the animal would be led thrice round the altar, stabbed with a spear, and burned on a pyre. Now at the Syrian Hierapolis the greatest festival of the year bore the name of the Pyre or the Torch. It was held at the beginning of spring. Great trees were then cut down and planted in the court of the temple : sheep, goats, birds, and other creatures were hung upon them : sacrificial victims were led round : then fire was set to the whole, and everything was consumed in the flames.[2] Perhaps here also the burning of animals was a substitute for the burning of men. When the practice of human sacrifice becomes too revolting to humanity to be tolerated, its abolition is commonly effected by substituting

[1] Porphyry, *De abstinentia*, ii. 54 sq. ; Lactantius, *Divin. Inst.* i. 21. As to the date when the custom was abolished, Lactantius says that it was done "recently in the reign of Hadrian." Porphyry says that the practice was put down by Diphilus, king of Cyprus, "in the time of Seleucus the Theologian." As nothing seems to be known as to the date of King Diphilus and Seleucus the Theologian, I have ventured to assume, on the strength of Lactantius's statement, that they were contemporaries of Hadrian. But it is curious to find kings of Cyprus reigning so late.

Beside the power of the Roman governors, their authority can have been little more than nominal, like that of native rajahs in British India. Seleucus the Theologian may be, as J. A. Fabricius supposed (*Bibliotheca Graeca*,[4] Hamburg, 1780–1809, vol. i. p. 86, compare p. 522), the Alexandrian grammarian who composed a voluminous work on the gods (Suidas, *s.v.* Σέλευκος). Suetonius tells an anecdote (*Tiberius*, 56) about a grammarian named Seleucus who flourished, and faded prematurely, at the court of Tiberius.

[2] Lucian, *De dea Syria*, 49.

either animals or images for living men or women.   At
Salamis certainly, and perhaps at Hierapolis, the substitutes
were animals : at Tarsus, if I am right, they were images.
In this connexion the statement of a Greek writer as to the   Burnt
worship of Adonis in Cyprus deserves attention.   He says   sacrifice
of doves
that as Adonis had been honoured by Aphrodite, the   to Adonis.
Cyprians after his death cast live doves on a pyre to him,
and that the birds, flying away from the flames, fell into
another pyre and were consumed.[1]   The statement seems to
be a description of an actual custom of burning doves in
sacrifice to Adonis.   Such a mode of honouring him would
be very remarkable, since doves were commonly sacred to
his divine mistress Aphrodite or Astarte.   For example, at
the Syrian Hierapolis, one of the chief seats of her worship,
these birds were so holy that they might not even be
touched.   If a man inadvertently touched a dove, he was
unclean or tabooed for the rest of the day.   Hence the
birds, never being molested, were so tame that they lived
with the people in their houses, and commonly picked up
their food fearlessly on the ground.[2]   Can the burning of
the sacred bird of Aphrodite in the Cyprian worship of
Adonis have been a substitute for the burning of a sacred
man who personated the lover of the goddess ?

If, as many scholars think, Tark or Tarku was the name,   The
or part of the name, of a great Hittite deity, sometimes   priestly
Teucers
identified as the god of the sky and the lightning,[3] we may   of Olba

---

[1] Diogenianus, *Praefatio*, in *Paroemiographi Graeci*, ed. E. L. Leutsch
et F. G. Schneidewin (Göttingen,
1839–1851), i. 180.   Raoul-Rochette
regarded the custom as part of the
ritual of the divine death and resurrection.   He compared it with the burning
of Melcarth at Tyre.   See his memoir,
"Sur l'Hercule Assyrien et Phénicien,"
*Mémoires de l'Académie des Inscriptions
et Belles-Lettres*, xvii. Deuxième Partie
(1848), p. 32.
[2] Lucian, *De dea Syria*, 54.
[3] A. H. Sayce, in W. Wright's
Empire of the Hittites,[2] p. 186 ; W.
M. Ramsay, "Pre-Hellenic Monuments of Cappadocia," *Recueil de
Travaux relatifs à la Philologie et
à l'Archéologie Égyptiennes et Assy-*

riennes, xiv. (1903) pp. 81 *sq.* ; C. P.
Tiele, *Geschichte der Religion im Altertum*, i. 251 ; W. Max Müller,
Asien und Europa, p. 333 ; P. Jensen, *Hittiter und Armenier*, pp. 70,
150 *sqq.*, 155 *sqq.* ; F. Hommel,
*Grundriss der Geographie und Ge-
schichte des alten Orients*, pp. 44, 51
sq. ; L. Messerschmidt, *The Hittites*,
p. 40.   Sir W. M. Ramsay thinks
(*l.c.*) that Tark was the native name
of the god who had his sanctuary at
Dastarkon in Cappadocia and who was
called by the Greeks the Cataonian
Apollo : his sanctuary was revered all
over Cappadocia (Strabo, xiv. 2. 5,
p. 537).   Prof. Hommel holds that
Tarku or Tarchu was the chief Hittite
deity, worshipped all over the south of

conjecture that Tark or Tarku was the native name of the god of Olba, whom the Greeks called Zeus, and that the priestly kings who bore the name of Teucer represented the god Tark or Tarku in their own persons. This conjecture is confirmed by the observation that Olba, the ancient name of the city, is itself merely a Grecized form of Oura, the name which the place retains to this day.[1] The situation of the town, moreover, speaks strongly in favour of the view that it was from the beginning an aboriginal settlement, though in after days, like so many other Asiatic cities, it took on a varnish of Greek culture. For it stood remote from the sea on a lofty and barren tableland, with a rigorous winter climate, in the highlands of Cilicia.

Great indeed is the contrast between the bleak windy uplands of Western or Rugged Cilicia, as the ancients called it, and the soft luxuriant lowlands of Eastern Cilicia, where winter is almost unknown and summer annually drives the population to seek in the cool air of the mountains a refuge from the intolerable heat and deadly fevers of the plains. In Western Cilicia, on the other hand, a lofty tableland, ending in a high sharp edge on the coast, rises steadily inland till it passes gradually into the chain of heights which divide it from the interior. Looked at from the sea it resembles a great blue wave swelling in one uniform sweep till its crest breaks into foam in the distant snows of the Taurus. The surface of the tableland is almost everywhere rocky and overgrown, in the intervals of the rocks, with dense, thorny, almost impenetrable scrub. Only here and there in a hollow or glen the niggardly soil allows of a patch of cultivation ; and here and there fine oaks and

---

Asia Minor. Prof. W. Max Müller is of opinion that Targh or Tarkh did not designate any particular deity, but was the general Hittite name for "god." There are grounds for holding that the proper name of the Hittite thunder-god was Teshub or Teshup. See above, p. 135 note.

[1] J. T. Bent, "Explorations in Cilicia Tracheia," *Proceedings of the Royal Geographical Society*, N.S. xii.

(1890) p. 458 ; *id.*, "A Journey in Cilicia Tracheia," *Journal of Hellenic Studies*, xii. (1891) p. 222 ; W. M. Ramsay, *Historical Geography of Asia Minor* (London, 1890), pp. 22, 364. Sir W. M. Ramsay had shown grounds for thinking that Olba was a Grecized form of a native name Ourba (pronounced Ourwa) before Mr. J. T. Bent discovered the site and the name.

planes, towering over the brushwood, clothe with a richer
foliage the depth of the valleys.   None but wandering
herdsmen with their flocks now maintain a precarious
existence in this rocky wilderness.   Yet the ruined towns
which stud the country prove that a dense population lived
and throve here in antiquity, while numerous remains of
wine-presses and wine-vats bear witness to the successful
cultivation of the grape.   The chief cause of the present
desolation is lack of water ; for wells are few and brackish,
perennial streams hardly exist, and the ancient aqueducts,
which once brought life and fertility to the land, have long
been suffered to fall into disrepair.

But for ages together the ancient inhabitants of these The
uplands earned their bread by less reputable means than Cilician
the toil of the husbandman and the vinedresser.   They pirates.
were buccaneers and slavers, scouring the high seas with
their galleys and retiring with their booty to the inaccessible fastnesses of their mountains.   In the decline of Greek
power all over the East the pirate communities of Cilicia
grew into a formidable state, recruited by gangs of desper-
adoes and broken men who flocked to it from all sides.
The holds of these robbers may still be seen perched on
the brink of the profound ravines which cleave the tableland at frequent intervals.   With their walls of massive
masonry, their towers and battlements, overhanging dizzy
depths, they are admirably adapted to bid defiance to the
pursuit of justice.   In antiquity the dark forests of cedar,
which clothed much of the country and supplied the pirates
with timber for their ships, must have rendered access to
these fastnesses still more difficult.   The great gorge of the
Lamas River, which eats its way like a sheet of forked
lightning into the heart of the mountains, is dotted every
few miles with fortified towns, some of them still magnificent in their ruins, dominating sheer cliffs high above the
stream.   They are now the haunt only of the ibex and the
bear.   Each of these communities had its own crest or
badge, which may still be seen carved on the corners of the
mouldering towers.   No doubt, too, it blazoned the same
crest on the hull, the sails, or the streamers of the galley
which, manned with a crew of ruffians, it sent out to prey

upon the rich merchantmen in the Golden Sea, as the corsairs called the highway of commerce between Crete and Africa.

A staircase cut in the rock connects one of these ruined castles with the river in the glen, a thousand feet below. But the steps are worn and dangerous, indeed impassable. You may go for miles along the edge of these stupendous cliffs before you find a way down. The paths keep on the heights, for in many of its reaches the gully affords no foothold even to the agile nomads who alone roam these solitudes. At evening the winding course of the river may be traced for a long distance by a mist which, as the heat of the day declines, rises like steam from the deep gorge and hangs suspended in a wavy line of fleecy cloud above it. But even more imposing than the ravine of the Lamas is the terrific gorge known as the *Sheitan dere* or Devil's Glen near the Corycian cave. Prodigious walls of rock, glowing in the intense sunlight, black in the shadow, and spanned by a summer sky of the deepest blue, hem in the dry bed of a winter torrent, choked with rocks and tangled with thickets of evergreens, among which the oleanders with their slim stalks, delicate taper leaves, and bunches of crimson blossom stand out conspicuous.[1]

---

[1] J. Theodore Bent, "Explorations in Cilicia Tracheia," *Proceedings of the Royal Geographical Society*, N.S. xii. (1890) pp. 445, 450-453; *id.*, "A Journal in Cilicia Tracheia," *Journal of Hellenic Studies*, xii. (1891) pp. 208, 210-212, 217-219; R. Heberdey und A. Wilhelm, "Reisen in Kilikien," *Denkschriften der kaiser. Akademie der Wissenschaften, Philosoph.-historische Classe*, xliv. (Vienna, 1896) No. vi. pp. 49, 70; D. G. Hogarth and J. A. R. Munro, "Modern and Ancient Roads in Eastern Asia Minor," *Royal Geographical Society, Supplementary Papers*, vol. iii. part 5 (London, 1893), pp. 653 *sq.* As to the Cilician pirates see Strabo, xiv. 5. 2, pp. 668 *sq.*; Plutarch, *Pompeius*, 24; Appian, *Bellum Mithridat.* 92 *sq.*; Dio Cassius, xxxvi. 20-24 [3-6], ed. L. Dindorf; Cicero, *De imperio Cn. Pompeii*, 11 *sq.*; Th. Mommsen, *Roman History* (London, 1868), iii. 68-70, iv. 40-45, 118-120. As to the crests carved on their towns see J. T. Bent, "Cilician Symbols," *Classical Review*, iv. (1890) pp. 321 *sq.* Among these crests are a club (the badge of Olba), a bunch of grapes, the caps of the Dioscuri, the three-legged symbol, and so on. As to the cedars and shipbuilding timber of Cilicia in antiquity see Theophrastus, *Historia Plantarum*, iii. 2. 6, iv. 5. 5. The cedars and firs have now retreated to the higher slopes of the Taurus. Great destruction is wrought in the forests by the roving Yuruks with their flocks; for they light their fires under the trees, tap the firs for turpentine, bark the cedars for their huts and bee-hives, and lay bare whole tracts of country that the grass may grow for their sheep and goats. See J. T. Bent, in *Proceedings of the Royal Geographical Society*, N.S. xii. (1890) pp. 453-458.

The ruins of Olba, among the most extensive and The site
and ruins
of Olba.
remarkable in Asia Minor, were discovered in 1890 by
Mr. J. Theodore Bent.   But three years before another
English traveller had caught a distant view of its battlements and towers outlined against the sky like a city of
enchantment or dreams.[1]   Standing at a height of nearly
six thousand feet above the sea, the upper town commands
a free, though somewhat uniform, prospect for immense
distances in all directions.   The sea is just visible far away
to the south.   On these heights the winter is long and
severe.   Snow lies on the ground for months.   No Greek
would have chosen such a site for a city, so bleak and chill,
so far from blue water ; but it served well for a fastness
of brigands.   Deep gorges, one of them filled for miles with
tombs, surround it on all sides, rendering fortification walls
superfluous.   But a great square tower, four stories high,
rises conspicuous on the hill, forming a landmark and
earning for this upper town the native name of *Jebel Hissar*,
or the . Mountain of the Castle.   A Greek inscription cut
on the tower proves that it was built by Teucer, son of
Tarkuaris, one of the priestly potentates of Olba.   Among
other remains of public buildings the most notable are forty
tall Corinthian columns of the great temple of Olbian Zeus.
Though coarse in style and corroded by long exposure to The
temple of
Olbian
Zeus.
frost and snow, these massive pillars, towering above the
ruins, produce an imposing effect.   That the temple of
which they formed part belonged indeed to Olbian Zeus
is shown by a Greek inscription found within the sacred
area, which records that the pent-houses on the inner side
of the boundary wall were built by King Seleucus Nicator
and repaired for Olbian Zeus by " the great high-priest
Teucer, son of Zenophanes." About two hundred yards
from this great temple are standing five elegant granite
columns of a small temple dedicated to the goddess Fortune.
Further, the remains of two theatres and many other public
buildings attest the former splendour of this mountain city.
An arched colonnade, of which some Corinthian columns
are standing with their architraves, ran through the town ;

[1] D. G. Hogarth, *A Wandering Scholar in the Levant* (London, 1896),
pp. 57 *sq.*

and an ancient paved road, lined with tombs and ruins, leads down hill to a lower and smaller city two or three miles distant.   It is this lower town which retains the ancient name of Oura.   Here the principal ruins occupy an isolated fir-clad height bounded by two narrow ravines full of rock-cut tombs.   Below the town the ravines unite and form a fine gorge, down which the old road passed seaward.[1]

§ 7. *The God of the Corycian Cave*

Limestone caverns of Western Cilicia.

Nothing yet found at Olba throws light on the nature of the god who was worshipped there under the Greek name of Zeus.   But at two places near the coast, distant only some fourteen or fifteen miles from Olba, a deity also called Zeus by the Greeks was revered in natural surroundings of a remarkable kind, which must have stood in close relation with the worship, and are therefore fitted to illustrate it.   In both places the features of the landscape are of the same general cast, and at one of them the god was definitely identified with the Zeus of Olba.   The country here consists of a tableland of calcareous rock rent at intervals by those great chasms which are characteristic of a limestone formation.   Similar fissures, with the accompaniment of streams or rivers which pour into them and vanish under ground, are frequent in Greece, and may be observed in our own country near Ingleborough in Yorkshire. Fossil bones of extinct animals are often found embedded in

[1] J. Theodore Bent, " Explorations in Cilicia Tracheia," *Proceedings of the Royal Geographical Society*, N.S. xii. (1890) pp. 445 *sq.*, 458-460 ; *id.*, "A Journey in Cilicia Tracheia," *Journal of Hellenic Studies*, xii. (1890) pp. 220-222 ; E. L. Hicks, "Inscriptions from Western Cilicia," *ib.* pp. 262-270 ; R. Heberdey und A. Wilhelm, " Reisen in Kilikien," *Denkschriften der kaiser. Akademie der Wissenschaften, Philos.-histor. Classe*, xliv. (Vienna, 1896) No. vi. pp. 83-91 ; W. M. Ramsay and D. G. Hogarth, in *American Journal of Archaeology*, vi. (1890) p. 345 ; Ch. Michel, *Recueil d'Inscriptions Grecques*, p. 858, No. 1231.   In one place (*Journal of Hellenic Studies*, xii. 222) Bent gives the height of Olba as 3800 feet ; but this is a misprint, for elsewhere (*Proceedings of the Royal Geographical Society*, N.S. xii. 446, 458) he gives the height as exactly 5850 or roughly 6000 feet.   The misprint has unfortunately been repeated by Messrs. Heberdey and Wilhelm (*op. cit.* p. 84 note [1]).   The tall tower of Olba is figured on the coins of the city.   See G. F. Hill, *Catalogue of the Greek Coins of Lycaonia, Isauria, and Cilicia* (London, 1900), pl. xxii. 8.

the stalagmite or breccia of limestone caves. For example, the famous Kent's Hole near Torquay contained bones of the mammoth, rhinoceros, lion, hyaena, and bear; and red osseous breccias, charged with the bones of quadrupeds which have long disappeared from Europe, are common in almost all the countries bordering on the Mediterranean.[1] Western Cilicia is richer in Miocene deposits than any other part of Anatolia, and the limestone gorges of the coast near Olba are crowded with fossil oysters, corals, and other shells.[2] Here, too, within the space of five miles the limestone plateau is rent by three great chasms, which Greek religion associated with Zeus and Typhon. One of these fissures is the celebrated Corycian cave.

To visit this spot, invested with the double charm of natural beauty and legendary renown, you start from the dead Cilician city of Corycus on the sea, with its ruined walls, towers, and churches, its rock-hewn houses and cisterns, its shattered mole, its island-fortress, still imposing in decay. Viewed from the sea, this part of the Cilician coast, with its long succession of white ruins, relieved by the dark wooded hills behind, presents an appearance of populousness and splendour. But a nearer approach reveals the nakedness and desolation of the once prosperous land.[3] Following the shore westward from Corycus for about an hour you come to a pretty cove enclosed by wooded heights, where a spring of pure cold water bubbles up close to the sea, giving to the spot its name of *Tatlu-su*, or the Sweet Water. From this bay a steep ascent of about a mile along an ancient paved road leads inland to a plateau. Here, threading your way through a labyrinth or petrified sea of jagged calcareous rocks, you suddenly find yourself on the brink of a vast chasm which yawns at your feet. This is the Corycian cave. In reality it is not a cave but an immense hollow or trough in the plateau, of oval shape and perhaps half a mile in circumference. The cliffs which

The city of Corycus.

The Corycian cave.

---

[1] Sir Charles Lyell, *Principles of Geology*[12] (London, 1875), ii. 518 *sqq.*; *Encyclopaedia Britannica*, Ninth Edition, *s.v.* "Caves," v. 265 *sqq.* Compare my notes on Pausanias, i. 35. 7, viii. 29. 1.

[2] J. T. Bent, in *Proceedings of the Royal Geographical Society*, N.S. xii. (1890) p. 447.

[3] Fr. Beaufort, *Karmania* (London, 1817), pp. 240 *sq.*

enclose it vary from one hundred to over two hundred feet in depth. Its uneven bottom slopes throughout its whole length from north to south, and is covered by a thick jungle of trees and shrubs—myrtles, pomegranates, carobs, and many more, kept always fresh and green by rivulets, underground water, and the shadow of the great cliffs. A single narrow path leads down into its depths. The way is long and rough, but the deeper you descend the denser grows the vegetation, and it is under the dappled shade of whispering leaves and with the purling of brooks in your ears that you at last reach the bottom. The saffron which of old grew here among the bushes is no longer to be found, though it still flourishes in the surrounding district. This luxuriant bottom, with its rich verdure, its refreshing moisture, its grateful shade, is called Paradise by the wandering herdsmen. They tether their camels and pasture their goats in it and come hither in the late summer to gather the ripe pomegranates. At the southern and deepest end of this great cliff-encircled hollow you come to the cavern proper. The ruins of a Byzantine church, which replaced a heathen temple, partly block the entrance. Inwards the cave descends with a gentle slope into the bowels of the earth. The old path paved with polygonal masonry still runs through it, but soon disappears under sand. At about two hundred feet from its mouth the cave comes to an end, and a tremendous roar of subterranean water is heard. By crawling on all fours you may reach a small pool arched by a dripping stalactite-hung roof, but the stream which makes the deafening din is invisible. It was otherwise in antiquity. A river of clear water burst from the rock, but only to vanish again into a chasm. Such changes in the course of streams are common in countries subject to earthquakes and to the disruption caused by volcanic agency. The ancients believed that this mysterious cavern was haunted ground. In the rumble and roar of the waters they seemed to hear the clash of cymbals touched by hands divine.[1]

[1] Strabo, xiv. 5. 5, pp. 670 *sq.*; Mela, i. 72-75, ed. G. Parthey; J. T. Bent, "Explorations in Cilicia Tracheia," *Proceedings of the Royal Geographical Society*, N.S. xii. (1890) pp. 446-448; *id.*, "A Journey in Cilicia Tracheia," *Journal of Hellenic Studies*, xii. (1891) pp. 212-214; R.

If now, quitting the cavern, we return by the same path to the summit of the cliffs, we shall find on the plateau the ruins of a town and of a temple at the western edge of the great Corycian chasm.   The wall of the holy precinct was built within a few feet of the precipices, and the sanctuary must have stood right over the actual cave and its subterranean waters.   In later times the temple was converted into a Christian church.   By pulling down a portion of the sacred edifice Mr. Bent had the good fortune to discover a Greek inscription containing a long list of names, probably those of the priests who superintended the worship.   One name which meets us frequently in the list is Zas, and it is tempting to regard this as merely a dialectical form of Zeus.   If that were so, the priests who bore the name might be supposed to personate the god.[1] But many strange and barbarous-looking names, evidently foreign, occur in the list, and Zas may be one of them. However, it is certain that Zeus was worshipped at the Corycian cave ; for about half a mile from it, on the summit of a hill, are the ruins of a larger temple, which an inscription proves to have been dedicated to Corycian Zeus.[2]

But Zeus, or whatever native deity masqueraded under his name, did not reign alone in the deep dell.   A more dreadful being haunted a still more awful abyss which opens in the ground only a hundred yards to the east of the great Corycian chasm.   It is a circular cauldron, about a quarter

---

Heberdey und A. Wilhelm, " Reisen in Kilikien," *Denkschriften der kaiser. Akademie der Wissenschaften, Philos.- histor. Classe*, xliv. (1896) No. vi. pp. 70-79.   Mr. D. G. Hogarth was so good as to furnish me with some notes embodying his recollections of the Corycian cave.   All these modern writers confirm the general accuracy of the descriptions of the cave given by Strabo and Mela.   Mr. Hogarth indeed speaks of exaggeration in Mela's account, but this is not admitted by Mr. A. Wilhelm.   As to the ruins of the city of Corycus the coast, distant about three miles from the cave, see Fr. Beaufort, *Karmania* (London,

1817), pp. 232-238 ; R. Heberdey und A. Wilhelm, *op. cit.* pp. 67-70.

[1] The suggestion is Mr. A. B. Cook's.   See his article, " The European Sky-god," *Classical Review*, xvii. (1903) p. 418, note [2].

[2] J. T. Bent, in *Proceedings of the Royal Geographical Society*, N.S. xii. (1890) p. 448 ; *id.*, in *Journal of Hellenic Studies*, xii. (1891) pp. 214-216.   For the inscription containing the names of the priests see R. Heberdey und A. Wilhelm, *op. cit.* pp. 71-79 ; Ch. Michel, *Recueil d'Inscriptions Grecques*, pp. 718 *sqq.*, No. 878 ; above, p. 145.

of a mile in circumference, resembling the Corycian chasm
in its general character, but smaller, deeper, and far more
terrific in appearance. Its sides overhang and stalactites
droop from them. There is no way down into it. The
only mode of reaching the bottom, which is covered with
vegetation, would be to be lowered at the end of a long
rope. The nomads call this chasm Purgatory, to distinguish
it from the other which they name Paradise. They say
that there is a subterranean passage between the two, and
that the smoke of a fire kindled in the Corycian cave may
be seen curling out of the other. The one ancient writer
who expressly mentions this second and more grisly cavern
is Mela, who says that it was the lair of the giant Typhon,
and that no animal let down into it could live.[1] Aeschylus
puts into the mouth of Prometheus an account of "the
earth-born Typhon, dweller in Cilician caves, dread monster,
hundred-headed," who in his pride rose up against the gods,
hissing destruction from his dreadful jaws, while from his
Gorgon eyes the lightning flashed. But him a flaming levin
bolt, crashing from heaven, smote to the very heart, and
now he lies, shrivelled and scorched, under the weight of
Etna by the narrow sea. Yet one day he will belch a fiery
hail, a boiling angry flood, rivers of flame, to devastate the
fat Sicilian fields.[2] This poetical description of the monster,
confirmed by a similar passage of Pindar,[3] clearly proves
that Typhon was conceived as a personification of those
active volcanoes which spout fire and smoke to heaven as
if they would assail the celestial gods. The Corycian caverns
are not volcanic, but the ancients apparently regarded them
as such, else they would hardly have made them the den of
Typhon.

Battle of
Zeus and
Typhon.

According to one legend Typhon was a monster, half
man and half brute, begotten in Cilicia by Tartarus upon
the goddess Earth. The upper part of him was human, but
from the loins downward he was an enormous snake. In
the battle of the gods and giants, which was fought out in
Egypt, Typhon hugged Zeus in his snaky coils, wrested

[1] Mela, i. 76, ed. G. Parthey (Berlin,
1867). The cave of Typhon is
described by J. T. Bent, *ll.cc.*
[2] Aeschylus, *Prometheus Vinctus*,
351-372.
[3] Pindar, *Pyth.* i. 30 *sqq.*, who
speaks of the giant as "bred in the
many-named Cilician cave."

from him his crooked sword, and with the blade cut the sinews of the god's hands and feet.   Then taking him on his back he conveyed the mutilated deity across the sea to Cilicia, and deposited him in the Corycian cave.   Here, too, he hid the severed sinews, wrapt in a bear's skin.   But Hermes and Aegipan contrived to steal the missing thews and restore them to their divine owner.   Thus made whole and strong again, Zeus pelted his beaten adversary with thunderbolts, drove him from place to place, and at last overwhelmed him under Mount Etna.   And the spots where the hissing bolts fell are still marked by jets of flame.[1]

It is possible that the discovery of fossil bones of large extinct animals may have helped to localize the story of the giant at the Corycian cave.   Such bones, as we have seen, are often found in limestone caverns, and the limestone gorges of Cilicia are in fact rich in fossils.   The Arcadians laid the scene of the battle of the gods and the giants in the plain of Megalopolis, where many bones of mammoths have come to light, and where, moreover, flames have been seen to burst from the earth and even to burn for years.[2]   These natural conditions would easily suggest a fable of giants who had fought the gods and had been slain by thunderbolts ; the smouldering earth or jets of flame would be regarded as the spots where the divine lightnings had struck the ground.   Hence the Arcadians sacrificed to thunder and lightning.[3]   In Sicily, too, great quantities of bones of mammoths, elephants, hippopotamuses, and other animals long extinct in the island have been found, and have been appealed to with confidence by patriotic Sicilians as conclusive evidence of the gigantic stature of their ancestors or predecessors.[4]   These remains of huge unwieldy creatures which once trampled through the jungle or splashed in the rivers of Sicily may have contributed with the fires of Etna to build up the story of giants imprisoned under the volcano and vomiting smoke and flame from its crater.   " Tales of

Fossil bones of extinct animals give rise to stories of giants.

[1] Apollodorus, *Bibliotheca*, i. 6. 3.
[2] Pausanias, viii. 29. 1, with my notes.   Pausanias mentions (viii. 32. 5) bones of superhuman size which were preserved at Megalopolis, and which popular superstition identified as the bones of the giant Hopladamus.

[3] Pausanias, viii. 29. 1.

[4] A. Holm, *Geschichte Siciliens im Alterthum* (Leipsic, 1870–1874), i. 57, 356.

giants and monsters, which stand in direct connexion with the finding of great fossil bones, are scattered broadcast over the mythology of the world. Huge bones, found at Punto Santa Elena, in the north of Guayaquil, have served as a foundation for the story of a colony of giants who dwelt there. The whole area of the Pampas is a great sepulchre of enormous extinct animals ; no wonder that one great plain should be called the 'Field of the giants,' and that such names as 'the hill of the giant,' 'the stream of the animal,' should be guides to the geologist in his search for fossil bones." [1]

Chasm of Olbian Zeus at Kanytelideis.

About five miles to the north-east of the Corycian caverns, but divided from them by many deep gorges and impassable rocks, is another and very similar chasm. It may be reached in about an hour and a quarter from the sea by an ancient paved road, which ascends at first very steeply and then gently through bush-clad and wooded hills. Thus you come to a stretch of level ground covered with the well-preserved ruins of an ancient town. Remains of fortresses constructed of polygonal masonry, stately churches, and many houses, together with numerous tombs and reliefs, finely chiselled in the calcareous limestone of the neighbourhood, bear witness to the extent and importance of the place. Yet it is mentioned by no ancient writer. Inscriptions prove that its name was Kanyteldeis or Kanytelideis, which still survives in the modern form of Kanidiwan. The great chasm opens in the very heart of the city. So crowded are the ruins that you do not perceive the abyss till you are within a few yards of it. It is almost a complete circle, about a quarter of a mile wide, three-quarters of a mile in circumference, and uniformly two hundred feet or more in depth. The cliffs go sheer down and remind the traveller of the great quarries at Syracuse. But like the Corycian caves, the larger of which it closely resembles, the huge fissure is natural ; and its bottom, like theirs, is overgrown with trees and vegetation. Two ways led down into it in antiquity, both cut through the rock. One of them was a tunnel, which is now obstructed ; the other is still open.

---

[1] (Sir) Edward B. Tylor, *Researches into the Early History of Mankind* [3] (London, 1878), p. 322, who adduces much more evidence of the same sort.

Remains of columns and hewn stones in the bottom of the chasm seem to show that a temple once stood there. But there is no cave at the foot of the cliffs, and no stream flows in the deep hollow or can be heard to rumble underground. A ruined tower of polygonal masonry, which stands on the southern edge of the chasm, bears a Greek inscription stating that it was dedicated to Olbian Zeus by the priest Teucer, son of Tarkuaris. The letters are beautifully cut in the style of the third century before Christ. We may infer that at the time of the dedication the town belonged to the priestly kings of Olba, and that the great chasm was sacred to Olbian Zeus.[1]

What, then, was the character of the god who was worshipped under the name of Zeus at these two great natural chasms? The depth of the fissures, opening suddenly and as it were without warning in the midst of a plateau, was well fitted to impress and awe the spectator; and the sight of the rank evergreen vegetation at their bottom, fed by rivulets or underground water, must have presented a striking contrast to the grey, barren, rocky wilderness of the surrounding tableland. Such a spot must have seemed to simple folk a paradise, a garden of God, the abode of higher powers who caused the wilderness to blossom, if not with roses, at least with myrtles and pomegranates for man, and with grass and underwood for his flocks. So to the Semite, as we saw, the Baal of the land is he who fertilizes it by subterranean water rather than by rain from the sky, and who therefore dwells in the depths of earth rather than in the height of heaven.[2] In rainless countries the sky-god is deprived of one of the principal functions which he discharges in cool cloudy climates like that of Europe. He has, in fact, little or nothing to do with the water-supply, and has therefore small excuse for levying a water-rate on his worshippers. Not, indeed, that Cilicia is rainless; but in countries border-

The deity of these great chasms was called Zeus by the Greeks, but he was probably a god of fertility embodied in vegetation and water.

[1] J. T. Bent, "Explorations in Cilicia Tracheia," *Proceedings of the Royal Geographical Society*, N.S. xii. (1890) pp. 448 *sq.*; *id.*, "A Journey in Cilicia Tracheia," *Journal of Hellenic Studies*, xii. (1891) pp. 208-210; R.

Heberdey und A. Wilhelm, "Reisen in Kilikien," *Denkschriften der kaiserlichen Akademie der Wissenschaften, Philosophisch-historische Classe*, xliv. (Vienna, 1896) No. vi. pp. 51-61.

[2] See above, pp. 26 *sq.*

ing on the Mediterranean the drought is almost unbroken through the long months of summer. Vegetation then withers: the face of nature is scorched and brown: most of the rivers dry up; and only their white stony beds, hot to the foot and dazzling to the eye, remain to tell where they flowed. It is at such seasons that a green hollow, a shady rock, a murmuring stream, are welcomed by the wanderer in the South with a joy and wonder which the untravelled Northerner can hardly imagine. Never do the broad slow rivers of England, with their winding reaches, their grassy banks, their grey willows mirrored with the soft English sky in the placid stream, appear so beautiful as when the traveller views them for the first time after leaving behind him the aridity, the heat, the blinding glare of the white southern landscape, set in seas and skies of caerulean blue.

Analogy of the Corycian and Olbian caverns to Ibreez and the vale of the Adonis.
We may take it, then, as probable that the god of the Corycian and Olbian caverns was worshipped as a source of fertility. In antiquity, when the river, which now roars underground, still burst from the rock in the Corycian cave, the scene must have resembled Ibreez, where the god of the corn and the vine was adored at the source of the stream; and we may compare the vale of Adonis in the Lebanon, where the divinity who gave his name to the river was revered at its foaming cascades. The three landscapes had in common the elements of luxuriant vegetation and copious streams leaping full-born from the rock. We shall hardly err in supposing that these features shaped the conception of the deities who were supposed to haunt the favoured spots. At the Corycian cave the existence of a second chasm, of a frowning and awful aspect, might well suggest the presence of an evil being who lurked in it and sought to undo the beneficent work of the good god. Thus we should have a fable of a conflict between the two, a battle of Zeus and Typhon.

Two gods at Olba, perhaps a father and a son, corresponding to the
On the whole we conclude that the Olbian Zeus, worshipped at one of these great limestone chasms, and clearly identical in nature with the Corycian Zeus, was also identical with the Baal of Tarsus, the god of the corn and the vine, who in his turn can hardly be separated from

the god of Ibreez. If my conjecture is right the native name of the Olbian Zeus was Tark or Trok, and the priestly Teucers of Olba represented him in their own persons. On that hypothesis the Olbian priests who bore the name of Ajax embodied another native deity of unknown name, perhaps the father or the son of Tark. A comparison of the coin-types of Tarsus with the Hittite monuments of Ibreez and Boghaz-Keui led us to the conclusion that the people of Tarsus worshipped at least two distinct gods, a father and a son, the father-god being known to the Semites as Baal and to the Greeks as Zeus, while the son was called Sandan by the natives, but Hercules by the Greeks. We may surmise that at Olba the names of Teucer and Ajax designated two gods who corresponded in type to the two gods of Tarsus ; and if the lesser figure at Ibreez, who appears in an attitude of adoration before the deity of the corn and the vine, could be interpreted as the divine Son in presence of the divine Father, we should have in all three places the same pair of deities, represented probably in the flesh by successive generations of priestly kings. But the evidence is far too slender to justify us in advancing this hypothesis as anything more than a bare conjecture.

§ 8. *Cilician Goddesses*

So far, the Cilician deities discussed have been males ; we have as yet found no trace of the great Mother Goddess who plays so important a part in the religion of Cappadocia and Phrygia, beyond the great dividing range of the Taurus. Yet we may suspect that she was not unknown in Cilicia, though her worship certainly seems to have been far less prominent there than in the centre of Asia Minor. The difference may perhaps be interpreted as evidence that mother-kin and hence the predominance of Mother Goddesses survived, in the bleak highlands of the interior, long after a genial climate and teeming soil had fostered the growth of a higher civilization, and with it the advance from female to male kinship, in the rich lowlands of Cilicia. Be that as it may, Cilician goddesses with or without a male partner are known to have been revered in various parts of the country.

The
goddess
'Atheh,
partner of
Baal at
Tarsus,
seems to
have been
a form of
Atargatis.

Thus at Tarsus itself the goddess 'Atheh was worshipped along with Baal ; their effigies are engraved on the same coins of the city. She is represented wearing a veil and seated upon a lion, with her name in Aramaic letters engraved beside her.[1] Hence it would seem that at Tarsus, as at Boghaz-Keui, the Father God mated with a lion-goddess like the Phrygian Cybele or the Syrian Atargatis. Now the name Atargatis is a Greek rendering of the Aramaic 'Athar-'atheh, a compound word which includes the name of the goddess of Tarsus.[2] Thus in name as well as in attributes the female partner of the Baal of Tarsus appears to correspond to

The lion-
goddess
and the
bull-god.

Atargatis, the Syrian Mother Goddess whose image, seated on a lion or lions, was worshipped with great pomp and splendour at Hierapolis - Bambyce near the Euphrates.[3]

[1] B. V. Head, *Historia Numorum* (Oxford, 1887), p. 616. [However, Mr. G. F. Hill writes to me : " The attribution to Tarsus of the 'Atheh coins is unfounded. Head himself only gives it as doubtful. I should think they belong further East." In the uncertainty which prevails on this point I have left the text unchanged. *Note to Second Edition.*]

[2] The name 'Athar-'atheh occurs in a Palmyrene inscription. See G. A. Cooke, *Text-book of North-Semitic Inscriptions*, No. 112, pp. 267-270. In analysing Atargatis into 'Athar-'atheh ('Atar-'ata) I follow E. Meyer (*Geschichte des Altertums*,[2] i. 2. pp. 605, 650 *sq.*), F. Baethgen (*Beiträge zur semitischen Religionsgeschichte*, pp. 68-75), Fr. Cumont (*s.v.* " Atargatis," Pauly-Wissowa, *Real-Encyclopädie der classischen Altertumswissenschaft*, ii. 1896), G. A. Cooke (*l.c.*), C. P. Tiele (*Geschichte der Religion im Altertum*, i. 245), F. Hommel (*Grundriss der Geographie und Geschichte des alten Orients*, pp. 43 *sq.*), Father Lagrange (*Études sur les Religions Sémitiques*,[2] p. 130), and L. B. Paton (*s.v.* " Atargatis," J. Hastings's *Encyclopaedia of Religion and Ethics*, ii. 164 *sq.*). In the great temple at Hierapolis - Bambyce a mysterious golden image stood between the images of Atargatis and her male partner. It resembled neither of them, yet combined the attributes of other

gods. Some interpreted it as Dionysus, others as Deucalion, and others as Semiramis ; for a golden dove, traditionally associated with Semiramis, was perched on the head of the figure. The Syrians called the image by a name which Lucian translates " sign ' (σημήιον). See Lucian, *De dea Syria*, 33. It has been plausibly conjectured by F. Baethgen that the name which Lucian translates " sign " was really 'Atheh (עתה), which could easily be confused with the Syriac word for "sign" (אתא). See F. Baethgen, *op. cit.* p. 73. A coin of Hierapolis, dating from the third century A.D., exhibits the images of the god and goddess seated on bulls and lions respectively, with the mysterious object between them enclosed in a shrine, which is surmounted by a bird, probably a dove. See J. Garstang, *The Syrian Goddess* (London, 1913), pp. 22 *sqq.*, 70 *sq.*, with fig. 7.

The modern writers cited at the beginning of this note have interpreted the Syrian 'Atheh as a male god, the lover of Atargatis, and identical in name and character with the Phrygian Attis. They may be right ; but none of them seems to have noticed that the same name 'Atheh (עתה) is applied to a goddess at Tarsus.

[3] As to the image, see above, p. 137.

May we go a step farther and find a correspondence between the Baal of Tarsus and the husband - god of Atargatis at Hierapolis-Bambyce? That husband-god, like the Baal of Tarsus, was identified by the Greeks with Zeus, and Lucian tells us that the resemblance of his image to the images of Zeus was in all respects unmistakable. But his image, unlike those of Zeus, was seated upon bulls.[1] In point of fact he was probably Hadad, the chief male god of the Syrians, who appears to have been a god of thunder and fertility; for at Baalbec in the Lebanon, where the ruined temple of the Sun is the most imposing monument bequeathed to the modern world by Greek art in its decline, his image grasped in his left hand a thunderbolt and ears of corn,[2] and a colossal statue of the deity, found near Zenjirli in Northern Syria, represents him with a bearded human head and horns, the emblem of strength and fertility.[3] A similar god of thunder and lightning was worshipped from early times by the Babylonians and Assyrians; he bore the similar name of Adad and his emblems appear to have been a thunderbolt and a bull. On an Assyrian relief his image is represented as that of a bearded man clad in a short tunic, wearing a cap with two pairs of horns, and grasping an axe in his right hand and a thunderbolt in his left. His resemblance to the Hittite god of the thundering sky was therefore very close. An alternative name for this Babylonian and Assyrian deity was Ramman, an appropriate

---

[1] Lucian, *De dea Syria*, 31.

[2] Macrobius, *Saturn.* i. 23. 12 and 17-19. The Greek name of Baalbec was Heliopolis, "the City of the Sun."

[3] G. A. Cooke, *Text-book of North-Semitic Inscriptions*, pp. 163, 164. The statue bears a long inscription, which in the style of its writing belongs to the archaic type represented by the Moabite Stone. The contents of the inscription show that it is earlier than the time of Tiglath-Pileser III. (745–727 B.C.). On Hadad, the Syrian thunder-god, see F. Baethgen, *Beiträge zur semitischen Religionsgeschichte*, pp. 66-68; C. P. Tiele, *Geschichte der Religion im Altertum*, i. 248 *sq.*; M. J. Lagrange, *Études sur les Religions Sémitiques*,[2] pp. 92 *sq.* That Hadad was the consort of Atargatis at Hiera-polis-Bambyce is the opinion of P. Jensen (*Hittiter und Armenier*, p. 171), who also indicates his character as a god both of thunder and of fertility (*ib.*, p. 167). The view of Prof. J. Garstang is similar (*The Syrian Goddess*, pp. 25 *sqq.*). That the name of the chief male god of Hierapolis-Bambyce was Hadad is rendered almost certain by coins of the city which were struck in the time of Alexander the Great by a priestly king Abd - Hadad, whose name means "Servant of Hadad." See B. V. Head, *Historia Numorum* (Oxford, 1887), p. 654; J. Garstang, *The Syrian Goddess*, p. 27, with fig. 5.

term, derived from a verb *ramâmu* to "scream" or "roar."[1]
Now we have seen that the god of Ibreez, whose attributes
tally with those of the Baal of Tarsus, wears a cap adorned
with bull's horns;[2] that the Father God at Boghaz-Keui,
meeting the Mother Goddess on her lioness, is attended by
an animal which according to the usual interpretation is a
bull;[3] and that the bull itself was worshipped, apparently as
an emblem of fertility, at Euyuk near Boghaz-Keui.[4] Thus
at Tarsus and Boghaz-Keui, as at Hierapolis-Bambyce, the
Father God and the Mother Goddess would seem to have
had as their sacred animals or emblems the bull and the lion

In later
times the
old
goddess
became the
Fortune of
the City.

respectively. In later times, under Greek influence, the
goddess was apparently exchanged for, or converted into,
the Fortune of the City, who appears on coins of Tarsus as
a seated woman with veiled and turreted head, grasping ears
of corn and a poppy in her hand. Her lion is gone, but a
trace of him perhaps remains on a coin which exhibits the
throne of the goddess adorned with a lion's leg.[5] In general
it would seem that the goddess Fortune, who figures commonly as the guardian of cities in the Greek East, especially
in Syria, was nothing but a disguised form of Gad, the
Semitic god of fortune or luck, who, though the exigencies of
grammar required him to be masculine, is supposed to have
been often merely a special aspect of the great goddess
Astarte or Atargatis conceived as the patroness and protector
of towns.[6] In Oriental religion such permutations or com-
binations need not surprise us. To the gods all things are

---

[1] H. Zimmern, in E. Schrader's *Die Keilinschriften und das Alte Testament*,[3] pp. 442-449; M. Jastrow, *Die Religion Babyloniens und Assyriens* (Giessen, 1905-1912), i. 146-150, with *Bildermappe*, plate 32, fig. 97. The Assyrian relief is also figured in W. H. Roscher's *Lexikon der griech. und röm. Mythologie*, s.v. "Marduk," ii. 2350. The Babylonian *ramâmu* "to scream, roar" has its equivalent in the Hebrew *ra'am* (רעם) "to thunder." The two names Adad (Hadad) and Ramman occur together in the form Hadadrimmon in Zechariah, xii. 11 (with S. R. Driver's note, *Century Bible*).

[2] See above, pp. 121, 123.

[3] See above, p. 130. However, the animal seems to be rather a goat. See above, p. 133 note.

[4] See above, p. 132.

[5] G. F. Hill, *Catalogue of the Greek Coins of Lycaonia, Isauria, and Cilicia*, pp. 181, 182, 185, 188, 190, 228.

[6] E. Meyer, *Geschichte des Alterthums*, i. (Stuttgart, 1884) pp. 246 *sq.*; F. Baethgen, *Beiträge zur semitischen Religionsgeschichte*, pp. 76 *sqq.* The idolatrous Hebrews spread tables for Gad, that is, for Fortune (Isaiah lxv. 11, Revised Version).

possible.   In Cyprus the goddess of love wore a beard,[1] and
Alexander the Great sometimes disported himself in the
costume of Artemis, while at other times he ransacked the
divine wardrobe to figure in the garb of Hercules, of Hermes,
and of Ammon.[2]   The change of the goddess Atheh of
Tarsus into Gad or Fortune would be easy if we suppose
that she was known as Gad- Atheh, " Luck of 'Atheh," which
occurs as a Semitic personal name.[3]   In like manner the
goddess of Fortune at Olba, who had her small temple
beside the great temple of Zeus,[4] may have been originally
the consort of the native god Tark or Tarku.

Another town in Cilicia where an Oriental god and
goddess appear to have been worshipped together was Mallus.
The city was built on a height in the great Cilician plain
near the mouth of the river Pyramus.[5]   Its coins exhibit
two winged deities, a male and a female, in a kneeling or
running attitude.   On some of the coins the male deity is
represented, like Janus, with two heads facing opposite ways,
and with two pairs of wings, while beneath him is the fore-
part of a bull with a human head.   The obverse of the
coins which bear the female deity displays a conical stone,
sometimes flanked by two bunches of grapes.[6]   This
conical stone, like those of other Asiatic cities,[7] was probably
the emblem of a Mother Goddess, and the bunches of grapes
indicate her fertilizing powers.   The god with the two heads

*The
Phoenician
god El and
his wife at
Mallus in
Cilicia.*

---

[1] Macrobius, *Saturn.* iii. 8. 2 ;
Servius on Virgil, *Aen.* ii. 632.

[2] Ephippus, cited by Athenaeus, xii.
53, p. 537.

[3] F. Baethgen, *op. cit.* p. 77 ; G.
A. Cooke, *Text-book of North-Semitic
Inscriptions*, p. 269.

[4] See above, p. 151.

[5] Strabo, xiv. 5. 16, p. 675.

[6] B. V. Head, *Historia Numorum*
(Oxford, 1887), pp. 605 *sq.*; G. F. Hill,
*Catalogue of the Greek Coins of Lycaonia,
Isauria, and Cilicia*, pp. cxvii. *sqq.*, 95-
98, plates xv. xvi. xl. 9 ; G. Macdonald,
*Catalogue of Greek Coins in the
Hunterian Collection*, ii. 536 *sq.*, pl.
lix. 11-14.   The male and female
figures appear on separate coins.   The
attribution to Mallus of the coins with

the female figure and conical stone has
been questioned by Messrs. J. P. Six
and G. F. Hill.   I follow the view
of Messrs. F. Imhoof-Blumer and
B. V. Head. [However, Mr. G. F. Hill
writes to me that the attribution of these
coins to Mallus is no longer maintained
by any one.   Imhoof-Blumer himself
now conjecturally assigns them to
Aphrodisias in Cilicia, and Mr. Hill
regards this conjecture as very plausible.
See F. Imhoof-Blumer, *Kleinasiatische
Münzen* (Vienna, 1901–1902), ii. 435
sq.   In the uncertainty which still prevails on the subject I have left the text
unchanged.   For my purpose it matters
little whether this Cilician goddess was
worshipped at Mallus or at Aphrodisias.   *Note to Second Edition.*]

[7] See above, pp. 34 *sq.*

and four wings can hardly be any other than the Phoenician El, whom the Greeks called Cronus ; for El was characterized by four eyes, two in front and two behind, and by three pairs of wings.[1] A discrepancy in the number of wings can scarcely be deemed fatal to the identification.   The god may easily have moulted some superfluous feathers on the road from Phoenicia to Mallus.   On later coins of Mallus these quaint Oriental deities disappear, and are replaced by corresponding Greek deities, particularly by a head of Cronus on one side and a figure of Demeter, grasping ears of corn, on the other.[2] The change doubtless sprang from a wish to assimilate the ancient native divinities to the new and fashionable divinities of the Greek pantheon.   If Cronus and Demeter, the harvest god and goddess, were chosen to supplant El and his female consort, the ground of the choice must certainly have been a supposed resemblance between the two pairs of deities. We may assume, therefore, that the discarded couple, El and his wife, had also been worshipped by the husbandman as sources of fertility, the givers of corn and wine.   One of these later coins of Mallus exhibits Dionysus sitting on a vine laden with ripe clusters, while on the obverse is seen a male figure guiding a yoke of oxen as if in the act of ploughing.[3] These types of the vine-god and the ploughman probably represent another attempt to adapt the native religion to changed conditions, to pour the old Asiatic wine into new Greek bottles.   The barbarous monster with the multiplicity of heads and wings has been reduced to a perfectly human Dionysus.   The sacred but deplorable old conical stone no longer flaunts proudly on the coins ; it has retired to a decent obscurity in favour of a natural and graceful vine.   It is thus that a truly progressive theology keeps pace with the march of intellect.   But if these things were done by the apostles of culture at Mallus, we cannot suppose that the clergy of Tarsus, the capital, lagged behind their pro-

[1] Philo of Byblus, in *Fragmenta Historicorum Graecorum*, ed. C. Müller, iii. 569. El is figured with three pairs of wings on coins of Byblus. See G. Maspero, *Histoire Ancienne des Peuples de l'Orient Classique*, ii. 174 ; M. J. Lagrange, *Études sur les Religions Sémitiques*,[2] p. 72.

[2] Imhoof-Blumer, *s.v.* "Kronos," in W. H. Roscher's *Lexikon der griech. und röm. Mythologie*, ii. 1572 ; G. F. Hill, *Catalogue of Greek Coins of Lycaonia, Isauria, and Cilicia*, pp. cxxii. 99, pl. xvii. 2.

[3] G. F. Hill, *op. cit.* pp. cxxi. *sq.*, 98, pl. xvii. 1.

vincial brethren in their efforts to place the ancient faith upon a sound modern basis. The fruit of their labours seems to have been the more or less nominal substitution of Zeus, Fortune, and Hercules for Baal, 'Atheh, and Sandan.[1]

We may suspect that in like manner the Sarpedonian Artemis, who had a sanctuary in South-Eastern Cilicia, near the Syrian border, was really a native goddess parading in borrowed plumes. She gave oracular responses by the mouth of inspired men, or more probably of women, who in their moments of divine ecstasy may have been deemed incarnations of her divinity.[2] Another even more transparently Asiatic goddess was Perasia, or Artemis Perasia, who was worshipped at Hieropolis-Castabala in Eastern Cilicia. The extensive ruins of the ancient city, now known as Bodroum, cover the slope of a hill about three-quarters of a mile to the north of the river Pyramus. Above them towers the acropolis, built on the summit of dark grey precipices, and divided from the neighbouring mountain by a deep cutting in the rock. A mediaeval castle, built of hewn blocks of reddish-yellow limestone, has replaced the ancient citadel. The city possessed a large theatre, and was traversed by two handsome colonnades, of which some columns are still standing among the ruins. A thick growth of brushwood and grass now covers most of the site, and the place is wild and solitary. Only the wandering herdsmen encamp near the deserted city in winter and spring. The neighbourhood is treeless; yet in May magnificent fields of wheat and barley gladden the eye, and in the valleys the

Sarpedonian Artemis.

The goddess Perasia at Hieropolis-Castabala.

---

[1] Another native Cilician deity who masqueraded in Greek dress was probably the Olybrian Zeus of Anazarba or Anazarbus, but of his true nature and worship we know nothing. See W. Dittenberger, *Orientis Graeci Inscriptiones Selectae* (Leipsic, 1903–1905), ii. p. 267, No. 577 ; Stephanus Byzantius, *s.v.* Ἄδανα (where the MS. reading Ὀλυμβρος was wrongly changed by Salmasius into Ὄλυμπος).

[2] Strabo, xiv. 5. 19, p. 676. The expression of Strabo leaves it doubtful whether the ministers of the goddess were men or women. There was a headland called Sarpedon near the mouth of the Calycadnus River in Western Cilicia (Strabo, xiii. 4. 6, p. 627, xiv. 5. 4, p. 670), where Sarpedon or Sarpedonian Apollo had a temple and an oracle. The temple was hewn in the rock, and contained an image of the god. See R. Heberdey und A. Wilhelm, "Reisen in Kilikien," *Denkschriften der kaiser. Akademie der Wissenschaften, Philosoph.-histor. Classe*, xliv. (Vienna, 1896) No. vi. pp. 100, 107. Probably this Sarpedonian Apollo was a native deity akin to Sarpedonian Artemis.

clover grows as high as the horses' knees.[1]   The ambiguous nature of the goddess who presided over this City of the Sanctuary (*Hieropolis*)[2] was confessed by a puzzled worshipper, a physician named Lucius Minius Claudianus, who confided his doubts to the deity herself in some very indifferent Greek verses.   He wisely left it to the goddess to say whether she was Artemis, or the Moon, or Hecate, or Aphrodite, or Demeter.[3]   All that we know about her is that her true name was Perasia, and that she was in the enjoyment of certain revenues.[4]   Further, we may reasonably conjecture that at the Cilician Castabala she was worshipped with rites like those which were held in honour of her namesake Artemis Perasia at another city of the same name, Castabala in Cappadocia.   There, as we saw, the priestesses of the goddess walked over fire with bare feet unscathed.[5]   Probably the

The fire-walk in the worship of Perasia.

[1] E. J. Davis, *Life in Asiatic Turkey*, pp. 128-134; J. T. Bent, "Recent Discoveries in Eastern Cilicia," *Journal of Hellenic Studies*, xi. (1890) pp. 234 *sq.*; E. L. Hicks, "Inscriptions from Eastern Cilicia," *ibid.* pp. 243 *sqq.*; R. Heberdey und A. Wilhelm, *op. cit.* pp. 25 *sqq.* The site of Hieropolis-Castabala was first identified by J. T. Bent by means of inscriptions.   As to the coins of the city, see Fr. Imhoof-Blumer, "Zur Münzkunde Kilikiens," *Zeitschrift für Numismatik*, x. (1883) pp. 267-290; G. F. Hill, *Catalogue of the Greek Coins of Lycaonia, Isauria, and Cilicia*, pp. c.-cii. 82-84, pl. xiv. 1-6; G. Macdonald, *Catalogue of Greek Coins in the Hunterian Collection*, ii. 534 *sq.*

[2] On the difference between Hieropolis and Hierapolis see (Sir) W. M. Ramsay, *Historical Geography of Asia Minor*, pp. 84 *sq.*   According to him, the cities designated by such names grew up gradually round a sanctuary; where Greek influence prevailed the city in time eclipsed the sanctuary and became known as Hierapolis, or the Sacred City, but where the native element retained its predominance the city continued to be known as Hieropolis, or the City of the Sanctuary.

[3] E. L. Hicks, "Inscriptions from Eastern Cilicia," *Journal of Hellenic Studies*, xi. (1890) pp. 251-253; R. Heberdey und A. Wilhelm, *op. cit.* p. 26.   These writers differ somewhat in their reading and restoration of the verses, which are engraved on a limestone basis among the ruins.   I follow the version of Messrs. Heberdey and Wilhelm.

[4] J. T. Bent and E. L. Hicks, *op. cit.* pp. 235, 246 *sq.*; R. Heberdey und A. Wilhelm, *op. cit.* p. 27.

[5] Strabo, xii. 2. 7, p. 537.   See above, p. 115.   The Cilician Castabala, the situation of which is identified by inscriptions, is not mentioned by Strabo. It is very unlikely that, with his intimate knowledge of Asia Minor, he should have erred so far as to place the city in Cappadocia, to the north of the Taurus mountains, instead of in Cilicia, to the south of them.   It is more probable that there were two cities of the same name, and that Strabo has omitted to mention one of them.   Similarly, there were two cities called Comana, one in Cappadocia and one in Pontus; at both places the same goddess was worshipped with similar rites.   See Strabo, xii. 2. 3, p. 535, xii. 3. 32, p. 557.   The situation of the various Castabalas mentioned by ancient writers is discussed by F. Imhoof-Blumer, "Zur Münzkunde Kilikiens," *Zeitschrift für Numismatik*, x. (1883) pp. 285-288.

same impressive ceremony was performed before a crowd of worshippers in the Cilician Castabala also. Whatever the exact meaning of the rite may have been, the goddess was in all probability one of those Asiatic Mother Goddesses to whom the Greeks often applied the name of Artemis.[1] The immunity enjoyed by the priestess in the furnace was attributed to her inspiration by the deity. In discussing the nature of inspiration or possession by a deity, the Syrian philosopher Jamblichus notes as one of its symptoms a total insensibility to pain. Many inspired persons, he tells us, " are not burned by fire, the fire not taking hold of them by reason of the divine inspiration ; and many, though they are burned, perceive it not, because at the time they do not live an animal life. They pierce themselves with skewers and feel nothing. They gash their backs with hatchets, they slash their arms with daggers, and know not what they do, because their acts are not those of mere men. For impassable places become passable to those who are filled with the spirit. They rush into fire, they pass through fire, they cross rivers, like the priestess at Castabala. These things prove that under the influence of inspiration men are beside themselves, that their senses, their will, their life are those neither of man nor of beast, but that they lead another and a diviner life instead, whereby they are inspired and wholly possessed."[2] Thus in traversing the fiery furnace the priestesses of Perasia were believed to be beside themselves, to be filled with the goddess, to be in a real sense incarnations of her divinity.[3]

A similar touchstone of inspiration is still applied by some villagers in the Himalayan districts of North-Western

Insensibility to pain regarded as a mark of inspiration.

---

[1] See *The Magic Art and the Evolution of Kings*, i. 37 *sq.*

[2] Jamblichus, *De mysteriis*, iii. 4.

[3] Another Cilician goddess was Athena of Magarsus, to whom Alexander the Great sacrificed before the battle of Issus. See Arrian, *Anabasis*, ii. 5. 9 ; Stephanus Byzantius, *s.v.* Μάγαρσος ; J. Tzetzes, *Schol. on Lycophron*, 444. The name of the city seems to be Oriental, perhaps derived from the Semitic word for " cave " (מְעָרָה). As to the importance of caves in Semitic religion, see W. Robertson Smith,

Religion of the Semites,[2] pp. 197 *sqq.* The site of Magarsus appears to be at Karatash, a hill rising from the sea at the southern extremity of the Cilician plain, about forty-five miles due south of Adana. The walls of the city, built of great limestone blocks, are standing to a height of several courses, and an inscription which mentions the priests of Magarsian Athena has been found on the spot. See R. Heberdey und A. Wilhelm, " Reisen in Kilikien," *Denkschriften der kaiser. Akademie der Wissenschaften, Philosoph.-histor. Classe*, xliv. (1896) No. vi. pp. 6-10.

India.   Once a year they worship Airi, a local deity, who is
represented by a trident and has his temples on lonely hills
and desolate tracts.   At his festival the people seat themselves in a circle about a bonfire.   A kettle-drum is beaten,
and one by one his worshippers become possessed by the
god and leap with shouts round the flames.   Some brand
themselves with heated iron spoons and sit down in the fire.
Such as escape unhurt are believed to be truly inspired,
while those who burn themselves are despised as mere pre-
tenders to the divine frenzy.   Persons thus possessed by the
spirit are called Airi's horses or his slaves.   During the
revels, which commonly last about ten days, they wear
red scarves round their heads and receive alms from the
faithful.   These men deem themselves so holy that they
will let nobody touch them, and they alone may touch
the sacred trident, the emblem of their god.[1]   In Western
Asia itself modern fanatics still practise the same austerities
which were practised by their brethren in the days of
Jamblichus.   " Asia Minor abounds in dervishes of different
orders, who lap red-hot iron, calling it their ' rose,' chew
coals of living fire, strike their heads against solid walls,
stab themselves in the cheek, the scalp, the temple, with
sharp spikes set in heavy weights, shouting ' Allah, Allah,'
and always consistently avowing that during such frenzy
they are entirely insensible to pain." [2]

§ 9. *The Burning of Cilician Gods*

The divine
triad, Baal,
'Atheh,
and
Sandan, at
Tarsus may
have been
personated
by priests
and
priestesses.

On the whole, then, we seem to be justified in concluding
that under a thin veneer of Greek humanity the barbarous
native gods of Cilicia continued long to survive, and that
among them the great Asiatic goddess retained a place,
though not the prominent place which she held in the
highlands of the interior down at least to the beginning of
our era.   The principle that the inspired priest or priestess
represents the deity in person appears, if I am right, to

[1] E. T. Atkinson, *The Himalayan
Districts of the North-Western Provinces of India*, ii. (Allahabad, 1884)
pp. 826 *sq.*

[2] The Rev. G. E. White (Missionary
at Marsovan, in the ancient Pontus), in
a letter to me dated 19 Southmoor
Road, Oxford, February 11, 1907.

have been recognized at Castabala and at Olba, as well
as at the sanctuary of Sarpedonian Artemis.   There
can be no intrinsic improbability, therefore, in the view
that at Tarsus also the divine triad of Baal, 'Atheh,
and Sandan may also have been personated by priests and
priestesses, who, on the analogy of Olba and of the great
sanctuaries in the interior of Asia Minor, would originally
be at the same time kings and queens, princes and princesses.
Further, the burning of Sandan in effigy at Tarsus would,
on this hypothesis, answer to the walk of the priestess of
Perasia through the furnace at Castabala.   Both were
perhaps mitigations of a custom of putting the priestly
king or queen, or another member of the royal family, to
death by fire.

CHAPTER VII

SARDANAPALUS AND HERCULES

§ 1. *The Burning of Sardanapalus*

Tarsus said to have been founded by the Assyrian king Sardanapalus, who burned himself on a pyre.

THE theory that kings or princes were formerly burned to death at Tarsus in the character of gods is singularly confirmed by another and wholly independent line of argument. For, according to one account, the city of Tarsus was founded not by Sandan but by Sardanapalus, the famous Assyrian monarch whose death on a great pyre was one of the most famous incidents in Oriental legend. Near the sea, within a day's march of Tarsus, might be seen in antiquity the ruins of a great ancient city named Anchiale, and outside its walls stood a monument called the monument of Sardanapalus, on which was carved in stone the figure of the monarch. He was represented snapping the fingers of his right hand, and the gesture was explained by an accompanying inscription, engraved in Assyrian characters, to the following effect :—" Sardanapalus, son of Anacyndaraxes, built Anchiale and Tarsus in one day. Eat, drink, and play, for everything else is not worth that," by which was implied that all other human affairs were not worth a snap of the fingers.[1] The gesture may have been misin-

[1] Strabo, xiv. 5. 9, pp. 671 *sq.*; Arrian, *Anabasis*, ii. 5; Athenaeus, xii. 39, p. 530 A, B. Compare Stephanus Byzantius, *s.v.* Ἀγχιάλη; Georgius Syncellus, *Chronographia*, vol. i. p. 312, ed. G. Dindorf (Bonn, 1829). The site of Anchiale has not yet been discovered. At Tarsus itself the ruins of a vast quadrangular structure have sometimes been identified with the monument of Sardanapalus. See E. J. Davis, *Life in Asiatic Turkey*, pp. 37-39; G. Perrot et Ch. Chipiez, *Histoire de l'Art dans l'Antiquité*, iv. 536 *sqq.* But Mr. D. G. Hogarth tells me that the ruins in question seem to be the concrete foundations of a Roman temple. The mistake had already been pointed out by Mr. R. Koldewey. See his article, "Das sogenannte Grab des Sardanapal zu Tarsus," *Aus der Anomia* (Berlin, 1890), pp. 178-185.

terpreted and the inscription mistranslated,[1] but there is no
reason to doubt the existence of such a monument, though
we may conjecture that it was of Hittite rather than
Assyrian origin ; for, not to speak of the traces of Hittite
art and religion which we have found at Tarsus, a group of
Hittite monuments has been discovered at Marash, in the
upper valley of the Pyramus.[2] The Assyrians may have
ruled over Cilicia for a time, but Hittite influence was
probably much deeper and more lasting.[3] The story that
Tarsus was founded by Sardanapalus may well be
apocryphal,[4] but there must have been some reason for
his association with the city. On the present hypothesis
that reason is to be found in the traditional manner of his
death. To avoid falling into the hands of the rebels, who
laid siege to Nineveh, he built a huge pyre in his palace,
heaped it up with gold and silver and purple raiment, and
then burnt himself, his wife, his concubines, and his eunuchs
in the fire.[5] The story is false of the historical Sardanapalus,
that is, of the great Assyrian king Ashurbanipal, but it is
true of his brother Shamashshumukin. Being appointed
king of Babylon by Ashurbanipal, he revolted against his
suzerain and benefactor, and was besieged by him in his
capital. The siege was long and the resistance desperate,
for the Babylonians knew that they had no mercy to expect
from the ruthless Assyrians. But they were decimated by
famine and pestilence, and when the city could hold out no
more, King Shamashshumukin, determined not to fall alive
into the hands of his offended brother, shut himself up in his

Deaths of Babylonian and Assyrian kings on the pyre.

---

[1] See G. Perrot et Ch. Chipiez, *Histoire de l'Art dans l'Antiquité*, iv. 542 *sq*. They think that the figure probably represented the king in a common attitude of adoration, his right arm raised and his thumb resting on his forefinger.

[2] L. Messerschmidt, *Corpus Inscriptionum Hettiticarum*, pp. 17-19, plates xxi.-xxv. ; G. Perrot et Ch. Chipiez, *Histoire de l'Art dans l'Antiquité*, iv. 492, 494 *sq*., 528-530, 547 ; J. Garstang, *The Land of the Hittites*, pp. 107-122.

[3] Prof. W. Max Müller is of opinion that the Hittite civilization and the Hittite system of writing were developed in Cilicia rather than in Cappadocia (*Asien und Europa*, p. 350).

[4] According to Berosus and Abydenus it was not Sardanapalus (Ashurbanipal) but Sennacherib who built or rebuilt Tarsus after the fashion of Babylon, causing the river Cydnus to flow through the midst of the city. See *Fragmenta Historicorum Graecorum*, ed. C. Müller, ii. 504, iv. 282 ; C. P. Tiele, *Babylonisch-assyrische Geschichte*, pp. 297 *sq*.

[5] Diodorus Siculus, ii. 27 ; Athenaeus, xii. 38, p. 529 ; Justin, i. 3.

palace, and there burned himself to death, along with his wives, his children, his slaves, and his treasures, at the very moment when the conquerors were breaking in the gates.[1] Not many years afterwards the same tragedy was repeated at Nineveh itself by Saracus or Sinsharishkun, the last king of Assyria. Besieged by the rebel Nabopolassar, king of Babylon, and by Cyaxares, king of the Medes, he burned himself in his palace. That was the end of Nineveh and of the Assyrian empire.[2] Thus Greek history preserved the memory of the catastrophe, but transferred it from the real victims to the far more famous Ashurbanipal, whose figure in after ages loomed vast and dim against the setting sun of Assyrian glory.

§ 2. *The Burning of Croesus*

Story that Cyrus intended to burn Croesus alive.

Another Oriental monarch who prepared at least to die in the flames was Croesus, king of Lydia. Herodotus tells how the Persians under Cyrus captured Sardes, the Lydian capital, and took Croesus alive, and how Cyrus caused a great pyre to be erected, on which he placed the captive monarch in fetters, and with him twice seven Lydian youths. Fire was then applied to the pile, but at the last moment Cyrus relented, a sudden shower extinguished the flames, and Croesus was spared.[3] But it is most improbable that the Persians, with their profound reverence for the sanctity of fire, should have thought of defiling the sacred element with the worst of all pollutions, the contact of dead bodies.[4] Such an act would have seemed to them sacrilege of the deepest dye. For to them fire was the earthly form of the

It is unlikely that the Persians would thus have polluted the sacred element of fire.

[1] G. Maspero, *Histoire Ancienne des Peuples de l'Orient Classique*, iii. 422 *sq.* For the inscriptions referring to him and a full discussion of them, see C. F. Lehmann (-Haupt), *Šamaš-šumukîn, König von Babylonien, 668–648 v. Chr.* (Leipsic, 1892).

[2] Abydenus, in *Fragmenta Historico-rum Graecorum*, ed. C. Müller, iv. 282; Georgius Syncellus, *Chronographia*, i. p. 396, ed. G. Dindorf; E. Meyer, *Geschichte des Alterthums*, i. (Stuttgart, 1884) pp. 576 *sq.*; G. Maspero, *Histoire Ancienne des Peuples de l'Orient Classique*, iii. 482-485. C. P. Tiele

thought that the story of the death of Saracus might be a popular but mistaken duplicate of the death of Shamash-shumukin (*Babylonisch-assyrische Geschichte*, pp. 410 *sq.*). Zimri, king of Israel, also burned himself in his palace to escape falling into the hands of his enemies (1 Kings xvi. 18).

[3] Herodotus, i. 86 *sq.*

[4] Raoul-Rochette, "Sur l'Hercule Assyrien et Phénicien," *Mémoires de l'Académie des Inscriptions et Belles-Lettres*, xvii. Deuxième Partie (Paris, 1848), p. 274.

heavenly light, the eternal, the infinite, the divine ; death, on the other hand, was in their opinion the main source of corruption and uncleanness.   Hence they took the most stringent precautions to guard the purity of fire from the defilement of death.[1]   If a man or a dog died in a house where the holy fire burned, the fire had to be removed from the house and kept away for nine nights in winter or a month in summer before it might be brought back ; and if any man broke the rule by bringing back the fire within the appointed time, he might be punished with two hundred stripes.[2]   As for burning a corpse in the fire, it was the most heinous of all sins, an invention of Ahriman, the devil ; there was no atonement for it, and it was punished with death.[3]   Nor did the law remain a dead letter.   Down to the beginning of our era the death penalty was inflicted on all who threw a corpse or cow-dung on the fire, nay, even on such as blew on the fire with their breath.[4]   It is hard, therefore, to believe that a Persian king should have commanded his subjects to perpetrate a deed which he and they viewed with horror as the most flagitious sacrilege conceivable.

Another and in some respects truer version of the story of Croesus and Cyrus has been preserved by two older witnesses—namely, by the Greek poet Bacchylides, who was born some forty years after the event,[5] and by a Greek artist who painted the scene on a red-figured vase about, or soon after, the time of the poet's birth.   Bacchylides tells us that when the Persians captured Sardes, Croesus, unable to brook the thought of slavery, caused a pyre to be erected in front of his courtyard, mounted it with his wife and daughters, and bade a page apply a light to the wood.   A bright blaze shot up, but Zeus extinguished it with rain from heaven, and

The older and truer tradition was that in the extremity of his fortunes Croesus attempted to burn himself.

---

[1] J. Darmesteter, *The Zend-Avesta*, vol. i. (Oxford, 1880) pp. lxxxvi., lxxxviii-xc. (*Sacred Books of the East*, vol. iv.).

[2] *Zend-Avesta*, *Vendîdâd*, Fargard, v. 7. 39-44 (*Sacred Books of the East*, iv. 60 *sq.*).

[3] *Zend-Avesta*, translated by J. Darmesteter, i. pp. xc. 9, 110 *sq.* (*Sacred Books of the East*, iv.).

[4] Strabo, xv. 3. 14, p. 732. Even gold, on account of its resemblance to fire, might not be brought near a corpse (*id.* xv. 3. 18, p. 734).

[5] Sardes fell in the autumn of 546 B.C. (E. Meyer, *Geschichte des Alterthums*, i. (Stuttgart, 1884), p. 604). Bacchylides was probably born between 512 and 505 B.C. See R. C. Jebb, *Bacchylides, the Poems and Fragments* (Cambridge, 1905), pp. 1 *sq.*

Apollo of the Golden Sword wafted the pious king and his daughters to the happy land beyond the North Wind.[1]   In like manner the vase-painter clearly represents the burning of Croesus as a voluntary act, not as a punishment inflicted on him by the conqueror.   He lets us see the king enthroned upon the pyre with a wreath of laurel on his head and a sceptre in one hand, while with the other he is pouring a libation.   An attendant is in the act of applying to the pile two objects which have been variously interpreted as torches to kindle the wood or whisks to sprinkle holy water.   The demeanour of the king is solemn and composed : he seems to be performing a religious rite, not suffering an ignominious death.[2]

Thus we may fairly conclude with some eminent modern scholars[3] that in the extremity of his fortunes Croesus prepared to meet death like a king or a god in the flames.   It was thus that Hercules, from whom the old kings of Lydia claimed to be sprung,[4] ascended from earth to heaven : it was thus that Zimri, king of Israel, passed beyond the reach of his enemies : it was thus that Shamashshumukin, king of Babylon, escaped a brother's vengeance : it was thus that the last king of Assyria expired in the ruins of his capital ; and it was thus that, sixty-six years after the capture of Sardes, the Carthaginian king Hamilcar sought to retrieve a lost battle by a hero's death.[5]

Legend that Semiramis burnt herself on a pyre.

Semiramis herself, the legendary queen of Assyria, is said to have burnt herself on a pyre out of grief at the death of a favourite horse.[6]   Since there are strong grounds for regard-

[1] Bacchylides, iii. 24-62.

[2] F. G. Welcker, *Alte Denkmäler* (Göttingen, 1849–1864), iii. pl. xxxiii. ; A. Baumeister, *Denkmäler des klassischen Altertums* (Munich and Leipsic, 1885–1888), ii. 796, fig. 860 ; A. H. Smith, "Illustrations to Bacchylides," *Journal of Hellenic Studies*, xviii. (1898) pp. 267-269 ; G. Maspero, *Histoire Ancienne des Peuples de l'Orient Classique*, iii. 618 *sq.*   It is true that Cambyses caused the dead body of the Egyptian king Amasis to be dragged from the tomb, mangled, and burned ; but the deed is expressly branded by the ancient historian as an

outrage on Persian religion (Herodotus, iii. 16).

[3] Raoul-Rochette, "Sur l'Hercule Assyrien et Phénicien," *Mémoires de l'Académie des Inscriptions et Belles-Lettres*, xvii. Deuxième Partie (Paris, 1848), pp. 277 *sq.* ; M. Duncker, *Geschichte des Alterthums*, iv.[5] 330-332 ; E. Meyer, *Geschichte des Alterthums*, i. (Stuttgart, 1884) p. 604 ; G. Maspero, *Histoire Ancienne des Peuples de l'Orient Classique*, iii. 618.

[4] Herodotus, i. 7.

[5] See above, pp. 115 *sq.*, 173 *sq.*

[6] Hyginus, *Fab.* 243 ; Pliny, viii. 155.

ing the queen in her mythical aspect as a form of Ishtar or Astarte,[1] the legend that Semiramis died for love in the flames furnishes a remarkable parallel to the traditionary death of the love-lorn Dido, who herself appears to be simply an Avatar of the same great Asiatic goddess.[2]   When we compare these stories of the burning of Semiramis and Dido with each other and with the historical cases of the burning of Oriental monarchs, we may perhaps conclude that there was a time when queens as well as kings were expected under certain circumstances, perhaps on the death of their consort, to perish in the fire.   The conclusion can hardly be deemed extravagant when we remember that the practice of burning widows to death survived in India under English rule down to a time within living memory.[3]

At Jerusalem itself a reminiscence of the practice of burning kings, alive or dead, appears to have lingered as late as the time of Isaiah, who says : " For Tophet is prepared of old ; yea, for the king it is made ready ; he hath made it deep and large : the pile thereof is fire and much wood ; the breath of the Lord, like a stream of brimstone, doth kindle it." [4]   We know that "great burnings" were

The " great burnings " for Jewish kings.

---

[1] See W. Robertson Smith, " Ctesias and the Semiramis Legend," *English Historical Review*, ii. (1887) pp. 303-317.   But the legend of Semiramis appears to have gathered round the person of a real Assyrian queen, by name Shammuramat, who lived towards the end of the ninth century B.C. and is known to us from historical inscriptions.   See C. F. Lehmann-Haupt, *Die historische Semiramis und ihre Zeit* (Tübingen, 1910), pp. 1 *sqq.* ; *id.*, *s.v.* " Semiramis," in W. H. Roscher's *Lexikon der griech. und röm. Mythologie*, iv. 678 *sqq.*; *The Scapegoat*, pp. 369 *sqq.*

[2] See above, p. 114.

[3] In ancient Greece we seem to have a reminiscence of widow-burning in the legend that when the corpse of Capaneus was being consumed on the pyre, his wife Evadne threw herself into the flames and perished.   See Euripides, *Supplices*, 980 *sqq.* ; Apollodorus, *Bibliotheca*, iii. 7. 1 ; Zenobius, *Cent.* i. 30 ; Ovid, *Tristia*, v. 14. 38.

[4] Isaiah xxx. 33.   The Revised Version has " a Topheth " instead of " Tophet."   But Hebrew does not possess an indefinite article (the few passages of the Bible in which the Aramaic הת is so used are no exception to the rule), and there is no evidence that Tophet (Topheth) was ever employed in a general sense. The passage of Isaiah has been rightly interpreted by W. Robertson Smith in the sense indicated in the text, though he denies that it contains any reference to the sacrifice of the children. See his *Lectures on the Religion of the Semites*,[2] pp. 372 *sq.*   He observes (p. 372, note 3) : " Saul's body was burned (1 Sam. xxxi. 12), possibly to save it from the risk of exhumation by the Philistines, but perhaps rather with a religious intention, and almost as an act of worship, since his bones were buried under the sacred tamarisk at Jabesh."   In 1 Chronicles x. 12 the tree under which the bones of Saul were buried is not a tamarisk but a terebinth or an oak.

regularly made for dead kings of Judah,[1] and it can hardly be accidental that the place assigned by Isaiah to the king's pyre is the very spot in the Valley of Hinnom where the first-born children were actually burned by their parents in honour of Moloch "the King." The exact site of the Valley of Hinnom is disputed, but all are agreed in identifying it with one of the ravines which encircle or intersect Jerusalem ; and according to some eminent authorities it was the one called by Josephus the Tyropoeon.[2] If this last identification is correct, the valley where the children were burned on a pyre lay immediately beneath the royal palace and the temple. Perhaps the young victims died for God and the king.[3]

The great burnings for Jewish Rabbis at Meiron in Galilee.

With the "great burnings" for dead Jewish kings it seems worth while to compare the great burnings still annually made for dead Jewish Rabbis at the lofty village of Meiron in Galilee, the most famous and venerated place of pilgrimage for Jews in modern Palestine. Here the tombs of the Rabbis are hewn out of the rock, and here on the thirtieth of April, the eve of May Day, multitudes of pilgrims, both men and women, assemble and burn their offerings, which consist of shawls, scarfs, handkerchiefs, books, and the like. These are placed in two stone basins on the top of two low pillars, and being drenched with oil and ignited they are consumed to ashes amid the loud applause, shouts, and cries of the spectators. A man has been known to pay as much as

---

[1] 2 Chronicles xvi. 14, xxi. 19 ; Jeremiah xxxiv. 5. There is no ground for assuming, as the Authorized version does in Jeremiah xxxiv. 5, that only spices were burned on these occasions ; indeed the burning of spices is not mentioned at all in any of the three passages. The "sweet odours and divers kinds of spices prepared by the apothecaries' art," which were laid in the dead king's bed (2 Chronicles xvi. 14), were probably used to embalm him, not to be burned at his funeral. For though "great burnings" were regularly made for the dead kings of Judah, there is no evidence (apart from the doubtful case of Saul) that their bodies were cremated. They are

regularly said to have been buried, not burnt. The passage of Isaiah seems to show that what was burned at a royal funeral was a great, but empty, pyre. That the burnings for the kings formed part of a heathen custom was rightly perceived by Renan (*Histoire du peuple d'Israel*, iii. 121, note).

[2] Josephus, *Bell. Jud.* v. 4. 1. See *Encyclopaedia Biblica*, s.v. "Jerusalem," vol. ii. 2423 *sq.*

[3] As to the Moloch worship, see Note I. at the end of the volume. I have to thank the Rev. Professor R. H. Kennett for indicating to me the inference which may be drawn from the identification of the Valley of Hinnom with the Tyropoeon.

two thousand piastres for the privilege of being allowed to open the ceremony by burning a costly shawl. On such occasions the solemn unmoved serenity of the Turkish officials, who keep order, presents a striking contrast to the intense excitement of the Jews.[1] This curious ceremony may be explained by the widespread practice of burning property for the use and benefit of the dead. So, to take a single instance, the tyrant Periander collected the finest raiment of all the women in Corinth and burned it in a pit for his dead wife, who had sent him word by necromancy that she was cold and naked in the other world, because the clothes he buried with her had not been burnt.[2] In like manner, perhaps, garments and other valuables may have been consumed on the pyre for the use of the dead kings of Judah. In Siam, the corpse of a king or queen is burned in a huge structure resembling a permanent palace, which with its many-gabled and high-pitched roofs and multitudinous tinselled spires, soaring to a height of over two hundred feet, sometimes occupies an area of about an acre.[3] The blaze of such an enormous catafalque may resemble, even if it far surpasses, the "great burnings" for the Jewish kings.

§ 3. *Purification by Fire*

These events and these traditions seem to prove that under certain circumstances Oriental monarchs deliberately chose to burn themselves to death. What were these circumstances? and what were the consequences of the act? If the intention had merely been to escape from the hands of a conqueror, an easier mode of death would naturally have been chosen. There must have been a special reason for electing to die by fire. The legendary death of Hercules, the historical death of Hamilcar, and the picture of Croesus enthroned in state on the pyre and pouring a libation, all combine to indicate that to be burnt alive was regarded as a solemn sacrifice, nay, more than that, as an apotheosis which

Death by fire regarded by the ancients as a kind of apotheosis.

[1] W. M. Thomson, *The Land and the Book, Central Palestine and Phoenicia* (London, 1883), pp. 575-579; Ed. Robinson, *Biblical Researches in Palestine* [3] (London, 1867), ii. 430 *sq.* ; K. Baedeker, *Palestine and Syria* [4] (Leipsic, 1906), p. 255.

[2] Herodotus, v. 92. 7.

[3] C. Bock, *Temples and Elephants* (London, 1884), pp. 73-76.

Fire was
supposed
to purge
away the
mortal
parts
of men,
leaving the
immortal.
raised the victim to the rank of a god.[1] For it is to be
remembered that Hamilcar as well as Hercules was worshipped after death. Fire, moreover, was regarded by the
ancients as a purgative so powerful that properly applied it
could burn away all that was mortal of a man, leaving only
the divine and immortal spirit behind. Hence we read of
goddesses who essayed to confer immortality on the infant
sons of kings by burning them in the fire by night ; but their
beneficent purpose was always frustrated by the ignorant
interposition of the mother or father, who peeping into the
room saw the child in the flames and raised a cry of horror,
thus disconcerting the goddess at her magic rites. This
story is told of Isis in the house of the king of Byblus, of
Demeter in the house of the king of Eleusis, and of Thetis
in the house of her mortal husband Peleus.[2] In a slightly

---

[1] This view was maintained long
ago by Raoul-Rochette in regard to
the deaths both of Sardanapalus and
of Croesus. He supposed that "the
Assyrian monarch, reduced to the last
extremity, wished, by the mode of
death which he chose, to give to his
sacrifice the form of an apotheosis and
to identify himself with the national
god of his country by allowing himself
to be consumed, like him, on a pyre.
. . . Thus mythology and history
would be combined in a legend in
which the god and the monarch would
finally be confused. There is nothing
in this which is not conformable to the
ideas and habits of Asiatic civilization."
See his memoir, "Sur l'Hercule
Assyrien et Phénicien," *Mémoires de
l'Académie des Inscriptions et Belles-
Lettres*, xvii. Deuxième Partie (Paris,
1848), pp. 247 *sq.*, 271 *sqq.* The
notion of regeneration by fire was fully
recognized by Raoul-Rochette (*op. cit.*
pp. 30 *sq.*). It deserves to be noted
that Croesus burned on a huge pyre
the great and costly offerings which he
dedicated to Apollo at Delphi. He
thought, says Herodotus (i. 50), that
in this way the god would get possession of the offerings.

[2] As to Isis see Plutarch, *Isis et
Osiris*, 16. As to Demeter see
Homer, *Hymn to Demeter*, 231-262 ;
Apollodorus, *Bibliotheca*, i. 5. 1 ; Ovid,

Fasti, iv. 547-560. As to Thetis see
Apollonius Rhodius, *Argon.* iv. 865-
879 ; Apollodorus, *Bibl.* iii. 13. 6.
Most of these writers express clearly
the thought that the fire consumed the
mortal element, leaving the immortal.
Thus Plutarch says, περικαίειν τὰ θνητὰ
τοῦ σώματος. Apollodorus says (i. 5. 1),
εἰς πῦρ κατετίθει τὸ βρέφος καὶ περιήρει
τὰς θνητὰς σάρκας αὐτοῦ, and again (iii.
13. 6), εἰς τὸ πῦρ ἐγκρυβοῦσα τῆς νυκτὸς
ἔφθειρεν ὃ ἦν αὐτῷ θνητὸν πατρῷον.
Apollonius Rhodius says,

ἡ μὲν γὰρ βροτέας αἰεὶ περὶ σάρκας ἔδαιεν
νύκτα διὰ μέσσην φλογμῷ πυρός.

And Ovid has,
"*Inque foco pueri corpus vivente favilla
Obruit, humanum purget ut ignis
onus.*"

On the custom of passing children
over a fire as a purification, see my
note, "The Youth of Achilles,"
Classical Review, vii. (1893) pp. 293
sq. On the purificatory virtue which the
Greeks ascribed to fire see also Erwin
Rohde, *Psyche*[3] (Tübingen and Leipsic,
1903), ii. 101, note[2]. The Warramunga of Central Australia have a
tradition of a great man who "used
to burn children in the fire so as to
make them grow strong" (B. Spencer
and F. J. Gillen, *The Northern Tribes
of Central Australia*, London, 1904,
p. 429).

different way the witch Medea professed to give back to the old their lost youth by boiling them with a hell-broth in her magic cauldron ;[1] and when Pelops had been butchered and served up at a banquet of the gods by his cruel father Tantalus, the divine beings, touched with pity, plunged his mangled remains in a kettle, from which after decoction he emerged alive and young.[2] - " Fire," says Jamblichus, " destroys the material part of sacrifices, it purifies all things that are brought near it, releasing them from the bonds of matter and, in virtue of the purity of its nature, making them meet for communion with the gods. So, too, it releases us from the bondage of corruption, it likens us to the gods, it makes us meet for their friendship, and it converts our material nature into an immaterial." [3]   Thus we can understand why kings and commoners who claimed or aspired to divinity should choose death by fire. It opened to them the gates of heaven. The quack Peregrinus, who ended his disreputable career in the flames at Olympia, gave out that after death he would be turned into a spirit who would guard men from the perils of the night ; and, as Lucian remarked, no doubt there were plenty of fools to believe him.[4] According to one account, the Sicilian philosopher Empedocles, who set up for being a god in his lifetime, leaped into the crater of Etna in order to establish his claim to godhead.[5] There is nothing incredible in the tradition. The crack-brained philosopher, with his itch for notoriety, may well have done what Indian fakirs [6] and the brazen-faced mountebank Peregrinus did in antiquity, and what Russian peasants and Chinese Buddhists have done in modern times.[7] There is no extremity to which fanaticism or vanity, or a mixture of the two, will not impel its victims.

[1] She is said to have thus restored the youth of her husband Jason, her father-in-law Aeson, the nurses of Dionysus, and all their husbands (Euripides, *Medea*, Argum. ; Scholiast on Aristophanes, *Knights*, 1321 ; compare Plautus, *Pseudolus*, 879 *sqq.*) ; and she applied the same process with success to an old ram (Apollodorus, *Bibl.* i. 9. 27 ; Pausanias, viii. 11: 2 ; Hyginus, *Fab.* 24).

[2] Pindar, *Olymp.* i. 40 *sqq.*, with the Scholiast ; J. Tzetzes, *Schol. on Lycophron*, 152.

[3] Jamblichus, *De mysteriis*, v. 12.

[4] Lucian, *De morte Peregrini*, 27 sq.

[5] Diogenes Laertius, viii. 2. 69 *sq.*

[6] Lucian, *De morte Peregrini*, 25 ; Strabo, xv. 1. 64 and 68, pp. 715, 717 ; Arrian, *Anabasis*, vii. 3.

[7] *The Dying God*, pp. 42 *sqq.*

§ 4. *The Divinity of Lydian Kings*

But apart from any general notions of the purificatory virtues of fire, the kings of Lydia seem to have had a special reason for regarding death in the flames as their appropriate end.   For the ancient dynasty of the Heraclids which preceded the house of Croesus on the throne traced their descent from a god or hero whom the Greeks called Hercules ;[1] and this Lydian Hercules appears to have been identical in name and in substance with the Cilician Hercules, whose effigy was regularly burned on a great pyre at Tarsus.   The Lydian Hercules bore the name of Sandon ;[2] the Cilician Hercules bore the name of Sandan, or perhaps rather of Sandon, since Sandon is known from inscriptions and other evidence to have been a Cilician name.[3]   The characteristic emblems of the Cilician Hercules were the lion and the double-headed axe ; and both these emblems meet us at Sardes in connexion with the dynasty of the Heraclids.   For the double-headed axe was carried as part of the sacred regalia by Lydian kings from the time of the legendary queen Omphale down to the reign of Candaules, the last of the Heraclid kings.   It is said to have been given to Omphale by Hercules himself, and it was apparently regarded as a palladium of the Heraclid sovereignty ; for after the dotard Candaules ceased to carry the axe himself, and had handed it over to the keeping of a courtier, a rebellion broke out, and the ancient dynasty of the Heraclids came to an end.   The new king Gyges did not attempt to carry the old emblem of sovereignty ; he dedicated it with other spoils to Zeus in Caria.   Hence the image of the Carian Zeus bore an axe in his hand and received the epithet of Labrandeus, from *labrys*, the Lydian word for "axe."[4]   Such is Plutarch's account ; but we may

---

[1] Herodotus, i. 7.

[2] Joannes Lydus, *De magistratibus*, iii. 64.

[3] See above, p. 144, note [2].

[4] Plutarch, *Quaestiones Graecae*, 45. Zeus Labrandeus was worshipped at the village of Labraunda, situated in a pass over the mountains, near Mylasa in Caria.   The temple was ancient. A road called the Sacred Way led downhill for ten miles to Mylasa, a city of white marble temples and colonnades which stood in a fertile plain at the foot of a precipitous mountain, where the marble was quarried.   Processions bearing the holy emblems

suspect that Zeus, or rather the native god whom the Greeks identified with Zeus, carried the axe long before the time of Candaules. If, as is commonly supposed, the axe was the symbol of the Asiatic thunder-god,[1] it would be an appropriate emblem in the hand of kings, who are so often expected to make rain, thunder, and lightning for the good of their people. Whether the kings of Lydia were bound to make thunder and rain we do not know; but at all events, like many early monarchs, they seem to have been held responsible for the weather and the crops. In the reign of Meles the country suffered severely from dearth, so the people consulted an oracle, and the deity laid the blame on the kings, one of whom had in former years incurred the guilt of murder. The soothsayers accordingly declared that King Meles, though his own hands were clean, must be banished for three years in order that the taint of bloodshed should be purged away. The king obeyed and retired to Babylon, where he lived three years. In his absence the kingdom was administered by a deputy, a certain Sadyattes, son of Cadys, who traced his descent from Tylon.[2] As to this Tylon we shall hear more presently. Again, we read that the Lydians rejoiced greatly at the assassination of Spermus, another of their kings, "for he was very wicked, and the land suffered from drought in his reign."[3] Apparently, like the ancient Irish and many modern Africans, they laid the drought at the king's door, and thought that he only got what he deserved under the knife of the assassin.

Lydian kings held responsible for the weather and the crops.

---

went to and fro along the Sacred Way from Mylasa to Labraunda. See Strabo, xiv. 2. 23, pp. 658 *sq.* The double-headed axe figures on the ruins and coins of Mylasa (Ch. Fellows, *An Account of Discoveries in Lycia*, London, 1841, p. 75; B. V. Head, *Historia Numorum*, Oxford, 1887, pp. 528 *sq.*). A horseman carrying a double-headed axe is a type which occurs on the coins of many towns in Lydia and Phrygia. At Thyatira this axe-bearing hero was called Tyrimnus, and games were held in his honour. He was identified with Apollo and the sun. See B. V. Head, *Catalogue of the Greek Coins of Lydia* (London, 1901), p. cxxviii. On a coin of Mostene in Lydia the double-headed axe is represented between a bunch of grapes and ears of corn, as if it were an emblem of fertility (B. V. Head, *op. cit.* p. 162, pl. xvii. 11).

[1] L. Preller, *Griechische Mythologie*, i.[4] (Berlin, 1894) pp. 141 *sq.* As to the Hittite thunder-god and his axe see above, pp. 134 *sqq.*

[2] Nicolaus Damascenus, in *Fragmenta Historicorum Graecorum*, ed. C. Müller, iii. 382 *sq.*

[3] *Ibid.* iii. 381.

The
lion-god
of Lydia.
With regard to the lion, the other emblem of the
Cilician Hercules, we are told that the same king Meles,
who was banished because of a dearth, sought to make the
acropolis of Sardes impregnable by carrying round it a lion
which a concubine had borne to him.   Unfortunately at a
single point, where the precipices were such that it seemed
as if no human foot could scale them, he omitted to carry
the beast, and sure enough at that very point the Persians
afterwards clambered up into the citadel.[1]   Now Meles was
one of the old Heraclid dynasty[2] who boasted their descent
from the lion-hero Hercules ; hence the carrying of a lion
round the acropolis was probably a form of consecration intended to place the stronghold under the guardianship of the
lion-god, the hereditary deity of the royal family.   And the
story that the king's concubine gave birth to a lion's whelp
suggests that the Lydian kings not only claimed kinship
with the beast, but posed as lions in their own persons and
passed off their sons as lion-cubs.   Croesus dedicated at
Delphi a lion of pure gold, perhaps as a badge of Lydia,[3]
and Hercules with his lion's skin is a common type on coins
of Sardes.[4]

Identity
of the
Lydian and
Cilician
Hercules.
Thus the death, or the attempted death, of Croesus on
the pyre completes the analogy between the Cilician and
the Lydian Hercules.   At Tarsus and at Sardes we find
the worship of a god whose symbols were the lion and the
double-headed axe, and who was burned on a great pyre,
either in effigy or in the person of a- human representative.
The Greeks called him Hercules, but his native name was
Sandan or Sandon.   At Sardes he seems to have been
personated by the kings, who carried the double-axe and
perhaps wore, like their ancestor Hercules, the lion's skin.
We may conjecture that at Tarsus also the royal family
aped the lion-god.   At all events we know that Sandan,
the name of the god, entered into the names of Cilician

---

[1] Herodotus, i. 84.

[2] Eusebius, *Chronic.* i. 69, ed. A.
Schoene (Berlin, 1866–1875).

[3] Herodotus, i. 50.   At Thebes
there was a stone lion which was said
to have been dedicated by Hercules
(Pausanias, ix. 17. 2).

[4] B. V. Head, *Historia Numorum*
(Oxford, 1887), p. 553 ; *id.*, *Catalogue
of the Greek Coins of Lydia* (London,
1901), pp. xcviii, 239, 240, 241, 244,
247, 253, 254, 264, with plates xxiv.
9-11, 13, xxv. 2, 12, xxvii. 8.

kings, and that in later times the priests of Sandan at Tarsus wore the royal purple.[1]

§ 5. *Hittite Gods at Tarsus and Sardes*

Now we have traced the religion of Tarsus back by a double thread to the Hittite religion of Cappadocia. One thread joins the Baal of Tarsus, with his grapes and his corn, to the god of Ibreez. The other thread unites the Sandan of Tarsus, with his lion and his double axe, to the similar figure at Boghaz - Keui. Without being unduly fanciful, therefore, we may surmise that the Sandon-Hercules of Lydia was also a Hittite god, and that the Heraclid dynasty of Lydia were of Hittite blood. Certainly the influence, if not the rule, of the Hittites extended to Lydia ; for at least two rock - carvings accompanied by Hittite inscriptions are still to be seen in the country. Both of them attracted the attention of the ancient Greeks. One of them represents a god or warrior in Hittite costume armed with a spear and bow. It is carved on the face of a grey rock, which stands out conspicuous on a bushy hillside, where an old road runs through a glen from the valley of the Hermus to the valley of the Cayster. The place is now called Kara - Bel. Herodotus thought that the figure represented the Egyptian king and conqueror Sesostris.[2] The other monument is a colossal seated figure of the Mother of the Gods, locally known in antiquity as Mother Plastene. It is hewn out of the solid rock and occupies a large niche in the face of a cliff at the steep northern foot of Mount Sipylus.[3] Thus it would seem that at some time or other the Hittites carried their arms to the shores of the Aegean. There is no improbability, therefore, in the view that a Hittite dynasty may have reigned at Sardes.[4]

The Cilician and Lydian Hercules (Sandan or Sandon) seems to have been a Hittite deity.

[1] See above, p. 143.

[2] Herodotus, ii. 106; G. Perrot et Ch. Chipiez, *Histoire de l'Art dans l'Antiquité*, iv. 742-752 ; L. Messerschmidt, *Corpus Inscriptionum Hettiticarum*, pp. 33-37, with plates xxxvii., xxxviii. ; J. Garstang, *The Land of the Hittites*, pp. 170-173, with plate liv.

[3] Pausanias, iii. 24. 2, v. 13. 7 with my note ; G. Perrot et Ch. Chipiez, *op.*

cit. iv. 752-759 ; L. Messerschmidt, *op. cit.* pp. 37 *sq.*, pl. xxxix. 1 ; J. Garstang, *The Land of the Hittites*, pp. 167-170, with plate liii. Unlike most Hittite sculptures the figure of Mother Plastene is carved almost in the round. The inscriptions which accompany both these Lydian monuments are much defaced.

[4] The suggestion that the Heraclid

§ 6. *The Resurrection of Tylon*

The burning of Sandan, like that of Melcarth,[1] was probably followed by a ceremony of his resurrection or awakening, to indicate that the divine life was not extinct, but had only assumed a fresher and purer form. Of that resurrection we have, so far as I am aware, no direct evidence. In default of it, however, there is a tale of a local Lydian hero called Tylon or Tylus, who was killed and brought to life again. The story runs thus. Tylon or Tylus was a son of Earth.[2] One day as he was walking on the banks of the Hermus a serpent stung and killed him. His distressed sister Moire had recourse to a giant named Damasen, who attacked and slew the serpent. But the serpent's mate culled a herb, "the flower of Zeus," in the woods, and bringing it in her mouth put it to the lips of the dead serpent, which immediately revived. In her turn Moire took the hint and restored her brother Tylon to life by touching him with the same plant.[3] A similar incident occurs in many folk-tales. Serpents are often credited with a knowledge of life-giving plants.[4] But Tylon seems to have been more than a mere hero of fairy-tales. He was closely associated with Sardes, for he figures on the coins of the city along with his champion Damasen or Masnes, the dead serpent, and the life-giving branch.[5] And

(marginal note) Death and resurrection of the Lydian hero Tylon.

kings of Lydia were Hittites, or under Hittite influence, is not novel. See W. Wright, *Empire of the Hittites*, p. 59; E. Meyer, *Geschichte des Alterthums*, i. (Stuttgart, 1884) p. 307, § 257; Fr. Hommel, *Grundriss der Geographie und Geschichte des alten Orients*, p. 54, note[2]; L. Messerschmidt, *The Hittites*, p. 22.

[1] See above, pp. 110 *sqq.*

[2] Dionysius Halicarnasensis, *Antiquit. Roman.* i. 27. 1.

[3] Nonnus, *Dionys.* xxv. 451-551; Pliny, *Nat. Hist.* xxv. 14. The story, as we learn from Pliny, was told by Xanthus, an early historian of Lydia.

[4] Thus Glaucus, son of Minos, was restored to life by the seer Polyidus, who learned the trick from a serpent.

See Apollodorus, *Bibliotheca*, iii. 3. 1. For references to other tales of the same sort see my note on Pausanias, ii. 10. 3 (vol. iii. pp. 65 *sq.*). The serpent's acquaintance with the tree of life in the garden of Eden perhaps belongs to the same cycle of stories.

[5] B. V. Head, *Catalogue of the Greek Coins of Lydia*, pp. cxi-cxiii, with pl. xxvii. 12. On the coins the champion's name appears as Masnes or Masanes, but the reading is doubtful. The name Masnes occurred in Xanthus's history of Lydia (*Fragmenta Historicorum Graecorum*, ed. C. Müller, iv. 629). It is probably the same with Manes, the name of a son of Zeus and Earth, who is said to have been the first king of Lydia (Dionysius

he was related in various ways to the royal family of Lydia ; for his daughter married Cotys, one of the earliest kings of the country,[1] and a descendant of his acted as regent during the banishment of King Meles.[2]   It has been suggested that the story of his death and resurrection was acted as a pageant to symbolize the revival of plant life in spring.[3] At all events, a festival called the Feast of the Golden Flower was celebrated in honour of Persephone at Sardes,[4] probably in one of the vernal months, and the revival of the hero and of the goddess may well have been represented together.   The Golden Flower of the Festival would then be the "flower of Zeus" of the legend, perhaps the yellow crocus of nature or rather her more gorgeous sister, the Oriental saffron.   For saffron grew in great abundance at the Corycian cave of Zeus ;[5] and it is an elegant conjecture, if it is nothing more, that the very name of the place meant "the Crocus Cave."[6]   However, on the coins of Sardes the magical plant seems to be a branch rather than a blossom, a Golden Bough rather than a Golden Flower.

Feast of the Golden Flower at Sardes.

Halicarnasensis, *Ant. Rom.* i. 27. 1). Manes was the father of King Atys (Herodotus, i. 94).   Thus Tylon was connected with the royal family of Lydia through his champion as well as in the ways mentioned in the text.

[1] Dionysius Halicarnasensis, *l.c.*

[2] See above, p. 183.

[3] B. V. Head, *Catalogue of the Greek Coins of Lydia*, p. cxiii.

[4] B. V. Head, *Catalogue of the Greek Coins of Lydia*, pp. cx, cxiii.   The festival seems to be mentioned only on coins.

[5] See above, p. 154.

[6] V. Hehn, *Kulturpflanzen und Haustiere*[7] (Berlin, 1902), p. 261. He would derive the name from the Semitic, or at all events the Cilician language.   The Hebrew word for saffron is *karkôm*.   As to the spring flowers of North-Western Asia Minor, W. M. Leake remarks (April 1, 1800)

that "primroses, violets, and crocuses, are the only flowers to be seen" (*Journal of a Tour in Asia Minor*, London, 1824, p. 143).   Near Mylasa in Caria, Fellows saw (March 20, 1840) the broom covered with yellow blossoms and a great variety of anemones, like "a rich Turkey carpet, in which the green grass did not form a prominent colour amidst the crimson, lilac, blue, scarlet, white, and yellow flowers" (Ch. Fellows, *An Account of Discoveries in Lycia*, London, 1841, pp. 65, 66).   In February the yellow stars of *Gagea arvensis* cover the rocky and grassy grounds of Lycia, and the field-marigold often meets the eye.   At the same season in Lycia the shrub *Colutea arborescens* opens its yellow flowers.   See T. A. B. Spratt and E. Forbes, *Travels in Lycia* (London, 1847), ii. 133.   I must leave it to others to identify the Golden Flower of Sardes.

CHAPTER VIII

VOLCANIC RELIGION

§ 1. *The Burning of a God*

The
custom of
burning a
god may
have been
intended to
recruit his
divine
energies. THUS it appears that a custom of burning a god in effigy or in the person of a human representative was practised by at least two peoples of Western Asia, the Phoenicians and the Hittites. Whether they both developed the custom independently, or whether one of them adopted it from the other, we cannot say. And their reasons for celebrating a rite which to us seems strange and monstrous are also obscure. In the preceding inquiry some grounds have been adduced for thinking that the practice was based on a conception of the purifying virtue of fire, which, by destroying the corruptible and perishable elements of man, was supposed to fit him for union with the imperishable and the divine. Now to people who created their gods in their own likeness, and imagined them subject to the same law of decadence and death, the idea would naturally occur that fire might do for the gods what it was believed to do for men, that it could purge them of the taint of corruption and decay, could sift the mortal from the immortal in their composition, and so endow them with eternal youth. Hence a custom might arise of subjecting the deities themselves, or the more important of them, to an ordeal of fire for the purpose of refreshing and renovating those creative energies on the maintenance of which so much depended. To the coarse apprehension of the uninstructed and unsympathetic observer the solemn rite might easily wear a very different aspect. According as he was of a pious or of a sceptical turn of mind, he might

denounce it as a sacrilege or deride it as an absurdity. "To burn the god whom you worship," he might say, "is the height of impiety and of folly. If you succeed in the attempt, you kill him and deprive yourselves of his valuable services. If you fail, you have mortally offended him, and sooner or later he will visit you with his severe displeasure." To this the worshipper, if he was patient and polite, might listen with a smile of indulgent pity for the ignorance and obtuseness of the critic. "You are much mistaken," he might observe, "in imagining that we expect or attempt to kill the god whom we adore. The idea of such a thing is as repugnant to us as to you. Our intention is precisely the opposite of that which you attribute to us. Far from wishing to destroy the deity, we desire .to make him live for ever, to place him beyond the reach of that process of degeneration and final- dissolution to which all things here below appear by their nature to be subject. He does not die in the fire. Oh no ! Only the corruptible and mortal part of him perishes in the flames : all that is incorruptible and immortal of him will survive the purer and stronger for being freed from the contagion of baser elements. That little heap of ashes which you see there is not our god. It is only the skin which he has sloughed, the husk which he has cast. He himself is far away, in the clouds of heaven, in the depths of earth, in the running waters, in the tree and the flower, in the corn and the vine. We do not see him face to face, but every year he manifests his divine life afresh in the blossoms of spring and the fruits of autumn. We eat of his broken body in bread. We drink of his shed blood in the juice of the grape."

§ 2. *The Volcanic Region of Cappadocia*

Some such train of reasoning may suffice to explain, though naturally not to justify, the custom which we bluntly call the burning of a god. Yet it is worth while to ask whether in the development of the practice these general considerations may not have been reinforced or modified by special circumstances ; for example, by the natural features of the country where the custom grew up. For the history

The custom of burning a god may have stood in some relation to volcanic phenomena.

of religion, like that of all other human institutions, has been profoundly affected by local conditions, and cannot be fully understood apart from them. Now Asia Minor, the region where the practice in question appears to have been widely diffused, has from time immemorial been subjected to the action of volcanic forces on a great scale. It is true that, so far as the memory of man goes back, the craters of its volcanoes have been extinct, but the vestiges of their dead or slumbering fires are to be seen in many places, and the country has been shaken and rent at intervals by tremendous earthquakes. These phenomena cannot fail to have impressed the imagination of the inhabitants, and thereby to have left some mark on their religion.

The great extinct volcano Mount Argaeus in Cappadocia.

Among the extinct volcanoes of Anatolia the greatest is Mount Argaeus, in the centre of Cappadocia, the heart of the old Hittite country. It is indeed the highest point of Asia Minor, and one of the loftiest mountains known to the ancients; for in height it falls not very far short of Mount Blanc. Towering abruptly in a huge pyramid from the plain, it is a conspicuous object for miles on miles. Its top is white with eternal snow, and in antiquity its lower slopes were clothed with dense forests, from which the inhabitants of the treeless Cappadocian plains drew their supply of timber. In these woods, and in the low grounds at the foot of the mountain, the languishing fires of the volcano manifested themselves as late as the beginning of our era. The ground was treacherous. Under a grassy surface there lurked pits of fire, into which stray cattle and unwary travellers often fell. Experienced woodmen used great caution when they went to fell trees in the forest. Elsewhere the soil was marshy, and flames were seen to play over it at night.[1] Superstitious fancies no doubt

---

[1] Strabo, xii. 2. 7, p. 538. Mount Argaeus still retains its ancient name in slightly altered forms (*Ardjeh, Erdjich, Erjäus*). Its height is about 13,000 feet. In the nineteenth century it was ascended by at least two English travellers, W. J. Hamilton and H. F. Tozer. See W. J. Hamilton, *Researches in Asia Minor, Pontus, and Armenia*, ii. 269-281; H. F. Tozer, *Turkish Armenia and Eastern Asia Minor*, pp. 94, 113-131; Élisée Reclus, *Nouvelle Géographie Universelle* (Paris, 1879–1894), ix. 476-478. A Hittite inscription is carved at a place called Tope Nefezi, near Asarjik, on the slope of Mount Argaeus. See J. Garstang, *The Land of the Hittites*, pp. 152 *sq.*

gathered thick around these perilous spots, but what shape they took we cannot say. Nor do we know whether sacrifices were offered on the top of the mountain, though a curious discovery may perhaps be thought to indicate that they were. Sharp and lofty pinnacles of red porphyry, inaccessible to the climber, rise in imposing grandeur from the eternal snow of the summit, and here Mr. Tozer found that the rock had been perforated in various places with human habitations. One such rock-hewn dwelling winds inward for a considerable distance; rude niches are hollowed in its sides, and on its roof and walls may be seen the marks of tools.[1] The ancients certainly did not climb mountains for pleasure or health, and it is difficult to imagine that any motive but superstition should have led them to provide dwellings in such a place. These rock-cut chambers may have been shelters for priests charged with the performance of religious or magical rites on the summit.

§ 3. *Fire-Worship in Cappadocia*

Under the Persian rule Cappadocia became, and long continued to be, a great seat of the Zoroastrian fire-worship. In the time of Strabo, about the beginning of our era, the votaries of that faith and their temples were still numerous in the country. The perpetual fire burned on an altar, surrounded by a heap of ashes, in the middle of the temple; and the priests daily chanted their liturgy before it, holding in their hands a bundle of myrtle rods and wearing on their heads tall felt caps with cheek-pieces which covered their lips, lest they should defile the sacred flame with their breath.[2] It is reasonable to suppose that the natural fires which burned perpetually on the outskirts of Mount Argaeus attracted the devotion of the disciples of Zoroaster, for elsewhere similar fires have been the object of religious

Persian fire-worship in Cappadocia.

Worship of natural fires which burn perpetually.

---

[1] H. F. Tozer, *op. cit.* pp. 125-127.

[2] Strabo, xv. 3. 14 *sq.*, pp. 732 *sq.* A bundle of twigs, called the Barsom (*Beresma* in the Avesta), is still used by the Parsee priests in chanting their liturgy. See M. Haug, *Essays on the Sacred Language, Writings and Religion of the Parsis* [3] (London, 1884), pp. 4, note [1], 283. When a potter in Southern India is making a pot which is to be worshipped as a household deity, he " should close his mouth with a bandage, so that his breath may not defile the pot." See E. Thurston, *Castes and Tribes of Southern India* (Madras, 1909), iv. 151.

reverence down to modern times. Thus at Jualamukhi, on the lower slopes of the Himalayas, jets of combustible gas issue from the earth; and a great Hindu temple, the resort of many pilgrims, is built over them. The perpetual flame, which is of a reddish hue and emits an aromatic perfume, rises from a pit in the fore-court of the sanctuary. The worshippers deliver their gifts, consisting usually of flowers, to the attendant fakirs, who first hold them over the flame and then cast them into the body of the temple.[1]

Again, Hindu pilgrims make their way with great difficulty to Baku on the Caspian, in order to worship the everlasting fires which there issue from the beds of petroleum. The sacred spot is about ten miles to the north-east of the city. An English traveller, who visited Baku in the middle of the eighteenth century, has thus described the place and the worship. "There are several ancient temples built with stone, supposed to have been all dedicated to fire; most of them are arched vaults, not above ten to fifteen feet high. Amongst others there is a little temple, in which the Indians now worship; near the altar, about three feet high, is a large hollow cane, from the end of which issues a blue flame, in colour and gentleness not unlike a lamp that burns with spirits, but seemingly more pure. These Indians affirm that this flame has continued ever since the flood, and they believe it will last to the end of the world; that if it was resisted or suppressed in that place, it would rise in some other. Here are generally forty or fifty of these poor devotees, who come on a pilgrimage from their own country, and subsist upon wild sallary, and a kind of Jerusalem artichokes, which are very good food, with other herbs and roots, found a little to the northward. Their business is to make expiation, not for their own sins only, but for those of others; and they continue the longer time, in proportion to the number of persons for whom they have engaged to pray. They mark their foreheads with saffron, and have a great veneration for a red cow."[2] Thus it

---

[1] Baron Charles Hügel, *Travels in Kashmir and the Panjab* (London, 1845), pp. 42-46; W. Crooke, *Things Indian* (London, 1906), p. 219.

[2] Jonas Hanway, *An Historical Account of the British Trade over the Caspian Sea: with the Author's Journal of Travels*, Second Edition (London, 1754), i. 263. For later descriptions of the fires and fire-worshippers of

would seem that a purifying virtue is attributed to the sacred flame, since pilgrims come to it from far to expiate sin.

§ 4. *The Burnt Land of Lydia*

Another volcanic region of Asia Minor is the district of Lydia, to which, on account of its remarkable appearance, the Greeks gave the name of the Burnt Land. It lies to the east of Sardes in the upper valley of the Hermus, and covers an area of about fifty miles by forty. As described by Strabo, the country was wholly treeless except for the vines, which produced a wine inferior to none of the most famous vintages of antiquity. The surface of the plains was like ashes ; the hills were composed of black stone, as if they had been scorched by fire. Some people laid the scene of Typhon's battle with the gods in this Black Country, and supposed that it had been burnt by the thunderbolts hurled from heaven at the impious monster. The philosophic Strabo, however, held that the fires which had wrought this havoc were subterranean, not celestial, and he pointed to three craters, at intervals of about four miles, each in a hill of scoriae which he supposed to have been once molten matter ejected by the volcanoes.[1] His observation and his theory have both been confirmed by modern science. The three extinct volcanoes to which he referred are still conspicuous features of the landscape. Each is a black cone of loose cinders, scoriae, and ashes, with steep sides and a deep crater. From each a flood of rugged black lava has flowed forth, bursting out at the foot of the cone, and then rushing down the dale to the bed of the Hermus. The dark streams follow all the sinuosities of the valleys, their sombre hue contrasting with the rich verdure of the surrounding landscape. Their surface, broken into a thousand fantastic forms, resembles a sea lashed into fury by a gale, and then suddenly hardened into

The Burnt Land of Lydia.

Baku, see J. Reinegg, *Beschreibung des Kaukasus* (Gotha, Hildesheim, and St. Petersburg, 1796–1797), i. 151-159 ; A. von Haxthausen, *Transkaukasia* (Leipsic, 1856), ii. 80-85. Compare

W. Crooke, *Things Indian*, p. 219.
[1] Strabo, xii. 8. 18 *sq*., p. 579 ; xiii. 4. 11, p. 628. The wine of the district is mentioned by Vitruvius (viii. 3. 12) and Pliny (*Nat. Hist.* xiv. 75).

stone. Regarded from the geological point of view, these black cones of cinders and these black rivers of lava are of comparatively recent formation. Exposure to the weather for thousands of years has not yet softened their asperities and decomposed them into vegetable mould; they are as hard and ungenial as if the volcanic stream had ceased to flow but yesterday. But in the same district there are upwards of thirty other volcanic cones, whose greater age is proved by their softened forms, their smoother sides, and their mantle of vegetation. Some of them are planted with vineyards to their summits.[1] Thus the volcanic soil is still as favourable to the cultivation of the vine as it was in antiquity. The relation between the two was noted by the ancients. Strabo compares the vines of the Burnt Land with the vineyards of Catania fertilized by the ashes of Mount Etna; and he tells us that some ingenious persons explained the fire-born Dionysus as a myth of the grapes fostered by volcanic agency.[2]

§ 5. *The Earthquake God*

Earth-
quakes
in Asia
Minor.

But the inhabitants of these regions were reminded of the slumbering fires by other and less agreeable tokens than the generous juice of their grapes. For not the Burnt Land only but the country to the south, including the whole valley of the Maeander, was subject to frequent and violent shocks of earthquake. The soil was loose, friable, and full of salts, the ground hollow, undermined by fire and water. In particular the city of Philadelphia was a great centre of disturbance. The shocks there, we are told, were continuous. The houses rocked, the walls cracked and gaped; the few inhabitants were kept busy repairing the breaches or buttressing and propping the edifices which threatened to tumble

---

[1] W. J. Hamilton, *Researches in Asia Minor, Pontus, and Armenia,* i. 136-140, ii. 131-138. One of the three recent cones described by Strabo is now called the *Kara Devlit,* or Black Inkstand. Its top is about 2500 feet above the sea, but only 500 feet above the surrounding plain. The adjoining town of Koula, built of the black lava on which it stands, has a sombre and dismal look. Another of the cones, almost equally high, has a crater of about half a mile in circumference and three or four hundred feet deep.

[2] Strabo, xiii. 4. 11, p. 628. Compare his account of the Catanian vineyards (vi. 2. 3, p. 269).

about their ears.   Most of the citizens, indeed, had the prudence to dwell dispersed on their farms.   It was a marvel, says Strabo, that such a city should have any inhabitants at all, and a still greater marvel that it should ever have been built.[1]   However, by a wise dispensation of Providence, the earthquakes which shook the foundations of their houses only strengthened those of their faith.   The people of Apameia, whose town was repeatedly devastated, paid their devotions with great fervour to Poseidon, the earthquake god.[2]   Again, the island of Santorin, in the Greek Archipelago, has been for thousands of years a great theatre of volcanic activity.   On one occasion the waters of the bay boiled and flamed for four days, and an island composed of red-hot matter rose gradually, as if hoisted by machinery, above the waves.   It happened that the sovereignty of the seas was then with the Rhodians, those merchant-princes whose prudent policy, strict but benevolent oligarchy, and beautiful island-city, rich with accumulated treasures of native art, rendered them in a sense the Venetians of the ancient world. So when the ebullition and heat of the eruption had subsided, their sea-captains landed in the new island, and founded a sanctuary of Poseidon the Establisher or Securer,[3] a complimentary epithet often bestowed on him as a hint not to shake the earth more than he could conveniently help.[4]   In many

Worship of Poseidon, the earth-quake god.

---

[1] Strabo, xii. 8. 16-18, pp. 578 sq.; xiii. 4. 10 sq., p. 628.

[2] Strabo, xii. 8. 18, p. 579. Compare Tacitus, Annals, xii. 58.

[3] Strabo, i. 3. 16, p. 57. Compare Plutarch, De Pythiae oraculis, 11 ; Pliny, Nat. Hist. ii. 202 ; Justin, xxx. 4.   The event seems to have happened in 197 B.C.   Several other islands are known to have appeared in the same bay both in ancient and modern times.   So far as antiquity is concerned, the dates of their appearance are given by Pliny, but some confusion on the subject has crept into his mind, or rather, perhaps, into his text.   See the discussion of the subject in W. Smith's Dictionary of Greek and Roman Geography (London, 1873), ii. 1158-1160.   As to the eruptions in the bay of Santorin, the last of which occurred in 1866 and produced a

new island, see Sir Charles Lyell, Principles of Geology [12] (London, 1875), i. 51, ii. 65 sqq.; C. Neumann und J. Partsch, Physikalische Geographie von Griechenland (Breslau, 1885), pp. 272 sqq.   There is a monograph on Santorin and its eruptions (F. Fouqué, Santorin et ses éruptions, Paris, 1879).   Strabo has given a brief but striking account of Rhodes, its architecture, its art-treasures, and its constitution (xiv. 2. 5, pp. 652 sq.). As to the Rhodian schools of art see H. Brunn, Geschichte der griechischen Künstler (Stuttgart, 1857–1859), i. 459 sqq., ii. 233 sqq., 286 sq.

[4] Aristophanes, Acharn. 682 ; Pausanias, iii. 11. 9, vii. 21. 7 ; Plutarch, Theseus, 36 ; Aristides, Isthmic. vol. i. p. 29, ed. G. Dindorf (Leipsic, 1829); Appian, Bell. Civ. v. 98 ; Macrobius, Saturn. i. 17. 22 ; G. Dittenberger,

places people sacrificed to Poseidon the Establisher, in the hope that he would be as good as his name and not bring down their houses on their heads.[1]

Spartan propitiation of Poseidon during an earthquake.

Another instance of a Greek attempt to quiet the perturbed spirit underground is instructive, because similar efforts are still made by savages in similar circumstances. Once when a Spartan army under King Agesipolis had taken the field, it chanced that the ground under their feet was shaken by an earthquake. It was evening, and the king was at mess with the officers of his staff. No sooner did they feel the shock than, with great presence of mind, they rose from their dinner and struck up a popular hymn in honour of Poseidon. The soldiers outside the tent took up the strain, and soon the whole army joined in the sacred melody.[2] It is not said whether the flute-band, which always played the Spartan redcoats into action,[3] accompanied the deep voices of the men with its shrill music. At all events, the intention of this service of praise, addressed to the earth-shaking god, can only have been to prevail on him to stop. I have spoken of the Spartan redcoats because the uniform of Spartan soldiers was red.[4] As they fought in an extended, not a deep, formation, a Spartan line of battle must always have been, what the British used to be, a thin red line. It was in this order, and no doubt with the music

---

Sylloge Inscriptionum Graecarum[2] (Leipsic, 1898–1901), ii. p. 230, No. 543.

[1] Cornutus, *Theologiae Graecae Compendium*, 22.

[2] Xenophon, *Hellenica*, iv. 7. 4. As to the Spartan headquarters staff (οἱ περὶ δαμοσίαν), see *id.* iv. 5. 8, vi. 4. 14; Xenophon, *Respublica Lacedaem.* xiii. 1, xv. 4. Usually the Spartans desisted from any enterprise they had in hand when an earthquake happened (Thucydides, iii. 59. 1, v. 50. 5, vi. 95. 1).

[3] Thucydides, v. 70. 1. The use of the music, Thucydides tells us, was not to inspire the men, but to enable them to keep step, and so to march in close order. Without music a long line of battle was apt to straggle in advancing to the charge. As missiles were little

used in Greek warfare, there was no need to hurry the advance over the intervening ground ; so it was made deliberately and with the bands playing. The air to which the Spartans charged was called Castor's tune. It was the king in person who gave the word for the flutes to strike up. See Plutarch, *Lycurgus*, 22.

[4] Xenophon, *Respublica Lacedaem.* xi. 3; Aristophanes, *Lysistrata*, 1140 ; Aristotle, cited by a scholiast on Aristophanes, *Acharn.* 320 ; Plutarch, *Instituta Laconica*, 24. When a great earthquake had destroyed the city of Sparta and the Messenians were in revolt, the Spartans sent a messenger to Athens asking for help. Aristophanes (*Lysistrata*, 1138 *sqq.*) describes the man as if he had seen him, sitting as a suppliant on the altar with his pale face and his red coat.

playing and the sun flashing on their arms, that they advanced to meet the Persians at Thermopylae. Like Cromwell's Ironsides, these men could fight as well as sing psalms.[1]

If the Spartans imagined that they could stop an earthquake by a soldiers' chorus, their theory and practice resembled those of many other barbarians. Thus the people of Timor, in the East Indies, think that the earth rests on the shoulder of a mighty giant, and that when he is weary of bearing it on one shoulder he shifts it to the other, and so causes the ground to quake. At such times, accordingly, they all shout at the top of their voices to let him know that there are still people on the earth; for otherwise they fear lest, impatient of his burden, he might tip it into the sea.[2] The Manichaeans held a precisely similar theory of earthquakes, except that according to them the weary giant transferred his burden from one shoulder to the other at the end of every thirty years,[3] a view which, at all events, points to the observation of a cycle in the recurrence of earthquake shocks. But we are not told that these heretics reduced an absurd theory to an absurd practice by raising a shout in

Modes of stopping an earthquake by informing the god or giant that there are still men on the earth.

---

[1] I have assumed that the sun shone on the Spartans at Thermopylae. For the battle was fought in the height of summer, when the Greek sky is generally cloudless, and on that particular morning the weather was very still. The evening before, the Persians had sent round a body of troops by a difficult pass to take the Spartans in the rear; day was breaking when they neared the summit, and the first intimation of their approach which reached the ears of the Phocian guards posted on the mountain was the loud crackling of leaves under their feet in the oak forest. Moreover, the famous Spartan saying about fighting in the shade of the Persian arrows, which obscured the sun, points to bright, hot weather. It was at high noon, and therefore probably in the full blaze of the mid-day sun, that the last march-out took place. See Herodotus, vii. 215-226; and as to the date of the battle (about the time of the Olympic games) see Herodotus, vii. 206, viii. 12 and 26; G. Busolt, *Griechische Geschichte*, ii.[2] (Gotha,

1895) p. 673, note [9].

[2] S. Müller, *Reizen en Onderzoekingen in den Indischen Archipel* (Amsterdam, 1857), ii. 264 *sq.* Compare A. Bastian, *Indonesien* (Berlin, 1884-1889), ii. 3. The beliefs and customs of the East Indian peoples in regard to earthquakes have been described by G. A. Wilken, *Het animisme bij de volken van den Indischen Archipel*, Tweede Stuk (Leyden, 1885), pp. 247-254; *id.*, *Verspreide Geschriften* (The Hague, 1912), iii. 274-281. Compare *id.*, *Handleiding voor de vergelijkende Volkenkunde van Nederlandsch-Indië* (Leyden, 1893), pp. 604 *sq.*; and on primitive conceptions of earthquakes in general, E. B. Tylor, *Primitive Culture*[2] (London, 1873), i. 364-366; R. Lasch, "Die Ursache und Bedeutung der Erdbeben im Volksglauben und Volksbrauch," *Archiv für Religionswissenschaft*, v. (1902) pp. 236-257, 369-383.

[3] Epiphanius, *Adversus Haereses*, ii. 2. 23 (Migne's *Patrologia Graeca*, xlii. 68).

order to remind the earth-shaker of the inconvenience he was putting them to. However, both the theory and the practice are to be found in full force in various parts of the East Indies. When the Balinese and the Sundanese feel an earthquake they cry out, " Still alive," or " We still live," to acquaint the earth-shaking god or giant with their existence.[1] The natives of Leti, Moa, and Lakor, islands of the Indian Archipelago, imagine that earthquakes are caused by Grandmother Earth in order to ascertain whether her descendants are still to the fore. So they make loud noises for the purpose of satisfying her grandmotherly solicitude.[2] The Tami of German New Guinea ascribe earthquakes to a certain old Panku who sits under a great rock ; when he stirs, the earth quakes. If the shock lasts a long time they beat on the ground with palm-branches, saying, " You down there ! easy a little ! We men are still here." [3] The Shans of Burma are taught by Buddhist monks that under the world there sleeps a great fish with his tail in his mouth, but sometimes he wakes, bites his tail, and quivering with pain causes the ground to quiver and shake likewise. That is the cause of great earthquakes. But the cause of little earthquakes is different. These are produced by little men who live underground and sometimes feeling lonely knock on the roof of the world over their heads ; these knockings we perceive as slight shocks of earthquakes. When Shans feel such a shock, they run out of their houses, kneel down, and answer the little men saying, " We are here ! We are here ! " [4] Earthquakes are common in the Pampa del Sacramento of Eastern Peru. The Conibos, a tribe of Indians on the left bank of the great Ucayali River, attribute these disturbances to the creator, who usually resides in heaven, but comes down from time to time to see whether the work of his hands still exists. The result of his descent is an earthquake. So when one happens, these Indians rush out

[1] H. N. van der Tuuk, "Notes on the Kawi Language and Literature," *Journal of the Royal Asiatic Society*, N.S. xiii. (1881) p. 50.

[2] J. G. F. Riedel, *De sluik- en kroesharige rassen tusschen Selebes en Papua* (The Hague, 1886), p. 398 ; compare *id.* pp. 330, 428.

[3] G. Bamler, "Tami," in R. Neuhauss's *Deutsch Neu - Guinea*, iii. (Berlin, 1911) p. 492.

[4] Mrs. Leslie Milne, *Shans at Home* (London, 1910), p. 54.

of their huts with extravagant gestures shouting, as if in answer to a question, "A moment, a moment, here I am, father, here I am!" Their intention is, no doubt, to assure their heavenly father that they are still alive, and that he may return to his mansion on high with an easy mind. They never remember the creator nor pay him any heed except at an earthquake.[1] In Africa the Atonga tribe of Lake Nyassa used to believe that an earthquake was the voice of God calling to inquire whether his people were all there. So when the rumble was heard underground they all shouted in answer, "*Ye, ye*," and some of them went to the mortars used for pounding corn and beat on them with pestles. They thought that if any one of them did not thus answer to the divine call he would die.[2] In Ourwira the people think that an earthquake is caused by a dead sultan marching past underground; so they stand up to do him honour, and some raise their hands to the salute. Were they to omit these marks of respect to the deceased, they would run the risk of being swallowed up alive.[3] The Baganda of Central Africa used to attribute earthquakes to a certain god named Musisi, who lived underground and set the earth in a tremor when he moved about. At such times persons who had fetishes to hand patted them and begged the god to be still; women who were with child patted their bellies to keep the god from taking either their own life or that of their unborn babes; others raised a shrill cry to induce him to remain quiet.[4]

When the Bataks of Sumatra feel an earthquake they shout "The handle! The handle!" The meaning of the cry is variously explained. Some say that it contains a delicate allusion to the sword which is thrust up to the hilt into the body of the demon or serpent who shakes the earth. Thus explained the words are a jeer or taunt levelled at that mischievous being.[5] Others say that when Batara-guru, the

Conduct of the Bataks during an earthquake.

---

[1] De St. Cricq, "Voyage du Pérou au Brésil par les fleuves Ucayali et Amazone, Indiens Conibos," *Bulletin de la Société de Géographie* (Paris), ive Série, vi. (1853) p. 292.

[2] Miss Alice Werner, *The Natives of British Central Africa* (London, 1906), p. 56.

[3] Mgr. Lechaptois, *Aux Rives du Tanganika* (Algiers, 1913), p. 217.

[4] Rev. J. Roscoe, *The Baganda* (London, 1911), pp. 313 *sq.*

[5] W. Ködding, "Die batakschen Götter und ihr Verhältniss zum Brahmanismus," *Allgemeine Missions-Zeitschrift*, xii. (1885) p. 405.

creator, was about to fashion the earth he began by building
a raft, which he commanded a certain Naga-padoha to support. While he was hard at work his chisel broke, and at
the same moment Naga-padoha budged under his burden.
Therefore Batara-guru said, "Hold hard a moment! The
handle of the chisel is broken off." And that is why the
Bataks call out " The handle of the chisel " during an earthquake. They believe that the deluded Naga-padoha will
take the words for the voice of the creator, and that he will
hold hard accordingly.[1]

Various
modes of
prevailing
upon the
earthquake
god to
stop.
When the earth quakes in some parts of Celebes, it is
said that all the inhabitants of a village will rush out of their
houses and grub up grass by handfuls in order to attract
the attention of the earth-spirit, who, feeling his hair thus
torn out by the roots, will be painfully conscious that there
are still people above ground.[2] So in Samoa, during
shocks of earthquake, the natives sometimes ran and threw
themselves on the ground, gnawed the earth, and shouted
frantically to the earthquake god Mafuie to desist lest he
should shake the earth to pieces.[3] They consoled themselves with the thought that Mafuie has only one arm,
saying, "If he had two, what a shake he would give!"[4]
The Bagobos of the Philippine Islands believe that the
earth rests on a great post, which a large serpent is trying
to remove. When the serpent shakes the post, the earth
quakes. At such times the Bagobos beat their dogs to
make them howl, for the howling of the animals frightens
the serpent, and he stops shaking the post. Hence so long
as an earthquake lasts the howls of dogs may be heard to
proceed from every house in a Bagobo village.[5] The
Tongans think that the earth is supported on the prostrate

[1] G. A. Wilken, "Het Animisme
bij de volken van den Indischen Archipel," *Verspreide Geschriften*, ii. 279 ;
H. N. van der Tuuk, *op. cit.* pp. 49 *sq.*

[2] J. G. F. Riedel, "De Topan-
tunuasu of oorspronkelijke Volkstam-
men van Central Selebes," *Bijdragen
tot de Taal- Land- en Volkenkunde
van Nederlandsch-Indië*, xxxv. (1886)
p. 95.

[3] John Williams, *Narrative of Mis-*

*sionary Enterprises in the South Sea
Islands* (London, 1838), p. 379.

[4] G. Turner, *Samoa* (London, 1884),
p. 211 ; Ch. Wilkes, *Narrative of the
United States Exploring Expedition*,
New Edition (New York, 1851), ii.
131.

[5] A. Schadenburg, " Die Bewohner
von Süd - Mindanao und der Insel
Samal," *Zeitschrift für Ethnologie*,
xvii. (1885) p. 32.

form of the god Móooi.   When he is tired of lying in one posture, he tries to turn himself about, and that causes an earthquake.   Then the people shout and beat the ground with sticks to make him lie still.[1]   During an earthquake the Burmese make a great uproar, beating the walls of their houses and shouting, to frighten away the evil genius who is shaking the earth.[2]   On a like occasion and for a like purpose · some natives of the Gazelle Peninsula in New Britain beat drums and blow on shells.[3]   The Dorasques, an Indian tribe of Panama, believed that the volcano of Chiriqui was inhabited by a powerful spirit, who, in his anger, caused an earthquake.   At such times the Indians shot volleys of arrows in the direction of the volcano to terrify him and make him desist.[4]   Some of the Peruvian Indians regarded an earthquake as a sign that the gods were thirsty, so they poured water on the ground.[5]   In Ashantee several persons used to be put to death after an earthquake ; they were slain as a sacrifice to Sasabonsun, the earthquake god, in the hope of satiating his cruelty for a time.   Houses which had been thrown down or damaged by an earthquake were sprinkled with human blood before they were rebuilt.   When part of the wall of the king's house at Coomassie was knocked down by an earthquake, fifty young girls were slaughtered, and the mud to be used in the repairs was kneaded with their blood.[6]

An English resident in Fiji attributed a sudden access of piety in Kantavu, one of the islands, to a tremendous earthquake which destroyed many of the natives.   The Fijians think that their islands rest on a god, who causes earthquakes by turning over in his sleep.   So they sacrifice to him things of great value in order that he may turn as gently as possible.[7]   In Nias a violent earthquake has a salutary

Religious and moral effects of earthquakes.

[1] W. Mariner, *Account of the Natives of the Tonga Islands*, Second Edition (London, 1818), ii. 112 *sq.*

[2] Sangermano, *Description of the Burmese Empire* (Rangoon, 1885), p. 130.

[3] P. A. Kleintitschen, *Die Küstenbewohner der Gazellehalbinsel* (Hiltrup bei Münster, N.D.), p. 336.

[4] A. Pinart, " Les Indiens de l'État de Panama," *Revue d'Ethnographie,*

vi. (1887) p. 119.

[5] E. J. Payne, *History of the New World called America*, i. (Oxford, 1892) p. 469.

[6] A. B. Ellis, *The Tshi-speaking Peoples of the Gold Coast* (London, 1887), pp. 35 *sq.*

[7] J. Jackson, in J. E. Erskine's *Journal of a Cruise among the Islands of the Western Pacific* (London, 1853), p. 473.   My friend, the late Mr.

effect on the morals of the natives. They suppose that it is
brought about by a certain Batoo Bedano, who intends to
destroy the earth because of the iniquity of mankind. So
they assemble and fashion a great image out of the trunk of
a tree. They make offerings, they confess their sins, they
correct the fraudulent weights and measures, they vow to
do better in the future, they implore mercy, and if the
earth has gaped, they throw a little gold into the fissure.
But when the danger is over, all their fine vows and
promises are soon forgotten.[1]

The god of the sea and of the earthquake naturally conceived as one.

We may surmise that in those Greek lands which have
suffered severely from earthquakes, such as Achaia and the
western coasts of Asia Minor, Poseidon was worshipped not
less as an earthquake god than as a sea-god.[2] It is to be
remembered that an earthquake is often accompanied by a
tremendous wave which comes rolling in like a mountain
from the sea, swamping the country far and wide; indeed
on the coasts of Chili and Peru, which have often been
devastated by both, the wave is said to be even more
dreaded than the earthquake.[3] The Greeks often experienced this combination of catastrophes, this conspiracy,
as it were, of earth and sea against the life and works of man.[4]

Lorimer Fison, wrote to me (December 15, 1906) that the name of the
Fijian earthquake god is Maui, not
A Dage, as Jackson says. Mr. Fison
adds, "I have seen Fijians stamping
and smiting the ground and yelling at
the top of their voices in order to
rouse him."

[1] J. T. Nieuwenhuisen en H. C. B.
von Rosenberg, "Verslag omtrent het
eiland Nias," *Verhandelingen van het
Bataviaasch Genootschap van Kunsten
en Wetenschappen*, xxx. (Batavia, 1863)
p. 118; Th. C. Rappard, "Het eiland
Nias en zijne bewoners," *Bijdragen tot
de Taal-, Land- en Volkenkunde van
Nederlandsch-Indië*, lxii. (1909) p. 582.
In Soerakarta, a district of Java, when
an earthquake takes place the people
lie flat on their stomachs on the ground,
and lick it with their tongues so long
as the earthquake lasts. This they do
in order that they may not lose their
teeth prematurely. See J. W. Winter,

"Beknopte Beschrijving van het hof
Soerokarta in 1824," *Bijdragen tot
de Taal-, Land- en Volkenkunde van
Nederlandsch-Indië*, liv. (1902) p. 85.
The connexion of ideas in this custom
is not clear.

[2] On this question see C. Neumann
und J. Partsch, *Physikalische Geographie von Griechenland* (Breslau,
1885), pp. 332-336. As to the
frequency of earthquakes in Achaia
and Asia Minor see Seneca, *Epist.*
xiv. 3. 9; and as to Achaia in
particular see C. Neumann und J.
Partsch, *op. cit.* pp. 324-326. On
the coast of Achaia there was a chain
of sanctuaries of Poseidon (L. Preller,
Griechische Mythologie, i.[4] 575).

[3] See Sir Ch. Lyell, *Principles of
Geology*,[12] ii. 147 *sqq.*; J. Milne,
Earthquakes (London, 1886), pp. 165
sqq.

[4] See, for example, Thucydides,
iii. 89.

It was thus that Helice, on the coast of Achaia, perished with all its inhabitants on a winter night, overwhelmed by the billows; and its destruction was set down to the wrath of Poseidon.[1] Nothing could be more natural than that to people familiar with the twofold calamity the dreadful god of the earthquake and of the sea should appear to be one and the same. The historian Diodorus Siculus observes that Peloponnese was deemed to have been in ancient days the abode of Poseidon, that the whole country was in a manner sacred to him, and that every city in it worshipped him above all the gods. The devotion to Poseidon he explains partly by the earthquakes and floods by which the land has been visited, partly by the remarkable chasms and subterranean rivers which are a conspicuous feature of its limestone mountains.[2]

§ 6. *The Worship of Mephitic Vapours*

But eruptions and earthquakes, though the most tremendous, are not the only phenomena of volcanic regions which have affected the religion of the inhabitants. Poisonous mephitic vapours and hot springs, which abound especially in volcanic regions,[3] have also had their devotees, and both are, or were formerly, to be found in those western districts of Asia Minor with which we are here concerned. To begin with vapours, we may take as an illustration of their deadly effect the Guevo Upas, or Valley of Poison, near Batur in Java. It is the crater of an extinct volcano, about half a mile in circumference, and from thirty to thirty-

Poisonous mephitic vapours.

---

[1] Strabo, viii. 7. 1 *sq.*, pp. 384 *sq.*; Diodorus Siculus, xv. 49; Aelian, *Nat. Anim.* xi. 19; Pausanias, vii. 24. 5 *sq.* and 12, vii. 25. 1 and 4.

[2] Diodorus Siculus, xv. 49. 4 *sq.* Among the most famous seats of the worship of Poseidon in Peloponnese were Taenarum in Laconia, Helice in Achaia, Mantinea in Arcadia, and the island of Calauria, off the coast of Troezen. See Pausanias, ii. 33. 2, iii. 25. 4-8, vii. 24. 5 *sq.*, viii. 10. 2-4. Laconia as well as Achaia has suffered much from earthquakes, and it contained many sanctuaries of Poseidon.

We may suppose that the deity was worshipped here chiefly as the earthquake god, since the rugged coasts of Laconia are ill adapted to maritime enterprise, and the Lacedaemonians were never a seafaring folk. See C. Neumann und J. Partsch, *Physikalische Geographie von Griechenland*, pp. 330 *sq.*, 335 *sq.* For Laconian sanctuaries of Poseidon see Pausanias, iii. 11. 9, iii. 12. 5, iii. 14. 2 and 7, iii. 15. 10, iii. 20. 2, iii. 21. 5, iii. 25. 4.

[3] Sir Ch. Lyell, *Principles of Geology*,[12] i. 391 *sqq.*, 590.

five feet deep. Neither man nor beast can descend to the bottom and live. The ground is covered with the carcases of tigers, deer, birds, and even the bones of men, all killed by the abundant emanations of carbonic acid gas which exhale from the soil. Animals let down into it die in a few minutes. The whole range of hills is volcanic. Two neighbouring craters constantly emit smoke.[1] In another crater of Java, near the volcano Talaga Bodas, the sulphureous exhalations have proved fatal to tigers, birds, and countless insects ; and the soft parts of these creatures, such as fibres, muscles, hair, and skin, are well preserved, while the bones are corroded or destroyed.[2]

Places of Pluto or Charon.

The ancients were acquainted with such noxious vapours in their own country, and they regarded the vents from which they were discharged as entrances to the infernal regions.[3] The Greeks called them places of Pluto (*Plutonia*) or places of Charon (*Charonia*).[4] In Italy the vapours were personified as a goddess, who bore the name of Mefitis and was worshipped in various parts of the peninsula.[5] She had a temple in the famous valley of Amsanctus in the land of the Hirpini, where the exhalations, supposed to be the breath of Pluto himself, were of so deadly a character that all who set foot on the spot died.[6] The place is a glen, partly wooded with chestnut trees, among limestone hills, distant about four miles from the town of Frigento. Here, under a steep shelving bank of decomposed limestone, there is a pool of dark ash-coloured water, which continually bubbles up with an explosion like distant thunder. A rapid stream of the same blackish water rushes into the pool from under the

The valley of Amsanctus.

1 "Extract from a Letter of Mr. Alexander Loudon," *Journal of the Royal Geographical Society*, ii. (1832) pp. 60-62 ; Sir Ch. Lyell, *Principles of Geology*,[12] i. 590.

2 Sir Ch. Lyell, *l.c.*

3 Lucretius, vi. 738 *sqq.*

4 Strabo, v. 4. 5, p. 244, xii. 8. 17, p. 579, xiii. 4. 14, p. 629, xiv. 1. 11 and 44, pp. 636, 649 ; Cicero, *De divinatione*, i. 36. 79 ; Pliny, *Nat. Hist.* ii. 208. Compare [Aristotle,] *De mundo*, 4, p. 395 B, ed. Bekker.

5 Servius on Virgil, *Aen.* vii. 84,

who says that some people looked on Mefitis as a god, the male partner of Leucothoë, to whom he stood as Adonis to Venus or as Virbius to Diana. As to Mefitis see L. Preller, *Römische Mythologie*[3] (Berlin, 1881–1883), ii. 144 *sq.* ; R. Peter, *s.v.* "Mefitis" in W. H. Roscher's *Lexikon der griech. und röm. Mythologie*, ii. 2519 *sqq.*

6 Virgil, *Aen.* vii. 563-571, with the commentary of Servius ; Cicero, *De divinatione*, i. 36. 79 ; Pliny, *Nat. Hist.* ii. 208.

barren rocky hill, but the fall is not more than a few feet. A little higher up are apertures in the ground, through which warm blasts of sulphuretted hydrogen are constantly issuing with more or less noise, according to the size of the holes. These blasts are no doubt what the ancients deemed the breath of Pluto. The pool is now called *Mefite* and the holes *Mefitinelle*. On the other side of the pool is a smaller pond called the *Coccaio*, or Cauldron, because it appears to be perpetually boiling. Thick masses of mephitic vapour, visible a hundred yards off, float in rapid undulations on its surface. The exhalations given off by these waters are sometimes fatal, especially when they are borne on a high wind. But as the carbonic acid gas does not naturally rise more than two or three feet from the ground, it is possible in calm weather to walk round the pools, though to stoop is difficult and to fall would be dangerous. The ancient temple of Mefitis has been replaced by a shrine of the martyred Santa Felicita.[1]

Similar discharges of poisonous vapours took place at various points in the volcanic district of Caria, and were the object of superstitious veneration in antiquity. Thus at the village of Thymbria there was a sacred cave which gave out deadly emanations, and the place was deemed a sanctuary of Charon.[2] A similar cave might be seen at the village of Acharaca near Nysa, in the valley of the Maeander. Here, below the cave, there was a fine grove with a temple dedicated to Pluto and Persephone. The place was sacred to Pluto, yet sick people resorted to it for the restoration of their health. They lived in the neighbouring village, and the priests prescribed for them according to the revelations which they received from the two deities in dreams. Often the priests would take the patients to the cave and leave them there for days without food. Sometimes the sufferers themselves were favoured with revelations in dreams, but

Sanctuaries of Charon or Pluto in Caria.

[1] Letter of Mr. Hamilton (British Envoy at the Court of Naples), in *Journal of the Royal Geographical Society*, ii. (1832) pp. 62-65; W. Smith's *Dictionary of Greek and Roman Geography*, i. 127; H. Nissen, *Italische Landeskunde* (Berlin, 1883–1902), i. 242, 271, ii. 819 *sq.* Another place in Italy infested by poisonous exhalations is the grotto called *dei cani* at Naples. It is described by Addison in his "Remarks on Several Parts of Italy" (*Works*, London, 1811, vol. ii. pp. 89-91).

[2] Strabo, xiv. 1. 11, p. 636.

they always acted under the spiritual direction of the priests. To all but the sick the place was unapproachable and fatal. Once a year a festival was held in the village, and then afflicted folk came in crowds to be rid of their ailments. About the hour of noon on that day a number of athletic young men, their naked bodies greased with oil, used to carry a bull up to the cave and there let it go. But the beast had not taken a few steps into the cavern before it fell to the ground and expired: so deadly was the vapour.[1]

Sanctuary of Pluto at the Lydian or Phrygian Hierapolis.

Another Plutonian sanctuary of the same sort existed at Hierapolis, in the upper valley of the Maeander, on the borders of Lydia and Phrygia.[2] Here under a brow of the hill there was a deep cave with a narrow mouth just large enough to admit the body of a man. A square space in front of the cave was railed off, and within the railing there hung so thick a cloudy vapour that it was hardly possible to see the ground. In calm weather people could step up to the railing with safety, but to pass within it was instant death. Bulls driven into the enclosure fell to the earth and were dragged out lifeless; and sparrows, which spectators by way of experiment allowed to fly into the mist, dropped dead at once. Yet the eunuch priests of the Great Mother Goddess could enter the railed-off area with impunity; nay more, they used to go up to the very mouth of the cave, stoop, and creep into it for a certain distance, holding their breath; but there was a look on their faces as if they were being choked. Some people ascribed the immunity of the priests to the divine protection, others to the use of antidotes.[3]

§ 7. The Worship of Hot Springs

The mysterious chasm of Hierapolis, with its deadly mist, has not been discovered in modern times; indeed it

---

[1] Strabo, xiv. 1. 44, pp. 649 sq. A coin of Nysa shows the bull carried to the sacrifice by six naked youths and preceded by a naked flute-player. See B. V. Head, Catalogue of the Greek Coins of Lydia, pp. lxxxiii. 181, pl. xx. 10. Strabo was familiar with this neighbourhood, for he tells us (xiv. 1. 48, p. 650) that in his youth he studied at Nysa under the philosopher Aristodemus.

[2] Some of the ancients assigned Hierapolis to Lydia, and others to Phrygia (W. M. Ramsay, Cities and Bishoprics of Phrygia, i. (Oxford, 1895) pp. 84 sq.

[3] Strabo, xiii. 4. 14, pp. 629 sq.; Dio Cassius, lxviii. 27. 3; Pliny, Nat. Hist. ii. 208; Ammianus Marcellinus, xxiii. 6. 18.

would seem to have vanished even in antiquity.[1] It may have been destroyed by an earthquake. But another marvel of the Sacred City remains to this day. The hot springs with their calcareous deposit, which, like a wizard's wand, turns all that it touches to stone, excited the wonder of the ancients, and the course of ages has only enhanced the fantastic splendour of the great transformation scene. The stately ruins of Hierapolis occupy a broad shelf or terrace on the mountain-side commanding distant views of extraordinary beauty and grandeur, from the dark precipices and dazzling snows of Mount Cadmus away to the burnt summits of Phrygia, fading in rosy tints into the blue of the sky. Hills, broken by wooded ravines, rise behind the city. In front the terrace falls away in cliffs three hundred feet high into the desolate treeless valley of the Lycus. Over the face of these cliffs the hot streams have poured or trickled for thousands of years, encrusting them with a pearly white substance like salt or driven snow. The appearance of the whole is as if a mighty river, some two miles broad, had been suddenly arrested in the act of falling over a great cliff and transformed into white marble. It is a petrified Niagara. The illusion is strongest in winter or in cool summer mornings when the mist from the hot springs hangs in the air, like a veil of spray resting on the foam of the waterfall. A closer inspection of the white cliff, which attracts the traveller's attention at a distance of twenty miles, only adds to its beauty and changes one illusion for another. For now it seems to be a glacier, its long pendent stalactites looking like icicles, and the snowy whiteness of its smooth expanse being tinged here and there with delicate hues of blue, rose and green, all the colours of the rainbow. These petrified cascades of Hierapolis are among the wonders of the world. Indeed they have probably been without a rival in their kind ever since the famous white and pink terraces or staircases of Rotomahana in New Zealand were destroyed by a volcanic eruption.

The hot springs which have wrought these miracles at

---

[1] Ammianus Marcellinus (*l.c.*) speaks as if the cave no longer existed in his time.

Hierapolis rise in a large deep pool among the vast and imposing ruins of the ancient city. The water is of a greenish-blue tint, but clear and transparent. At the bottom may be seen the white marble columns of a beautiful Corinthian colonnade, which must formerly have encircled the sacred pool. Shimmering through the green-blue water they look like the ruins of a Naiad's palace. Clumps of oleanders and pomegranate-trees overhang the little lake and add to its charm. Yet the enchanted spot has its dangers. Bubbles of carbonic acid gas rise incessantly from the bottom and mount like flickering particles of silver to the surface. Birds and beasts which come to drink of the water are sometimes found dead on the bank, stifled by the noxious vapour; and the villagers tell of bathers who have been overpowered by it and drowned, or dragged down, as they say, to death by the water-spirit.

The streams of hot water, no longer regulated by the care of a religious population, have for centuries been allowed to overflow their channels and to spread unchecked over the tableland. By the deposit which they leave behind they have raised the surface of the ground many feet, their white ridges concealing the ruins and impeding the footstep, except where the old channels, filled up solidly to the brim, now form hard level footpaths, from which the traveller may survey the strange scene without quitting the saddle. In antiquity the husbandmen used purposely to lead the water in rills round their lands, and thus in a few years their fields and vineyards were enclosed with walls of solid stone. The water was also peculiarly adapted for the dyeing of woollen stuffs. Tinged with dyes extracted from certain roots, it imparted to cloths dipped in it the finest shades of purple and scarlet.[1]

---

[1] Strabo, xiii. 4. 14, pp. 629, 630; Vitruvius, viii. 3. 10. For modern descriptions of Hierapolis see R. Chandler, *Travels in Asia Minor* [2] (London, 1776), pp. 228-235; Ch. Fellows, *Journal written during an Excursion in Asia Minor* (London, 1839), pp. 283-285; W. J. Hamilton, *Researches in Asia Minor, Pontus, and Armenia*, i. 517-521; E. Renan, *Saint Paul*, pp. 357 *sq.*; E. J. Davis, *Anatolica* (London, 1874), pp. 97-112; É. Reclus, *Nouvelle Géographie Universelle*, ix. 510-512; W. Cochran, *Pen and Pencil Sketches in Asia Minor* (London, 1887), pp. 387-390; W. M. Ramsay, *Cities and Bishoprics of Phrygia*, i. 84 *sqq.* The temperature of the hot pool varies from 85 to 90 degrees Fahrenheit. The volcanic district of Tuscany which skirts the Apennines abounds in hot calcareous springs which have produced phenomena like those of Hierapolis. Indeed the

We cannot doubt that Hierapolis owed its reputation as a holy city in great part to its hot springs and mephitic vapours.   The curative virtue of mineral and thermal springs was well known to the ancients, and it would be interesting, if it were possible, to trace the causes which have gradually eliminated the superstitious element from the use of such waters, and so converted many old seats of volcanic religion into the medicinal baths of modern times.   It was an article of Greek faith that all hot springs were sacred to Hercules.[1] "Who ever heard of cold baths that were sacred to Hercules?" asks Injustice in Aristophanes ; and Justice admits that the brawny hero's patronage of hot baths was the excuse alleged by young men for sprawling all day in the steaming water when they ought to have been sweating in the gymnasium.[2] Hot springs were said to have been first produced for the refreshment of Hercules after his labours ; some ascribed the kindly thought and deed to Athena, others to Hephaestus, and others to the nymphs.[3]   The warm water of these sources appears to have been used especially to heal diseases of the skin ; for a Greek proverb, "the itch of Hercules," was applied to persons in need of hot baths for the scab.[4] On the strength of his connexion with medicinal springs Hercules set up as a patron of the healing art.   In heaven, if we can trust Lucian, he even refused to give place to Aesculapius himself, and the difference between the two deities led to a very unseemly brawl.   "Do you mean to say," demanded Hercules of his father Zeus, in a burst of indignation, "that this apothecary is to sit down to table

Hercules the patron of hot springs.

---

whole ground is in some places coated over with tufa and travertine, which have been deposited by the water, and, like the ground at Hierapolis, it sounds hollow under the foot. See Sir Ch. Lyell, *Principles of Geology*,[12] i. 397 *sqq.* As to the terraces of Rotomahana in New Zealand, which were destroyed by an eruption of Mount Taravera in 1886, see R. Taylor, *Te Ika A Maui, or New Zealand and its Inhabitants*[2] (London, 1870), pp. 464-469.

[1] Athenaeus, xii. 6. p. 512.

[2] Aristophanes, *Clouds*, 1044-1054.

[3] Scholiast on Aristophanes, *Clouds*, 1050; Scholiast on Pindar, *Olymp.* xii. 25 ; Suidas and Hesychius, *s.v.* Ἡράκλεια λουτρά ; Apostolius, viii. 66 ; Zenobius, vi. 49 ; Diogenianus, v. 7 ; Plutarch, *Proverbia Alexandrinorum*, 21 ; Diodorus Siculus, iv. 23. 1, v. 3. 4.   Another story was that Hercules, like Moses, produced the water by smiting the rock with his club (Antoninus Liberalis, *Transform.* 4).

[4] Apostolius, viii. 68 ; Zenobius, vi. 49 ; Diogenianus, v. 7 ; Plutarch, *Proverbia Alexandrinorum*, 21.

before me?" To this the apothecary replied with much acrimony, recalling certain painful episodes in the private life of the burly hero. Finally the dispute was settled by Zeus, who decided in favour of Aesculapius on the ground that he died before Hercules, and was therefore entitled to rank as senior god.[1]

Hot springs of Hercules at Thermopylae.

Among the hot springs sacred to Hercules the most famous were those which rose in the pass of Thermopylae, and gave to the defile its name of the Hot Gates.[2] The warm baths, called by the natives "the Pots," were enlarged and improved for the use of invalids by the wealthy sophist Herodes Atticus in the second century of our era. An altar of Hercules stood beside them.[3] According to one story, the hot springs were here produced for his refreshment by the goddess Athena.[4] They exist to this day apparently unchanged, although the recession of the sea has converted what used to be a narrow pass into a wide, swampy flat, through which the broad but shallow, turbid stream of the Sperchius creeps sluggishly seaward. On the other side the rugged mountains descend in crags and precipices to the pass, their grey rocky sides tufted with low wood or bushes wherever vegetation can find a foothold, and their summits fringed along the sky-line with pines. They remind a Scotchman of the "crags, knolls, and mounds confusedly hurled" in which Ben Venue comes down to the Silver Strand of Loch Katrine. The principal spring bursts from the rocks just at the foot of the steepest and loftiest part of the range. After forming a small pool it flows in a rapid stream eastward, skirting the foot of the mountains. The water is so hot that it is almost painful to hold the hands in it, at least near the source, and steam rises thickly from its surface along the course of the brook. Indeed the clouds of white steam and the strong sulphurous smell acquaint the traveller with his approach to the famous spot before he comes in sight of the springs. The water is clear, but has the appearance of being of a deep sea-blue or sea-green

---

[1] Lucian, *Dialogi Deorum*, 13.

[2] Strabo, ix. 4. 13, p. 428.

[3] Herodotus, vii. 176 ; Pausanias, iv. 35. 9 ; Philostratus, *Vit. Sophist.* ii. 1. 9.

[4] Scholiast on Aristophanes, *Clouds*, 1050.

colour. This appearance it takes from the thick, slimy deposits of blue-green sulphur which line the bed of the stream. From its source the blue, steaming, sulphur-reeking brook rushes eastward for a few hundred yards at the foot of the mountain, and is then joined by the water of another spring, which rises much more tranquilly in a sort of natural bath among the rocks. The sides of this bath are not so thickly coated with sulphur as the banks of the stream; hence its water, about two feet deep, is not so blue. Just beyond it there is a second and larger bath, which, from its square shape and smooth sides, would seem to be in part artificial. These two baths are probably the Pots mentioned by ancient writers. They are still used by bathers, and a few wooden dressing-rooms are provided for the accommodation of visitors. Some of the water is conducted in an artificial channel to turn a mill about half a mile off at the eastern end of the pass. The rest crosses the flat to find its way to the sea. In its passage it has coated the swampy ground with a white crust, which sounds hollow under the tread.[1]

We may conjecture that these remarkable springs furnished the principal reason for associating Hercules with this district, and for laying the scene of his fiery death on the top of the neighbouring Mount Oeta. The district is volcanic, and has often been shaken by earthquakes.[2] Across the strait the island of Euboea has suffered from the same cause and at the same time; and on its southern shore sulphureous springs, like those of Thermopylae, but much hotter and more powerful, were in like manner dedicated to Hercules.[3] The strong medicinal qualities of the

Hot springs of Hercules at Aedepsus.

---

[1] I have described Thermopylae as I saw it in November 1895. Compare W. M. Leake, *Travels in Northern Greece* (London, 1835), ii. 33 *sqq.*; E. Dodwell, *Classical and Topographical Tour through Greece* (London, 1819), ii. 66 *sqq.*; K. G. Fiedler, *Reise durch alle Theile des Königreichs Griechenland* (Leipsic, 1840–1841), i. 207 *sqq.*; L. Ross, *Wanderungen in Griechenland* (Halle, 1851), i. 90 *sqq.*; C. Bursian, *Geographie von Griechenland* (Leipsic, 1862–1872), i. 92 *sqq.*

[2] Thucydides, iii. 87 and 89; Strabo, i. 3. 20, pp. 60 *sq.*; C. Neumann und J. Partsch, *Physikalische Geographie von Griechenland*, pp. 321-323.

[3] Aristotle, *Meteora*, ii. 8, p. 366 A, ed. Bekker; Strabo, ix. 4. 2, p. 425. Aristotle expressly recognized the connexion of the springs with earthquakes, which he tells us were very common in this district. As to the earthquakes of Euboea see also Thucydides, iii. 87, 89; Strabo, i. 3. 16 and 20, pp. 58, 60 *sq.*

waters, which are especially adapted for the cure of skin diseases and gout, have attracted patients in ancient and modern times.   Sulla took the waters here for his gout ;[1] and in the days of Plutarch the neighbouring town of Aedepsus, situated in a green valley about two miles from the springs, was one of the most fashionable resorts of Greece.   Elegant and commodious buildings, an agreeable country, and abundance of fish and game united with the health-giving properties of the baths to draw crowds of idlers to the place, especially in the prime of the glorious Greek spring, the height of the season at Aedepsus.   While some watched the dancers dancing or listened to the strains of the harp, others passed the time in discourse, lounging in the shade of cloisters or pacing the shore of the beautiful strait with its prospect of mountains beyond mountains immortalized in story across the water.[2]   Of all this Greek elegance and luxury hardly a vestige remains.   Yet the healing springs flow now as freely as of old.   In the course of time the white and yellow calcareous deposit which the water leaves behind it, has formed a hillock at the foot of the mountains, and the stream now falls in a steaming cascade from the face of the rock into the sea.[3]   Once, after an earthquake, the springs ceased to flow for three days, and at the same time the hot springs of Thermopylae dried up.[4]   The incident proves the relation of these Baths of Hercules on both sides of the strait to each other and to volcanic agency.   On another occasion a cold spring suddenly burst out beside the hot springs of Aedepsus, and as its water was supposed to be peculiarly beneficial to health, patients hastened from far and near to drink of it.   But the generals of King Antigonus, anxious to raise a revenue, imposed a tax on the use of the water ; and the spring, as if in disgust at being turned to so base a use, disappeared as suddenly as it had come.[5]

[1] Plutarch, *Sulla*, 26.

[2] Plutarch, *Quaest. Conviviales*, iv. 4. 1 ; *id.*, *De fraterno Amore*, 17.

[3] As to the hot springs of Aedepsus (the modern *Lipso*) see K. G. Fiedler, *Reise durch alle Theile des Königreichs Griechenland*, i. 487 - 492 ; H. N. Ulrichs, *Reisen und Forschungen in Griechenland* (Bremen, 1840—Berlin, 1863), ii. 233-235 ; C. Bursian, *Geographie von Griechenland*, ii. 409 ; C. Neumann und J. Partsch, *Physikalische Geographie von Griechenland*, pp. 342-344.

[4] Strabo, i. 3. 20, p. 60.

[5] Athenaeus, iii. 4, p. 73 E, D.

The association of Hercules with hot springs was not Reasons
confined to Greece itself. Greek influence extended it to for the
Sicily,[1] Italy,[2] and even to Dacia.[3] Why the hero should of Hercules
have been chosen as the patron of thermal waters, it is hard with hot
to say. Yet it is worth while, perhaps, to remember that springs.
such springs combine in a manner the twofold and seemingly
discordant principles of water and fire,[4] of fertility and
destruction, and that the death of Hercules in the flames
seems to connect him with the fiery element. Further, the
apparent conflict of the two principles is by no means as
absolute as at first sight we might be tempted to suppose ;
for heat is as necessary as moisture to the support of animal
and vegetable life. Even volcanic fires have their beneficent
aspect, since their products lend a more generous flavour
to the juice of the grape. The ancients themselves, as we
have seen, perceived the connexion between good wine and
volcanic soil, and proposed more or less seriously to interpret the vine-god Dionysus as a child of the fire.[5] As a
patron of hot springs Hercules combined the genial elements
of heat and moisture, and may therefore have stood, in one
of his many aspects, for the principle of fertility.

In Syria childless women still resort to hot springs in order
to procure offspring from the saint or the jinnee of the waters.[6]

[1] The hot springs of Himera (the
modern *Termini*) were said to have
been produced for the refreshment of
the weary Hercules. See Diodorus
Siculus, iv. 23. 1, v. 3. 4 ; Scholiast
on Pindar, *Olymp.* xii. 25. The hero
is said to have taught the Syracusans
to sacrifice a bull annually to Persephone at the Blue Spring (*Cyane*) near
Syracuse ; the beasts were drowned in
the water of the pool. See Diodorus
Siculus, iv. 23. 4, v. 4. 1 *sq.* As to
the spring, which is now thickly surrounded by tall papyrus-plants introduced by the Arabs, see K. Baedeker,
Southern Italy[7] (Leipsic, 1880), pp.
356, 357.

[2] The splendid baths of Allifae in
Samnium, of which there are considerable remains, were sacred to Hercules. See G. Wilmanns, *Exempla
Inscriptionum Latinarum* (Berlin,
1873), vol. i. p. 227, No. 735 C;
H. Nissen, *Italische Landeskunde*,

ii. 798. It is characteristic of the
volcanic nature of the springs that the
same inscription which mentions these
baths of Hercules records their destruction by an earthquake.

[3] H. Dessau, *Inscriptiones Latinae
Selectae*, vol. ii. Pars i. (Berlin, 1902)
p. 113, No. 3891.

[4] Speaking of thermal springs Lyell
observes that the description of them
" might almost with equal propriety
have been given under the head of
' igneous causes,' as they are agents of
a mixed nature, being at once igneous
and aqueous " (*Principles of Geology*,[12]
i. 392).

[5] See above, p. 194.

[6] S. I. Curtiss, *Primitive Semitic
Religion To-day* (Chicago, New York,
and Toronto, 1902), pp. 116 *sq.* ;
Mrs. H. H. Spoer, "The Powers of
Evil in Jerusalem," *Folk-lore*, xviii.
(1907) p. 55. See above, p. 78.

This, for example, they do at the famous hot springs in the land of Moab which flow through a wild gorge into the Dead Sea. In antiquity the springs went by the Greek name of Callirrhoe, the Fair-flowing. It was to them that the dying Herod, weighed down by a complication of disorders which the pious Jews traced to God's vengeance, repaired in the vain hope of arresting or mitigating the fatal progress of disease. The healing waters brought no alleviation of his sufferings, and he retired to Jericho to die.[1] The hot springs burst in various places from the sides of a deep romantic ravine to form a large and rapid stream of lukewarm water, which rushes down the depths of the lynn, dashing and foaming over boulders, under the dense shade of tamarisk-trees and cane-brakes, the rocks on either bank draped with an emerald fringe of maidenhair fern. One of the springs falls from a high rocky shelf over the face of a cliff which is tinted bright yellow by the sulphurous water. The lofty crags which shut in the narrow chasm are bold and imposing in outline and varied in colour, for they range from red sandstone through white and yellow limestone to black basalt. The waters issue from the line where the sandstone and limestone meet. Their temperature is high, and from great clefts in the mountain-sides you may see clouds of steam rising and hear the rumbling of the running waters. The bottom of the glen is clothed and half choked with rank vegetation; for, situated far below the level of the sea, the hot ravine is almost African in climate and flora. Here grow dense thickets of canes with their feathery tufts that shake and nod in every passing breath of wind: here the oleander flourishes with its dark-green glossy foliage and its beautiful pink blossoms: here tall date-palms rear their stately heads wherever the hot springs flow. Gorgeous flowers, too, carpet the ground. Splendid orobanches, some pinkish purple, some bright yellow, grow in large tufts, each flower-stalk more than three feet high, and covered with blossoms from the ground upwards. An exquisite rose-coloured geranium abounds among the stones; and where the soil is a little richer than

---

[1] Josephus, *Antiquit. Jud.* xvii. 6. 5. The medical properties of the spring are mentioned by Pliny (*Nat. Hist.* v. 72).

usual it is a mass of the night-scented stock, while the
crannies of the rocks are gay with scarlet ranunculus and
masses of sorrel and cyclamen. Over all this luxuriant
vegetation flit great butterflies of brilliant hues. Looking
down the far-stretching gorge to its mouth you see in the
distance the purple hills of Judah framed between walls
of black basaltic columns on the one side and of bright red
sandstone on the other.[1]

Every year in the months of April and May the Arabs
resort in crowds to the glen to benefit by the waters. They
take up their quarters in huts made of the reeds which they
cut in the thickets. They bathe in the steaming water,
or allow it to splash on their bodies as it gushes in a powerful jet from a crevice in the rocks. But before they indulge
in these ablutions, the visitors, both Moslem and Christian,
propitiate the spirit or genius of the place by sacrificing
a sheep or goat at the spring and allowing its red blood
to tinge the water. Then they bathe in what they call the
Baths of Solomon. Legend runs that Solomon the Wise
made his bathing-place here, and in order to keep the water
always warm he commanded the jinn never to let the fire
die down. The jinn obey his orders to this day, but sometimes they slacken their efforts, and then the water runs
low and cool. When the bathers perceive that, they say,
" O Solomon, bring green wood, dry wood," and no sooner
have they said so than the water begins to gurgle and steam
as before. Sick people tell the saint or sheikh, who lives
invisible in the springs, all about their ailments ; they point
out to him the precise spot that is the seat of the malady,
it may be the back, or the head, or the legs ; and if the heat
of the water diminishes, they call out, " Thy bath is cold,
O sheikh, thy bath is cold ! " whereupon the obliging sheikh
stokes up the fire, and out comes the water boiling. But if
in spite of their remonstrances the temperature of the spring

*Prayers
and sacri-
fices offered
to the hot
springs of
Callirrhoe.*

---

[1] C. L. Irby and J. Mangles,
*Travels in Egypt and Nubia, Syria
and the Holy Land* (London, 1844),
pp. 144 *sq.* ; W. Smith, *Dictionary of
Greek and Roman Geography* (London,
1873), i. 482, *s.v.* " Callirrhoë " ;
K. Baedeker, *Syria and Palestine*[4]
(Leipsic, 1906), p. 148 ; H. B.

Tristram, *The Land of Moab* (London,
1873), pp. 233-250, 285 *sqq.* ; Jacob
E. Spafford, " Around the Dead Sea
by Motor Boat," *The Geographical
Journal*, xxxix. (1912) pp. 39 *sq.*
The river formed by the springs is
now called the Zerka.

continues low, they say that the sheikh has gone on pilgrimage, and they shout to him to hasten his return. Barren Moslem women also visit these hot springs to obtain children, and they do the same at the similar baths near Kerak. At the latter place a childless woman has been known to address the spirit of the waters saying, " O sheikh Solomon, I am not yet an old woman ; give me children." [1] The respect thus paid by Arab men and women to the sheikh Solomon at his hot springs may help us to understand the worship which at similar spots Greek men and women used to render to the hero Hercules. As the ideal of manly strength he may have been deemed the father of many of his worshippers, and Greek wives may have gone on pilgrimage to his steaming waters in order to obtain the wish of their hearts.

§ 8. *The Worship of Volcanoes in other Lands*

Worship of volcanic phenomena in other lands.

How far these considerations may serve to explain the custom of burning Hercules, or gods identified with him, in effigy or in the person of a human being, is a question which deserves to be considered. It might be more easily answered if we were better acquainted with analogous customs in other parts of the world, but our information with regard to the worship of volcanic phenomena in general appears to be very scanty. However, a few facts may be noted.

The great volcano of Kirauea in Hawaii.

The largest active crater in the world is Kirauea in Hawaii. It is a huge cauldron, several miles in circumference and hundreds of feet deep, the bottom of which is filled with boiling lava in a state of terrific ebullition ; from the red surge rise many black cones or insulated craters belching columns of grey smoke or pyramids of brilliant flame from their roaring mouths, while torrents of blazing lava roll down their sides to flow into the molten, tossing sea of fire below. The scene is especially impressive by night,

---

[1] Antonin Jaussen, *Coutumes des Arabes au pays de Moab* (Paris, 1908), pp. 359 *sq.* The Arabs think that the evil spirits let the hot water out of hell, lest its healing properties should assuage the pains of the damned. See H. B. Tristram, *The Land of Moab* (London, 1873), p. 247.

when flames of sulphurous blue or metallic red sweep across the heaving billows of the infernal lake, casting a broad glare on the jagged sides of the insulated craters, which shoot up eddying streams of fire with a continuous roar, varied at frequent intervals by loud detonations, as spherical masses of fusing lava or bright ignited stones are hurled into the air.[1] It is no wonder that so appalling a spectacle should have impressed the imagination of the natives and filled it with ideas of the dreadful beings who inhabit the fiery abyss. They considered the great crater, we are told, as the primaeval abode of their volcanic deities : the black cones that rise like islands from the burning lake appeared to them the houses where the gods often amused themselves by playing at draughts : the roaring of the furnaces and the crackling of the flames were the music of their dance ; and the red flaming surge was the surf wherein they played, sportively swimming on the rolling wave.[2]

For these fearful divinities they had appropriate names ; one was the King of Steam or Vapour, another the Rain of Night, another the Husband of Thunder, another the Child of War with a Spear of Fire, another the Fiery-eyed Canoe-breaker, another the Red-hot Mountain holding or lifting Clouds, and so on. But above them all was the great goddess Pélé. All were dreaded : they never journeyed on errands of mercy but only to receive offerings or to execute vengeance ; and their arrival in any place was announced by the convulsive trembling of the earth, by the lurid light of volcanic eruption, by the flash of lightning, and the clap of thunder. The whole island was bound to pay them tribute or support their temples and devotees ; and whenever the chiefs or people failed to send the proper offerings, or incurred their displeasure by insulting them or their priests or breaking the taboos which should be observed round about the craters, they filled the huge cauldron on the top of Kirauea with molten lava, and spouted the fiery liquid on the surrounding country ; or they would

The divinities of the volcano.

Offerings to the volcano.

---

[1] W. Ellis, *Polynesian Researches*, Second Edition (London, 1832–1836), iv. 235 *sqq.* Mr. Ellis was the first European to visit and describe the tremendous volcano. His visit was paid in the year 1823. Compare *The Encyclopaedia Britannica*,[9] xi. 531.

[2] W. Ellis, *op. cit.* iv. 246 *sq.*

march to some of their other houses, which mortals call
craters, in the neighbourhood of the sinners, and rushing
forth in a river or column of fire overwhelm the guilty.   If
fishermen did not bring them enough fish from the sea, they
would go down, kill all the fish, fill the shoals with lava, and
so destroy the fishing-grounds.   Hence, when the volcano
was in active eruption or threatened to break out, the people
used to cast vast numbers of hogs, alive or dead, into the
craters or into the rolling torrent of lava in order to appease
the gods and arrest the progress of the fiery stream.[1]   To
pluck certain sacred berries, which grow on the mountain, to
dig sand on its slopes, or to throw stones into the crater were
acts particularly offensive to the deities, who would instantly
rise in volumes of smoke, crush the offender under a shower
of stones, or so involve him in thick darkness and rain that
he could never find his way home.   However, it was lawful
to pluck and eat of the sacred berries, if only a portion of
them were first offered to the goddess Pélé.   The offerer
would take a branch laden with clusters of the beautiful red
and yellow berries, and standing on the edge of the abyss
and looking towards the place where the smoke rose in
densest volumes, he would say, " Pélé, here are your berries :
I offer some to you, some I also eat."   With that he would
throw some of the berries into the crater and eat the rest.[2]
A kind of brittle volcanic glass, of a dark-olive colour and
semi-transparent, is found on the mountain in the shape of
filaments as fine as human hair ; the natives call it the hair
of the goddess Pélé.[3]   Worshippers used to cast locks of
their own hair into the crater of Kirauea as an offering to
the dreadful goddess who dwelt in it.   She had also a temple
at the bottom of a valley, where stood a number of rude
stone idols wrapt in white and yellow cloth.   Once a year
the priests and devotees of Pélé assembled there to perform
certain rites and to feast on hogs, dogs, and fruit, which the

---

[1] W. Ellis, *op. cit.* iv. 248-250.

[2] W. Ellis, *op. cit.* iv. 207, 234-
236.   The berries resemble currants in
shape and size and grow on low bushes.
" The branches small and clear, leaves
alternate, obtuse with a point, and
serrated ; the flower was monopetalous,

and, on being examined, determined
the plant to belong to the class
decandria and order *monogynia*.   The
native name of the plant is *ohelo* "
(W. Ellis, *op. cit.* iv. 234).

[3] W. Ellis, *op. cit.* iv. 263.

pious inhabitants of Hamakua brought to the holy place in great abundance. This annual festival was intended to propitiate the volcanic goddess and thereby to secure the country from earthquakes and floods of molten lava.[1] The goddess of the volcano was supposed to inspire people, though to the carnal eye the inspiration resembled intoxication. One of these inspired priestesses solemnly affirmed to an English missionary that she was the goddess Pélé herself and as such immortal. Assuming a haughty air, she said, " I am Pélé ; I shall never die ; and those who follow me, when they die, if part of their bones be taken to Kirauea (the name of the volcano), will live with me in the bright fires there." [2] For " the worshippers of Pélé threw a part of bones of their dead into the volcano, under the impression that the spirits of the deceased would then be admitted to the society of the volcanic deities, and that their influence would preserve the survivors from the ravages of volcanic fire." [3]

Priestess impersonating the goddess of the volcano.

This last belief may help to explain a custom, which some peoples have observed, of throwing human victims into volcanoes. The intention of such a practice need not be simply to appease the dreadful volcanic spirits by ministering to their fiendish lust of cruelty ; it may be a notion that the souls of the men or women who have been burnt to death in the crater will join the host of demons in the fiery furnace, mitigate their fury, and induce them to spare the works and the life of man. But, however we may explain the custom, it has been usual in various parts of the world to throw human beings as well as less precious offerings into the craters of active volcanoes. Thus the Indians of Nicaragua used to sacrifice men, women, and children to the active volcano Massaya, flinging them into the craters : we are told that the victims went willingly to their fate.[4] In the island of Siao, to the north of Celebes, a child was formerly sacrificed every year in order to keep the volcano Goowoong Awoo quiet. The poor wretch was tortured to death at a festival which lasted nine days. In later times the place of the child has

Sacrifices to volcanoes.

Human victims thrown into volcanoes.

---

[1] W. Ellis, *op. cit.* iv. 350.
[2] W. Ellis, *op. cit.* iv. 309-311.
[3] W. Ellis, *op. cit.* iv. 361.

[4] Fernandez de Oviedo y Valdés, *Historia General y Natural de las Indias* (Madrid, 1851–1855), iv. 74.

been taken by a wooden puppet, which is hacked to pieces
in the same way. The Galelareese of Halmahera say that
the Sultan of Ternate used annually to require some human
victims, who were cast into the crater of the volcano to save
the island from its ravages.[1] In Java the volcano Bromo or
Bromok is annually worshipped by people who throw offerings
of coco-nuts, plantains, mangoes, rice, chickens, cakes, cloth,
money, and so forth into the crater.[2] To the Tenggereese,
an aboriginal heathen tribe inhabiting the mountains of which
Bromo is the central crater, the festival of making offerings to
the volcano is the greatest of the year. It is held at full moon
in the twelfth month, the day being fixed by the high priest.
Each household prepares its offerings the night before. Very
early in the morning the people set out by moonlight for
Mount Bromo, men, women, and children all arrayed in their
best. Before they reach the mountain they must cross a
wide sandy plain, where the spirits of the dead are supposed
to dwell until by means of the Festival of the Dead they
obtain admittance to the volcano. It is a remarkable sight
to see thousands of people streaming across the level sands
from three different directions. They have to descend into
it from the neighbouring heights, and the horses break into
a gallop when, after the steep descent, they reach the level.
The gay and varied colours of the dresses, the fantastic
costumes of the priests, the offerings borne along, the whole lit
up by the warm beams of the rising sun, lend to the spectacle
a peculiar charm. All assemble at the foot of the crater,
where a market is held for offerings and refreshments. The
scene is a lively one, for hundreds of people must now pay
the vows which they made during the year. The priests sit
in a long row on mats, and when the high priest appears the
people pray, saying, " Bromo, we thank thee for all thy gifts
and benefits with which thou ever blessest us, and for which
we offer thee our thank-offerings to-day. Bless us, our
children, and our children's children." The prayers over, the
high priest gives a signal, and the whole multitude arises
and climbs the mountain. On reaching the edge of the

[1] A. C. Kruijt, *Het Animisme in
den Indischen Archipel* (The Hague,
1906), pp. 497 *sq.*

[2] W. B. d'Almeida, *Life in Java*
(London, 1864), i. 166-173.

Annual
sacrifices to
the volcano
Bromo in
Java.

crater, the pontiff again blesses the offerings of food, clothes, and money, which are then thrown into the crater. Yet few of them reach the spirits for whom they are intended ; for a swarm of urchins now scrambles down into the crater, and at more or less risk to life and limb succeeds in appropriating the greater part of the offerings. The spirits, defrauded of their dues, must take the will for the deed.[1] Tradition says that once in a time of dearth a chief vowed to sacrifice one of his children to the volcano, if the mountain would bless the people with plenty of food. His prayer was answered, and he paid his vow by casting his youngest son as a thank-offering into the crater.[2]

On the slope of Mount Smeroe, another active volcano in Java, there are two small idols, which the natives worship and pray to when they ascend the mountain. They lay food before the images to obtain the favour of the god of the volcano.[3] In antiquity people cast into the craters of Etna vessels of gold and silver and all kinds of victims. If the fire swallowed up the offerings, the omen was good ; but if it rejected them, some evil was sure to befall the offerer.[4] Other sacrifices to volcanoes.

These examples suggest that a custom of burning men or images may possibly be derived from a practice of throwing them into the craters of active volcanoes in order to appease the dreaded spirits or gods who dwell there. But unless we reckon the fires of Mount Argaeus in Cappadocia[5] and of Mount Chimaera in Lycia,[6] there is apparently no record of any mountain in Western Asia which has been in No evidence that the Asiatic custom of burning kings or gods was connected with volcanic phenomena.

---

[1] J. H. F. Kohlbrugge, " Die Tĕnggĕresen, ein alter Javanischer Volksstamm," *Bijdragen tot de Taal- Land- en Volkenkunde van Nederlandsch-Indië*, liii. (1901) pp. 84, 144-147.

[2] J. H. F. Kohlbrugge, *op. cit.* pp. 100 *sq.*

[3] I. A. Stigand, " The Volcano of Smeroe, Java," *The Geographical Journal*, xxviii. (1906) pp. 621, 624.

[4] Pausanias, iii. 23. 9. Some have thought that Pausanias confused the crater of Etna with the *Lago di Naftia*, a pool near Palagonia in the interior of Sicily, of which the water, impregnated with naphtha and sulphur, is thrown into violent ebullition by jets of volcanic gas. See [Aristotle,] *Mirab. Auscult.*

57 ; Macrobius, *Saturn.* v. 19. 26 *sqq.*; Diodorus Siculus, xi. 89 ; Stephanus Byzantius, *s.v.* Παλική ; E. H. Bunbury, *s.v.* " Palicorum lacus," in W. Smith's *Dictionary of Greek and Roman Geography*, ii. 533 *sq.* The author of the ancient Latin poem *Aetna* says (vv. 340 *sq.*) that people offered incense to the celestial deities on the top of Etna.

[5] See above,. pp. 190 *sq.*

[6] On Mount Chimaera in Lycia a flame burned perpetually which neither earth nor water could extinguish. See Pliny, *Nat. Hist.* ii. 236, v. 100 ; Servius on Virgil, *Aen.* vi. 288 ; Seneca, *Epist.* x. 3. 3 ; Diodorus, quoted by Photius, *Bibliotheca*, p. 212

eruption within historical times. On the whole, then, we conclude that the Asiatic custom of burning kings or gods was probably in no way connected with volcanic phenomena. Yet it was perhaps worth while to raise the question of the connexion, even though it has received only a negative answer. The whole subject of the influence which physical environment has exercised on the history of religion deserves to be studied with more attention than it has yet received.[1]

B, 10 *sqq.*, ed. Im. Bekker (Berlin, 1824). This perpetual flame was rediscovered by Captain Beaufort near Porto Genovese on the coast of Lycia. It issues from the side of a hill of crumbly serpentine rock, giving out an intense heat, but no smoke. "Trees, brushwood, and weeds grow close round this little crater, a small stream trickles down the hill hard bye, and the ground does not appear to feel the effect of its heat at more than a few feet distance." The fire is not accompanied by earthquakes or noises; it ejects no stones and emits no noxious vapours. There is nothing but a brilliant and perpetual flame, at which the shepherds often cook their food. See Fr. Beaufort, *Karmania* (London, 1817), p. 46; compare T. A. B. Spratt and E. Forbes, *Travels in Lycia* (London, 1847), ii. 181 *sq.*

[1] In the foregoing discussion I have confined myself, so far as concerns Asia, to the volcanic regions of Cappadocia, Lydia, and Caria. But Syria and Palestine, the home of Adonis and Melcarth, "abound in volcanic appearances, and very extensive areas have been shaken, at different periods, with great destruction of cities and loss of lives. Continual mention is made in history of the ravages committed by earthquakes in Sidon, Tyre, Berytus, Laodicea, and Antioch, and in the island of Cyprus. The country around the Dead Sea exhibits in some spots layers of sulphur and bitumen, forming a superficial deposit, supposed by Mr. Tristram to be of volcanic origin" (Sir Ch. Lyell, *Principles of Geology*,[12] i. 592 *sq.*). As to the earthquakes of Syria and Phoenicia see Strabo, i. 3. 16, p. 58; Lucretius, vi. 585; Josephus, *Antiquit. Jud.* xv. 5. 2; *id.*, *Bell. Jud.* i. 19. 3; W. M. Thomson, *The Land and the Book, Central Palestine and Phoenicia*, pp. 568-574; Ed. Robinson, *Biblical Researches in Palestine*,[3] ii. 422-424; S. R. Driver, on Amos iv. 11 (Cambridge *Bible for Schools and Colleges*). It is said that in the reign of the Emperor Justin the city of Antioch was totally destroyed by a dreadful earthquake, in which three hundred thousand people perished (Procopius, *De Bello Persico*, ii. 14). The destruction of Sodom and Gomorrah (Genesis xix. 24-28) has been plausibly explained as the effect of an earthquake liberating large quantities of petroleum and inflammable gases. See H. B. Tristram, *The Land of Israel*, Fourth Edition (London, 1882), pp. 350-354; S. R. Driver, *The Book of Genesis*[4] (London, 1905), pp. 202 *sq.*

CHAPTER IX

THE RITUAL OF ADONIS

THUS far we have dealt with the myth of Adonis and the legends which associated him with Byblus and Paphos. A discussion of these legends led us to the conclusion that among Semitic peoples in early times, Adonis, the divine lord of the city, was often personated by priestly kings or other members of the royal family, and that these his human representatives were of old put to death, whether periodically or occasionally, in their divine character. Further, we found that certain traditions and monuments of Asia Minor seem to preserve traces of a similar practice. As time went on, the cruel custom was apparently mitigated in various ways ; for example, by substituting an effigy or an animal for the man, or by allowing the destined victim to escape with a merely make-believe sacrifice. The evidence of all this is drawn from a variety of scattered and often ambiguous indications : it is fragmentary, it is uncertain, and the conclusions built upon it inevitably partake of the weakness of the foundation. Where the records are so imperfect, as they happen to be in this branch of our subject, the element of hypothesis must enter largely into any attempt to piece together and interpret the disjointed facts. How far the interpretations here proposed are sound, I leave to future inquiries to determine.

Results of the preceding inquiry.

From dim regions of the past, where we have had to grope our way with small help from the lamp of history, it is a relief to pass to those later periods of classical antiquity on which contemporary Greek writers have shed the light of their clear intelligence. To them we owe

Our knowledge of the rites of Adonis derived chiefly from Greek writers.

223

almost all that we know for certain about the rites of Adonis. The Semites who practised the worship have said little about it; at all events little that they said has come down to us. Accordingly, the following account of the ritual is derived mainly from Greek authors who saw what they describe; and it applies to ages in which the growth of humane feeling had softened some of the harsher features of the worship.

Festivals of the death and resurrection of Adonis.

At the festivals of Adonis, which were held in Western Asia and in Greek lands, the death of the god was annually mourned, with a bitter wailing, chiefly by women; images of him, dressed to resemble corpses, were carried out as to burial and then thrown into the sea or into springs;[1] and in some places his revival was celebrated on the following day.[2] But at different places the ceremonies varied somewhat in the manner and apparently also in the season of their celebration. At Alexandria images of Aphrodite and Adonis were displayed on two couches; beside them were set ripe fruits of all kinds, cakes, plants growing in flower-pots, and green bowers twined with anise. The marriage of the lovers was celebrated one day, and on the morrow women attired as mourners, with streaming hair and bared

The festival at Alexandria.

---

[1] Plutarch, *Alcibiades*, 18; *id.*, *Nicias*, 13; Zenobius, *Centur.* i. 49; Theocritus, xv. 132 *sqq.*; Eustathius on Homer, *Od.* xi. 590.

[2] Besides Lucian (cited below) see Origen, *Selecta in Ezechielem* (Migne's *Patrologia Graeca*, xiii. 800), δοκοῦσι γὰρ κατ' ἐνιαυτὸν τελετάς τινας ποιεῖν πρῶτον μὲν ὅτι θρηνοῦσιν αὐτὸν [scil. Ἄδωνιν] ὡς τεθνηκότα, δεύτερον δὲ ὅτι χαίρουσιν ἐπ' αὐτῷ ὡς ἀπὸ νεκρῶν ἀναστάντι. Jerome, *Commentar. in Ezechielem*, viii. 13, 14 (Migne's *Patrologia Latina*, xxv. 82, 83): "*Quem nos* Adonidem *interpretati sumus, et Hebraeus et Syrus sermo* THAMUZ (תמוז) *vocat: unde quia juxta gentilem fabulam, in mense Junis amasius Veneris et pulcherrimus juvenis occisus, et deinceps revixisse narratur, eundem Junium mensem eodem appellant nomine, et anniversariam ei celebrant solemni-* tatem, *in qua plangitur a mulieribus quasi mortuus, et postea reviviscens canitur atque laudatur . . . inter- fectionem et resurrectionem Adonidis planctu et gaudio prosequens.*" Cyril of Alexandria, *In Isaiam*, lib. ii. tomus iii. (Migne's *Patrologia Graeca*, lxx. 441), ἐπλάττοντο τοίνυν Ἕλληνες ἑορτὴν ἐπὶ τούτῳ τοιαύτην. Προσεποιοῦντο μὲν γὰρ λυπουμένη τῇ Ἀφροδίτῃ, διὰ τὸ τεθνάναι τὸν Ἄδωνιν, συνολοφύρεσθαι καὶ θρηνεῖν· ἀνελθούσης δὲ ἐξ ᾅδου, καὶ μὴν καὶ ηὑρῆσθαι λεγούσης τὸν ζητούμενον, συνήδεσθαι καὶ ἀνασκιρτᾶν· καὶ μέχρι τῶν καθ' ἡμᾶς καιρῶν ἐν τοῖς κατ' Ἀλεξάνδρειαν ἱεροῖς ἐτελεῖτο τὸ παίγνιον τοῦτο. From this testimony of Cyril we learn that the festival of the death and resurrection of Adonis was celebrated at Alexandria down to his time, that is, down to the fourth or even the fifth century, long after the official establishment of Christianity.

breasts, bore the image of the dead Adonis to the sea-shore and committed it to the waves. Yet they sorrowed not without hope, for they sang that the lost one would come back again.[1] The date at which this Alexandrian ceremony was observed is not expressly stated ; but from the mention of the ripe fruits it has been inferred that it took place in late summer.[2] In the great Phoenician sanctuary of Astarte at Byblus the death of Adonis was annually mourned, to the shrill wailing notes of the flute, with weeping, lamentation, and beating of the breast ; but next day he was believed to come to life again and ascend up to heaven in the presence of his worshippers. The disconsolate believers, left behind on earth, shaved their heads as the Egyptians did on the death of the divine bull Apis ; women who could not bring themselves to sacrifice their beautiful tresses had to give themselves up to strangers on a certain day of the festival, and to dedicate to Astarte the wages of their shame.[3]

The festival at Byblus.

This Phoenician festival appears to have been a vernal one, for its date was determined by the discoloration of the river Adonis, and this has been observed by modern travellers to occur in spring. At that season the red earth washed down from the mountains by the rain tinges the water of the river, and even the sea, for a great way with a blood-red hue, and the crimson stain was believed to be the blood of Adonis, annually wounded to death by the boar on Mount Lebanon.[4] Again, the

Date of the festival at Byblus.

---

[1] Theocritus, xv.

[2] W. Mannhardt, *Antike Wald- und Feldkulte* (Berlin, 1877), p. 277.

[3] Lucian, *De dea Syria*, 6. See above, p. 38. The flutes used by the Phoenicians in the lament for Adonis are mentioned by Athenaeus (iv. 76, p. 174 F), and by Pollux (iv. 76), who say that the same name *gingras* was applied by the Phoenicians both to the flute and to Adonis himself. Compare F. C. Movers, *Die Phoenizier*, i. 243 *sq.* We have seen that flutes were also played in the Babylonian rites of Tammuz (above, p. 9). Lucian's words, ἐς τὸν ἠέρα πέμπουσι, imply that the ascension of the god was supposed to take place in the

presence, if not before the eyes, of the worshipping crowds. The devotion of Byblus to Adonis is noticed also by Strabo (xvi. 2. 18, p. 755).

[4] Lucian, *De dea Syria*, 8. The discoloration of the river and the sea was observed by H. Maundrell on $\frac{17}{27}$ March $\frac{1696}{1697}$. See his *Journey from Aleppo to Jerusalem, at Easter, A.D. 1697*, Fourth Edition (Perth, 1800), pp. 59 *sq.* ; *id.*, in Bohn's *Early Travels in Palestine*, edited by Thomas Wright (London, 1848), pp. 411 *sq.* Renan remarked the discoloration at the beginning of February (*Mission de Phénicie*, p. 283). In his well-known lines on the subject

The
anemone
and the
red rose
the flowers
of Adonis.
scarlet anemone is said to have sprung from the blood of
Adonis, or to have been stained by it ;[1] and as the anemone
blooms in Syria about Easter, this may be thought to show
that the festival of Adonis, or at least one of his festivals,
was held in spring.   The name of the flower is probably
derived from Naaman (" darling "), which seems to have been
an epithet of Adonis.   The Arabs still call the anemone
" wounds of the Naaman."[2]   The red rose also was said to
owe its hue to the same sad occasion ; for Aphrodite,
hastening to her wounded lover, trod on a bush of white
roses ; the cruel thorns tore her tender flesh, and her sacred
blood dyed the white roses for ever red.[3]   It would be idle,
perhaps, to lay much weight on evidence drawn from the
calendar of flowers, and in particular to press an argument
so fragile as the bloom of the rose.   Yet so far as it
counts at all, the tale which links the damask rose with
the death of Adonis points to a summer rather than to
a spring celebration of his passion.   In Attica, certainly,
the festival fell at the height of summer.   For the fleet
which Athens fitted out against Syracuse, and by the destruction of which her power was permanently crippled,
sailed at midsummer, and by an ominous coincidence the
sombre rites of Adonis were being celebrated at the very
time.   As the troops marched down to the harbour to
embark, the streets through which they passed were lined
with coffins and corpse-like effigies, and the air was rent
with the noise of women wailing for the dead Adonis.   The
circumstance cast a gloom over the sailing of the most
splendid armament that Athens ever sent to sea.[4]   Many

Milton has laid the mourning in
summer :—

> " *Thammuz came next behind,*
> *Whose annual wound in Lebanon*
>   *allur'd*
> *The Syrian damsels to lament his fate*
> *In amorous ditties all a summer's day.*"

[1] Ovid, *Metam.* x. 735 ; Servius on
Virgil, *Aen.* v. 72 ; J. Tzetzes, *Schol.
on Lycophron*, 831.   Bion, on the other
hand, represents the anemone as sprung
from the tears of Aphrodite (*Idyl.* i. 66).
[2] W. Robertson Smith, " Ctesias
and the Semiramis Legend," *English*

Historical Review, ii. (1887) p. 307,
following Lagarde.   Compare W. W.
Graf Baudissin, *Adonis und Esmun*,
pp. 88 *sq.*
[3] J. Tzetzes, *Schol. on Lycophron*,
831 ; *Geoponica*, xi. 17 ; *Mythographi
Graeci*, ed. A. Westermann, p. 359.
Compare Bion, *Idyl.* i. 66 ; Pausanias,
vi. 24. 7 ; Philostratus, *Epist.* i. and
iii.
[4] Plutarch, *Alcibiades*, 18 ; *id.*,
Nicias, 13.   The date of the sailing
of the fleet is given by Thucydides
(vi. 30, θέρους μεσοῦντος ἤδη), who, with
his habitual contempt for the supersti-

ages afterwards, when the Emperor Julian made his first entry into Antioch, he found in like manner the gay, the luxurious capital of the East plunged in mimic grief for the annual death of Adonis : and if he had any presentiment of coming evil, the voices of lamentation which struck upon his ear must have seemed to sound his knell.[1]

The resemblance of these ceremonies to the Indian and European ceremonies which I have described elsewhere is obvious. In particular, apart from the somewhat doubtful date of its celebration, the Alexandrian ceremony is almost identical with the Indian.[2] In both of them the marriage of two divine beings, whose affinity with vegetation seems indicated by the fresh plants with which they are surrounded, is celebrated in effigy, and the effigies are afterwards mourned over and thrown into the water.[3] From the similarity of these customs to each other and to the spring and midsummer customs of modern Europe we should naturally expect that they all admit of a common explanation. Hence, if the explanation which I have adopted of the latter is correct, the ceremony of the death and resurrection of Adonis must also have been a dramatic representation of the decay and revival of plant life. The inference thus based on the resemblance of the customs is confirmed by the following features in the legend and ritual of Adonis. His affinity with vegetation comes out at once in the common story of his birth. He was said to have been born from a myrrh-tree, the bark of which bursting, after a ten months' gestation, allowed the lovely infant to come forth. According to some, a boar rent the bark with his tusk and so opened a passage for the babe. A faint rationalistic colour was given to the legend by saying that his mother was a woman named Myrrh, who had been

Marginal notes: Resemblance of these rites to Indian and European ceremonies.

The death and resurrection of Adonis a mythical expression for the annual decay and revival of plant life.

---

tion of his countrymen, disdains to notice the coincidence. Adonis was also bewailed by the Argive women (Pausanias, ii. 20. 6), but we do not know at what season of the year the lamentation took place. Inscriptions prove that processions in honour of Adonis were held in the Piraeus, and that a society of his worshippers existed at Loryma in Caria. See G.

Dittenberger, *Sylloge Inscriptionum Graecarum,*[2] Nos. 726, 741 (vol. ii. pp. 564, 604).

[1] Ammianus Marcellinus, xxii. 9. 15.

[2] *The Dying God*, pp. 261-266.

[3] In the Alexandrian ceremony, however, it appears to have been the image of Adonis only which was thrown into the sea.

turned into a myrrh-tree soon after she had conceived the child.[1] The use of myrrh as incense at the festival of Adonis may have given rise to the fable.[2] We have seen that incense was burnt at the corresponding Babylonian rites,[3] just as it was burnt by the idolatrous Hebrews in honour of the Queen of Heaven,[4] who was no other than Astarte. Again, the story that Adonis spent half, or according to others a third, of the year in the lower world and the rest of it in the upper world,[5] is explained most simply and naturally by supposing that he represented vegetation, especially the corn, which lies buried in the earth half the year and reappears above ground the other half. Certainly of the annual phenomena of nature there is none which suggests so obviously the idea of death and resurrection as the disappearance and reappearance of vegetation in autumn and spring. Adonis has been taken for the sun ; but there is nothing in the sun's annual course within the temperate and tropical zones to suggest that he is dead for half or a third of the year and alive for the other half or two-thirds. He might, indeed, be conceived as weakened in winter, but dead he could not be thought to be ; his daily reappearance contradicts the supposition.[6] Within the Arctic Circle, where the sun annually disappears for a continuous period which varies from twenty-four hours to six months according to the latitude, his yearly death and resurrection would certainly be an obvious idea ; but no one except the unfortunate

Adonis sometimes taken for the sun.

---

[1] Apollodorus, *Bibliotheca*, iii. 14.4 ; Scholiast on Theocritus, i. 109 ; Antoninus Liberalis, *Transform.* 34 ; J. Tzetzes, *Scholia on Lycophron*, 829 ; Ovid, *Metamorph.* x. 489 *sqq.* ; Servius on Virgil, *Aen.* v. 72, and on *Bucol.* x. 18 ; Hyginus, *Fab.* 58, 164 ; Fulgentius, iii. 8. The word Myrrha or Smyrna is borrowed from the Phoenician (Liddell and Scott, *Greek Lexicon, s.v.* σμύρνα). Hence the mother's name. as well as the son's, was taken directly from the Semites.

[2] W. Mannhardt, *Antike Wald- und Feldkulte*, p. 383, note [2].

[3] Above, p. 9.

[4] Jeremiah xliv. 17-19.

[5] Scholiast on Theocritus, iii. 48 ; Hyginus, *Astronom.* ii. 7 ; Lucian, *Dialog. deor.* xi. 1 ; Cornutus, *Theologiae Graecae Compendium*, 28, p. 54, ed. C. Lang (Leipsic, 1881) ; Apollodorus, *Bibliotheca*, iii. 14. 4.

[6] The arguments which tell against the solar interpretation of Adonis are stated more fully by the learned and candid scholar Graf Baudissin (*Adonis und Esmun*, pp. 169 *sqq.*), who himself formerly accepted the solar theory but afterwards rightly rejected it in favour of the view "*dass Adonis die Frühlingsvegetation darstellt, die im Sommer abstirbt*" (*op. cit.* p. 169).

astronomer Bailly [1] has maintained that the Adonis worship came from the Arctic regions. On the other hand, the annual death and revival of vegetation is a conception which readily presents itself to men in every stage of savagery and civilization ; and the vastness of the scale on which this ever-recurring decay and regeneration takes place, together with man's intimate dependence on it for subsistence, combine to render it the most impressive annual occurrence in nature, at least within the temperate zones. It is no wonder that a phenomenon so important, so striking, and so universal should, by suggesting similar ideas, have given rise to similar rites in many lands. We may, therefore, accept as probable an explanation of the Adonis worship which accords so well with the facts of nature and with the analogy of similar rites in other lands. Moreover, the explanation is countenanced by a considerable body of opinion amongst the ancients themselves, who again and again interpreted the dying and reviving god as the reaped and sprouting grain.[2]

[1] Bailly, *Lettres sur l' Origine des Sciences* (London and Paris, 1777), pp. 255 *sq.* ; *id.*, *Lettres sur l' Atlantide de Platon* (London and Paris, 1779), pp. 114-125. Carlyle has described how through the sleety drizzle of a dreary November day poor innocent Bailly was dragged to the scaffold amid the howls and curses of the Parisian mob (*French Revolution*, bk. v. ch. 2). My friend the late Professor C. Bendall showed me a book by a Hindoo gentleman in which it is seriously maintained that the primitive home of the Aryans was within the Arctic regions. See Bâl Gangâdhar Tilak, *The Arctic Home in the Vedas* (Poona and Bombay, 1903).

[2] Cornutus, *Theologiae Graecae Compendium*, 28, pp. 54 *sq.*, ed. C. Lang (Leipsic, 1881), τοιοῦτον γάρ τι καὶ παρ' Αἰγυπτίοις ὁ ζητούμενος καὶ ἀνευρισκόμενος ὑπὸ τῆς Ἴσιδος Ὄσιρις ἐμφαίνει καὶ παρὰ Φοίνιξιν ὁ ἀνὰ μέρος παρ' ἓξ μῆνας ὑπὲρ γῆν τε καὶ ὑπὸ γῆν γινόμενος Ἄδωνις, ἀπὸ τοῦ ἀδεῖν τοῖς ἀνθρώποις οὕτως ὠνομασμένου τοῦ Δημητριακοῦ καρποῦ. τοῦτον δὲ πλήξας κάπρος ἀνελεῖν λέγεται διὰ τὸ τὰς ὗς δοκεῖν ληιβότειρας εἶναι ἢ τὸν τῆς ὕνεως ὀδόντα αἰνιττομένων αὐτῶν, ὑφ' οὗ κατὰ γῆς κρύπτεται τὸ σπέρμα. Scholiast on Theocritus, iii. 48, ὁ Ἄδωνις, ἤγουν ὁ σῖτος ὁ σπειρόμενος, ἓξ μῆνας ἐν τῇ γῇ ποιεῖ ἀπὸ τῆς σπορᾶς καὶ ἓξ μῆνας ἔχει αὐτὸν ἡ Ἀφροδίτη, τουτέστιν ἡ εὐκρασία τοῦ ἀέρος. καὶ ἐκτότε λαμβάνουσιν αὐτὸν οἱ ἄνθρωποι. Origen, *Selecta in Ezechielem* (Migne's *Patrologia Graeca*, xiii. 800), οἱ δὲ περὶ τὴν ἀναγωγὴν τῶν Ἑλληνικῶν μύθων δεινοὶ καὶ μυθικῆς νομιζομένης θεολογίας, φασὶ τὸν Ἄδωνιν σύμβολον εἶναι τῶν τῆς γῆς καρπῶν, θρηνουμένων μὲν ὅτε σπείρονται, ἀνισταμένων δέ, καὶ διὰ τοῦτο χαίρειν ποιούντων τοὺς γεωργοὺς ὅτε φύονται. Jerome, *Commentar. in Ezechielem*, viii. 13, 14 (Migne's *Patrologia Latina*, xxv. 83), "*Eadem gentilitas hujuscemodi fabulas poetarum, quae habent turpitudinem, interpretatur subtiliter, interfectionem et resurrectionem Adonidis planctu et gaudio prosequens : quorum alterum in seminibus, quae moriuntur in terra, alterum in*

Tammuz
or Adonis
as a
corn-spirit
bruised and
ground in
a mill.

The character of Tammuz or Adonis as a corn-spirit comes out plainly in an account of his festival given by an Arabic writer of the tenth century. In describing the rites and sacrifices observed at the different seasons of the year by the heathen Syrians of Harran, he says : "Tammuz (July). In the middle of this month is the festival of el-Bûgât, that is, of the weeping women, and this is the Tâ-uz festival, which is celebrated in honour of the god Tâ-uz. The women bewail him, because his lord slew him so cruelly, ground his bones in a mill, and then scattered them to the wind. The women (during this festival) eat nothing which has been ground in a mill, but limit their diet to steeped wheat, sweet vetches, dates, raisins, and the like." [1] Tâ-uz, who is no other than Tammuz, is here like Burns's John Barleycorn—

---

segetibus, quibus mortua semina renascuntur, ostendi putat." Ammianus Marcellinus, xix. 1. 11, "*in sollemnibus Adonidis sacris, quod simulacrum aliquod esse frugum adultarnm religiones mysticae docent.*" *Id.* xxii. 9. 15, "*amato Veneris, ut fabulae fingunt, apri dente ferali deleto, quod in adulto flore sectarum est indicium frugum.*" Clement of Alexandria, *Hom.* 6. 11 (quoted by W. Mannhardt, *Antique Wald- und Feldkulte*, p. 281), λαμβάνουσι δὲ καὶ Ἄδωνιν εἰς ὡραίους καρπούς. *Etymologieum Magnum s.v.* Ἄδωνις κύριον· δύναται καὶ ὁ καρπὸς εἶναι ἄδωνις· οἷον ἀδώνειος καρπός, ἀρέσκων. Eusebius, *Praepar. Evang.* iii. 11. 9, Ἄδωνις τῆς τῶν τελείων καρπῶν ἐκτομῆς σύμβολον. Sallustius philosophus, "De diis et mundo," iv. *Fragmenta Philosophorum Graecorum*, ed. F. G. A. Mullach, iii. 32, οἱ Αἰγύπτιοι . . . αὐτὰ τὰ σώματα θεοὺς νομίσαντες . . . Ἴσιν μὲν τὴν γῆν . . . Ἄδωνιν δὲ καρπούς. Joannes Lydus, *De mensibus*, iv. 4, τῷ Ἀδώνιδι, τουτέστι τῷ Μαΐῳ . . . ἢ ὡς ἄλλοις, δοκεῖ, Ἄδωνις μέν ἐστιν ὁ καρπός, κτλ. The view that Tammuz or Adonis is a personification of the dying and reviving vegetation is now accepted by

many scholars. See P. Jensen, *Kosmologie der Babylonier* (Strasburg, 1890), p. 480 ; *id., Assyrisch-babylonische Mythen und Epen*, pp. 411, 560 ; H. Zimmern, in E. Schrader's *Keilinschriften und das Alte Testament*,[3] p. 397 ; A. Jeremias, *s.v.* "Nergal," in W. H. Roscher's *Lexikon der griech. und röm. Mythologie*, iii. 265 ; R. Wünsch, *Das Frühlingsfest der Insel Malta* (Leipsic, 1902), p. 21; M. J. Lagrange, *Études sur les Religions Sémitiques*,[2] pp. 306 *sqq.* ; W. W. Graf Baudissin, "Tammuz," *Realencyclopädie für protestantische Theologie und Kirchengeschichte*; *id., Esmun und Adonis*, pp. 81, 141, 169, etc. ; and Ed. Meyer, *Geschichte des Altertums*,[2] i. 2. pp. 394, 427. Prof. Jastrow regards Tammuz as a god both of the sun and of vegetation (*Religion of Babylonia and Assyria*, pp. 547, 564, 574, 588). But such a combination of disparate qualities seems artificial and unlikely.

[1] D. Chwolsohn, *Die Ssabier und der Ssabismus* (St. Petersburg, 1856), ii. 27 ; *id., Ueber Tammûz und die Menschenverehrung bei den alten Babyloniern* (St. Petersburg, 1860), p. 38. Compare W. W. Graf Baudissin, *Adonis und Esmun*, pp. 111 *sqq.*

" They wasted o'er a scorching flame
  The marrow of his bones ;
  But a miller us'd him worst of all—
  For he crush'd him between two stones."

This concentration, so to say, of the nature of Adonis upon the cereal crops is characteristic of the stage of culture reached by his worshippers in historical times. They had left the nomadic life of the wandering hunter and herdsman far behind them ; for ages they had been settled on the land, and had depended for their subsistence mainly on the products of tillage. The berries and roots of the wilderness, the grass of the pastures, which had been matters of vital importance to their ruder forefathers, were now of little moment to them : more and more their thoughts and energies were engrossed by the staple of their life, the corn ; more and more accordingly the propitiation of the deities of fertility in general and of the corn-spirit in particular tended to become the central feature of their religion. The aim they set before themselves in celebrating the rites was thoroughly practical. It was no vague poetical sentiment which prompted them to hail with joy the rebirth of vegetation and to mourn its decline. Hunger, felt or feared, was the mainspring of the worship of Adonis.

It has been suggested by Father Lagrange that the mourning for Adonis was essentially a harvest rite designed to propitiate the corn-god, who was then either perishing under the sickles of the reapers, or being trodden to death under the hoofs of the oxen on the threshing-floor. While the men slew him, the women wept crocodile tears at home to appease his natural indignation by a show of grief for his death.[2] The theory fits in well with the dates of the festivals, which fell in spring or summer ; for spring and summer, not autumn, are the seasons of the barley and wheat harvests in the lands which worshipped Adonis.[3]

The mourning for Adonis interpreted as a harvest rite.

---

[1] The comparison is due to Felix Liebrecht (*Zur Volkskunde*, Heilbronn, 1879, p. 259).

[2] M. J. Lagrange, *Études sur les Religions Sémitiques*[2] (Paris, 1905), pp. 307 *sq.*

[3] Hence Philo of Alexandria dates the corn-reaping in the middle of spring (Μεσοῦντος δὲ ἔαρος ἄμητος ἐνίσταται, *De special. legibus*, i. 183, vol. v. p. 44, ed. L. Cohn). On this subject Professor W. M. Flinders Petrie writes to me : "The Coptic calendar puts on April 2 beginning of wheat harvest in Upper Egypt, May 2 wheat harvest, Lower Egypt.

Further, the hypothesis is confirmed by the practice of the Egyptian reapers, who lamented, calling upon Isis, when they cut the first corn;[1] and it is recommended by the analogous customs of many hunting tribes, who testify great respect for the animals which they kill and eat.[2]

But probably Adonis was a spirit of fruits, edible roots, and grass before he became a spirit of the cultivated corn.

Thus interpreted the death of Adonis is not the natural decay of vegetation in general under the summer heat or the winter cold; it is the violent destruction of the corn by man, who cuts it down on the field, stamps it to pieces on the threshing-floor, and grinds it to powder in the mill. That this was indeed the principal aspect in which Adonis presented himself in later times to the agricultural peoples of the Levant, may be admitted; but whether from the beginning he had been the corn and nothing but the corn,

---

Barley is two or three weeks earlier than wheat in Palestine, but probably less in Egypt. The Palestine harvest is about the time of that in North Egypt." With regard to Palestine we are told that "the harvest begins with the barley in April; in the valley of the Jordan it begins at the end of March. Between the end of the barley harvest and the beginning of the wheat harvest an interval of two or three weeks elapses. Thus as a rule the business of harvest lasts about seven weeks" (J. Benzinger, *Hebräische Archäologie*, Freiburg i. B. and Leipsic, 1894, p. 209). "The principal grain crops of Palestine are barley, wheat, lentils, maize, and millet. Of the latter there is very little, and it is all gathered in by the end of May. The maize is then only just beginning to shoot. In the hotter parts of the Jordan valley the barley harvest is over by the end of March, and throughout the country the wheat harvest is at its height at the end of May, excepting in the highlands of Galilee, where it is about a fortnight later" (H. B. Tristram, *The Land of Israel*, Fourth Edition, London, 1882, pp. 583 *sq.*). As to Greece, Professor E. A. Gardner tells me that harvest is from April to May in the plains and about a month later in the mountains. He adds that "barley may, then, be assigned to the latter

part of April, wheat to May in the lower ground, but you know the great difference of climate between different parts; there is the same difference of a month in the vintage." Mrs. Hawes (Miss Boyd), who excavated at Gournia, tells me that in Crete the barley is cut in April and the beginning of May, and that the wheat is cut and threshed from about the twentieth of June, though the dates naturally vary somewhat with the height of the place above the sea. June is also the season when the wheat is threshed in Euboea (R. A. Arnold, *From the Levant*, London, 1868, i. 250). Thus it seems possible that the spring festival of Adonis coincided with the cutting of the first barley in March, and his summer festival with the threshing of the last wheat in June. Father Lagrange (*op. cit.* pp. 305 *sq.*) argues that the rites of Adonis were always celebrated in summer at the solstice of June or soon afterwards. Baudissin also holds that the summer cèlebration is the only one which is clearly attested, and that if there was a celebration in spring it must have had a different signification than the death of the god. See his *Adonis und Esmun*, pp. 132 *sq.*

[1] Diodorus Siculus, i. 14. 2. See below, vol. ii. pp. 45 *sq.*

[2] *Spirits of the Corn and of the Wild*, ii. 180 *sqq.*, 204 *sqq.*

may be doubted.   At an earlier period he may have been
to the herdsman, above all, the tender herbage which
sprouts after rain, offering rich pasture. to the lean and
hungry cattle.   Earlier still he may have embodied the
spirit of the nuts and berries which the autumn woods
yield to the savage hunter and his squaw.   And just as
the husbandman must propitiate the spirit of the corn
which he consumes, so the herdsman must appease the
spirit of the grass and leaves which his cattle munch, and
the hunter must soothe the spirit of the roots which he digs,
and of the fruits which he gathers from the bough.   In
all cases the propitiation of the injured and angry sprite
would naturally comprise elaborate excuses and apologies,
accompanied by loud lamentations at his decease whenever,
through some deplorable accident or necessity, he happened
to be murdered as well as robbed.   Only we must bear in
mind that the savage hunter and herdsman of those early
days had probably not yet attained to the abstract idea of
vegetation in general ; and that accordingly, so far as Adonis
existed for them at all, he must have been the *Adon* or lord
of each individual tree and plant rather than a personification of vegetable life as a whole.   Thus there would be as
many Adonises as there were trees and shrubs, and each
of them might expect to receive satisfaction for any damage
done to his person or property.   And year by year, when
the trees were deciduous, every Adonis would seem to bleed
to death with the red leaves of autumn and to come to life
again with the fresh green of spring.

We have seen reason to think that in early times
Adonis was sometimes personated by a living man who
died a violent death in the character of the god.   Further,
there is evidence which goes to show that among the
agricultural peoples of the Eastern Mediterranean, the corn-
spirit, by whatever name he was known, was often represented, year by year, by human victims slain on the harvest-
field.[1]   If that was so, it seems likely that the propitiation
of the corn-spirit would tend to fuse to some extent with
the worship of the dead.   For the spirits of these victims

The propitiation of the corn-spirit may have fused with the worship of the dead.

[1] W. Mannhardt, *Mythologische For-*   *Spirits of the Corn and of the Wild,*
schungen (Strasburg, 1884), pp. 1 *sqq.*;   i. 216 *sqq.*

might be thought to return to life in the ears which they had fattened with their blood, and to die a second death at the reaping of the corn. Now the ghosts of those who have perished by violence are surly and apt to wreak their vengeance on their slayers whenever an opportunity offers. Hence the attempt to appease the souls of the slaughtered victims would naturally blend, at least in the popular conception, with the attempt to pacify the slain corn-spirit. And as the dead came back in the sprouting corn, so they might be thought to return in the spring flowers, waked from their long sleep by the soft vernal airs. They had been laid to their rest under the sod. What more natural than to imagine that the violets and the hyacinths, the roses and the anemones, sprang from their dust, were empurpled or incarnadined by their blood, and contained some portion of their spirit?

> " *I sometimes think that never blows so red*
> *The Rose as where some buried Caesar bled;*
> *That every Hyacinth the Garden wears*
> *Dropt in her Lap from some once lovely Head.*

> " *And this reviving Herb whose tender Green*
> *Fledges the River-Lip on which we lean—*
> *Ah, lean upon it lightly, for who knows*
> *From what once lovely Lip it springs unseen ?* "

In the summer after the battle of Landen, the most sanguinary battle of the seventeenth century in Europe, the earth, saturated with the blood of twenty thousand slain, broke forth into millions of poppies, and the traveller who passed that vast sheet of scarlet might well fancy that the earth had indeed given up her dead.[1] At Athens the great Commemoration of the Dead fell in spring about the middle of March, when the early flowers are in bloom. Then the dead were believed to rise from their graves and go about the streets, vainly endeavouring to enter the temples and the dwellings, which were barred against these perturbed spirits with ropes, buckthorn, and pitch. The name of the festival, according to the most obvious and natural interpretation, means the Festival of Flowers, and the title would

The festival of the dead a festival of flowers.

[1] T. B. Macaulay, *History of England*, chapter xx. vol. iv. (London, 1855) p. 410.

fit well with the substance of the ceremonies if at that
season the poor ghosts were indeed thought to creep from
the narrow house with the opening flowers.[1]   There may
therefore be a measure of truth in the theory of Renan,
who saw in the Adonis worship a dreamy voluptuous cult
of death, conceived not as the King of Terrors, but as an
insidious enchanter who lures his victims to himself and
lulls them into an eternal sleep.   The infinite charm of
nature in the Lebanon, he thought, lends itself to religious
emotions of this sensuous, visionary sort, hovering vaguely
between pain and pleasure, between slumber and tears.[2]   It
would doubtless be a mistake to attribute to Syrian peasants
the worship of a conception so purely abstract as that of
death in general.   Yet it may be true that in their simple
minds the thought of the reviving spirit of vegetation was
blent with the very concrete notion of the ghosts of the
dead, who come to life again in spring days with the early
flowers, with the tender green of the corn and the many-
tinted blossoms of the trees.   Thus their views of the death
and resurrection of nature would be coloured by their views
of the death and resurrection of man, by their personal sorrows
and hopes and fears.   In like manner we cannot doubt that
Renan's theory of Adonis was itself deeply tinged by
passionate memories, memories of the slumber akin to death
which sealed his own eyes on the slopes of the Lebanon,
memories of the sister who sleeps in the land of Adonis
never again to wake with the anemones and the roses.

---

[1] This explanation of the name
Anthesteria, as applied to a festival of
the dead, is due to Mr. R. Wünsch
(*Das Frühlingsfest der Insel Malta*,
Leipsic, 1902, pp. 43 *sqq.*).   I cannot
accept the late Dr. A. W. Verrall's
ingenious derivation of the word from
a verb ἀναθέσσασθαι in the sense of
"to conjure up" ("The Name Anthesteria," *Journal of Hellenic Studies*,
xx. (1900) pp. 115-117).   As to
the festival see E. Rohde, *Psyche* [3]
(Tübingen and Leipsic, 1903), i. 236

sqq. ; Miss J. E. Harrison, *Prolego-
mena to the Study of Greek Religion* [2]
(Cambridge, 1908), pp. 32 *sqq.*   In
Annam people offer food to their dead
on the graves when the earth begins
to grow green in spring.   The ceremony takes place on the third day of
the third month, the sun then entering
the sign of Taurus.   See Paul Giran,
Magie et Religion Annamites (Paris,
1912), pp. 423 *sq.*

[2] E. Renan, *Mission de Phénicie*
(Paris, 1864), p. 216.

CHAPTER X

THE GARDENS OF ADONIS

Pots of corn, herbs, and flowers, called the gardens of Adonis.
PERHAPS the best proof that Adonis was a deity of vegetation, and especially of the corn, is furnished by the gardens of Adonis, as they were called. These were baskets or pots filled with earth, in which wheat, barley, lettuces, fennel, and various kinds of flowers were sown and tended for eight days, chiefly or exclusively by women. Fostered by the sun's heat, the plants shot up rapidly, but having no root they withered as rapidly away, and at the end of eight days were carried out with the images of the dead Adonis, and flung with them into the sea or into springs.[1]

These gardens of Adonis were charms to promote the growth of vegetation.
These gardens of Adonis are most naturally interpreted as representatives of Adonis or manifestations of his power; they represented him, true to his original nature, in vegetable form, while the images of him, with which they were carried out and cast into the water, portrayed him in his later human shape. All these Adonis ceremonies, if I am right, were originally intended as charms to promote the growth

---

[1] For the authorities see Raoul Rochette, "Mémoire sur les jardins d'Adonis," *Revue Archéologique*, viii. (1851) pp. 97-123; W. Mannhardt, *Antike Wald- und Feldkulte*, p. 279, note [2], and p. 280, note [2]. To the authorities cited by Mannhardt add Theophrastus, *Hist. Plant.* vi. 7. 3; *id., De Causis Plant.* i. 12. 2; Gregorius Cyprius, i. 7; Macarius, i. 63; Apostolius, i. 34; Diogenianus, i. 14; Plutarch, *De sera num. vind.* 17. Women only are mentioned as planting the gardens of Adonis by Plutarch, *l.c.*; Julian, *Convivium*, p. 329 ed. Spanheim (p. 423 ed. Hertlein); Eustathius on Homer, *Od.* xi. 590. On the other hand, Apostolius and Diogenianus (*ll.cc.*) say φυτεύοντες ἢ φυτεύουσαι. The earliest extant Greek writer who mentions the gardens of Adonis is Plato (*Phaedrus*, p. 276 B). The procession at the festival of Adonis is mentioned in an Attic inscription of 302 or 301 B.C. (G. Dittenberger, *Sylloge Inscriptionum Graecarum*,[2] vol. ii. p. 564, No. 726). Gardens of Adonis are perhaps alluded to by Isaiah (xvii. 10, with the commentators).

or revival of vegetation; and the principle by which they were supposed to produce this effect was homoeopathic or imitative magic. For ignorant people suppose that by mimicking the effect which they desire to produce they actually help to produce it; thus by sprinkling water they make rain, by lighting a fire they make sunshine, and so on. Similarly, by mimicking the growth of crops they hope to ensure a good harvest. The rapid growth of the wheat and barley in the gardens of Adonis was intended to make the corn shoot up; and the throwing of the gardens and of the images into the water was a charm to secure a due supply of fertilizing rain.[1] The same, I take it, was the object of throwing the effigies of Death and the Carnival into water in the corresponding ceremonies of modern Europe.[2] Certainly the custom of drenching with water a leaf-clad person, who undoubtedly personifies vegetation, is still resorted to in Europe for the express purpose of producing rain.[3] Similarly the custom of throwing water on the last corn cut at harvest, or on the person who brings it home (a custom observed in Germany and France, and till quite lately in England and Scotland), is in some places practised with the avowed intent to procure rain for the next year's crops. Thus in Wallachia and amongst the Roumanians in Transylvania, when a girl is bringing home a crown made of the last ears of corn cut at harvest, all who meet her hasten to throw water on her, and two farm-servants are placed at the door for the purpose; for they believe that if this were not done, the crops next year would perish from drought.[4] So

The throwing of the "gardens" into water was a rain-charm.

Parallel European customs of drenching the corn with water at harvest or sowing.

---

[1] In hot southern countries like Egypt and the Semitic regions of Western Asia, where vegetation depends chiefly or entirely upon irrigation, the purpose of the charm is doubtless to secure a plentiful flow of water in the streams. But as the ultimate object and the charms for securing it are the same in both cases, I have not thought it necessary always to point out the distinction.

[2] *The Dying God*, pp. 232, 233 *sqq.*

[3] *The Magic Art and the Evolution of Kings*, i. 272 *sqq.*

[4] W. Mannhardt, *Der Baumkultus der Germanen und ihrer Nachbar-*

stämme (Berlin, 1875), p. 214; W. Schmidt, *Das Jahr und seine Tage in Meinung und Branch der Romänen Siebenbürgens* (Hermannstadt, 1866), pp. 18 *sq.* The custom of throwing water on the last wagon-load of corn returning from the harvest-field has been practised within living memory in Wigtownshire, and at Orwell in Cambridgeshire. See J. G. Frazer, "Notes on Harvest Customs," *Folk-lore Journal,* vii. (1889) pp. 50, 51. (In the first of these passages the Orwell at which the custom used to be observed is said to be in Kent; this was a mistake of mine, which my informant, the Rev.

Use of
water as a
rain-charm
at harvest
and
sowing.

amongst the Saxons of Transylvania, the person who wears
the wreath made of the last corn cut is drenched with water
to the skin ; for the wetter he is, the better will be next
year's harvest, and the more grain there will be threshed out.
Sometimes the wearer of the wreath is the reaper who cut
the last corn.[1] In Northern Euboea, when the corn-sheaves
have been piled in a stack, the farmer's wife brings a pitcher
of water and offers it to each of the labourers that he may
wash his hands. Every man, after he has washed his hands,
sprinkles water on the corn and on the threshing-floor,
expressing at the same time a wish that the corn may last
long. Lastly, the farmer's wife holds the pitcher slantingly
and runs at full speed round the stack without spilling a
drop, while she utters a wish that the stack may endure as
long as the circle she has just described.[2] At the spring
ploughing in Prussia, when the ploughmen and sowers
returned in the evening from their work in the fields, the
farmer's wife and the servants used to splash water over
them. The ploughmen and sowers retorted by seizing every
one, throwing them into the pond, and ducking them under
the water. The farmer's wife might claim exemption on
payment of a forfeit, but every one else had to be ducked.
By observing this custom they hoped to ensure a due
supply of rain for the seed.[3] Also after harvest in Prussia,
the person who wore a wreath made of the last corn cut
was drenched with water, while a prayer was uttered that
"as the corn had sprung up and multiplied through the
water, so it might spring up and multiply in the barn and
granary."[4] At Schlanow, in Brandenburg, when the sowers

E. B. Birks, formerly Fellow of Trinity
College, Cambridge, afterwards corrected.) Mr. R. F. Davis writes to
me (March 4, 1906) from Campbell
College, Belfast : " Between 30 and
40 years ago I was staying, as a very
small boy, at a Nottinghamshire farmhouse at harvest-time, and was allowed
—as a great privilege—to ride home
on the top of the last load. All the
harvesters followed the waggon, and
on reaching the farmyard we found the
maids of the farm gathered near the
gate, with bowls and buckets of water,
which they proceeded to throw on the

men, who got thoroughly drenched."
[1] G. A. Heinrich, *Agrarische Sitten
und Gebräuche unter den Sachsen
Siebenbürgens* (Hermanstadt, 1880), p.
24 ; H. von Wlislocki, *Sitten und
Brauch der Siebenbürger Sachsen* (Hamburg, 1888), p. 32.
[2] G. Drosinis, *Land und Leute in
Nord-Euböa* (Leipsic, 1884), p. 53.
[3] Matthäus Prätorius, *Deliciae Prussicae* (Berlin, 1871), p. 55 ; W. Mannhardt, *Baumkultus*, pp. 214 *sq.*, note.
[4] M. Prätorius, *op. cit.* p. 60 ; W.
Mannhardt, *Baumkultus*, p. 215,
note.

return home from the first sowing they are drenched with water "in order that the corn may grow."[1] In Anhalt on the same occasion the farmer is still often sprinkled with water by his family; and his men and horses, and even the plough, receive the same treatment. The object of the custom, as people at Arensdorf explained it, is "to wish fertility to the fields for the whole year."[2] So in Hesse, when the ploughmen return with the plough from the field for the first time, the women and girls lie in wait for them and slyly drench them with water.[3] Near Naaburg, in Bavaria, the man who first comes back from sowing or ploughing has a vessel of water thrown over him by some one in hiding.[4] At Hettingen in Baden the farmer who is about to begin the sowing of oats is sprinkled with water, in order that the oats may not shrivel up.[5] Before the Tusayan Indians of North America go out to plant their fields, the women sometimes pour water on them; the reason for doing so is that "as the water is poured on the men, so may water fall on the planted fields."[6] The Indians of Santiago Tepehuacan steep the seed of the maize in water before they sow it, in order that the god of the waters may bestow on the fields the needed moisture.[7]

The opinion that the gardens of Adonis are essentially charms to promote the growth of vegetation, especially of the crops, and that they belong to the same class of customs as those spring and midsummer folk-customs of modern Europe which I have described elsewhere,[8] does not rest for its evidence merely on the intrinsic probability of the case. Fortunately we are able to show that gardens of Adonis (if we may use the expression in a general sense) are still planted, first, by a primitive race at their sowing season,

Gardens of Adonis among the Oraons and Mundas of Bengal.

[1] H. Prahn, "Glaube und Brauch in der Mark Brandenburg," *Zeitschrift des Vereins für Volkskunde,* i. (1891) p. 186.

[2] O. Hartung, "Zur Volkskunde aus Anhalt," *Zeitschrift des Vereins für Volkskunde,* vii. (1897) p. 150.

[3] W. Kolbe, *Hessische Volks-Sitten und Gebräuche* (Marburg, 1888), p. 51.

[4] *Bavaria, Landes- und Volkskunde des Königreichs Bayern,* ii. (Munich, 1863) p. 297.

[5] E. H. Meyer, *Badisches Volksleben* (Strasburg, 1900), p. 420.

[6] J. Walter Fewkes, "The Tusayan New Fire Ceremony," *Proceedings of the Boston Society of Natural History,* xxvi. (1895) p. 446.

[7] "Lettre du curé de Santiago Tepehuacan à son évêque," *Bulletin de la Société de Géographie* (Paris), Deuxième Série, ii. (1834) pp. 181 *sq.*

[8] *The Magic Art and the Evolution of Kings,* ii. 59 *sqq.*

and, second, by European peasants at midsummer. Amongst the Oraons and Mundas of Bengal, when the time comes for planting out the rice which has been grown in seed-beds, a party of young people of both sexes go to the forest and cut a young Karma-tree, or the branch of one. Bearing it in triumph they return dancing, singing, and beating drums, and plant it in the middle of the village dancing-ground. A sacrifice is offered to the tree; and next morning the youth of both sexes, linked arm-in-arm, dance in a great circle round the Karma-tree, which is decked with strips of coloured cloth and sham bracelets and necklets of plaited straw. As a preparation for the festival, the daughters of the headman of the village cultivate blades of barley in a peculiar way. The seed is sown in moist, sandy soil, mixed with turmeric, and the blades sprout and unfold of a pale-yellow or primrose colour. On the day of the festival the girls take up these blades and carry them in baskets to the dancing-ground, where, prostrating themselves reverentially, they place some of the plants before the Karma-tree. Finally, the Karma-tree is taken away and thrown into a stream or tank.[1] The meaning of planting these barley blades and then presenting them to the Karma-tree is hardly open to question. Trees are supposed to exercise a quickening influence upon the growth of crops, and amongst the very people in question — the Mundas or Mundaris — "the grove deities are held responsible for the crops." [2] Therefore, when at the season for planting out the rice the Mundas bring in a tree and treat it with so much respect, their object can only be to foster thereby the growth of the rice which is about to be planted out; and the custom of causing barley blades to sprout rapidly and then presenting them to the tree must be intended to subserve the same purpose, perhaps by reminding the tree-spirit of his duty towards the crops, and stimulating his activity by this visible example of rapid vegetable growth. The throwing of the Karma-tree into the water is to be interpreted as a rain-

[1] E. T. Dalton, *Descriptive Ethnology of Bengal* (Calcutta, 1872), p. 259.

[2] E. T. Dalton, *op. cit.* p. 188.

As to the influence which trees are supposed to exercise on the crops, see *The Magic Art and the Evolution of Kings*, ii. 47 *sqq.*

charm. Whether the barley blades are also thrown into the water is not said ; but if my interpretation of the custom is right, probably they are so. A distinction between this Bengal custom and the Greek rites of Adonis is that in the former the tree-spirit appears in his original form as a tree ; whereas in the Adonis worship he appears in human form, represented as a dead man, though his vegetable nature is indicated by the gardens of Adonis, which are, so to say, a secondary manifestation of his original power as a tree-spirit.

Gardens of Adonis are cultivated also by the Hindoos, with the intention apparently of ensuring the fertility both of the earth and of mankind. Thus at Oodeypoor in Rajputana a festival is held " in honour of Gouri, or Isani, the goddess of abundance, the Isis of Egypt, the Ceres of Greece. Like the Rajpoot Saturnalia, which it follows, it belongs to the vernal equinox, when nature in these regions proximate to the tropic is in the full expanse of her charms, and the matronly Gouri casts her golden mantle over the verdant Vassanti, personification of spring. Then the fruits exhibit their promise to the eye ; the kohil fills the ear with melody ; the air is impregnated with aroma, and the crimson poppy contrasts with the spikes of golden grain to form a wreath for the beneficent Gouri. Gouri is one of the names of Isa or Parvati, wife of the greatest of the gods, Mahadeva or Iswara, who is conjoined with her in these rites, which almost exclusively appertain to the women. The meaning of *gouri* is ' yellow,' emblematic of the ripened harvest, when the votaries of the goddess adore her effigies, which are those of a matron painted the colour of ripe corn." The rites begin when the sun enters the sign of the Ram, the opening of the Hindoo year. An image of the goddess Gouri is made of earth, and a smaller one of her husband Iswara, and the two are placed together. A small trench is next dug, barley is sown in it, and the ground watered and heated artificially till the grain sprouts, when the women dance round it hand in hand, invoking the blessing of Gouri on their husbands. After that the young corn is taken up and distributed by the women to the men, who wear it in their turbans. Every wealthy family, or at least every sub-division of the city, has its own image. These and other

Gardens of Adonis in Rajputana.

rites, known only to the initiated, occupy several days, and are performed within doors. Then the images of the goddess and her husband are decorated and borne in procession to a beautiful lake, whose deep blue waters mirror the cloudless Indian sky, marble palaces, and orange groves. Here the women, their hair decked with roses and jessamine, carry the image of Gouri down a marble staircase to the water's edge, and dance round it singing hymns and lovesongs. Meantime the goddess is supposed to bathe in the water. No men take part in the ceremony; even the image of Iswara, the husband-god, attracts little attention.[1] In these rites the distribution of the barley shoots to the men, and the invocation of a blessing on their husbands by the wives, point clearly to the desire of offspring as one motive for observing the custom. The same motive probably explains the use of gardens of Adonis at the marriage of Brahmans in the Madras Presidency. Seeds of five or nine sorts are mixed and sown in earthen pots, which are made specially for the purpose and are filled with earth. Bride and bridegroom water the seeds both morning and evening for four days; and on the fifth day the seedlings are thrown, like the real gardens of Adonis, into a tank or river.[2]

Gardens of Adonis in North-Western and Central India.

In the Himalayan districts of North-Western India the cultivators sow barley, maize, pulse, or mustard in a basket of earth on the twenty-fourth day of the fourth month (*Asárh*), which falls about the middle of July. Then on the last day of the month they place amidst the new sprouts small clay images of Mahadeo and Parvati and worship them in remembrance of the marriage of those deities. Next day they cut down the green stalks and wear them in their head-dress.[3] Similar is the barley feast known as Jâyî or Jawâra in Upper India and as Bhujariya in the Central Provinces. On the seventh day of the light half of the month Sâwan grains of barley are sown in a pot of manure, and spring up so quickly that by the end of the

---

[1] Lieut.-Col. James Tod, *Annals and Antiquities of Rajast'han*, i. (London, 1829) pp. 570-572.

[2] G. F. D'Penha, "A Collection of Notes on Marriage Customs in the Madras Presidency," *Indian Anti-*

quary, xxv. (1896) p. 144; E. Thurston, *Ethnographic Notes in Southern India* (Madras, 1906), p. 2.

[3] E. T. Atkinson, *The Himalayan Districts of the North-Western Provinces of India*, ii. (Allahabad, 1884) p. 870.

month the vessel is full of long, yellowish-green stalks. On the first day of the next month, Bhâdon, the women and girls take the stalks out, throw the earth and manure into water, and distribute the plants among their male friends, who bind them in their turbans and about their dress.[1] At Sargal in the Central Provinces of India this ceremony is observed about the middle of September. None but women may take part in it, though crowds of men come to look on. Some little time before the festival wheat or other grain has been sown in pots ingeniously constructed of large leaves, which are held together by the thorns of a species of acacia. Having grown up in the dark, the stalks are of a pale colour. On the day appointed these gardens of Adonis, as we may call them, are carried towards a lake which abuts on the native city. The women of every family or circle of friends bring their own pots, and having laid them on the ground they dance round them. Then taking the pots of sprouting corn they descend to the edge of the water, wash the soil away from the pots, and distribute the young plants among their friends.[2] At the temple of the goddess Padma-vati, near Pandharpur in the Bombay Presidency, a Nine Nights' festival is held in the bright half of the month Ashvin (September—October). At this time a bamboo frame is hung in front of the image, and from it depend garlands of flowers and strings of wheaten cakes. Under the frame the floor in front of the pedestal is strewn with a layer of earth in which wheat is sown and allowed to sprout.[3] A similar rite is observed in the same month before the images of two other goddesses, Ambabai and Lakhubai, who also have temples at Pandharpur.[4]

[1] W. Crooke, *Popular Religion and Folk-lore of Northern India* (Westminster, 1896), ii. 293 *sq.* Compare Baboo Ishuree Dass, *Domestic Manners and Customs of the Hindoos of Northern India* (Benares, 1860), pp. 111 *sq.* According to the latter writer, the festival of Salono [not Salonan] takes place in August, and the barley is planted by women and girls in baskets a few days before the festival, to be thrown by them into a river or tank when the grain has sprouted to the height of a few inches.

[2] Mrs. J. C. Murray - Aynsley, "Secular and Religious Dances," *Folklore Journal*, v. (1887) pp. 253 *sq.* The writer thinks that the ceremony "probably fixes the season for sowing some particular crop."

[3] *Gazetteer of the Bombay Presidency*, xx. (Bombay, 1884) p. 454. This passage was pointed out to me by my friend Mr. W. Crooke.

[4] *Gazetteer of the Bombay Presidency*, xx. 443, 460.

Gardens of
Adonis in
Bavaria.

In some parts of Bavaria it is customary to sow flax
in a pot on the last three days of the Carnival ; from the
seed which grows best an omen is drawn as to whether the
early, the middle, or the late sowing will produce the best

Gardens of
Adonis on
St. John's
Day in
Sardinia.

crop.[1] In Sardinia the gardens of Adonis are still planted
in connexion with the great Midsummer festival which bears
the name of St. John.   At the end of March or on the first
of April a young man of the village presents himself to a girl,
and asks her to be his *comare* (gossip or sweetheart), offering
to be her *compare*.   The invitation is considered as an honour
by the girl's family, and is gladly accepted.   At the end of
May the girl makes a pot of the bark of the cork-tree, fills
it with earth, and sows a handful of wheat and barley in it.
The pot being placed in the sun and often watered, the corn
sprouts rapidly and has a good head by Midsummer Eve
(St. John's Eve, the twenty-third of June).   The pot is then
called *Erme* or *Nenneri*.   On St. John's Day the young man
and the girl, dressed in their best, accompanied by a long
retinue and preceded by children gambolling and frolicking,
move in procession to a church outside the village.   Here
they break the pot by throwing it against the door of the
church.   Then they sit down in a ring on the grass and eat
eggs and herbs to the music of flutes.   Wine is mixed in a
cup and passed round, each one drinking as it passes.
Then they join hands and sing " Sweethearts of St. John "
(*Compare e comare di San Giovanni*) over and over again,
the flutes playing the while.   When they tire of singing
they stand up and dance gaily in a ring till evening.   This
is the general, Sardinian custom.   As practised at Ozieri it
has some special features.   In May the pots are made of
cork - bark and planted with corn, as already described.
Then on the Eve of St. John the window-sills are draped
with rich cloths, on which the pots are placed, adorned with
crimson and blue silk and ribbons of various colours.   On
each of the pots they used formerly to place a statuette or
cloth doll dressed as a woman, or a Priapus-like figure made
of paste ; but this custom, rigorously forbidden by the
Church, has fallen into disuse.   The village swains go about

---

[1] *Bavaria, Landes- und Volkskunde des Königreichs Bayern* (Munich, 1860-
1867), ii. 298.

in a troop to look at the pots and their decorations and to
wait for the girls, who assemble on the public square to
celebrate the festival.   Here a great bonfire is kindled,
round which they dance and make merry.   Those who wish
to be " Sweethearts of St. John " act as follows.   The young
man stands on one side of the bonfire and the girl on the
other, and they, in a manner, join hands by each grasping
one end of a long stick, which they pass three times backwards and forwards across the fire, thus thrusting their hands
thrice rapidly into the flames.   This seals their relationship
to each other.   Dancing and music go on till late at night.[1]
The correspondence of these Sardinian pots of grain to the
gardens of Adonis seems complete, and the images formerly
placed in them answer to the images of Adonis which
accompanied his gardens.

Customs of the same sort are observed at the same
season in Sicily.   Pairs of boys and girls become gossips of
St. John on St. John's Day by drawing each a hair from his
or her head and performing various ceremonies over them.
Thus they tie the hairs together and throw them up in
the air, or exchange them over a potsherd, which they
afterwards break in two, preserving each a fragment with
pious care.   The tie formed in the latter way is supposed
to last for life.   In some parts of Sicily the gossips of St.
John present each other with plates of sprouting corn, lentils,
and canary seed, which have been planted forty days before
the festival.   The one who receives the plate pulls a stalk
of the young plants, binds it with a ribbon, and preserves it
among his or her greatest treasures, restoring the platter to
the giver.   At Catania the gossips exchange pots of basil
and great cucumbers ; the girls tend the basil, and the
thicker it grows the more it is prized.[2]

*Gardens of
Adonis on
St. John's
Day in
Sicily.*

---

[1] Antonio Bresciani, *Dei costumi
dell' isola di Sardegna comparati cogli
antichissimi popoli orientali* (Rome
and Turin, 1866), pp. 427 *sq.* ; R.
Tennant, *Sardinia and its Resources*
(Rome and London, 1885), p. 187 ; S.
Gabriele, " Usi dei contadini della
Sardegna," *Archivio per lo Studio delle
Tradizioni Popolari*, vii. (1888) pp.
469 *sq.*   Tennant says that the pots

are kept in a dark warm place, and
that the children leap across the fire.

[2] G. Pitrè, *Usi e Costumi, Credenze
e Pregiudizi del Popolo Siciliano*
(Palermo, 1889), ii. 271-278.   Compare *id., Spettacoli e Feste Popolari
Siciliane* (Palermo, 1881), pp. 297 *sq.*
In the Abruzzi also young men and
young women become gossips by ex-
changing nosegays on St. John's Day,

In these
Sardinian
and Sicilian
ceremonies
St. John
may have
taken the
place of
Adonis.

In these midsummer customs of Sardinia and Sicily it is possible that, as Mr. R. Wünsch supposes,[1] St. John has replaced Adonis. We have seen that the rites of Tammuz or Adonis were commonly celebrated about midsummer; according to Jerome, their date was June.[2] And besides their date and their similarity in respect of the pots of herbs and corn, there is another point of affinity between the two festivals, the heathen and the Christian. In both of them water plays a prominent part. At his midsummer festival in Babylon the image of Tammuz, whose name is said to mean " true son of the deep water," was bathed with pure water : at his summer festival in Alexandria the image of Adonis, with that of his divine mistress Aphrodite, was committed to the waves ; and at the midsummer celebration in Greece the gardens of Adonis were thrown into the sea or into springs. Now a great feature of the midsummer festival associated with the name of St. John is, or used to be, the custom of bathing in the sea, springs, rivers, or the dew on Midsummer Eve or the morning of Midsummer Day. Thus, for example, at Naples there is a church dedicated to St. John the Baptist under the name of St. John of the Sea (*S. Giovan a mare*) ; and 'it was an old practice for men and women to bathe in the sea on St. John's Eve, that is, on Midsummer Eve, believing that thus all their sins were washed away.[3] In the Abruzzi water is still supposed to acquire certain marvellous and beneficent properties on St. John's Night. They say that on that night the sun and moon bathe in the water. Hence many people take a bath in the sea or in a river at that season, especially at the moment of sunrise. At Castiglione a Casauria they go before sunrise to the Pescara River or to springs, wash their faces and hands, then gird themselves with twigs of bryony (*vitalba*) and twine the plant round their brows, in order that they may be free from pains. At Pescina boys and girls wash each other's faces in a river or a spring, then exchange kisses, and become gossips. The dew, also, that

Custom of
bathing in
water or
washing in
dew on
the Eve or
Day of St.
John (Midsummer
Eve or Midsummer
Day).

and the tie thus formed is regarded as sacred. See G. Finamore, *Credenze, Usi e Costumi Abruzzesi* (Palermo, 1890), pp. 165 *sq.*

[1] R. Wünsch, *Das Frühlingsfest der Insel Malta*, pp. 47-57.

[2] See above, pp. 10, note [1], 224 *sq.*, 226.

[3] J. Grimm, *Deutsche Mythologie*,[4] i. 490.

falls on St. John's Night is supposed in the Abruzzi to benefit whatever it touches, whether it be water, flowers, or the human body.   For that reason people put out vessels of water on the window-sills or the terraces, and wash themselves with the water in the morning in order to purify themselves and escape headaches and colds.   A still more efficacious mode of accomplishing the same end is to rise at the peep of dawn, to wet the hands in the dewy grass, and then to rub the moisture on the eyelids, the brow, and the temples, because the dew is believed to cure maladies of the head and eyes.   It is also a remedy for diseases of the skin. Persons who are thus afflicted should roll on the dewy grass.   When patients are prevented by their infirmity or any other cause from quitting the house, their friends will gather the dew in sheets or tablecloths and so apply it to the suffering part.[1]   At Marsala in Sicily there is a spring of water in a subterranean grotto called the Grotto of the Sibyl.   Beside it stands a church of St. John, which has been supposed to occupy the site of a temple of Apollo. On St. John's Eve, the twenty-third of June, women and girls visit the grotto, and by drinking of the prophetic water learn whether their husbands have been faithful to them in the year that is past, or whether they themselves will wed in the year that is to come.   Sick people, too, imagine that by bathing in the water, drinking of it, or ducking thrice in it in the name of the Trinity, they will be made whole.[2]   At Chiaramonte in Sicily the following custom is observed on St. John's Eve.   The men repair to one fountain and the women to another, and dip their heads thrice in the water, repeating at each ablution certain verses in honour of St. John.   They believe that this is a cure or preventive of the scald.[3]   When Petrarch visited Cologne, he chanced to

---

[1] G. Finamore, *Credenze, Usi e Costumi Abruzzesi*, pp. 156-160.   A passage in Isaiah (xxvi. 19) seems to imply that dew possessed the magical virtue of restoring the dead to life. In this passage of Isaiah the customs which I have cited in the text perhaps favour the ordinary interpretation of טַל אוֹרֹת as "dew of herbs" (compare 2 Kings iv. 39) against the interpretation

"dew of lights," which some modern commentators (Dillmann, Skinner, Whitehouse), following Jerome, have adopted.

[2] G. Pitrè, *Feste patronali in Sicilia* (Turin and Palermo, 1900), pp. 488, 491-493.

[3] G. Pitrè, *Spettacoli e Feste Popolari Siciliane*, p. 307.

arrive in the town on St. John's Eve. The sun was nearly
setting, and his host at once led him to the Rhine. A
strange sight there met his eyes, for the banks of the
river were covered with pretty women. The crowd was great
but good-humoured. From a rising ground on which he
stood the poet saw many of the women, girt with fragrant
herbs, kneel down on the water's edge, roll their sleeves
up above their elbows, and wash their white arms and hands
in the river, murmuring softly some words which the Italian
did not understand. He was told that the custom was a
very old one, much honoured in the observance ; for the
common folk, especially the women, believed that to wash
in the river on St. John's Eve would avert every misfortune
in the coming year.[1] On St. John's Eve the people of
Copenhagen used to go on pilgrimage to a neighbouring
spring, there to heal and strengthen themselves in the
water.[2] In Spain people still bathe in the sea or roll naked
in the dew of the meadows on St. John's Eve, believing that
this is a sovereign preservative against diseases of the skin.[3]
To roll in the dew on the morning of St. John's Day is also
esteemed a cure for diseases of the skin in Normandy and
Perigord. In Perigord a field of hemp is especially recommended for the purpose, and the patient should rub himself
with the plants on which he has rolled.[4] At Ciotat in
Provence, while the midsummer bonfire blazed, young people
used to plunge into the sea and splash each other vigorously.
At Vitrolles they bathed in a pond in order that they might
not suffer from fever during the year, and at Saint-Maries
they watered the horses to protect them from the itch.[5] A
custom of drenching people on this occasion with water
formerly prevailed in Toulon, Marseilles, and other towns of
the south of France. The water was squirted from syringes,
poured on the heads of passers-by from windows, and so

---

[1] Petrarch, *Epistolae de rebus fami-
liaribus*, i. 4 (vol. i. pp. 44-46 ed. J.
Fracassetti, Florence, 1859–1862).
The passage is quoted by J. Grimm,
Deutsche Mythologie,[4] i. 489 *sq*.

[2] J. Grimm, *op. cit.* i. 489.

[3] Letter of Dr. Otero Acevado, of
Madrid, *Le Temps*, September 1898.

[4] J. Lecœur, *Esquisses du Bocage*

Normand (Condé-sur-Noireau, 1883–
1887), ii. 8 ; A. de Nore, *Coutumes,
Mythes et Traditions des provinces de
France* (Paris and Lyons, 1846), p.
150.

[5] A. de Nore, *op. cit.* p. 20 ;
Bérenger-Féraud, *Réminiscences populaires de la Provence* (Paris, 1885),
pp. 135-141.

forth.[1] From Europe the practice of bathing in rivers and springs on St. John's Day appears to have passed with the Spaniards to the New World.[2]

It may perhaps be suggested that this wide-spread custom of bathing in water or dew on Midsummer Eve or Midsummer Day is purely Christian in origin, having been adopted as an appropriate mode of celebrating the day dedicated to the Baptist. But in point of fact the custom is older than Christianity, for it was denounced and forbidden as a heathen practice by Augustine,[3] and to this day it is practised at midsummer by the Mohammedan peoples of North Africa.[4] We may conjecture that the Church, unable to put down this relic of paganism, followed its usual policy of accommodation by bestowing on the rite of a Christian name and acquiescing, with a sigh, in its observance. And casting about for a saint to supplant a heathen patron of bathing, the Christian doctors could hardly have hit upon a more appropriate successor than St. John the Baptist.

But into whose shoes did the Baptist step? Was the displaced deity really Adonis, as the foregoing evidence seems to suggest? In Sardinia and Sicily it may have been so, for in these islands Semitic influence was certainly deep and probably lasting. The midsummer pastimes of Sardinian and Sicilian children may therefore be a direct continuation of the Carthaginian rites of Tammuz. Yet the midsummer festival seems too widely spread and too deeply rooted in Central and Northern Europe to allow us to trace it everywhere to an Oriental origin in general and to the cult of Adonis in particular. It has the air of a native of the soil rather than of an exotic imported from the East. We shall

[marginal note: The custom of bathing at midsummer is pagan, not Christian, in its origin.]

[marginal note: Old heathen festival of midsummer in Europe and the East.]

---

[1] A. Breuil, "Du Culte de St. Jean Baptiste," *Mémoires de la Société des Antiquaires de Picardie*, viii. (1845) pp. 237 *sq.* Compare *Balder the Beautiful*, i. 193 *sq.*

[2] Diego Duran, *Historia de las Indias de Nueva España*, edited by J. F. Ramirez (Mexico, 1867–1880), ii. 293.

[3] Augustine, *Opera*, v. (Paris, 1683) col. 903 ; *id.*, Pars Secunda, coll. 461 *sq.* The second of these passages occurs in a sermon of doubtful authen-

ticity. Both have been quoted by J. Grimm, *Deutsche Mythologie*,[4] i. 490.

[4] E. Doutté, *Magie et Religion dans l'Afrique du Nord* (Algiers, 1908), pp. 567 *sq.* ; E. Westermarck, "Midsummer Customs in Morocco," *Folklore*, xvi. (1905) pp. 31 *sq.* ; *id.*, *Ceremonies and Beliefs connected with Agriculture, Certain Dates of the Solar Year, and the Weather* (Helsingfors, 1913), pp. 84-86. See *Balder the Beautiful*, i. 216.

do better, therefore, to suppose that at a remote period similar modes of thought, based on similar needs, led men independently in many distant lands, from the North Sea to the Euphrates, to celebrate the summer solstice with rites which, while they differed in some things, yet agreed closely in others ; that in historical times a wave of Oriental influence, starting perhaps from Babylonia, carried the Tammuz or Adonis form of the festival westward till it met with native forms of a similar festival ; and that under pressure of the Roman civilization these different yet kindred festivals fused with each other and crystallized into a variety of shapes, which subsisted more or less separately side by side, till the Church, unable to suppress them altogether, stripped them so far as it could of their grosser features, and dexterously changing the names allowed them to pass muster as Christian. And what has just been said of the midsummer festivals probably applies, with the necessary modifications, to the spring festivals also. They, too, seem to have originated independently in Europe and the East, and after ages of separation to have amalgamated under the sway of the Roman Empire and the Christian Church. In Syria, as we have seen, there appears to have been a vernal celebration of Adonis ; and we shall presently meet with an undoubted instance of an Oriental festival of spring in the rites of Attis. Meantime we must return for a little to the midsummer festival which goes by the name of St. John.

Midsummer fires and midsummer couples in relation to vegetation.

The Sardinian practice of making merry round a great bonfire on St. John's Eve is an instance of a custom which has been practised at the midsummer festival from time immemorial in many parts of Europe. That custom has been more fully dealt with by me elsewhere.[1] The instances which I have cited in other parts of this work seem to indicate a connexion of the midsummer bonfire with vegetation. For example, both in Sweden and Bohemia an essential part of the festival is the raising of a May-pole or Midsummer-tree, which in Bohemia is burned in the bonfire.[2] Again, in a Russian midsummer ceremony a straw figure of Kupalo,

---

[1] *Balder the Beautiful*, i. 160 *sqq.*
[2] *The Magic Art and the Evolution of Kings*, ii. 65 *sq.*

the representative of vegetation, is placed beside a May-pole or Midsummer-tree and then carried to and fro across a bonfire.[1] Kupalo is here represented in duplicate, in tree-form by the Midsummer-tree, and in human form by the straw effigy, just as Adonis was represented both by an image and a garden of Adonis; and the duplicate representatives of Kupalo, like those of Adonis, are finally cast into water. In the Sardinian and Sicilian customs the Gossips or Sweethearts of St. John probably answer, on the one hand to Adonis and Astarte, on the other to the King and Queen of May. In the Swedish province of Blekinge part of the midsummer festival is the election of a Midsummer Bride, who chooses her bridegroom; a collection is made for the pair, who for the time being are looked upon as man and wife.[2] Such Midsummer pairs may be supposed, like the May pairs, to stand for the powers of vegetation or of fertility in general: they represent in flesh and blood what the images of Siva or Mahadeo and Parvati in the Indian ceremonies, and the images of Adonis and Aphrodite in the Alexandrian ceremony, set forth in effigy.

The reason why ceremonies whose aim is to foster the growth of vegetation should thus be associated with bonfires; why in particular the representative of vegetation should be burned in the likeness of a tree, or passed across the fire in effigy or in the form of a living couple, has been discussed by me elsewhere.[3] Here it is enough to have adduced evidence of such association, and therefore to have obviated the objection which might have been raised to my theory of the Sardinian custom, on the ground that the bonfires have nothing to do with vegetation. One more piece of evidence may here be given to prove the contrary. In some parts of Germany and Austria young men and girls leap over midsummer bonfires for the express purpose of making the hemp or flax grow tall.[4] We may, therefore, assume that in the Sardinian custom the blades of wheat and barley which are

Gardens of Adonis intended to foster the growth of vegetation, and especially of the crops.

---

[1] *The Dying God*, p. 262.

[2] L. Lloyd, *Peasant Life in Sweden* (London, 1870), p. 257.

[3] *Balder the Beautiful*, i. 328 *sqq.*, ii. 21 *sqq.*

[4] W. Mannhardt, *Baumkultus*, p. 464; K. von Leoprechting, *Aus dem Lechrain* (Munich, 1855), p. 183. For more evidence see *Balder the Beautiful*, i. 165, 166, 166 *sq.*, 168, 173, 174.

forced on in pots for the midsummer festival, and which correspond so closely to the gardens of Adonis, form one of those widely-spread midsummer ceremonies, the original object of which was to promote the growth of vegetation, and especially of the crops. But as, by an easy extension of ideas, the spirit of vegetation was believed to exercise a beneficent and fertilizing influence on human as well as animal life, the gardens of Adonis would be supposed, like the May-trees or May-boughs, to bring good luck, and more particularly perhaps offspring,[1] to the family or to the person who planted them ; and even after the idea had been abandoned that they operated actively to confer prosperity, they

Modes of divination at midsummer like the gardens of Adonis.

might still be used to furnish omens of good or evil. It is thus that magic dwindles into divination. Accordingly we find modes of divination practised at midsummer which resemble more or less closely the gardens of Adonis. Thus an anonymous Italian writer of the sixteenth century has recorded that it was customary to sow barley and wheat a few days before the festival of St. John (Midsummer Day) and also before that of St. Vitus ; and it was believed that the person for whom they were sown would be fortunate, and get a good husband or a good wife, if the grain sprouted well ; but if it sprouted ill, he or she would be unlucky.[2] In various parts of Italy and all over Sicily it is still customary to put plants in water or in earth on the Eve of St. John, and from the manner in which they are found to be blooming or fading on St. John's Day omens are drawn, especially as to fortune in love. Amongst the plants used for this purpose are *Ciuri di S. Giuvanni* (St. John's wort ?) and nettles.[3] In Prussia two hundred years ago the farmers used to send out their servants, especially their maids, to gather St. John's

[1] The use of gardens of Adonis to fertilize the human sexes appears plainly in the corresponding Indian practices. See above, pp. 241, 242, 243.

[2] G. Pitrè, *Spettacoli e Feste Popolari Siciliane*, pp. 296 *sq.*

[3] G. Pitrè, *op. cit.* pp. 302 *sq.* ; Antonio de Nino, *Usi e Costumi Abruzzesi* (Florence, 1879–1883), i. 55 *sq.* ; A. de Gubernatis, *Usi Nuziali in Italia e presso gli altri Popoli Indo-Europei* (Milan, 1878), pp. 39 *sq.* Compare

L. Passarini, "Il Comparatico e la Festa di S. Giovanni nelle Marche e in Roma," *Archivio per lo Studio delle Tradizioni Popolari*, i. (1882) p. 135. At Smyrna a blossom of the *Agnus castus* is used on St. John's Day for a similar purpose, but the mode in which the omens are drawn is somewhat different. See Teofilo, "La notte di San Giovanni in Oriente," *Archivio per lo Studio delle Tradizioni Popolari*, vii. (1888) pp. 128-130.

wort on Midsummer Eve or Midsummer Day (St. John's Day). When they had fetched it, the farmer took as many plants as there were persons and stuck them in the wall or between the beams ; and it was thought that he or she whose plant did not bloom would soon fall sick or die. The rest of the plants were tied in a bundle, fastened to the end of a pole, and set up at the gate or wherever the corn would be brought in at the next harvest. The bundle was called *Kupole* : the ceremony was known as Kupole's festival ; and at it the farmer prayed for a good crop of hay, and so forth.[1] This Prussian custom is particularly notable, inasmuch as it strongly confirms the opinion that Kupalo (doubtless identical with Kupole) was originally a deity of vegetation.[2] For here Kupalo is represented by a bundle of plants specially associated with midsummer in folk-custom ; and her influence over vegetation is plainly signified by placing her vegetable emblem over the place where the harvest is brought in, as well as by the prayers for a good crop which are uttered on the occasion. This furnishes a fresh argument in support of the view that the Death, whose analogy to Kupalo, Yarilo, and the rest I have shown elsewhere, originally personified vegetation, more especially the dying or dead vegetation of winter.[3] Further, my interpretation of the gardens of Adonis is confirmed by finding that in this Prussian custom the very same kind of plants is used to form the gardens of Adonis (as we may call them) and the image of the deity. Nothing could set in a stronger light the truth of the theory that the gardens of Adonis are merely another manifestation of the god himself.

In Sicily gardens of Adonis are still sown in spring as well as in summer, from which we may perhaps infer that Sicily as well as Syria celebrated of old a vernal festival of the dead and risen god. At the approach of Easter, Sicilian women sow wheat, lentils, and canary-seed in plates, which they keep in the dark and water every two days. The plants soon shoot up ; the stalks are tied together with red ribbons, and the plates containing them are placed on

Sicilian gardens of Adonis in spring.

---

[1] Matthäus Prätorius, *Deliciae Prussicae* (Berlin, 1871), p. 56.

[2] *The Dying God*, pp. 261 *sq.*

[3] *The Dying God*, pp. 233 *sqq.*, 261 *sqq.*

the sepulchres which, with the effigies of the dead Christ, are made up in Catholic and Greek churches on Good Friday,[1] just as the gardens of Adonis were placed on the grave of the dead Adonis.[2] The practice is not confined to Sicily, for it is observed also at Cosenza in Calabria,[3] and perhaps in other places. The whole custom—sepulchres as well as plates of sprouting grain—may be nothing but a continuation, under a different name, of the worship of Adonis.

Resemblance of the Easter ceremonies in the Greek Church to the rites of Adonis.

Nor are these Sicilian and Calabrian customs the only Easter ceremonies which resemble the rites of Adonis. " During the whole of Good Friday a waxen effigy of the dead Christ is exposed to view in the middle of the Greek churches and is covered with fervent kisses by the thronging crowd, while the whole church rings with melancholy, monotonous dirges. Late in the evening, when it has grown quite dark, this waxen image is carried by the priests into the street on a bier adorned with lemons, roses, jessamine, and other flowers, and there begins a grand procession of the multitude, who move in serried ranks, with slow and solemn step, through the whole town. Every man carries his taper and breaks out into doleful lamentation. At all the houses which the procession passes there are seated women with censers to fumigate the marching host. Thus the community solemnly buries its Christ as if he had just died. At last the waxen image is again deposited in the church, and the same lugubrious chants echo anew. These lamentations, accompanied by a strict fast, continue till midnight on Saturday. As the clock strikes twelve, the bishop appears and announces the glad tidings that ' Christ is risen,' to which the crowd replies, ' He is risen indeed,' and at once the whole city bursts into an uproar of joy, which finds vent in shrieks and shouts, in the endless discharge of carronades and muskets, and the explosion of fire-works of every sort. In the very same hour people plunge from the extremity of the fast into the enjoyment of the Easter lamb and neat wine." [4]

[1] G. Pitrè, *Spettacoli e Feste Popolari Siciliane*, p. 211.

[2] Κήπους ώσίουν ἐπιταφίους ᾿Αδώνιδι, Eustathius on Homer, *Od.* xi. 590.

[3] Vincenzo Dorsa, *La tradizione Greco-Latina negli usi e nelle credenze popolari della Calabria Citeriore* (Cosenza, 1884), p. 50.

[4] C. Wachsmuth, *Das alte Griechenland im neuem* (Bonn, 1864), pp. 26

In like manner the Catholic Church has been accustomed to bring before its followers in a visible form the death and resurrection of the Redeemer.   Such sacred dramas are well fitted to impress the lively imagination and to stir the warm feelings of a susceptible southern race, to whom the pomp and pageantry of Catholicism are more congenial than to the colder temperament of the Teutonic peoples.   The solemnities observed in Sicily on Good Friday, the official anniversary of the Crucifixion, are thus described by a native Sicilian writer.   " A truly moving ceremony is the procession which always takes place in the evening in every commune of Sicily, and further the Deposition from the Cross.   The brotherhoods took part in the procession, and the rear was brought up by a great many boys and girls representing saints, both male and female, and carrying the emblems of Christ's Passion.   The Deposition from the Cross was managed by the priests.   The coffin with the dead Christ in it was flanked by Jews armed with swords, an object of horror and aversion in the midst of the profound pity excited by the sight not only of Christ but of the Mater Dolorosa, who followed behind him.   Now and then the 'mysteries' or symbols of the Crucifixion went in front. Sometimes the procession followed the 'three hours of agony' and the 'Deposition from the Cross.'   The 'three hours' commemorated those which Jesus Christ passed upon the Cross.   Beginning at the eighteenth and ending at the twenty‐first hour of Italian time two priests preached alternately on the Passion.   Anciently the sermons were delivered in the open air on the place called the Calvary : at last, when the third hour was about to strike, at the words

Resemblance of the Easter ceremonies in the Catholic Church to the rites of Adonis.

---

sq. The writer compares these ceremonies with the Eleusinian rites.   But I agree with Mr. R. Wünsch (*Das Frühlingsfest der Insel Malta*, pp. 49 *sq.*) that the resemblance to the Adonis festival is still closer.   Compare V. Dorsa, *La tradizione Greco‐Latina negli usi e nelle credenze popolari della Calabria Citeriore*, pp. 49 *sq.*   Prof. Wachsmuth's description seems to apply to Athens.   In the country districts the ritual is apparently similar.

See R. A. Arnold, *From the Levant* (London, 1868), pp. 251 *sq.*, 259 *sq.* So in the Church of the Holy Sepulchre at Jerusalem the death and burial of Christ are acted over a life‐like effigy. See Henry Maundrell, *Journey from Aleppo to Jerusalem at Easter*, A.D. *1697*, Fourth Edition (Perth, 1800), pp. 110 *sqq.* ; *id.*, in Th. Wright's *Early Travels in Palestine* (London, 1848), pp. 443‐445.

emisit spiritum Christ died, bowing his head amid the sobs
and tears of the bystanders. Immediately afterwards in
some places, three hours afterwards in others, the sacred
body was unnailed and deposited in the coffin. In Castro-
nuovo, at the Ave Maria, two priests clad as Jews, representing Joseph of Arimathea and Nicodemus, with their
servants in costume, repaired to the Calvary, preceded by
the Company of the Whites. There, with doleful verses
and chants appropriate to the occasion, they performed the
various operations of the Deposition, after which the procession took its way to the larger church. . . . In Salaparuta
the Calvary is erected in the church. At the preaching of
the death, the Crucified is made to bow his head by means
of machinery, while guns are fired, trumpets sound, and
amid the silence of the people, impressed by the death of
the Redeemer, the strains of a melancholy funeral march
are heard. Christ is removed from the Cross and deposited
in the coffin by three priests. After the procession of the
dead Christ the burial is performed, that is, two priests lay
Christ in a fictitious sepulchre, from which at the mass of
Easter Saturday the image of the risen Christ issues and is
elevated upon the altar by means of machinery."[1] Scenic
representations of the same sort, with variations of detail, are
exhibited at Easter in the Abruzzi,[2] and probably in many
other parts of the Catholic world.[3]

The
Christian
festival of
Easter
perhaps
grafted on
a festival
of Adonis.

When we reflect how often the Church has skilfully contrived to plant the seeds of the new faith on the old stock
of paganism, we may surmise that the Easter celebration of
the dead and risen Christ was grafted upon a similar celebration of the dead and risen Adonis, which, as we have seen
reason to believe, was celebrated in Syria at the same season.
The type, created by Greek artists, of the sorrowful goddess
with her dying lover in her arms, resembles and may have

---

[1] G. Pitrè, *Spettacoli e Feste Popolari
Siciliane*, pp. 217 *sq.*

[2] G. Finamore, *Credenze, Usi e
Costumi Abruzzesi*, pp. 118-120 ; A.
de Nino, *Usi e Costumi Abruzzesi*,
i. 64 *sq.*, ii. 210-212. At Roccacara-
manico part of the Easter spectacle is
the death of Judas, who, personated by
a living man, pretends to hang himself

upon a tree or a great branch, which
has been brought into the church and
planted near the high altar for the purpose (A. de Nino, *op. cit.* ii. 211).

[3] The drama of the death and resurrection of Christ was formerly celebrated at Easter in England. See
Abbot Gasquet, *Parish Life in Mediaeval England*, pp. 177 *sqq.*, 182 *sq.*

been the model of the *Pietà* of Christian art, the Virgin with the dead body of her divine Son in her lap, of which the most celebrated example is the one by Michaél Angelo in St. Peter's. That noble group, in which the living sorrow of the mother contrasts so wonderfully with the languor of death in the son, is one of the finest compositions in marble. Ancient Greek art has bequeathed to us few works so beautiful, and none so pathetic.[1]

In this connexion a well-known statement of Jerome may not be without significance. He tells us that Bethlehem, the traditionary birthplace of the Lord, was shaded by a grove of that still older Syrian Lord, Adonis, and that where the infant Jesus had wept, the lover of Venus was bewailed.[2] Though he does not expressly say so, Jerome seems to have thought that the grove of Adonis had been planted by the heathen after the birth of Christ for the purpose of defiling the sacred spot. In this he may have been mistaken. If Adonis was indeed, as I have argued, the spirit of the corn, a more suitable name for his dwelling-place could hardly be found than Bethlehem, "the House of Bread,"[3] and he may well have been worshipped there at his House of Bread long ages before the birth of Him who said, "I am the bread of life."[4] Even on the hypothesis that Adonis followed rather than preceded Christ at Bethlehem, the choice of his sad figure to divert the allegiance of Christians from their Lord cannot but strike us as eminently appropriate when we remember the similarity of the rites which commemorated the death and resurrection of the two. One of the earliest seats of the worship of the new god was Antioch, and at Antioch,

The
worship of
Adonis at
Bethlehem.

---

[1] The comparison has already been made by A. Maury, who also compares the Easter ceremonies of the Catholic Church with the rites of Adonis (*Histoire des Religions de la Grèce Antique*, Paris, 1857–1859, vol. iii. p. 221).

[2] Jerome, *Epist.* lviii. 3 (Migne's *Patrologia Latina*, xxii. 581).

[3] Bethlehem is בֵּית־לֶחֶם, literally "House of Bread." The name is appropriate, for "the immediate neighbourhood is very fertile, bearing, besides wheat and barley, groves of olive and almond, and vineyards. The wine of Bethlehem ('Talḥamī') is among the best of Palestine. So great fertility must mean that the site was occupied, in spite of the want of springs, from the earliest times" (George Adam Smith, *s.v.* "Bethlehem," *Encyclopaedia Biblica*, i. 560). It was in the harvest-fields of Bethlehem that Ruth, at least in the poet's fancy, listened to the nightingale "amid the alien corn."

[4] John vi. 35.

The
Morning
Star,
identified
with
Venus,
may have
been the
signal for
the festival
of Adonis.

as we have seen,[1] the death of the old god was annually celebrated with great solemnity. A circumstance which attended the entrance of Julian into the city at the time of the Adonis festival may perhaps throw some light on the date of its celebration. When the emperor drew near to the city he was received with public prayers as if he had been a god, and he marvelled at the voices of a great multitude who cried that the Star of Salvation had dawned upon them in the East.[2] This may doubtless have been no more than a fulsome compliment paid by an obsequious Oriental crowd to the Roman emperor. But it is also possible that the rising of a bright star regularly gave the signal for the festival, and that as chance would have it the star emerged above the rim of the eastern horizon at the very moment of the emperor's approach. The coincidence, if it happened, could hardly fail to strike the imagination of a superstitious and excited multitude, who might thereupon hail the great man as the deity whose coming was announced by the sign in the heavens. Or the emperor may have mistaken for a greeting to himself the shouts which were addressed to the star. Now Astarte, the divine mistress of Adonis, was identified with the planet Venus, and her changes from a morning to an evening star were carefully noted by the Babylonian astronomers, who drew omens from her alternate appearance and disappearance.[3] Hence we may conjecture that the festival of Adonis was regularly timed to coincide with the appearance of Venus as

---

[1] Above, p. 227.

[2] Ammianus Marcellinus, xxii. 9. 14, " *Urbique propinquans in speciem alicujus numinis votis excipitur publicis, miratus voces multitudinis magnae, salutare sidus inluxisse eois partibus adclamantis.*" We may compare the greeting which a tribe of South American Indians used to give to a worshipful star after its temporary disappearance. " The Abipones think that the Pleiades, composed of seven stars, is an image of their ancestor. As the constellation is invisible for some months in the sky of South America, they believe that their ancestor is ill, and every year they are mortally afraid that he will die. But when the said

stars reappear in the month of May, they imagine that their ancestor is recovered from his sickness and has returned ; so they hail him with joyous shouts and the glad music of pipes and war-horns. They congratulate him on his recovery. ' How we thank you ! At last you have come back ? Oh, have you happily recovered ? ' With such cries they fill the air, attesting at once their gladness and their folly." See M. Dobrizhoffer, *Historia de Abiponibus* (Vienna, 1784), ii. 77.

[3] M. Jastrow, *The Religion of Babylonia and Assyria*, pp. 370 *sqq.*; H. Zimmern, in E. Schrader's *Die Keilinschriften und das Alte Testament*,[3] p. 424.

the Morning or Evening Star. But the star which the
people of Antioch saluted at the festival was seen in the
East; therefore, if it was indeed Venus, it can only have
been the Morning Star.   At Aphaca in Syria, where there
was a famous temple of Astarte, the signal for the celebration of the rites was apparently given by the flashing of a
meteor, which on a certain day fell like a star from the top
of Mount Lebanon into the river Adonis.   The meteor was
thought to be Astarte herself,[1] and its flight through the air
might naturally be interpreted as the descent of the amorous
goddess to the arms of her lover.   At Antioch and elsewhere
the appearance of the Morning Star on the day of the festival
may in like manner have been hailed as the coming of the
goddess of love to wake her dead leman from his earthy bed.
If that were so, we may surmise that it was the Morning
Star which guided the wise men of the East to Bethlehem,[2]   The Star of
the hallowed spot which heard, in the language of Jerome, the   Bethlehem.
weeping of the infant Christ and the lament for Adonis.

[1] Sozomenus, *Historia Ecclesiastica,*
ii. 5 (Migne's *Patrologia Graeca,* lxvii.
948).   The connexion of the meteor
with the festival of Adonis is not
mentioned by Sozomenus, but is confirmed by Zosimus, who says (*Hist.* i.
58) that a light like a torch or a globe
of fire was seen on the sanctuary at the

seasons when the people assembled to
worship the goddess and to cast their
offerings of gold, silver, and fine
raiment into a lake beside the temple.
As to Aphaca and the grave of Adonis
see above, pp. 28 *sq.*

[2] Matthew ii. 1-12.

BOOK SECOND

ATTIS

CHAPTER I

THE MYTH AND RITUAL OF ATTIS

ANOTHER of those gods whose supposed death and resurrec- Attis the tion struck such deep roots into the faith and ritual of Phrygian Western Asia is Attis. He was to Phrygia what Adonis part of was to Syria. Like Adonis, he appears to have been a god Adonis. of vegetation, and his death and resurrection were annually mourned and rejoiced over at a festival in spring.[1] The legends and rites of the two gods were so much alike that the ancients themselves sometimes identified them.[2] Attis His was said to have been a fair young shepherd or herdsman relation beloved by Cybele, the Mother of the Gods, a great Asiatic goddess of fertility, who had her chief home in Phrygia.[3] Some held that Attis was her son.[4] His birth, His like that of many other heroes, is said to have been miraculous birth. miraculous. His mother, Nana, was a virgin, who conceived by putting a ripe almond or a pomegranate in her bosom. Indeed in the Phrygian cosmogony an almond figured

---

[1] Diodorus Siculus, iii. 59. 7 ; Sallustius philosophus, "De diis et mundo," iv., *Fragmenta Philosophorum Graecorum*, ed. F. G. A. Mullach, iii. 33 ; Scholiast on Nicander, *Alexipharmaca*, 8 ; Firmicus Maternus, *De errore profanarum religionum*, 3 and 22. The ancient evidence, literary and inscriptional, as to the myth and ritual of Attis has been collected and discussed by Mr. H. Hepding in his monograph, *Attis, seine Mythen und sein Kult* (Giessen, 1903).

[2] Hippolytus, *Refutatio omnium haeresium*, v. 9, p. 168 ed. L. Duncker and F. G. Schneidewin (Göttingen, 1859); Socrates, *Historia Ecclesiastica*,

iii. 23. 51 *sqq.*

[3] Ovid, *Fasti*, iv. 223 *sqq.*; Tertullian, *Apologeticus*, 15 ; *id.*, *Ad Nationes*, i. 10 ; Arnobius, *Adversus Nationes*, iv. 35. As to Cybele, the Great Mother, the Mother of the Gods, conceived as the source of all life, both animal and vegetable, see Rapp, in W. H. Roscher's *Lexikon der griech. und röm. Mythologie*, s.v. "Kybele," ii. 1638 *sqq.*

[4] Scholiast on Lucian, *Jupiter Tragoedus*, 8, p. 60 ed. H. Rabe (Leipsic, 1906), (vol. iv. p. 173 ed. C. Jacobitz) ; Hippolytus, *Refutatio omnium haeresium*, v. 9, pp. 168, 170 ed. Duncker and Schneidewin.

as the father of all things,[1] perhaps because its delicate lilac blossom is one of the first heralds of the spring, appearing on the bare boughs before the leaves have opened. Such tales of virgin mothers are relics of an age of childish ignorance when men had not yet recognized the intercourse of the sexes as the true cause of offspring. That ignorance, still shared by the lowest of existing savages, the aboriginal tribes of central Australia,[2] was doubtless at one time universal among mankind. Even in later times, when people are better acquainted with the laws of nature, they sometimes imagine that these laws may be subject to exceptions, and that miraculous beings may be born in miraculous ways by women who have never known a man. In Palestine to this day it is believed that a woman may conceive by a jinnee or by the spirit of her dead husband. There is, or was lately, a man at Nebk who is currently supposed to be the offspring of such a union, and the simple folk have never suspected his mother's virtue.[3] Two different accounts

The death of Attis.

of the death of Attis were current. According to the one he was killed by a boar, like Adonis. According to the other he unmanned himself under a pine-tree, and bled to death on the spot. The latter is said to have been the local story told by the people of Pessinus, a great seat of the worship of Cybele, and the whole legend of which the story forms a part is stamped with a character of rudeness and savagery that speaks strongly for its antiquity.[4] Both tales might claim the support of custom,

---

[1] Pausanias, vii. 17. 11; Hippolytus, *Refutatio omnium haeresium*, v. 9, pp. 166, 168 ed. Duncker and Schneidewin; Arnobius, *Adversus Nationes*, v. 6.

[2] See above, pp. 99 *sqq.*

[3] S. I. Curtiss, *Primitive Semitic Religion To-day*, pp. 115 *sq.* See above, pp. 78, 213 *sqq.*

[4] That Attis was killed by a boar was stated by Hermesianax, an elegiac poet of the fourth century B.C. (Pausanias, vii. 17); compare Scholiast on Nicander, *Alexipharmaca*, 8. The other story is told by Arnobius (*Adversus Nationes*, v. 5 *sqq.*) on the authority of Timotheus, who professed to derive it from recondite antiquarian works and from the very heart of the mysteries. It is obviously identical with the account which Pausanias (*l.c.*) mentions as the story current in Pessinus. According to Servius (on Virgil, *Aen.* ix. 115), Attis was found bleeding to death under a pine-tree, but the wound which robbed him of his virility and his life was not inflicted by himself. The Timotheus cited by Pausanias may be the Timotheus who was consulted by Ptolemy Soter on religious matters and helped to establish the worship of Serapis. See Plutarch, *Isis et Osiris*, 28; Franz Cumont, *Les Religions Orientales dans le Paganisme Romain*[2] (Paris, 1909), pp. 77, 113, 335.

or rather both were probably invented to explain certain customs observed by the worshippers. The story of the self-mutilation of Attis is clearly an attempt to account for the self-mutilation of his priests, who regularly castrated themselves on entering the service of the goddess. The story of his death by the boar may have been told to explain why his worshippers, especially the people of Pessinus, abstained from eating swine.[1] In like manner the worshippers of Adonis abstained from pork, because a boar had killed their god.[2] After his death Attis is said to have been changed into a pine-tree.[3]

The worship of the Phrygian Mother of the Gods was adopted by the Romans in 204 B.C. towards the close of their long struggle with Hannibal. For their drooping spirits had been opportunely cheered by a prophecy, alleged to be drawn from that convenient farrago of nonsense, the Sibylline Books, that the foreign invader would be driven from Italy if the great Oriental goddess were brought to Rome. Accordingly ambassadors were despatched to her sacred city Pessinus in Phrygia. The small black stone which embodied the mighty divinity was entrusted to them and conveyed to Rome, where it was received with great respect and installed in the temple of Victory on the Palatine Hill. It was the middle of April when the goddess arrived,[4] and she went to work at once. For the harvest that year was such as had not been seen for many a long day,[5] and in the very next year Hannibal and his veterans embarked for Africa. As he looked his last on the coast of Italy, fading behind him in the distance, he could not foresee that Europe, which had repelled the arms, would yet yield to the gods, of the Orient. The vanguard of the conquerors had already encamped in

Worship of Cybele introduced into Rome in 204 B.C.

---

[1] Pausanias, vii. 17. 10; Julian, *Orat.* v. 177 B, p. 229 ed. F. C. Hertlein (Leipsic, 1875–1876). Similarly at Comana in Pontus, the seat of the worship of the goddess Ma, pork was not eaten, and swine might not even be brought into the city (Strabo, xii. 8. 9, p. 575). As to Comana see above, p. 39.

[2] S. Sophronius, " SS. Cyri et Joannis Miracula," Migne's *Patrologia Graeca*, lxxxvii. Pars Tertia, col. 3624,

πρὸς πλάνην Ἑλληνικὴν ἀποκλίνουσαν [*scil.* τὴν 'Ιουλίαν] καὶ ταύτῃ διὰ τὸν 'Αδώνιδος θάνατον τὰ κρέα παραιτεῖσθαι τὰ ὕεια.

[3] Ovid, *Metam.* x. 103 *sqq.*

[4] Livy, xxix. chs. 10, 11, and 14; Ovid, *Fasti*, iv. 259 *sqq.*; Herodian, ii. 11. As to the stone which represented the goddess see Arnobius, *Adversus Nationes*, vii. 49.

[5] Pliny, *Nat. Hist.* xviii. 16.

the heart of Italy before the rearguard of the beaten army fell sullenly back from its shores.

We may conjecture, though we are not told, that the Mother of the Gods brought with her the worship of her youthful lover or son to her new home in the West. Certainly the Romans were familiar with the Galli, the emasculated priests of Attis, before the close of the Republic. These unsexed beings, in their Oriental costume, with little images suspended on their breasts, appear to have been a familiar sight in the streets of Rome, which they traversed in procession, carrying the image of the goddess and chanting their hymns to the music of cymbals and tambourines, flutes and horns, while the people, impressed by the fantastic show and moved by the wild strains, flung alms to them in abundance, and buried the image and its bearers under showers of roses.[1] A further step was taken by the Emperor Claudius when he incorporated the Phrygian worship of the sacred tree, and with it probably the orgiastic rites of Attis, in the established religion of Rome.[2] The great

[1] Lucretius, ii. 598 *sqq.*; Catullus, lxiii. ; Varro, *Satir. Menipp.*, ed. F. Bücheler (Berlin, 1882), pp. 176, 178 ; Ovid, *Fasti*, iv. 181 *sqq.*, 223 *sqq.*, 361 *sqq.*; Dionysius Halicarnasensis, *Antiquit. Rom.* ii. 19, compare Polybius, xxii. 18 ed. L. Dindorf (Leipsic, 1866–1868).

[2] Joannes Lydus, *De mensibus*, iv. 41. See Robinson Ellis, *Commentary on Catullus* (Oxford, 1876), pp. 206 *sq.*; H. Hepding, *Attis*, pp. 142 *sqq.*; Fr. Cumont, *Les Religions Orientales dans le Paganisme Romain*[2] (Paris, 1909), pp. 83 *sq.*

It is held by Prof. A. von Domaszewski that the Claudius who incorporated the Phrygian worship of the sacred tree in the Roman ritual was not the emperor of the first century but the emperor of the third century, Claudius Gothicus, who came to the throne in 268 A.D.   See A. von Domaszewski, "Magna Mater in Latin Inscriptions," *The Journal of Roman Studies*, i. (1911) p. 56. The later date, it is said, fits better with the slow development of the worship. But on the other hand this view is open to

certain objections. (1) Joannes Lydus, our only authority on the point, appears to identify the Claudius in question with the emperor of the first century. (2) The great and widespread popularity of the Phrygian worship in the Roman empire long before 268 A.D. is amply attested by an array of ancient writers and inscriptions, especially by a great series of inscriptions referring to the colleges of Tree-bearers (*Dendrophori*), from which we learn that one of these colleges, devoted to the worship of Cybele and Attis, existed at Rome in the age of the Antonines, about a century before the accession of Claudius Gothicus.   (3) Passages of the Augustan historians (Aelius Lampridius, *Alexander Severus*, 37 ; Trebellius Pollio, *Claudius*, iv. 2) refer to the great spring festival of Cybele and Attis in a way which seems to imply that the festival was officially recognized by the Roman government before Claudius Gothicus succeeded to the purple ; and we may hesitate to follow Prof. von Domaszewski in simply excising these passages as the work of an "impudent forger."   (4) The spring festival of Cybele and Attis is best known to us in the form in which it was celebrated at Rome ; but as we are informed that the Roman ceremonies were also Phrygian,[1] we may assume that they differed hardly, if at all, from their Asiatic original. The order of the festival seems to have been as follows.[2]

On the twenty-second day of March, a pine-tree was cut in the woods and brought into the sanctuary of Cybele, where it was treated as a great divinity. The duty of carrying the sacred tree was entrusted to a guild of Tree-bearers. The trunk was swathed like a corpse with woollen bands and decked with wreaths of violets, for violets were said to have sprung from the blood of Attis, as roses and anemones from the blood of Adonis ; and the effigy of a young man, doubtless Attis himself, was tied to the middle of the stem.[3]   On the second day of the festival, the twenty-

The spring festival of Cybele and Attis at Rome.

---

official establishment of the bloody Phrygian superstition suits better the life and character of the superstitious, timid, cruel, pedantic Claudius of the first century than the gallant soldier his namesake in the third century. The one lounged away his contemptible days in the safety of the palace, surrounded by a hedge of lifeguards. The other spent the two years of his brief but glorious reign in camps and battlefields on the frontier, combating the barbarian enemies of the empire ; and it is probable that he had as little leisure as inclination to pander to the superstitions of the Roman populace. For these reasons it seems better with Mr. Hepding and Prof. Cumont to acquiesce in the traditional view that the rites of Attis were officially celebrated at Rome from the first century onward.

An intermediate view is adopted by Prof. G. Wissowa, who, brushing aside the statement of Joannes Lydus altogether, would seemingly assign the public institution of the rites to the middle of the second century A.D. on the ground that the earliest extant evidence of their public celebration refers to that period (*Religion und Kultus der Römer,*[2] Munich, 1912, p. 322). But, considering the extremely imperfect evi-

dence at our disposal for the history of these centuries, it seems rash to infer that an official cult cannot have been older than the earliest notice of it which has chanced to come down to us.

[1] Arrian, *Tactica,* 33 ; Servius on Virgil, *Aen.* xii. 836.

[2] On the festival see J. Marquardt, *Römische Staatsverwaltung,* iii.[2] (Leipsic, 1885) pp. 370 *sqq.* ; the calendar of Philocalus, in *Corpus Inscriptionum Latinarum,* vol. i.[2] Pars prior (Berlin, 1893), p. 260, with Th. Mommsen's commentary (pp. 313 *sq.*) ; W. Mannhardt, *Antike Wald- und Feldkulte,* pp. 291 *sqq.,* ; *id., Baumkultus,* pp. 572 *sqq.* ; G. Wissowa, *Religion und Kultus der Römer,*[2] pp. 318 *sqq.* ; H. Hepding, *Attis,* pp. 147 *sqq.* ; J. Toutain, *Les Cultes Païens dans l'Empire Romain,* ii. (Paris, 1911) pp. 82 *sqq.*

[3] Julian, *Orat.* v. 168 C, p. 218 ed. F. C. Hertlein (Leipsic, 1875–1876) ; Joannes Lydus, *De mensibus,* iv. 41 ; Arnobius, *Adversus Nationes,* v. chs. 7, 16, 39 ; Firmicus Maternus, *De errore profanarum religionum,* 27 ; Sallustius philosophus, "De diis et mundo," iv., *Fragmenta Philosophorum Graecorum,* ed. F. G. A. Mullach, iii. 33.   As to the guild of

third of March, the chief ceremony seems to have been a blowing of trumpets.[1]   The third day, the twenty-fourth of March, was known as the Day of Blood : the Archigallus or high-priest drew blood from his arms and presented it as an offering.[2]   Nor was he alone in making this bloody sacrifice. Stirred by the wild barbaric music of clashing cymbals, rumbling drums, droning horns, and screaming flutes, the inferior clergy whirled about in the dance with waggling heads and streaming hair, until, rapt into a frenzy of excitement and insensible to pain, they gashed their bodies with potsherds or slashed them with knives in order to bespatter the altar and the sacred tree with their flowing blood.[3]   The ghastly rite probably formed part of the mourning for Attis and may have been intended to strengthen him for the resurrection.   The Australian aborigines cut themselves in like manner over the graves of their friends for the purpose, perhaps, of enabling them to be born again.[4]   Further, we may conjecture, though we are not expressly told, that it was on the same Day of Blood and for the same purpose that the novices sacrificed their virility. Wrought up to the highest pitch of religious excitement they dashed the severed portions of themselves against the image of the cruel goddess.   These broken instruments of fertility were afterwards reverently wrapt up and buried in the earth or in subterranean chambers sacred to Cybele,[5] where, like the

Tree-bearers (*Dendrophori*) see Joannes Lydus, *l.c.* ; H. Dessau, *Inscriptiones Latinae Selectae*, Nos. 4116 *sq.*, 4171-4174, 4176; H. Hepding, *Attis*, pp. 86, 92, 93, 96, 152 *sqq.*; F. Cumont, *s.v.* "Dendrophori," in Pauly-Wissowa's *Real - Encyclopädie der classischen Altertumswissenschaft*, v. I. coll. 216-219; J. Toutain, *Les Cultes Païens dans l'Empire Romain*, ii. 82 *sq.*, 92 *sq.*

[1] Julian, *l.c.* and 169 c, p. 219 ed. F. C. Hertlein.   The ceremony may have been combined with the old *tubilustrium* or purification of trumpets, which fell on this day.   See Joannes Lydus, *De mensibus*, iv. 42 ; Varro, *De lingua Latina*, vi. 14 ; Festus, pp. 352, 353 ed. C. O. Müller ; W. Warde Fowler, *Roman Festivals of the Period*

of the Republic (London, 1899), p. 62.

[2] Trebellius Pollio, *Claudius*, 4 ; Tertullian, *Apologeticus*, 25.

[3] Lucian, *Deorum dialogi*, xii. I ; Seneca, *Agamemnon*, 686 *sqq.*; Martial, xi. 84. 3 *sq.* ; Valerius Flaccus, *Argonaut.* viii. 239 *sqq.*; Statius, *Theb.* x. 170 *sqq.*; Apuleius, *Metam.* viii. 27; Lactantius, *Divinarum Institutionum Epitome*, 23 (18, vol. i. p. 689 ed. Brandt and Laubmann) ; H. Hepding, *Attis*, pp. 158 *sqq.* As to the music of these dancing dervishes see also Lucretius, ii. 618 *sqq.*

[4] *The Magic Art and the Evolution of Kings*, i. 90 *sq.*, 101 *sq.*

[5] Minucius Felix, *Octavius*, 22 and 24 ; Lactantius, *Divin. Instit.* i. 21. 16; *id.*, *Epitoma*, 8 ; Schol. on Lucian,

offering of blood, they may have been deemed instrumental in recalling Attis to life and hastening the general resurrection of nature, which was then bursting into leaf and blossom in the vernal sunshine.   Some confirmation of this conjecture is furnished by the savage story that the mother of Attis conceived by putting in her bosom a pomegranate sprung from the severed genitals of a man-monster named Agdestis, a sort of double of Attis.[1]

If there is any truth in this conjectural explanation of the custom, we can readily understand why other Asiatic goddesses of fertility were served in like manner by eunuch priests.   These feminine deities required to receive from their male ministers, who personated the divine lovers, the means of discharging their beneficent functions: they had themselves to be impregnated by the life-giving energy before they could transmit it to the world.   Goddesses thus ministered to by eunuch priests were the great Artemis of Ephesus [2] and the great Syrian Astarte of Hierapolis,[3] whose sanctuary, frequented by swarms of pilgrims and enriched by the offerings of Assyria and Babylonia, of Arabia and Phoenicia, was perhaps in the days of its glory the most popular in the East.[4]   Now the unsexed priests of this Syrian goddess resembled those of Cybele so closely that some people took them to be the same.[5]   And the mode in which they dedicated themselves to the religious life was similar.   The

Eunuch priests in the service of Asiatic goddesses.

Jupiter Tragoedus, 8 (p. 60 ed. H. Rabe) ; Servius on Virgil, *Aen.* ix. 115 ; Prudentius, *Peristephan.* x. 1066 *sqq.* ; " Passio Sancti Symphoriani," chs. 2 and 6 (Migne's *Patrologia Graeca*, v. 1463, 1466) ; Arnobius, *Adversus Nationes*, v. 14 ; Scholiast on Nicander, *Alexipharmaca*, 8 ; H. Hepding, *Attis*, pp. 163 *sq.* A story told by Clement of Alexandria (*Protrept.* ii. 15, p. 13 ed. Potter) suggests that weaker brethren may have been allowed to sacrifice the virility of a ram instead of their own. We know from inscriptions that rams and bulls were regularly sacrificed at the mysteries of Attis and the Great Mother, and that the testicles of the bulls were used for a special purpose, probably as a fertility charm. May not the testicles

of the rams have been employed for the same purpose? and may not those of both animals have been substitutes for the corresponding organs in men? As to the sacrifices of rams and bulls see G. Zippel, " Das Taurobolium," *Festschrift zum fünfzigjährigen Doctorjubiläum L. Friedlaender* (Leipsic, 1895), pp. 498 *sqq.* ; H. Dessau, *Inscriptiones Latinae Selectae*, Nos. 4118 *sqq.* ; J. Toutain, *Les Cultes Païens dans l'Empire Romain*, ii. 84 *sqq.*

[1] Arnobius, *Adversus Nationes*, v. 5 *sq.*

[2] Strabo, xiv. 1. 23, p. 641.

[3] Lucian, *De dea Syria*, 15, 27, 50-53.

[4] Lucian, *op. cit.* 10.

[5] Lucian, *op. cit.* 15.

greatest festival of the year at Hierapolis fell at the beginning of spring, when multitudes thronged to the sanctuary from Syria and the regions round about. While the flutes played, the drums beat, and the eunuch priests slashed themselves with knives, the religious excitement gradually spread like a wave among the crowd of onlookers, and many a one did that which he little thought to do when he came as a holiday spectator to the festival. For man after man, his veins throbbing with the music, his eyes fascinated by the sight of the streaming blood, flung his garments from him, leaped forth with a shout, and seizing one of the swords which stood ready for the purpose, castrated himself on the spot. Then he ran through the city, holding the bloody pieces in his hand, till he threw them into one of the houses which he passed in his mad career. The household thus honoured had to furnish him with a suit of female attire and female ornaments, which he wore for the rest of his life.[1] When the tumult of emotion had subsided, and the man had come to himself again, the irrevocable sacrifice must often have been followed by passionate sorrow and lifelong regret. This revulsion of natural human feeling after the frenzies of a fanatical religion is powerfully depicted by Catullus in a celebrated poem.[2]

---

[1] Lucian, *De dea Syria*, 49-51.

[2] Catullus, *Carm*. lxiii. I agree with Mr. H. Hepding (*Attis*, p. 140) in thinking that the subject of the poem is not the mythical Attis, but one of his ordinary priests, who bore the name and imitated the sufferings of his god. Thus interpreted the poem gains greatly in force and pathos. The real sorrows of our fellow-men touch us more nearly than the imaginary pangs of the gods.

As the sacrifice of virility and the institution of eunuch priests appear to be rare, I will add a few examples. At Stratonicea in Caria a eunuch held a sacred office in connexion with the worship of Zeus and Hecate (*Corpus Inscriptionum Graecarum*, No. 2715). According to Eustathius (on Homer, *Iliad*, xix. 254, p. 1183) the Egyptian priests were eunuchs who had sacrificed their virility as a first-

fruit to the gods. In Corea "during a certain night, known as *Chu-il*, in the twelfth moon, the palace eunuchs, of whom there are some three hundred, perform a ceremony supposed to ensure a bountiful crop in the ensuing year. They chant in chorus prayers, swinging burning torches around them the while. This is said to be symbolical of burning the dead grass, so as to destroy the field mice and other vermin." See W. Woodville Rockhill, "Notes on some of the Laws, Customs, and Superstitions of Korea," *The American Anthropologist*, iv. (Washington, 1891) p. 185. Compare Mrs. Bishop, *Korea and her Neighbours* (London, 1898), ii. 56 *sq.* It appears that among the Ekoi of Southern Nigeria both men and women are, or used to be, mutilated by the excision of their genital organs at an annual festival, which is celebrated in order to produce plentiful

The parallel of these Syrian devotees confirms the view The sacri-
that in the similar worship of Cybele the sacrifice of virility virility.
took place on the Day of Blood at the vernal rites of the
goddess, when the violets, supposed to spring from the red
drops of her wounded lover, were in bloom among the pines.
Indeed the story that Attis unmanned himself under a pine-
tree [1] was clearly devised to explain why his priests did the
same beside the sacred violet-wreathed tree at his festival.

harvests and immunity from thunderbolts. The victims apparently die from
loss of blood. See P. Amaury Talbot,
In the Shadow of the Bush (London,
1912), pp. 74 *sqq.* Mr. Talbot writes
to me : "A horrible case has just
happened at Idua, where, at the new
yam planting, a man cut off his own
membrum virile" (letter dated Eket,
N[r] Calabar, Southern Nigeria, Feb.
7th, 1913). Amongst the Ba-sundi
and Ba-bwende of the Congo many
youths are castrated "in order to more
fittingly offer themselves to the phallic
worship, which increasingly prevails
as we advance from the coast to the
interior. At certain villages between
Manyanga and Isangila there are curious eunuch dances to celebrate the
new moon, in which a white cock is
thrown up into the air alive, with
clipped wings, and as it falls towards
the ground it is caught and plucked
by the eunuchs. I was told that
originally this used to be a human
sacrifice, and that a young boy or girl
was thrown up into the air and torn
to pieces by the eunuchs as he or
she fell, but that of late years slaves
had got scarce or manners milder, and
a white cock was now substituted"
(H. H. Johnston, "On the Races of
the Congo," *Journal of the Anthropological Institute*, xiii. (1884) p. 473 ;
compare *id.*, *The River Congo*, London,
1884, p. 409). In India, men who
are born eunuchs or in some way
deformed are sometimes dedicated to
a goddess named Huligamma. They
wear female attire and might be mistaken for women. Also men who are
or believe themselves impotent will
vow to dress as women and serve the
goddess in the hope of recovering

their virility. See F. Fawcett, "On
Basivis," *Journal of the Anthropological
Society of Bombay*, ii. 343 *sq.* In
Pegu the English traveller, Alexander
Hamilton, witnessed a dance in honour
of the gods of the earth. "Herma-
phrodites, who are numerous in this
country, are generally chosen, if there
are enough present to make a set for
the dance. I saw nine dance like mad
folks for above half-an-hour ; and
then some of them fell in fits, foaming
at the mouth for the space of half-an-
hour ; and, when their senses are restored, they pretend to foretell plenty
or scarcity of corn for that year, if the
year will prove sickly or salutary to
the people, and several other things of
moment; and all by that half hour's
conversation that the furious dancer
had with the gods while she was in a
trance" (A. Hamilton, "A New Account
of the East Indies," in J. Pinkerton's *Voyages and Travels*, viii. 427).
So in the worship of Attis the Archigallus or head of the eunuch priests
prophesied ; perhaps he in like manner
worked himself up to the pitch of inspiration by a frenzied dance. See H.
Dessau, *Inscriptiones Latinae Selectae*,
vol. ii. Pars i. pp. 142, 143, Nos.
4130, 4136 ; G. Wilmanns, *Exempla
Inscriptionum Latinarum* (Berlin,
1873), vol. i. p. 36, Nos. 119a, 120 ;
J. Toutain, *Les Cultes Païens dans
l'Empire Romain*, ii. 93 *sq.* As to
the sacrifice of virility in the Syrian
religion compare Th. Nöldeke, "Die
Selbstentmannung bei den Syrern,"
Archiv für Religionswissenschaft, x.
(1907) pp. 150-152.

[1] Arnobius, *Adversus Nationes*, v. 7
and 16 ; Servius on Virgil, *Aen.* ix.
115.

The mourning for Attis.

At all events, we can hardly doubt that the Day of Blood witnessed the mourning for Attis over an effigy of him which was afterwards buried.[1] The image thus laid in the sepulchre was probably the same which had hung upon the tree.[2] Throughout the period of mourning the worshippers fasted from bread, nominally because Cybele had done so in her grief for the death of Attis,[3] but really perhaps for the same reason which induced the women of Harran to abstain from eating anything ground in a mill while they wept for Tammuz.[4] To partake of bread or flour at such a season might have been deemed a wanton profanation of the bruised and broken body of the god. Or the fast may possibly have been a preparation for a sacramental meal.[5]

The Festival of Joy (*Hilaria*) for the resurrection of Attis on March 25th.

But when night had fallen, the sorrow of the worshippers was turned to joy. For suddenly a light shone in the darkness: the tomb was opened: the god had risen from the dead; and as the priest touched the lips of the weeping mourners with balm, he softly whispered in their ears the glad tidings of salvation. The resurrection of the god was hailed by his disciples as a promise that they too would issue triumphant from the corruption of the grave.[6] On the

---

[1] Diodorus Siculus, iii. 59; Arrian, *Tactica*, 33; Scholiast on Nicander, *Alexipharmaca*, 8; Firmicus Maternus, *De errore profanarum religionum*, 3 and 22; Arnobius, *Adversus Nationes*, v. 16; Servius on Virgil, *Aen.* ix. 115.

[2] See above, p. 267.

[3] Arnobius, *l.c.*; Sallustius philosophus, "De diis et mundo," iv., *Fragmenta Philosophorum Graecorum*, ed. F. G. A. Mullach, iii. 33.

[4] Above, p. 230.

[5] See below, p. 274.

[6] Firmicus Maternus, *De errore profanarum religionum*, 22, " *Nocte quadam simulacrum in lectica supinum ponitur et per numeros digestis fletibus plangitur : deinde cum se ficta lamentatione satiaverint, lumen infertur : tunc a sacerdote omnium qui flebant fauces unguentur, quibus perunctis hoc lento murmure susurrat :*

θαρρεῖτε μύσται τοῦ θεοῦ σεσωσμένου·
ἔσται γὰρ ἡμῖν ἐκ πόνων σωτηρία.

Quid miseros hortaris gaudeant ? quid deceptos homines laetari compellis ? quam illis spem, quam salutem funesta persuasione promittis ? Dei tui mors nota est, vita non paret. . . . Idolum sepelis, idolum plangis, idolum de sepultura proferis, et miser cum haec feceris, gaudes. Tu deum tuum liberas, tu jacentia lapidis membra componis, tu insensibile corrigis saxum." In this passage Firmicus does not expressly mention Attis, but that the reference is to his rites is made probable by a comparison with chapter 3 of the same writer's work. Compare also Damascius, in Photius's *Bibliotheca*, p. 345 A, 5 *sqq.*, ed. I. Bekker (Berlin, 1824), τότε τῇ Ἱεραπόλει ἐγκαθευδήσας ἐδόκουν ὄναρ ὁ Ἄττης γένεσθαι, καί μοι ἐπιτελεῖσθαι παρὰ τῆς μητρὸς τῶν θεῶν τὴν τῶν ἱλαρίων καλουμένων ἑορτήν· ὅπερ ἐδήλου τὴν ἐξ ᾅδου γεγονυῖαν ἡμῶν σωτηρίαν. See furthei Fr. Cumont, *Les Religions Orientales dans le Paganisme Romain*[2] (Paris, 1909), pp. 89 *sq.*

morrow, the twenty-fifth day of March, which was reckoned the vernal equinox, the divine resurrection was celebrated with a wild outburst of glee. At Rome, and probably elsewhere, the celebration took the form of a carnival. It was the Festival of Joy (*Hilaria*). A universal licence prevailed. Every man might say and do what he pleased. People went about the streets in disguise. No dignity was too high or too sacred for the humblest citizen to assume with impunity. In the reign of Commodus a band of conspirators thought to take advantage of the masquerade by dressing in the uniform of the Imperial Guard, and so, mingling with the crowd of merrymakers, to get within stabbing distance of the emperor. But the plot miscarried.[1] Even the stern Alexander Severus used to relax so far on the joyous day as to admit a pheasant to his frugal board.[2] The next day, the twenty-sixth of March, was given to repose, which must have been much needed after the varied excitements and fatigues of the preceding days.[3] Finally, the Roman festival closed on the twenty-seventh of March with a procession to the brook Almo. The silver image of the goddess, with its face of jagged black stone, sat in a wagon drawn by oxen. Preceded by the nobles walking barefoot, it moved slowly, to the loud music of pipes and tambourines, out by the Porta Capena, and so down to the banks of the Almo, which flows into the Tiber just below the walls of Rome. There the high-priest, robed in purple, washed the wagon, the image, and the other sacred objects in the water of the stream. On returning from their bath, the wain and the oxen were strewn with fresh spring flowers. All was mirth and gaiety. No one thought of the blood that had flowed so lately. Even the eunuch priests forgot their wounds.[4]

The procession to the Almo.

---

[1] Macrobius, *Saturn.* i. 21. 10; Flavius Vopiscus, *Aurelianus*, i. 1; Julian, *Or.* v. pp. 168 D, 169 D; Damascius, *l.c.*; Herodian, i. 10. 5-7; Sallustius philosophus, "De diis et mundo," *Fragmenta Philosophorum Graecorum*, ed. F. G. A. Mullach, iii. 33. In like manner Easter Sunday, the Resurrection-day of Christ, was called by some ancient writers the Sunday of Joy (*Dominica Gaudii*). The emperors used to celebrate the happy day by releasing from prison all but the worst offenders. See J. Bingham, *The Antiquities of the Christian Church*, bk. xx. ch. vi. §§ 5 *sq.* (Bingham's *Works* (Oxford, 1855), vii. 317 *sqq.*).

[2] Aelius Lampridius, *Alexander Severus*, 37.

[3] *Corpus Inscriptionum Latinarum*, i.² Pars prior (Berlin, 1893), pp. 260, 313 *sq.*; H. Hepding, *Attis*, pp. 51, 172.

[4] Ovid, *Fasti*, iv. 337-346; Silius Italicus, *Punic.* viii. 365; Valerius

The mysteries of Attis.

Such, then, appears to have been the annual solemniza-tion of the death and resurrection of Attis in spring.   But besides these public rites, his worship is known to have comprised certain secret or mystic ceremonies, which prob-ably aimed at bringing the worshipper, and especially the novice, into closer communication with his god.   Our informa-tion as to the nature of these mysteries and the date of their celebration is unfortunately very scanty, but they seem to have included a sacramental meal and a baptism of

The sacrament.

blood.   In the sacrament the novice became a partaker of the mysteries by eating out of a drum and drinking out of a cymbal, two instruments of music which figured pro-minently in the thrilling orchestra of Attis.[1]   The fast which accompanied the mourning for the dead god[2] may perhaps have been designed to prepare the body of the communicant for the reception of the blessed sacrament by purging it of all that could defile by contact the sacred

The baptism of blood.

elements.[3]   In the baptism the devotee, crowned with gold and wreathed with fillets, descended into a pit, the mouth of which was covered with a wooden grating.   A bull, adorned with garlands of flowers, its forehead glittering with gold leaf, was then driven on to the grating and there stabbed to death with a consecrated spear.   Its hot reeking blood poured in torrents through the apertures, and was received with devout eagerness by the worshipper on every part of his person and garments, till he emerged from the pit, drenched, dripping, and scarlet from head to foot, to receive the homage, nay the adoration, of his fellows as one who had been born again to eternal life and had washed

Flaccus, *Argonaut.* viii. 239 *sqq.* ; Martial, iii. 47. 1 *sq.* ; Ammianus Marcellinus, xxiii. 3. 7 ; Arnobius, *Adversus Nationes*, vii. 32 ; Pruden-tius, *Peristephan.* x. 154 *sqq.*   For the description of the image of the goddess see Arnobius, *Adversus Nationes*, vii. 49.   At Carthage the goddess was carried to her bath in a litter, not in a wagon (Augustine, *De civitate Dei*, ii. 4).   The bath formed part of the festival in Phrygia, whence the custom was borrowed by the Romans (Arrian, *Tactica*, 33).   At Cyzicus the Placi-anian Mother, a form of Cybele, was

served by women called "marine" (θαλάσσιαι), whose duty it probably was to wash her image in the sea (Ch. Michel, *Recueil d'Inscriptions Grecques* Brussels, 1900, pp. 403 *sq.*, No. 537).   See further J. Marquardt, *Römische Staatsverwaltung*, iii.² 373 ; H. Hepding, *Attis*, pp. 133 *sq.*

[1] Clement of Alexandria, *Protrept.* ii. 15, p. 13 ed. Potter; Firmicus Maternus, *De errore profanarum re-ligionum*, 18.

[2] Above, p. 272.

[3] H. Hepding, *Attis*, p. 185.

away his sins in the blood of the bull.[1]   For some time
afterwards the fiction of a new birth was kept up by
dieting him on milk like a new-born babe.[2]   The regeneration of the worshipper took place at the same time as the
regeneration of his god, namely at the vernal equinox.[3]   At
Rome the new birth and the remission of sins by the
shedding of bull's blood appear to have been carried out
above all at the sanctuary of the Phrygian goddess on the
Vatican Hill, at or near the spot where the great basilica of
St. Peter's now stands ; for many inscriptions relating to
the rites were found when the church was being enlarged in
1608 or 1609.[4]   From the Vatican as a centre this barbarous
system of superstition seems to have spread to other parts

The Vatican a centre of the worship of Attis.

---

[1] Prudentius, *Peristephan.* x. 1006-
1050 ; compare Firmicus Maternus,
De errore profanarum religionum, 28. 8.
That the bath of bull's blood (*taurobolium*) was believed to regenerate the
devotee for eternity is proved by an
inscription found at Rome, which records that a certain Sextilius Agesilaus
Aedesius, who dedicated an altar to
Attis and the Mother of the Gods, was
*taurobolio criobolioque in aeternum
renatus* (*Corpus Inscriptionum Latinarum*, vi. No. 510 ; H. Dessau, *Inscriptiones Latinae Selectae*, No. 4152).
The phrase *arcanis perfusionibus in
aeternum renatus* occurs in a dedication to Mithra (*Corpus Inscriptionum
Latinarum*, vi. No. 736), which, however, is suspected of being spurious.
As to the inscriptions which refer to
the *taurobolium* see G. Zippel, "Das
Taurobolium," in *Festschrift zum
fünfzigjährigen Doctorjubiläum L.
Friedlaender dargebracht von seinen
Schülern* (Leipsic, 1895), pp. 498-520 ;
H. Dessau, *Inscriptiones Latinae
Selectae*, vol. ii. Pars i. pp. 140-147,
Nos. 4118-4159. As to the origin of
the *taurobolium* and the meaning of
the word, see Fr. Cumont, *Textes et
Monuments Figurés relatifs aux Mystères de Mithra* (Brussels, 1896-1899),
i. 334 *sq.*; *id.*, *Les Religions Orientales
dans le Paganisme Romain*,[2] pp. 100
sqq. ; J. Toutain, *Les Cultes Païens
dans l'Empire Romain*, ii. 84 *sqq.* ;
G. Wissowa, *Religion und Kultus der

Römer,[2] pp. 322 *sqq.* The *taurobolium* seems to have formed no part
of the original worship of Cybele and
to have been imported into it at a comparatively late date, perhaps in the
second century of our era. Its origin
is obscure. In the majority of the
older inscriptions the name of the rite
appears as *tauropolium*, and it has been
held that this is the true form, being
derived from the worship of the Asiatic
goddess Artemis Tauropolis (Strabo,
xii. 2. 7, p. 537). This was formerly
the view of Prof. F. Cumont (*s.v.*
"Anaitis," in Pauly-Wissowa's *Real-
Encyclopädie der classischen Altertumswissenschaft*, i. 2. col. 2031) ; but
he now prefers the form *taurobolium*,
and would deduce both the name and
the rite from an ancient Anatolian
hunting custom of lassoing wild bulls.

[2] Sallustius philosophus, "De diis
et mundo," iv., *Fragmenta Philosophorum Graecorum*, ed. F. G. A.
Mullach, iii. 33.

[3] Sallustius philosophus, *l.c.*

[4] *Corpus Inscriptionum Latinarum*,
vi. Nos. 497-504 ; H. Dessau, *Inscriptiones Latinae Selectae*, Nos. 4145,
4147-4151, 4153 ; *Inscriptiones
Graecae Siciliae et Italiae*, ed. G.
Kaibel (Berlin, 1890), p. 270, No.
1020 ; G. Zippel, *op. cit.* pp. 509 *sq.*,
519 ; H. Hepding, *Attis*, pp. 83, 86-
88, 176 ; Ch. Huelsen, *Topographie
der Stadt Rom im Alterthum, von H.
Jordan*, i. 3 (Berlin, 1907), pp. 658 *sq.*

of the Roman empire. Inscriptions found in Gaul and Germany prove that provincial sanctuaries modelled their ritual on that of the Vatican.[1] From the same source we learn that the testicles as well as the 'blood of the bull played an important part in the ceremonies.[2] Probably they were regarded as a powerful charm to promote fertility and hasten the new birth.

[1] *Corpus Inscriptionum Latinarum,* xiii. No. 1751; H. Dessau, *Inscriptiones Latinae Selectae,* No. 4131; G. Wilmanns, *Exempla Inscriptionum Latinarum* (Berlin, 1873), vol. ii. p. 125, No. 2278; G. Wissowa, *Religion und Kultus der Römer,*[2] p. 267; H. Hepding, *Attis,* pp. 169-171, 176.

[2] *Corpus Inscriptionum Latinarum,* xiii. No. 1751; G. Wilmanns, *Exempla Inscriptionum Latinarum,* vol. i. pp. 35-37, Nos. 119, 123, 124; H. Dessau, *Inscriptiones Latinae Selectae,* Nos. 4127, 4129, 4131, 4140; G. Wissowa, *Religion und Kultus der Römer,*[2] pp. 322 *sqq.*; H. Hepding, *Attis,* p. 191.

CHAPTER II

ATTIS AS A GOD OF VEGETATION

THE original character of Attis as a tree-spirit is brought The sanctity of the pine-tree in the worship of Attis. out plainly by the part which the pine-tree plays in his legend, his ritual, and his monuments.[1] The story that he was a human being transformed into a pine-tree is only one of those transparent attempts at rationalizing old beliefs which meet us so frequently in mythology. The bringing in of the pine-tree from the woods, decked with violets and woollen bands, is like bringing in the May-tree or Summer-tree in modern folk-custom ; and the effigy which was attached to the pine-tree was only a duplicate representative of the tree-spirit Attis. After being fastened to the tree, the effigy was kept for a year and then burned.[2] The same thing appears to have been sometimes done with the May-pole ; and in like manner the effigy of the corn-spirit, made at harvest, is often preserved till it is replaced by a new effigy at next year's harvest.[3] The original intention of such customs was no doubt to maintain the spirit of vegetation in life throughout the year. Why the Phrygians should have worshipped the pine above other trees we can only guess. Perhaps the sight of its changeless, though sombre, green cresting the ridges of the high hills above the fading splendour of the autumn woods in the valleys may have seemed to their eyes to mark it out as the seat of a diviner life, of something exempt from the sad vicissitudes of the

[1] As to the monuments see H. Dessau, *Inscriptiones Latinae Selectae*, Nos. 4143, 4152, 4153 ; H. Hepding, *Attis*, pp. 82, 83, 88, 89.

[2] Firmicus Maternus, *De errore profanarum religionum*, 27.

[3] *The Magic Art and the Evolution of Kings*, ii. 47 *sq.*, 71 ; *Spirits of the Corn and of the Wild*, i. 138, 143, 152, 153, 154, 155, 156, 157, 158.

seasons, constant and eternal as the sky which stooped to meet it. For the same reason, perhaps, ivy was sacred to Attis ; at all events, we read that his eunuch priests were tattooed with a pattern of ivy leaves.[1] Another reason for the sanctity of the pine may have been its usefulness. The cones of the stone-pine contain edible nut-like seeds, which have been used as food since antiquity, and are still eaten, for example, by the poorer classes in Rome.[2] Moreover, a wine was brewed from these seeds,[3] and this may partly account for the orgiastic nature of the rites of Cybele, which the ancients compared to those of Dionysus.[4] Further, pine-cones were regarded as symbols or rather instruments of fertility. Hence at the festival of the Thesmophoria they were thrown, along with pigs and other agents or emblems of fecundity, into the sacred vaults of Demeter for the purpose of quickening the ground and the wombs of women.[5]

---

[1] Etymologicum Magnum, p. 220, line 20, Γάλλος, ὁ φιλοπάτωρ Πτολεμαῖος· διὰ τὸ φύλλα κισσοῦ κατέστιχθαι, ὡς οἱ γάλλοι. Ἀεὶ γὰρ ταῖς Διονυσιακαῖς τελεταῖς κισσῷ ἐστεφανοῦντο. But there seems to be some confusion here between the rites of Dionysus and those of Attis ; ivy was certainly sacred to Dionysus (Pausanias, i. 31. 6 with my note). Compare C. A. Lobeck, *Agla-ophamus* (Königsberg, 1829), i. 657, who, in the passage quoted, rightly defends the readings κατέστιχθαι and ἐστεφανοῦντο.

[2] *Encyclopaedia Britannica*,[9] xix. 105. Compare Athenaeus, ii. 49, p. 57. The nuts of the silver-pine (*Pinus edulis*) are a favourite food of the Californian Indians (S. Powers, *Tribes of California* (Washington, 1877), p. 421) ; the Wintun Indians hold a pine-nut dance when the nuts are fit to be gathered (*ib.* p. 237). The Shuswap Indians of British Columbia collect the cones of various sorts of pines and eat the nutlets which they extract from them. See G. M. Dawson, "Notes on the Shuswap People of British Columbia," *Proceedings and Trans-actions of the Royal Society of Canada*, ix. (Montreal, 1892) Transactions, section ii. p. 22. With regard to the Araucanian Indians of South America we read that "the great staple food,

the base of all their subsistence, save among the coast tribes, was the *piñon*, the fruit of the Araucanian pine (*Arau-caria imbricata*). Every year during the autumn months excursions are made by the whole tribe to the pine forests, where they remain until they have collected sufficient for the following year. Each tribe has its own district, inherited by custom from generation to generation and inviolate, by unwritten law, from other tribes, even in time of warfare. This harvest was formerly of such supreme importance, that all inter-tribal quarrels and warfares were suspended by mutual accord during this period." See R. E. Latcham, "Ethnology of the Araucanos," *Journal of the Royal Anthropological Institute,* xxxix. (1909) p. 341. The Gilyaks of the Amoor valley in like manner eat the nutlets of the Siberian stone-pine (L. von Schrenk, *Die Völker des Amur-Landes*, iii. 440). See also the commentators on Herodotus, iv. 109 φθειροτραγέουσι.

[3] Pliny, *Nat. Hist.* xiv. 103.

[4] Strabo, x. 3. 12 *sqq.*, pp. 469 *sqq.* However, tipsy people were excluded from the sanctuary of Attis (Arnobius, *Adversus Nationes*, v. 6).

[5] Scholiast on Lucian, *Dial. Meretr.* ii. 1, p. 276 ed. H. Rabe (Leipsic, 1906).

Like tree-spirits in general, Attis was apparently thought Attis as a
corn-god. to wield power over the fruits of the earth or even to be identical with the corn. One of his epithets was "very fruitful" : he was addressed as the "reaped green (or yellow) ear of corn"; and the story of his sufferings, death, and resurrection was interpreted as the ripe grain wounded by the reaper, buried in the granary, and coming to life again when it is sown in the ground.[1] A statue of him in the Lateran Museum at Rome clearly indicates his relation to the fruits of the earth, and particularly to the corn ; for it represents him with a bunch of ears of corn and fruit in his hand, and a wreath of pine-cones, pomegranates, and other fruits on his head, while from the top of his Phrygian cap ears of corn are sprouting.[2] On a stone urn, which con- Cybele as a tained the ashes of an Archigallus or high-priest of Attis, goddess of
fertility. the same idea is expressed in a slightly different way. The top of the urn is adorned with ears of corn carved in relief, and it is surmounted by the figure of a cock, whose tail consists of ears of corn.[3] Cybele in like manner was conceived as a goddess of fertility who could make or mar the fruits of the earth ; for the people of Augustodunum (Autun) in Gaul used to cart her image about in a wagon for the good of the fields and vineyards, while they danced and sang before it,[4] and we have seen that in Italy an unusually

[1] Hippolytus, *Refutatio omnium haeresium*, v. 8 and 9, pp. 162, 168 ed. Duncker and Schneidewin ; Firmicus Maternus, *De errore profanarum religionum*, 3 ; Sallustius philosophus, "De diis et mundo," *Fragmenta Philosophorum Graecorum*, ed. F. G. A. Mullach, iii. 33. Others identified him with the spring flowers. See Eusebius, *Praeparatio Evangelii*, iii. 11. 8 and 12, iii. 13. 10 ed. F. A. Heinichen (Leipsic, 1842–1843) ; Augustine, *De civitate Dei*, vii. 25.

[2] W. Helbig, *Führer durch die öffentlichen Sammlungen klassischer Altertümer in Rom* [2] (Leipsic, 1899), i. 481, No. 721.

[3] The urn is in the Lateran Museum at Rome (No. 1046). It is not described by W. Helbig in his *Führer*.[2] The inscription on the urn (*M. Modius Maxximus archigallus coloniae Ostiens*)

is published by H. Dessau (*Inscriptiones Latinae Selectae*, No. 4162), who does not notice the curious and interesting composition of the cock's tail. The bird is chosen as an emblem of the priest with a punning reference to the word *gallus*, which in Latin means a cock as well as a priest of Attis.

[4] Gregory of Tours, *De gloria confessorum*, 77 (Migne's *Patrologia Latina*, lxxi. 884). That the goddess here referred to was Cybele and not a native Gallic deity, as I formerly thought (*Lectures on the Early History of the Kingship*, p. 178), seems proved by the "Passion of St. Symphorian," chs. 2 and 6 (Migne s *Patrologia Graeca*, v. 1463, 1466). Gregory and the author of the "Passion of St. Symphorian" call the goddess simply Berecynthia, the latter writer adding "the Mother of the

The
bathing of
her image
either a
rain-charm
or a
marriage-
rite.

fine harvest was attributed to the recent arrival of the Great Mother.[1] The bathing of the image of the goddess in a river may well have been a rain-charm to ensure an abundant supply of moisture for the crops. Or perhaps, as Mr. Hepding has suggested, the union of Cybele and Attis, like that of Aphrodite and Adonis, was dramatically represented at the festival, and the subsequent bath of the goddess was a ceremonial purification of the bride, such as is often observed at human marriages.[2] In like manner Aphrodite is said to have bathed after her union with Adonis,[3] and so did Demeter after her intercourse with Poseidon.[4] Hera washed in the springs of the river Burrha after her marriage with Zeus ;[5] and every year she recovered her virginity by bathing in the spring of Canathus.[6] However that may be, the rules of diet observed by the worshippers of Cybele and Attis at their solemn fasts are clearly dictated by a belief that the divine life of these deities manifested itself in the fruits of the earth, and especially in such of them as are actually hidden by the soil. For while the devotees were allowed to partake of flesh, though not of pork or fish, they were forbidden to eat seeds and the roots of vegetables, but they might eat the stalks and upper parts of the plants.[7]

Demons," which is plainly a Christian version of the title "Mother of the Gods."

[1] Above, p. 265. In the island of Thera an ox, wheat, barley, wine, and "other first-fruits of all that the seasons produce" were offered to the Mother of the Gods, plainly because she was deemed the source of fertility. See G. Dittenberger, *Sylloge Inscriptionum Graecarum,*[2] vol. ii. p. 426, No. 630.

[2] H. Hepding, *Attis,* pp. 215-217; compare *id.* p. 175 note [7].

[3] Ptolemaeus, *Nov. Hist.* i. p. 183 of A. Westermann's *Mythographi Graeci* (Brunswick, 1843).

[4] Pausanias, viii. 25. 5 *sq.*

[5] Aelian, *Nat. Anim.* xii. 30. The place was in Mesopotamia, and the goddess was probably Astarte. So Lucian (*De dea Syria*) calls the Astarte of Hierapolis "the Assyrian Hera."

[6] Pausanias, ii. 38. 2.

[7] Julian, *Orat.* v. 173 *sqq.* (pp. 225 *sqq.* ed. F. C. Hertlein) ; H. Hepding, *Attis,* pp. 155-157. However, apples, pomegranates, and dates were also forbidden. The story that the mother of Attis conceived him through contact with a pomegranate (above, pp. 263, 269) might explain the prohibition of that fruit. But the reasons for tabooing apples and dates are not apparent, though Julian tried to discover them. He suggested that dates may have been forbidden because the date-palm does not grow in Phrygia, the native land of Cybele and Attis.

CHAPTER III

ATTIS AS THE FATHER GOD

THE name Attis appears to mean simply "father."[1] This explanation, suggested by etymology, is confirmed by the observation that another name for Attis was Papas;[2] for Papas has all the appearance of being a common form of that word for "father" which occurs independently in many distinct families of speech all the world over. Similarly the mother of Attis was named Nana,[3] which is itself a form of the world-wide word for "mother." "The immense list of such words collected by Buschmann shows that the types *pa* and *ta*, with the similar forms *ap* and *at*, preponderate in the world as names for 'father,' while *ma* and *na*, *am* and *an*, preponderate as names for 'mother.'"[4]

The name Attis seems to mean "father."

Thus the mother of Attis is only another form of his divine mistress the great Mother Goddess,[5] and we are brought back to the myth that the lovers were mother and son. The story that Nana conceived miraculously without commerce with the other sex shows that the Mother Goddess of Phrygia herself was viewed, like other goddesses of the same primitive type, as a Virgin Mother.[6] That view of

Relation of Attis to the Mother Goddess.

[1] P. Kretschmer, *Einleitung in die Geschichte der griechischen Sprache* (Göttingen, 1896), p. 355.

[2] Diodorus Siculus, iii. 58. 4; Hippolytus, *Refutatio omnium haeresium*, i. 9, p. 168 ed. Duncker and Schneidewin. A Latin dedication to *Atte Papa* has been found at Aquileia (F. Cumont, in Pauly-Wissowa's *Realencyclopädie der classischen Altertumswissenschaft*, ii. 2180, *s.v.* "Attepata"; H. Hepding, *Attis*, p. 86). Greek dedications to Papas or to Zeus Papas

occur in Phrygia (H. Hepding, *Attis*, pp. 78 *sq.*). Compare A. B. Cook, "Zeus, Jupiter, and the Oak," *Classical Review*, xviii. (1904) p. 79.

[3] Arnobius, *Adversus Nationes*, v. 6 and 13.

[4] (Sir) Edward B. Tylor, *Primitive Culture*[2] (London, 1873), i. 223.

[5] Rapp, *s.v.* "Kybele," in W. H. Roscher's *Lexikon der griech. und röm. Mythologie*, ii. 1648.

[6] She is called a "motherless virgin" by Julian (*Or.* v. 166 B, p.

her character does not rest on a perverse and mischievous theory that virginity is more honourable than matrimony. It is derived, as I have already indicated, from a state of savagery in which the mere fact of paternity was unknown. That explains why in later times, long after the true nature of paternity had been ascertained, the Father God was often a much less important personage in mythology than his divine partner the Mother Goddess. With regard to Attis in his paternal character it deserves to be noticed that the Bithynians used to ascend to the tops of the mountains and there call upon him under the name of Papas. The custom is attested by Arrian,[1] who as a native of Bithynia must have had good opportunities of observing it. We may perhaps infer from it that the Bithynians conceived Attis as a sky-god or heavenly father, like Zeus, with whom indeed Arrian identifies him. If that were so, the story of the loves of Attis and Cybele, the Father God and the Mother Goddess, might be in one of its aspects a particular version of the widespread myth which represents Mother Earth fertilized by Father Sky;[2] and, further, the story of the

Attis as a Sky-god or Heavenly Father.

---

215 ed. F. C. Hertlein), and there was a *Parthenon* or virgin's chamber in her sanctuary at Cyzicus (Ch. Michel, *Recueil d'Inscriptions Grecques*, p. 404, No. 538). Compare Rapp, in W. H. Roscher's *Lexikon der griech. und röm. Mythologie*, ii. 1648; Wagner, *s.v.* "Nana," *ibid.* iii. 4 *sq.* Another great goddess of fertility who was conceived as a Virgin Mother was the Egyptian Neith or Net. She is called "the Great Goddess, the Mother of All the Gods," and was believed to have brought forth Ra, the Sun, without the help of a male partner. See C. P. Tiele, *Geschichte der Religion im Altertum*, i. 111; E. A. Wallis Budge, *The Gods of the Egyptians* (London, 1904), i. 457-462. The latter writer says (p. 462); "In very early times Net was the personification of the eternal female principle of life which was self-sustaining and self-existent, and was secret and unknown, and all-pervading; the more material thinkers, whilst admitting that she brought forth her son Rā without the aid of a

husband, were unable to divorce from their minds the idea that a male germ was necessary for its production, and finding it impossible to derive it from a being external to the goddess, assumed that she herself provided not only the substance which was to form the body of Rā but also the male germ which fecundated it. Thus Net was the type of partheno-genesis."

[1] Quoted by Eustathius on Homer, *Il.* v. 408; *Fragmenta Historicorum Graecorum*, ed. C. Müller, iii. 592, Frag. 30.

[2] (Sir) Edward B. Tylor, *Primitive Culture*,[2] i. 321 *sqq.*, ii. 270 *sqq.* For example, the Ewe people of Togo-land, in West Africa, think that the Earth is the wife of the Sky, and that their marriage takes place in the rainy season, when the rain causes the seeds to sprout and bear fruit. These fruits they regard as the children of Mother Earth, who in their opinion is the mother also of men and of gods. See J. Spieth, *Die Ewe-Stämme* (Berlin, 1906), pp. 464, 548. In the

emasculation of Attis would be parallel to the Greek legend
that Cronus castrated his father, the old sky-god Uranus,[1]
and was himself in turn castrated by his own son, the
younger sky-god Zeus.[2] The tale of the mutilation of
the sky-god by his son has been plausibly explained as a
myth of the violent separation of the earth and sky, which
some races, for example the Polynesians, suppose to have
originally clasped each other in a close embrace.[3] Yet it
seems unlikely that an order of eunuch priests like the Galli
should have been based on a purely cosmogonic myth : why
should they continue for all time to be mutilated because
the sky-god was so in the beginning ? The custom of
castration must surely have been designed to meet a constantly recurring need, not merely to reflect a mythical
event which happened at the creation of the world. Such
a need is the maintenance of the fruitfulness of the earth,
annually imperilled by the changes of the seasons. Yet

---

regions of the Senegal and the Niger
it is believed that the Sky-god and the
Earth-goddess are the parents of the
principal spirits who dispense life and
death, weal and woe, among mankind.
The eldest son of Sky and Earth is
represented in very various forms,
sometimes as a hermaphrodite, sometimes in semi-animal shape, with the
head of a bull, a crocodile, a fish, or
a serpent. His name varies in the
different tribes, but the outward form
of his ceremonies is everywhere similar.
His rites, which are to some extent
veiled in mystery, are forbidden to
women. See Maurice Delafosse, *Haut-
Sénégal-Niger* (Paris, 1912), iii. 173-
175.

[1] Hesiod, *Theogony*, 159 *sqq.*

[2] Porphyry, *De antro nympharum*,
16 ; Aristides, *Or.* iii. (vol. i. p. 35 ed.
G. Dindorf, Leipsic, 1829) ; Scholiast
on Apollonius Rhodius, *Argon.* iv.
983.

[3] A. Lang, *Custom and Myth*
(London, 1884), pp. 45 *sqq.* ; *id.,
Myth, Ritual, and Religion* (London,
1887), i. 299 *sqq.* In Egyptian
mythology the separation of heaven
and earth was ascribed to Shu, the
god of light, who insinuated himself

between the bodies of Seb (Keb) the
earth-god and of Nut the sky-goddess.
On the monuments Shu is represented
holding up the star-spangled body of
Nut on his hands, while Seb reclines
on the ground. See A. Wiedemann,
Religion of the Ancient Egyptians (London, 1897), pp. 230 *sq.* ; E. A. Wallis
Budge, *The Gods of the Egyptians*, ii.
90, 97 *sq.*, 100, 105 ; A. Erman, *Die
ägyptische Religion*[2] (Berlin, 1909),
pp. 35 *sq.* ; C. P. Tiele, *Geschichte der
Religion im Altertum*, i. 33 *sq.* Thus
contrary to the usual mythical conception the Egyptians regarded the earth
as male and the sky as female. An
allusion in the *Book of the Dead* (ch.
69, vol. ii. p. 235, E. A. Wallis
Budge's translation, London, 1901) has
been interpreted as a hint that Osiris
mutilated his father Seb at the separation of earth and heaven, just as Cronus
mutilated his father Uranus. See H.
Brugsch, *Religion und Mythologie der
alten Aegypter* (Leipsic, 1885–1888),
p. 581 ; E. A. Wallis Budge, *op. cit.*
ii. 99 *sq.* Sometimes the Egyptians
conceived the sky as a great cow standing with its legs on the earth. See A.
Erman, *Die ägyptische Religion*,[2] pp.
7, 8.

the theory that the mutilation of the priests of Attis and the burial of the severed parts were designed to fertilize the ground may perhaps be reconciled with the cosmogonic myth if we remember the old opinion, held apparently by many peoples, that the creation of the world is year by year repeated in that great transformation which depends ultimately on the annual increase of the sun's heat.[1] However, the evidence for the celestial aspect of Attis is too slight to allow us to speak with any confidence on this subject. A trace of that aspect appears to survive in the star-spangled cap which he is said to have received from Cybele,[2] and which is figured on some monuments supposed to represent him.[3] His identification with the Phrygian moon-god Men Tyrannus[4] points in the same direction, but is probably due rather to the religious speculation of a later age than to genuine popular tradition.[5]

---

[1] Compare *The Dying God*, pp. 105 *sqq.*

[2] Julian, *Or.* v. pp. 165 B, 170 D (pp. 214, 221, ed. F. C. Hertlein); Sallustius philosophus, "De diis et mundo," iv. *Fragmenta Philosophorum Graecorum*, ed. F. G. A. Mullach, iii. 33.

[3] Drexler, *s.v.* "Men," in W. H. Roscher's *Lexikon der griech. und röm. Mythologie*, ii. 2745; H. Hepding, *Attis*, p. 120, note [8].

[4] H. Dessau, *Inscriptiones Latinae Selectae*, vol. ii. Pars i. pp. 145 *sq.*,

Nos. 4146-4149; H. Hepding, *Attis*, pp. 82, 86 *sq.*, 89 *sq.* As to Men Tyrannus, see Drexler, *s.v.* "Men," in W. H. Roscher's *Lexikon der griech. und röm. Myth.* ii. 2687 *sqq.*

[5] On the other hand Sir W. M. Ramsay holds that Attis and Men are deities of similar character and origin, but differentiated from each other by development in different surroundings (*Cities and Bishoprics of Phrygia*, i. 169); but he denies that Men was a moon-god (*op. cit.* i. 104, note [4]).

CHAPTER IV

HUMAN REPRESENTATIVES OF ATTIS

FROM inscriptions it appears that both at Pessinus and Rome the high-priest of Cybele regularly bore the name of Attis.[1] It is therefore a reasonable conjecture that he played the part of his namesake, the legendary Attis, at the annual festival.[2] We have seen that on the Day of Blood he drew blood from his arms, and this may have been an imitation of the self-inflicted death of Attis under the pine-tree. It is not inconsistent with this supposition that Attis was also represented at these ceremonies by an effigy; for instances can be shown in which the divine being is first represented by a living person and afterwards by an effigy, which is then burned or otherwise destroyed.[3] Perhaps we may go a step farther and conjecture that this mimic killing of the priest, accompanied by a real effusion of his blood, was in Phrygia, as it has been elsewhere, a substitute for a human sacrifice which in earlier times was actually offered. Sir W. M. Ramsay, whose authority on all questions relating to Phrygia no one will dispute, is

[1] In letters of Eumenes and Attalus, preserved in inscriptions at Sivrihissar, the priest at Pessinus is addressed as Attis. See A. von Domaszewski, "Briefe der Attaliden an den Priester von Pessinus," *Archaeologische - epigraphische Mittheilungen aus Oesterreich - Ungarn*, viii. (1884) pp. 96, 98; Ch. Michel, *Recueil d'Inscriptions Grecques*, pp. 57 *sq.* No. 45; W. Dittenberger, *Orientis Graeci Inscriptiones Selectae* (Leipsic, 1903-1905), vol. i. pp. 482 *sqq.* No. 315. For more evidence of inscriptions see H.

Hepding, *Attis*, p. 79; Rapp, *s.v.* "Attis," in W. H. Roscher's *Lexikon der griech. und röm. Mythologie*, i. 724. See also Polybius, xxii. 18 (20), (ed. L. Dindorf), who mentions a priest of the Mother of the Gods named Attis at Pessinus.

[2] The conjecture is that of Henzen, in *Annal. d. Inst.* 1856, p. 110, referred to by Rapp, *l.c.*

[3] *The Magic Art and the Evolution of Kings*, ii. 75 *sq.*; *The Dying God*, pp. 151 *sq.*, 209.

The high priest of Attis bore the god's name and seems to have personated him.

The drawing of the high priest's blood may have been a substitute for putting him to

of opinion that at these Phrygian ceremonies "the representative of the god was probably slain each year by a cruel
death, just as the god himself died."[1] We know from
Strabo[2] that the priests of Pessinus were at one time
potentates as well as priests ; they may, therefore, have
belonged to that class of divine kings or popes whose duty
it was to die each year for their people and the world.

The name
of Attis in
the royal
families of
Phrygia
and Lydia.

The name of Attis, it is true, does not occur among the
names of the old kings of Phrygia, who seem to have borne
the names of Midas and Gordias in alternate generations ;
but a very ancient inscription carved in the rock above a
famous Phrygian monument, which is known as the Tomb
of Midas, records that the monument was made for, or
dedicated to, King Midas by a certain Ates, whose name
is doubtless identical with .Attis, and who, if not a king
himself, may have been one of the royal family.[3] It is
worthy of note also that the name Atys, which, again,
appears to be only another form of Attis, is recorded as
that of an early king of Lydia ;[4] and that a son of Croesus,
king of Lydia, not only bore the name Atys but was said
to have been killed, while he was hunting a boar, by a
member of the royal Phrygian family, who traced his lineage
to King Midas and had fled to the court of Croesus because
he had unwittingly slain his own brother.[5] Scholars have
recognized in this story of the death of Atys, son of Croesus,
a mere double of the myth of Attis ;[6] and in view of the
facts which have come before us in the present inquiry[7] it

[1] Article "Phrygia," in *Encyclopaedia Britannica*, 9th ed. xviii. (1885) p. 853. Elsewhere, speaking of the religions of Asia Minor in general, the same writer says : "The highest priests and priest-esses played the parts of the great gods in the mystic ritual, wore their dress, and bore their names" (*Cities and Bishoprics of Phrygia*, i. 101).

[2] Strabo, xii. 5. 3, p. 567.

[3] (Sir) W. M. Ramsay, "A Study of Phrygian Art," *Journal of Hellenic Studies*, ix. (1888) pp. 379 *sqq.* ; *id.*, "A Study of Phrygian Art," *Journal of Hellenic Studies*, x. (1889) pp. 156 *sqq.*; G. Perrot et Ch. Chipiez, *Histoire de l'Art dans l'Antiquité*, v. 82 *sqq.*

[4] Herodotus, i. 94. According to Sir W. M. Ramsay, the conquering and ruling caste in Lydia belonged to the Phrygian stock (*Journal of Hellenic Studies*, ix. (1888) p. 351).

[5] Herodotus, i. 34-45. The tradition that Croesus would allow no iron weapon to come near Atys suggests that a similar taboo may have been imposed on the Phrygian priests named Attis. For taboos of this sort see *Taboo and the Perils of the Soul*, pp. 225 *sqq.*

[6] H. Stein on Herodotus, i. 43 ; Ed. Meyer, *s.v.* "Atys," in Pauly-Wissowa's *Real-Encyclopädie der clas-sischen Altertumswissenschaft*, ii. 2 col. 2262.

[7] See above, pp. 13, 16 *sq.*, 48 *sqq.*

1905

8770

2.10

14355

1.9 1.905

1 1945

IMPORTANT SAFETY INFORMATION

Any tire no matter how well constructed, may fail in use as a result of punctures, impact damage, improper inflation or other conditions resulting from use. Tire failures may create a risk of property damage or personal injury. To reduce the risk of tire failure we strongly recommend the following:

1. CHECK the pressure in your tires, including your spare, at least monthly when the tires are cool (after the vehicle has been stopped three hours and then driven less than one mile). Do not reduce pressure when tires are hot; use a tire gauge to check pressure and maintain it at the level recommended by the vehicle manufacturer. If a tire loses more than 1 pound of air pressure per month have it checked.

2. NEVER overload your tires. The maximum load carrying capability of your tires is molded on the sidewall of the tire.

3. CHECK your tires frequently for scrapes, bulges, separations, cuts or snags resulting from use. See your Duralon dealer immediately if any such condition is discovered.

4. NEVER operate your vehicle in excess of lawful speeds or the maximum speeds justified by driving conditions or in excess of speeds recommended for the tire you are using.

5. MAKE every effort to avoid running over objects that may damage the tire through impact or cutting such as chuckholes, glass, metal, etc.

6. NEVER drive on smooth tires. Tires should be removed when 2/32" of tread depth remains.

7. A Consumer Tire Guide with tips on auto tire care, safety and mileage performance is available free by writing

Duralon Tires, P.O. Box 26601, Akron, Ohio 44319

is a remarkable circumstance that the myth of a slain god should be told of a king's son.   May we conjecture that the Phrygian priests who bore the name of Attis and represented the god of that name were themselves members, perhaps the eldest sons, of the royal house, to whom their fathers, uncles, brothers, or other kinsmen deputed the honour of dying a violent death in the character of gods, while they reserved to themselves the duty of living, as long as nature allowed them, in the humbler character of kings?   If this were so, the Phrygian dynasty of Midas may have presented a close parallel to the Greek dynasty of Athamas, in which the eldest sons seem to have been regularly destined to the altar.[1]   But it is also possible that the divine priests who bore the name of Attis may have belonged to that indigenous race which the Phrygians, on their irruption into Asia from Europe, appear to have found and conquered in the land afterwards known as Phrygia.[2]   On the latter hypothesis the priests may have represented an older and higher civilization than that of their barbarous conquerors.   Be that as it may, the god they personated was a deity of vegetation whose divine life manifested itself especially in the pine-tree and the violets of spring ; and if they died in the character of that divinity, they corresponded to the mummers who are still slain in mimicry by European peasants in spring, and to the priest who was slain long ago in grim earnest on the wooded shore of the Lake of Nemi.

The Phrygian priests of Attis may have been members of the royal family.

[1] *The Dying God*, pp. 161 *sqq.*

[2] See (Sir) W. M. Ramsay, *s.v.* " Phrygia," *Encyclopaedia Britannica*, 9th ed. xviii. 849 *sq.* ; *id.*, " A Study of Phrygian Art," *Journal of Hellenic Studies*, ix. (1888) pp. 350 *sq.*   Prof. P. Kretschmer holds that both Cybele and Attis were gods of the indigenous Asiatic population, not of the Phrygian invaders (*Einleitung in die Geschichte der griechischen Sprache*, Göttingen, 1896, pp. 194 *sq.*).

CHAPTER V

THE HANGED GOD

The way in which the representatives of Attis were put to death is perhaps shown by the legend of Marsyas, who was hung on a pine-tree and flayed by Apollo.

A REMINISCENCE of the manner in which these old representatives of the deity were put to death is perhaps preserved in the famous story of Marsyas. He was said to be a Phrygian satyr or Silenus, according to others a shepherd or herdsman, who played sweetly on the flute. A friend of Cybele, he roamed the country with the disconsolate goddess to soothe her grief for the death of Attis.[1] The composition of the Mother's Air, a tune played on the flute in honour of the Great Mother Goddess, was attributed to him by the people of Celaenae in Phrygia.[2] Vain of his skill, he challenged Apollo to a musical contest, he to play on the flute and Apollo on the lyre. Being vanquished, Marsyas was tied up to a pine-tree and flayed or cut limb from limb either by the victorious Apollo or by a Scythian slave.[3] His skin was shown at Celaenae in historical times. It

---

[1] Diodorus Siculus, iii. 58 *sq.* As to Marsyas in the character of a shepherd or herdsman see Hyginus, *Fab.* 165 ; Nonnus, *Dionys.* i. 41 *sqq.* He is called a Silenus by Pausanias (i. 24. 1).

[2] Pausanias, x. 30. 9.

[3] Apollodorus, *Bibliotheca*, i. 4. 2 ; Hyginus, *Fab.* 165. Many ancient writers mention that the tree on which Marsyas suffered death was a pine. See Apollodorus, *l.c.* ; Nicander, *Alexipharmaca*, 301 *sq.*, with the Scholiast's note ; Lucian, *Tragodopodagra*, 314 *sq.* ; Archias Mitylenaeus, in *Anthologia Palatina*, vii. 696 ; Philostratus, Junior, *Imagines*, i. 3 ; Longus, *Pastor.* iv. 8 ; Zen-

obius, *Cent.* iv. 81 ; J. Tzetzes, *Chiliades*, i. 353 *sqq.* Pliny alone declares the tree to have been a plane, which according to him was still shown at Aulocrene on the way from Apamea to Phrygia (*Nat. Hist.* xvi. 240). On a candelabra in the Vatican the defeated Marsyas is represented hanging on a pine-tree (W. Helbig, *Führer*,[2] i. 225 *sq.*) ; but the monumental evidence is not consistent on this point (Jessen, *s.v.* "Marsyas," in W. H. Roscher's *Lexikon der griech. und röm. Mythologie*, ii. 2442). The position which the pine held in the myth and ritual of Cybele supports the preponderance of ancient testimony in favour of that tree.

hung at the foot of the citadel in a cave from which the river Marsyas rushed with an impetuous and noisy tide to join the Maeander.[1] So the Adonis bursts full-born from the precipices of the Lebanon ; so the blue river of Ibreez leaps in a crystal jet from the red rocks of the Taurus ; so the stream, which now rumbles deep underground, used to gleam for a moment on its passage from darkness to darkness in the dim light of the Corycian cave. In all these copious fountains, with their glad promise of fertility and life, men of old saw the hand of God and worshipped him beside the rushing river with the music of its tumbling waters in their ears. At Celaenae, if we can trust tradition, the piper Marsyas, hanging in his cave, had a soul for harmony even in death ; for it is said that at the sound of his native Phrygian melodies the skin of the dead satyr used to thrill, but that if the musician struck up an air in praise of Apollo it remained deaf and motionless.[2]

In this Phrygian satyr, shepherd, or herdsman who enjoyed the friendship of Cybele, practised the music so characteristic of her rites,[3] and died a violent death on her sacred tree, the pine, may we not detect a close resemblance to Attis, the favourite shepherd or herdsman of the goddess, who is himself described as a piper,[4] is said to have perished under a pine-tree, and was annually represented by an effigy hung, like Marsyas, upon a pine? We may conjecture that in old days the priest who bore the name and played the part of Attis at the spring festival of Cybele was regularly hanged or otherwise slain upon the sacred tree, and that this barbarous custom was afterwards mitigated into the form in which it is known to us in later times, when the priest merely drew blood from his body under the tree and attached an effigy instead of himself to its trunk. In the holy grove at Upsala men and animals were sacrificed by

Marsyas apparently a double of Attis.

---

[1] Herodotus, vii. 26 ; Xenophon, *Anabasis*, i. 2. 8 ; Livy, xxxviii. 13. 6 : Quintus Curtius, iii. 1. 1-5 ; Pliny, *Nat. Hist.* v. 106. Herodotus calls the river the Catarrhactes.

[2] Aelian, *Var. Hist.* xiii. 21.

[3] Catullus, lxiii. 22 ; Lucretius, ii. 620 ; Ovid, *Fasti*, iv. 181 *sq.*,

341 ; Polyaenus, *Stratagem.* viii. 53. 4. Flutes or pipes often appear on her monuments. See H. Dessau, *Inscriptiones Latinae Selectae*, Nos. 4100, 4143, 4145, 4152, 4153.

[4] Hippolytus, *Refutatio omnium haeresium*, v. 9, p. 168, ed. Duncker and Schneidewin.

The
hanging
and spear-
ing of Odin
and his
human
victims on
sacred
trees.

being hanged upon the sacred trees.[1] The human victims dedicated to Odin were regularly put to death by hanging or by a combination of hanging and stabbing, the man being strung up to a tree or a gallows and then wounded with a spear. Hence Odin was called the Lord of the Gallows or the God of the Hanged, and he is represented sitting under a gallows tree.[2] Indeed he is said to have been sacrificed to himself in the ordinary way, as we learn from the weird verses of the *Havamal*, in which the god describes how he acquired his divine power by learning the magic runes :

> " *I know that I hung on the windy tree*
> *For nine whole nights,*
> *Wounded with the spear, dedicated to Odin,*
> *Myself to myself.*" [3]

The hang-
ing and
spearing

The Bagobos of Mindanao, one of the Philippine Islands, used annually to sacrifice human victims for the good of the crops in a similar way. Early in December, when the

---

[1] Adam of Bremen, *Descriptio insularum Aquilonis*, 27 (Migne's *Patrologia Latina*, cxlvi. 643).

[2] S. Bugge, *Studien über die Entstehung der nördischen Götter- und Heldensagen* (Munich, 1889), pp. 339 *sqq.* ; K. Simrock, *Die Edda*[8] (Stuttgart, 1882), p. 382 ; K. Müllenhoff, *Deutsche Altertumskunde* (Berlin, 1870–1900), iv. 244 *sq.* ; H. M. Chadwick, *The Cult of Othin* (London, 1899), pp. 3-20. The old English custom of hanging and disembowelling traitors was probably derived from a practice of thus sacrificing them to Odin ; for among many races, including the Teutonic and Latin peoples, capital punishment appears to have been originally a religious rite, a sacrifice or consecration of the criminal to the god whom he had offended. See F. Liebrecht, *Zur Volkskunde* (Heilbronn, 1879), pp. 8 *sq.* ; K. von Amira, in H. Paul's *Grundriss der germanischen Philologie*,[2] iii. (Strasburg, 1900) pp. 197 *sq.* ; G. Vigfusson and F. York Powell, *Corpus Poeticum Boreale* (Oxford, 1883), i. 410 ; W. Golther, *Handbuch der germanischen Mythologie* (Leipsic,

1895), pp. 548 *sq.* ; Th. Mommsen, *Roman History*, bk. i. ch. 12 (vol. i. p. 192, ed. 1868) ; *id.*, *Römisches Strafrecht* (Leipsic, 1899), pp. 900 *sqq.* ; F. Granger, *The Worship of the Romans* (London, 1895), pp. 259 *sqq.* ; E. Westermarck, *The Origin and Development of the Moral Ideas*, i. (London, 1906) pp. 439 *sq.* So, too, among barbarous peoples the slaughter of prisoners in war is often a sacrifice offered by the victors to the gods to whose aid they ascribe the victory. See A. B. Ellis, *The Tshi-speaking Peoples of the Gold Coast* (London, 1887), pp. 169 *sq.* ; W. Ellis, *Polynesian Researches*[2] (London, 1832–1836), i. 289 ; Diodorus Siculus, xx. 65 ; Strabo, vii. 2. 3, p. 294 ; Caesar, *De bello Gallico*, vi. 17 ; Tacitus, *Annals*, i. 61, xiii. 57 ; Procopius, *De bello Gothico*, ii. 15. 24, ii. 25. 9 ; Jornandes, *Getica*, vi. 41 ; J. Grimm, *Deutsche Mythologie*[4] (Berlin, 1875–1878), i. 36 *sq.* ; Fr. Schwally, *Semitische Kriegsaltertümer* (Leipsic, 1901), pp. 29 *sqq.*

[3] *Havamal*, 139 *sqq.* (K. Simrock, *Die Edda*,[8] p. 55 ; K. Müllenhoff, *Deutsche Altertumskunde*, v. 270 *sq.*).

constellation Orion appeared at seven o'clock in the evening, of human victims among the Bagobos. the people knew that the time had come to clear their fields for sowing and to sacrifice a slave. The sacrifice was presented to certain powerful spirits as payment for the good year which the people had enjoyed, and to ensure the favour of the spirits for the coming season. The victim was led to a great tree in the forest ; there he was tied with his back to the tree and his arms stretched high above his head, in the attitude in which ancient artists portrayed Marsyas hanging on the fatal tree. While he thus hung by the arms, he was slain by a spear thrust through his body at the level of the armpits. Afterwards the body was cut clean through the middle at the waist, and the upper part was apparently allowed to dangle for a little from the tree, while the under part wallowed in blood on the ground. The two portions were finally cast into a shallow trench beside the tree. Before this was done, anybody who wished might cut off a piece of flesh or a lock of hair from the corpse and carry it to the grave of some relation whose body was being consumed by a ghoul. Attracted by the fresh corpse, the ghoul would leave the mouldering old body in peace. These sacrifices have been offered by men now living.[1]

In Greece the great goddess Artemis herself appears The hanging of Artemis. to have been annually hanged in effigy in her sacred grove of Condylea among the Arcadian hills, and there accordingly she went by the name of the Hanged One.[2] Indeed a trace of a similar rite may perhaps be detected even at Ephesus, the most famous of her sanctuaries, in the legend of a woman who hanged herself and was thereupon dressed by the compassionate goddess in her own divine garb and called by the name of Hecate.[3] Similarly, at Melite in Phthia, a story

---

[1] Fay-Cooper Cole, *The Wild Tribes of Davao District, Mindanao* (Chicago, 1913), pp. 114 *sqq.* (*Field Museum of Natural History, Publication* 170).

[2] Pausanias, viii. 23. 6 *sq.* The story, mentioned by Pausanias, that some children tied a rope round the neck of the image of Artemis was probably invented to explain a ritual practice of the same sort, as scholars have rightly perceived. See L. Preller, *Griechische Mythologie*, i.[4] 305, note [2] ; L. R. Farnell, *The Cults of the Greek States* (Oxford, 1896–1909), ii. 428 *sq.*; M. P. Nilsson, *Griechische Feste* (Leipsic, 1906), pp. 232 *sqq.* The Arcadian worship of the Hanged Artemis was noticed by Callimachus. See Clement of Alexandria, *Protrept.* ii. 38, p. 32, ed. Potter.

[3] Eustathius on Homer, *Od.* xii. 85, p. 1714 ; I. Bekker, *Anecdota Graeca*

was told of a girl named Aspalis who hanged herself, but who appears to have been merely a form of Artemis. For after her death her body could not be found, but an image of her was discovered standing beside the image of Artemis, and the people bestowed on it the title of Hecaerge or Far-shooter, one of the regular epithets of the goddess. Every year the virgins sacrificed a young goat to the image by hanging it, because Astypalis was said to have hanged herself.[1] The sacrifice may have been a substitute for hang-

The hanging of Helen.

ing an image or a human representative of Artemis. Again, in Rhodes the fair Helen was worshipped under the title of Helen of the Tree, because the queen of the island had caused her handmaids, disguised as Furies, to string her up to a bough.[2] That the Asiatic Greeks sacrificed animals in

The hanging of animal victims.

this fashion is proved by coins of Ilium, which represent an ox or cow hanging on a tree and stabbed with a knife by a man, who sits among the branches or on the animal's back.[3] At Hierapolis also the victims were hung on trees before they were burnt.[4] With these Greek and Scandinavian parallels before us we can hardly dismiss as wholly improb-

---

(Berlin, 1814–1821), i. 336 sq., s.v. Ἄγαλμα Ἑκάτης. The goddess Hecate was sometimes identified with Artemis, though in origin probably she was quite distinct. See L. R. Farnell, The Cults of the Greek States, ii. 499 sqq.

[1] Antoninus Liberalis, Transform. xiii.

[2] Pausanias, iii. 19. 9 sq.

[3] H. von Fritze, "Zum griechischer Opferritual," Jahrbuch des kaiser. deutsch. Archäologischen Instituts, xviii. (1903) pp. 58-67. In the ritual of Eleusis the sacrificial oxen were sometimes lifted up by young men from the ground. See G. Dittenberger, Sylloge Inscriptionum Graecarum,[2] vol. ii. pp. 166 sq. No. 521 (ἤραντο δὲ καὶ τοῖς μυστηρίοις τοὺς βοῦς ἐν Ἐλευσῖνι τῇ θυσίαι, κτλ.); E. S. Roberts and E. A. Gardner, Introduction to Greek Epigraphy, ii. (Cambridge, 1905) pp. 176 sq., No. 65. In this inscription the word ἤραντο is differently interpreted by P. Stengel, who supposes that it refers merely to

turning backwards and upwards the head of the victim. See P. Stengel, "Zum griechischen Opferritual," Jahrbuch des kaiser. deutsch. Archäologischen Instituts, xviii. (1903) pp. 113-123. But it seems highly improbable that so trivial an act should be solemnly commemorated in an inscription among the exploits of the young men (epheboi) who performed it. On the other hand, we know that at Nysa the young men did lift and carry the sacrificial bull, and that the act was deemed worthy of commemoration on the coins. See above, p. 206. The Wajagga of East Africa dread the ghosts of suicides; so when a man has hanged himself they take the rope from his neck and hang a goat in the fatal noose, after which they slay the animal. This is supposed to appease the ghost and prevent him from tempting human beings to follow his bad example. See B. Gutmann, "Trauer und Begrabnissitten der Wadschagga," Globus, lxxxix. (1906) p. 200.

[4] See above, p. 146.

able the conjecture that in Phrygia a man-god may have hung year by year on the sacred but fatal tree.

The tradition that Marsyas was flayed and that his skin was exhibited at Celaenae down to historical times may well reflect a ritual practice of flaying the dead god and hanging his skin upon the pine as a means of effecting his resurrection, and with it the revival of vegetation in spring. Similarly, in ancient Mexico the human victims who personated gods were often flayed and their bloody skins worn by men who appear to have represented the dead deities come to life again.[1] When a Scythian king died, he was buried in a grave along with one of his concubines, his cup-bearer, cook, groom, lacquey, and messenger, who were all killed for the purpose, and a great barrow was heaped up over the grave. A year afterwards fifty of his servants and fifty of his best horses were strangled ; and their bodies, having been disembowelled and cleaned out, were stuffed with chaff, sewn up, and set on scaffolds round about the barrow, every dead man bestriding a dead horse, which was bitted and bridled as in life.[2] These strange horsemen were no doubt supposed to mount guard over the king. The setting up of their stuffed skins might be thought to ensure their ghostly resurrection.

That some such notion was entertained by the Scythians is made probable by the account which the mediaeval traveller de Plano Carpini gives of the funeral customs of the Mongols. The traveller tells us that when a noble Mongol died, the custom was to bury him seated in the middle of a tent, along with a horse saddled and bridled, and a mare and her foal. Also they used to eat another horse, stuff the carcase with straw, and set it up on poles. All this they did in order that in the other world the dead man might have a tent to live in, a mare to yield milk, and a steed to ride, and that he might be able to breed horses. Moreover, the bones of the horse which they ate were burned for the good of his soul.[3] When the Arab traveller Ibn Batuta visited Peking in the fourteenth century,

---

[1] *The Scapegoat*, pp. 294 *sqq.*

[2] Herodotus, iv. 71 *sq.*

[3] Jean du Plan de Carpin, *Historia Mongalorum*, ed. D'Avezac (Paris, 1838), cap. iii. § iii.

he witnessed the funeral of an emperor of China who had been killed in battle. The dead sovereign was buried along with four young female slaves and six guards in a vault, and an immense mound like a hill was piled over him. Four horses were then made to run round the hillock till they could run no longer, after which they were killed, impaled, and set up beside the tomb.[1] When an Indian of Patagonia dies, he is buried in a pit along with some of his property. Afterwards his favourite horse, having been killed, skinned, and stuffed, is propped up on sticks with its head turned towards the grave. At the funeral of a chief four horses are sacrificed, and one is set up at each corner of the burial-place. The clothes and other effects of the deceased are burned ; and to conclude all, a feast is made of the horses' flesh.[2] The Scythians certainly believed in the existence of the soul after death and in the possibility of turning it to account. This is proved by the practice of one of their tribes, the Taurians of the Crimea, who used to cut off the heads of their prisoners and set them on poles over their houses, especially over the chimneys, in order that the spirits of the slain men might guard the dwellings.[3]

Some of the savages of Borneo allege a similar reason for their favourite custom of taking human heads. " The custom," said a Kayan chief, " is not horrible. It is an ancient custom, a good, beneficent custom, bequeathed to us

Some tribes of Borneo use the skulls of their enemies to

---

[1] *Voyages d'Ibn Batoutah, texte Arabe accompagné d'une traduction,* par C. Défrémery et B. R. Sanguinetti (Paris, 1853–1858), iv. 300 *sq.* For more evidence of similar customs, observed by Turanian peoples, see K. Neumann, *Die Hellenen im Skythenlande* (Berlin, 1855), pp. 237-239.

[2] Captain R. Fitz-roy, *Narrative of the Surveying Voyages of His Majesty's Ships " Adventure" and "Beagle"* (London, 1839), ii. 155 *sq.*

[3] Herodotus, iv. 103. Many Scythians flayed their dead enemies, and, stretching the skin on a wooden framework, carried it about with them on horseback (Herodotus, iv. 64). The souls of the dead may have been thought to attend on and serve the man who thus bore their remains about with him. It is also possible that

the custom was nothing more than a barbarous mode of wreaking vengeance on the dead. Thus a Persian king has been known to flay an enemy, stuff the skin with chaff, and hang it on a high tree (Procopius, *De bello Persico,* i. 5. 28). This was the treatment which the arch-heretic Manichaeus is said to have received at the hands of the Persian king whose son he failed to cure (Socrates, *Historia Ecclesiastica,* i. 22 ; Migne's *Patrologia Graeca,* lxvii. 137, 139). Still such a punishment may have been suggested by a religious rite. The idea of crucifying their human victims appears to have been suggested to the negroes of Benin by the crucifixes of the early Portuguese missionaries. See H. Ling Roth, *Great Benin* (Halifax, 1903), pp. 14 *sq.*

by our fathers and our fathers' fathers ; it brings us blessings, ^{ensure the} plentiful harvests, and keeps off sickness and pains. Those fertility of the ground who were once our enemies, hereby become our guardians, our and of friends, our benefactors." [1] Thus to convert dead foes into women, the abund- friends and allies all that is necessary is to feed and other- ance of wise propitiate their skulls at a festival when they are game, and so forth. brought into the village. "An offering of food is made to the heads, and their spirits, being thus appeased, cease to entertain malice against, or to seek to inflict injury upon, those who have got possession of the skull which formerly adorned the now forsaken body." [2] When the Sea Dyaks of Sarawak return home successful from a head-hunting expedition, they bring the head ashore with much ceremony, wrapt in palm leaves. "On shore and in the village, the head, for months after its arrival, is treated with the greatest consideration, and all the names and terms of endearment of which their language is capable are abundantly lavished on it ; the most dainty morsels, culled from their abundant though inelegant repast, are thrust into its mouth, and it is instructed to hate its former friends, and that, having been now adopted into the tribe of its captors, its spirit must be always with them ; sirih leaves and betel-nut are given to it, and finally a cigar is frequently placed between its ghastly and pallid lips. None of this disgusting mockery is performed with the intention of ridicule, but all to propitiate the spirit by kindness, and to procure its good wishes for the tribe, of whom it is now supposed to have become a member." [3] Amongst these Dyaks the "Head-Feast," which has been just described, is supposed to be the most beneficial in its

---

[1] W. H. Furness, *Home-Life of Borneo Head-Hunters* (Philadelphia, 1902), p. 59. According to Messrs. Hose and McDougall, the spirits which animate the skulls appear not to be those of the persons from whose shoulders the heads were taken. However, the spirits (called *Toh*) reside in or about the heads, and "it is held that in some way their presence in the house brings prosperity to it, especially in the form of good crops ; and so essential to the welfare of the house are the heads held to be that, if through fire a house has lost its heads and has no occasion for war, the people will beg a head, or even a fragment of one, from some friendly house, and will instal it in their own with the usual ceremonies." See Ch. Hose and W. McDougall, *The Pagan Tribes of Borneo* (London, 1912), ii. 20, 23.

[2] Spenser St. John, *Life in the Forests of the Far East* [2] (London, 1863), i. 197.

[3] Hugh Low, *Sarawak* (London, 1848), pp. 206 *sq.* In quoting this passage I have taken the liberty to correct a grammatical slip.

influence of all their feasts and ceremonies. "The object of them all is to make their rice grow well, to cause the forest to abound with wild animals, to enable their dogs and snares to be successful in securing game, to have the streams swarm with fish, to give health and activity to the people themselves, and to ensure fertility to their women. All these blessings, the possessing and feasting of a fresh head are supposed to be the most efficient means of securing. The very ground itself is believed to be benefited and rendered fertile, more fertile even than when the water in which fragments of gold presented by the Rajah have been washed, has been sprinkled over it." [1]

The stuffed skin of the human representative of the Phrygian god may have been used for like purposes.

In like manner, if my conjecture is right, the man who represented the father-god of Phrygia used to be slain and his stuffed skin hung on the sacred pine in order that his spirit might work for the growth of the crops, the multiplication of animals, and the fertility of women. So at Athens an ox, which appears to have embodied the corn-spirit, was killed at an annual sacrifice, and its hide, stuffed with straw and sewn up, was afterwards set on its feet and yoked to a plough as if it were ploughing, apparently in order to represent, or rather to promote, the resurrection of the slain

---

[1] Spenser St. John, *op. cit.* i. 204. See further G. A. Wilken, "Iets over de schedelvereering," *Bijdragen tot de Taal- Land- en Volkenkunde van Nederlandsch-Indië*, xxxviii. (1889) pp. 89-129; *id.*, *Verspreide Geschriften* (The Hague, 1912), iv. 37-81. A different view of the purpose of head-hunting is maintained by Mr. A. C. Kruyt, in his essay, "Het koppensnellen der Toradja's van Midden-Celebes, en zijne Beteekenis," *Verslagen en Mededeelingen der koninklijke Akademie van Wetenschappen*, Afdeeling Letterkunde, Vierde Reeks, iii. 2 (Amsterdam, 1899), pp. 147 *sqq.*

The natives of Nias, an island to the west of Sumatra, think it necessary to obtain the heads of their enemies for the purpose of celebrating the final obsequies of a dead chief. Their notion seems to be that the ghost of the deceased ruler demands this sacrifice in his honour, and will punish the omission of it by sending sickness or

other misfortunes on the survivors. Thus among these people the custom of head-hunting is based on their belief in human immortality and on their conception of the exacting demands which the dead make upon the living. When the skulls have been presented to a dead chief, the priest prays to him for his blessing on the sowing and harvesting of the rice, on the fruitfulness of women, and so forth. See C. Fries, "Das 'Koppensnellen' auf Nias," *Allgemeine Missions-Zeitschrift*, February, 1908, pp. 73-88. From this account it would seem that it is not the spirits of the slain men, but the ghost of the dead chief from whom the blessings of fertility and so forth are supposed to emanate. Compare Th. C. Rappard, "Het eiland Nias en zijne bewoners," *Bijdragen tot de Taal- Land- en Volkenkunde van Nederlandsch-Indië*, lxii. (1909) pp. 609-611.

corn-spirit at the end of the threshing.[1]   This employment
of the skins of divine animals for the purpose of ensuring
the revival of the slaughtered divinity might be illustrated by
other examples.[2]   Perhaps the hide of the bull which was
killed to furnish the regenerating bath of blood in the rites
of Attis may have been put to a similar use.

[1] *Spirits of the Corn and of the Wild*, ii. 4-7.

[2] *Spirits of the Corn and of the Wild*, ii. 169 *sqq.*

CHAPTER VI

ORIENTAL RELIGIONS IN THE WEST

Popularity of the worship of Cybele and Attis in the Roman Empire. THE worship of the Great Mother of the Gods and her lover or son was very popular under the Roman Empire. Inscriptions prove that the two received divine honours, separately or conjointly, not only in Italy, and especially at Rome, but also in the provinces, particularly in Africa, Spain, Portugal, France, Germany, and Bulgaria.[1] Their worship survived the establishment of Christianity by Constantine ; for Symmachus records the recurrence of the festival of the Great Mother,[2] and in the days of Augustine her effeminate priests still paraded the streets and squares of Carthage with whitened faces, scented hair, and mincing gait, while, like the mendicant friars of the Middle Ages, they begged alms from the passers-by.[3] In Greece, on the other hand, the bloody orgies of the Asiatic goddess and her consort appear to have found little favour.[4] The barbarous and cruel character of the worship, with its frantic excesses, was doubtless repugnant to the good taste and humanity of the Greeks, who seem to have preferred the kindred but gentler rites of Adonis. Yet the same features which shocked and repelled the Greeks may have positively

---

[1] H. Dessau, *Inscriptiones Latinae Selectae*, Nos. 4099, 4100, 4103, 4105, 4106, 4116, 4117, 4119, 4120, 4121, 4123, 4124, 4127, 4128, 4131, 4136, 4139, 4140, 4142, 4156, 4163, 4167 ; H. Hepding, *Attis*, pp. 85, 86, 93, 94, 95, Inscr. Nos. 21-24, 26, 50, 51, 52, 61, 62, 63. See further, J. Toutain, *Les Cultes Païens dans l'Empire Romain* (Paris, 1911), pp. 73 *sqq.*, 103 *sqq.*

[2] S. Dill, *Roman Society in the Last*

Century of the Western Empire[2] (London, 1899), p. 16.

[3] Augustine, *De civitate Dei*, vii. 26.

[4] But the two were publicly worshipped at Dyme and Patrae in Achaia (Pausanias, vii. 17. 9, vii. 20. 3), and there was an association for their worship at Piraeus. See P. Foucart, *Des Associations Religieuses chez les Grecs* (Paris, 1873), pp. 85 *sqq.*, 196 ; Ch. Michel, *Recueil d'Inscriptions Grecques*, p. 772, No. 982.

attracted the less refined Romans and barbarians of the West. The ecstatic frenzies, which were mistaken for divine inspiration,[1] the mangling of the body, the theory of a new birth and the remission of sins through the shedding of blood, have all their origin in savagery,[2] and they naturally appealed to peoples in whom the savage instincts were still strong. Their true character was indeed often disguised under a decent veil of allegorical or philosophical interpretation,[3] which probably sufficed to impose upon the rapt and enthusiastic worshippers, reconciling even the more cultivated of them to things which otherwise must have filled them with horror and disgust.

The religion of the Great Mother, with its curious blending of crude savagery with spiritual aspirations, was only one of a multitude of similar Oriental faiths which in the later days of paganism spread over the Roman Empire, and by saturating the European peoples with alien ideals of

The spread of Oriental faiths over the Roman Empire contributed to under-

---

[1] Rapp, *s.v.* "Kybele," in W. H. Roscher's *Lexikon der griech. und röm. Mythologie*, ii. 1656.

[2] As to the savage theory of inspiration or possession by a deity see (Sir) Edward B. Tylor, *Primitive Culture*,[2] ii. 131 *sqq.* As to the savage theory of a new birth see *Balder the Beautiful*, ii. 251 *sqq.* As to the use of blood to wash away sins see *The Magic Art and the Evolution of Kings*, ii. 107 *sqq.* ; *Psyche's Task*, Second Edition, pp. 44 *sq.*, 47 *sqq.*, 116 *sq.* Among the Cameroon negroes accidental homicide can be expiated by the blood of an animal. The relations of the slayer and of the slain assemble. An animal is killed and every person present is smeared with its blood on his face and breast. They think that the guilt of manslaughter is thus atoned for, and that no punishment will overtake the homicide. See Missionary Autenrieth, "Zur Religion der Kamerun-Neger," in *Mitteilungen der geographischen Gesellschaft zu Jena*, xii. (1893) pp. 93 *sq.* In Car Nicobar a man possessed by devils is cleansed of them by being rubbed all over with pig's blood and beaten with leaves.

The devils are thus transferred to the leaves, which are thrown into the sea before daybreak. See V. Solomon, "Extracts from diaries kept in Car Nicobar," in *Journal of the Anthropological Institute*, xxxii. (1902) p. 227. Similarly the ancient Greeks purified a homicide by means of pig's blood and laurel leaves. See my note on Pausanias, ii. 31. 8 (vol. iii. pp. 276-279). The original idea of thus purging a manslayer was probably to rid him of the angry ghost of his victim, just as in Car Nicobar a man is rid of devils in the same manner. The purgative virtue ascribed to the blood in these ceremonies may be based on the notion that the offended spirit accepts it as a substitute for the blood of the guilty person. This was the view of C. Meiners (*Geschichte der Religionen*, Hanover, 1806–1807, ii. 137 *sq.*) and of E. Rohde (*Psyche*,[3] Tübingen and Leipsic, 1903, ii. 77 *sq.*).

[3] A good instance of such an attempt to dress up savagery in the garb of philosophy is the fifth speech of the emperor Julian, "On the Mother of the Gods" (pp. 206 *sqq.* ed. F. C. Hertlein, Leipsic, 1875–1876).

life gradually undermined the whole fabric of ancient
civilization.[1]   Greek and Roman society was built on the
conception of the subordination of the individual to the
community, of the citizen to the state ; it set the safety of
the commonwealth, as the supreme aim of conduct, above
the safety of the individual whether in this world or in a
world to come.   Trained from infancy in this unselfish
ideal, the citizens devoted their lives to the public service
and were ready to lay them down for the common good ;
or if they shrank from the supreme sacrifice, it never
occurred to them that they acted otherwise than basely in
preferring their personal existence to the interests of their
country.   All this was changed by the spread of Oriental
religions which inculcated the communion of the soul
with God and its eternal salvation as the only objects
worth living for, objects in comparison with which the
prosperity and even the existence of the state sank into
insignificance.   The inevitable result of this selfish and
immoral doctrine was to withdraw the devotee more
and more from the public service, to concentrate his
thoughts on his own spiritual emotions, and to breed in
him a contempt for the present life which he regarded
merely as a probation for a better and an eternal.   The
saint and the recluse, disdainful of earth and rapt in ecstatic
contemplation of heaven, became in popular opinion the
highest ideal of humanity, displacing the old ideal of the
patriot and hero who, forgetful of self, lives and is ready to
die for the good of his country.   The earthly city seemed
poor and contemptible to men whose eyes beheld the City
of God coming in the clouds of heaven.   Thus the centre
of gravity, so to say, was shifted from the present to a
future life, and however much the other world may have
gained, there can be little doubt that this one lost heavily
by the change.   A general disintegration of the body
politic set in.   The ties of the state and the family were
loosened : the structure of society tended to resolve itself

[1] As to the diffusion of Oriental
religions in the Roman Empire see
G. Boissier, *La Religion Romaine
d'Auguste aux Antonins*[5] (Paris, 1900),
i. 349 *sqq.* ; J. Reville, *La Religion à*
Rome sous les Sévères (Paris, 1886), pp.
47 *sqq.* ; S. Dill, *Roman Society in the
Last Century of the Western Empire*[2]
(London, 1899), pp. 76 *sqq.*

into its individual elements and thereby to relapse into
barbarism ; for civilization is only possible through the
active co-operation of the citizens and their willingness to
subordinate their private interests to the common good.
Men refused to defend their country and even to continue
their kind.[1]   In their anxiety to save their own souls and
the souls of others, they were content to leave the material
world, which they identified with the principle of evil, to
perish around them.   This obsession lasted for a thousand
years.   The revival of Roman law, of the Aristotelian
philosophy, of ancient art and literature at the close of the
Middle Ages, marked the return of Europe to native ideals
of life and conduct, to saner, manlier views of the world.
The long halt in the march of civilization was over.   The
tide of Oriental invasion had turned at last.   It is ebbing
still.[2]

Among the gods of eastern origin who in the decline
of the ancient world competed against each other for the
allegiance of the West was the old Persian deity Mithra.

Popularity of the worship of Mithra ;

---

[1] Compare Servius on Virgil, *Aen.*
ii. 604, vi. 661; Origen, *Contra
Celsum*, viii. 73 (Migne's *Patrologia
Graeca*, xi. 1628) ; G. Boissier, *La
Religion Romaine d'Auguste aux
Antonins*[5] (Paris, 1900), i. 357 *sq.* ;
E. Westermarck, *The Origin and Development of the Moral Ideas* (London,
1906–1908), i. 345 *sq.* ; H. H.
Milman, *History of Latin Christianity*,[4] i. 150-153, ii. 90.   In the
passage just cited Origen tells us that
the Christians refused to follow the
Emperor to the field of battle even
when he ordered them to do so ; but
he adds that they gave the emperor
the benefit of their prayers and thus
did him more real service than if they
had fought for him with the sword.
On the decline of the civic virtues
under the influence of Christian asceti-
cism see W. E. H. Lecky, *History of
European Morals from Augustus to
Charlemagne*[3] (London, 1877), ii. 139
sqq.

[2] To prevent misapprehension I will
add that the spread of Oriental religions
was only one of many causes which
contributed to the downfall of ancient
civilization. Among these contributory
causes a friend, for whose judgment and
learning I entertain the highest respect,
counts bad government and a ruinous
fiscal system, two of the most powerful
agents to blast the prosperity of nations,
as may be seen in our own day by the
blight which has struck the Turkish
empire.   It is probable, too, as my
friend thinks, that the rapid diffusion
of alien faiths was as much an effect
as a cause of widespread intellectual
decay.   Such unwholesome growths
could hardly have fastened upon the
Graeco-Roman mind in the days of
its full vigour.   We may remember
the energy with which the Roman
Government combated the first outbreak of the Bacchic plague (Th.
Mommsen, *Roman History*, iii. 115
sq., ed. 1894).   The disastrous effects
of Roman financial oppression on the
industries and population of the empire,
particularly of Greece, are described
by George Finlay (*Greece under the
Romans*,[2] Edinburgh and London, 1857,
pp. 47 *sqq.*).

its resemblance to Christianity and its rivalry with that religion.

The immense popularity of his worship is attested by the monuments illustrative of it which have been found scattered in profusion all over the Roman Empire.[1]   In respect both of doctrines and of rites the cult of Mithra appears to have presented many points of resemblance not only to the religion of the Mother of the Gods[2] but also to Christianity.[3] The similarity struck the Christian doctors themselves and was explained by them as a work of the devil, who sought to seduce the souls of men from the true faith by a false and insidious imitation of it.[4]   So to the Spanish conquerors of Mexico and Peru many of the native heathen rites appeared to be diabolical counterfeits of the Christian sacraments.[5]   With more probability the modern student of comparative religion traces such resemblances to the similar and independent workings of the mind of man in his sincere, if crude, attempts to fathom the secret of the universe, and to adjust his little life to its awful mysteries. However that may be, there can be no doubt that the Mithraic religion proved a formidable rival to Christianity, combining as it did a solemn ritual with aspirations after moral purity and a hope of immortality.[6]   Indeed the issue of the conflict between the two faiths appears for a time to have hung in the balance.[7]   An instructive relic of the long

[1] See Fr. Cumont, *Textes et Monuments figurés relatifs aux Mystères de Mithra* (Brussels, 1896–1899); *id., s.v.* " Mithras," in W. H. Roscher's *Lexikon der griech. und röm. Mythologie*, ii. 3028 *sqq.* Compare *id., Les Religions Orientales dans le Paganisme Romain*[2] (Paris, 1909), pp. 207 *sqq.*

[2] Fr. Cumont, *Textes et Monuments*, i. 333 *sqq.*

[3] E. Renan, *Marc-Aurèle et la Fin du Monde Antique* (Paris, 1882), pp. 576 *sqq.*; Fr. Cumont, *Textes et Monuments*, i. 339 *sqq.*

[4] Tertullian, *De corona*, 15; *id., De praescriptione haereticorum*, 40; Justin Martyr, *Apologia*, i. 66; *id., Dialogus cum Tryphone*, 78 (Migne's *Patrologia Graeca*, vi. 429, 660). Tertullian explained in like manner the resemblance of the fasts of Isis and Cybele to the fasts of Christianity (*De jejunio*, 16). Justin Martyr thought that by

listening to the words of the inspired prophets the devils discovered the divine intentions and anticipated them by a series of profane and blasphemous imitations. Among these travesties of Christian truth he enumerates the death, resurrection, and ascension of Dionysus, the virgin birth of Perseus, and Bellerophon mounted on Pegasus, whom he regards as a parody of Christ riding on an ass. See Justin Martyr, *Apology*, i. 54.

[5] J. de Acosta, *Natural and Moral History of the Indies*, translated by E. Grimston (London, 1880), bk. v. chs. 11, 16, 17, 18, 24-28, vol. ii. pp. 324 *sq.*, 334 *sqq.*, 356 *sqq.*

[6] Compare S. Dill, *Roman Society in the Last Century of the Western Empire*[2] (London, 1899), pp. 80 *sqq.*; *id., Roman Society from Nero to Marcus Aurelius* (London, 1904), pp. 619 *sqq.*

[7] E. Renan, *Marc-Aurèle et la Fin*

struggle is preserved in our festival of Christmas, which the The festival of Christmas borrowed by the Church from the religion of Mithra.
Church seems to have borrowed directly from its heathen
rival.   In the Julian calendar the twenty-fifth of December
was reckoned the winter solstice,[1] and it was regarded as the
Nativity of the Sun, because the day begins to lengthen
and the power of the sun to increase from that turning-
point of the year.[2]   The ritual of the nativity, as it appears
to have been celebrated in Syria and Egypt, was remarkable.
The celebrants retired into certain inner shrines, from which
at midnight they issued with a loud cry, " The Virgin has
brought forth !   The light is waxing ! "[3]   The Egyptians
even represented the new-born sun by the image of an infant
which on his birthday, the winter solstice, they brought forth
and exhibited to his worshippers.[4]   No doubt the Virgin
who thus conceived and bore a son on the twenty-fifth of
December was the great Oriental goddess whom the Semites
called the Heavenly Virgin or simply the Heavenly Goddess ; in Semitic lands she was a form of Astarte.[5]   Now

---

du Monde Antique (Paris, 1882), pp.
579 *sq.* ; Fr. Cumont, *Textes et Monuments,* i. 338.

[1] Pliny, *Nat. Hist.* xviii. 221 ;
Columella, *De re rustica,* ix. 14. 12 ;
L. Ideler, *Handbuch der mathematischen
und· technischen Chronologie* (Berlin,
1825–1826), ii. 124 ; G. F. Unger, in
Iwan Müller's *Handbuch der klassischen
Altertumswissenschaft,* i.[1] (Nördlingen,
1886) p. 649.

[2] In the calendar of Philocalus the
twenty-fifth of December is marked *N.
Invicti,* that is, *Natalis Solis Invicti.*
See *Corpus Inscriptionum Latinarum,*
i.[2] Pars prior (Berlin, 1893), p. 278,
with Th. Mommsen's commentary,
pp. 338 *sq.*

[3] Cosmas Hierosolymitanus, *Com-
mentarii in Sancti Gregorii Nazianzeni
Carmina* (Migne's *Patrologia Graeca,*
xxxviii. 464) : ταύτην [Christmas] ἦγον
ἔκπαλαι δὲ τὴν ἡμέραν ἑορτὴν Ἕλληνες,
καθ' ἣν ἐτελοῦντο κατὰ τὸ μεσονύκτιον,
ἐν ἀδύτοις τισὶν ὑπεισερχόμενοι, ὅθεν
ἐξιόντες ἔκραζον· "Ἡ παρθένος ἔτεκεν,
αὔξει φῶς." ταύτην Ἐπιφάνιος ὁ μέγας
τῆς Κυπρίων ἱερεύς φησι τὴν ἑορτὴν καὶ
Σαρρακηνοὺς ἄγειν τῇ παρ' αὐτῶν σεβομένῃ

Ἀφροδίτῃ, ἣν δὴ Χαμαρᾷ τῇ αὐτῶν
προσαγορεύουσι γλώττῃ. The passage
is quoted, with some verbal variations,
by Ch. Aug. Lobeck, *Aglaophamus*
(Königsberg, 1829), ii. 1227 note[z].
See Franz Cumont, " Le Natalis Invicti," *Comptes Rendus de l'Académie
des Inscriptions et Belles-Lettres, 1911*
(Paris, 1911), pp. 292-298, whose
learned elucidations I follow in the
text.   That the festival of the Nativity
of the Sun was similarly celebrated in
Egypt may be inferred from a Greek
calendar drawn up by the astrologer
Antiochus in Lower Egypt at the end
of the second or the beginning of the
third century A.D. ; for under the
25th December the calendar has the
entry, " Birthday of the Sun, the light
waxes " (Ἡλίου γενέθλιον· αὔξει φῶς).
See F. Cumont, *op. cit.* p. 294.

[4] Macrobius, *Saturnalia,* i. 18. 10.

[5] F. Cumont, *s.v.* " Caelestis," in
Pauly - Wissowa's *Real - Encyclopädie
der classischen Altertumswissenschaft,*
v. i. 1247 *sqq.*   She was called the
Queen of Heaven (Jeremiah vii. 18,
xliv. 18), the Heavenly Goddess
(Herodotus, iii. 8 ; Pausanias, i. 14.

Mithra was regularly identified by his worshippers with the Sun, the Unconquered Sun, as they called him ;[1] hence his nativity also fell on the twenty-fifth of December.[2] The Gospels say nothing as to the day of Christ's birth, and accordingly the early Church did not celebrate it. In time, however, the Christians of Egypt came to regard the sixth of January as the date of the Nativity, and the custom of commemorating the birth of the Saviour on that day gradually spread until by the fourth century it was universally established in the East. But at the end of the third or the beginning of the fourth century the Western Church, which had never recognized the sixth of January as the day of the Nativity, adopted the twenty-fifth of December as the true date, and in time its decision was accepted also by the Eastern Church. At Antioch the change was not introduced till about the year 375 A.D.[3]

Motives for the institution of Christmas. What considerations led the ecclesiastical authorities to institute the festival of Christmas? The motives for the innovation are stated with great frankness by a Syrian writer, himself a Christian. "The reason," he tells us, "why the fathers transferred the celebration of the sixth of January to the twenty-fifth of December was this. It was a custom of the heathen to celebrate on the same twenty-fifth of December the birthday of the Sun, at which they kindled

---

7), or the Heavenly Virgin (Tertullian, *Apologeticus*, 23 ; Augustine, *De civitate Dei*, ii. 4). The Greeks spoke of her as the Heavenly Aphrodite (Herodotus, i. 105 ; Pausanias, i. 14. 7). A Greek inscription found in Delos contains a dedication to Astarte Aphrodite ; and another found in the same island couples Palestinian Astarte and Heavenly Aphrodite. See G. Dittenberger, *Sylloge Inscriptionum Graecorum*,[2] vol. ii. pp. 619 *sq.*, No. 764 ; R. A. Stewart Macalister, *The Philistines, their History and Civilization* (London, 1913), p. 94.

[1] Dedications to Mithra the Unconquered Sun (*Soli invicto Mithrae*) have been found in abundance. See Fr. Cumont, *Textes et Monuments*, ii. 99 *sqq.* As to the worship of the Unconquered Sun (*Sol Invictus*) see

H. Usener, *Das Weihnachtsfest*[2] (Bonn, 1911), pp. 348 *sqq.*

[2] Fr. Cumont, *op. cit.* i. 325 *sq.*, 339.

[3] J. Bingham, *The Antiquities of the Christian Church*, bk. xx. ch. iv. (Bingham's *Works*, vol. vii. pp. 279 *sqq.*, Oxford, 1855) ; C. A. Credner, "De natalitiorum Christi origine," *Zeitschrift für die historische Theologie*, iii. 2 (1833), pp. 236 *sqq.* ; Mgr. L. Duchesne, *Origines du Culte Chrétien*[3] (Paris, 1903), pp. 257 *sqq.* ; Th. Mommsen, in *Corpus Inscriptionum Latinarum*, i.[2] Pars prior, p. 338. The earliest mention of the festival of Christmas is in the calendar of Philocalus, which was drawn up at Rome in 336 A.D. The words are *VIII. kal. jan., natus Christus in Betleem Judee* (L. Duchesne, *op. cit.* p. 258).

lights in token of festivity.   In these solemnities and festivities the Christians also took part.   Accordingly when the doctors of the Church perceived that the Christians had a leaning to this festival, they took counsel and resolved that the true Nativity should be solemnized on that day and the festival of the Epiphany on the sixth of January. Accordingly, along with this custom, the practice has prevailed of kindling fires till the sixth." [1]   The heathen origin of Christmas is plainly hinted at, if not tacitly admitted, by Augustine when he exhorts his Christian brethren not to celebrate that solemn day like the heathen on account of the sun, but on account of him who made the sun. [2]   In like manner Leo the Great rebuked the pestilent belief that Christmas was solemnized because of the birth of the new sun, as it was called, and not because of the nativity of Christ. [3]

Thus it appears that the Christian Church chose to celebrate the birthday of its Founder on the twenty-fifth of December in order to transfer the devotion of the heathen from the Sun to him who was called the Sun of Righteousness. [4]   If that was so, there can be no intrinsic improba-

The Easter celebration of the death and resurrection of Christ

[1] Quoted by C. A. Credner, *op. cit.* p. 239, note [46]; by Th. Mommsen, *Corpus Inscriptionum Latinarum*, i. [2] Pars prior, pp. 338 *sq.* ; and by H. Usener, *Das Weihnachtsfest* [2] (Bonn, 1911), pp. 349 *sq.*

[2] Augustine, *Serm.* cxc. 1 (Migne's *Patrologia Latina*, xxxviii. 1007).

[3] Leo the Great, *Serm.* xxii. (*al.* xxi.) 6 (Migne's *Patrologia Latina*, liv. 198).   Compare St. Ambrose, *Serm.* vi. 1 (Migne's *Patrologia Latina*, xvii. 614).

[4] A. Credner, *op. cit.* pp. 236 *sqq.* ; E. B. Tylor, *Primitive Culture*, [2] ii. 297 *sq.* ; Fr. Cumont, *Textes et Monuments*, i. 342, 355 *sq.*; Th. Mommsen, in *Corpus Inscriptionum Latinarum*, i. [2] Pars prior, pp. 338 *sq.* ; H. Usener, *Das Weihnachtsfest* [2] (Bonn, 1911), pp. 348 *sqq.*   A different explanation of Christmas has been put forward by Mgr. Duchesne.   He shows that among the early Christians the death of Christ was commonly supposed to have fallen on the twenty-fifth of March, that day

having been "chosen arbitrarily, or rather suggested by its coincidence with the official equinox of spring." It would be natural to assume that Christ had lived an exact number of years on earth, and therefore that his incarnation as well as his death took place on the twenty-fifth of March.   In point of fact the Church has placed the Annunciation and with it the beginning of his mother's pregnancy on that very day.   If that were so, his birth would in the course of nature have occurred nine months later, that is, on the twenty-fifth of December.   Thus on Mgr. Duchesne's theory the date of the Nativity was obtained by inference from the date of the Crucifixion, which in its turn was chosen because it coincided with the official equinox of spring. Mgr. Duchesne does not notice the coincidence of the vernal equinox with the festival of Attis.   See his work, *Origines du Culte Chrétien* [3] (Paris, 1903), pp. 261-265, 272.   The tradition that both the conception and the

bility in the conjecture that motives of the same sort may
have led the ecclesiastical authorities to assimilate the
Easter festival of the death and resurrection of their Lord
to the festival of the death and resurrection of another
Asiatic god which fell at the same season.   Now the Easter
rites still observed in Greece, Sicily, and Southern Italy bear
in some respects a striking resemblance to the rites of
Adonis, and I have suggested that the Church may have
consciously adapted the new festival to its heathen predecessor for the sake of winning souls to Christ.[1]   But this
adaptation probably took place in the Greek-speaking
rather than in the Latin-speaking parts of the ancient
world ; for the worship of Adonis, while it flourished among
the Greeks, appears to have made little impression on Rome
and the West.[2]   Certainly it never formed part of the official
Roman religion.   The place which it might have taken in
the affections of the vulgar was already occupied by the
similar but more barbarous worship of Attis and the Great
Mother.   Now the death and resurrection of Attis were
officially celebrated at Rome on the twenty-fourth and
twenty-fifth of March,[3] the latter being regarded as the
spring equinox,[4] and therefore as the most appropriate day
for the revival of a god of vegetation who had been dead
or sleeping throughout the winter.   But according to an
ancient and widespread tradition Christ suffered on the
twenty-fifth of March, and accordingly some Christians
regularly celebrated the Crucifixion on that day without
any regard to the state of the moon.   This custom was
certainly observed in Phrygia, Cappadocia, and Gaul, and
there seem to be grounds for thinking that at one time it
was followed also in Rome.[5]   Thus the tradition which

---

death of Christ fell on the twenty-fifth
of March is mentioned and apparently
accepted by Augustine (*De Trinitate*,
iv. 9, Migne's *Patrologia Latina*, xlii.
894).

[1] See above, pp. 253 *sqq.*

[2] However, the lament for Adonis
is mentioned by Ovid (*Ars Amat.* i.
75 *sq.*) along with the Jewish observance of the Sabbath.

[3] See above, pp. 268 *sqq.*

[4] Columella, *De re rustica*, ix. 14. 1 ;
Pliny, *Nat. Hist.* xviii. 246 ; Macrobius, *Saturn.* i. 21. 10 ; L. Ideler,
*Handbuch der mathematischen und
technischen Chronologie*, ii. 124.

[5] Mgr. L. Duchesne, *Origines du
Culte Chrétien*,[3] pp. 262 *sq.*   That
Christ was crucified on the twenty-
fifth of March in the year 29 is ex-
pressly affirmed by Tertullian (*Adversus
Judaeos*, 8, vol. ii. p. 719, ed. F.

placed the death of Christ on the twenty-fifth of March was ancient and deeply rooted. It is all the more remarkable because astronomical considerations prove that it can have had no historical foundation.[1] The inference appears to be inevitable that the passion of Christ must have been arbitrarily referred to that date in order to harmonize with an older festival of the spring equinox. This is the view of the learned ecclesiastical historian Mgr. Duchesne, who points out that the death of the Saviour was thus made to fall upon the very day on which, according to a widespread belief, the world had been created.[2] But the resur-

---

Oehler), Hippolytus (*Commentary on Daniel*, iv. 23, vol. i. p. 242, ed. Bonwetsch and Achelis), and Augustine (*De civitate Dei*, xviii. 54; *id.*, *De Trinitate*, iv. 9). See also *Thesaurus Linguae Latinae*, iv. (Leipsic, 1906–1909) col. 1222, *s.v.* "Crucimissio": "*POL. SILV. fast. Mart 25 aequinoctium. principium veris. crucimissio gentilium. Christus passus hoc die.*" From this last testimony we learn that there was a gentile as well as a Christian crucifixion at the spring equinox. The gentile crucifixion was probably the affixing of the effigy of Attis to the tree, though at Rome that ceremony appears to have taken place on the twenty-second rather than on the twenty-fifth of March. See above, p. 267. The Quartodecimans of Phrygia celebrated the twenty-fifth of March as the day of Christ's death, quoting as their authority certain acts of Pilate; in Cappadocia the adherents of this sect were divided between the twenty-fifth of March and the fourteenth of the moon. See Epiphanius, *Adversus Haeres.* l. 1 (vol. ii. p. 447, ed. G. Dindorf; Migne's *Patrologia Graeca*, xli. 884 *sq.*). In Gaul the death and resurrection of Christ were regularly celebrated on the twenty-fifth and twenty-seventh of March as late as the sixth century. See Gregory of Tours, *Historia Francorum*, viii. 31. 6 (Migne's *Patrologia Latina*, lxxi. 566); S. Martinus Dumiensis (bishop of Braga), *De Pascha*, 1 (Migne's *Patrologia Latina*, lxxii. 50), who says: "*A plerisque Gallicanis episcopis usque*

ante non multum tempus custoditum est, ut semper VIII. Kal. April. diem Paschae celebrent, in quo facta Christi resurrectio traditur." According to this last testimony, it was the resurrection, not the crucifixion, of Christ that was celebrated on the twenty-fifth of March; but Mgr. Duchesne attributes the statement to a mistake of the writer. With regard to the Roman practice the twenty-fifth and twenty-seventh of March are marked in ancient Martyrologies as the dates of the Crucifixion and Resurrection. See *Vetustius Occidentalis Ecclesiae Martyrologium*, ed. Franciscus Maria Florentinus (Lucca, 1667), pp. 396 *sq.*, 405 *sq.* On this subject Mgr. Duchesne observes: "Hippolytus, in his Paschal Table, marks the Passion of Christ in a year in which the fourteenth of Nisan falls on Friday twenty-fifth March. In his commentary on Daniel he expressly indicates Friday the twenty-fifth of March and the consulship of the two Gemini. The Philocalien Catalogue of the Popes gives the same date as to day and year. It is to be noted that the cycle of Hippolytus and the Philocalien Catalogue are derived from official documents, and may be cited as evidence of the Roman ecclesiastical usage" (*Origines du Culte Chrétien*,[3] p. 262).

[1] Mgr. L. Duchesne, *op. cit.* p. 263.

[2] Mgr. L. Duchesne, *l.c.* A sect of the Montanists held that the world began and that the sun and moon were created at the spring equinox, which, however, they dated on the twenty-

Heathen
festivals
displaced
by
Christian.

rection of Attis, who combined in himself the characters of the divine Father and the divine Son,[1] was officially celebrated at Rome on the same day.   When we remember that the festival of St. George in April has replaced the ancient pagan festival of the Parilia ;[2] that the festival of St. John the Baptist in June has succeeded to a heathen Midsummer festival of water ;[3] that the festival of the Assumption of the Virgin in August has ousted the festival of Diana ;[4] that the feast of All Souls in November is a continuation of an old heathen feast of the dead ;[5] and that the Nativity of Christ himself was assigned to the winter solstice in December because that day was deemed the Nativity of the Sun ;[6] we can hardly be thought rash or unreasonable in conjecturing that the other cardinal festival of the Christian church — the solemnization of Easter — may have been in like manner, and from like motives of edification, adapted to a similar celebration of the Phrygian god Attis at the vernal equinox.[7]

Coinci-
dence be-
tween the
pagan
and the
Christian
festivals of
the divine
death and
resurrec-
tion.

At least it is a remarkable coincidence, if it is nothing more, that the Christian and the heathen festivals of the divine death and resurrection should have been solemnized at the same season and in the same places.   For the places which celebrated the death of Christ at the spring equinox were Phrygia, Gaul, and apparently Rome, that is, the very regions in which the worship of Attis either originated or

---

fourth of March (Sozomenus, *Historia Ecclesiastica*, vii. 18).   At Henen-Su in Egypt there was celebrated a festival of the "hanging out of the heavens," that is, the supposed reconstituting of the heavens each year in the spring (E. A. Wallis Budge, *The Gods of the Egyptians*, ii. 63).   But the Egyptians thought that the creation of the world took place at the rising of Sirius (Porphyry, *De antro nympharum*, 24 ; Solinus, xxxii. 13), which in antiquity fell on the twentieth of July (L. Ideler, *Handbuch der mathematischen und technischen Chronologie*, i. 127 *sqq.*).

[1] See above, pp. 263, 281 *sqq.*
[2] *The Magic Art and the Evolution of Kings*, ii. 324 *sqq.*
[3] Above, pp. 246 *sqq.*
[4] *The Magic Art and the Evolution*

of *Kings*, i. 14 *sqq.*
[5] See below, vol. ii. pp. 81 *sqq.*
[6] Above, pp. 302 *sqq.*
[7] Another instance of the substitution of a Christian for a pagan festival may be mentioned.   On the first of August the people of Alexandria used to commemorate the defeat of Mark Antony by Augustus and the entrance of the victor into their city.   The heathen pomp of the festival offended Eudoxia, wife of Theodosius the Younger, and she decreed that on that day the Alexandrians should thenceforth celebrate the deliverance of St. Peter from prison instead of the deliverance of their city from the yoke of Antony and Cleopatra.   See L. Ideler, *Handbuch der mathematischen und technischen Chronologie*, i. 154.

struck deepest root.   It is difficult to regard the coincidence as purely accidental.   If the vernal equinox, the season at which in the temperate regions the whole face of nature testifies to a fresh outburst of vital energy, had been viewed from of old as the time when the world was annually created afresh in the resurrection of a god, nothing could be more natural than to place the resurrection of the new deity at the same cardinal point of the year.   Only it is to be observed that if the death of Christ was dated on the twenty-fifth of March, his resurrection, according to Christian tradition, must have happened on the twenty-seventh of March, which is just two days later than the vernal equinox of the Julian calendar and the resurrection of Attis.   A similar displacement of two days in the adjustment of Christian to heathen celebrations occurs in the festivals of St. George and the Assumption of the Virgin.   However, another Christian tradition, followed by Lactantius and perhaps by the practice of the Church in Gaul, placed the death of Christ on the twenty-third and his resurrection on the twenty-fifth of March.[1]   If that was so, his resurrection coincided exactly with the resurrection of Attis.

In point of fact it appears from the testimony of an anonymous Christian, who wrote in the fourth century of our era, that Christians and pagans alike were struck by the remarkable coincidence between the death and resurrection of their respective deities, and that the coincidence formed a theme of bitter controversy between the adherents of the rival religions, the pagans contending that the resurrection of Christ was a spurious imitation of the resurrection of Attis, and the Christians asserting with equal warmth that the resurrection of Attis was a diabolical counterfeit of the resurrection of Christ.   In these unseemly bickerings the heathen took what to a superficial observer might seem strong ground by arguing that their god was the older and therefore presumably the original, not the counterfeit, since as a general rule an original is older than its copy. This feeble argument the Christians easily rebutted.   They

---

[1] Lactantius, *De mortibus perse-cutorum*, 2 ; *id.*, *Divin. Institut.* iv. 10. 18.   As to the evidence of the Gallic usage see S. Martinus Dumi-ensis, quoted above, p. 307 note.

admitted, indeed, that in point of time Christ was the junior
deity, but they triumphantly demonstrated his real seniority
by falling back on the subtlety of Satan, who on so
important an occasion had surpassed himself by inverting
the usual order of nature.[1]

Com-
promise of
Christi-
anity with
paganism.

Taken altogether, the coincidences of the Christian with
the heathen festivals are too close and too numerous to be
accidental. They mark the compromise which the Church
in the hour of its triumph was compelled to make with
its vanquished yet still dangerous rivals. The inflexible
Protestantism of the primitive missionaries, with their fiery
denunciations of heathendom, had been exchanged for the
supple policy, the easy tolerance, the comprehensive
charity of shrewd ecclesiastics, who clearly perceived
that if Christianity was to conquer the world it could
do so only by relaxing the too rigid principles of its
Founder, by widening a little the narrow gate which leads

Parallel
with
Buddhism.

to salvation. In this respect an instructive parallel might
be drawn between the history of Christianity and the

---

[1] The passage occurs in the 84th
of the *Quaestiones Veteris et Novi
Testamenti* (Migne's *Patrologia Latina*,
xxxv. 2279), which are printed in the
works of Augustine, though internal
evidence is said to shew that they
cannot be by that Father, and that they
were written three hundred years after
the destruction of Jerusalem. The
writer's words are as follows : "*Diabolus
autem, qui est satanas, ut fallaciae suae
auctoritatem aliquam possit adhibere,
et mendacia sua commentitia veritate
colorare, primo mense quo sacramenta
dominica scit celebranda, quia non
mediocris potentiae est, Paganis quae
observarent instituit mysteria, ut
animas eorum duabus ex causis in
errore detineret : ut quia praevenit
veritatem fallacia, melius quiddam
fallacia videretur, quasi antiquitate
praejudicans veritati. Et quia in
primo mense, in quo aequinoctium
habent Romani, sicut et nos, ea ipsa
observatio ab his custoditur ; ita etiam
per sanguinem dicant expiationem fieri,
sicut et nos per crucem : hac versutia
Paganos detinet in errore, ut putent*

*veritatem nostram imitationem potius
videri quam veritatem, quasi per
aemulationem superstitione quadam
inventam. Nec enim verum potest,
inquiunt, aestimari quod postea est
inventum. Sed quia apud nos pro
certo veritas est, et ab initio haec est,
virtutum atque prodigiorum signa per-
hibent testimonium, ut, teste virtute,
diaboli improbitas innotescat.*" I have
to thank my learned friend Professor
Franz Cumont for pointing out this
passage to me. He had previously
indicated and discussed it ("La
Polémique de l'Ambrosiaster contre les
Païens," *Revue d'Histoire et de Littéra-
ture religieuses*, viii. (1903) pp. 419
sqq.). Though the name of Attis is
not mentioned in the passage, I agree
with Prof. Cumont in holding that
the bloody expiatory rites at the spring
equinox, to which the writer refers,
can only be those of the Day of Blood
which formed part of the great aequi-
noctial festival of Attis. Compare F.
Cumont, *Les Religions Orientales dans
le Paganisme Romain*[2] (Paris, 1909),
pp. 106 *sq.*, 333 *sq.*

history of Buddhism.[1] Both systems were in their origin essentially ethical reforms born of the generous ardour, the lofty aspirations, the tender compassion of their noble Founders, two of those beautiful spirits who appear at rare intervals on earth like beings come from a better world to support and guide our weak and erring nature.[2] Both preached moral virtue as the means of accomplishing what they regarded as the supreme object of life, the eternal salvation of the individual soul, though by a curious antithesis the one sought that salvation in a blissful eternity, the other in a final release from suffering, in annihilation. But the austere ideals of sanctity which they inculcated were too deeply opposed not only to the frailties but to the natural instincts of humanity ever to be carried out in practice by more than a small number of disciples, who consistently renounced the ties of the family and the state in order to work out their own salvation in the still seclusion of the cloister. If such faiths were to be nominally accepted by whole nations or even by the world, it was essential that they should first be modified or transformed so as to accord in some measure with the prejudices, the passions, the superstitions of the vulgar. This process of accommodation was carried out in after ages by followers who, made of less ethereal stuff than their masters, were for that reason the better fitted to mediate between them and the common herd. Thus as time went on, the two religions, in exact proportion to their growing popularity, absorbed more and more of those baser elements which they had been instituted for the very purpose of suppressing. Such spiritual decadences are

---

[1] On the decadence of Buddhism and its gradual assimilation to those popular Oriental superstitions against which it was at first directed, see Monier Williams, *Buddhism* [2] (London, 1890), pp. 147 *sqq.*

[2] The historical reality both of Buddha and of Christ has sometimes been doubted or denied. It would be just as reasonable to question the historical existence of Alexander the Great and Charlemagne on account of the legends which have gathered round them. The great religious movements which have stirred humanity to its depths and altered the beliefs of nations spring ultimately from the conscious and deliberate efforts of extraordinary minds, not from the blind unconscious co-operation of the multitude. The attempt to explain history without the influence of great men may flatter the vanity of the vulgar, but it will find no favour with the philosophic historian.

inevitable.   The world cannot live at the level of its great men.   Yet it would be unfair to the generality of our kind to ascribe wholly to their intellectual and moral weakness the gradual divergence of Buddhism and Christianity from their primitive patterns.   For it should never be forgotten that by their glorification of poverty and celibacy both these religions struck straight at the root not merely of civil society but of human existence.   The blow was parried by the wisdom or the folly of the vast majority of mankind, who refused to purchase a chance of saving their souls with the certainty of extinguishing the species.

CHAPTER VII

HYACINTH

ANOTHER mythical being who has been supposed to belong to the class of gods here discussed is Hyacinth. He too has been interpreted as the vegetation which blooms in spring and withers under the scorching heat of the summer sun.[1] Though he belongs to Greek, not to Oriental mythology, some account of him may not be out of place in the present discussion. According to the legend, Hyacinth was the youngest and handsomest son of the ancient king Amyclas, who had his capital at Amyclae in the beautiful vale of Sparta. One day playing at quoits with Apollo, he was accidentally killed by a blow of the god's quoit. Bitterly the god lamented the death of his friend. The hyacinth—"that sanguine flower inscribed with woe"—sprang from the blood of the hapless youth, as anemones and roses from the blood of Adonis, and violets from the blood of Attis:[2] like these vernal flowers it heralded the advent of another spring and gladdened the hearts of men with the promise of a joyful resurrection. The flower is usually supposed to be not what we call a hyacinth, but a little purple iris with the letters of lamentation (AI, which in

The Greek Hyacinth interpreted as the vegetation which blooms and withers away.

---

[1] G. F. Schömann, *Griechische Alterthümer*[4] (Berlin, 1897-1902), ii. 473; L. Preller, *Griechische Mythologie*, i.[4] (Berlin, 1894) pp. 248 *sq.*; Greve, *s.v.* "Hyakinthos," in W. H. Roscher's *Lexikon der griech. und röm. Mythologie*, i. 2763 *sq.* Other views of Hyacinth have been expressed by G. F. Welcker (*Griechische Götterlehre*, Göttingen, 1857-1862, i. 472), G. F. Unger ("Der Isthmientag und die Hyakin-thien," *Philologus*, xxxvii. (1877) pp. 20 *sqq.*), E. Rohde (*Psyche*,[3] i. 137 *sqq.*) and S. Wide (*Lakonische Kulte*, Leipsic, 1893, p. 290).

[2] Apollodorus, *Bibliotheca*, i. 3. 3, iii. 10. 3; Nicander, *Ther.* 901 *sqq.*, with the Scholiast's note; Lucian, *De saltatione*, 45; Pausanias, iii. 1. 3, iii. 19. 5; J. Tzetzes, *Chiliades*, i. 241 *sqq.*; Ovid, *Metam.* x. 161-219; Pliny, *Nat. Hist.* xxi. 66.

Greek means " alas ") clearly inscribed in black on its petals.
In Greece it blooms in spring after the early violets but
before the roses.[1]   One spring, when the hyacinths were in
bloom, it happened that the red-coated Spartan regiments
lay encamped under the walls of Corinth.   Their com-
mander gave the Amyclean battalion leave to go home
and celebrate as usual the festival of Hyacinth in their
native town.   But the sad flower was to be to these men
an omen of death ; for they had not gone far before they
were enveloped by clouds of light-armed foes and cut to
pieces.[2]

The tomb
and the
festival of
Hyacinth
at
Amyclae.

The tomb of Hyacinth was at Amyclae under a massive
altar-like pedestal, which supported an archaic bronze image
of Apollo.   In the left side of the pedestal was a bronze
door, and through it offerings were passed to Hyacinth, as
to a hero or a dead man, not as to a god, before sacrifices
were offered to Apollo at the annual Hyacinthian festival.
Bas-reliefs carved on the pedestal represented Hyacinth
and his maiden sister Polyboea caught up to heaven by
a company of goddesses.[3]   The annual festival of the
Hyacinthia was held in the month of Hecatombeus, which
seems to have corresponded to May.[4]   The ceremonies
occupied three days.   On the first the people mourned for

[1] Theophrastus, *Histor. Plant.* vi.
8. 1 *sq.*   That the hyacinth was a
spring flower is plainly indicated also
by Philostratus (*Imag.* i. 23. 1) and
Ovid (*Metam.* x. 162-166). See further
Greve, *s.v.* " Hyakinthos," in W. H.
Roscher's *Lexikon der griech. und
röm. Mythologie,* i. 2764 ; J. Murr,
*Die Pflanzenwelt in der griechi-
schen Mythologie* (Innsbruck, 1890),
pp. 257 *sqq.* ; O. Schrader, *Reallexikon der Indogermanischen Altertumskunde* (Strasburg, 1901), pp. 383 *sq.*
Miss J. E. Harrison was so kind as to
present me with two specimens of the
flower (*Delphinium Ajacis*) on which
the woful letters were plainly visible.
A flower similarly marked, of a colour
between white and red, was associated
with the death of Ajax (Pausanias,
i. 35. 4).   But usually the two flowers
were thought to be the same (Ovid,
Metam. xiii. 394 *sqq.* ; Scholiast on

Theocritus, x. 28 ; Pliny, *Nat. Hist.*
xxi. 66 ; Eustathius on Homer, *Iliad,*
ii. 557, p. 285).
[2] Xenophon, *Hellenica,* iv. 5. 7-17 ;
Pausanias, iii. 10. 1.
[3] Pausanias, iii. 1. 3, iii. 19. 1-5.
[4] Hesychius, *s.v.* Ἑκατομβεύς ; G.
F. Unger in *Philologus,* xxxvii. (1877)
pp. 13-33 ; Greve, *s.v.* " Hyakinthos,"
in W. H. Roscher's *Lexikon der griech.
und röm. Mythologie,* i. 2762 ; W.
Smith, *Dictionary of Greek and
Roman Antiquities,*[3] i. 339.   From
Xenophon (*Hellenica,* iv. 5) we learn
that in 390 B.C. the Hyacinthian
followed soon after the Isthmian
festival, which that year fell in spring.
Others, however, identifying Hecatombeus with the Attic month Hecatom-
baeon, would place the Hyacinthia in
July (K. O. Müller, *Dorier,*[2] Breslau,
1844, i. 358).   In Rhodes, Cos, and
other Greek states there was a month

Hyacinth, wearing no wreaths, singing no paeans, eating no bread, and behaving with great gravity. It was on this day probably that the offerings were made at Hyacinth's tomb. Next day the scene was changed. All was joy and bustle. The capital was emptied of its inhabitants, who poured out in their thousands to witness and share the festivities at Amyclae. Boys in high girt tunics sang hymns in honour of the god to the accompaniment of flutes and lyres. Others, splendidly attired, paraded on horseback in the theatre: choirs of youths chanted their native ditties: dancers danced: maidens rode in wicker carriages or went in procession to witness the chariot races: sacrifices were offered in profusion: the citizens feasted their friends and even their slaves.[1] This outburst of gaiety may be supposed to have celebrated the resurrection of Hyacinth and perhaps also his ascension to heaven, which, as we have seen, was represented on his tomb. However, it may be that the ascension took place on the third day of the festival; but as to that we know nothing. The sister who went to heaven with him was by some identified with Artemis or Persephone.[2]

It is highly probable, as Erwin Rohde perceived,[3] that Hyacinth was an old aboriginal deity of the underworld who had been worshipped at Amyclae long before the Dorians invaded and conquered the country. If that was so, the story of his relation to Apollo must have been a comparatively late invention, an attempt of the newcomers to fit the ancient god of the land into their own mythical system, in order that he might extend his protection to them. On this theory it may not be without significance

[margin:] Hyacinth an aboriginal god, perhaps a king, who was worshipped in Laconia before the invasion of the Dorians.

---

called Hyacinthius, which probably took its name from the Hyacinthian festival. The month is thought to correspond to the Athenian Scirophorion and therefore to June. See E. Bischof, "De fastis Graecorum antiquioribus," *Leipziger Studien für classische Philologie*, vii. (1884) pp. 369 *sq*., 381, 384, 410, 414 *sq*.; G. Dittenberger, *Sylloge Inscriptionum Graecarum*,[2] vol. i. pp. 396, 607, Nos. 614, note [3], 744, note [1]. If this latter identification of

the month is correct, it would furnish an argument for dating the Spartan festival of Hyacinth in June also. The question is too intricate to be discussed here.

[1] Athenaeus, iv. 17, pp. 139 *sq*. Strabo speaks (vi. 3. 2, p. 278) of a contest at the Hyacinthian festival. It may have been the chariot races mentioned by Athenaeus.

[2] Hesychius, *s.v.* Πολύβοια.

[3] E. Rohde, *Psyche*,[3] i. 137 *sqq*.

that sacrifices at the festival were offered to Hyacinth, as to
a hero, before they were offered to Apollo.[1] Further, on
the analogy of similar deities elsewhere, we should expect
to find Hyacinth coupled, not with a male friend, but with a
female consort. That consort may perhaps be detected in
his sister Polyboea, who ascended to heaven with him. The
new myth, if new it was, of the love of Apollo for Hyacinth
would involve a changed conception of the aboriginal god,
which in its turn must have affected that of his spouse.
For when Hyacinth came to be thought of as young and
unmarried there was no longer room in his story for a wife,
and she would have to be disposed of in some other way.
What was easier for the myth-maker than to turn her into
his unmarried sister? However we may explain it, a
change seems certainly to have come over the popular idea
of Hyacinth ; for whereas on his tomb he was portrayed as
a bearded man, later art represented him as the pink of
youthful beauty.[2] But it is perhaps needless to suppose
that the sisterly relation of Polyboea to him was a late
modification of the myth. The stories of Cronus and Rhea,
of Zeus and Hera, of Osiris and Isis, remind us that in old
days gods, like kings, often married their sisters, and probably for the same reason, namely, to ensure their own title
to the throne under a rule of female kinship which treated
women and not men as the channel in which the blood royal
flowed.[3] It is not impossible that Hyacinth may have been
a divine king who actually reigned in his lifetime at Amyclae
and was afterwards worshipped at his tomb. The representation of his triumphal ascent to heaven in company with
his sister suggests that, like Adonis and Persephone, he may
have been supposed to spend one part of the year in the

His sister Polyboea may perhaps have been his spouse.

---

[1] Pausanias, iii. 19. 3. The Greek
word here used for sacrifice (ἐναγίζειν)
properly denotes sacrifices offered to
the heroic or worshipful dead ; another
word (θύειν) was employed for sacrifices
offered to gods. The two terms are
distinguished by Pausanias here and
elsewhere (ii. 10. 1, ii. 11. 7). Compare Herodotus, ii. 44. Sacrifices to
the worshipful dead were often annual.
See Pausanias, iii. 1. 8, vii. 19. 10,
vii. 20. 9, viii. 14. 11, viii. 41. 1, ix.
38. 5, x. 24. 6. It has been observed
by E. Rohde (*Psyche*,[3] i. 139, note [2])
that sacrifices were frequently offered
to a hero before a god, and he suggests
with much probability that in these
cases the worship of the hero was
older than that of the deity.

[2] Pausanias, iii. 19. 14.

[3] See above, p. 44 ; and below, vol.
ii. pp. 213 *sqq.*

under-world of darkness and death, and another part in the upper-world of light and life.   And as the anemones and the sprouting corn marked the return of Adonis and Persephone, so the flowers to which he gave his name may have heralded the ascension of Hyacinth.

Volume Two

BOOK THIRD
OSIRIS

CHAPTER I

THE MYTH OF OSIRIS

IN ancient Egypt the god whose death and resurrection were annually celebrated with alternate sorrow and joy was Osiris, the most popular of all Egyptian deities; and there are good grounds for classing him in one of his aspects with Adonis and Attis as a personification of the great yearly vicissitudes of nature, especially of the corn. But the immense vogue which he enjoyed for many ages induced his devoted worshippers to heap upon him the attributes and powers of many other gods; so that it is not always easy to strip him, so to say, of his borrowed plumes and to restore them to their proper owners. In the following pages I do not pretend to enumerate and analyse all the alien elements which thus gathered round the popular deity. All that I shall attempt to do is to peel off these accretions and to exhibit the god, as far as possible, in his primitive simplicity. The discoveries of recent years in Egypt enable us to do so with more confidence now than when I first addressed myself to the problem many years ago. *Osiris the Egyptian counterpart of Adonis and Attis.*

The story of Osiris is told in a connected form only by Plutarch, whose narrative has been confirmed and to some extent amplified in modern times by the evidence of the monuments.[1] Of the monuments which illustrate *The myth of Osiris.*

[1] See Plutarch, *Isis et Osiris*, 12-20; R. V. Lanzone, *Dizionario di Mitologia Egizia* (Turin, 1881–1884), vol. ii. pp. 692 *sqq.*; A. Erman, *Aegypten und aegyptisches Leben im Altertum* (Tübingen, N.D.), pp. 365-369; *id.*, *Die ägyptische Religion*[2] (Berlin, 1909), pp. 38 *sqq.*; A. Wiedemann, *Die Religion der alten Ägypter* (Münster i. w. 1890), pp. 109 *sqq.*; *id.*, *Religion of the Ancient Egyptians* (London, 1897), pp. 207 *sqq.*; G. Maspero, *Histoire ancienne des Peuples de l'Orient Classique*, i. 172

The
Pyramid
Texts.

the myth or legend of Osiris the oldest are a long
series of hymns, prayers, incantations, and liturgies, which
have been found engraved in hieroglyphics on the walls,
passages, and galleries of five pyramids at Sakkara. From
the place where they were discovered these ancient religious records are known as the Pyramid Texts. They
date from the fifth and sixth dynasties, and the period
of time during which they were carved on the pyramids
is believed to have been roughly a hundred and fifty
years from about the year 2625 B.C. onward. But from
their contents it appears that many of these documents
were drawn up much earlier; for in some of them there
are references to works which have perished, and in others
there are political allusions which seem to show that the
passages containing them must have been composed at
a time when the Northern and Southern Kingdoms
were still independent and hostile states and had not yet
coalesced into a single realm under the sway of one powerful monarch. As the union of the kingdoms appears
to have taken place about three thousand four hundred
years before our era, the whole period covered by the composition of the Pyramid Texts probably did not fall short of
a thousand years. Thus the documents form the oldest
body of religious literature surviving to us from the ancient
world, and occupy a place in the history of Egyptian language and civilization like that which the Vedic hymns and
incantations occupy in the history of Aryan speech and
culture.[1]

The
Pyramid
Texts
intended
to ensure

The special purpose for which these texts were engraved
on the pyramids was to ensure the eternal life and felicity
of the dead kings who slept beneath these colossal monu-

---

sqq.; E. A. Wallis Budge, *The Gods
of the Egyptians* (London, 1904), ii.
123 *sqq.*; *id.*, *Osiris and the Egyptian
Resurrection* (London, 1911). i. 1 *sqq.*

[1] J. H. Breasted, *Development of
Religion and Thought in Ancient
Egypt* (London, 1912), pp. vii. *sq.*, 77
sqq., 84 *sqq.*, 91 *sqq.* Compare *id.*, *History of the Ancient Egyptians* (London,
1908), p. 68; Ed. Meyer, *Geschichte des
Altertums*,[2] i. 2. pp. 116 *sq.*; E. A.

Wallis Budge, *Osiris and the Egyptian
Resurrection* (London, 1911), i. 100
sqq. The first series of the texts was
discovered in 1880 when Mariette's
workmen penetrated into the pyramid
of King Pepi the First. Till then it
had been thought by modern scholars
that the pyramids were destitute of
inscriptions. The first to edit the
Pyramid Texts was Sir Gaston Maspero.

ments.   Hence the dominant note that sounds through them all is an insistent, a passionate protest against the reality of death : indeed the word death never occurs in the Pyramid Texts except to be scornfully denied or to be applied to an enemy.   Again and again the indomitable assurance is repeated that the dead man did not die but lives.   "King Teti has not died the death, he has become a glorious one in the horizon."   "Ho!   King Unis!   Thou didst not depart dead, thou didst depart living."   "Thou hast departed that thou mightest live, thou hast not departed that thou mightest die."   "Thou diest not."   "This King Pepi dies not."   "Have ye said that he would die ? He dies not ; this King Pepi lives for ever."   "Live!   Thou shalt not die."   "Thou livest, thou livest, raise thee up." "Thou diest not, stand up, raise thee up."   "O lofty one among the Imperishable Stars, thou perishest not eternally." [1]   Thus for Egyptian kings death was swallowed up in victory ; and through their tears Egyptian mourners might ask, like Christian mourners thousands of years afterwards, "O death, where is thy sting?   O grave, where is thy victory ? "

Now it is significant that in these ancient documents, though the myth or legend of Osiris is not set forth at length, it is often alluded to as if it were a matter of common knowledge.   Hence we may legitimately infer the great antiquity of the Osirian tradition in Egypt.   Indeed so numerous are the allusions to it in the Pyramid Texts that by their help we could reconstruct the story in its main outlines even without the narrative of Plutarch.[2]   Thus the discovery of these texts has confirmed our belief in the accuracy and fidelity of the Greek writer, and we may accept his account with confidence even when it records incidents or details which have not yet been verified by a

---

[1] J. H. Breasted, *Development of Religion and Thought in Ancient Egypt*, pp. 91 *sq.*   Among the earlier works referred to in the Pyramid Texts are "the chapter of those who ascend" and "the chapter of those who raise themselves up" (J. H. Breasted, *op. cit.* p. 85).   From their titles these works would seem to have recorded a belief in the resurrection and ascension of the dead.

[2] This has been done by Professor J. H. Breasted in his *Development of Religion and Thought in Ancient Egypt*, pp. 18 *sqq.*

comparison with original Egyptian sources. The tragic
tale runs thus :

Osiris was the offspring of an intrigue between the
earth-god Seb (Keb or Geb, as the name is sometimes trans-
literated) and the sky-goddess Nut. The Greeks identified
his parents with their own deities Cronus and Rhea. When
the sun-god Ra perceived that his wife Nut had been un-
faithful to him, he declared with a curse that she should be
delivered of the child in no month and no year. But the
goddess had another lover, the god Thoth or Hermes, as the
Greeks called him, and he playing at draughts with the
moon won from her a seventy-second part[1] of every day,
and having compounded five whole days out of these parts
he added them to the Egyptian year of three hundred and
sixty days. This was the mythical origin of the five supplementary days which the Egyptians annually inserted at the
end of every year in order to establish a harmony between
lunar and solar time.[2] On these five days, regarded as
outside the year of twelve months, the curse of the sun-god
did not rest, and accordingly Osiris was born on the first of
them. At his nativity a voice rang out proclaiming that the
Lord of All had come into the world. Some say that a
certain Pamyles heard a voice from the temple at Thebes
bidding him announce with a shout that a great king, the
beneficent Osiris, was born. But Osiris was not the only
child of his mother. On the second of the supplementary
days she gave birth to the elder Horus, on the third to the
god Set, whom the Greeks called Typhon, on the fourth to
the goddess Isis, and on the fifth to the goddess Nephthys.[3]

---

[1] In Plutarch, *Isis et Osiris*, 12, we
must clearly read ἑβδομηκοστὸν δεύτερον
with Scaliger and Wyttenbach for the
ἑβδομηκοστόν of the MSS.

[2] Herodotus, ii. 4, with A. Wiedemann's note ; L. Ideler, *Handbuch der
mathematischen und technischen Chronologie* (Berlin, 1825–1826), i. 94 *sqq.* ;
A. Erman, *Aegypten und aegyptisches
Leben im Altertum*, pp. 468 *sq.* ; G.
Maspero, *Histoire ancienne des Peuples
de l'Orient Classique*, i. 208 *sq.*

[3] The birth of the five deities on the
five supplementary days is mentioned

by Diodorus Siculus (i. 13. 4) as well
as by Plutarch (*Isis et Osiris*, 12).
The memory of the five supplementary
days seems to survive in the modern
Coptic calendar of Egypt. The days
from the first to the sixth of Amshir
(February) are called "the days outside
the year" and they are deemed unlucky. "Any child begotten during
these days will infallibly be misshapen
or abnormally tall or short. This also
applies to animals so that cattle and
mares are not covered during these
days ; moreover, some say (though

Afterwards Set married his sister Nephthys, and Osiris married his sister Isis.

Reigning as a king on earth, Osiris reclaimed the Egyptians from savagery, gave them laws, and taught them to worship the gods. Before his time the Egyptians had been cannibals. But Isis, the sister and wife of Osiris, discovered wheat and barley growing wild, and Osiris introduced the cultivation of these grains amongst his people, who forthwith abandoned cannibalism and took kindly to a corn diet. Moreover, Osiris is said to have been the first to gather fruit from trees, to train the vine to poles, and to tread the grapes. Eager to communicate these beneficent discoveries to all mankind, he committed the whole government of Egypt to his wife Isis, and travelled over the world, diffusing the blessings of civilization and agriculture wherever he went. In countries where a harsh climate or niggardly soil forbade the cultivation of the vine, he taught the inhabitants to console themselves for the want of wine by brewing beer from barley. Loaded with the wealth that had been showered upon him by grateful nations, he returned to Egypt, and on account of the benefits he had conferred on mankind he was unanimously hailed and worshipped as a deity.[1] But his brother Set (whom the Greeks called Typhon) with seventy-two others plotted against him. Having taken the measure of his good brother's body by stealth, the bad brother Typhon fashioned and highly decorated a coffer of the same size, and once when they were all drinking and making merry he brought in the coffer and jestingly promised to give it to the one whom it should fit exactly. Well, they all tried one after the other, but it fitted none of them. Last of all Osiris stepped into it and lay down. On that the conspirators ran and slammed the lid down on him, nailed it fast, soldered it with molten lead, and flung the

Osiris introduces the cultivation of corn and of the vine.

His violent death.

---

others deny) that neither sowing nor planting should be undertaken." However, these unlucky days are not the true intercalary days of the Coptic calendar, which occur in the second week of September at the end of the Coptic year. See C. G. Seligmann, " Ancient Egyptian Beliefs in Modern

Egypt," *Essays and Studies presented to William Ridgeway* (Cambridge, 1913), p. 456. As to the unluckiness of intercalary days in general, see *The Scapegoat*, pp. 339 *sqq.*

[1] Plutarch, *Isis et Osiris*, 13 ; Diodorus Siculus, i. 14, 17, 20 ; Tibullus, i. 7. 29 *sqq.*

coffer into the Nile. This happened on the seventeenth day of the month Athyr, when the sun is in the sign of the Scorpion, and in the eight-and-twentieth year of the reign or

the life of Osiris. When Isis heard of it she sheared off a lock of her hair, put on mourning attire, and wandered disconsolately up and down, seeking the body.[1]

By the advice of the god of wisdom she took refuge in the papyrus swamps of the Delta. Seven scorpions accompanied her in her flight. One evening when she was weary she came to the house of a woman, who, alarmed at the sight of the scorpions, shut the door in her face. Then one of the scorpions crept under the door and stung the child of the woman that he died. But when Isis heard the mother's lamentation, her heart was touched, and she laid her hands on the child and uttered her powerful spells; so the poison was driven out of the child and he

lived. Afterwards Isis herself gave birth to a son in the swamps. She had conceived him while she fluttered in the form of a hawk over the corpse of her dead husband. The infant was the younger Horus, who in his youth bore the name of Harpocrates, that is, the child Horus. Him Buto, the goddess of the north, hid from the wrath of his wicked uncle Set. Yet she could not guard him from all mishap; for one day when Isis came to her little son's hiding-place she found him stretched lifeless and rigid on the ground: a scorpion had stung him. Then Isis prayed to the sun-god Ra for help. The god hearkened to her and staid his bark in the sky, and sent down Thoth to teach her the spell by which she might restore her son to life. She uttered the words of power, and straightway the poison flowed from the body of Horus, air passed into him, and he lived. Then Thoth ascended up into the sky and took his place once more in the bark of the sun, and the bright pomp passed onward jubilant.[2]

[1] Plutarch, *Isis et Osiris*, 13 *sq.*

[2] A. Erman, *Aegypten und aegyptisches Leben im Altertum*, p. 366; *id.*, *Die ägyptische Religion*[2] (Berlin, 1909), p. 40; A. Wiedemann, *Religion of the Ancient Egyptians* (London, 1897), pp. 213 *sq.*; E. A. Wallis Budge, *The Gods of the Egyptians*, i. 487 *sq.*,

ii. 206-211; *id.*, *Osiris and the Egyptian Resurrection* (London, 1911), i. 92-96, ii. 84, 274-276. These incidents of the scorpions are not related by Plutarch but are known to us from Egyptian sources. The barbarous legend of the begetting of Horus by the dead Osiris is told in unambiguous language in the

Meantime the coffer containing the body of Osiris had The body of Osiris floats to Byblus, where it is recovered by Isis. floated down the river and away out to sea, till at last it drifted ashore at Byblus, on the coast of Syria.   Here a fine *erica*-tree shot up suddenly and enclosed the chest in its trunk.   The king of the country, admiring the growth of the tree, had it cut down and made into a pillar of his house ; but he did not know that the coffer with the dead Osiris was in it.   Word of this came to Isis and she journeyed to Byblus, and sat down by the well, in humble guise, her face wet with tears.   To none would she speak till the king's handmaidens came, and them she greeted kindly, and braided their hair, and breathed on them from her own divine body a wondrous perfume.   But when the queen beheld the braids of her handmaidens' hair and smelt the sweet smell that emanated from them, she sent for the stranger woman and took her into her house and made her the nurse of her child.   But Isis gave the babe her finger instead of her breast to suck, and at night she began to burn all that was mortal of him away, while she herself in the likeness of a swallow fluttered round the pillar that contained her dead brother, twittering mournfully.   But the queen spied what she was doing and shrieked out when she saw her child in flames, and thereby she hindered him from becoming immortal.   Then the goddess revealed herself and begged for the pillar of the roof, and they gave it her, and she cut the coffer out of it, and fell upon it and embraced it and lamented so loud that the younger of the king's children died of fright on the spot.   But the trunk of the tree she wrapped in fine linen, and poured ointment on it, and gave it to the king and queen, and the wood stands in a temple of

---

Pyramid Texts, and it is illustrated by a monument which represents the two sister goddesses hovering in the likeness of hawks over the god, while Hathor sits at his head and the Frog-goddess Heqet squats in the form of a huge frog at his feet. See J. H. Breasted, *Development of Religion and Thought in Ancient Egypt,* p. 28, with note[2] ; E. A. Wallis Budge, *Osiris and the Egyptian Resurrection,* i. 280. Harpocrates is in Egyptian *Her-pe-khred,* "Horus the child" (A. Wiede-

mann, *Religion of the Ancient Egyptians,* p. 223).   Plutarch, who appears to distinguish him from Horus, says that Harpocrates was begotten by the dead Osiris on Isis, and that he was born untimely and was weak in his lower limbs (*Isis et Osiris,* 19).   Elsewhere he tells us that Harpocrates "was born, incomplete and youthful, about the winter solstice along with the early flowers and blossoms" (*Isis et Osiris,* 65).

Isis and is worshipped by the people of Byblus to this day. And Isis put the coffer in a boat and took the eldest of the king's children with her and sailed away. As soon as they were alone, she opened the chest, and laying her face on the face of her brother she kissed him and wept. But the child came behind her softly and saw what she was about, and she turned and looked at him in anger, and the child could not bear her look and died ; but some say that it was not so, but that he fell into the sea and was drowned. It is he whom the Egyptians sing of at their banquets under the name of Maneros. But Isis put the coffer by and went to see her son Horus at the city of Buto, and Typhon found the coffer as he was hunting a boar one night by the light of a full moon.[1] And he knew the body, and rent it into fourteen pieces, and scattered them abroad. But Isis sailed up and down the marshes in a shallop made of papyrus, looking for the pieces ; and that is why when people sail in shallops made of papyrus, the crocodiles do not hurt them, for they fear or respect the goddess. And that is the reason, too, why there are many graves of Osiris in Egypt, for she buried each limb as she found it. But others will have it that she buried an image of him in every city, pretending it was his body, in order that Osiris might be worshipped in many places, and that if Typhon searched for the real grave he might not be able to find it.[2] However, the genital member of Osiris had been eaten by the fishes, so Isis made an image of it instead, and the image is used by the Egyptians at their festivals to this day.[3] " Isis," writes the historian Diodorus Siculus, " recovered all the parts of the body except the genitals ; and because she wished that her husband's grave should be unknown and honoured by all who dwell in the land of Egypt, she resorted to the following device. She moulded human images out of wax and spices, corresponding to the stature of Osiris, round each one of the parts of his body. Then she called in the priests according to their families and took an oath of them all that

The body of Osiris dismembered by Typhon, and the pieces recovered by Isis.

Diodorus Siculus on the burial of Osiris.

---

[1] Plutarch, *Isis et Osiris*, 8, 18.

[2] Plutarch, *Isis et Osiris*, 18.

[3] Plutarch, *Isis et Osiris*, 18. Compare Hippolytus, *Refutatio omnium haeresium*, v. 7, p. 142, ed. L. Duncker and F. G. Schneidewin (Göttingen, 1859).

they would reveal to no man the trust she was about to repose in them.   So to each of them privately she said that
to them alone she entrusted the burial of the body, and reminding them of the benefits they had received she exhorted
them to bury the body in their own land and to honour
Osiris as a god.   She also besought them to dedicate one of
the animals of their country, whichever they chose, and to
honour it in life as they had formerly honoured Osiris, and
when it died to grant it obsequies like his.   And because she
would encourage the priests in their own interest to bestow
the aforesaid honours, she gave them a third part of the land
to be used by them in the service and worship of the gods.
Accordingly it is said that the priests, mindful of the benefits
of Osiris, desirous of gratifying the queen, and moved by the
prospect of gain, carried out all the injunctions of Isis.
Wherefore to this day each of the priests imagines that
Osiris is buried in his country, and they honour the beasts
that were consecrated in the beginning, and when the
animals die the priests renew at their burial the mourning
for Osiris.   But the sacred bulls, the one called Apis and
the other Mnevis, were dedicated to Osiris, and it was
ordained that they should be worshipped as gods in common
by all the Egyptians ; since these animals above all others
had helped the discoverers of corn in sowing the seed
and procuring the universal benefits of agriculture." [1]

Such is the myth or legend of Osiris, as told by Greek
writers and eked out by more or less fragmentary notices or
allusions in native Egyptian literature.   A long inscription
in the temple at Denderah has preserved a list of the god's
graves, and other texts mention the parts of his body which
were treasured as holy relics in each of the sanctuaries.
Thus his heart was at Athribis, his backbone at Busiris, his
neck at Letopolis, and his head at Memphis.   As often
happens in such cases, some of his divine limbs were miraculously multiplied.   His head, for example, was at Abydos as
well as at Memphis, and his legs, which were remarkably
numerous, would have sufficed for several ordinary mortals. [2]

The various members of Osiris treasured as relics in various parts of Egypt.

---

[1] Diodorus Siculus, i. 21. 5 - 11 ;
compare *id.*, iv. 6. 3 ; Strabo, xvii. 1.
23, p. 803.

[2] H. Brugsch, "Das Osiris-Mysterium von Tentyra," *Zeitschrift für
ägyptische Sprache und Alterthums-*

In this respect, however, Osiris was nothing to St. Denys, of whom no less than seven heads, all equally genuine, are extant.[1]

Osiris mourned by Isis and Nephthys.

According to native Egyptian accounts, which supplement that of Plutarch, when Isis had found the corpse of her husband Osiris, she and her sister Nephthys sat down beside it and uttered a lament which in after ages became the type of all Egyptian lamentations for the dead. "Come to thy house," they wailed, "Come to thy house. O god On ! come to thy house, thou who hast no foes. O fair youth, come to thy house, that thou mayest see me. I am thy sister, whom thou lovest ; thou shalt not part from me. O fair boy, come to thy house. . . . I see thee not, yet doth my heart yearn after thee and mine eyes desire thee. Come to her who loves thee, who loves thee, Unnefer, thou blessed one ! Come to thy sister, come to thy wife, to thy wife, thou whose heart stands still. Come to thy housewife. I am thy sister by the same mother, thou shalt not be far from me. Gods and men have turned their faces towards thee and weep for thee together. . . . I call after thee and weep, so that my cry is heard to heaven, but thou hearest not my voice ; yet am I thy sister, whom thou didst love on earth ; thou didst love none but me, my brother ! my brother !"[2] This lament for the fair youth cut off in his prime reminds us of the laments for Adonis. The title of Unnefer or "the Good Being" bestowed on him marks the beneficence which tradition universally ascribed to Osiris ; it was at once his commonest title and one of his names as king.[3]

Being brought to life again, Osiris

The lamentations of the two sad sisters were not in vain. In pity for her sorrow the sun-god Ra sent down from heaven the jackal-headed god Anubis, who, with the

---

kunde, xix. (1881) pp. 77 *sqq.* ; V. Loret, " Les fêtes d'Osiris au mois de Khoiak," *Recueil de Travaux relatifs à la Philologie et à l'Archéologie Égyptiennes et Assyriennes*, iii. (1882) pp. 43 *sqq.* ; R. V. Lanzone, *Dizionario di Mitologia Egizia*, pp. 697 *sqq.* ; A. Wiedemann, *Herodots zweites Buch* (Leipsic, 1890), pp. 584 *sqq.* ; *id.*, *Die Religion der alten Ägypter*, p. 115 ; *id.*, *Religion of the Ancient Egyptians*, pp. 215 *sqq.* ; A. Erman,

Aegypten und aegyptisches Leben im Altertum, pp. 367 *sq.*

[1] J. Rendel Harris, *The Annotators of the Codex Bezae* (London, 1901), p. 104, note [2], referring to Dulaure.

[2] A. Erman, *Die ägyptische Religion*[2] (Berlin, 1909), pp. 39 *sq.* ; E. A. Wallis Budge, *Osiris and the Egyptian Resurrection*, ii. 59 *sqq.*

[3] A. Wiedemann, *Religion of the Ancient Egyptians*, p. 211.

aid of Isis and Nephthys, of Thoth and Horus, pieced
together the broken body of the murdered god, swathed it
in linen bandages, and observed all the other rites which
the Egyptians were wont to perform over the bodies of the
departed. Then Isis fanned the cold clay with her wings:
Osiris revived, and thenceforth reigned as king over the
dead in the other world.[1] There he bore the titles of Lord
of the Underworld, Lord of Eternity, Ruler of the Dead.[2]
There, too, in the great Hall of the Two Truths, assisted by
forty-two assessors, one from each of the principal districts of
Egypt, he presided as judge at the trial of the souls of the
departed, who made their solemn confession before him, and,
their heart having been weighed in the balance of justice, received the reward of virtue in a life eternal or the appropriate
punishment of their sins.[3] The confession or rather profession
which the *Book of the Dead* puts in the mouth of the deceased
at the judgment-bar of Osiris [4] sets the morality of the
ancient Egyptians in a very favourable light. In rendering
an account of his life the deceased solemnly protested that he
had not oppressed his fellow-men, that he had made none
to weep, that he had done no murder, neither committed
fornication nor borne false witness, that he had not falsified
the balance, that he had not taken the milk from the mouths
of babes, that he had given bread to the hungry and water
to the thirsty, and had clothed the naked. In harmony

marginal notes: reigns as king and judge of the dead in the other world.

The confession of the dead.

---

[1] A. Erman, *Die ägyptische Religion*,[2]
pp. 39 *sq.*; G. Maspero, *Histoire
ancienne des Peuples de l'Orient
Classique*, i. 176; E. A. Wallis
Budge, *The Gods of the Egyptians*, ii.
140, 262; *id.*, *Osiris and the Egyptian
Resurrection*, i. 70-75, 80-82. On
Osiris as king of the dead see Plutarch,
Isis et Osiris, 79.

[2] Miss Margaret A. Murray, *The
Osireion at Abydos* (London, 1904),
pp. 8, 17, 18.

[3] On Osiris as judge of the dead
see A. Wiedemann, *Die Religion der
alten Ägypter*, pp. 131 *sqq.*; *id.*,
Religion of the Ancient Egyptians,
pp. 248 *sqq.*; G. Maspero, *Histoire
ancienne des Peuples de l'Orient
Classique*, i. 187 *sqq.*; E. A. Wallis
Budge, *The Book of the Dead* [2] (London,
1909), i. pp. liii. *sqq.*; *id.*, *The Gods of

the Egyptians*, ii. 141 *sqq.*; *id.*, *Osiris
and the Egyptian Resurrection*, i. 305
sqq.; A. Erman, *Die ägyptische Religion*,[2] pp. 116 *sqq.*

[4] *The Book of the Dead*, ch. cxxv.
(vol. ii. pp. 355 *sqq.* of Budge's
translation; P. Pierret, *Le Livre des
Morts*, Paris, 1882, pp. 369 *sqq.*);
R. V. Lanzone, *Dizionario di Mitologia
Egizia*, pp. 788 *sqq.*; A. Wiedemann,
Die Religion der alten Ägypter, pp.
132-134; *id.*, *Religion of the Ancient
Egyptians*, pp. 249 *sqq.*; G. Maspero,
*Histoire ancienne des Peuples de l'Orient
Classique*, i. 188-191; A. Erman,
Die ägyptische Religion,[2] pp. 117-121;
E. A. Wallis Budge, *Osiris and the
Egyptian Resurrection*, i. 337 *sqq.*; J.
H. Breasted, *Development of Religion
and Thought in Ancient Egypt*, pp.
297 *sqq.*

with these professions are the epitaphs on Egyptian graves, which .reveal, if not the moral practice, at least the moral ideals of those who slept beneath them. Thus, for example, a man says in his epitaph: "I gave bread to the hungry and clothes to the naked, and ferried across in my own boat him who could not pass the water. I was a father to the orphan, a husband to the widow, a shelter from the wind to them that were cold. I am one that spake good and told good. I earned my substance in righteousness."[1] Those who had done thus in their mortal life and had been acquitted at the Great Assize, were believed to dwell thenceforth at ease in a land where the corn grew higher than on earth, where harvests never failed, where trees were always green, and wives for ever young and fair.[2]

The fate of the wicked.

We are not clearly informed as to the fate which the Egyptians supposed to befall the wicked after death. In the scenes which represent the Last Judgment there is seen crouching beside the scales, in which the heart of the dead is being weighed, a monstrous animal known as the "Eater of the Dead." It has the head of a crocodile, the trunk of a lion, and the hinder parts of a hippopotamus. Some think that the souls of those whose hearts had been weighed in the balance and found wanting were delivered over to this grim monster to be devoured; but this view appears to be conjectural. "Generally the animal seems to have been placed there simply as guardian of the entrance to the Fields of the Blessed, but sometimes it is likened to Set. Elsewhere it is said that the judges of the dead slay the wicked and drink their blood. In brief, here also we have conflicting statements, and can only gather that there seems to have been no general agreement among the dwellers in the Valley of the Nile as to the ultimate lot of the wicked."[3]

[1] A. Erman, *Die ägyptische Religion*,[2] p. 121. Compare A. Wiedemann, *Die Religion der alten Ägypter*, pp. 134 *sq.*; *id.*, *Religion of the Ancient Egyptians*, p. 253.

[2] A. Wiedemann, *Religion of the Ancient Egyptians*, p. 254; E. A. Wallis Budge, *Osiris and the Egyptian Resurrection*, i. 305 *sqq.*; G. Maspero, *op. cit.* i. 194 *sq.*; A. Erman, *Die ägyptische Religion*,[2] pp. 121 *sqq.*; E.

A. Wallis Budge, *Osiris and the Egyptian Resurrection*, i. 97 *sq.*, 100 *sqq.*; E. Lefébure, "Le Paradis Égyptien," *Sphinx*, iii. (Upsala, 1900) pp. 191 *sqq.*

[3] A. Wiedemann, *Religion of the Ancient Egyptians*, p. 249. Compare A. Erman, *Die ägyptische Religion*,[2] pp. 117, 121; E. A. Wallis Budge, *Osiris and the Egyptian Resurrection*, i. 317, 328.

In the resurrection of Osiris the Egyptians saw the pledge of a life everlasting for themselves beyond the grave. They believed that every man would live eternally in the other world if only his surviving friends did for his body what the gods had done for the body of Osiris. Hence the ceremonies observed by the Egyptians over the human dead were an exact copy of those which Anubis, Horus, and the rest had performed over the dead god. "At every burial there was enacted a representation of the divine mystery which had been performed of old over Osiris, when his son, his sisters, his friends were gathered round his mangled remains and succeeded by their spells and manipulations in converting his broken body into the first mummy, which they afterwards reanimated and furnished with the means of entering on a new individual life beyond the grave. The mummy of the deceased was Osiris ; the professional female mourners were his two sisters Isis and Nephthys ; Anubis, Horus, all the gods of the Osirian legend gathered about the corpse." In this solemn drama of death and resurrection the principal part was played by the celebrant, who represented Horus the son of the dead and resuscitated Osiris.[1] He formally opened the eyes and mouth of the dead man by rubbing or pretending to rub them four times with the bleeding heart and thigh of a sacrificed bull ; after which a pretence was made of actually opening the mouth of the mummy or of the statue with certain instruments specially reserved for the purpose. Geese and gazelles were also sacrificed by being decapitated ; they were supposed to represent the enemies of Osiris, who after the murder of the divine man had sought to evade the righteous punishment of their crime but had been detected and beheaded.[2]

[1] G. Maspero, "Le rituel du sacrifice funéraire," *Études de Mythologie et d'Archéologie Égyptiennes* (Paris, 1893–1912), i. 291 *sq.*

[2] G. Maspero, *op. cit.* pp. 300-316. Compare A. Wiedemann, *Die Religion der alten Ägypter*, pp. 123 *sqq.* ; *id., Religion of the Ancient Egyptians*, pp. 234 *sqq.* ; E. A. Wallis Budge, *The Book of the Dead*[2] (London, 1909), i. pp. liii. *sqq.* ; *id., The Gods of the Egyptians*, ii. 126, 140 *sq.* ; *id., Osiris and the Egyptian Resurrection*, i. 66 *sqq.*, 101 *sq.*, 176, 305, 399 *sq.* ; A. Moret, *Du Caractère religieux de la Royauté Pharaonique* (Paris, 1902), p. 312 ; *id., Kings and Gods of Egypt* (New York and London, 1912), pp. 91 *sqq.* ; *id., Mystères Égyptiens* (Paris, 1913), pp. 37 *sqq.* "In one of the ceremonies of the 'Opening of the Mouth' the deceased was temporarily

Every dead Egyptian identified with Osiris.

Thus every dead Egyptian was identified with Osiris and bore his name. From the Middle Kingdom onwards it was the regular practice to address the deceased as " Osiris So-and-So," as if he were the god himself, and to add the standing epithet " true of speech," because true speech was characteristic of Osiris.[1] The thousands of inscribed and pictured tombs that have been opened in the valley of the Nile prove that the mystery of the resurrection was performed for the benefit of every dead Egyptian ;[2] as Osiris died and rose again from the dead, so all men hoped to arise like him from death to life eternal. In an Egyptian text it is said of the departed that " as surely as Osiris lives, so shall he live also; as surely as Osiris did not die, so shall he not die; as surely as Osiris is not annihilated, so shall he too not be annihilated." The dead man, conceived to be lying, like Osiris, with mangled body, was comforted by being told that the heavenly goddess Nut, the mother of Osiris, was coming to gather up his poor scattered limbs and mould them with her own hands into a form immortal and divine. " She gives thee thy head, she brings thee thy bones, she sets thy limbs together and puts thy heart in thy body." Thus the resurrection of the dead was conceived, like that of Osiris, not merely as spiritual but also as bodily. " They possess their heart, they possess their senses, they possess their mouth, they possess their feet, they possess their arms, they possess all their limbs."[3]

Combat between Set and

If we may trust Egyptian legend, the trials and contests of the royal house did not cease with the restoration of Osiris

---

placed in a bull's skin, which was probably that of one of the bulls which were offered up during the celebration of the service. From this skin the deceased obtained further power, and his emergence from it was the visible symbol of his resurrection and of his entrance into everlasting life with all the strength of Osiris and Horus " (E. A. Wallis Budge, *Osiris and the Egyptian Resurrection*, i. 400).

[1] A. Erman, *Aegypten und aegyptisches Leben im Altertum*, p. 416 ; J. H. Breasted, *History of the Ancient Egyptians*, pp. 149 *sq.*; Margaret A.

Murray, *The Osireion at Abydos* (London, 1904), p. 31. Under the earlier dynasties only kings appear to have been identified with Osiris.

[2] A. Moret, *Mystères Égyptiens* (Paris, 1913), p. 40.

[3] A. Erman, *Die ägyptische Religion*,[2] pp. 111-113. However, in later times the body with which the dead came to life was believed to be a spiritual, not a material body ; it was called *sāhu*. See E. A. Wallis Budge, *The Book of the Dead*,[2] i. pp. lvii. *sqq.*; *id.*, *Osiris and the Egyptian Resurrection*, ii. 123 *sq.*

to life and his elevation to the rank of presiding deity in the world of the dead. When Horus the younger, the son of Osiris and Isis, was grown to man's estate, the ghost of his royal and murdered father appeared to him and urged him, like another Hamlet, to avenge the foul unnatural murder upon his wicked uncle. Thus encouraged, the youth attacked the miscreant. The combat was terrific and lasted many days. Horus lost an eye in the conflict and Set suffered a still more serious mutilation. At last Thoth parted the combatants and healed their wounds ; the eye of Horus he restored by spitting on it. According to one account the great battle was fought on the twenty-sixth day of the month of Thoth. Foiled in open war, the artful uncle now took the law of his virtuous nephew. He brought a suit of bastardy against Horus, hoping thus to rob him of his inheritance and to get possession of it himself; nay, not content with having murdered his good brother, the unnatural Set carried his rancour even beyond the grave by accusing the dead Osiris of certain high crimes and misdemeanours. The case was tried before the supreme court of the gods in the great hall at Heliopolis. Thoth, the god of wisdom, pleaded the cause of Osiris, and the august judges decided that " the word of Osiris was true." Moreover, they pronounced Horus to be the true-begotten son of his father. So that prince assumed the crown and mounted the throne of the lamented Osiris. However, according to another and perhaps later version of the story, the victory of Horus over his uncle was by no means so decisive, and their struggles ended in a compromise, by which Horus reigned over the Delta, while Set became king of the upper valley of the Nile from near Memphis to the first cataract. Be that as it may, with the accession of Horus began for the Egyptians the modern period of the world, for on his throne all the kings of Egypt sat as his successors.[1]

These legends of a contest for the throne of Egypt

Horus, the brother and the son of Osiris, for the crown of Egypt.

---

[1] Plutarch, *Isis et Osiris*, 19 and 55; A. Erman, *Aegypten und aegyptisches Leben im Altertum*, p. 368 ; *id.*, *Die ägyptische Religion*,[2] pp. 41 *sq.* ; A. Wiedemann, *Die Religion der alten Ägypter*, p. 114 ; *id.*, *Religion of the Ancient Egyptians*, pp. 214 *sq.*; G. Maspero, *Histoire ancienne des Peuples de l'Orient Classique*, i. 176-178 ; E. A. Wallis Budge, *Osiris and the Egyptian Resurrection*, i. 62 *sq.*, 64, 89 *sqq.*, 309 *sqq.*

The legend of their contest may be a reminiscence of dynastic struggles.

may perhaps contain a reminiscence of real dynastical struggles which attended an attempt to change the right of succession from the female to the male line. For under a rule of female kinship the heir to the throne is either the late king's brother, or the son of the late king's sister, while under a rule of male kinship the heir to the throne is the late king's son. In the legend of Osiris the rival heirs are Set and Horus, Set being the late king's brother, and Horus the late king's son ; though Horus indeed united both claims to the crown, being the son of the king's sister as well as of the king. A similar attempt to shift the line of succession seems to have given rise to similar contests at Rome.[1]

Osiris represented as a king in tradition and art.

Thus according to what seems to have been the general native tradition Osiris was a good and beloved king of Egypt, who suffered a violent death but rose from the dead and was henceforth worshipped as a deity. In harmony with this tradition he was regularly represented by sculptors and painters in human and regal form as a dead king, swathed in the wrappings of a mummy, but wearing on his head a kingly crown and grasping in one of his hands, which were left free from the bandages, a kingly sceptre.[2] Two cities above all others were associated with his myth or memory. One of them was Busiris in Lower Egypt, which claimed to possess his backbone ; the other was Abydos in Upper Egypt, which gloried in

The tomb of Osiris at Abydos.

the possession of his head.[3] Encircled by the nimbus of the dead yet living god, Abydos, originally an obscure place, became from the end of the Old Kingdom the holiest spot in Egypt ; his tomb there would seem to have been to the Egyptians what the Church of the Holy

---

[1] *The Magic Art and the Evolution of Kings*, ii. 290 *sqq.*

[2] A. Wiedemann, *Religion of the Ancient Egyptians*, p. 217. For details see E. A. Wallis Budge, *Osiris and the Egyptian Resurrection*, i. 30 *sqq.*

[3] J. H. Breasted, *History of the Ancient Egyptians* (London, 1908), p. 61 ; *id.*, *Development of Religion and Thought in Ancient Egypt*, p. 38 ; E. A. Wallis Budge, *Osiris and the Egyptian Resurrection*, i. 37, 67, 81, 210, 212, 214, 290, ii. 1, 2, 8-13, 82-85 ; A. Erman, *Die ägyptische Religion*,[2] pp. 21, 23, 110 ; A. Wiedemann, *Religion of the Ancient Egyptians*, p. 289 ; Ed. Meyer, *Geschichte des Altertums*,[2] i. 2. pp. 70, 96, 97. It appears to be now generally held that the original seat of the worship of Osiris was at Busiris, but that at Abydos the god found a second home, which in time eclipsed the old one in glory. According to Professors Ed. Meyer and A. Erman, the god whom Osiris displaced at Abydos was Anubis.

Sepulchre at Jerusalem is to Christians. It was the wish of every pious man that his dead body should rest in hallowed earth near the grave of the glorified Osiris. Few indeed were rich enough to enjoy this inestimable privilege; for, apart from the cost of a tomb in the sacred city, the mere transport of mummies from great distances was both difficult and expensive. Yet so eager were many to absorb in death the blessed influence which radiated from the holy sepulchre that they caused their surviving friends to convey their mortal remains to Abydos, there to tarry for a short time, and then to be brought back by river and interred in the tombs which had been made ready for them in their native land. Others had cenotaphs built or memorial tablets erected for themselves near the tomb of their dead and risen Lord, that they might share with him the bliss of a joyful resurrection.[1]

Hence from the earliest ages of Egyptian history Abydos would seem to have been a city of the dead rather than of the living; certainly there is no evidence that the place was ever of any political importance.[2] No less than nine of the most ancient kings of Egypt known to us were buried here, for their tombs have been discovered and explored within recent years.[3] The royal necropolis lies on the edge of the desert about a mile and a half from the temple of Osiris.[4] Of the graves the oldest is that of King Khent, the second or third king of the first dynasty. His reign, which fell somewhere between three thousand four hundred

The tombs of the old kings at Abydos.

The tomb of King Khent identified

[1] Plutarch, *Isis et Osiris*, 20; A. Erman, *Aegypten und aegyptisches Leben im Altertum*, p. 417; J. H. Breasted, *History of the Ancient Egyptians* (London, 1908), pp. 148 *sq.*; Ed. Meyer, *Geschichte des Altertums*,[2] i. 2. p. 209; E. A. Wallis Budge, *Osiris and the Egyptian Resurrection*, i. 68 *sq.*, ii. 3.

[2] Ed. Meyer, *Geschichte des Altertums*,[2] i. 2. p. 125.

[3] J. H. Breasted, *History of the Ancient Egyptians*, pp. 43, 50 *sq.* The excavations were begun by E. Amélineau and continued by W. M. Flinders Petrie (Ed. Meyer, *Geschichte des Altertums*,[2] i. 2. p. 119). See

E. Amélineau, *Le Tombeau d'Osiris* (Paris, 1899); W. M. Flinders Petrie, *The Royal Tombs of the Earliest Dynasties*, Part ii. (London, 1901). The excavations of the former have been criticized by Sir Gaston Maspero (*Études de Mythologie et d'Archéologie Égyptiennes*, vi. (Paris, 1912) pp. 153-182).

[4] Ed. Meyer, *Geschichte des Altertums*,[2] i. 2. pp. 119, 124; E. A. Wallis Budge, *Osiris and the Egyptian Resurrection*, ii. 8. The place is now known by the Arabic name of Umm al-Ka'âb or "Mother of Pots" on account of the large quantity of pottery that has been found there.

with the
tomb of
Osiris.

and three thousand two hundred years before our era, seems to have marked an epoch in the history of Egypt, for under him the costume, the figure drawing, and the hieroglyphics all assumed the character which they thenceforth preserved to the very end of Egyptian nationality.[1] Later ages identified him with Osiris in a more intimate sense than that in which the divine title was lavished on every dead king and indeed on every dead man; for his tomb was actually converted into the tomb of Osiris and as such received in great profusion the offerings of the faithful. Somewhere between the twenty-second and the twenty-sixth dynasty a massive bier of grey granite was placed in the sepulchral chamber. On it, cut in high relief,

The sculptured effigy of Osiris.

reposes a shrouded figure of the dead Osiris. He lies at full length, with bare and upturned face. On his head is the White Crown of Upper Egypt; in his hands, which issue from the shroud, he holds the characteristic emblems of the god, the sceptre and the scourge. At the four corners of the bier are perched four hawks, representing the four children of Horus, each with their father's banner, keeping watch over the dead god, as they kept watch over the four quarters of the world. A fifth hawk seems to have been perched on the middle of the body of Osiris, but it had been broken off before the tomb was discovered in recent years, for only the bird's claws remain in position. Finely carved heads of lions, one at each corner of the bier, with the claws to match below, complete the impressive monument. The scene represented is unquestionably the impregnation of Isis in the form of a hawk by the dead Osiris; the Copts who dismantled the shrine appear to have vented their pious rage on the figure of the hawk Isis by carrying it off or smashing it. If any doubt could exist as to the meaning of these sculptured figures, it would be set at rest by the ancient inscriptions attached to them. Over against the right shoulder of the shrouded figure, who lies stretched on the bier, are carved in hieroglyphics the words, " Osiris, the

---

[1] Ed. Meyer, *Geschichte des Altertums*,[2] i. 2. pp. 119, 125, 127, 128, 129, 209. The king's Horus name has sometimes been read Zer, but according to Professor Meyer (*op. cit.* p. 128) and Dr. Budge (*Osiris and the Egyptian Resurrection*, ii. 83) the true reading is Khent (Chent). The king's personal name was perhaps Ka (Ed. Meyer, *op. cit.* p. 128).

Good Being, true of speech"; and over against the place where the missing hawk perched on the body of the dead god is carved the symbol of Isis.   Two relics of the ancient human occupants of the tomb escaped alike the fury of the fanatics and the avarice of the plunderers who pillaged and destroyed it.   One of the relics is a human skull, from which the lower jawbone is missing ; the other is an arm encircled by gorgeous jewelled bracelets of gold, turquoises, amethysts, and dark purple lapis lazuli.   The former may be the head of King Khent himself ; the latter is almost certainly the arm of his queen.   One of the bracelets is composed of alternate plaques of gold and turquoise, each ornamented with the figure of a hawk perched on the top of it.[1]   The hawk was the sacred bird or crest of the earliest dynasties of Egyptian kings.   The figure of a hawk was borne before the king as a standard on solemn occasions : the oldest capital of the country known to us was called Hawk-town : there the kings of the first dynasty built a temple to the hawk : there in modern times has been found a splendid golden head of a hawk dating from the Ancient Empire ; and on the life-like statue of King Chephren of the third dynasty we see a hawk with outspread wings protecting the back of the monarch's head.

The hawk the crest of the earliest dynasties.

---

[1] E. Amélineau, *Le Tombeau d'Osiris* (Paris, 1899), pp. 107-115 ; W. M. Flinders Petrie, *The Royal Tombs of the Earliest Dynasties*, Part ii. (London, 1901) pp. 8 *sq.*, 16-19, with the frontispiece and plates lx. lxi.; G. Maspero, *Études de Mythologie et d'Archéologie Égyptiennes* (Paris, 1893–1912), vi. 167-173 ; J. H. Breasted, *History of the Ancient Egyptians* (London, 1908), pp. 50 *sq.*, 148 ; E. A. Wallis Budge, *Osiris and the Egyptian Resurrection*, ii. 8-10, 13, 83-85.   The tomb, with its interesting contents, was discovered and excavated by Monsieur E. Amélineau. The masses, almost the mountains, of broken pottery, under which the tomb was found to be buried, are probably remains of the vessels in which pious pilgrims presented their offerings at the shrine.   See E. Amélineau, *op. cit.* pp. 85 *sq.* ; J. H.

Breasted, *op. cit.* pp. 51, 148.   The high White Crown, worn by Osiris, was the symbol of the king's dominion over Upper Egypt ; the flat Red Crown, with a high backpiece and a projecting spiral, was the symbol of his dominion over Lower Egypt.   On the monuments the king is sometimes represented wearing a combination of the White and the Red Crown to symbolize his sovereignty over both the South and the North.   White was the distinctive colour of Upper, as red was of Lower, Egypt.   The treasury of Upper Egypt was called "the White House" ; the treasury of Lower Egypt was called "the Red House." See Ed. Meyer, *Geschichte des Altertums*,[2] i. 2. pp. 103 *sq.*; J. H. Breasted, *History of the Ancient Egyptians* (London, 1908), pp. 34 *sq.*, 36, 41.

From the earliest to the latest times of Egyptian civilization "the Hawk" was the epithet of the king of Egypt
and of the king alone; it took the first place in the list of
his titles.[1] The sanctity of the bird may help us to understand why Isis took the form of a hawk in order to mate
with her dead husband; why the queen of Egypt wore on
her arm a bracelet adorned with golden hawks; and why in
the holy sepulchre the four sons of Horus were represented
in the likeness of hawks keeping watch over the effigy of
their divine grandfather.[2]

The asso-
ciation of
Osiris with
Byblus.

The legend recorded by Plutarch which associated the
dead Osiris with Byblus in Phoenicia [3] is doubtless late and
probably untrustworthy. It may have been suggested by
the resemblance which the worship of the Egyptian Osiris
bore to the worship of the Phoenician Adonis in that city.
But it is possible that the story has no deeper foundation
than a verbal misunderstanding. For Byblus is not only
the name of a city, it is the Greek word for papyrus; and
as Isis is said after the death of Osiris to have taken refuge
in the papyrus swamps of the Delta, where she gave birth to
and reared her son Horus, a Greek writer may perhaps have
confused the plant with the city of the same name.[4] How-

---

[1] A. Moret, *Mystères Égyptiens*
(Paris, 1913), pp. 159-162, with
plate iii. Compare Victor Loret,
"L'Égypte au temps du totémisme,"
*Conférences faites au Musée Guimet,
Bibliothèque de Vulgarisation*, xix.
(Paris, 1906) pp. 179-186. Both
these writers regard the hawk as the
totem of the royal clan. This view is
rejected by Prof. Ed. Meyer, who,
however, holds that Horus, whose
emblem was the hawk, was the oldest
national god of Egypt (*Geschichte des
Altertums*,[2] i. 2. pp. 102-106). He
prefers to suppose that the hawk, or
rather the falcon, was the emblem of a
god of light because the bird flies high
in the sky (*op. cit.* p. 73; according
to him the bird is not the sparrow-
hawk but the falcon, *ib.* p. 75). A
similar view is adopted by Professor
A. Wiedemann (*Religion of the
Ancient Egyptians*, p. 26). Compare
A. Erman, *Die ägyptische Religion*,[2]

pp. 10, 11. The native Egyptian
name of Hawk-town was Nechen, in
Greek it was Hieraconpolis (Ed. Meyer,
op. cit. p. 103). Hawks were worshipped by the inhabitants (Strabo,
xvii. 1. 47, p. 817).

[2] According to the legend the four
sons of Horus were set by Anubis to
protect the burial of Osiris. They
washed his dead body, they mourned
over him, and they opened his cold
lips with their fingers. But they disappeared, for Isis had caused them to
grow out of a lotus flower in a pool of
water. In that position they are sometimes represented in Egyptian art
before the seated effigy of Osiris. See
A. Erman, *Die ägyptische Religion*,[2]
p. 43; E. A. Wallis Budge, *Osiris
and the Egyptian Resurrection*, i. 40,
41, 327.

[3] See above, pp. 9 *sq.*

[4] E. A. Wallis Budge, *Osiris and
the Egyptian Resurrection*, i. 16 *sq.*

ever that may have been, the association of Osiris with Adonis at Byblus gave rise to a curious tale. It is said that every year the people beyond the rivers of Ethiopia used to write a letter to the women of Byblus informing them that the lost and lamented Adonis was found. This letter they enclosed in an earthen pot, which they sealed and sent floating down the river to the sea. The waves carried the pot to Byblus, where every year it arrived at the time when the Syrian women were weeping for their dead Lord. The pot was taken up from the water and opened : the letter was read ; and the weeping women dried their tears, because the lost Adonis was found.[1]

[1] Cyril of Alexandria, *In Isaiam*, lib. ii. Tomus iii. (Migne's *Patrologia Graeca*, lxx. 441).

CHAPTER II

THE OFFICIAL EGYPTIAN CALENDAR

The date
of a
festival
sometimes
furnishes
a clue to
the nature
of the god.

A USEFUL clue to the original nature of a god or goddess is often furnished by the season at which his or her festival is celebrated. Thus, if the festival falls at the new or the full moon, there is a certain presumption that the deity thus honoured either is the moon or at least has lunar affinities. If the festival is held at the winter or summer solstice, we naturally surmise that the god is the sun, or at all events that he stands in some close relation to that luminary. Again, if the festival coincides with the time of sowing or harvest, we are inclined to infer that the divinity is an embodiment of the earth or of the corn. These presumptions or inferences, taken by themselves, are by no means conclusive ; but if they happen to be confirmed by other indications, the evidence may be regarded as fairly strong.

The year
of the
Egyptian
calendar
a vague or
movable
one.

Unfortunately, in dealing with the Egyptian gods we are in a great measure precluded from making use of this clue. The reason is not that the dates of the festivals are always unknown, but that they shifted from year to year, until after a long interval they had revolved through the whole course of the seasons. This gradual revolution of the festal Egyptian cycle resulted from the employment of a calendar year which neither corresponded exactly to the solar year nor was periodically corrected by intercalation.[1]

[1] As to the Egyptian calendar see L. Ideler, *Handbuch der mathematischen und technischen Chronologie* (Berlin, 1825–1826), i. 93 *sqq.* ; Sir J. G. Wilkinson, *Manners and Customs of the Ancient Egyptians* (London, 1878), ii. 368 *sqq.* ; R. Lepsius, *Die Chronologie der Aegypter*, i. (Berlin, 1849) pp. 125 *sqq.* ; H. Brugsch, *Die Ägyptologie* (Leipsic, 1891), pp. 347-366 ; A. Erman, *Aegypten und aegyptisches Leben im Altertum*, pp. 468 *sq.* ; G. Maspero, *Histoire ancienne des Peuples de l'Orient Clas-*

The solar year is equivalent to about three hundred and sixty-five and a quarter days ; but the ancient Egyptians, ignoring the quarter of a day, reckoned the year at three hundred and sixty-five days only.[1] Thus each of their calendar years was shorter than the true solar year by about a quarter of a day. In four years the deficiency amounted to one whole day ; in forty years it amounted to ten days ; in four hundred years it amounted to a hundred days; and so it went on increasing until after a lapse of four times three hundred and sixty-five, or one thousand four hundred and sixty solar years, the deficiency amounted to three hundred and sixty-five days, or a whole Egyptian year. Hence one thousand four hundred and sixty solar years, or their equivalent, one thousand four hundred and sixty-one Egyptian years, formed a period or cycle at the end of which the Egyptian festivals returned to those points of the solar year at which they had been celebrated in the beginning.[2] In the meantime they had been held successively on every day of the solar year, though always on the same day of the calendar.

Thus the official calendar was completely divorced, except at rare and long intervals, from what may be called the natural calendar of the shepherd, the husbandman, and the sailor—that is, from the course of the seasons in which the times for the various labours of cattle-breeding, tillage, and navigation are marked by the position of the sun in the sky, the rising or setting of the stars, the fall of rain, the growth of pasture, the ripening of the corn, the blowing of certain winds, and so forth. Nowhere, perhaps, are the events of this natural calendar better marked or more regular in their recurrence than in Egypt ; nowhere accordingly could their divergence from the corresponding dates of the official calendar be more readily observed. The

Thus the official calendar was divorced from the natural calendar, which is marked by the course of the seasons.

---

sique, i. 207 - 210 ; Ed. Meyer, "Aegyptische Chronologie," *Abhandlungen der königl. Preuss. Akademie der Wissenschaften*, 1904, pp. 2 *sqq.* ; *id.*, "Nachträge zur ägyptischen Chronologie," *Abhandlungen der königl. Preuss. Akademie der Wissenschaften*, 1907, pp. 3 *sqq.* ; *id.*, *Geschichte des Altertums*,[2] i. 2. pp. 28 *sqq.*, 98 *sqq.* ; F. K. Ginzel,

Handbuch der mathematischen und technischen Chronologie, i. (Leipsic, 1906) pp. 150 *sqq.*

[1] Herodotus, ii. 4, with A. Wiedemann's note ; Geminus, *Elementa Astronomiae*, 8, p. 106, ed. C. Manitius (Leipsic, 1898) ; Censorinus, *De die natali*, xviii. 10.

[2] Geminus, *Elementa Astronomiae*, 8, pp. 106 *sqq.*, ed. C. Manitius.

divergence certainly did not escape the notice of the Egyptians themselves, and some of them apparently attempted successfully to correct it. Thus we are told that the Theban priests, who particularly excelled in astronomy, were acquainted with the true length of the solar year, and harmonized the calendar with it by intercalating a day every few, probably every four, years.[1] But this scientific improvement was too deeply opposed to the religious conservatism of the Egyptian nature to win general acceptance. "The Egyptians," said Geminus, a Greek astronomer writing about 77 B.C., "are of an opposite opinion and purpose from the Greeks. For they neither reckon the years by the sun nor the months and days by the moon, but they observe a peculiar system of their own. They wish, in fact, that the sacrifices should not always be offered to the gods at the same time of the year, but that they should pass through all the seasons of the year, so that the summer festival should in time be celebrated in winter, in autumn, and in spring. For that purpose they employ a year of three hundred and sixty-five days, composed of twelve months of thirty days each, with five supplementary days added. But they do not add the quarter of a day for the reason I have given— namely, in order that their festivals may revolve."[2] So attached, indeed, were the Egyptians to their old calendar, that the kings at their consecration were led by the priest of Isis at Memphis into the holy of holies, and there made to swear that they would maintain the year of three hundred and sixty-five days without intercalation.[3]

The practical inconvenience of a calendar which marked true time only once in about fifteen hundred years might be

[1] Diodorus Siculus, i. 50. 2 ; Strabo, xvii. i. 46, p. 816. According to H. Brugsch (*Die Ägyptologie*, pp. 349 *sq.*), the Egyptians would seem to have denoted the movable year of the calendar and the fixed year of the sun by different written symbols. For more evidence that they were acquainted with a four years' period, corrected by intercalation, see R. Lepsius, *Chronologie der Aegypter*, i. 149 *sqq.*

[2] Geminus, *Elementa Astronomiae*, 8, p. 106, ed. C. Manitius. The same writer further (p. 108) describes as a popular Greek error the opinion that the Egyptian festival of Isis coincided with the winter solstice. In his day, he tells us, the two events were separated by an interval of a full month, though they had coincided a hundred and twenty years before the time he was writing.

[3] *Scholia in Caesaris Germanici Aratea*, p. 409, ed. Fr. Eyssenhardt, in his edition of Martianus Capella (Leipsic, 1866).

calmly borne by a submissive Oriental race like the ancient Egyptians, but it naturally proved a stumbling-block to the less patient temperament of their European conquerors. Accordingly in the reign of King Ptolemy III. Euergetes a decree was passed that henceforth the movable Egyptian year should be converted into a fixed solar year by the intercalation of one day at the end of every four years, " in order that the seasons may do their duty perpetually according to the present constitution of the world, and that it may not happen, through the shifting of the star by one day in four years, that some of the public festivals which are now held in the winter should ever be celebrated in the summer, and that other festivals now held in the summer should hereafter be celebrated in the winter, as has happened before, and must happen again if the year of three hundred and sixty-five days be retained."   The decree was passed in the year 239 or 238 B.C. by the high priests, scribes, and other dignitaries of the Egyptian church assembled in convocation at Canopus ; but we cannot doubt that the measure, though it embodied native Egyptian science, was prompted by the king or his Macedonian advisers.[1]   This sage attempt to reform the erratic calendar was not permanently successful. The change may indeed have been carried out during the reign of the king who instituted it, but it was abandoned by the year 196 B.C. at latest, as we learn from the celebrated inscription known as the Rosetta stone, in which a month of the Macedonian calendar is equated to the corresponding month of the movable Egyptian year.[2]   And the testimony of Geminus, which I have cited, proves that in the following century the festivals were still revolving in the old style.

The reform which the Macedonian king had vainly attempted to impose upon his people was accomplished by the practical Romans when they took over the administra-

Attempt of Ptolemy III. to reform the Egyptian calendar by intercalation.

Institution of the fixed Alexandrian year by the Romans.

[1] Copies of the decree in hieroglyphic, demotic, and Greek have been found inscribed on stones in Egypt. See Ch. Michel, *Recueil d'Inscriptions Grecques* (Brussels, 1900), pp. 415 *sqq.*, No. 551 ; W. Dittenberger, *Orientis Graeci Inscriptiones Selectae* (Leipsic, 1903–1905), vol. i. pp. 91 *sqq.*, No. 56 ; J. P. Mahaffy, *The Empire of the Ptolemies* (London, 1895), pp. 205 *sqq.*, 226 *sqq.*   The star mentioned in the decree is the Dog-star (Sirius). See below, pp. 34 *sqq.*

[2] W. Dittenberger, *Orientis Graeci Inscriptiones Selectae*, vol. i. pp. 140 *sqq.*, No. 90, with note 25 of the editor.

tion of the country.   The expedient by which they effected
the change was a simple one ; indeed it was no other than
that to which Ptolemy Euergetes had resorted for the same
purpose.   They merely intercalated one day at the end of
every four years, thus equalizing within a small fraction four
calendar years to four solar years.   Henceforth the official
and the natural calendars were in practical agreement.   The
movable Egyptian year had been converted into the fixed
Alexandrian year, as it was called, which agreed with the
Julian year in length and in its system of intercalation,
though it differed from that year in retaining the twelve
equal Egyptian months and five supplementary days.[1]   But
while the new calendar received the sanction of law and
regulated the business of government, the ancient calendar
was too firmly established in popular usage to be at once
displaced.   Accordingly it survived for ages side by side with
its modern rival.[2]   The spread of Christianity, which required
a fixed year for the due observance of its festivals, did much
to promote the adoption of the new Alexandrian style, and
by the beginning of the fifth century the ancient movable year
of Egypt appears to have been not only dead but forgotten.[3]

---

[1] On the Alexandrian year see L.
Ideler, *Handbuch der mathematischen
und technischen Chronologie*, i. 140
sqq.   That admirable chronologer
argued (pp. 153-161) that the innovation was introduced not, as had
been commonly supposed, in 25 B.C.,
but in 30 B.C., the year in which
Augustus defeated Mark Antony under
the walls of Alexandria and captured
the city.   However, the question seems
to be still unsettled.   See F. K. Ginzel,
*Handbuch der mathematischen und
technischen Chronologie*, i. 226 *sqq.*,
who thinks it probable that the change
was made in 26 B.C.   For the purposes
of this study the precise date of the
introduction of the Alexandrian year is
not material.

[2] In demotic the fixed Alexandrian
year is called "the year of the
Ionians," while the old movable year
is styled "the year of the Egyptians."
Documents have been found which are
dated by the day and the month of

both years.   See H. Brugsch, *Die
Ägyptologie*, pp. 354 *sq.*

[3] L. Ideler, *op. cit.* i. 149-152.
Macrobius thought that the Egyptians
had always employed a solar year of
$365\frac{1}{4}$ days (*Saturn.* i. 12. 2, i. 14. 3).
The ancient calendar of the Mexicans
resembled that of the Egyptians except
that it was divided into eighteen months
of twenty days each (instead of twelve
months of thirty days each), with five
supplementary days added at the end
of the year.   These supplementary
days (*nemontemi*) were deemed unlucky : nothing was done on them :
they were dedicated to no deity ; and
persons born on them were considered
unfortunate.   See B. de Sahagun,
*Histoire générale des choses de la
Nouvelle - Espagne*, traduite par D.
Jourdanet et R. Simeon (Paris, 1880),
pp. 50, 164 ; F. S. Clavigero, *History
of Mexico* (London, 1807), i. 290.
Unlike the Egyptian calendar, however, the Mexican appears to have

been regularly corrected by intercalation so as to bring it into harmony
with the solar year.   But as to the
mode of intercalation our authorities
differ.   According to the positive
statement of Sahagun, one of the
earliest and best authorities, the
Mexicans corrected the deficiency of
their year by intercalating one day in
every fourth year, which is precisely the
correction adopted in the Alexandrian
and the Julian calendar.   See B. de
Sahagun, *op. cit.* pp. 286 *sq.*, where
he expressly asserts the falsehood of
the view that the bissextile year was
unknown to the Mexicans.   This
weighty statement is confirmed by the
practice of the Indians of Yucatan.
Like the Aztecs, they reckoned a year
to consist of 360 days divided into
18 months of 20 days each, with 5
days added so as to make a total of
365 days, but every fourth year they
intercalated a day so as to make a

total of 366 days.   See Diego de
Landa, *Relation des choses de Yucatan*
(Paris, 1864), pp. 202 *sqq.*   On the
other hand the historian Clavigero,
who lived in the eighteenth century,
but used earlier authorities, tells us
that the Mexicans " did not interpose
a day every four years, but thirteen
days (making use here even of this
favourite number) every fifty-two years ;
which produces the same regulation of
time " (*History of Mexico*, Second
Edition, London, 1807, vol. i. p. 293).
However, the view that the Mexicans
corrected their year by intercalation is
rejected by Professor E. Seler.   See his
" Mexican Chronology," in *Bulletin 28*
of the Bureau of American Ethnology
(Washington, 1904), pp. 13 *sqq.* ; and
on the other side Miss Zelia Nuttall,
" The Periodical Adjustments of the
Ancient Mexican Calendar," *American
Anthropologist*, N.S. vi. (1904) pp
486-500.

CHAPTER III

THE CALENDAR OF THE EGYPTIAN FARMER

§ 1. *The Rise and Fall of the Nile*

In Egypt the operations of husbandry are dependent on the annual rise and fall of the Nile.

IF the Egyptian farmer of the olden time could thus get no help, except at the rarest intervals, from the official or sacerdotal calendar, he must have been compelled to observe for himself those natural signals which marked the times for the various operations of husbandry. In all ages of which we possess any records the Egyptians have been an agricultural people, dependent for their subsistence on the growth of the corn. The cereals which they cultivated were wheat, barley, and apparently sorghum (*Holcus sorghum*, Linnaeus), the *doora* of the modern fellaheen.[1] Then as now the whole country, with the exception of a fringe on the coast of the Mediterranean, was almost rainless, and owed its immense fertility entirely to the annual inundation of the Nile, which, regulated by an elaborate system of dams and canals, was distributed over the fields, renewing the soil year by year with a fresh deposit of mud washed down from the great equatorial lakes and the mountains of Abyssinia. Hence the rise of the river has always been watched by the inhabitants with the utmost anxiety; for if it either falls short of or exceeds a certain height, dearth and famine are the inevitable consequences.[2] The water begins to rise early in

---

[1] Herodotus, ii. 36, with A. Wiedemann's note; Diodorus Siculus, i. 14. 1, i. 17. 1; Pliny, *Nat. Hist.* v. 57 *sq.*, xviii. 60; Sir J. Gardiner Wilkinson, *Manners and Customs of the Ancient Egyptians* (London, 1878), ii. 398, 399, 418, 426 *sq.*; A. Erman, *Aegypten und aegyptisches Leben im Altertum*, pp. 577 *sqq.*; A. de Candolle, *Origin of Cultivated Plants* (London, 1884), pp. 354 *sq.*, 369, 381; G. Maspero, *Histoire ancienne des Peuples de l'Orient Classique*, i. 66.

[2] Herodotus, ii. 14; Diodorus Siculus, i. 36; Strabo, xvii. 1. 3, pp. 786-788; Pliny, *Nat. Hist.* xviii. 167·

June, but it is not until the latter half of July that it swells to a mighty tide. By the end of September the inundation is at its greatest height. The country is now submerged, and presents the appearance of a sea of turbid water, from which the towns and villages, built on higher ground, rise like islands. For about a month the flood remains nearly stationary, then sinks more and more rapidly, till by December or January the river has returned to its ordinary bed. With the approach of summer the level of the water continues to fall. In the early days of June the Nile is reduced to half its ordinary breadth ; and Egypt, scorched by the sun, blasted by the wind that has blown from the Sahara for many days, seems a mere continuation of the desert. The trees are choked with a thick layer of grey dust. A few meagre patches of vegetables, watered with difficulty, struggle painfully for existence in the immediate neighbourhood of the villages. Some appearance of verdure lingers beside the canals and in the hollows from which the moisture has not wholly evaporated. The plain appears to pant in the pitiless sunshine, bare, dusty, ash-coloured, cracked and seamed as far as the eye can see with a network of fissures. From the middle of April till the middle of June the land of Egypt is but half alive, waiting for the new Nile.[1]

For countless ages this cycle of natural events has determined the annual labours of the Egyptian husbandman. The first work of the agricultural year is the cutting

Irrigation, sowing, and harvest in Egypt.

170; Seneca, *Natur. Quaest.* iv. 2. 1-10; E. W. Lane, *Manners and Customs of the Modern Egyptians* (Paisley and London, 1895), pp. 17 *sq.*, 495 *sqq.*; A. Erman, *op. cit.* pp. 21-25; G. Maspero, *op. cit.* i. 22 *sqq.* However, since the Suez Canal was cut, rain has been commoner in Lower Egypt (A. H. Sayce on Herodotus, ii. 14).

[1] G. Maspero, *Histoire ancienne des Peuples de l'Orient Classique,* i. 22-26 ; A. Erman, *Aegypten und aegyptisches Leben im Altertum,* p. 23. According to Lane (*op. cit.* pp. 17 *sq.*) the Nile rises in Egypt about the summer solstice (June 21) and reaches its greatest height by the autumnal equinox (Sep-

tember 22). This agrees exactly with the statement of Diodorus Siculus (i. 36. 2). Herodotus says (ii. 19) that the rise of the river lasted for a hundred days from the summer solstice. Compare Pliny, *Nat. Hist.* v. 57, xviii. 167 ; Seneca, *Nat. Quaest.* iv. 2. 1. According to Prof. Ginzel the Nile does not rise in Egypt till the last week of June (*Handbuch der mathematischen und technischen Chronologie,* i. 154). For ancient descriptions of Egypt in time of flood see Herodotus, ii. 97 ; Diodorus Siculus, i. 36. 8 *sq.* ; Strabo, xvii. 1. 4, p. 788 ; Aelian, *De natura animalium,* x. 43 ; Achilles Tatius, iv. 12 ; Seneca, *Natur. Quaest.* iv. 2. 8 and 11.

of the dams which have hitherto prevented the swollen river from flooding the canals and the fields.   This is done, and the pent-up waters released on their beneficent mission, in the first half of August.[1]   In November, when the inundation has subsided, wheat, barley, and sorghum are sown. The time of harvest varies with the district, falling about a month later in the north than in the south.   In Upper or Southern Egypt barley is reaped at the beginning of March, wheat at the beginning of April, and sorghum about the end of that month.[2]

The events of the agricultural year were probably celebrated with religious rites.   It is natural to suppose that these various events of the agricultural year were celebrated by the Egyptian farmer with some simple religious rites designed to secure the blessing of the gods upon his labours.   These rustic ceremonies he would continue to perform year after year at the same season, while the solemn festivals of the priests continued to shift, with the shifting calendar, from summer through spring to winter, and so backward through autumn to summer.   The rites of the husbandman were stable because they rested on direct observation of nature : the rites of the priest were unstable because they were based on a false calculation.   Yet many of the priestly festivals may have been nothing but the old rural festivals disguised in the course of ages by the pomp of sacerdotalism and severed, by the error of the calendar, from their roots in the natural cycle of the seasons.

[1] Sir J. Gardiner Wilkinson, *Manners and Customs of the Ancient Egyptians* (London, 1878), ii. 365 *sq.* ; E. W. Lane, *Manners and Customs of the Modern Egyptians* (Paisley and London, 1895), pp. 498 *sqq.* ; G. Maspero, *Histoire ancienne des Peuples de l'Orient Classique*, i. 23 *sq.*, 69.   The last-mentioned writer says (p. 24) that the dams are commonly cut between the first and sixteenth of July, but apparently he means August.

[2] Sir J. D. Wilkinson, *op. cit.* ii. 398 *sq.* ; Prof. W. M. Flinders Petrie, cited above, vol. i. p. 231, note [3].   According to Pliny (*Nat. Hist.* xviii. 60) barley was reaped in Egypt in the sixth month from sowing, and wheat in the seventh month.   Diodorus Siculus, on the other hand, says (i. 36. 4) that the corn was reaped after four or five months.   Perhaps Pliny refers to Lower, and Diodorus to Upper Egypt.   Elsewhere Pliny affirms (*Nat. Hist.* xviii. 169) that the corn was sown at the beginning of November, and that the reaping began at the end of March and was completed in May.   This certainly applies better to Lower than to Upper Egypt.

§ 2. *Rites of Irrigation*

These conjectures are confirmed by the little we know both of the popular and of the official Egyptian religion. Thus we are told that the Egyptians held a festival of Isis at the time when the Nile began to rise.   They believed that the goddess was then mourning for the lost Osiris, and that the tears which dropped from her eyes swelled the impetuous tide of the river.[1]   Hence in Egyptian inscriptions Isis is spoken of as she " who maketh the Nile to swell and overflow, who maketh the Nile to swell in his season." [2] Similarly the Toradjas of Central Celebes imagine that showers of rain are the tears shed by the compassionate gods in weeping for somebody who is about to die ; a shower in the morning is to them an infallible omen of death.[3]   However, an uneasy suspicion would seem to have occurred to the Egyptians that perhaps after all the tears of the goddess might not suffice of themselves to raise the water to the proper level ; so in the time of Rameses II. the king used on the first day of the flood to throw into the Nile a written order commanding the river to do its duty, and the submissive stream never failed to obey the royal mandate.[4]   Yet the ancient belief survives in a modified form to this day.   For the Nile, as we saw, begins to rise in June about the time of the summer solstice, and the people still attribute its increased volume to a miraculous drop which falls into the river on the night of the seventeenth of the month.   The charms and divinations which they practise on that mystic night in order to ascertain the length of their own life and to rid the houses of bugs may well date from a remote antiquity.[5]   Now if Osiris was in one of his aspects

Mourning for Osiris at mid-summer when the Nile begins to rise.

---

[1] Pausanias, x. 32. 18.

[2] E. A. Wallis Budge, *Osiris and the Egyptian Resurrection*, ii. 278.

[3] N. Adriani en Alb. C. Kruijt, *De Bare'e-sprekende Toradjas van Midden-Celebes* (Batavia, 1912), i. 273. The more civilized Indians of tropical America, who practised agriculture and had developed a barbaric art, appear to have commonly represented the rain-god in human form with tears

streaming down from his eyes. See T. A. Joyce, "The Weeping God," *Essays and Studies presented to William Ridgeway* (Cambridge, 1913), pp. 365-374.

[4] This we learn from inscriptions at Silsilis. See A. Moret, *Mystères Égyptiens* (Paris, 1913), p. 180.

[5] E. W. Lane, *Manners and Customs of the Modern Egyptians* (Paisley and London, 1895), ch. xxvi. pp. 495 *sq.*

a god of the corn, nothing could be more natural than that he should be mourned at midsummer. For by that time the harvest was past, the fields were bare, the river ran low, life seemed to be suspended, the corn-god was dead. At such a moment people who saw the handiwork of divine beings in all the operations of nature might well trace the swelling of the sacred stream to the tears shed by the goddess at the death of the beneficent corn-god her husband.

And the sign of the rising waters on earth was accompanied by a sign in heaven. For in the early days of Egyptian history, some three or four thousand years before the beginning of our era, the splendid star of Sirius, the brightest of all the fixed stars, appeared at dawn in the east just before sunrise about the time of the summer solstice, when the Nile begins to rise.[1] The Egyptians called it Sothis, and regarded it as the star of Isis,[2] just as the

---

[1] L. Ideler, *Handbuch der mathematischen und technischen Chronologie*, i. 124 *sqq.*; R. Lepsius, *Die Chronologie der Aegypter*, i. 168 *sq.*; F. K. Ginzel, *Handbuch der mathematischen und technischen Chronologie*, i. 190 *sq.*; Ed. Meyer, " Nachträge zur ägyptischen Chronologie," *Abhandlungen der königl. Preuss. Akademie der Wissenschaften*, 1907 (Berlin, 1908), pp. 11 *sq.*; *id.*, *Geschichte des Altertums*,[2] i. 28 *sq.*, 99 *sqq.* The coincidence of the rising of Sirius with the swelling of the Nile is mentioned by Tibullus (i. 7. 21 *sq.*) and Aelian (*De natura animalium*, x. 45). In later times, as a consequence of the precession of the equinoxes, the rising of Sirius gradually diverged from the summer solstice, falling later and later in the solar year. In the sixteenth and fifteenth century B.C. Sirius rose seventeen days after the summer solstice, and at the date of the Canopic decree (238 B.C.) it rose a whole month after the first swelling of the Nile. See L. Ideler, *op. cit.* i. 130; F. K. Ginzel, *op. cit.* i. 190; Ed. Meyer, "Nachträge zur ägyptischen Chronologie," pp. 11 *sq.* According to Censorinus (*De die natali*, xxi. 10), Sirius regularly rose in Egypt on the twentieth of July (Julian calendar);

and this was true of latitude 30° in Egypt (the latitude nearly of Heliopolis and Memphis) for about three thousand years of Egyptian history. See L. Ideler, *op. cit.* i. 128-130. But the date of the rising of the star is not the same throughout Egypt; it varies with the latitude, and the variation within the limits of Egypt amounts to seven days or more. Roughly speaking, Sirius rises nearly a whole day earlier for each degree of latitude you go south. Thus, whereas near Alexandria in the north Sirius does not rise till the twenty-second of July, at Syene in the south it rises on the sixteenth of July. See R. Lepsius, *op. cit.* i. 168 *sq.*; F. K. Ginzel, *op. cit.* i. 182 *sq.* Now it is to be remembered that the rising of the Nile, as well as the rising of Sirius, is observed earlier and earlier the further south you go. The coincident variation of the two phenomena could hardly fail to confirm the Egyptians in their belief of a natural or supernatural connexion between them.

[2] Diodorus Siculus, i. 27. 4; Plutarch, *Isis et Osiris*, 21, 22, 38, 61; Porphyry, *De antro nympharum*, 24; Scholiast on Apollonius Rhodius, ii. 517; Canopic decree, lines 36 *sq.*, in W. Dittenberger's *Orientis Graeci In-*

Babylonians deemed the planet Venus the star of Astarte. To both peoples apparently the brilliant luminary in the morning sky seemed the goddess of life and love come to mourn her departed lover or spouse and to wake him from the dead.   Hence the rising of Sirius marked the beginning of the sacred Egyptian year,[1] and was regularly celebrated by a festival which did not shift with the shifting official year.[2]   The

scriptiones Selectae, vol. i. p. 102, No. 56 (lines 28 *sq.* in Ch. Michel's *Recueil d'Inscriptions Grecques*, p. 417, No. 551) ; R. V. Lanzone, *Dizionario di Mitologia Egizia*, pp. 825 *sq*. On the ceiling of the Memnonium at Thebes the heliacal rising of Sirius is represented under the form and name of Isis (Sir J. G. Wilkinson, *Manners and Customs of the Ancient Egyptians*, London, 1878, iii. 102).

[1] Porphyry and the Canopic decree, *ll.cc.* ; Censorinus, *De die natali*, xviii. 10, xxi. 10. In inscriptions on the temple at Syene, the modern Assuan, Isis is called "the mistress of the beginning of the year," the goddess "who revolves about the world, near to the constellation of Orion, who rises in the eastern sky and passes to the west perpetually" (R. V. Lanzone, *op. cit.* p. 826). According to some, the festival of the rising of Sirius and the beginning of the sacred year was held on the nineteenth, not the twentieth of July.   See Ed. Meyer, "Ägyptische Chronologie," *Abhandlungen der königl. Preuss. Akademie der Wissenschaften*, 1904, pp. 22 *sqq.* ; *id.*, "Nachträge zur ägyptischen Chronologie," *Abhandlungen der königl. Preuss. Akademie der Wissenschaften*, 1907, pp. 7 *sqq.* ; *id.*, *Geschichte des Altertums*,[2] i. 2. pp. 28 *sqq.*, 98 *sqq.*

[2] *Eudoxi ars astronomica, qualis in charta Aegyptiaca superest*, ed. F. Blass (Kiliae, 1887), p. 14, οἱ δὲ ἀσ[τρο]λ[ό]γοι καὶ οἱ ἱερογραμμ[ατεῖς] χ[ρῶν]ται ταῖς κατὰ σελή[ν]η[ν] ἡμ[έ]ραις καὶ ἄγουσι πανδημ[ι]κὰς ἑ[ορ]τας τινὰς μὲν ὡς ἐνομί[σθ]η τὰ δὲ καταχυτήρια καὶ κυνὸς ἀνατολὴν καὶ σεληναῖα κατὰ θεό[ν], ἀναλεγόμενοι τὰς ἡμέρας ἐκ τῶν Αἰγυπτίων. This statement of Eudoxus or of one of his pupils is

important, since it definitely proves that, besides the shifting festivals of the shifting official year, the Egyptians celebrated other festivals, which were dated by direct observation of natural phenomena, namely, the annual inundation, the rise of Sirius, and the phases of the moon.   The same distinction of the fixed from the movable festivals is indicated in one of the Hibeh papyri, but the passage is unfortunately mutilated.   See *The Hibeh Papyri*, part i., edited by B. P. Grenfell and A. S. Hunt (London, 1906), pp. 145, 151 (pointed out to me by my friend Mr. W. Wyse).   The annual festival in honour of Ptolemy and Berenice was fixed on the day of the rising of Sirius.   See the Canopic decree, in W. Dittenberger's *Orientis Graeci Inscriptiones Selectae*, No. 56 (vol. i. pp. 102 *sq.*).

The rise of Sirius was carefully observed by the islanders of Ceos, in the Aegean.   They watched for it with arms in their hands and sacrificed on the mountains to the star, drawing from its aspect omens of the salubrity or unhealthiness of the coming year. The sacrifice was believed to secure the advent of the cool North winds (the Etesian winds as the Greeks call them), which regularly begin to blow about this time of the year, and mitigate the oppressive heat of summer in the Aegean.   See Apollonius Rhodius, *Argon.* ii. 516-527, with the notes of the Scholiast on vv. 498, 526 ; Theophrastus, *De ventis*, ii. 14 ; Clement of Alexandria, *Strom.* vi. 3. 29, p. 753, ed. Potter ; Nonnus, *Dionys.* v. 269-279 ; Hyginus, *Astronomica*, ii. 4 ; Cicero, *De divinatione*, i. 57. 130 ; M. P. Nilsson, *Griechische Feste* (Leipsic, 1906), pp. 6-8 ; C. Neu-

first day of the first month Thoth was theoretically supposed
to date from the heliacal rising of the bright star, and in all
probability it really did so when the official or civil year of
three hundred and sixty-five days was first instituted. But
the miscalculation which has been already explained [1] had
the effect of making the star to shift its place in the calendar
by one day in four years. Thus if Sirius rose on the first
of Thoth in one year, it would rise on the second of Thoth
four years afterwards, on the third of Thoth eight years
afterwards, and so on until after the lapse of a Siriac or
Sothic period of fourteen hundred and sixty solar years the
first of Thoth again coincided with the heliacal rising of
Sirius.[2] This observation of the gradual displacement of

mann und J. Partsch, *Physikalische
Geographie von Griechenland* (Breslau,
1885), pp. 96 *sqq.* On the top of
Mount Pelion in Thessaly there was a
sanctuary of Zeus, where sacrifices were
offered at the rising of Sirius, in the
height of the summer, by men of rank,
who were chosen by the priest and
wore fresh sheep-skins. See [Dicae-
archus,] "Descriptio Graeciae," *Geographi Graeci Minores*, ed. C. Müller,
i. 107; *Historicorum Graecorum Fragmenta*, ed. C. Müller, ii. 262.

[1] Above, pp. 24 *sq.*

[2] We know from Censorinus (*De die
natali*, xxi. 10) that the first of Thoth
coincided with the heliacal rising of
Sirius on July 20 (Julian calendar) in
the year 139 A.D. Hence reckoning
backwards by Sothic periods of 1460
solar years we may infer that Sirius
rose on July 20th (Julian calendar) in
the years 1321 B.C., 2781 B.C., and
4241 B.C.; and accordingly that the
civil or vague Egyptian year of 365
days was instituted in one of these
years. In favour of supposing that it
was instituted either in 2781 B.C. or
4241 B.C., it may be said that in both
these years the rising of Sirius nearly
coincided with the summer solstice and
the rising of the Nile; whereas in the
year 1321 B.C. the summer solstice,
and with it the rising of the Nile, fell
nineteen days before the rising of Sirius
and the first of Thoth. Now when we
consider the close causal connexion

which the Egyptians traced between
the rising of Sirius and the rising of
the Nile, it seems probable that they
started the new calendar on the first
of Thoth in a year in which the two
natural phenomena coincided rather
than in one in which they diverged
from each other by nineteen days.
Prof. Ed. Meyer decides in favour of
the year 4241 B.C. as the date of the
introduction of the Egyptian calendar
on the ground that the calendar was
already well known in the Old Kingdom. See L. Ideler, *op. cit.* i. 125
sqq.; F. K. Ginzel, *op. cit.* i. 192 *sqq.*;
Ed. Meyer, "Nachträge zur ägyp-
tischen Chronologie," *Abhandlungen
der königl. Preuss. Akademie der
Wissenschaften*, 1907 (Berlin, 1908),
pp. 11 *sq.*; *id., Geschichte des Altertums*,[2] i. 2. pp. 28 *sqq.*, 98 *sqq.*
When the fixed Alexandrian year was
introduced in 30 B.C. (see above, pp.
27 *sq.*) the first of Thoth fell on
August 29, which accordingly was
thenceforth reckoned the first day of
the year in the Alexandrian calendar.
See L. Ideler, *op. cit.* i. 153 *sqq.* The
period of 1460 solar or 1461 movable
Egyptian years was variously called a
Sothic period (Clement of Alexandria,
Strom. i. 21. 136, p. 401 ed. Potter),
a Canicular year (from *Canicula*, "the
Dog-star," that is, Sirius), a heliacal
year, and a year of God (Censorinus,
De die natali, xviii. 10). But there is
no evidence or probability that the

the star in the calendar has been of the utmost importance for the progress of astronomy, since it led the Egyptians directly to the determination of the approximately true length of the solar year and thus laid the basis of our modern calendar ; for the Julian calendar, which we owe to Caesar, was founded on the Egyptian theory, though not on the Egyptian practice.[1] It was therefore a fortunate moment for the world when some pious Egyptian, thousands of years ago, identified for the first time the bright star of Sirius with his goddess ; for the identification induced his countrymen to regard the heavenly body with an attention which they would never have paid to it if they had known it to be nothing but a world vastly greater than our own and separated from it by an inconceivable, if not immeasurable, abyss of space.

The observation of the gradual displacement of Sirius in the calendar led to the determination of the true length of the solar year.

The cutting of the dams and the admission of the water

---

period was recognized by the Egyptian astronomers who instituted the movable year of 365 days. Rather, as Ideler pointed out (*op. cit.* i. 132), it must have been a later discovery based on continued observations of the heliacal rising of Sirius and of its gradual displacement through the whole length of the official calendar. Brugsch, indeed, went so far as to suppose that the period was a discovery of astronomers of the second century A.D., to which they were led by the coincidence of the first of Thoth with the heliacal rising of Sirius in 139 A.D. (*Die Ägyptologie*, p. 357). But the discovery, based as it is on a very simple calculation (365 × 4 = 1460), could hardly fail to be made as soon as astronomers estimated the length of the solar year at $365\frac{1}{4}$ days, and that they did so at least as early as 238 B.C. is proved conclusively by the Canopic decree. See above, pp. 25 *sq.*, 27. As to the Sothic period see further R. Lepsius, *Die Chronologie der Aegypter*, i. 165 *sqq.* ; F. K. Ginzel, *op. cit.* i. 187 *sqq.*

For the convenience of the reader I subjoin a table of the Egyptian months, with their dates, as these fell, (1) in a year when the first of Thoth coincided with July 20 of the Julian calendar, and (2) in the fixed Alexandrian year.

Egyptian Months.	Sothic Year beginning July 20	Alexandrian Year.
1 Thoth .	. 20 July .	. 29 August
1 Phaophi .	. 19 August .	28 September
1 Athyr .	. 18 September	28 October
1 Khoiak .	. 18 October .	27 November
1 Tybi . .	. 17 November	27 December
1 Mechir .	. 17 December .	26 January
1 Phamenoth	16 January .	25 February
1 Pharmuthi .	15 February .	27 March
1 Pachon .	. 17 March .	26 April
1 Payni . .	16 April . .	26 May
1 Epiphi .	. 16 May . .	25 June
1 Mesori .	. 15 June . .	25 July
1 Supplement-ary day	15 July . .	24 August

See L. Ideler, *op. cit.* i. 143 *sq.* ; F. K. Ginzel, *op. cit.* i. 200.

[1] The Canopic decree (above, p. 27) suffices to prove that the Egyptian astronomers, long before Caesar's time, were well acquainted with the approximately exact length of the solar year, although they did not use their knowledge to correct the calendar except for a short time in the reign of Ptolemy Euergetes. With regard to Caesar's debt to the Egyptian astronomers see Dio Cassius, xliii. 26 ; Macrobius, *Saturn.* i. 14. 3, i. 16. 39; L. Ideler, *Handbuch der mathematischen und technischen Chronologie*, i. 166 *sqq.*

Cere-
monies
observed in
Egypt at
the cutting
of the
dams early
in August.

into the canals and fields is a great event in the Egyptian year. At Cairo the operation generally takes place between the sixth and the sixteenth of August, and till lately was attended by ceremonies which deserve to be noticed, because they were probably handed down from antiquity. An ancient canal, known by the name of the Khalíj, formerly passed through the native town of Cairo. Near its entrance the canal was crossed by a dam of earth, very broad at the bottom and diminishing in breadth upwards, which used to be constructed before or soon after the Nile began to rise. In front of the dam, on the side of the river, was reared a truncated cone of earth called the 'arooseh or

The Bride
of the Nile.

"bride," on the top of which a little maize or millet was generally sown. This " bride " was commonly washed down by the rising tide a week or a fortnight before the cutting of the dam. Tradition runs that the old custom was to deck a young virgin in gay apparel and throw her into the river as a sacrifice to obtain a plentiful inundation.[1]

Sacrifices
offered by
savages at
the cutting
of dams.

Certainly human sacrifices were offered for a similar purpose by the Wajagga of German East Africa down to recent years. These people irrigate their fields by means of skil-fully constructed channels, through which they conduct the water of the mountain brooks and rivers to the thirsty land. They imagine that the spirits of their forefathers dwell in the rocky basins of these rushing streams, and that they would resent the withdrawal of the water to irrigate the fields if compensation were not offered to them. The water-rate paid to them consisted of a child, uncircumcised and of unblemished body, who was decked with ornaments and bells and thrown into the river to drown, before they ventured to draw off the water into the irrigation channel. Having thrown him in, his executioners shewed a clean pair of heels, because they expected the river to rise in flood at once on receipt of the water-rate.[2] In similar circum-stances the Njamus of British East Africa sacrifice a sheep before they let the water of the stream flow into the ditch

---

[1] E. W. Lane, *Manners and Customs of the Modern Egyptians* (Paisley and London, 1895), ch. xxvi. pp. 499 *sq.*

[2] Bruno Gutmann, " Feldbausitten und Wachstumsbräuche der Wads-chagga," *Zeitschrift für Ethnologie*, xlv. (1913) pp. 484 *sq.*

or artificial channel. The fat, dung, and blood of the animal are sprinkled at the mouth of the ditch and in the water ; thereupon the dam is broken down and the stream pours into the ditch. The sacrifice may only be offered by a man of the Il Mayek clan, and for two days afterwards he wears the skin of the beast tied round his head. No one may quarrel with this man while the water is irrigating the crops, else the people believe that the water would cease to flow in the ditch ; more than that, if the men of the Il Mayek clan were angry and sulked for ten days, the water would dry up permanently for that season. Hence the Il Mayek clan enjoys great consideration in the tribe, since the crops are thought to depend on their good will and good offices. Ten elders assist at the sacrifice of the sheep, though they may take no part in it. They must all be of a particular age ; and after the ceremony they may not cohabit with their wives until harvest, and they are obliged to sleep at night in their granaries. Curiously enough, too, while the water is irrigating the fields, nobody may kill waterbuck, eland, oryx, zebra, rhinoceros, or hippopotamus. Anybody caught red-handed in the act of breaking this game-law would at once be cast out of the village.[1]

Whether the " bride " who used to figure at the ceremony of cutting the dam in Cairo was ever a live woman or not, the intention of the practice appears to have been to marry the river, conceived as a male power, to his bride the corn-land, which was soon to be fertilized by his water.˙ The ceremony was therefore a charm to ensure the growth of the crops. As such it probably dated, in one form or another, from ancient times. Dense crowds assembled to witness the cutting of the dam. The operation was performed before sunrise, and many people spent the preceding night on the banks of the canal or in boats lit with lamps on the river, while fireworks were displayed and guns discharged at frequent intervals. Before sunrise a great number of workmen began to cut the dam, and the task was accomplished about an hour before the sun appeared on the

Modern Egyptian ceremony at the cutting of the dams.

[1] Hon. K. R. Dundas, "Notes on the tribes inhabiting the Baringo District, East Africa Protectorate," *Journal of the Royal Anthropological Institute*, xl. (1910) p. 54.

horizon. When only a thin ridge of earth remained, a boat with an officer on board was propelled against it, and breaking through the slight barrier descended with the rush of water into the canal. The Governor of Cairo flung a purse of gold into the boat as it passed. Formerly the custom was to throw money into the canal. The populace used to dive after it, and several lives were generally lost in the scramble.[1] This practice also would seem to have been ancient, for Seneca tells us that at a place called the Veins of the Nile, not far from Philae, the priests used to cast money and offerings of gold into the river at a festival which apparently took place at the rising of the water.[2] At Cairo the time-honoured ceremony came to an end in 1897, when the old canal was filled up. An electric tramway now runs over the spot where for countless ages crowds of worshippers or holiday-makers had annually assembled to witness the marriage of the Nile.[3]

§ 3. *Rites of Sowing*

The next great operation of the agricultural year in Egypt is the sowing of the seed in November, when the water of the inundation has retreated from the fields. With the Egyptians, as with many peoples of antiquity, the committing of the seed to the earth assumed the character of a solemn and mournful rite. On this subject I will let Plutarch speak for himself. " What," he asks, " are we to make of the gloomy, joyless, and mournful sacrifices, if it is wrong either to omit the established rites or to confuse and disturb our conceptions of the gods by absurd suspicions? For the Greeks also perform many rites which resemble those of the Egyptians and are observed about the same time. Thus at the festival of the Thesmophoria in Athens

The sowing of the seed in November.

Plutarch on the mournful character of the rites of sowing.

[1] E. W. Lane, *op. cit.* pp. 500-504; Sir Auckland Colvin, *The Making of Modern Egypt* (London, 1906), pp. 278 *sq.* According to the latter writer, a dressed dummy was thrown into the river at each cutting of the dam.

[2] Seneca, *Naturales Quaestiones*, iv. 2. 7. The cutting of the dams is mentioned by Diodorus Siculus (i. 36. 3), and the festival on that occasion (τὰ καταχυτήρια) is noticed by Eudoxus (or one of his pupils) in a passage which has already been quoted. See above, p. 35, note [2].

[3] Sir Auckland Colvin, *l.c.*

women sit on the ground and fast. And the Boeotians open the vaults of the Sorrowful One,[1] naming that festival sorrowful because Demeter is sorrowing for the descent of the Maiden. The month is the month of sowing about the setting of the Pleiades.[2] The Egyptians call it Athyr, the Athenians Pyanepsion, the Boeotians the month of Demeter. Theopompus informs us that the western peoples consider and call the winter Cronus, the summer Aphrodite, and the spring Persephone, and they believe that all things are brought into being by Cronus and Aphrodite. The Phrygians imagine that the god sleeps in winter and wakes in summer, and accordingly they celebrate with Bacchic rites the putting him to bed in winter and his awakening in summer. The Paphlagonians allege that he is bound fast and shut up in winter, but that he stirs and is set free in spring. And the season furnishes a hint that the sadness is for the hiding of those fruits of the earth which the ancients esteemed, not indeed gods, but great and necessary gifts bestowed by the gods in order that men might not lead the life of savages and of wild beasts. For it was that time of year when they saw some of the fruits vanishing and failing from the trees, while they sowed others grudgingly and with difficulty, scraping the earth with their hands and huddling it up again, on the uncertain chance that what they deposited in the ground would ever ripen and come to maturity. Thus they did in many respects like those who bury and mourn their dead. And just as we say that a purchaser of Plato's books purchases Plato, or that an actor who plays the comedies of Menander plays Menander, so the men of old did not hesitate to call the gifts and products of the gods by the names of the gods themselves, thereby honouring and glorifying the things on account of their utility. But in

The sadness of autumn

[1] Τῆς Ἀχαίας. Plutarch derives the name from ἄχος, "pain," "grief." But the etymology is uncertain. It has lately been proposed to derive the epithet from ὀχή, "nourishment." See M. P. Nilsson, *Griechische Feste* (Leipsic, 1906), p. 326. As to the vaults (μέγαρα) of Demeter see Pausanias, ix. 8. 1 ; Scholiast on Lucian, *Dial. Meretr.* ii. pp. 275 *sq.*, ed. H. Rabe (Leipsic, 1906).

[2] In antiquity the Pleiades set at dawn about the end of October or early in November. See L. Ideler, *Handbuch der mathematischen und technischen Chronologie*, i. 242 ; Aug. Mommsen, *Chronologie* (Leipsic, 1883), pp. 16, 27 ; G. F. Unger, " Zeitrechnung der Griechen und Römer," in Iwan Müller's *Handbuch der klassischen Altertumswissenschaft*, i.[1] (Nördlingen, 1886) pp. 558, 585.

after ages simple folk in their ignorance applied to the gods statements which only held true of the fruits of the earth, and so they came not merely to say but actually to believe that the growth and decay of plants, on which they subsisted,[1] were the birth and the death of gods.   Thus they fell into absurd, immoral, and confused ways of thinking, though all the while the absurdity of the fallacy was manifest.   Hence Xenophanes of Colophon declared that if the Egyptians deemed their gods divine they should not weep for them, and that if they wept for them they should not deem them divine.   ' For it is ridiculous,' said he, ' to lament and pray that the fruits would be good enough to grow and ripen again in order that they may again be eaten and lamented.'   But he was wrong, for though the lamentations are for the fruits, the prayers are addressed to the gods, as the causes and givers of them, that they would be pleased to make fresh fruits to spring up instead of those that perish." [2]

Plutarch's view that the worship of the fruits of the earth sprang from a verbal misunderstanding.   In this interesting passage Plutarch expresses his belief that the worship of the fruits of the earth was the result of a verbal misapprehension or disease of language, as it has been called by a modern school of mythologists, who explain the origin of myths in general on the same easy principle of metaphors misunderstood.   Primitive man, on Plutarch's theory, firmly believed that the fruits of the earth on which he subsisted were not themselves gods but merely the gifts of the gods, who were the real givers of all good things. Yet at the same time men were in the habit of bestowing on these divine products the names of their divine creators, either out of gratitude or merely for the sake of brevity, as when we say that a man has bought a Shakespeare or acted Molière, when we mean that he has bought the works of Shakespeare or acted the plays of Molière.   This abbreviated mode of expression was misunderstood in later times, and so

---

[1] Τὰς παρουσίας τῶν ἀναγκαίων καὶ ἀποκρύψεις.

[2] Plutarch, *Isis et Osiris*, 69-71.   With the sleep of the Phrygian gods we may compare the sleep of Vishnu.   The toils and anxieties of the Indian farmer "are continuous, and his only period of comparative rest is in the heavy rain time, when, as he says, the god Vishnu goes to sleep, and does not wake till October is well advanced and the time has come to begin cutting and crushing the sugar-cane and boiling down the juice "   (W. Crooke, *Natives of Northern India*, London, 1907, p. 159).

people came to look upon the fruits of the earth as themselves divine instead of as being the work of divinities : in short, they mistook the creature for the creator.   In like manner Plutarch would explain the Egyptian worship of animals as reverence done not so much to the beasts themselves as to the great god who displays the divine handiwork in sentient organisms even more than in the most beautiful and wonderful works of inanimate nature.[1]

The comparative study of religion has proved that these theories of Plutarch are an inversion of the truth.   Fetishism, or the view that the fruits of the earth and things in general are divine or animated by powerful spirits, is not, as Plutarch imagined, a late corruption of a pure and primitive theism, which regarded the gods as the creators and givers of all good things.   On the contrary, fetishism is early and theism is late in the history of mankind.   In this respect Xenophanes, whom Plutarch attempts to correct, displayed a much truer insight into the mind of the savage.   To weep crocodile tears over the animals and plants which he kills and eats, and to pray them to come again in order that they may be again eaten and again lamented—this may seem absurd to us, but it is precisely what the savage does.   And from his point of view the proceeding is not at all absurd but perfectly rational and well calculated to answer his ends. For he sincerely believes that animals and fruits are tenanted by spirits who can harm him if they please, and who cannot but be put to considerable inconvenience by that destruction of their bodies which is unfortunately inseparable from the processes of mastication and digestion.   What more natural, therefore, than that the savage should offer excuses to the beasts and the fruits for the painful necessity he is under of consuming them, and that he should endeavour to alleviate their pangs by soft words and an air of respectful sympathy, in order that they may bear him no grudge, and may in due time come again to be again eaten and again lamented ? Judged by the standard of primitive manners the attitude of the walrus to the oysters was strictly correct :—

His theory is an inversion of the truth : for fetishism is the antecedent, not the corruption, of theism.

Lamentations of the savage for the animals and plants which he kills and eats.

---

[1] Plutarch, *Isis et Osiris*, 77.

" ' I weep for you,' the Walrus said:
    ' I deeply sympathize.'
With sobs and tears he sorted out
    Those of the largest size,
    Holding his pocket-handkerchief
    Before his streaming eyes."

Respect
shown by
savages
for the
fruits and
the animals
which
they eat.

Many examples of such hypocritical lamentations for animals, drawn not from the fancy of a playful writer but from the facts of savage life, could be cited.[1]   Here I shall quote the general statement of a writer on the Indians of British Columbia, because it covers the case of vegetable as well as of animal food.   After describing the respectful welcome accorded by the Stlatlum Indians to the first " sock-eye " salmon which they have caught in the season, he goes on : " The significance of these ceremonies is easy to perceive when we remember the attitude of the Indians towards nature generally, and recall their myths relating to the salmon, and their coming to their rivers and streams. Nothing that the Indian of this region eats is regarded by him as mere food and nothing more.   Not a single plant, animal, or fish, or other object upon which he feeds, is looked upon in this light, or as something he has secured for himself by his own wit and skill.   He regards it rather as something which has been voluntarily and compassionately placed in his hands by the goodwill and consent of the ' spirit' of the object itself, or by the intercession and magic of his culture-heroes ; to be retained and used by him only upon the fulfilment of certain conditions.   These conditions include respect and reverent care in the killing or plucking of the animal or plant and proper treatment of the parts he has no use for, such as the bones, blood, and offal ; and the depositing of the same in some stream or lake, so that the object may by that means renew its life and physical form. The practices in connection with the killing of animals and the gathering of plants and fruits all make this quite clear, and it is only when we bear this attitude of the savage towards nature in mind that we can hope to rightly understand the motives and purposes of many of his strange customs and beliefs."[2]

[1] *Spirits of the Corn and of the Wild,* **ii.** 204 *sqq.*

[2] C. Hill Tout, " Report on the Ethnology of the Stlatlum Indians of

We can now understand why among many peoples of
antiquity, as Plutarch tells us, the time of sowing was a
time of sorrow. The laying of the seed in the earth was
a burial of the divine element, and it was fitting that like a
human burial it should be performed with gravity and the
semblance, if not the reality, of sorrow. Yet they sorrowed
not without hope, perhaps a sure and certain hope, that the
seed which they thus committed with sighs and tears to
the ground would yet rise from the dust and yield fruit a
hundredfold to the reaper. "They that sow in tears shall
reap in joy. He that goeth forth and weepeth, bearing
precious seed, shall doubtless come again with rejoicing,
bringing his sheaves with him." [1]

§ 4. *Rites of Harvest*

The Egyptian harvest, as we have seen, falls not in
autumn but in spring, in the months of March, April, and
May. To the husbandman the time of harvest, at least in a
good year, must necessarily be a season of joy: in bringing
home his sheaves he is requited for his long and anxious
labours. Yet if the old Egyptian farmer felt a secret joy
at reaping and garnering the grain, it was essential that he
should conceal the natural emotion under an air of profound
dejection. For was he not severing the body of the corn-
god with his sickle and trampling it to pieces under the
hoofs of his cattle on the threshing-floor? [2] Accordingly we
are told that it was an ancient custom of the Egyptian corn-
reapers to beat their breasts and lament over the first sheaf
cut, while at the same time they called upon Isis. [3] The
invocation seems to have taken the form of a melancholy
chant, to which the Greeks gave the name of Maneros.
Similar plaintive strains were chanted by corn-reapers in

British Columbia," *Journal of the
Anthropological Institute*, xxxv. (1905)
pp. 140 *sq.*

[1] Psalm cxxvi. 5 *sq.* Firmicus
Maternus asks the Egyptians (*De
errore profanarum religionum*, ii. 7),
" *Cur plangitis fruges terrae et cre-
scentia lugetis semina?* "

[2] As to the Egyptian modes of
reaping and threshing see Sir J.
Gardiner Wilkinson, *Manners and
Customs of the Ancient Egyptians*
(London, 1878), ii. 419 *sqq*; A.
Erman, *Aegypten und aegyptisches
Leben im Altertum*, pp. 572 *sqq.*

[3] Diodorus Siculus, i. 14. 2.

Phoenicia and other parts of Western Asia.[1] Probably all
these doleful ditties were lamentations for the corn-god
killed by the sickles of the reapers. In Egypt the slain
deity was Osiris, and the name *Maneros* applied to the dirge
appears to be derived from certain words meaning " Come
to thy house," which often occur in the lamentations for the
dead god.[2]

Similar
ceremonies
observed
by the
Cherokee
Indians
in the
cultivation
of the
corn.

Ceremonies of the same sort have been observed by
other peoples, probably for the same purpose. Thus we are
told that among all vegetables corn (*selu*), by which is
apparently meant maize, holds the first place in the household economy and the ceremonial observance of the
Cherokee Indians, who invoke it under the name of " the
Old Woman " in allusion to a myth that it sprang from
the blood of an old woman killed by her disobedient sons.
" Much ceremony accompanied the planting and tending of
the crop. Seven grains, the sacred number, were put into
each hill, and these were not afterwards thinned out. After
the last working of the crop, the priest and an assistant—
generally the owner of the field—went into the field and
built a small enclosure in the centre. Then entering it,
they seated themselves upon the ground, with heads bent
down, and while the assistant kept perfect silence the priest,
with rattle in hand, sang songs of invocation to the spirit of
the corn. Soon, according to the orthodox belief, a loud
rustling would be heard outside, which they would know

The Old
Woman of
the corn
and the
laments for
her death.

was caused by the ' Old Woman ' bringing the corn into the
field, but neither must look up until the song was finished.
This ceremony was repeated on four successive nights, after
which no one entered the field for seven other nights, when
the priest himself went in, and, if all the sacred regulations
had been properly observed, was rewarded by finding young
ears upon the stalks. The corn ceremonies could be performed by the owner of the field himself, provided he was
willing to pay a sufficient fee to the priest in order to learn
the songs and ritual. Care was always taken to keep a

---

[1] Herodotus, ii. 79 ; Julius Pollux,
iv. 54 ; Pausanias, ix. 29. 7 ; Athenaeus, xiv. 11 *sq.*, pp. 618-620. As to
these songs see *Spirits of the Corn and
of the Wild*, i. 214 *sqq.*

[2] H. Brugsch, *Adonisklage und
Linoslied* (Berlin, 1852), p. 24, corrected by A. Wiedemann, *Herodots
zweites Buch*, p. 336. As to the lamentations for Osiris see above, p. 12.

clean trail from the field to the house, so that the corn might be encouraged to stay at home and not go wandering elsewhere. Most of these customs have now fallen into disuse excepting among the old people, by many of whom they are still religiously observed. Another curious ceremony, of which even the memory is now almost forgotten, was enacted after the first working of the corn, when the owner or priest stood in succession at each of the four corners of the field and wept and wailed loudly. Even the priests are now unable to give a reason for this performance, which may have been a lament for the bloody death of Selu," the Old Woman of the Corn.[1] In these Cherokee practices the lamentations and the invocations of the Old Woman of the Corn resemble the ancient Egyptian customs of lamenting over the first corn cut and calling upon Isis, herself probably in one of her aspects an Old Woman of the Corn. Further, the Cherokee precaution of leaving a clear path from the field to the house resembles the Egyptian invitation to Osiris, "Come to thy house." So in the East Indies to this day people observe elaborate ceremonies for the purpose of bringing back the Soul of the Rice from the fields to the barn.[2] The Nandi of British East Africa perform a ceremony in September when the eleusine grain is ripening. Every woman who owns a plantation goes out with her daughters into the cornfields and makes a bonfire of the branches and leaves of certain trees (the *Solanum campylanthum* and *Lantana salvifolia*). After that they pluck some of the eleusine, and each of them puts one grain in her necklace, chews another and rubs it on her forehead, throat, and breast. " No joy is shown by the womenfolk on this occasion, and they sorrowfully cut a basketful of the corn which they take home with them and place in the loft to dry."[3]

Just as the Egyptians lamented at cutting the corn, so the Karok Indians of California lament at hewing the

---

[1] J. Mooney, "Myths of the Cherokee," *Nineteenth Annual Report of the Bureau of American Ethnology* (Washington, 1900), pp. 423 *sq.* I do not know what precisely the writer means by "the last working of the crop" and "the first working of the corn."

[2] *Spirits of the Corn and of the Wild*, i. 180 *sqq.*

[3] A. C. Hollis, *The Nandi* (Oxford, 1909), p. 46.

Lamentations of Indians at cutting sacred wood.

sacred wood for the fire in the assembly-room. The wood must be cut from a tree on the top of the highest hill. In lopping off the boughs the Indian weeps and sobs piteously, shedding real tears, and at the top of the tree he leaves two branches and a top-knot, resembling a man's head and outstretched arms. Having descended from the tree, he binds the wood in a faggot and carries it back to the assembly-room, blubbering all the way. If he is asked why he thus weeps at cutting and fetching the sacred fuel, he will either give no answer or say simply that he does it for luck.[1] We may suspect that his real motive is to appease the wrath of the tree-spirit, many of whose limbs he has amputated, though he took care to leave him two arms and a head.

Arab ceremony of burying " the old man " at harvest.

The conception of the corn-spirit as old and dead at harvest is very clearly embodied in a custom observed by the Arabs of Moab. When the harvesters have nearly finished their task and only a small corner of the field remains to be reaped, the owner takes a handful of wheat tied up in a sheaf. A hole is dug in the form of a grave, and two stones are set upright, one at the head and the other at the foot, just as in an ordinary burial. Then the sheaf of wheat is laid at the bottom of the grave, and the sheikh pronounces these words, " The old man is dead." Earth is afterwards thrown in to cover the sheaf, with a prayer, " May Allah bring us back the wheat of the dead." [2]

---

[1] S. Powers, *Tribes of California* (Washington, 1877), p. 25.

[2] A. Jaussen, "Coutumes Arabes," *Revue Biblique,* 1er avril 1903, p. 258; *id., Coutumes des Arabes au pays de Moab* (Paris 1908), pp. 252 *sq.*

CHAPTER IV

THE OFFICIAL FESTIVALS OF OSIRIS

§ 1. *The Festival at Sais*

SUCH, then, were the principal events of the farmer's calendar in ancient Egypt, and such the simple religious rites by which he celebrated them. But we have still to consider the Osirian festivals of the official calendar, so far as these are described by Greek writers or recorded on the monuments. In examining them it is necessary to bear in mind that on account of the movable year of the old Egyptian calendar the true or astronomical dates of the official festivals must have varied from year to year, at least until the adoption of the fixed Alexandrian year in 30 B.C. From that time onward, apparently, the dates of the festivals were determined by the new calendar, and so ceased to rotate throughout the length of the solar year. At all events Plutarch, writing about the end of the first century, implies that they were then fixed, not movable; for though he does not mention the Alexandrian calendar, he clearly dates the festivals by it.[1] Moreover, the long festal calendar of

[1] Thus with regard to the Egyptian month of Athyr he tells us that the sun was then in the sign of the Scorpion (*Isis et Osiris*, 13), that Athyr corresponded to the Athenian month Pyanepsion and the Boeotian month Damatrius (*op. cit.* 69), that it was the month of sowing (*ib.*), that in it the Nile sank, the earth was laid bare by the retreat of the inundation, the leaves fell, and the nights grew longer than the days (*op. cit.* 39). These indications agree on the whole with the date of Athyr in the Alexandrian calendar, namely October 28-November 26. Again, he says (*op. cit.* 43) that the festival of the beginning of spring was held at the new moon of the month Phamenoth, which, in the Alexandrian calendar, corresponded to February 24-March 26. Further, he tells us that a festival was celebrated on the 23rd of Phaophi after the autumn equinox (*op. cit.* 52), and in the Alexandrian calendar Phaophi began on September 28, a few days after the autumn equinox.

Esne, an important document of the Imperial age, is obviously based on the fixed Alexandrian year; for it assigns the mark for New Year's Day to the day which corresponds to the twenty-ninth of August, which was the first day of the Alexandrian year, and its references to the rising of the Nile, the position of the sun, and the operations of agriculture are all in harmony with this supposition.[1] Thus we may take it as fairly certain that from 30 B.C. onwards the Egyptian festivals were stationary in the solar year.

The sufferings of Osiris displayed as a mystery at Sais.

Herodotus tells us that the grave of Osiris was at Sais in Lower Egypt, and that there was a lake there upon which the sufferings of the god were displayed as a mystery by night.[2] This commemoration of the divine passion was held once a year: the people mourned and beat their breasts at it to testify their sorrow for the death of the god; and an image of a cow, made of gilt wood with a golden sun between its horns, was carried out of the chamber in which it stood the rest of the year.[3] The cow no doubt represented Isis herself, for cows were sacred to her, and she was regularly depicted with the horns of a cow on her head,[4] or even as a woman with the head of a cow.[5] It is probable that the carrying out of her cow-shaped image symbolized the goddess searching for the dead body of Osiris; for this was the native Egyptian interpretation of a similar ceremony observed in Plutarch's time about the winter solstice, when the gilt cow was carried seven times round the temple.[6] A great feature of the festival was the

---

Once more, he observes that another festival was held after the spring equinox (*op. cit.* 65), which implies the use of a fixed solar year. See G. Parthey in his edition of Plutarch's *Isis et Osiris* (Berlin, 1850), pp. 165-169.

[1] H. Brugsch, *Die Ägyptologie*, p. 355.

[2] Herodotus, ii. 170.

[3] Herodotus, ii. 129-132.

[4] Herodotus, ii. 41, with Prof. A. Wiedemann's note (*Herodots zweites Buch*, pp. 187 *sqq.*); Diodorus Siculus, i. 11. 4; Aelian, *De natura animalium*, x. 27; Plutarch, *Isis et Osiris*, 19 and 39. According to Prof. Wiedemann "the Egyptian name of the cow of Isis was *ḥes-t*, and

this is one of the rare cases in which the name of the sacred animal agrees with that of the deity." *Hest* was the usual Egyptian form of the name which the Greeks and Romans represented as Isis. See R. V. Lanzone, *Dizionario di Mitologia Egizia*, pp. 813 *sqq.*

[5] In this form she is represented on a relief at Philae pouring a libation in honour of the soul of Osiris. See E. A. Wallis Budge, *Osiris and the Egyptian Resurrection*, i. 8. She is similarly portrayed in a bronze statuette, which is now in the Louvre. See G. Perrot et Ch. Chipiez, *Histoire de l'Art dans l'Antiquité*, i. (Paris, 1882) p. 60, fig. 40.

[6] Plutarch, *Isis et Osiris*, 52. The

nocturnal illumination. People fastened rows of oil-lamps to the outside of their houses, and the lamps burned all night long. The custom was not confined to Sais, but was observed throughout the whole of Egypt.[1]

This universal illumination of the houses on one night of the year suggests that the festival may have been a commemoration not merely of the dead Osiris but of the dead in general, in other words, that it may have been a night of All Souls.[2] For it is a widespread belief that the souls of the dead revisit their old homes on one night of the year; and on that solemn occasion people prepare for the reception of the ghosts by laying out food for them to eat, and lighting lamps to guide them on their dark road from and to the grave. The following instances will illustrate the custom.

§ 2. Feasts of All Souls

The Esquimaux of St. Michael and the lower Yukon River in Alaska hold a festival of the dead every year at the end of November or the beginning of December, as well as a greater festival at intervals of several years. At these seasons, food, drink, and clothes are provided for the returning ghosts in the *kashim* or clubhouse of the village, which is illuminated with oil lamps. Every man or woman who wishes to honour a dead friend sets up a lamp on a stand in front of the place which the deceased used to occupy in the clubhouse. These lamps, filled with seal oil, are kept burning day and night till the festival is over. They are believed to light the shades on their return to

The illumination of houses throughout Egypt on the night of the festival suggests that the rite was a Feast of All Souls.

Annual festival of the dead among the Esquimaux.

The lighting of the lamps for the dead.

---

interpretation is accepted by Prof. A. Wiedemann (*Herodots zweites Buch*, p. 482).

[1] Herodotus, ii. 62. In one of the Hibeh papyri (No. 27, lines 165-167) mention is made of the festival and of the lights which were burned throughout the district. See *The Hibeh Papyri*, part i., ed. B. P. Grenfell and A. S. Hunt (London, 1906), p. 149 (pointed out to me by Mr. W. Wyse). In the papyrus the festival is said to have been held in honour of Athena (*i.e.* Neith), the great goddess of Sais, who

was there identified with Isis. See A. Wiedemann, *Die Religion der alten Ägypter*, pp. 77 *sq.*; *id.*, *Religion of the Ancient Egyptians*, pp. 140 *sq.*

[2] In the period of the Middle Kingdom the Egyptians of Siut used to light lamps for the dead on the last day and the first day of the year. See A. Erman, "Zehn Vorträge aus dem mittleren Reich," *Zeitschrift für ägyptische Sprache und Alterthumskunde*, xx. (1882) p. 164; *id.*, *Ägypten und aegyptisches Leben im Altertum*, pp. 434 *sq.*

their old home and back again to the land of the dead. If any one fäils to put up a lamp in the clubhouse and to keep it burning, the shade whom he or she desires to honour could not find its way to the place and so would miss the feast. On the eve of the festival the nearest male relation goes to the grave and summons the ghost by planting there a small model of a seal spear or of a wooden dish, according as the deceased was a man or a woman. The badges of the dead are marked on these implements. When all is ready, the ghosts gather in the fire-pit under the clubhouse, and ascending through the floor at the proper moment take possession of the bodies of their namesakes, to whom the offerings of food, drink, and clothing are made for the benefit of the dead. Thus each shade obtains the supplies he needs in the other world. The dead who have none to make offerings to them are believed to suffer great destitution. Hence the Esquimaux fear to die without leaving behind them some one who will sacrifice to their spirits, and childless people generally adopt children lest their shades should be forgotten at the festivals. When a person has been much disliked, his ghost is sometimes purposely ignored, and that is deemed the severest punishment that could be inflicted upon him. After the songs of invitation to the dead have been sung, the givers of the feast take a small portion of food from every dish and cast it down as an offering to the shades ; then each pours a little water on the floor so that it runs through the cracks. In this way they believe that the spiritual essence of all the food and water is conveyed to the souls. The remainder of the food is afterwards distributed among the people present, who eat of it heartily. Then with songs and dances the feast comes to an end, and the ghosts are dismissed to their own place. Dances form a conspicuous feature of the great festival of the dead, which is held every few years. The dancers dance not only in the clubhouse but also at the graves and on the ice, if the deceased met their death by drowning.[1]

The Indians of California used to observe annual cere-

Esquimaux festival of the dead.

---

[1] E. W. Nelson, " The Eskimo about Bering Strait," *Eighteenth Annual Report of the Bureau of Ethnology,* Part i. (Washington, 1899) pp. 363 *sqq.*

monies of mourning for the dead,[1] at some of which the souls of the departed were represented by living persons. Ten or more men would prepare themselves to play the part of the ghosts by fasting for several days, especially by abstaining from flesh. Disguised with paint and soot, adorned with feathers and grasses, they danced and sang in the village or rushed about in the forest by night with burning torches in their hands. After a time they presented themselves to the relations of the deceased, who looked upon these maskers as in very truth their departed friends and received them accordingly with an outburst of lamentation, the old women scratching their own faces and smiting their breasts with stones in token of mourning. These masquerades were generally held in February. During their continuance a strict fast was observed in the village.[2] Among the Konkaus of California the dance of the dead is always held about the end of August and marks their New Year's Day. They collect a large quantity of food, clothing, baskets, ornaments, and whatever else the spirits are supposed to need in the other world. These they hang on a semicircle of boughs or small trees, cut and set in the ground leafless. In the centre burns a great fire, and hard by are the graves. The ceremony begins at evening and lasts till daybreak. As darkness falls, men and women sit on the graves and wail for the dead of the year. Then they dance round the fire with frenzied yells and whoops, casting from time to time the offerings into the flames. All must be consumed before the first faint streaks of dawn glimmer in the East.[3] The Choctaws used to have a great respect for their dead. They did not bury their bodies but laid them on biers made of bark and supported by forked sticks about fifteen feet high.

[1] S. Powers, *Tribes of California* (Washington, 1877), pp. 328, 355, 356, 384.

[2] Kostromitonow, " Bemerkungen über die Indianer in Ober-Kalifornien," in K. F. v. Baer and Gr. v. Helmersen's *Beiträge zur Kenntniss des russischen Reiches*, i. (St. Petersburg, 1839) pp. 88 *sq.* The natives of the western islands of Torres Straits used to hold a great death-dance at which disguised men personated the ghosts of the lately deceased, mimicking their characteristic gait and gestures. Women and children were supposed to take these mummers for real ghosts. See A. C. Haddon, in *Reports of the Cambridge Anthropological Expedition to Torres Straits*, v. (Cambridge, 1904) pp. 252-256; *The Belief in Immortality and the Worship of the Dead*, i. 176 *sqq.*

[3] S. Powers, *Tribes of California*, pp. 437 *sq.*

When the worms had consumed the flesh, the skeleton was dismembered, any remains of muscles and sinews were buried, and the bones were deposited in a box, the skull being reddened with ochre. The box containing the bones was then carried to the common burial ground. In the early days of November the tribe celebrated a great festival which they called the Festival of the Dead or of the Souls; every family then gathered in the common burial ground, and there with weeping and lamentation visited the boxes which contained the mouldering relics of their dead. On returning from the graveyard they held a great banquet, which ended the festival.[1] Some of the Pueblo Indians of New Mexico "believe that on a certain day (in August, I think) the dead rise from their graves and flit about the neighbouring hills, and on that day all who have lost friends carry out quantities of corn, bread, meat, and such other good things of this life as they can obtain, and place them in the haunts frequented by the dead, in order that the departed spirits may once more enjoy the comforts of this nether world. They have been encouraged in this belief by the priests, who were in the habit of sending out and appropriating to themselves all these things, and then making the poor simple Indians believe that the dead had eaten them."[2]

Annual festival of the dead among the Miztecs of Mexico.

The Miztecs of Mexico believed that the souls of the dead came back in the twelfth month of every year, which corresponded to our November. On this day of All Souls the houses were decked out to welcome the spirits. Jars of food and drink were set on a table in the principal room, and the family went forth with torches to meet the ghosts and invite them to enter. Then returning themselves to the house they knelt around the table, and with eyes bent on the ground prayed the souls to accept of the offerings and to procure the blessings of the gods upon the family. Thus they remained on bended knees and with downcast eyes till the morning, not daring to look at the table lest they

[1] Bossu, *Nouveaux Voyages aux Indes Occidentales* (Paris, 1768), ii. 95 *sq.*

[2] T. G. S. Ten Broeck, in H. R. Schoolcraft's *Indian Tribes of the United States* (Philadelphia, 1853–1856), iv. 78. The Pueblo village to which the writer particularly refers is Laguna.

should offend the spirits by spying on them at their meal. With the first beams of the sun they rose, glad at heart. The jars of food which had been presented to the dead were given to the poor or deposited in a secret place.[1] The Indians of Santiago Tepehuacan believe that the souls of their dead return to them on the night of the eighteenth of October, the festival of St. Luke, and they sweep the roads in order that the ghosts may find them clean on their passage.[2]

Again, the natives of Sumba, an East Indian island, celebrate a New Year's festival, which is at the same time a festival of the dead. The graves are in the middle of the village, and at a given moment all the people repair to them and raise a loud weeping and wailing. Then after indulging for a short time in the national pastimes they disperse to their houses, and every family calls upon its dead to come back. The ghosts are believed to hear and accept the invitation. Accordingly betel and areca nuts are set out for them. Victims, too, are sacrificed in front of every house, and their hearts and livers are offered with rice to the dead. After a decent interval these portions are distributed amongst the living, who consume them and banquet gaily on flesh and rice, a rare event in their frugal lives. Then they play, dance, and sing to their heart's content, and the festival which began so lugubriously ends by being the merriest of the year. A little before daybreak the invisible guests take their departure. All the people turn out of their houses to escort them a little way. Holding in one hand the half of a coco-nut, which contains a small packet of provisions for the dead, and in the other hand a piece of smouldering wood, they march in procession, singing a drawling song to the accompaniment of a gong and waving the lighted brands in time to the music. So they move through the darkness till with the last words of the song

Annual
festival of
the dead
in Sumba

---

[1] Brasseur de Bourbourg, *Histoire des nations civilisées du Mexique et de l'Amérique - Centrale* (Paris, 1857–1859), iii. 23 *sq.* ; H. H. Bancroft, *Native Races of the Pacific States* (London, 1875–1876), ii. 623. Similar customs are still practised by the Indians of a great part of Mexico and Central America (Brasseur de Bourbourg, *op. cit.* iii. 24, note [1]).

[2] "Lettre du curé de Santiago Tepehuacan à son évêque," *Bulletin de la Société de Géographie* (Paris), IIme Série, ii. (1834) p. 179.

they throw away the coco-nuts and the brands in the direction of the spirit-land, leaving the ghosts to wend their way thither, while they themselves return to the village.[1]

Annual
festival of
the dead in
Kiriwina.

In Kiriwina, one of the Trobriand Islands, to the east of New Guinea, the spirits of the ancestors are believed to revisit their native village in a body once a year after the harvest has been got in. At this time the men perform special dances, the people openly display their valuables, spread out on platforms, and great feasts are made for the spirits. On a certain night, when the moon is at the full, all the people raise a great shout and so drive away the spirits to the spirit land.[2] The Sea Dyaks of Borneo celebrate a great festival in honour of the dead at irregular intervals, it may be one or more years after the death of a particular person. All who have died since the last feast was held, and have not yet been honoured by such a celebration, are remembered at this time ; hence the number of persons commemorated may be great, especially if many years have elapsed since the last commemoration service. The preparations last many weeks : food and drink and all other necessaries are stored in plenty, and the whole neighbourhood for miles round is invited to attend. On the eve of the feast the women take bamboo splints and fashion out of them little models of various useful articles, and these models are hung over the graves for the use of the dead in the other world. If the feast is held in honour of a man, the things manufactured in his behoof will take the form of a bamboo gun, a shield, a war-cap, and so on ; if it is a woman who is commemorated, little models of a loom, a fish-basket, a winnowing-fan and such like things will be provided for her spirit ; and if it is a child for whom the rite is performed, toys of various kinds will be made ready for the childish ghost. Finally, to stay the appetite of ghosts who may be too sharp-set to wait for the formal banquet in the house,

Festival of
the dead
among the
Sea Dyaks
of Borneo.

---

[1] S. Roos, "Bijdrage tot de kennis van taal, land en volk op het eiland Soemba," *Verhandelingen van het Bataviaasch Genootschap van Kunsten en Wetenschappen*, xxxvi. (1872) pp. 63-65.

[2] Rev. S. B. Fellows, quoted by George Brown, D.D., *Melanesians and Polynesians* (London, 1910), p. 237.

a supply of victuals is very considerately placed outside the house on which the hungry spirits may fall to without delay. The dead arrive in a boat from the other world ; for living Dyaks generally travel by river, from which it necessarily follows that Dyak ghosts do so likewise. The ship in which the ghostly visitors voyage to the land of the living is not much to look at, being in appearance nothing but a tiny boat made out of a bamboo which has been used to cook rice. Even this is not set floating on the river but is simply thrown away under the house. Yet through the incantations uttered by the professional wailing-woman the bark is wafted away to the spirit world and is there converted into a large war-canoe. Gladly the ghosts embark and sail away as soon as the final summons comes. It always comes in the evening, for it is then that the wailer begins to croon her mournful ditties ; but the way is so long that the spirits do not arrive in the house till the day is breaking. To refresh them after their weary journey a bamboo full of rice-spirit awaits them ; and this they partake of by deputy, for a brave old man, who does not fear the face of ghosts, quaffs the beverage in their stead amid the joyful shouts of the spectators. On the morning after the feast the living pay the last offices of respect to the dead. Monuments made of ironwood, the little bamboo articles, and food of all kinds are set upon the graves. In consideration of these gifts the ghosts now relinquish all claims on their surviving relatives, and henceforth earn their own living by the sweat of their brow. Before they take their final departure they come to eat and drink in the house for the last time.[1]

Thus the Dyak festival of the dead is not an annual welcome accorded to all the souls of ancestors ; it is a propitiatory ceremony designed to secure once for all the eternal welfare of the recently departed, or at least to prevent their ghosts from returning to infest and importune the living. The same is perhaps the intention of the " soul departure" (*Kathi Kasham*) festival which the Tangkul

Annual festival of the dead among the Nagas of Manipur.

---

[1] E. H. Gomes, *Seventeen Years among the Sea Dyaks of Borneo* (London, 1911), pp. 216-218. For another and briefer account of this festival see *The Scapegoat*, p. 154.

Nagas of Manipur, in Assam, celebrate every year about the end of January. At this great feast the dead are represented by living men, chosen on the ground of their likeness to the departed, who are decked with ornaments and treated as if they were in truth the deceased persons come to life again. In that character they dance together in the large open space of the village, they are fed by the female relations, and they go from house to house, receiving presents of cloth. The festival lasts ten days, but the great day is the ninth. Huge torches of pinewood are made ready to be used that evening when darkness has fallen. The time of departure of the dead is at hand. Their living representatives are treated to a last meal in the houses, and they distribute farewell presents to the sorrowing kinsfolk, who have come to bid them good-bye. When the sun has set, a procession is formed. At the head of it march men holding aloft the flaring, sputtering torches. Then follow the elders armed and in martial array, and behind them stalk the representatives of the dead, with the relations of the departed crowding and trooping about them. Slowly and mournfully the sad procession moves, with loud lamentations, through the darkness to a spot at the north end of the village which is overshadowed by a great tree. The light of the torches is to guide the souls of the dead to their place of rest; the warlike array of the elders is to guard them from the perils and dangers of the way. At the village boundary the procession stops and the torch-bearers throw down their torches. At the same moment the spirits of the dead are believed to pass into the dying flambeaux and in that guise to depart to the far country. There is therefore no further need for their living representatives, who are accordingly stripped of all their finery on the spot. When the people return home, each family is careful to light a pine torch and set it burning on a stone in the house just inside the front door; this they do as a precaution to prevent their own souls from following the spirits of the dead to the other world. The expense of thus despatching the dead to their long home is very great; when the head of a family dies, debts may be incurred and rice-fields and houses sold to defray the cost of carriage. Thus the living impoverish themselves in order to enrich the dead.[1]

The Oraons or Uraons of Bengal feast their dead every year on a day in January. This ceremony is called the Great Marriage, because by it the bones of the deceased are believed to be mysteriously reunited to each other. The Oraons treat the bones of the dead differently according to the dates of their death in the agricultural year. The bones of those who died before the seeds have sprouted in the fields are burnt, and the few charred bones which have not been reduced to ashes are gathered in an earthen pot. With the bones in the pot are placed offerings of rice, native gin, and money, and then they carry the urn to the river, where the bones of their forefathers repose. But the bones of all who die after the seeds have sprung up and before the end of harvest may not be taken to the river, because the people believe that were that to be done the crops would suffer. These bones are therefore put away in a pot under a stone near the house till the harvest is over. Then on the appointed day in January they are all collected. A banquet is given in honour of the dead, and then both men and women form a procession to accompany the bones to their last resting-place in the sands of the river. But first the relics of mortality are carried from house to house in the village, and each family pours rice and gin into the urn which contains the bones of its dead. Then the procession sets out for the river, men and women dancing, singing, beating drums, and weeping, while the earthen pots containing the bones are passed from hand to hand and dance with the jigging steps of the dancers. When they are yet some way from the spot, the bearers of the urns run forward and bury them in the sand of the river. When the rest come up, they all bathe and the Great Marriage is over.[2]

Annual festival of the dead among the Oraons of Bengal.

[1] Rev. Wm. Pettigrew, "Kathi Kasham, the 'Soul Departure' feast as practised by the Tangkkul Nagas, Manipur, Assam," *Journal and Proceedings of the Asiatic Society of Bengal*, N.S. vol. v. 1909 (Calcutta, 1910), pp. 37-46; T. C. Hodson, *The Naga Tribes of Manipur* (London, 1911), pp. 153-158.

[2] Rev. P. Dehon, S.J., "Religion and Customs of the Uraons," *Memoirs of the Asiatic Society of Bengal*, vol. i. No. 9 (Calcutta, 1906), p. 136. Compare Rev. F. Hahn, "Some Notes on the Religion and Superstition of the Orāōs," *Journal of the Asiatic Society of Bengal*, lxxii. Part iii. (Calcutta, 1904) pp. 12 *sq.* According to the latter

In the Bila..pore district of the Central Provinces, India, " the festival known as the Fortnight of the Manes—*Pitr Pāk*—occurs about September. It is believed that during this fortnight it is the practice of all the departed to come and visit their relatives. The homes are therefore cleaned, and the spaces in front of the house are plastered and painted in order to be pleasing to those who are expected. It is believed that the departed will return on the very date on which they went away. A father who left on the fourth, be it the fourth of the dark half or the light half of the moon, will return to visit his family on the fourth of the Fortnight of the Manes. On that day cakes are prepared, and with certain ceremony these are offered to the unseen hovering spirit. Their implicit belief is that the spirit will partake of the essence of the food, and that which remains— the material portion—may be eaten by members of the family. The souls of women, it is said, will all come on the ninth of the fortnight. On the thirteenth come those who have met with a violent death and who lost their lives by a fall, by snake-bite, or any other unusual cause. During the Fortnight of the Manes a woman is not supposed to put on new bangles and a man is not permitted to shave. In short, this is a season of sad remembrances, an annual festival for the departed." [1]

Annual
festival of
the dead
among the
Bghais and
Hkamies.
The Bghais, a Karen tribe of Burma, hold an annual feast for the dead at the new moon which falls near the end of August or the beginning of September. All the villagers who have lost relatives within the last three years take part in it. Food and drink are set out on tables for the ghosts, and new clothes for them are hung up in the room. All being ready, the people beat gongs and begin to weep. Each one calls upon the relation whom he has lost to come and eat. When the dead are thought to have arrived, the

---

writer the pots containing the relics of the dead are buried, not in the sand of the river, but in a pit, generally covered with huge stones, which is dug for the purpose in some field or grove.

[1] E. M. Gordon, *Indian Folk Tales* (London, 1908), p. 18. According to Mr. W. Crooke, the Hindoo Feast of Lamps (*Diwālī*) seems to have been based on " the idea that on this night the spirits of the dead revisit their homes, which are cleaned and lighted for their reception." See W. Crooke, *The Popular Religion and Folk-lore of Northern India* (Westminster, 1896), ii. 295 *sq.*

living address them, saying, "You have come to me, you have returned to me. It has been raining hard, and you must be wet. Dress yourselves, clothe yourselves with these new garments, and all the companions that are with you. Eat betel together with all that accompany you, all your friends and associates, and the long dead. Call them all to eat and drink." The ghosts having finished their repast, the people dry their tears and sit down to eat what is left. More food is then prepared and put into a basket, and at cock-crow next morning the contents of the basket are thrown out of the house, while the living weep and call upon their dead as before.[1] The Hkamies, a hill tribe of North Aracan, hold an important festival every year in honour of departed spirits. It falls after harvest and is called "the opening of the house of the dead." When a person dies and has been burnt, the ashes are collected and placed in a small house in the forest together with his spear or gun, which has first been broken. These little huts are generally arranged in groups near a village, and are some-times large enough to be mistaken for one. After harvest all the relations of the deceased cook various kinds of food and take them with pots of liquor distilled from rice to the village of the dead. There they open the doors of the houses, and having placed the food and drink inside they shut them again. After that they weep, eat, drink, and return home.[2]

The great festival of the dead in Cambodia takes place on the last day of the month Phatrabot (September-October), but ever since the moon began to wane everybody has been busy preparing for it. In every house cakes and sweet-meats are set out, candles burn, incense sticks smoke, and the whole is offered to the ancestral shades with an invocation which is thrice repeated: "O all you our ancestors who are departed, deign to come and eat what we have prepared

Annual festival of the dead in Cambodia.

---

[1] Rev. F. Mason, D.D., "Physical Character of the Karens," *Journal of the Asiatic Society of Bengal*, 1866, Part ii. pp. 29 *sq.* Lights are not men-tioned by the writer, but the festival being nocturnal we may assume that they are used for the convenience of the living as well as of the dead. In other respects the ceremonies are typical.

[2] R. F. St. Andrew St. John, "A Short Account of the Hill Tribes of North Aracan," *Journal of the Anthropological Institute*, ii. (1873) p. 238. At this festival the dead are apparently not supposed to return to the houses.

for you, and to bless your posterity and make it happy."
Fifteen days afterwards many little boats are made of bark
and filled with rice, cakes, small coins, smoking incense
sticks, and lighted candles.   At evening these are set floating on the river, and the souls of the dead embark in them
to return to their own place.   The living now bid them
farewell.   "Go to the lands," they say, "go to the fields
you inhabit, to the mountains, under the stones which are
your abodes.   Go away! return!   In due time your sons
and your grandsons will think of you.   Then you will
return, you will return, you will return."   The river is now
covered with twinkling points of fire.   But the current soon
bears them away, and as they vanish one by one in the
darkness the souls depart with them to the far country.[1]

Annual festival of the dead in Tonquin. In Tonquin, as in Sumba, the dead revisit their kinsfolk
and their old homes at the New Year.   From the hour of
midnight, when the New Year begins, no one dares to shut
the door of his house for fear of excluding the ghosts, who
begin to arrive at that time.   Preparations have been made
to welcome and refresh them after their long journey.   Beds
and mats are ready for their weary bodies to repose upon,
water to wash their dusty feet, slippers to comfort them, and
canes to support their feeble steps.   Candles burn on the
domestic altar, and pastilles diffuse a fragrant odour.   The
people bow before the unseen visitors and beseech them to
remember and bless their descendants in the coming year.
Having discharged this pious duty they abstain from sweeping the houses for three days lest the dust should incom-
mode the ghosts.[2]

Annual festival of the dead in Annam. In Annam one of the most important festivals of the
year is the festival of Têt, which falls on the first three days
of the New Year.   It is devoted to the worship of ancestors.
Everybody, even the poorest, must provide a good meal for
the souls of his dead at this time and must himself eat and

---

[1] E. Aymonier, *Notice sur le Cambodge* (Paris, 1875), p. 59; A. Leclère,
Le Buddhisme au Cambodge (Paris,
1899), pp. 374-376.   The departure
of the souls is described only by the
latter writer.   Compare E. Aymonier,
"Notes sur les coutumes et croyances

superstitieuses   des   Cambodgiens,"
*Cochinchine Française, Excursions et
Reconnaissances,*   No.   16   (Saigon,
1883), pp. 205 *sq.*
[2] Mariny, *Relation nouvelle et cu-
rieuse des royaumes de Tunquin et de
Lao* (Paris, 1666), pp. 251-253.

drink heartily. Some families, in order to discharge this pious duty, run into debt for the whole year. In the houses everything is put in order, washed, and scoured for the reception of the dear and distinguished guests. A tall bamboo pole is set up in the front of every house and allowed to stand there for seven days. A small basket containing areca, betel, and leaves of gilt paper is fastened to the pole. The erection of the pole is a sacred rite which no family omits to perform, though why they do so few people can say. Some, however, allege that the posts are intended to guide the ancestral spirits to their old homes. The ceremony of the reception of the shades takes place at nightfall on the last day of the year. The house of the head of the family is then decked with flowers, and in the room which serves as a domestic chapel the altar of the ancestors is surrounded with flowers, among which the lotus, the emblem of immortality, is most conspicuous. On a table are set red candles, perfumes, incense, sandal-wood, and plates full of bananas, oranges, and other fruits. The relations crouch before the altar, and kneeling at the foot of it the head of the house invokes the name of the family which he represents. Then in solemn tones he recites an incantation, mentioning the names of his most illustrious ancestors and marking time with the strokes of a hammer upon a gong, while crackers are exploded outside the room. After that, he implores the ancestral shades to protect their descendants and invites them to a repast, which is spread for them on a table. Round this table he walks, serving the invisible guests with his own hands. He distributes to them smoking balls of rice in little china saucers, and pours tea or spirits into each little cup, while he murmurs words of invitation and compliment. When the ghosts have eaten and drunk their fill, the head of the family returns to the altar and salutes them for the last time. Finally, he takes leaves of yellow paper, covered with gold and silver spangles, and throws them into a brazier placed at the foot of the ancestral tablets. These papers represent imaginary bars of gold and silver which the living send to the dead. Cardboard models of houses, furniture, jewels, clothes, of everything in short that the

ghosts can need in the other world, are despatched to
them in like manner in the flames. Then the family sits
down to table and feasts on the remains of the ghostly
banquet.[1]

Annual
festival of
friendless
ghosts in
Annam.

But in Annam it is not merely the spirits of ancestors
who are thus feasted and supplied with all the necessaries of
life. The poor ghosts of those who died without leaving
descendants or whose bodies were left unburied are not
forgotten by the pious Annamites. But these spirits come
round at a different time of year from the others. The
seventh month of the year is set apart for expiatory sacrifices destined to benefit these unhappy beings, and that
is why in Annam nobody should marry or be betrothed in
that month. The great day of the month is the fifteenth,
which is called the Festival of the Souls. On that day the
ghosts in question are set free by the lord of the underworld,
and they come prowling about among the living. They
are exceedingly dangerous, especially to children. Hence in
order to appease their wrath and prevent them from entering
the houses every family takes care to put out offerings for
them in the street. Before every house on that night you
may see candles lighted, paper garments of many colours,
paper hats, paper boots, paper furniture, ingots of gold and
silver paper, all hanging in tempting array from a string,
while plates of food and cups of tea and rice-spirit stand
ready for the use of hungry and thirsty souls. The theory
is that the ghosts will be so busy consuming the victuals,
appropriating the deceitful riches, and trying on the paper
coats, hats, and boots that they will have neither the leisure
nor the inclination to intrude upon the domestic circle
indoors. At seven o'clock in the evening fire is put to the
offerings, and the paper wardrobe, furniture, and money soon
vanish crackling in the flames. At the same moment,
peeping in at a door or window, you may see the domestic
ancestral altar brilliantly illuminated. As for the food, it is
supposed to be thrown on the fire or on the ground for the

[1] Le R. P. Cadière, "Coutumes
populaires de la vallée du Nguôn-So'n,"
Bulletin de l'École Française d'Extrême-
Orient, ii. (Hanoi, 1902) pp. 376-379;
P. d'Enjoy, "Du droit successoral en Annam," etc., Bulletins de la Société
d'Anthropologie de Paris, Ve Série, iv.
(1903) pp. 500-502; E. Diguet, Les
Annamites (Paris, 1906), pp. 372-
375.

use of the ghosts, but practically it is eaten by vagabonds and beggars, who scuffle for the booty.[1]

In Cochinchina the ancestral spirits are similarly pro- pitiated and fed on the first day of the New Year. The tablets which represent them are placed on the domestic altar, and the family prostrate themselves before these emblems of the departed. The head of the family lights sticks of incense on the altar and prays the shades of his forefathers to accept the offerings and be favourable to their descendants. With great gravity he waits upon the ghosts, passing dishes of food before the ancestral tablets and pour- ing out wine and tea to slake the thirst of the spirits. When the dead are supposed to be satisfied with the shadowy essence of the food, the living partake of its gross material substance.[2] In Siam and Japan also the souls of the dead revisit their families for three days in every year, and the lamps which the Japanese kindle in multitudes on that occasion to light the spirits on their way have procured for the festival the name of the Feast of Lanterns. It is to be observed that in Siam, as in Tonquin and Sumba, the return of the ghosts takes place at the New Year.[3]

Annual festivals of the dead in Cochin- china, Siam and Japan.

The Chewsurs of the Caucasus believe that the souls of the departed revisit their old homes on the Saturday night of the second week in Lent. This gathering of the dead is called the "Assembly of Souls." The people spare no expense to treat the unseen guests handsomely. Beer is brewed and loaves of various shapes baked specially for the occasion.[4] The Armenians celebrate the memory of the dead on many days of the year, burning incense and lighting tapers in their honour. One of their customs is to keep a "light of the dead" burning all night in the house in order that the ghosts may be able to enter. For if the

Annual festivals of the dead among the Chewsurs and Armenians.

---

[1] E. Diguet, *Les Annamites* (Paris, 1906), pp. 254 *sq.* ; Paul Giran, *Magie et Religion Annamites* (Paris, 1912), pp. 258 *sq.* According to the latter writer the offerings to the vagrant souls are made on the first and last days of the month, while sacrifices of a more domestic character are performed on the fifteenth.

[2] L. E. Louvet, *La Cochinchine religieuse* (Paris, 1885), pp. 149-151.

[3] *The Scapegoat*, pp. 149 *sqq.*

[4] C. v. Hahn, "Religiöse An-schauungen und Totengedächtnisfeier der Chewsuren," *Globus*, lxxvi. (1899) pp. 211 *sq.*

spirits find the house dark, they spit down the chimney and depart, cursing the churlish inmates.[1]

Annual festivals of the dead in Africa.

Early in April every year the Dahomans of West Africa " set a table, as they term it, and invite friends to eat with the deceased relatives, whose spirits are supposed to move round and partake of the good things of this life. Even my interpreter, Madi-Ki Lemon, who pretends to despise the belief in fetish, sets a table to his ancestors, and will tell you that his grand- or great-grandfather, Corporal Lemon, makes a meal on this occasion which will last him till the next annual feast." [2] The Barea and apparently the Kunama, two heathen tribes who lead a settled agricultural life to the north of Abyssinia, celebrate every year a festival in the month of November. It is a festival of thanksgiving for the completion of the harvest, and at the same time a commemoration and propitiation of the dead. Every house prepares much beer for the occasion, and a small pot of beer is set out for each deceased member of the household. After standing for two days in the house the beer which was devoted to the dead is drunk by the living. At these festivals all the people of a district meet in a special place, and there pass the time in games and dances. Among the Barea the festive gatherings are held in a sacred grove. We are told that " he who owes another a drubbing on this day can pay his debt with impunity ; for it is a day of peace when all feuds are in abeyance." Wild honey may not be gathered till the festival has been held.[3] Apparently the festival is a sort of Saturnalia, such as is celebrated elsewhere at the end of harvest.[4] At that season there is food and to spare for the dead as well as the living.

[1] M. Abeghian, *Der armenische Volksglaube* (Leipsic, 1899), pp. 23 sq.

[2] Fred. E. Forbes, *Dahomey and the Dahomans* (London, 1851), ii. 73. Compare John Duncan, *Travels in Western Africa* (London, 1847), i. 125 sq. ; A. B. Ellis, *The Ewe-speaking Peoples of the Slave Coast* (London, 1890), p. 108. The Tshi-speaking peoples of the Gold Coast and Ashantee celebrate an annual festival of eight days in honour of the dead. It falls towards the end of August. The offerings are presented to the departed at their graves. See A. B. Ellis, *The Tshi-speaking Peoples of the Gold Coast* (London, 1887), pp. 227 sq.; E. Perregaux, *Chez les Achanti* (Neuchâtel, 1906), pp. 136, 138. According to the latter writer the festival is celebrated at the time of the yam harvest.

[3] W. Munzinger, *Ostafrikanische Studien* (Schaffhausen, 1864), p. 473.

[4] *The Scapegoat*, pp. 136 sq.

Among peoples of the Aryan stock, so far back as we can trace their history, the worship and propitiation of the dead seem to have formed a principal element of the popular religion ;[1] and like so many other races they appear to have believed that once a year the souls of their departed kinsfolk revisited their old homes and expected to be refreshed with abundance of good cheer by their surviving relations. This belief gave rise to the custom of celebrating an annual Feast of All Souls, which has come down to us from a dateless antiquity and is still observed year by year, with rites of primitive simplicity, in some parts of Europe. Such a festival was held every year in spring by the old Iranians. The celebration fell at the end of the year and lasted ten days, namely the last five days of the last month and the five following supplementary days, which were regularly inserted to make up a year of three hundred and sixty-five days ; for the old Iranian, like the old Egyptian, year was a vague year of twelve months of thirty days each, with five supplementary days added at the end for the sake of bringing it into apparent, though not real, harmony with the sun's annual course in the sky. According to one calculation the ten days of the festival corresponded to the last days of February, but according to another they fell in March ; in later ages the Parsees assigned them to the time of the spring equinox. The name of the festival was Hamaspathmaedaya.[2] From a passage in the *Zend-Avesta*, the

Annual festivals of the dead among peoples of the Aryan stock.

Annual festival of the dead (the Fravashis) among the old Iranians.

---

[1] On the worship of the dead, and especially of ancestors, among Aryan peoples, see W. Caland, *Über Totenverehrung bei einigen der indo-germanischen Völker* (Amsterdam, 1888) ; O. Schrader, *Reallexikon der indogermanischen Altertumskunde* (Strasburg, 1901), pp. 21 *sqq.* ; *id.*, *s.v.* "Aryan Religion," in Dr. J. Hastings's *Encyclopaedia of Religion and Ethics*, ii. (Edinburgh, 1909) pp. 16 *sqq.*

[2] As to the Iranian calendar see W. Geiger, *Altiranische Kultur im Altertum* (Erlangen, 1882), pp. 314 *sqq.* ; as to the Iranian worship of the sainted dead (the Fravashis) see *id.* pp. 286 *sqq.* As to the annual festival of the dead (Hamaspathmaedaya) see W. Caland, *Über Totenverehrung bei*

einigen der indo-germanischen Völker (Amsterdam, 1888), pp. 64 *sq.* ; N. Söderblom, *Les Fravashis* (Paris, 1899), pp. 4 *sqq.* ; J. H. Moulton, *Early Zoroastrianism* (London, 1913), pp. 256 *sqq.* All these writers agree that the Fravashis of the *Zend-Avesta* were originally the souls of the dead. See also James Darmesteter, *Zend-Avesta*, Part ii. (Oxford, 1883) p. 179 : "The Fravashi is the inner power in every being that maintains it and makes it grow and subsist. Originally the Fravashis were the same as the *Pitris* of the Hindus or the *Manes* of the Latins, that is to say, the everlasting and deified souls of the dead ; but in course of time they gained a wider domain, and not only men, but gods

ancient sacred book of the Iranians, we learn that on the
ten nights of the festival the souls of the dead (the Fravashis)
were believed to go about the village asking the people to
do them reverence, to pray to them, to meditate on them,
and to furnish them with meat and clothes, while at the
same time they promised that blessings should rest on the

Annual
festival of
the dead
among the
Persians.

pious householder who complied with their request.[1]   The
Arab geographer Albiruni, who flourished about the year
one thousand of our era, tells us that among the Persians of
his time the last five days of the month Aban were called
Farwardajan.   " During this time," he says, " people put
food in the halls of the dead and drink on the roofs of the
houses, believing that the spirits of their dead during these
days come out from the places of their reward or their
punishment, that they go to the dishes laid out for them,
imbibe their strength and suck their taste.   They fumigate
their houses with juniper, that the dead may enjoy its smell.
The spirits of the pious men dwell among their families,
children, and relations, and occupy themselves with their
affairs, although invisible to them."   He adds that there
was a controversy among the Persians as to the date of this
festival of the dead, some maintaining that the five days
during which it lasted were the last five days of the month
Aban, whereas others held that they were the five supplementary days which were inserted between the months Aban
and Adhar.   The dispute, he continues, was settled by the
adoption of all ten days for the celebration of the feast.[2]

---

and even physical objects, like the
sky and the earth, etc., had each a
Fravashi." Compare *id.*, *Ormazd et
Ahriman* (Paris, 1877), pp. 130 *sqq.* ;
N. Söderblom, *La Vie Future d'après
Le Mazdéisme* (Paris, 1901), pp. 7 *sqq.*
A different view of the original nature
of the Fravashis was taken by C. P.
Tiele, according to whom they were
essentially guardian spirits. See C. P.
Tiele, *Geschichte der Religion im Alter-
tum* (Gotha, 1896–1903), ii. 256 *sqq.*

[1] *The Zend-Avesta*, translated by
James Darmesteter, Part ii. (Oxford,
1883) pp. 192 *sq.* (*Sacred Books of the
East*, vol. xxiii.).

[2] Albiruni, *The Chronology of*

Ancient Nations, translated and edited
by Dr. C. Edward Sachau (London,
1879), p. 210. In the *Dinkard*, a
Pahlavi work which seems to have
been composed in the first half of the
ninth century A.D., the festival is
spoken of as " those ten days which
are the end of the winter and termination of the year, because the five Gathic
days, among them, are for that purpose."
By " the five Gathic days " the writer
means the five supplementary days added
at the end of the twelfth month to
complete the year of 365 days. See
Pahlavi Texts translated by E.W.West,
Part iv. (Oxford, 1892) p. 17 (*The
Sacred Books of the East*, vol. xxxvii.).

Similar beliefs as to the annual return of the dead sur- vive to this day in many parts of Europe and find expression in similar customs. The day of the dead or of All Souls, as we call it, is commonly the second of November. Thus in Lower Brittany the souls of the departed come to visit the living on the eve of that day. After vespers are over, the priests and choir walk in procession, "the procession of the charnel-house," chanting a weird dirge in the Breton tongue. Then the people go home, gather round the fire, and talk of the departed. The housewife covers the kitchen table with a white cloth, sets out cider, curds, and hot pancakes on it, and retires with the family to rest. The fire on the hearth is kept up by a huge log known as "the log of the dead" (*kef ann Anaon*). Soon doleful voices outside in the darkness break the stillness of night. It is the "singers of death" who go about the streets waking the sleepers by a wild and melancholy song, in which they remind the living in their comfortable beds to pray for the poor souls in pain. All that night the dead warm themselves at the hearth and feast on the viands prepared for them. Sometimes the awe-struck listeners hear the stools creaking in the kitchen, or the dead leaves outside rustling under the ghostly footsteps.[1] In the Vosges Mountains on All Souls' Eve the solemn sound of the church bells invites good Christians to pray for the repose of the dead. While the bells are ringing, it is customary in some families to uncover the beds and open the windows, doubtless in order to let the poor souls enter and rest. No one that evening would dare to remain deaf to the appeal of the bells. The prayers are prolonged to a late hour of the night. When the last *De profundis* has been uttered, the head of the family gently covers up the beds, sprinkles them with holy water, and shuts the windows. In some villages fire is kept up on the hearth and a basket of nuts is placed beside it for the use of the ghosts.[2] Again, in some parts of Saintonge and Aunis a Candlemas candle used to be lit before the domestic

---

[1] A. le Braz, *La Légende de la Morten Basse-Bretagne* (Paris, 1893), pp. 280-287. Compare J. Lecœur, *Esquisses du Bocage Normand* (Condé-sur-Noir- eau, 1883–1887), ii. 283 *sqq.*

[2] L. F. Sauvé, *Le folk-lore des Hautes-Vosges* (Paris, 1889), pp. 295 *sq.*

crucifix on All Souls' Day at the very hour when the last member of the family departed this life ; and some people, just as in Tonquin, refrained from sweeping the house that day lest they should thereby disturb the ghostly visitors.[1]

In Bruges, Dinant, and other towns of Belgium holy candles burn all night in the houses on the Eve of All Souls, and the bells toll till midnight, or even till morning. People, too, often set lighted candles on the graves. At Scherpenheuvel the houses are illuminated, and the people walk in procession carrying lighted candles in their hands. A very common custom in Belgium is to eat " soul-cakes " or " soul-bread " on the eve or the day of All Souls. The eating of them is believed to benefit the dead in some way. Perhaps originally, as among the Esquimaux of Alaska to this day,[2] the ghosts were thought to enter into the bodies of their relatives and so to share the victuals which the survivors consumed. Similarly at festivals in honour of the dead in Northern India it is customary to feed Brahmans, and the food which these holy men partake of is believed to pass to the deceased and to refresh their languid spirits.[3] The same idea of eating and drinking by proxy may perhaps partly explain many other funeral feasts. Be that as it may, at Dixmude and elsewhere in Belgium they say that you deliver a soul from Purgatory for every cake you eat. At Antwerp they give a local colour to the soul-cakes by baking them with plenty of saffron, the deep yellow tinge being suggestive of the flames of Purgatory. People in Antwerp at the same season are careful not to slam doors or windows for fear of hurting the ghosts.[4]

In Lechrain, a district of Southern Bavaria which extends along the valley of the Lech from its source to near the point where the river flows into the Danube, the two festivals of All Saints and All Souls, on the first

---

[1] J. L. M. Noguès, *Les mœurs d'autrefois en Saintonge et en Aunis* (Saintes, 1891), p. 76. As to the observance of All Souls' Day in other parts of France see A. Meyrac, *Traditions, coutumes, légendes et contes des Ardennes* (Charleville, 1890), pp. 22-24 ; Ch. Beauquier, *Les mois en Franche-Comté* (Paris, 1900), pp. 123-125.

[2] Above, p. 52.

[3] W. Crooke, *The Natives of Northern India* (London, 1907), p. 219.

[4] Reinsberg-Düringsfeld, *Calendrier Belge* (Brussels, 1861–1862), ii. 236-240 ; id., *Das festliche Jahr* (Leipsic, 1863), pp. 229 *sq.*

and second of November, have significantly fused in popular usage into a single festival of the dead.   In fact, the people pay little or no heed to the saints and give all their thoughts to the souls of their departed kinsfolk. , The Feast of All Souls begins immediately after vespers on All Saints' Day.   Even on the eve of All Saints' Day, that is, on the thirty-first of October, which we call Hallowe'en, the graveyard is cleaned and every grave adorned.   The decoration consists in weeding the mounds, sprinkling a layer of charcoal on the bare earth, and marking out patterns on it in red service-berries.   The marigold, too, is still in bloom at that season in cottage gardens, and garlands of its orange blooms, mingled with other late flowers left by the departing summer, are twined about the grey mossgrown tombstones. The basin of holy water is filled with fresh water and a branch of box-wood put into it ; for box-wood in the popular mind is associated with death and the dead.   On the eve of All Souls' Day the people begin to visit the graves and to offer the soul-cakes to the hungry souls.   Next morning, before eight o'clock, commence the vigil, the requiem, and the solemn visitation of the graves.   On that day every household offers a plate of meal, oats, and spelt on a side-altar in the church ; while in the middle of the sacred edifice a bier is set, covered with a pall, and surrounded by lighted tapers and vessels of holy water.   The tapers burnt on that day and indeed generally in services for the departed are red.   In the evening people go, whenever they can do so, to their native village, where their dear ones lie in the churchyard ; and there at the graves they pray for the poor souls, and leave an offering of soul-cakes also on a side-altar in the church. The soul-cakes are baked of dough in the shape of a coil of hair and are made of all sizes up to three feet long.   They form a perquisite of the sexton.[1]

The custom of baking soul-cakes, sometimes called simply " souls," on All Souls' Day is widespread in Southern Germany and Austria ;[2] everywhere, we may assume, the cakes were originally intended for the benefit of the hungry dead, though

Soul-cakes and All Souls' Day in Southern Germany.

[1] Karl Freiherr von Leoprechting, *Aus dem Lechrain* (Munich, 1855), pp. 198-200.

[2] O. Freiherr von Reinsberg-Düringsfeld, *Das festliche Jahr* (Leipsic, 1863), p. 330.   As to these cakes

they are often eaten by the living. In the Upper Palatinate people throw food into the fire on All Souls' Day for the poor souls, set lights on the table for them, and pray on bended knees for their repose. On the graves, too, lights are kindled, vessels of holy water placed, and food deposited for the refreshment of the souls. All over the Upper Palatinate on All Souls' Day it is also customary to bake special cakes of fine bread and distribute them to the poor,[1] who eat them perhaps as the deputies of the dead.

The Germans of Bohemia observe All Souls' Day with much solemnity. Each family celebrates the memory of its dead. On the eve of the day it is customary to eat cakes and to drink cold milk for the purpose of cooling the poor souls who are roasting in purgatory ; from which it appears that spirits feel the soothing effect of victuals consumed vicariously by their friends on earth. The ringing of the church bells to prayer on that evening is believed to be the signal at which the ghosts, released from the infernal gaol, come trooping to the old familiar fire-side, there to rest from their pangs for a single night. So in many places people fill a lamp with butter, light it, and set it on the hearth, that with the butter the poor ghosts may anoint the burns they have received from the sulphureous and tormenting flames of purgatory. Next morning the chime of the church bells, ringing to early mass, is the knell that bids the souls return to their place of pain ; but such as have completed their penance take flight to heaven. So on the eve of All Saints' Day each family gathers in the parlour or the kitchen, speaks softly of those they have lost, recalls what they said and did in life, and prays for the repose of their souls. While the prayer is being said, the children kindle little wax lights which have been specially bought for the purpose that day. Next morning the families go to church, where mass is celebrated for the dead ; then they wend their way to the

---

(called "souls") in Swabia see E. Meyer, *Deutsche Sagen, Sitten und Gebräuche aus Schwaben* (Stuttgart, 1852), p. 452, § 174 ; Anton Birlinger, *Volksthümliches aus Schwaben* (Freiburg im Breisgau, 1861–1862), ii. 167 *sq.* The cakes are baked of white flour, and are of a longish rounded shape with two small tips at each end.

[1] Adalbert Kuhn, *Mythologische Studien*, ii. (Gütersloh, 1912) pp. 41 *sq.*, citing F. Schönwerth, *Aus der Oberpfalz*, i. 283.

churchyard, where they deck the graves of their kinsfolk with flowers and wreaths and set little lights upon them. This custom of illumining the graves and decking them with flowers on the Eve or Day of All Souls is common all over Bohemia; it is observed in Prague as well as in the country, by Czechs as well as by Germans. In some Czech villages four-cornered cakes of a special sort, baked of white wheaten meal with milk, are eaten on All Souls' Day or given to beggars that they may pray for the dead.[1] Among the Germans of Western Bohemia poor children go from house to house on All Souls' Day, begging for soul-cakes, and when they receive them they pray God to bless all poor souls. In the southern districts every farmer used to grind a great quantity of corn against the day and to bake it into five or six hundred little black soul-cakes which he gave away to the poor who came begging for them.[2]

All Souls' Day is celebrated with similar rites by the Germans of Moravia. "The festival of the farewell to summer," says a German writer on this subject, "was held by our heathen forefathers in the beginning of November, and with the memory of the departed summer they united the memory of the departed souls, and this last has survived in the Feast of All Souls, which is everywhere observed with great piety. On the evening of All Souls the relations of the departed assemble in the churchyards and adorn the graves of their dear ones with flowers and lights, while the children kindle little wax tapers, which have been bought for them, to light the 'poor souls.' According to the popular belief, the dead go in procession to the church about midnight, and any stout-hearted young man can there see all the living men who will die within the year."[3]

Feast of All Souls in Moravia.

In the Tyrol the beliefs and customs are similar. There, too, "soul-lights," that is, lamps filled with lard or butter are lighted and placed on the hearth on All Souls' Eve in order that poor souls, escaped from the fires of purgatory, may smear the melted grease on their burns and so alleviate their pangs.

Feast of All Souls in the Tyrol.

---

[1] O. Freiherr von Reinsberg-Düringsfeld, *Fest-Kalender aus Böhmen* (Prague, N.D.), pp. 493-495.

[2] Alois John, *Sitte, Brauch und Volksglaube im deutschen Westböhmen* (Prague, 1905), p. 97.

[3] Willibald Müller, *Beiträge zur Volkskunde der Deutschen in Mähren* (Vienna and Olmütz, 1893), p. 330.

Some people also leave milk and dough-nuts for them on the table all night. The graves also are illuminated with wax candles and decked with such a profusion of flowers that you might think it was springtime.[1] In the Italian Tyrol it is customary to give bread or money to the poor on All Souls' Day ; in the Val di Ledro children threaten to dirty the doors of houses if they do not get the usual dole. Some rich people treat the poor to bean-soup on that day. Others put pitchers full of water in the kitchen on All Souls'

Feast of
All Souls
in Baden. night that the poor souls may slake their thirst.[2] In Baden it is still customary to deck the graves with flowers and lights on All Saints' Day and All Souls' Day. The lights are sometimes kindled in hollow turnips, on the sides of which inscriptions are carved and shine out in the darkness. If any child steals a turnip-lantern or anything else from a grave, the indignant ghost who has been robbed appears to the thief the same night and reclaims his stolen property. A relic of the old custom of feeding the dead survives in the practice of giving soul-cakes to godchildren.[3]

Annual
festivals of
the dead
among the
Letts and
Samagi-
tians. The Letts used to entertain and feed the souls of the dead for four weeks from Michaelmas (September 29) to the day of St. Simon and St. Jude (October 28). They called the season *Wellalaick* or *Semlicka*, and regarded it as so holy that while it lasted they would not willingly thresh the corn, alleging that grain threshed at that time would be useless for sowing, since the souls of the dead would not allow it to sprout. But we may suspect that the original motive of the abstinence was a fear lest the blows of the flails should fall upon the poor ghosts swarming in the air. At this season the people were wont to prepare food of all sorts for the spirits and set it on the floor of a room, which had been well heated and swept for the purpose. Late in the evening the master of the house went into the room, tended the fire, and called upon his dead kinsfolk by their names to come and eat and drink. If he saw the ghosts, he would die within the year ; but if

[1] Ignaz V. Zingerle, *Sitten, Bräuche und Meiningen des Tiroler Volkes*[2] (Innsbruck, 1871), pp. 176-178.

[2] Christian Schneller, *Märchen und Sagen aus Wälschtirol* (Innsbruck, 1867), p. 238.

[3] Elard Hugo Meyer, *Badisches Volksleben im neunzehnten Jahrhundert* (Strasburg, 1900), p. 601.

he did not see them he would outlive it. When he thought
the souls had eaten and drunk enough, he took the staff
which served as a poker and laying it on the threshold cut
it in two with an axe. At the same time he bade the spirits
go their way, charging them to keep to the roads and paths
and not to tread upon the rye. If the crops turned out ill
next year, the people laid the failure at the door of the
ghosts, who fancied themselves scurvily treated and had
taken their revenge by trampling down the corn.[1] The
Samagitians annually invited the dead to come from their
graves and enjoy a bath and a feast. For their entertain-
ment they prepared a special hut, in which they set out
food and drink, together with a seat and a napkin for every
soul who had been invited. They left the souls to revel by
themselves for three days in the hut ; then they deposited
the remains of the banquet on the graves and bade the
ghosts farewell. The good things, however, were usually
consumed by charcoal burners in the forest. This feast of
the dead fell early in November.[2] The Esthonians prepare
a meal for their dead on All Souls' Day, the second of
November, and invite them by their names to come and
partake of it. The ghosts arrive in the early morning at
the first cock-crow, and depart at the second, being cere-
moniously lighted out of the house by the head of the
family, who waves a white cloth after them and bids them
come again next year.[3]

In some parts of the Russian Government of Olonets *Festival of*
the inhabitants of a village sometimes celebrate a joint *the dead*
festival in honour of all their dead. Having chosen a house *in Russia.*
for the purpose, they spread three tables, one outside the
front door, one in the passage, and one in the room which
is heated by a stove. Then they go out to meet their

[1] P. Einhorn, "Historia Lettica,"
in *Scriptores Rerum Livonicarum*, ii.
(Riga and Leipsic, 1848) pp. 587, 598,
630 *sq.*, 645 *sq.* See also the description of D. Fabricius in his "Livonicae
Historiae compendiosa series," *ib.* p.
441. Fabricius assigns the custom to
All Souls' Day.

[2] J. Lasicius, "De diis Samagita-
rum caeterorumque Sarmatarum," in

*Magazin herausgegeben von der let-
tisch-literärischen Gesellschaft*, xiv. 1.
(Mitau, 1868), p. 92.

[3] F. J. Wiedemann, *Aus dem
inneren und äussern Leben der Ehsten*
(St. Petersburg, 1876), pp. 366 *sq.* ;
Boecler-Kreutzwald, *Der Ehsten abergläubische Gebräuche, Weisen und Gewohnheiten* (St. Petersburg, 1854), p.
89.

unseen guests and usher them into the house with these words, " Ye are tired, our own ones ; take something to eat." The ghosts accordingly refresh themselves at each table in succession.   Then the master of the house bids them warm themselves at the stove, remarking that they must have grown cold in the damp earth.   After that the living guests sit down to eat at the tables.   Towards the end of the meal the host opens the window and lets the ghosts gently out of it by means of the shroud in which they were lowered into the grave.   As they slide down it from the warm room into the outer air, the people tell ˙them, " Now it is time for you to go home, and your feet must be tired ; the way is not a little one for you to travel.   Here it is softer for you.   Now, in God's name, farewell ! " [1]

Annual festivals of the dead among the Votiaks of Russia.   Among the Votiaks of Russia every family sacrifices to its dead once a year in the week before Palm Sunday.   The sacrifice is offered in the house about midnight.   Flesh, bread, or cakes and beer are set on the table, and on the floor beside the table stands a trough of bark with a lighted wax candle stuck on the rim.   The master of the house, having covered his head with his hat, takes a piece of meat in his hand and says, " Ye spirits of the long departed, guard and preserve us well.   Make none of us cripples.   Send no plagues upon us.   Cause the corn, the wine, and the food to prosper with us." [2]   The Votiaks of the Governments of Wjatka and Kasan celebrate two memorial festivals of the dead every year, one in autumn and the other in spring.   On a certain day koumiss is distilled, beer brewed, and potato scones baked in every house.   All the members of a clan, who trace their descent through women from one mythical ancestress, assemble in a single house, generally in one which lies at the boundary of the clan land.   Here an old man moulds wax candles ; and when the requisite number is made he sticks them on the shelf of the stove, and begins to mention the dead relations of the master of the house by name.   For each of them he crumbles a piece of bread,

---

[1] W. R. S. Ralston, *Songs of the Russian People*[2] (London, 1872), pp. 321 *sq.*   The date of the festival is not mentioned. Apparently it is celebrated at irregular intervals.

[2] M. Buch, *Die Wotjäken* (Stuttgart, 1882), p. 145.

gives each of them a piece of pancake, pours koumiss and beer, and puts a spoonful of soup into a trough made for the purpose. All persons present whose parents are dead follow his example. The dogs are then allowed to eat out of the trough. If they eat quietly, it is a sign that the dead live at peace; if they do not eat quietly, it argues the contrary. Then the company sit down to table and partake of the meal. Next morning both the dead and the living refresh themselves with a drink, and a fowl is boiled. The proceedings are the same as on the evening before. But now they treat the souls for the last time as a preparation for their journey, saying: "Eat, drink, and go home to your companions. Live at peace, be gracious to us, keep our children, guard our corn, our beasts and birds." Then the people banquet and indulge in all sorts of improprieties. The women refrain from feasting until the dead have taken their departure; but when the souls are gone, there is no longer any motive for abstinence, the koumiss circulates freely among the women, and they grow wanton. Yet at this, as at every other festival, the men and women eat in different parts of the room.[1]

On All Saints' Day, the first of November, shops and streets in the Abruzzi are filled with candles, which people buy in order to kindle them in the evening on the graves of their relations. For all the dead come to visit their homes that night, the Eve of All Souls, and they need lights to show them the way. For their use, too, lights are kept burning in the houses all night. Before people go to sleep they place on the table a lighted lamp or candle and a frugal meal of bread and water. The dead issue from their graves and stalk in procession through every street of the village. You can see them if you stand at a cross-road with your chin resting on a forked stick. First pass the souls of the good, and then the souls of the murdered and the damned. Once, they say, a man was thus peeping at the ghastly procession. The good souls told him he had

Feast of All Souls in the Abruzzi.

---

[1] J. Wasiljev, *Übersicht über die heidnischen Gebräuche, Aberglauben und Religion der Wotjäken* (Helsingfors, 1902), pp. 34 *sq.* (*Mémoires de la Société Finno-Ougrienne*, xviii.). As to the Votiak clans see the same work, pp. 42-44.

better go home.   He did not, and when he saw the tail of the procession he died of fright.[1]

Soul-cakes on All-Souls' Day in England. In our own country the old belief in the annual return of the dead long lingered in the custom of baking " soul-cakes " and eating them or distributing them to the poor on All Souls' Day.   Peasant girls used to go from farmhouse to farmhouse on that day, singing,

> " *Soul, soul, for a soul cake,*
> *Pray you, good mistress, a soul cake.*" [2]

In Shropshire down to the seventeenth century it was customary on All Souls' Day to set on the table a high heap of soul-cakes, and most visitors to the house took one of them.   The antiquary John Aubrey, who records the custom, mentions also the appropriate verses :

> " *A soul-cake, a soul-cake,*
> *Have mercy on all Christen soules for a soule-cake.*" [3]

Indeed the custom of soul-cakes survived in Shropshire down to the latter part of the nineteenth century and may
" Souling Day " in Shropshire. not be extinct even now.   " With us, All Saints' Day is known as ' Souling Day,' and up to the present time in many places, poor children, and sometimes men, go out ' souling ': which means that they go round to the houses of all the more well-to-do people within reach, reciting a ditty peculiar to the day, and looking for a dole of cakes, broken victuals, ale, apples, or money.   The two latter are now the usual rewards, but there are few old North Salopians who cannot remember when ' soul-cakes ' were made at all the farms and ' bettermost ' houses in readiness for the day, and were given to all who came for them.   We are told of

---

[1] G. Finamore, *Credenze, Usi e Costumi Abruzzesi* (Palermo, 1890), pp. 180-182.   Mr. W. R. Paton writes to me (12th December 1906) : " You do not mention the practice[s] on the modern Greek feast τῶν ψυχῶν (in May) which quite correspond.   The κόλυβα is made in every house and put on a table laid with a white tablecloth.   A glass of water and a taper are put on the table, and all is left so for the whole night.   Our Greek maid-servant says that when she was a child she remembers seeing the souls come and partake.   Almost the same rite is practised for the κόλυβα made on the commemoration of particular dead."

[2] John Brand, *Popular Antiquities of Great Britain* (London, 1882-1883), i. 393.

[3] John Aubrey, *Remaines of Gentilisme and Judaisme* (London, 1881), p. 23.

liberal housewives who would provide as many as a clothes-basket full."[1]   The same custom of going out "a-souling" on All Saints' Day or All Souls' Day used to be observed in the neighbouring counties of Staffordshire, Cheshire, Lancashire, Herefordshire, and Monmouthshire.   In Herefordshire the soul-cakes were made of oatmeal, and he or she who received one of them was bound to say to the giver :

> " *God have your saul,*
> *Beens and all.*" [2]

Thus the practice of "souling" appears to have prevailed especially in the English counties which border on Wales. In many parts of Wales itself down to the first half of the nineteenth century poor peasants used to go about begging for bread on All Souls' Day   The bread bestowed on them was called *bara ran* or dole-bread.   "This custom was a survival of the Middle Ages, when the poor begged bread for the souls of their departed relatives and friends."[3]   However, the custom was not confined to the west of England, for at Whitby in Yorkshire down to the early part of the nineteenth century it was usual to make "soul mass loaves" on or about All Souls' Day.   They were small round loaves, sold by bakers at a farthing apiece, chiefly for presents to children.   In former times people used to keep one or two of them for good luck.[4]   In Aberdeenshire, also, "on All Souls' Day, baked cakes of a particular sort are given away to those who may chance to visit the house, where they are

---

[1] Miss C. S. Burne and Miss G. F. Jackson, *Shropshire Folk-lore* (London, 1883), p. 381.   The writers record (pp. 382 *sqq.*) some of the ditties which were sung on this occasion by those who begged for soul-cakes.

[2] J. Brand, *Popular Antiquities of Great Britain*, i. 392, 393 ; W. Hone, *Year Book* (London, N.D.), col. 1288 ; T. F. Thiselton Dyer, *British Popular Customs* (London, 1876), pp. 405, 406, 407, 409 ; J. Harland and T. T. Wilkinson, *Lancashire Folk-lore* (London, 1882), p. 251 ; Elizabeth Mary Wright, *Rustic Speech and Folk-lore* (Oxford, 1913), p. 300.

[3] Marie Trevelyan, *Folk-lore and Folk-stories of Wales* (London, 1909), p. 255.   See also T. F. Thiselton Dyer, *British Popular Customs* (London, 1876), p. 410, who, quoting Pennant as his authority, says that the poor people who received soul-cakes prayed God to bless the next crop of wheat.

[4] *County Folk-lore*, vol. ii. *North Riding of Yorkshire, York, and the Ainsty* (London, 1901), quoting George Young, *A History of Whitby and Streoneshalth Abbey* (Whitby, 1817), ii. 882.

made. The cakes are called 'dirge-loaf.'"[1] Even in the remote island of St. Kilda it was customary on All Saints' Day to bake a large cake in the form of a triangle, furrowed round ; the cake must be all eaten that night.[2]

Feast of
All Souls
among the
Indians of
Ecuador.

The same mode of celebrating All Souls' Day has been transported by Catholicism to the New World and imparted to the aborigines of that continent. Thus in Carchi, a province of Ecuador, the Indians prepare foods of various sorts against All Souls' Day, and when the day has come they take some of the provisions to the church and there deposit them on tables set out for the purpose. These good things are the perquisite of the priest, who celebrates mass for the dead. After the service the Indians repair to the cemetery, where with burning candles and pots of holy water they prostrate themselves before the tombs of their relations, while the priest or the sacristan recites prayers for the souls of the departed. In the evening the Indians return to their houses. A table with four lights on it is spread with food and drink, especially with such things as the dead loved in their life. The door is left open all night, no doubt to let the spirits of the dead enter, and the family sits up, keeping the invisible guests company through the long hours of darkness. From seven o'clock and onwards troops of children traverse the village and its neighbourhood. They go from house to house ringing a bell and crying, "We are angels, we descend from the sky, we ask for bread." The people go to their doors and beg the children to recite a *Pater Noster* or an *Ave Maria* for the dead whom they name. When the prayer has been duly said, they give the children a little of the food from the table. All night long this goes on, band succeeding band of children. At five o'clock in the morning the family consumes the remainder of the food of the souls.[3] Here the children going from door to door during the night of All Souls appear to personate the souls of the dead who are also abroad at that time ; hence to give bread to the children is the same thing as to

---

[1] T. F. Thiselton Dyer, *British Popular Customs*, p. 410.

[2] M. Martin, "Description of the Western Islands of Scotland," in John Pinkerton's *Voyages and Travels* (Lon-don, 1808–1814), iii. 666.

[3] Dr. Rivet, "Le Christianisme et les Indiens de la République de l'Équateur," *L'Anthropologie*, xvii. (1906) pp. 93 *sq.*

give bread to the poor hungry souls.   Probably the same
explanation applies to the giving of soul-cakes to children
and the poor on All Souls' Day in Europe.

A comparison of these European customs with the
similar heathen rites can leave no room for doubt that the
nominally Christian feast of All Souls is nothing but an old
pagan festival of the dead which the Church, unable or
unwilling to suppress, resolved from motives of policy to
connive at.   But whence did it borrow the practice of
solemnizing the festival on that particular day, the second
of November ?   In order to answer this question we should
observe, first, that celebrations of this sort are often held at
the beginning of a New Year,[1] and, second, that the peoples
of North - Western Europe, the Celts and the Teutons,
appear to have dated the beginning of their year from the
beginning of winter, the Celts reckoning it from the first of
November[2] and the Teutons from the first of October.[3]
The difference of reckoning may be due to a difference of
climate, the home of the Teutons in Central and Northern
Europe being a region where winter sets in earlier than on
the more temperate and humid coasts of the Atlantic, the
home of the Celts.   These considerations suggest that the
festival of All Souls on the second of November originated
with the Celts, and spread from them to the rest of the
European peoples, who, while they preserved their old
feasts of the dead practically unchanged, may have transferred them to the second of November.   This conjecture
is supported by what we know of the ecclesiastical
institution, or rather recognition, of the festival.   For

*The
nominally
Christian
feast of
All Souls
on Nov. 2
appears
to be an
old Celtic
festival of
the dead
adopted
by the
Church in
998 A.D.*

---

[1] See above, pp. 53, 55, 62, 65.

[2] Sir John Rhys, *Celtic Heathendom*
(London and Edinburgh, 1888), pp.
460, 514 *sq.* ; *id.*, "Celtae and Galli,"
*Proceedings of the British Academy,
1905-1906* (London, N.D.), p. 78 ;
Balder the Beautiful, i. 224 *sq.*

[3] K. Müllenhoff, *Deutsche Altertumskunde*, iv. (Berlin, 1900) pp.
379 *sq.* The first of October seems
to have been a great festival among
the Saxons and also the Samagitians.
See Widukind, *Res gestae Saxonicae*,
i. 12 (Migne's *Patrologia Latina*,

cxxxvii. 135) ; M. A. Michov, "De
Sarmatia Asiana atque Europea," in
S. Grynaeus's *Novus Orbis Regionum
ac Insularum veteribus incognitarum*
(Bâle, 1532), p. 520. I have to
thank Professor H. M. Chadwick for
pointing out these two passages to
me.   Mr. A. Tille prefers to date the
Teutonic winter from Martinmas, the
eleventh of November. See A. Tille,
*Die Geschichte der deutschen Weih-
nacht* (Leipsic, N.D.), pp. 23 *sqq.* ;
O. Schrader, *Reallexikon der indogermanischen Altertumskunde* (Strasburg,
1901), p. 395.

that recognition was first accorded at the end of the tenth century in France, a Celtic country, from which the

Institution of the Feast of All Souls by the Abbot of Clugny.

Church festival gradually spread over Europe.   It was Odiio, abbot of the great Benedictine monastery of Clugny, who initiated the change in 998 A.D. by ordering that in all the monasteries over which he ruled, a solemn mass should be celebrated on the second of November for all the dead who sleep in Christ.   The example thus set was followed by other religious houses, and the bishops, one after another, introduced the new celebration into their dioceses.   Thus the festival of All Souls gradually established itself throughout Christendom, though in fact the Church has never formally sanctioned it by a general edict nor attached much weight to its observance.   Indeed, when objections were raised to the festival at the Reformation, the ecclesiastical authorities seemed ready to abandon it.[1]   These facts are explained very simply by the theory that an old Celtic commemoration of the dead lingered in France down to the end of the tenth century, and was then, as a measure of policy and a concession to ineradicable paganism, at last incorporated in the Catholic ritual.   The consciousness of the heathen origin of the practice would naturally prevent the supreme authorities from insisting strongly on its observance.   They appear rightly to have regarded it as an outpost which they could surrender to the forces of rationalism without endangering the citadel of the faith.

The feast of All Saints on Nov. 1 seems also to have displaced a heathen festival of the dead.

Perhaps we may go a step further and explain in like manner the origin of the feast of All Saints on the first of November.   For the analogy of similar customs elsewhere would lead us to suppose that the old Celtic festival of the dead was held on the Celtic New Year's Day, that is, on the first, not the second, of November.   May not then the institution of the feast of All Saints on that day have been the first attempt of the Church to give a colour of Christianity to the ancient heathen rite by substituting the saints for the souls of the dead as the true object of worship?

---

[1] A. J. Binterim, *Die vorzüglichsten Denkwürdigkeiten der Christ-Katholischen Kirche*, v. 1 (Mayence, 1829), pp. 493 *sq.* ; J. J. Herzog und G. F. Plitt, *Real-Encyclopädie für protestan-* *tische Theologie und Kirche*,[2] i.(Leipsic, 1877), pp. 303 *sq.* ; W. Smith and S. Cheetham, *Dictionary of Christian Antiquities* (London, 1875–1880), i. 57 *sq.*

The facts of history seem to countenance this hypothesis. For the feast of All Saints was instituted in France and Germany by order of the Emperor Lewis the Pious in 835 A.D., that is, about a hundred and sixty years before the introduction of the feast of All Souls. The innovation was made by the advice of the pope, Gregory IV., whose motive may well have been that of suppressing an old pagan custom which was still notoriously practised in France and Germany. The idea, however, was not a novel one, for the testimony of Bede proves that in Britain, another Celtic country, the feast of All Saints on the first of November was already celebrated in the eighth century.[1] We may conjecture that this attempt to divert the devotion of the faithful from the souls of the dead to the saints proved a failure, and that finally the Church reluctantly decided to sanction the popular superstition by frankly admitting a feast of All Souls into the calendar. But it could not assign the new, or rather the old, festival to the old day, the first of November, since that was already occupied by the feast of All Saints. Accordingly it placed the mass for the dead on the next day, the second of November. On this theory the feasts of All Saints and of All Souls mark two successive efforts of the Catholic Church to eradicate an old heathen festival of the dead. Both efforts failed. "In all Catholic countries the day of All Souls has preserved the serious character of a festival of the dead which no worldly gaieties are allowed to disturb. It is then the sacred duty of the survivors to visit the graves of their loved ones in the churchyard, to deck them with flowers and lights, and to utter a devout prayer—a pious custom with which in cities like Paris and Vienna even the gay and frivolous comply for the sake of appearance, if not to satisfy an impulse of the heart."[2]

[1] A. J. Binterim, *op. cit.* v. 1, pp. 487 *sqq.* ; J. J. Herzog und G. F. Plitt, *op. cit.* i. p. 303 ; W. Smith and S. Cheetham, *Dictionary of Christian Antiquities*, i. 57. In the last of these works a passage from the *Martyrologium Romanum Vetus* is quoted which states that a feast of Saints (*Festivitas Sanctorum*) on the first of November was celebrated at Rome. But the date of this particular Martyrology is disputed. See A. J. Binterim, *op. cit.* v. 1, pp. 52-54.

[2] J. J. Herzog und G. F. Plitt, *op. cit.* i. 304. A similar attempt to reform religion by diverting the devotion of the people from the spirits of their dead appears to have been made in

§ 3. *The Festival in the Month of Athyr*

Festival of
the death
and resur-
rection of
Osiris in
the month
of Athyr.

The foregoing evidence lends some support to the conjecture—for it is only a conjecture—that the great festival of Osiris at Sais, with its accompanying illumination of the houses, was a night of All Souls, when the ghosts of the dead swarmed in the streets and revisited their old homes, which were lit up to welcome them back again. Herodotus, who briefly describes the festival, omits to mention its date, but we can determine it with some probability from other sources. Thus Plutarch tells us that Osiris was murdered on the seventeenth of the month Athyr, and that the Egyptians accordingly observed mournful rites for four days from the seventeenth of Athyr.[1] Now in the Alexandrian calendar, which Plutarch used, these four days corresponded to the thirteenth, fourteenth, fifteenth, and sixteenth of November, and this date answers exactly to the other indications given by Plutarch, who says that at the time of the festival the Nile was sinking, the north winds dying away, the nights lengthening, and the leaves falling from the trees. During these four days a gilt cow swathed in a black pall was exhibited as an image of Isis.

---

antiquity by the doctors of the Persian faith. For that faith "in its most finished and purest form, in the *Gathas*, does not recognize the dead as objects worthy of worship and sacrifice. But the popular beliefs were too firmly rooted, and the Mazdeans, like the sectaries of many other ideal and lofty forms of religion, were forced to give way. As they could not suppress the worship and get rid of the primitive and crude ideas involved in it, they set about the reform in another way: they interpreted the worship in a new manner, and thus the worship of the dead became a worship of the gods or of a god in favour of the loved and lost ones, a pious commemoration of their names and their virtues." See N. Söderblom, *Les Fravashis* (Paris, 1899), pp. 6 *sq.* The *Gathas* form the oldest part of the *Zend-Avesta*. James Darmesteter, indeed, in his later life

startled the learned world by a theory that the *Gathas* were a comparatively late work based on the teaching of Philo of Alexandria. But this attempt of a Jew to claim for his race the inspiration of the Persian scriptures has been coldly received by Gentile scholars. See J. H. Moulton, *Early Zoroastrianism* (London, 1913), pp. 8 *sqq.*

[1] Plutarch, *Isis et Osiris*, 39. As to the death of Osiris on the seventeenth of Athyr see *ib.* 13 and 42. Plutarch's statement on this subject is confirmed by the evidence of the papyrus Sallier IV., a document dating from the 19th dynasty, which places the lamentation for Osiris at Sais on the seventeenth day of Athyr. See A. Wiedemann, *Herodots zweites Buch*, p. 262; *id.*, *Die Religion der alten Ägypter*, p. 112; *id.*, *Religion of the Ancient Egyptians*, pp. 211 *sq.*

This, no doubt, was the image mentioned by Herodotus in his account of the festival.[1] On the nineteenth day of the month the people went down to the sea, the priests carrying a shrine which contained a golden casket. Into this casket they poured fresh water, and thereupon the spectators raised a shout that Osiris was found. After that they took some vegetable mould, moistened it with water, mixed it with precious spices and incense, and moulded the paste into a small moon - shaped image, which was then robed and ornamented.[2] Thus it appears that the purpose of the ceremonies described by Plutarch was to represent dramatically, first, the search for the dead body of Osiris, and, second, its joyful discovery, followed by the resurrection of the dead god who came to life again in the new image of vegetable mould and spices. Lactantius tells us how on these occasions the priests, with their shaven bodies, beat their breasts and lamented, imitating the sorrowful search of Isis for her lost son Osiris, and how afterwards their sorrow was turned to joy when the jackal - headed god Anubis, or rather a mummer in his stead, produced a small boy, the living representative of the god who was lost and was found.[3] Thus Lactantius regarded Osiris as the son instead of the husband of Isis, and he makes no mention of the image of vegetable mould. It is probable that the boy who figured in the sacred drama played the part, not of Osiris, but of his son Horus;[4] but as the death and resurrection of the god were celebrated in many cities of Egypt, it is also possible that in some places the part of the god come to life was played by a living actor instead of by

The finding of Osiris.

---

[1] See above, p. 50.

[2] Plutarch, *Isis et Osiris*, 39. The words which I have translated "vegetable mould" are γῆν κάρπιμον, literally, "fruitful earth." The composition of the image was very important, as we shall see presently.

[3] Lactantius, *Divin. Institut.* i. 21; *id.*, *Epitome Inst. Divin.* 23 (18, ed. Brandt and Laubmann). The description of the ceremony which Minucius Felix gives (*Octavius*, xxii. 1) agrees closely with, and is probably copied from, that of Lactantius. We know from Appian (*Bell. Civ.* iv. 6. 47) that in the rites of Isis a priest personated Anubis, wearing a dog's, or perhaps rather a jackal's, mask on his head; for the historian tells how in the great proscription a certain Volusius, who was on the condemned list, escaped in the disguise of a priest of Isis, wearing a long linen garment and the mask of a dog over his head.

[4] The suggestion is due to Prof. A. Wiedemann (*Herodots zweites Buch*, p. 261).

an image.　Another Christian writer describes how the Egyptians, with shorn heads, annually lamented over a buried idol of Osiris, smiting their breasts, slashing their shoulders, ripping open their old wounds, until, after several days of mourning, they professed to find the mangled remains of the god, at which they rejoiced.[1]　However the details of the ceremony may have varied in different places, the pretence of finding the god's body, and probably of restoring it to life, was a great event in the festal year of the Egyptians. The shouts of joy which greeted it are described or alluded to by many ancient writers.[2]

§ 4. *The Festival in the Month of Khoiak*

The great Osirian inscription at Denderah.

The funeral rites of Osiris, as they were observed at his great festival in the sixteen provinces of Egypt, are described in a long inscription of the Ptolemaic period, which is engraved on the walls of the god's temple at Denderah, the Tentyra of the Greeks, a town of Upper Egypt situated on the western bank of the Nile about forty miles north of Thebes.[3]　Unfortunately, while the information thus furnished is remarkably full and minute on many points, the arrangement adopted in the inscription is so confused and the expression often so obscure that a clear and consistent account of the ceremonies as a whole can hardly be extracted from it.　Moreover, we learn from the document that the ceremonies varied somewhat in the several cities, the ritual of Abydos, for example, differing from that of Busiris.　Without attempting to trace all the particularities of local usage I shall briefly indicate what seem to have been the leading features of the festival, so far as these can be ascertained with tolerable certainty.[4]

---

[1] Firmicus Maternus, *De errore profanarum religionum*, 2.　Herodotus tells (ii. 61) how the Carians cut their foreheads with knives at the mourning for Osiris.

[2] In addition to the writers who have been already cited see Juvenal, viii. 29 *sq.* ; Athenagoras, *Supplicatio pro Christianis*, 22, pp. 112, 114, ed. J. C. T. Otto (Jena, 1857) ; Tertullian,

Adversus Marcionem, i. 13 ; Augustine, *De civitate Dei*, vi. 10.

[3] W. Smith, *Dictionary of Greek and Roman Geography*, ii. 1127.

[4] For complete translations of the inscription see H. Brugsch, "Das Osiris-Mysterium von Tentyra," *Zeitschrift für ägyptische Sprache und Alterthumskunde*, 1881, pp. 77-111 ; V. Loret, "Les fêtes d'Osiris au mois

The rites lasted eighteen days, from the twelfth to the thirtieth of the month Khoiak, and set forth the nature of Osiris in his triple aspect as dead, dismembered, and finally reconstituted by the union of his scattered limbs. In the first of these aspects he was called Chent-Ament (Khenti-Amenti), in the second Osiris-Sep, and in the third Sokari (Seker).[1] Small images of the god were moulded of sand or vegetable earth and corn, to which incense was sometimes added ; [2] his face was painted yellow and his cheek-bones green.[3] These images were cast in a mould of pure gold, which represented the god in the form of a mummy, with the white crown of Egypt on his head.[4] The festival opened on the twelfth day of Khoiak with a ceremony of ploughing and sowing. Two black cows were yoked to the plough, which was made of tamarisk wood, while the share was of black copper. A boy scattered the seed. One end of the field was sown with barley, the other with spelt, and the middle with flax. During the operation the chief celebrant recited the ritual chapter of "the sowing of the fields." [5] At Busiris on the twentieth of Khoiak sand and barley were put in the god's

The rites of Osiris in the month of Khoiak represented the god as dead, dismembered, and then reconstituted by the union of his scattered limbs.

---

de Khoiak," *Recueil de Travaux relatifs à la Philologie et à l'Archéologie Égyptiennes et Assyriennes*, iii. (1882) pp. 43-57, iv. (1883) pp. 21-33, v. (1884) pp. 85-103. On the document and the festivals described in it see further A. Mariette-Pacha, *Dendérah* (Paris, 1880), pp. 334-347 ; J. Dümichen, "Die dem Osiris im Denderatempel geweihten Räume," *Zeitschrift für ägyptische Sprache und Alterthumskunde*, 1882, pp. 88-101 ; H. Brugsch, *Religion und Mythologie der alten Aegypter* (Leipsic, 1885–1888), pp. 616-618 ; R. V. Lanzone, *Dizionario di Mitologia Egizia*, pp. 725-744 ; A. Wiedemann, *Herodots zweites Buch*, p. 262 ; *id.*, "Osiris végétant," *Le Muséon*, N.S. iv. (1903) p. 113 ; E. A. Wallis Budge, *The Gods of the Egyptians*, ii. 128 *sq.* ; *id.*, *Osiris and the Egyptian Resurrection*, ii. 21 *sqq.* ; Miss Margaret A. Murray, *The Osireion at Abydos* (London, 1904), pp. 27 *sq.*

[1] R. V. Lanzone, *op. cit.* p. 727.

[2] H. Brugsch, in *Zeitschrift für ägyptische Sprache und Alterthums-* kunde, 1881, pp. 80-82 ; A. Wiedemann, in *Le Muséon*, N.S. iv. (1903) p. 113. The corn used in the making of the images is called barley by Brugsch and Miss M. A. Murray (*l.c.*), but wheat (*blé*) by Mr. V. Loret.

[3] H. Brugsch, *op. cit.* pp. 99, 101.

[4] H. Brugsch, *op. cit.* pp. 82 *sq.* ; R. V. Lanzone, *op. cit.* p. 728 ; Miss Margaret A. Murray, *op. cit.* p. 27.

[5] H. Brugsch, *op. cit.* pp. 90 *sq.*, 96 *sq.*, 98 ; R. V. Lanzone, *op. cit.* pp. 743 *sq.* ; E. A. Wallis Budge, *The Gods of the Egyptians*, ii. 128. According to Lanzone, the ploughing took place, not on the first, but on the last day of the festival, namely, on the thirtieth of Khoiak ; and that certainly appears to have been the date of the ploughing at Busiris, for the inscription directs that there "the ploughing of the earth shall take place in the Serapeum of *Aa-n-beḥ* under the fine Persea-trees on the last day of the month Khoiak " (H. Brugsch, *op. cit.* p. 84).

"garden," which appears to have been a sort of large flower-pot. This was done in the presence of the cow-goddess Shenty, represented seemingly by the image of a cow made of gilt sycamore wood with a headless human image in its inside. "Then fresh inundation water was poured out of a golden vase over both the goddess and the 'garden,' and the barley was allowed to grow as the emblem of the resurrection of the god after his burial in the earth, 'for the growth of the garden is the growth of the divine substance.'" [1] On the twenty-second of Khoiak, at the eighth hour, the images of Osiris, attended by thirty-four images of deities, performed a mysterious voyage in thirty-four tiny boats made of papyrus, which were illuminated by three hundred and sixty-five lights.[2] On the twenty-fourth of Khoiak, after sunset, the effigy of Osiris in a coffin of mulberry wood was laid in the grave, and at the ninth hour of the night the effigy which had been made and deposited the year before was removed and placed upon boughs of sycamore.[3] Lastly, on the thirtieth day of Khoiak they repaired to the holy sepulchre, a subterranean chamber over which appears to have grown a clump of Persea-trees. Entering the vault by the western door, they laid the coffined effigy of the dead god reverently on a bed of sand in the chamber. So they left him to his rest, and departed from the sepulchre by the eastern door. Thus ended the ceremonies in the month of Khoiak.[4]

The burial of Osiris.

[1] Miss Margaret A. Murray, *The Osireion at Abydos*, p. 28 ; H. Brugsch, *op. cit.* pp. 83, 92. The headless human image in the cow may have stood for Isis, who is said to have been decapitated by her son Horus, and to have received from Thoth a cow's head as a substitute. See Plutarch, *Isis et Osiris*, 20 ; G. Maspero, *Histoire ancienne des Peuples de l'Orient Classique*, i. 177 ; Ed. Meyer, *s.v.* "Isis," in W. H. Roscher's *Lexikon der griech. und röm. Mythologie*, ii. 366.

[2] H. Brugsch, *op. cit.* pp. 92 *sq.* ; R. V. Lanzone, *op. cit.* pp. 738-740 ; A. Wiedemann, *Herodots zweites Buch*, p. 262 ; Miss M. A. Murray, *op. cit.* p. 35. An Egyptian calendar, written at Sais about 300 B.C., has under the date 26 Khoiak the following entry : "Osiris goes about and the golden

boat is brought forth." See *The Hibeh Papyri*, Part i., edited by B. P. Grenfell and A. S. Hunt (London, 1906), pp. 146, 153. In the Canopic decree "the voyage of the sacred boat of Osiris" is said to take place on the 29th of Khoiak from "the sanctuary in the Heracleum" to the Canopic sanctuary. See W. Dittenberger, *Orientis Graeci Inscriptiones Selectae*, No. 56 (vol. i. pp. 105, 108). Hence it would seem that the date of this part of the festival varied somewhat in different places or at different times.

[3] H. Brugsch, *op. cit.* p. 99 ; E. A. Wallis Budge, *The Gods of the Egyptians*, ii. 129 ; compare Miss Margaret A. Murray, *op. cit.* p. 28, who refers the ceremony to the twenty-fifth of Khoiak.

[4] H. Brugsch, *op. cit.* pp. 94, 99 ;

§ 5. *The Resurrection of Osiris*

In the foregoing account of the festival, drawn from the great inscription of Denderah, the burial of Osiris figures prominently, while his resurrection is implied rather than expressed. This defect of the document, however, is amply compensated by a remarkable series of bas-reliefs which accompany and illustrate the inscription. These exhibit in a series of scenes the dead god lying swathed as a mummy on his bier, then gradually raising himself up higher and higher, until at last he has entirely quitted the bier and is seen erect between the guardian wings of the faithful Isis, who stands behind him, while a male figure holds up before his eyes the *crux ansata*, the Egyptian symbol of life.[1] The resurrection of the god could hardly be portrayed more graphically. Even more instructive, however, is another representation of the same event in a chamber dedicated to Osiris in the great temple of Isis at Philae. Here we see the dead body of Osiris with stalks of corn springing from it, while a priest waters the stalks from a pitcher which he holds in his hand. The accompanying inscription sets forth that "this is the form of him whom one may not name, Osiris of the mysteries, who springs from the returning waters."[2] Taken together, the picture and the words seem to leave no doubt that Osiris was here conceived and represented as a personification of the corn which springs from

(marginal note) The resurrection of Osiris represented on the monuments.

[1] A. Mariette - Bey, *Dendérah*, iv. (Paris, 1873) plates 65, 66, 68, 69, 70, 71, 72, 88, 89, 90; R. V. Lanzone, *Dizionario di Mitologia Egizia*, pp. 757 *sqq.*, with plates cclxviii.-ccxcii.; E. A. Wallis Budge, *The Gods of the Egyptians*, ii. 131-138; *id.*, *Osiris and the Egyptian Resurrection*, ii. 31 *sqq.*

A. Mariette-Pacha, *Dendérah*, pp. 336 *sq.*; R. V. Lanzone, *op. cit.* p. 744. Mariette supposed that after depositing the new image in the sepulchre they carried out the old one of the preceding year, thus setting forth the resurrection as well as the death of the god. But this view is apparently not shared by Brugsch and Lanzone.

[2] H. Brugsch, *Religion und Mythologie der alten Aegypter*, p. 621; R. V. Lanzone, *Dizionario di Mitologia Egizia*, plate cclxi.; A. Wiedemann, "L'Osiris végétant," *Le Muséon*, N.S. iv. (1903) p. 112; E. A. Wallis Budge, *Osiris and the Egyptian Resurrection*, i. 58. According to Prof. Wiedemann, the corn springing from the god's body is barley. Similarly in a papyrus of the Louvre (No. 3377) Osiris is represented swathed as a mummy and lying on his back, while stalks of corn sprout from his body. See R. V. Lanzone, *op. cit.* pp. 801 *sq.*, with plate ccciii. 2; A. Wiedemann, "L'Osiris végétant," *Le Muséon*, N.S. iv. (1903) p. 112.

the fields after they have been fertilized by the inundation. This, according to the inscription, was the kernel of the mysteries, the innermost secret revealed to the initiated.   So in the rites of Demeter at Eleusis a reaped ear of corn was exhibited to the worshippers as the central mystery of their religion.[1]   We can now fully understand why at the great festival of sowing in the month of Khoiak the priests used to bury effigies of Osiris made of earth and corn.   When these effigies were taken up again at the end of a year or of a shorter interval, the corn would be found to have sprouted from the body of Osiris, and this sprouting of the grain would be hailed as an omen, or rather as the cause, of the growth of the crops.[2]   The corn-god produced the corn from himself : he gave his own body to feed the people : he died that they might live.

Corn-stuffed effigies of Osiris buried with the dead to ensure their resurrection.

And from the death and resurrection of their great god the Egyptians drew not only their support and sustenance in this life, but also their hope of a life eternal beyond the grave.   This hope is indicated in the clearest manner by the very remarkable effigies of Osiris which have come to light in Egyptian cemeteries.   Thus in the Valley of the Kings at Thebes there was found the tomb of a royal fan-bearer who lived about 1500 B.C.   Among the rich contents of the tomb there was a bier on which rested a mattress of reeds covered with three layers of linen.   On the upper side of the linen was painted a life-size figure of Osiris ; and the interior of the figure, which was waterproof, contained a mixture of vegetable mould, barley, and a sticky fluid.   The barley had sprouted and sent out shoots two or three inches long.[3]   Again, in the cemetery at Cynopolis "were numerous burials of Osiris figures.   These were made of grain wrapped up in cloth and roughly shaped like an Osiris, and placed inside a bricked-up recess at the side of the tomb, sometimes

[1] Hippolytus, *Refutatio omnium haeresium*, v. 8, p. 162 ed. L. Duncker and F. G. Schneidewin (Göttingen, 1859). See *Spirits of the Corn and of the Wild*, i. 38 *sq.*

[2] Prof. A. Erman rightly assumes (*Die ägyptische Religion*,[2] p. 234) that the images made in the month of Khoiak were intended to germinate as

a symbol of the divine resurrection.

[3] A. Wiedemann, " L'Osiris végé-tant," *Le Muséon*, N.S. iv. (1903) p. 111 ; *Egyptian Exploration Fund Archaeological Report*, 1898–1899, pp. 24 *sq.* ; A. Moret, *Kings and Gods of Egypt* (New York and London, 1912), p. 94, with plate xi. ; *id.*, *Mystères Égyptiens* (Paris, 1913), p. 41.

in small pottery coffins, sometimes in wooden coffins in the form of a hawk-mummy, sometimes without any coffins at all." [1]   These corn-stuffed figures were bandaged like mummies with patches of gilding here and there, as if in imitation of the golden mould in which the similar figures of Osiris were cast at the festival of sowing.[2]   Again, effigies of Osiris, with faces of green wax and their interior full of grain, were found buried near the necropolis of Thebes.[3]   Finally, we are told by Professor Erman that between the legs of mummies "there sometimes lies a figure of Osiris made of slime ; it is filled with grains of corn, the sprouting of which is intended to signify the resurrection of the god." [4]   We cannot doubt that, just as the burial of corn-stuffed images of Osiris in the earth at the festival of sowing was designed to quicken the seed, so the burial of similar images in the grave was meant to quicken the dead, in other words, to ensure their spiritual immortality.

§ 6. *Readjustment of Egyptian Festivals*

The festival of Osiris which Plutarch assigns to the month of Athyr would seem to be identical in substance with the one which the inscription of Denderah assigns to the following month, namely, to Khoiak.   Apparently the essence of both festivals was a dramatic representation of the death and resurrection of the god ; in both of them Isis was figured by a gilt cow, and Osiris by an image moulded of moist vegetable earth.   But if the festivals were the same, why were they held in different months ?   It is easy to suggest that different towns in Egypt celebrated the festival at different dates.   But when we remember that according to the great inscription of Denderah, the authority of which is indisputable, the festival fell in the month of Khoiak in

The festivals of Osiris in the months of Athyr and Khoiak seem to have been substantially the same.

---

[1] B. P. Grenfell and A. S. Hunt, in *Egyptian Exploration Fund Archaeological Report*, 1902–1903, p. 5.

[2] Miss Margaret A. Murray, *The Osireion at Abydos*, pp. 28 *sq.*

[3] Sir J. Gardiner Wilkinson, *A Second Series of the Manners and Customs of the Ancient Egyptians* (London, 1841), ii. 300, note §.   The writer seems to have doubted whether these effigies represented Osiris.   But the doubt has been entirely removed by subsequent discoveries.   Wilkinson's important note on the subject is omitted by his editor, S. Birch (vol. iii. p. 375, ed. 1878).

[4] A. Erman, *Die ägyptische Religion,*[2] pp. 209 *sq.*

every province of Egypt, we shall be reluctant to suppose that at some one place, or even at a few places, it was exceptionally held in the preceding month of Athyr, and that the usually well-informed Plutarch described the exception as if it had been the rule, of which on this supposition he must have been wholly ignorant.   More probably the discrepancy is to be explained by the great change which came over the Egyptian calendar between the date of the inscription and the lifetime of Plutarch.   For when the inscription was drawn up in the Ptolemaic age the festivals were dated by the old vague or movable year, and therefore rotated gradually through the whole circle of the seasons ; whereas at the time when Plutarch wrote, about the end of the first century, they were seemingly dated by the fixed Alexandrian year, and accordingly had ceased to rotate.[1]

The old festival of Khoiak may have been transferred to Athyr when the Egyptians adopted the fixed Alexandrian year in 30 B.C.

But even if we grant that in Plutarch's day the festivals had become stationary, still this would not explain why the old festival of Khoiak had been transferred to Athyr.   In order to understand that transference it seems necessary to suppose that when the Egyptians gave to their months fixed places in the solar year by accepting the Alexandrian system of intercalation, they at the same time transferred the festivals from what may be called their artificial to their natural dates.   Under the old system a summer festival was sometimes held in winter and a winter festival in summer ; a harvest celebration sometimes fell at the season of sowing, and a sowing celebration at the season of harvest.   People might reconcile themselves to such anomalies so long as they knew that they were only temporary, and that in the course of time the festivals would necessarily return to their proper seasons.   But it must have been otherwise when they adopted a fixed instead of a movable year, and so arrested the rotation of the festivals for ever.   For they could not but be aware that every festival would thenceforth continue to occupy for all time that particular place in the solar year which it chanced to occupy in the year 30 B.C., when the calendar became fixed.   If in that particular year it happened, as it might have happened, that the summer

---

[1] See above, pp. 24 *sq.*, 27 *sq.*, 49 *sq.*

festivals were held in winter and the winter festivals in summer, they would always be so held in future; the absurdity and anomaly would never again be rectified as it had been before. This consideration, which could not have escaped intelligent men, must have suggested the advisability of transferring the festivals from the dates at which they chanced to be celebrated in 30 B.C. to the dates at which they ought properly to be celebrated in the course of nature.

Now what in the year 30 B.C. was the actual amount of discrepancy between the accidental and the natural dates of the festivals? It was a little more than a month. In that year Thoth, the first month of the Egyptian calendar, happened to begin on the twenty-ninth of August,[1] whereas according to theory it should have begun with the heliacal rising of Sirius on the twentieth of July, that is, forty days or, roughly speaking, a month earlier. From this it follows that in the year 30 B.C. all the Egyptian festivals fell about a month later than their natural dates, and they must have continued to fall a month late for ever if they were allowed to retain those places in the calendar which they chanced to occupy in that particular year. In these circumstances it would be a natural and sensible thing to restore the festivals to their proper places in the solar year by celebrating them one calendar month earlier than before.[2] If this measure were adopted the

The transference would be intelligible if we suppose that in 30 B.C. the dates of all the Egyptian festivals were shifted backward by about a month in order to restore them to their natural places in the calendar.

---

[1] So it was reckoned at the time. But, strictly speaking, Thoth in that year began on August 31. The miscalculation originated in a blunder of the ignorant Roman pontiffs who, being charged with the management of the new Julian calendar, at first intercalated a day every third, instead of every fourth, year. See Solinus, *Collectanea*, i. 45-47 (p. 15, ed. Th. Mommsen, Berlin, 1864); Macrobius, *Saturn.* i. 14. 13 *sq.*; L. Ideler, *Handbuch der mathematischen und technischen Chronologie*, i. 157-161.

[2] Theoretically the shift should have been 40, or rather 42 days, that being the interval between July 20 and August 29 or 31 (see the preceding note). If that shift was actually made, the calendar date of any festival in the old vague

Egyptian year could be found by adding 40 or 42 days to its date in the Alexandrian year. Thus if the death of Osiris fell on the 17th of Athyr in the Alexandrian year, it should have fallen on the 27th or 29th of Khoiak in the old vague year; and if his resurrection fell on the 19th of Athyr in the Alexandrian year, it should have fallen on the 29th of Khoiak or the 1st of Tybi in the old vague year. These calculations agree nearly, but not exactly, with the somewhat uncertain indications of the Denderah calendar (above, p. 88), and also with the independent evidence which we possess that the resurrection of Osiris was celebrated on the 30th of Khoiak (below, pp. 108 *sq.*). These approximate agreements to some extent con-

festivals which had hitherto been held, for example, in the third month Athyr would henceforth be held in the second month Phaophi ; the festivals which had hitherto fallen in the fourth month Khoiak would thenceforth fall in the third month Athyr ; and so on. Thus the festal calendar would be reduced to harmony with the seasons instead of being in more or less flagrant discord with them, as it had generally been before, and must always have been afterwards if the change which I have indicated had not been introduced. It is only to credit the native astronomers and the Roman rulers of Egypt with common sense to suppose that they actually adopted the measure. On that supposition we can perfectly understand why the festival of sowing, which had formerly belonged to the month of Khoiak, was transferred to Athyr. For in the Alexandrian calendar Khoiak corresponds very nearly to December, and Athyr to November. But in Egypt the month of November, not the month of December, is the season of sowing. There was therefore every reason why the great sowing festival of the corn-god Osiris should be held in Athyr and not Khoiak, in November and not in December. In like manner we may suppose that all the Egyptian festivals were restored to their true places in the solar year, and that when Plutarch dates a festival both by its calendar month and by its relation to

---

firm my theory that, with the adoption of the fixed Alexandrian year, the dates of the official Egyptian festivals were shifted from their accidental places in the calendar to their proper places in the natural year.

Since I published in the first edition of this book (1906) my theory that with the adoption of the fixed Alexandrian year in 30 B.C. the Egyptian festivals were shifted about a month backward in the year, Professor Ed. Meyer has shown independent grounds for holding "that the festivals which gave rise to the later names of the (Egyptian) months were demonstrably held a month later in earlier ages, under the twentieth, eighteenth, indeed partly under the twelfth dynasty ; in other words, that after the end of the New Kingdom the festivals and the

corresponding names of the months were displaced one month backwards. It is true that this displacement can as yet be proved for only five months ; but as the names of these months and the festivals keep their relative position towards each other, the assumption is inevitable that the displacement affected not merely particular festivals but the whole system equally." See Ed. Meyer, *Nachträge zur ägyptischen Chronologie* (Berlin, 1908), pp. 3 *sqq.* (*Abhandlungen der königl. Preuss. Akademie der Wissenschaften vom Jahre 1907*). Thus it is possible that the displacement of the festivals by a month backward in the calendar took place a good deal earlier than I had supposed. In the uncertainty of the whole question I leave my theory as it stood.

the cycle of the seasons, he is perfectly right in doing so, and we may accept his evidence with confidence instead of having to accuse him of ignorantly confounding the movable Egyptian with the fixed Alexandrian year. Accusations of ignorance levelled at the best writers of antiquity are apt to recoil on those who make them.[1]

[1] If the results of the foregoing inquiry be accepted, the resurrection of Osiris was regularly celebrated in Egypt on the 15th of November from the year 30 B.C. onward, since the 15th of November corresponded to the 19th of Athyr (the resurrection day) in the fixed Alexandrian year. This agrees with the indications of the Roman Rustic Calendars, which place the resurrection (*heuresis*, that is, the discovery of Osiris) between the 14th and the 30th of November. Yet according to the calendar of Philocalus, the official Roman celebration of the resurrection seems to have been held on the 1st of November, not on the 15th. How is the discrepancy to be explained? Th. Mommsen supposed that the festival was officially adopted at Rome at a time when the 19th of Athyr of the vague Egyptian year corresponded to the 31st of October or the 1st of November of the Julian calendar, and that the Romans, overlooking the vague or shifting character of the Egyptian year, fixed the resurrection of Osiris permanently on the 1st of November. Now the 19th of Athyr of the vague year corresponded to the 1st of November in the years 32-35 A.D. and to the 31st of October in the years 36-39; and it appears that the festival was officially adopted at Rome some time before 65 A.D. (Lucan, *Pharsalia*, viii. 831 *sqq.*). It is unlikely that the adoption took place in the reign of Tiberius, who died in 37 A.D. ; for he is known to have persecuted the Egyptian religion (Tacitus, *Annals*, ii. 85; Suetonius, *Tiberius*, 36; Josephus, *Antiquit. Jud.* xviii. 3. 4) ; hence Mommsen concluded that the great festival of Osiris was officially adopted at Rome in the early years of the reign of Caligula, that is, in 37, 38, or 39 A.D. See Th. Mommsen, *Corpus Inscriptionum Latinarum*, i.[2] Pars prior (Berlin, 1893), pp. 333 *sq.*; H. Dessau, *Inscriptiones Latinae Selectae*, vol. ii. p. 995, No. 8745. This theory of Mommsen's assumes that in Egypt the festivals were still regulated by the old vague year in the first century of our era. It cannot, therefore, be reconciled with the conclusion reached in the text that the Egyptian festivals ceased to be regulated by the old vague year from 30 B.C. onward. How the difference of date between the official Roman and the Egyptian festival of the resurrection is to be explained, I do not pretend to say.

CHAPTER V

THE NATURE OF OSIRIS

§ 1. *Osiris a Corn-God*

Osiris in one of his aspects a personi-fication of the corn.

THE foregoing survey of the myth and ritual of Osiris may suffice to prove that in one of his aspects the god was a personification of the corn, which may be said to die and come to life again every year. Through all the pomp and glamour with which in later times the priests had invested his worship, the conception of him as the corn-god comes clearly out in the festival of his death and resurrection, which was celebrated in the month of Khoiak and at a later period in the month of Athyr. That festival appears to have been essentially a festival of sowing, which properly fell at the time when the husbandman actually committed the seed to the earth. On that occasion an effigy of the corn-god, moulded of earth and corn, was buried with funeral rites in the ground in order that, dying there, he might come to life again with the new crops. The ceremony was, in fact, a charm to ensure the growth of the corn by sympathetic magic, and we may conjecture that as such it was practised in a simple form by every Egyptian farmer on his fields long before it was adopted and transfigured by the priests in the stately ritual of the temple. In the modern, but doubtless ancient, Arab custom of burying " the Old Man," namely, a sheaf of wheat, in the harvest-field and praying that he may return from the dead,[1] we see the germ out of which the worship of the corn-god Osiris was probably developed.

The details of his myth fit in well with this interpretation of the god. He was said to be the offspring of Sky and

[1] See above, p. 48.

Earth.[1] What more appropriate parentage could be invented for the corn which springs from the ground that has been fertilized by the water of heaven? It is true that the land of Egypt owed its fertility directly to the Nile and not to showers; but the inhabitants must have known or guessed that the great river in its turn was fed by the rains which fell in the far interior. Again, the legend that Osiris was the first to teach men the use of corn[2] would be most naturally told of the corn-god himself. Further, the story that his mangled remains were scattered up and down the land and buried in different places may be a mythical way of expressing either the sowing or the winnowing of the grain. The latter interpretation is supported by the tale that Isis placed the severed limbs of Osiris on a corn-sieve.[3] Or more probably the legend may be a reminiscence of a custom of slaying a human victim, perhaps a representative of the corn-spirit and distributing his flesh or scattering his ashes over the fields to fertilize them. In modern Europe the figure of Death is sometimes torn in pieces, and the fragments are then buried in the ground to make the crops grow well,[4] and in other parts of the world human victims are treated is the same way.[5] With regard to the ancient Egyptians we have it on the authority of Manetho that they used to burn red-haired men and scatter their ashes with winnowing fans,[6] and it is highly significant that this barbarous sacrifice was offered by the kings at the grave of Osiris.[7] We may conjecture that the victims represented Osiris himself, who was annually slain, dismembered, and buried in their persons that he might quicken the seed in the earth.

Possibly in prehistoric times the kings themselves

Osiris a child of Sky and Earth.

The legend of the dismemberment of Osiris points to the dismemberment of human beings, perhaps of the kings, in the character of the corn-spirit

---

[1] See above, p. 6.

[2] See above, p. 7.

[3] Servius on Virgil, *Georg.* i. 166.

[4] *The Dying God*, p. 250.

[5] *Spirits of the Corn and of the Wild*, i. 236 *sqq.*

[6] Plutarch, *Isis et Osiris*, 73, compare 33.

[7] Diodorus Siculus, i. 88. 5. The slaughter may have been performed by the king with his own hand. On Egyptian monuments the king is often represented in the act of slaying prisoners before a god. See A. Moret, *Du caractère religieux de la royauté Pharaonique* (Paris, 1902), pp. 179, 224; E. A. Wallis Budge, *Osiris and the Egyptian Resurrection*, i. 197 *sqq.* Similarly the kings of Ashantee and Dahomey used often themselves to cut the throats of the human victims. See A. B. Ellis, *The Tshi-speaking Peoples of the Gold Coast* (London, 1887), p. 162; *id.*, *The Ewe-speaking Peoples of the Slave Coast* (London, 1890), pp. 125, 129.

Roman
and Greek
traditions
of the
dismem-
berment
of kings.

played the part of the god and were slain and dismembered
in that character. Set as well as Osiris is said to have
been torn in pieces after a reign of eighteen days, which
was commemorated by an annual festival of the same
length.[1] According to one story Romulus, the first
king of Rome, was cut in pieces by the senators, who
buried the fragments of him in the ground;[2] and
the traditional day of his death, the seventh of July,
was celebrated with certain curious rites, which were
apparently connected with the artificial fertilization of the
fig.[3] Again, Greek legend told how Pentheus, king of
Thebes, and Lycurgus, king of the Thracian Edonians,
opposed the vine-god Dionysus, and how the impious
monarchs were rent in pieces, the one by the frenzied
Bacchanals, the other by horses.[4] These Greek traditions
may well be distorted reminiscences of a custom of sacrificing human beings, and especially divine kings, in the
character of Dionysus, a god who resembled Osiris in many
points and was said like him to have been torn limb from
limb.[5] We are told that in Chios men were rent in pieces

---

[1] *Scholia in Caesaris Germanici
Aratea*, in F. Eyssenhardt's edition of
Martianus Capella, p. 408 (Leipsic,
1866).

[2] Dionysius Halicarnasensis, *Antiquit. Rom.* ii. 56. 4. Compare
Livy, i. 16. 4; Florus, i. 1. 16 *sq.*;
Plutarch, *Romulus*, 27. Mr. A. B.
Cook was, I believe, the first to interpret the story as a reminiscence of the
sacrifice of a king. See his article
"The European Sky-God," *Folk-lore*,
xvi. (1905) pp. 324 *sq.* However, the
acute historian A. Schwegler long ago
maintained that the tradition rested on
some very ancient religious rite, which
was afterwards abolished or misunderstood, and he rightly compared the
legendary deaths of Pentheus and
Orpheus (*Römische Geschichte*, Tübingen, 1853–1858, vol. i. pp. 534 *sq.*).
See further W. Otto, "Juno," *Philologus*, lxiv. (1905) pp. 187 *sqq.*

[3] *The Magic Art and the Evolution
of Kings*, ii. 313 *sqq.*

[4] Euripides, *Bacchae*, 43 *sqq.*, 1043
sqq.; Theocritus, xxvi.; Pausanias, ii.
2. 7; Apollodorus, *Bibliotheca*, iii. 5.

1 *sq.*; Hyginus, *Fab.* 132 and 184. The
destruction of Lycurgus by horses
seems to be mentioned only by Apollodorus. As to Pentheus see especially
A. G. Bather, "The Problem of the
Bacchae," *Journal of Hellenic Studies*,
xiv. (1904) pp. 244-263.

[5] Nonnus, *Dionys.* vi. 165-205;
Clement of Alexandria, *Protrept.* ii. 17
sq., p. 15 ed. Potter; Justin Martyr,
Apology, i. 54; Firmicus Maternus,
De errore profanarum religionum, 6;
Arnobius, *Adversus Nationes*, v. 19.
According to the Clementine *Recognitiones*, x. 24 (Migne's *Patrologia Graeca*,
i. 1434) Dionysus was torn in pieces
at Thebes, the very place of which
Pentheus was king. The description
of Euripides (*Bacchae*, 1058 *sqq.*)
suggests that the human victim was tied
or hung to a pine-tree before being rent
to pieces. We are reminded of the effigy
of Attis which hung on the sacred
pine (above, vol. i. p. 267), and of
the image of Osiris which was made
out of a pine-tree and then buried in
the hollow of the trunk (below, p. 108).
The pine-tree on which Pentheus was

as a sacrifice to Dionysus;[1] and since they died the same
death as their god, it is reasonable to suppose that they
personated him.   The story that the Thracian Orpheus was
similarly torn limb from limb by the Bacchanals seems to
indicate that he too perished in the character of the god whose
death he died.[2]   It is significant that the Thracian Lycurgus,
king of the Edonians, is said to have been put to death in
order that the ground, which had ceased to be fruitful, might
regain its fertility.[3]   In some Thracian villages at Carnival
time a custom is still annually observed, which may well be
a mitigation of an ancient practice of putting a man, perhaps
a king, to death in the character of Dionysus for the sake
of the crops.   A man disguised in goatskins and fawnskins,
the livery of Dionysus, is shot at and falls down as dead.
A pretence is made of flaying his body and of mourning
over him, but afterwards he comes to life again.   Further,
a plough is dragged about the village and seed is scattered,
while prayers are said that the wheat, rye, and barley may
be plentiful.   One town (Viza), where these customs are
observed, was the capital of the old Thracian kings.   In
another town (Kosti, near the Black Sea) the principal masker
is called the king.   He wears goatskins or sheepskins, and is
attended by a boy who dispenses wine to the people.   The
king himself carries seed, which he casts on the ground
before the church, after being invited to throw it on two

*Modern
Thracian
pretence
of killing
a man,
who is
sometimes
called a
king, for
the good of
the crops.*

---

pelted by the Bacchanals before they
tore him limb from limb is said to have
been worshipped as if it were the god
himself by the Corinthians, who made
two images of Dionysus out of it
(Pausanias, ii. 2. 7).   The tradition
points to an intimate connexion between the tree, the god, and the human
victim.

[1] Porphyry, *De abstinentia*, ii. 55.
At Potniae in Boeotia a priest of
Dionysus is said to have been killed by
the drunken worshippers (Pausanias,
ix. 8. 2).   He may have been sacrificed in the character of the god.

[2] Lucian, *De saltatione*, 51 ; Plato,
Symposium, 7, p. 179 D, E ; Pausanias,
ix. 30. 5 ; Ovid, *Metam.* xi. 1-43 ; O.
Gruppe, *s.v.* "Orpheus," in W. H.
Roscher's *Lexikon der griech. und röm.*

Mythologie, iii. 1165 *sq*.   That Orpheus
died the death of the god has been
observed both in ancient and modern
times.   See E. Rohde, *Psyche*[3] (Tübingen and Leipsic, 1903) ii. 118, note[2],
quoting Proclus on Plato ; S. Reinach,
" La mort d'Orphée," *Cultes, Mythes
et Religions*, ii. (1906) pp. 85 *sqq*.
According to Ovid, the Bacchanals
killed him with hoes, rakes, and
mattocks.   Similarly in West Africa
human victims used to be killed with
spades and hoes and then buried in
a field which had just been tilled
(J. B. Labat, *Relation historique de
l'Ethiopie occidentale*, Paris, 1732, i.
380).   Such a mode of sacrifice points
to the identification of the human
victim with the fruits of the earth.

[3] Apollodorus, *Bibliotheca*, iii. 5. 1.

bands of married and unmarried men respectively. Finally, he is stripped of the skins and thrown into the river.[1]

Further, we read of a Norwegian king, Halfdan the Black, whose body was cut up and buried in different parts of his kingdom for the sake of ensuring the fruitfulness of the earth. He is said to have been drowned at the age of forty through the breaking of the ice in spring. What followed his death is thus related by the old Norse historian Snorri Sturluson : " He had been the most prosperous (literally, blessed with abundance) of all kings. So greatly did men value him that when the news came that he was dead and his body removed to Hringariki and intended for burial there, the chief men from Raumariki and Westfold and Heithmörk came and all requested that they might take his body with them and bury it in their various provinces ; they thought that it would bring abundance to those who obtained it. Eventually it was settled that the body was distributed in four places. The head was laid in a barrow at Steinn in Hringariki, and each party took away their own share and buried it. All these barrows are called Halfdan's barrows." [2] It should be remembered that this Halfdan belonged to the family of the Ynglings, who traced their descent from Frey, the great Scandinavian god of fertility.[3] Frey himself is said to have reigned as king of Sweden at Upsala. The years of his reign were plenteous, and the people laid the plenty to his account. So when he

[1] R. M. Dawkins, "The Modern Carnival in Thrace and the Cult of Dionysus," *Journal of Hellenic Studies,* xxvi. (1906) pp. 191-206. See further *Spirits of the Corn and of the Wild*, i. 25 *sqq.*

[2] Snorri Sturluson, *Heimskringla, Saga Halfdanar Svarta*, ch. 9. I have to thank Professor H. M. Chadwick for referring me to this passage and translating it for me. See also *The Stories of the Kings of Norway* (*Heimskringla*), done into English by W. Morris and E. Magnússon (London, 1893–1905), i. 86 *sq.* Halfdan the Black was the father of Harold the Fair-haired, king of Norway (860–933 A.D.). Professor Chadwick tells me that, though the tradition as to the

death and mutilation of Halfdan was not committed to writing for three hundred years, he sees no reason to doubt its truth. He also informs me that the word translated "abundance" means literally "the produce of the season." "Plenteous years" is the rendering of Morris and Magnússon.

[3] As to the descent of Halfdan and the Ynglings from Frey, see *Heimskringla*, done into English by W. Morris and E. Magnússon, i. 23-71 (*The Saga Library*, vol. iii.). With regard to Frey, the god of fertility, both animal and vegetable, see E. H. Meyer, *Mythologie der Germanen* (Strasburg, 1903), pp. 366 *sq.* ; P. Hermann, *Nordische Mythologie* (Leipsic, 1903), pp. 206 *sqq.*

died, they would not burn him, as it had been customary to
do with the dead before his time ; but they resolved to
preserve his body, believing that, so long as it remained in
Sweden, the land would have abundance and peace.　Therefore they reared a great mound, and put him in it, and
sacrificed to him for plenty and peace ever afterwards.
And for three years after his death they poured the tribute
to him into the mound, as if he were alive ; the gold they
poured in by one window, the silver by a second, and the
copper by a third.[1]

The natives of Kiwai, an island lying off the mouth of
the Fly River in British New Guinea, tell of a certain
magician named Segera, who had sago for his totem.
When his son died, the death was set down to the magic
of an enemy, and the bereaved father was so angry that
by his spells he caused the whole crop of sago in the
country to fail ; only in his own garden the sago grew as
luxuriantly as ever.　When many had died of famine, the
people went to him and begged him to remove the spells
which he had cast on the sago palms, so that they might
eat food and live.　The magician, touched with remorse and
pity, went round planting a sago shoot in every garden, and
the shoots flourished, sago was plentiful once more, and the
famine came to an end.　When Segera was old and ill, he
told the people that he would soon die, but that, nevertheless, he would cause their gardens to thrive.　Accordingly,
he instructed them that when he was dead they should
cut him up and place pieces of his flesh in their gardens,
but his head was to be buried in his own garden.　Of him
it is said that he outlived the ordinary age, and that no man
knew his father, but that he made the sago good and no
one was hungry any more.　Old men who were alive a
few years ago affirmed that they had known Segera in their
youth, and the general opinion of the Kiwai people seems
to be that Segera died not more than two generations ago.[2]

Taken all together, these legends point to a widespread
practice of dismembering the body of a king or magician

Segera, a magician of Kiwai, said to have been cut up after death and the pieces buried in gardens to fertilize them.

---

[1] *Heimskringla*, done into English by W. Morris and E. Magnússon, i. 4, 22 24 (*The Saga Library*, vol. iii.).

[2] *Totemism and Exogamy*, ii. 32 *sq.*, from information supplied by Dr. C. G. Seligmann.

Apparently widespread custom of dismembering a king or magician and burying the pieces in different parts of the kingdom.

and burying the pieces in different parts of the country in order to ensure the fertility of the ground and probably also the fecundity of man and beast. Whether regarded as the descendant of a god, as himself divine, or simply as a mighty enchanter, the king was believed to radiate magical virtue for the good of his subjects, quickening the seed in the earth and in the womb. This radiation of reproductive energy did not cease with his life; hence the people deemed it essential to preserve his body as a pledge of the continued prosperity of the country. It would be natural to imagine that the spot where the dead king was buried would enjoy a more than ordinary share of his blessed influence, and accordingly disputes would almost inevitably arise between different districts for the exclusive possession of so powerful a talisman. These disputes could be settled and local jealousies appeased by dividing the precious body between the rival claimants, in order that all should benefit in equal measure by its life-giving properties. This was certainly done in Norway with the body of Halfdan the Black, the descendant of the harvest-god Frey; it appears to have been done with the body of Segera, the sago-magician of Kiwai; and we may conjecture that in prehistoric times it was done with the bodies of Egyptian kings, who personated Osiris, the god of fertility in general and of the corn in particular. At least such a practice would account for the legend of the mangling of the god's body and the distribution of the pieces throughout Egypt.

In this dismemberment a special virtue seems to have been ascribed to the genital organs.

In this connexion the story that the genital member of Osiris was missing when Isis pieced together his mutilated body,[1] may not be without significance. When a Zulu medicine-man wishes to make the crops grow well, he will take the body of a man who has died in full vigour and cut minute portions of tissue from the foot, the leg, the arm, the face, and the nail of a single finger in order to compound a fertilizing medicine out of them. But the most important part of the medicine consists of the dead man's generative organs, which are removed entire. All these pieces of the corpse are fried with herbs

[1] See above, p. 10.

on a slow fire, then ground to powder, and sown over the fields.[1]   We have seen that similarly the Egyptians scattered the ashes of human victims by means of winnowing-fans ;[2] and if my explanation of the practice is correct, it may well have been that they, like the Zulus, attributed a special power of reproduction to the genital organs, and therefore carefully excised them from the body of the victim in order to impart their virtue to the fields.   I have conjectured that a similar use was made of the severed portions of the priests of Attis.[3]

To an ancient Egyptian, with his firm belief in a personal immortality dependent on the integrity of the body, the prospect of mutilation after death must have been very repugnant ; and we may suppose that the kings offered a strenuous resistance to the custom and finally succeeded in abolishing it.   They may have represented to the people that they would attain their object better by keeping the royal corpse intact than by frittering it away in small pieces. Their subjects apparently acquiesced in the argument, or at all events in the conclusion ; yet the mountains of masonry beneath which the old Egyptian kings lay buried may have been intended to guard them from the superstitious devotion of their friends quite as much as from the hostile designs of their enemies, since both alike must have been under a strong temptation to violate the sanctity of the grave in order to possess themselves of bodies which were believed to be endowed with magical virtue of the most tremendous potency.   In antiquity the safety of the state was often believed to depend on the possession of a talisman, which sometimes consisted of the bones of a king or hero.   Hence the graves of such persons were sometimes kept secret.[4] The violation of royal tombs by a conqueror was not a mere insult : it was a deadly blow struck at the prosperity of the kingdom.   Hence Ashurbanipal carried off to Assyria the bones of the kings of Elam, believing that thus he gave their shades no repose and deprived them of food and

The Egyptian kings probably opposed the custom and succeeded in abolishing it.

Precautions taken to preserve the bodies of kings from mutilation.

---

[1] Dudley Kidd, *Savage Childhood* (London, 1906), p. 291.

[2] Above, p. 97.

[3] Above, pp. 268 *sq.*

[4] See my notes on Pausanias, i. 28. 7 and viii. 47. 5 (vol. ii. pp. 366 *sq.*, vol. iv. pp. 433 *sq.*).

drink.[1]   The Moabites burned the bones of the king of Edom into lime.[2]   Lysimachus is said to have opened the graves of the kings of Epirus and scattered the bones of the dead.[3]

Graves of kings and chiefs in Africa kept secret.With savage and barbarous tribes in like manner it is not unusual to violate the sanctity of the tomb either for the purpose of wreaking vengeance on the dead or more commonly perhaps for the sake of gaining possession of the bones and converting them to magical uses.   Hence the Mpongwe kings of the Gaboon region in West Africa are buried secretly lest their heads should fall into the hands of men of another tribe, who would make a powerful fetish out of the brains.[4]   Again, in Togoland, West Africa, the kings of the Ho tribe are buried with great secrecy in the forest, and a false grave is made ostentatiously in the king's house. None but his personal retainers and a single daughter know where the king's real grave is.   The intention of this secret burial is to prevent enemies from digging up the corpse and cutting off the head.[5]   "The heads of important chiefs in the Calabar districts are usually cut off from the body on burial and kept secretly for fear the head, and thereby the spirit, of the dead chief, should be stolen from the town.   If it were stolen it would be not only a great advantage to its new possessor, but a great danger to the chief's old town, because he would know all the peculiar ju-ju relating to it. For each town has a peculiar one, kept exceedingly secret, in addition to the general ju-jus, and this secret one would then be in the hands of the new owners of the spirit."[6]   The graves of Basuto chiefs are kept secret lest certain more or less imaginary witches and wizards called *Baloi*, who haunt tombs, should get possession of the bones and work evil magic with them.[7]   In the Thonga tribe of South Africa,

[1] R. F. Harper, *Assyrian and Baby-lonian Literature* (New York, 1901), p. 116 ; C. Fossey, *La Magie Assyri-enne* (Paris, 1902), pp. 34 *sq.*

[2] Amos ii. 1.

[3] Pausanias, i. 9. 7 *sq.*

[4] P. B. du Chaillu, *Explorations and Adventures in Equatorial Africa* (London, 1861), pp. 18 *sq.*

[5] J. Spieth, *Die Ewe-Stämme* (Ber-lin, 1906), p. 107.

[6] Mary H. Kingsley, *Travels in West Africa* (London, 1897), pp. 449 *sq.*   In West African jargon the word ju-ju means fetish or magic.

[7] Father Porte, "Les reminiscences d'un missionnaire du Basutoland," *Missions Catholiques*, xxviii. (1896) pp. 311 *sq.*   As to the *Baloi*, see A. Merensky, *Beiträge zur Kenntniss Süd-Afrikas* (Berlin, 1875), pp. 138 *sq.* ; E. Gottschling, "The Bawenda,"

when a chief dies, he is buried secretly by night in a sacred wood, and few people know the place of the grave. With some clans of the tribe it is customary to level the mound over the grave so that no sign whatever remains to show where the body has been buried. This is said to be done lest enemies should exhume the corpse and cut off the ears, the diaphragm, and other parts in order to make powerful war-charms out of them.[1] By many tribes in Fiji "the burial-place of their chief is kept a profound secret, lest those whom he injured during his lifetime should revenge themselves by digging up and insulting or even eating his body. In some places the dead chief is buried in his own house, and armed warriors of his mother's kin keep watch night and day over his grave. After a time his bones are taken up and carried by night to some far-away inaccessible cave in the mountains, whose position is known only to a few trustworthy men. Ladders are constructed to enable them to reach the cave, and are taken down when the bones have been deposited there. Many frightful stories are told in connection with this custom, and it is certain that not even decomposition itself avails to baulk the last revenge of cannibals if they can find the grave. The very bones of the dead chief are not secure from the revenge of those whose friends he killed during his lifetime, or whom he otherwise so exasperated by the tyrannous exercise of his power as to fill their hearts with a deadly hate. In one instance within my own knowledge, when the hiding-place was discovered, the bones were taken away, scraped, and stewed down into a horrible hell-broth."[2] When a Melanesian dies who enjoyed a reputation for magical powers in his lifetime, his friends will sometimes hold a sham burial and keep the real grave secret for fear that men might come and dig up the skull and bones to make charms with them.[3]

Burial-place of chiefs in Fiji kept secret.

Graves of Melanesian magicians kept secret.

Journal of the Anthropological Institute, xxxv. (1905) p. 375. For these two references I have to thank Mr. E. S. Hartland.

[1] Henri A. Junod, *The Life of a South African Tribe* (Neuchâtel, 1912–1913), i. 387 *sq*

[2] Lorimer Fison, "Notes on Fijian Burial Customs," *Journal of the Anthropological Institute*, x. (1881) pp. 141 *sq*.

[3] R. H. Codrington, *The Melanesians* (Oxford, 1891), p. 269.

Beliefs and practices of this sort are by no means
confined to agricultural peoples.   Among the Koniags of
Alaska " in ancient times the pursuit of the whale was
accompanied by numerous superstitious observances kept a
secret by the hunters.   Lieutenant Davidof states that the
whalers preserved the bodies of brave or distinguished men
in secluded caves, and before proceeding upon a whale-hunt
would carry these dead bodies into a stream and then drink
of the water thus tainted.   One famous whaler of Kadiak
who desired to flatter Baranof, the first chief manager of the
Russian colonies, said to him, ' When you die I shall try to
steal your body,' intending thus to express his great respect
for Baranof.   On the occasion of the death of a whaler his
fellows would cut the body into pieces, each man taking
one of them for the purpose of rubbing his spear-heads
therewith.   These pieces were dried or otherwise preserved,
and were frequently taken into the canoes as talismans." [1]

To return to the human victims whose ashes the Egyptians
scattered with winnowing-fans,[2] the red hair of these unfortunates was probably significant.   If I am right, the custom of
sacrificing such persons was not a mere way of wreaking
a national spite on fair-haired foreigners, whom the black-
haired Egyptians of old, like the black-haired Chinese of
modern times, may have regarded as red-haired devils.   For
in Egypt the oxen which were sacrificed had also to be red ;
a single black or white hair found on the beast would have
disqualified it for the sacrifice.[3]   If, as I conjecture, these
human sacrifices were intended to promote the growth of
the crops — and the winnowing of their ashes seems to
support this view—red-haired victims-were perhaps selected
as best fitted to personate the spirit of the ruddy grain.   For
when a god is represented by a living person, it is natural
that the human representative should be chosen on the
ground of his supposed resemblance to the divine original.

---

[1] Ivan Petroff, *Report on the Population, Industries, and Resources of
Alaska*, p. 142.   The account seems to
be borrowed from H. J. Holmberg, who
adds that pains were taken to preserve
the flesh from decay, " because they
believed that their own life depended

on it."   See H. J. Holmberg, " Über
die Völker des russischen Amerika,"
Acta Societatis Scientiarum Fennicae,
iv. (Helsingfors, 1856) p. 391.

[2] Above, p. 97.

[3] Plutarch, *Isis et Osiris*, 31 ; Herodotus, ii. 38.

Hence the ancient Mexicans, conceiving the maize as a
personal being who went through the whole course of life
between seed-time and harvest, sacrificed new-born babes
when the maize was sown, older children when it had
sprouted, and so on till it was fully ripe, when they sacrificed old men.[1]   A name for Osiris was the "crop" or
"harvest";[2] and the ancients sometimes explained him as
a personification of the corn.[3]

§ 2. *Osiris a Tree-Spirit*

But Osiris was more than a spirit of the corn; he was
also a tree-spirit, and this may perhaps have been his
primitive character, since the worship of trees is naturally
older in the history of religion than the worship of the
cereals.   However that may have been, to an agricultural
people like the Egyptians, who depended almost wholly on
their crops, the corn-god was naturally a far more important

*Osiris as a
tree-spirit.*

---

[1] Herrera, quoted by A. Bastian,
Die Culturländer des alten Amerika
(Berlin, 1878), ii. 639; *id.*, *General
History of the vast Continent and
Islands of America*, translated by Capt.
J. Stevens (London, 1725-26), ii. 379
sq (whose version of the passage is
inadequate).   Compare Brasseur de
Bourbourg, *Histoire des nations civi-
isées du Mexique et de l'Amérique
Centrale* (Paris, 1857-59), i. 327, iii.
525.

[2] E. Lefébure, *Le mythe Osirien*
(Paris, 1874-75), p. 188.

[3] Firmicus Maternus, *De errore profanarum religionum*, 2, "*Defen-
sores eorum volunt addere physicam
rationem, frugum semina Osirim
dicentes esse, Isim terram, Tyfonem
calorem : et quia maturatae fruges
calore ad vitam hominum colliguntur
et divisae a terrae consortio separantur
et rursus adpropinquante hieme semi-
nantur, hanc volunt esse mortem
Osiridis, cum fruges recondunt, in-
ventionem vero, cum fruges genitali
terrae fomento conceptae annua rursus
coeperint procreatione generari.*"   Tertullian, *Adversus Marcionem*, i. 13,
"*Sic et Osiris quod semper sepelitur*

*et in vivido quaeritur et cum gaudio
invenitur, reciprocarum frugum et
vividorum elementorum et recidivi anni
fidem argumentantur.*"   Plutarch, *Isis
et Osiris*, 65, οὕτω δὲ καὶ τοῖς πολλοῖς
καὶ φορτικοῖς ἐπιχειρήσομεν, εἴτε ταῖς
καθ' ὥραν μεταβολαῖς τοῦ περιέχοντος
εἴτε ταῖς καρπῶν γενέσεσι καὶ σποραῖς
καὶ ἀρότοις χαίρουσι τὰ περὶ τοὺς θεοὺς
τούτους συνοικειοῦντες, καὶ λέγοντες
θάπτεσθαι μὲν Ὄσιριν ὅτε κρύπτεται τῇ
γῇ σπειρόμενος ὁ καρπός, αὖθις δ' ἀνα-
βιοῦσθαι καὶ ἀναφαίνεσθαι ὅτε βλασ-
τήσεως ἀρχή. Eusebius, *Praeparatio
Evangelii*, iii. 11. 31, ὁ δὲ Ὄσιρις παρ'
Αἰγυπτίοις τὴν κάρπιμον παρίστησι
δύναμιν, ἣν θρήνοις ἀπομειλίσσονται εἰς
γῆν ἀφανιζομένην ἐν τῷ σπόρῳ καὶ ὑφ'
ἡμῶν καταναλισκομένην εἰς τὰς τροφάς.
Athenagoras, *Supplicatio pro Christianis*, 22, pp. 112, 114 ed. J. C. T.
Otto, τὰ δὲ στοιχεῖα καὶ τὰ μόρια αὐτῶν
θεοποιοῦσιν, ἄλλοτε ἄλλα ὀνόματα αὐτοῖς
τιθέμενοι, τὴν μὲν τοῦ σίτου σποράν
Ὄσιριν (ὅθεν φασὶ μυστικῶς ἐπὶ τῇ
ἀνευρέσει τῶν μελῶν ἢ τῶν καρπῶν
ἐπιλεχθῆναι τῇ Ἰσίδι·   Εὑρήκαμεν,
συγχαίρομεν).   See also the passage of
Cornutus quoted above, vol. i. p. 229,
note [2].

personage than the tree-god, and attracted a larger share of their devotion.   The character of Osiris as a tree-spirit was represented very graphically in a ceremony described by Firmicus Maternus.[1]   A pine-tree having been cut down, the centre was hollowed out, and with the wood thus excavated an image of Osiris was made, which was then buried like a corpse in the hollow of the tree.   It is hard to imagine how the conception of a tree as tenanted by a personal being could be more plainly expressed.   The image of Osiris thus made was kept for a year and then burned, exactly as was done with the image of Attis which was attached to the pine-tree.[2]   The ceremony of cutting the tree, as described by Firmicus Maternus, appears to be alluded to by Plutarch.[3] It was probably the ritual counterpart of the mythical discovery of the body of Osiris enclosed in the *erica*-tree.[4]

His image enclosed in a pine-tree.

Now we know from the monuments that at Busiris, Memphis, and elsewhere the great festival of Osiris closed on the thirtieth of Khoiak with the setting up of a remarkable pillar known as the *tatu*, *tat*, *tet*, *dad*, or *ded*.   This was a column with four or five cross-bars, like superposed capitals, at the top.   The whole roughly resembled a telegraph-post with the cross-pieces which support the wires.   Sometimes on the monuments a human form is given to the pillar by carving a grotesque face on it, robing the lower part, crowning the top with the symbols of Osiris, and adding two arms which hold two other characteristic emblems of the god, the crook and the scourge or flail.   On a Theban tomb the king himself, assisted by his relations and a priest, is represented hauling at the ropes by which the pillar is being raised, while the queen looks on and her sixteen daughters accompany the ceremony with the music of rattles and sistrums. Again, in the hall of the Osirian mysteries at Abydos the King Sety I. and the goddess Isis are depicted raising the column between them.   In Egyptian theology the pillar was interpreted as the backbone of Osiris, and whatever its meaning

The setting up of the *ded* pillar at the great festival of Osiris in the month of Khoiak.

---

[1] *De errore profanarum religionum*, 27.

[2] See above, vol. i. pp. 267, 277.

[3] Plutarch, *Isis et Osiris*, 21, αἰνῷ δὲ τομὴν ξύλου καὶ σχίσιν λίνου καὶ χοὰς

χεομένας, διὰ τὸ πολλὰ τῶν μυστικῶν ἀναμεμίχθαι τούτοις.   Again, *ibid.* 42, τὸ δὲ ξύλον ἐν ταῖς λεγομέναις Ὀσίριδος ταφαῖς τέμνοντες κατασκευάζουσι λάρνακε μηνοειδῆ.

[4] See above, p. 9.

may have been, it was one of the holiest symbols of the national religion. It might very well be a conventional way of representing a tree stripped of its leaves ; and if Osiris was a tree-spirit, the bare trunk and branches might naturally be described as his backbone. The setting up of the column would thus, as several modern scholars believe, shadow forth the resurrection of the god, and the importance of the occasion would explain and justify the prominent part which the king appears to have taken in the ceremony.[1] It is to be noted that in the myth of Osiris the *erica*-tree which shot up and enclosed his dead body, was cut down by a king and turned by him into a pillar of his house.[2] We can hardly doubt, therefore, that this incident of the legend was supposed to be dramatically set forth in the erection of the *ded* column by the king. Like the similar custom of cutting a pine-tree and fastening an image to it in the rites of Attis, the ceremony may have belonged to that class of customs of which the bringing· in of the May-pole is among the most familiar. The association of the king and queen of Egypt with the *ded* pillar reminds us of the association of a King and Queen of May with the May-pole.[3] The resemblance may be more than superficial.

The setting up of the pillar may have been an emblem of the god's resurrection.

[1] As to the *tet* or *ded* pillar and its erection at the festival see H. Brugsch in *Zeitschrift für ägyptische Sprache und Alterthumskunde*, 1881, pp. 84, 96 ; *id.*, *Religion und Mythologie der alten Aegypter*, p. 618 ; A. Erman, *Aegypten und aegyptisches Leben im Altertum*, pp. 377 *sq.* ; *id.*, *Die ägyptische Religion*,[2] pp. 22, 64 ; C. P. Tiele, *History of the Egyptian Religion* (London, 1882), pp. 46 *sq.* ; Sir J. Gardiner Wilkinson, *Manners and Customs of the Ancient Egyptians* (London, 1878), iii. pp. 67, note [3], and 82 ; A. Wiedemann, *Religion of the Ancient Egyptians*, pp. 289 *sq.* ; G. Maspero, *Histoire ancienne des Peuples de l' Orient Classique*, i. 130 *sq.* ; A. Moret, *Du caractère religieux de la royauté Pharaonique*, p. 153, note[1] ; *id.*, *Mystères Égyptiens*, pp. 12-16 ; E. A. Wallis Budge, *The Gods of the Egyptians*, ii. 122, 124, *sq.* ; *id. Osiris and the Egyptian Resurrection*, i. 6, 37, 48,

51 *sqq.* ; Miss Margaret A. Murray, *The Osireion at Abydos*, pp. 27, 28 ; Ed. Meyer, *Geschichte des Altertums*,[2] i. 2, p. 70. In a letter to me (dated 8th December, 1910) my colleague Professor P. E. Newberry tells me that he believes Osiris to have been originally a cedar-tree god imported into Egypt from the Lebanon, and he regards the *ded* pillar as a lopped cedar-tree. The flail, as a symbol of Osiris, he believes to be the instrument used to collect incense: A similar flail is used by peasants in Crete to extract the ladanum gum from the shrubs. See P. de Tournefort, *Relation d'un Voyage du Levant* (Amsterdam, 1718), i. 29, with the plate. For this reference I am indebted to Professor Newberry.

[2] Plutarch, *Isis et Osiris*, 15. See above, p. 9.

[3] *The Magic Art and the Evolution of Kings*, ii. 88-90.

In the hall of Osiris at Denderah the coffin containing the hawk-headed mummy of the god is clearly depicted as enclosed within a tree, apparently a conifer, the trunk and branches of which are seen above and below the coffin.[1] The scene thus corresponds closely both to the myth and to the ceremony described by Firmicus Maternus. In another scene at Denderah a tree of the same sort is represented growing between the dead and the reviving Osiris, as if on purpose to indicate that the tree was the symbol of the divine resurrection.[2] A pine-cone often appears on the monuments as an offering presented to Osiris, and a manuscript of the Louvre speaks of the cedar as sprung from him.[3] The sycamore and the tamarisk were also his trees. In inscriptions he is spoken of as residing in them;[4] and in tombs his mother Nut is often portrayed standing in the midst of a sycamore-tree and pouring a libation for the benefit of the dead.[5] In one of the Pyramid Texts we read, " Hail to thee, Sycamore, which enclosest the god " [6] and in certain temples the statue of Osiris used to be placed for seven days upon branches of sycamores. The explanation appended in the sacred texts declares that the placing of the image on the tree was intended to recall the seven months passed by Osiris in the womb of his mother Nut, the goddess of the sycamore.[7] The rite recalls the story that Adonis was born after ten months' gestation from a myrrh-tree.[8] Further, in a sepulchre at How (Diospolis Parva) a tamarisk is depicted overshadowing the tomb of Osiris, while a bird is perched among the branches with the significant legend "the soul of Osiris," [9]

---

[1] A. Mariette-Bey, *Dendérah*, iv. pl. 66.

[2] A. Mariette-Bey, *Dendérah*, iv. pl. 72. Compare E. Lefébure, *Le mythe Osirien*, pp. 194, 196, who regards the tree as a conifer. But it is perhaps a tamarisk.

[3] E. Lefébure, *op. cit.* pp. 195, 197.

[4] S. Birch, in Sir J. G. Wilkinson's *Manners and Customs of the Ancient Egyptians* (London, 1878), iii. 84.

[5] Sir J. G. Wilkinson; *op. cit.* iii. 62-64 ; E. A. Wallis Budge, *The Gods of the Egyptians*, ii. 106 *sq.* ; G.

Maspero, *Histoire ancienne des Peuples de l'Orient Classique*, i. 185.

[6] J. H. Breasted, *Development of Religion and Thought in Ancient Egypt* (London, 1912), p. 28.

[7] A. Moret, *Kings and Gods of Egypt* (New York and London, 1912), p. 83.

[8] Above, vol. i. pp. 227 *sq.*

[9] Sir J. G. Wilkinson, *op. cit.* iii. 349 *sq.* ; A. Erman, *Aegypten und aegyptisches Leben im Altertum*, p. 368 ; H. Brugsch, *Religion und Mythologie der alten Aegypter*, p. 621.

showing that the spirit of the dead god was believed to haunt his sacred tree.[1] Again, in the series of sculptures which illustrate the mystic history of Osiris in the great temple of Isis at Philae, a tamarisk is figured with two men pouring water on it. The accompanying inscription leaves no doubt, says Brugsch, that the verdure of the earth was believed to be connected with the verdure of the tree, and that the sculpture refers to the grave of Osiris at Philae, of which Plutarch tells us that it was overshadowed by a *methide* plant, taller than any olive-tree. This sculpture, it may be observed, occurs in the same chamber in which the god is represented as a corpse with ears of corn springing from him.[2] In inscriptions he is referred to as "the one in the tree," "the solitary one in the acacia," and so forth.[3] On the monuments he sometimes appears as a mummy covered with a tree or with plants ;[4] and trees are represented growing from his grave.[5]

It accords with the character of Osiris as a tree-spirit that his worshippers were forbidden to injure fruit-trees, and with his character as a god of vegetation in general that they were not allowed to stop up wells of water, which are so important for the irrigation of hot southern lands.[6]

Osiris in relation to fruit-trees, wells, the vine, and ivy.

[1] We may compare a belief of some of the Californian Indians that the owl is the guardian spirit and deity of the " California big tree," and that it is equally unlucky to fell the tree or to shoot the bird. See S. Powers, *Tribes of California* (Washington, 1877), p. 398. When a Maori priest desires to protect the life or soul (*hau*) of a tree against the insidious arts of magicians, he sets a bird-snare in the tree, and the first bird caught in the snare, or its right wing, embodies the life or soul of the tree. Accordingly the priest recites appropriate spells over the bird or its wing and hides it away in the forest. After that no evil-disposed magician can hurt the tree, since its life or soul is not in it but hidden away in the forest. See Elsdon Best, " Spiritual Concepts of the Maori," *Journal of the Polynesian Society*, ix. (1900) p. 195. Thus the bird or its wing is the depository of the external

soul of the tree. Compare *Balder the Beautiful*, ii. 95 *sqq.*

[2] Sir J. G. Wilkinson, *op. cit.* iii. 349 *sq.* ; H. Brugsch, *Religion und Mythologie der alten Aegypter*, p. 621 ; R. V. Lanzone, *Dizionario di Mitologia Egizia*, tav. cclxiii. ; Plutarch, *Isis et Osiris*, 20. In this passage of Plutarch it has been proposed by G. Parthey to read μυρίκης (tamarisk) for μηθίδης (*methide*), and the conjecture appears to be accepted by Wilkinson, *loc. cit.*

[3] E. Lefébure, *Le mythe Osirien*, p. 191.

[4] E. Lefébure, *op. cit.* p. 188.

[5] R. V. Lanzone, *Dizionario di Mitologia Egizia*, tav. ccciv. ; G. Maspero, *Histoire ancienne des Peuples de l'Orient Classique*, ii. 570, fig.

[6] Plutarch, *Isis et Osiris*, 35. One of the points in which the myths of Isis and Demeter agree is that both goddesses in the search for the loved and lost one are said to have sat down,

According to one legend, he taught men to train the vine to poles, to prune its superfluous foliage, and to extract the juice of the grape.[1] In the papyrus of Nebseni, written about 1550 B.C., Osiris is depicted sitting in a shrine, from the roof of which hang clusters of grapes ;[2] and in the papyrus of the royal scribe Nekht we see the god enthroned in front of a pool, from the banks of which a luxuriant vine, with many bunches of grapes, grows towards the green face of the seated deity.[3] The ivy was sacred to him, and was called his plant because it is always green.[4]

§ 3. *Osiris a God of Fertility*

Osiris
perhaps
conceived
as a god of
fertility in
general.

As a god of vegetation Osiris was naturally conceived as a god of creative energy in general, since men at a certain stage of evolution fail to distinguish between the reproductive powers of animals and of plants. Hence a striking feature in his worship was the coarse but expressive symbolism by which this aspect of his nature was presented to the eye not merely of the initiated but of the multitude. At his festival women used to go about the villages singing songs in his praise and carrying obscene images of him which they set in motion by means of strings.[5] The custom was probably a charm to ensure the growth of the crops. A similar image of him, decked with all the fruits of the earth, is said to have stood in a temple before a figure of Isis,[6] and in the chambers dedicated to him at Philae the dead god is portrayed lying on his bier in an attitude which indicates in the plainest way that even in death his generative virtue was not extinct but only suspended, ready to prove a source of life and fertility to the world when the opportunity should offer.[7] Hymns

---

sad at heart and weary, on the edge of a well. Hence those who had been initiated at Eleusis were forbidden to sit on a well. See Plutarch, *Isis et Osiris*, 15 ; Homer, *Hymn to Demeter*, 98 *sq.* ; Pausanias, i. 39. 1 ; Apollodorus, *Bibliotheca*, i. 5. 1 ; Nicander, *Theriaca*, 486 ; Clement of Alexandria, *Protrept.* ii. 20, p. 16 ed. Potter.

[1] Tibullus, i. 7. 33-36 ; Diodorus Siculus, i. 17. 1, i. 20. 4.

[2] E. A. Wallis Budge, *Osiris and the Egyptian Resurrection*, i. 38, 39.

[3] E. A. Wallis Budge, *op. cit.* i. 19, 45, with frontispiece.

[4] Diodorus Siculus, i. 17. 4 *sq.*

[5] Herodotus, ii. 48 ; Plutarch, *Isis et Osiris*, 12, 18, 36, 51 ; Diodorus Siculus, i. 21. 5, i. 22. 6 *sq.*, iv. 6. 3.

[6] Hippolytus, *Refutatio omnium haeresium*, v. 7, p. 144 ed. Duncker and Schneidewin.

[7] A. Mariette-Bey, *Dendérah*, iv. plates 66, 68, 69, 70, 88, 89, 90. Com-

addressed to Osiris contain allusions to this important side of his nature. In one of them it is said that the world waxes green in triumph through him ; and another declares, " Thou art the father and mother of mankind, they live on thy breath, they subsist on the flesh of thy body." [1] We may conjecture that in this paternal aspect he was supposed, like other gods of fertility, to bless men and women with offspring, and that the processions at his festival were intended to promote this object as well as to quicken the seed in the ground. It would be to misjudge ancient religion to denounce as lewd and profligate the emblems and the ceremonies which the Egyptians employed for the purpose of giving effect to this conception of the divine power. The ends which they proposed to themselves in these rites were natural and laudable ; only the means they adopted to compass them were mistaken. A similar fallacy induced the Greeks to adopt a like symbolism in their Dionysiac festivals, and the superficial but striking resemblance thus produced between the two religions has perhaps more than anything else misled inquirers, both ancient and modern, into identifying worships which, though certainly akin in nature, are perfectly distinct and independent in origin.[2]

§ 4. *Osiris a God of the Dead*

We have seen that in one of his aspects Osiris was the ruler and judge of the dead.[3] To a people like the Egyptians, who not only believed in a life beyond the grave but actually spent much of their time, labour, and money in preparing for it, this office of the god must have appeared hardly, if at all, less important than his function of making the earth to bring forth its fruits in due season. We may assume that in the faith of his worshippers the two provinces of the

As god of the corn Osiris came to be viewed as the god of the resurrection.

---

pare R. V. Lanzone, *Dizionario di Mitologia Egizia*, tavv. cclxxi., cclxxii., cclxxvi., cclxxxv., cclxxxvi., cclxxxvii., cclxxxix., ccxc. ; E. A. Wallis Budge, *The Gods of the Egyptians*, ii. 132, 136, 137.

[1] Miss Margaret A. Murray, *The Osireion at Abydos*, p. 27.

[2] That the Greek Dionysus was

nothing but a slightly disguised form of the Egyptian Osiris has been held by Herodotus in ancient and by Mr. P. Foucart in modern times. See Herodotus, ii. 49 ; P. Foucart, *Le culte de Dionysos en Attique* (Paris, 1904) (*Mémoires de l'Académie des Inscriptions et Belles-Lettres*, xxxvii.).

[3] Above, pp. 13 *sq.*

god were intimately connected. In laying their dead in the grave they committed them to his keeping who could raise them from the dust to life eternal, even as he caused the seed to spring from the ground. Of that faith the corn-stuffed effigies of Osiris found in Egyptian tombs furnish an eloquent and unequivocal testimony.[1] They were at once an emblem and an instrument of resurrection. Thus from the sprouting of the grain the ancient Egyptians drew an augury of human immortality. They are not the only people who have built the same towering hopes on the same slender foundation. "Thou fool, that which thou sowest, thou sowest not that body that shall be, but bare grain, it may chance of wheat, or of some other grain : but God giveth it a body as it hath pleased him, and to every seed his own body. So also is the resurrection of the dead. It is sown in corruption ; it is raised in incorruption : it is sown in weakness ; it is raised in power : it is sown a natural body ; it is raised a spiritual body." [2]

Great popularity of the worship of Osiris.

A god who thus fed his people with his own broken body in this life, and who held out to them a promise of a blissful eternity in a better world hereafter, naturally reigned supreme in their affections. We need not wonder, therefore, that in Egypt the worship of the other gods was overshadowed by that of Osiris, and that while they were revered each in his own district, he and his divine partner Isis were adored in all.[3]

---

[1] Above, pp. 90 *sq.*

[2] 1 Corinthians xv. 36-38, 42-44.

[c] Herodotus, ii. 42. Compare E.

A. Wallis Budge, *The Gods of the Egyptians*, ii. 115 *sq.*, 203 *sq.* ; *id.*, *Osiris and the Egyptian Resurrection,* i. 22 *sq.*

CHAPTER VI

ISIS

THE original meaning of the goddess Isis is still more
difficult to determine than that of her brother and husband
Osiris. Her attributes and epithets were so numerous that
in the hieroglyphics she is called " the many-named," " the
thousand-named," and in Greek inscriptions " the myriad-
named." [1] The late eminent Dutch scholar C. P. Tiele
confessed candidly that " it is now impossible to tell precisely to what natural phenomena the character of Isis at
first referred." Yet he adds, " Originally she was a goddess
of fecundity." [2] Similarly Dr. Budge writes that " Isis was
the great and beneficent goddess and mother, whose influence
and love pervaded all heaven and earth and the abode of
the dead, and she was the personification of the great
feminine, creative power which conceived, and brought forth
every living creature and thing, from the gods in heaven to
man on the earth, and to the insect on the ground ; what
she brought forth she protected, and cared for, and fed, and
nourished, and she employed her life in using her power
graciously and successfully, not only in creating new beings
but in restoring those that were dead. She was, besides
these things, the highest type of a faithful and loving wife

---

[1] H. Brugsch, *Religion und Mythologie der alten Aegypter*, p. 645 ; W.
Dittenberger, *Orientis Graeci Inscriptiones Selectae*, vol. ii. p. 433, No.
695 ; *Corpus Inscriptionum Graecarum*,
iii. p. 1232, No. 4941. Compare H.
Dessau, *Inscriptiones Latinae Selectae*,
vol. ii. Pars i. p. 179, No. 4376 A.

In Egyptian her name is *Hest* or *Ast*,
but the derivation and meaning of the
name are unknown. See A. Wiedemann, *The Religion of the Ancient
Egyptians*, pp. 218 *sq.*

[2] C. P. Tiele, *History of Egyptian
Religion* (London, 1882), p. 57.

and mother, and it was in this capacity that the Egyptians honoured and worshipped her most."[1]

How Isis resembled yet differed from the Mother Goddesses of Asia.

Thus in her character of a goddess of fecundity Isis answered to the great mother goddesses of Asia, though she differed from them in the chastity and fidelity of her conjugal life ; for while they were unmarried and dissolute, she had a husband and was a true wife to him as well as an affectionate mother to their son. Hence her beautiful Madonna-like figure reflects a more refined state of society and of morals than the coarse, sensual, cruel figures of Astarte, Anaitis, Cybele, and the rest of that crew. A clear trace, indeed, of an ethical standard very different from our own lingers in her double relation of sister and wife to Osiris ; but in most other respects she is rather late than primitive, the full-blown flower rather than the seed of a long religious development. The attributes ascribed to her were too various to be all her own. They were graces borrowed from many lesser deities, sweets rifled from a thousand humbler plants to feed the honey of her superb efflorescence. Yet in her complex nature it is perhaps still possible to detect the original nucleus round which by a slow process of accretion the other elements gathered.

Isis perhaps originally a goddess of the corn.

For if her brother and husband Osiris was in one of his aspects the corn-god, as we have seen reason to believe, she must surely have been the corn-goddess. There are at least some grounds for thinking so. For if we may trust Diodorus Siculus, whose authority appears to have been the Egyptian historian Manetho, the discovery of wheat and barley was attributed to Isis, and at her festivals stalks of these grains were carried in procession to commemorate the boon she had conferred on men.[2] A further detail is added by Augustine. He says that Isis made the discovery of barley at the moment when she was sacrificing to the common ancestors of her husband and herself, all of whom had been kings, and that she showed the newly discovered ears of barley to Osiris and his councillor Thoth or Mercury, as Roman writers called him. That is why,

[1] E. A. Wallis Budge, *The Gods of the Egyptians*, ii. 203 *sq.*

[2] Diodorus Siculus, i. 14. 1 *sq.* Eusebius (*Praeparatio Evangelii*, iii. 3) quotes from Diodorus a long passage on the early religion of Egypt, prefacing it with the remark that Diodorus's account of the subject was more concise than that of Manetho.

adds Augustine, they identify Isis with Ceres.[1] Further,
at harvest-time, when the Egyptian reapers had cut the first
stalks, they laid them down and beat their breasts, wailing
and calling upon Isis.[2] The custom has been already explained as a lament for the corn-spirit slain under the sickle.[3]
Amongst the epithets by which Isis is designated in the inscriptions are " Creatress of green things," " Green goddess,
whose green colour is like unto the greenness of the earth,"
" Lady of Bread," " Lady of Beer," " Lady of Abundance." [4]
According to Brugsch she is " not only the creatress of the
fresh verdure of vegetation which covers the earth, but is
actually the green corn-field itself, which is personified as a
goddess." [5] This is confirmed by her epithet *Sochit* or *Sochet*,
meaning " a corn-field," a sense which the word still retains
in Coptic.[6] The Greeks conceived of Isis as a corn-goddess,
for they identified her with Demeter.[7] In a Greek epigram
she is described as " she who has given birth to the fruits of
the earth," and " the mother of the ears of corn " ; [8] and in
a hymn composed in her honour she speaks of herself as
" queen of the wheat-field," and is described as " charged with
the care of the fruitful furrow's wheat-rich path." [9] Accordingly, Greek or Roman artists often represented her with ears
of corn on her head or in her hand.[10]

Such, we may suppose, was Isis in the olden time, a
rustic Corn-Mother adored with uncouth rites by Egyptian
swains. But the homely features of the clownish goddess
could hardly be traced in the refined, the saintly form which,
spiritualized by ages of religious evolution, she presented to
her worshippers of after days as the true wife, the tender

Refinement and spirit-ualization of Isis in later times the popu-larity of her worship in the Roman empire.

[1] Augustine, *De civitate Dei*, viii.
27. Tertullian says that Isis wore a
wreath of the corn she had discovered
(*De corona*, 7).

[2] Diodorus Siculus, i. 14. 2.

[3] See above, p. 45, and vol. i. p. 232.

[4] H. Brugsch, *Religion und Mytho-
logie der alten Aegypter*, p. 647 ;
E. A. Wallis Budge, *Osiris and the
Egyptian Resurrection*, ii. 277.

[5] H. Brugsch, *op. cit.* p. 649. Compare E. A. Wallis Budge, *The Gods of
the Egyptians*, ii. 216.

[6] H. Brugsch, *loc. cit.*

[7] Herodotus, ii. 59, 156 ; Diodorus
Siculus, i. 13, 25, 96 ; Apollodorus,
Bibliotheca, ii. 1. 3 ; J. Tzetzes, *Schol.
on Lycophron*, 212. See further W.
Drexler, *s.v.* "Isis," in W. H. Ros-
cher's *Lexikon der griech. und röm.
Mythologie*, ii. 443 *sq.*

[8] *Anthologia Planudea*, cclxiv. 1.

[9] *Epigrammata Graeca ex lapidibus
conlecta*, ed. G. Kaibel (Berlin, 1878),
No. 1028, pp. 437 *sq.* ; *Orphica*, ed.
E. Abel (Leipsic and Prague, 1885),
pp. 295 *sqq.*

[10] W. Drexler, *op. cit.* ii. 448 *sqq.*

mother, the beneficent queen of nature, encircled with the nimbus of moral purity, of immemorial and mysterious sanctity. Thus chastened and transfigured she won many hearts far beyond the boundaries of her native land. In that welter of religions which accompanied the decline of national life in antiquity her worship was one of the most popular at Rome and throughout the empire. Some of the Roman emperors themselves were openly addicted to it.[1] And however the religion of Isis may, like any other, have been often worn as a cloak by men and women of loose life, her rites appear on the whole to have been honourably distinguished by a dignity and composure, a solemnity and decorum well fitted to soothe the troubled mind, to ease the burdened heart. They appealed therefore to gentle spirits, and above all to women, whom the bloody and licentious rites of other Oriental goddesses only shocked and repelled. We need not wonder, then, that in a period of decadence, when traditional faiths were shaken, when systems clashed, when men's minds were disquieted, when the fabric of empire itself, once deemed eternal, began to show ominous rents and fissures, the serene figure of Isis with her spiritual calm, her gracious promise of immortality, should have appeared to many like a star in a stormy sky, and should have roused in their breasts a rapture of devotion not unlike that which was paid in the Middle Ages to the Virgin Mary. Indeed her stately ritual, with its shaven and tonsured priests, its matins and vespers, its tinkling music, its baptism and aspersions of holy water, its solemn processions, its jewelled images of the Mother of God, presented many points of similarity to the pomps and ceremonies of Catholicism.[2] The resemblance need not be purely acci-

Resemblance of Isis to the Madonna.

---

[1] Otho often celebrated, or at least attended, the rites of Isis, clad in a linen garment (Suetonius, *Otho*, 12). Commodus did the same, with shaven head, carrying the effigy of Anubis. See Lampridius, *Commodus*, 9; Spartianus, *Pescennius Niger*, 6; *id.*, *Caracallus*, 9.

[2] L. Preller, *Römische Mythologie*[3] (Berlin, 1881–1883), ii. 373-385; J. Marquardt, *Römische Staatsverwaltung* (Leipsic, 1885), iii.[2] 77-81; E. Renan, *Marc-Aurèle et la fin du Monde Antique* (Paris, 1882), pp. 570 *sqq.*; J. Reville, *La religion romaine à Rome sous les Sévères* (Paris, 1886), pp. 54-61; G. Lafaye, *Histoire du culte des divinités d'Alexandrie* (Paris, 1884); E. Meyer and W. Drexler, *s.v.* "Isis," in W. H. Roscher's *Lexikon der griech. und röm. Mythologie*, ii. 360 *sqq.*; S. Dill, *Roman Society in the Last Century of the Western Empire*[2] (London, 1899), pp. 79 *sq.*, 85 *sqq.*; *id.*, *Roman Society*

dental.   Ancient Egypt may have contributed its share
to the gorgeous symbolism of the Catholic Church as well
as to the pale abstractions of her theology.[1]   Certainly in
art the figure of Isis suckling the infant Horus is so like
that of the Madonna and child that it has sometimes
received the adoration of ignorant Christians.[2]   And to
Isis in her later character of patroness of mariners the
Virgin Mary perhaps owes her beautiful epithet of *Stella
Maris*, " Star of the Sea," under which she is adored by
tempest-tossed sailors.[3]   The attributes of a marine deity
may have been bestowed on Isis by the sea-faring Greeks
of Alexandria.   They are quite foreign to her original
character and to the habits of the Egyptians, who had no
love of the sea.[4]   On this hypothesis Sirius, the bright star
of Isis, which on July mornings rises from the glassy waves
of the eastern Mediterranean, a harbinger of halcyon weather
to mariners, was the true *Stella Maris*, " the Star of the
Sea."

---

from Nero to Marcus Aurelius (London, 1904), pp. 560 *sqq*. The chief passage on the worship of Isis in the West is the eleventh book of Apuleius's *Metamorphoses*.   On the reputation which the goddess enjoyed as a healer of the sick see Diodorus Siculus, i. 25 ; W. Drexler, *op. cit.* ii. 521 *sqq*. The divine partner of Isis in later times, especially outside of Egypt, was Serapis, that is Osiris-Apis (*Aśar-Hāpi*), the sacred Apis bull of Memphis, identified after death with Osiris.   His oldest sanctuary was at Memphis (Pausanias, i. 18. 4), and there was one at Babylon in the time of Alexander the Great (Plutarch, *Alexander*, 76 ; Arrian, *Anabasis*, vii. 26).   Ptolemy I. or II. built a great and famous temple in his honour at Alexandria, where he set up an image of the god which was commonly said to have been imported from Sinope in Pontus.   See Tacitus, *Histor.* iv. 83 *sq.*; Plutarch, *Isis et Osiris*, 27-29 ; Clement of Alexandria, *Protrept.* iv. 48, p. 42 ed. Potter.   In after ages the institution of the worship of Serapis

was attributed to this Ptolemy, but all that the politic Macedonian monarch appears to have done was to assimilate the Egyptian Osiris to the Greek Pluto, and so to set up a god whom Egyptians and Greeks could unite in worshipping. Serapis gradually assumed the attributes of Aesculapius, the Greek god of healing, in addition to those of Pluto, the Greek god of the dead. See G. Lafaye, *Histoire du culte des divinités d'Alexandrie*, pp. 16 *sqq.* ; A. Wiedemann, *Herodots zweites Buch*, p. 589 ; E. A. Wallis Budge, *The Gods of the Egyptians*, ii. 195 *sqq.* ; A. Erman, *Die ägyptische Religion*,[2] pp. 237 *sq.*

[1] The resemblance of Isis to the Virgin Mary has often been pointed out.   See W. Drexler, *s.v.* " Isis," in W. H. Roscher's *Lexikon der griech. und röm. Mythologie*, ii. 428 *sqq.*

[2] W. Drexler, *op. cit.* ii. 430 *sq.*

[3] Th. Trede, *Das Heidentum in der römischen Kirche* (Gotha, 1889–1891), iii. 144 *sq.*

[4] On this later aspect of Isis see W. Drexler, *op. cit.* ii. 474 *sqq.*

CHAPTER VII

OSIRIS AND THE SUN

OSIRIS has been sometimes interpreted as the sun-god; and in modern times this view has been held by so many distinguished writers that it deserves a brief examination. If we inquire on what evidence Osiris has been identified with the sun or the sun-god, it will be found on analysis to be minute in quantity and dubious, where it is not absolutely worthless, in quality. The diligent Jablonski, the first modern scholar to collect and sift the testimony of classical writers on Egyptian religion, says that it can be shown in many ways that Osiris is the sun, and that he could produce a cloud of witnesses to prove it, but that it is needless to do so, since no learned man is ignorant of the fact.[1] Of the writers whom he condescends to quote, the only two who expressly identify Osiris with the sun are Diodorus and Macrobius. The passage in Diodorus runs thus:[2] "It is said that the aboriginal inhabitants of Egypt, looking up to the sky, and smitten with awe and wonder at the nature of the universe, supposed that there were two gods, eternal and primaeval, the sun and the moon, of whom they named the sun Osiris and the moon Isis." Even if Diodorus's authority for this statement is Manetho, as there is some ground for believing,[3] little or no weight can be attached to it. For it is plainly a philosophical, and therefore a late, explanation of the first beginnings of Egyptian religion, reminding us of Kant's familiar saying about the starry heavens and the moral law rather than of the

Marginal note: Osiris interpreted as the sun by many modern writers.

[1] P. E. Jablonski, *Pantheon Aegyptiorum* (Frankfort, 1750–1752), i. 125 *sq.*

[2] Diodorus Siculus, i. 11. 1.

[3] See p. 116, note [2].

rude traditions of a primitive people. Jablonski's second
authority, Macrobius, is no better, but rather worse. For
Macrobius was the father of that large family of mythologists who resolve all or most gods into the sun. According to him Mercury was the sun, Mars was the sun, Janus
was the sun, Saturn was the sun, so was Jupiter, also
Nemesis, likewise Pan, and so on through a great part of
the pantheon.[1] It was natural, therefore, that he should
identify Osiris with the sun,[2] but his reasons for doing so
are exceedingly slight. He refers to the ceremonies of
alternate lamentation and joy as if they reflected the
vicissitudes of the great luminary in his course through the
sky. Further, he argues that Osiris must be the sun
because an eye was one of his symbols. It is true that
an eye was a symbol of Osiris,[3] and it is also true that the
sun was often called 'the eye of Horus'";[4] yet the coincidence hardly suffices to establish the identity of the two
deities. The opinion that Osiris was the sun is also
mentioned, but not accepted, by Plutarch,[5] and it is referred
to by Firmicus Maternus.[6]

Amongst modern scholars, Lepsius, in identifying Osiris
with the sun, appears to rely mainly on the passage of
Diodorus already quoted. But the monuments, he adds,
also show " that down to a late time Osiris was sometimes
conceived as *Ra*. In this quality he is named *Osiris-Ra*

The later
identifica-
tion of
Osiris with
Ra, the
sun-god,
does not

---

[1] See Macrobius, *Saturnalia*, bk. i.

[2] *Saturn*. i. 21. 11.

[3] Plutarch, *Isis et Osiris*, 10 and
51 ; Sir J. G. Wilkinson, *Manners
and Customs of the Ancient Egyptians*
(London, 1878), iii. 353 ; R. V.
Lanzone, *Dizionario di Mitologia
Egizia*, pp. 782 *sq.* ; E. A. Wallis
Budge, *The Gods of the Egyptians*,
ii. 113 *sq.* ; J. H. Breasted, *Development of Religion and Thought in
Ancient Egypt*, pp. 11 *sq.* Strictly
speaking, the eye was the eye of Horus,
which the dutiful son sacrificed in
behalf of his father Osiris. " This act
of filial devotion, preserved to us in
the Pyramid Texts, made the already
sacred Horus-eye doubly revered in
the tradition and feeling of the
Egyptians. It became the symbol
of all sacrifice ; every gift or offer-

ing might be called a 'Horus-eye,'
especially if offered to the dead. Excepting the sacred beetle, or scarab,
it became the commonest and the
most revered symbol known to
Egyptian religion, and the myriads
of eyes, wrought in blue or green
glaze, or even cut from costly stone,
which fill our museum collections, and
are brought home by thousands by the
modern tourist, are survivals of this
ancient story of Horus and his devotion to his father" (J. H. Breasted,
op. cit. p. 31).

[4] E. A. Wallis Budge, *The Gods of
the Egyptians*, i. 467 ; A. Erman,
Die ägyptische Religion,[2] p. 8.

[5] *Isis et Osiris*, 52.

[6] *De errore profanarum religionum*,
8.

prove that
Osiris was
originally
the sun.

even in the 'Book of the Dead,' and Isis is often called 'the royal consort of Ra.'"[1] That Ra was both the physical sun and the sun-god is undisputed; but with every deference for the authority of so great a scholar as Lepsius, we may doubt whether the identification of Osiris with Ra can be accepted as proof that Osiris was originally the sun.

Such
identifica-
tions
sprang
from
attempts to
unify and
amalga-
mate the
many
local cults
of Egypt.

For the religion of ancient Egypt[2] may be described as a confederacy of local cults which, while maintaining against each other a certain measure of jealous and even hostile independence, were yet constantly subjected to the fusing and amalgamating influence of political centralization and philosophic thought. The history of the religion appears to have largely consisted of a struggle between these opposite forces or tendencies. On the one side there was the conservative tendency to preserve the local cults with all their distinctive features, fresh, sharp, and crisp as they had been handed down from an immemorial past. On the other side there was the progressive tendency, favoured by the gradual fusion of the people under a powerful central government, first to dull the edge of these provincial distinctions, and finally to break them down completely and merge them in a single national religion. The conservative party probably mustered in its ranks the great bulk of the people, their prejudices and affections being warmly enlisted in favour of the local deity, with whose temple and rites they had been familiar from childhood; and the popular dislike of change, based on the endearing effect of old association, must have been strongly reinforced by the less disinterested opposition of the local clergy, whose material interests would necessarily suffer with any decay of their shrines. On the other hand the kings, whose power and glory rose with the political and ecclesiastical consolidation of the realm, were the natural champions of religious unity; and their efforts would be seconded by the refined and

[1] Lepsius, "Über den ersten ägyptischen Götterkreis und seine geschichtlich-mythologische Entstehung," in *Abhandlungen der königlichen Akademie der Wissenschaften zu Berlin*, 1851, pp. 194 *sq.*

[2] The view here taken of the history of Egyptian religion is based on the sketch in Ad. Erman's *Aegypten und aegyptisches Leben im Altertum*, pp. 351 *sqq.* Compare C. P. Tiele, *Geschichte der Religion im Altertum* (Gotha, 1896–1903), i. 79 *sq.*

thoughtful minority, who could hardly fail to be shocked by the many barbarous and revolting elements in the local rites.   As usually happens in such cases, the process of religious unification appears to have been largely effected by discovering points of similarity, real or imaginary, between the provincial deities, which were thereupon declared to be only different names or manifestations of the same god.

Of the deities who thus acted as centres of attraction, absorbing in themselves a multitude of minor divinities, by far the most important was the sun-god Ra.   There appear to have been few gods in Egypt who were not at one time or other identified with him.   Ammon of Thebes, Horus of the East, Horus of Edfu, Chnum of Elephantine, Tum of Heliopolis, all were regarded as one god, the sun.   Even the water-god Sobk, in spite of his crocodile shape, did not escape the same fate.   Indeed one king, Amenophis IV., undertook to sweep away all the old gods at a stroke and replace them by a single god, the " great living disc of the sun." [1]   In the hymns composed in his honour, this deity is referred to as " the living disc of the sun, besides whom there is none other."   He is said to have made " the far heaven " and " men, beasts, and birds ; he strengtheneth the eyes with his beams, and when he showeth himself, all flowers

Most Egyptian gods were at some time identified with the sun.

Attempt of Amenophis IV. to abolish all gods except the sun-god.

---

[1] On this attempted revolution in religion see Lepsius, in *Verhandlungen der königl. Akad. der Wissenschaften zu Berlin*, 1851, pp. 196-201 ; A. Erman, *Aegypten und aegyptisches Leben im Altertum*, pp. 74 *sq.*, 355-357 ; *id.*, *Die ägyptische Religion*,[2] pp. 76-84 ; H. Brugsch, *History of Egypt* (London, 1879), i. 441 *sqq.* ; A. Wiedemann, *Aegyptische Geschichte* (Gotha, 1884), pp. 396 *sqq.*; *id.*, *Die Religion der alten Ägypter*, pp. 20-22 ; *id.*, *Religion of the Ancient Egyptians*, pp. 35-43 ; C. P. Tiele, *Geschichte der Religion im Altertum*, i. 84-92 ; G. Maspero, *Histoire ancienne des Peuples de l'Orient Classique*, ii. 316 *sqq.*; E. A. Wallis Budge, *The Gods of the Egyptians*, ii. 68-84 ; J. H. Breasted, *History of the Ancient Egyptians* (London, 1908), pp. 264-289 ; A. Moret, *Kings and Gods of Egypt* (New York and London, 1912), pp. 41-68.

A very sympathetic account of this remarkable religious reformer is given by Professor J. H. Breasted (*Development of Religion and Thought in Ancient Egypt*, pp. 319 - 343). Amenophis IV. reigned from about 1375 to 1358 B.C.   His new capital, Akhetaton, the modern Tell-el-Amarna, was on the right bank of the Nile, between Memphis and Thebes.   The king has been described as " of all the Pharaohs the most curious and at the same time the most enigmatic figure." To explain his bodily and mental peculiarities some scholars conjectured that through his mother, Queen Tii, he might have had Semitic blood in his veins.   But this theory appears to have been refuted by the discovery in 1905 of the tomb of Queen Tii's parents, the contents of which are of pure Egyptian style.   See A. Moret, *op. cit.* pp. 46 *sq.*

live and grow, the meadows flourish at his upgoing and are drunken at his sight, all cattle skip on their feet, and the birds that are in the marsh flutter for joy." It is he "who bringeth the years, createth the months, maketh the days, calculateth the hours, the lord of time, by whom men reckon." In his zeal for the unity of god, the king commanded to erase the names of all other gods from the monuments, and to destroy their images. His rage was particularly directed against the god Ammon, whose name and likeness were effaced wherever they were found ; even the sanctity of the tomb was violated in order to destroy the memorials of the hated deity. In some of the halls of the great temples at Carnac, Luxor, and other places, all the names of the gods, with a few chance exceptions, were scratched out. The monarch even changed his own name, Amenophis, because it was compounded of Ammon, and took instead the name of Chu-en-aten, "gleam of the sun's disc." Thebes itself, the ancient capital of his glorious ancestors, full of the monuments of their piety and idolatry, was no longer a fit home for the puritan king. He deserted it, and built for himself a new capital in Middle Egypt at the place now known as Tell-el-Amarna. Here in a few years a city of palaces and gardens rose like an exhalation at his command, and here the king, his dearly loved wife and children, and his complaisant courtiers led a merry life. The grave and sombre ritual of Thebes was discarded. The sun-god was worshipped with songs and hymns, with the music of harps and flutes, with offerings of cakes and fruits and flowers. Blood seldom stained his kindly altars. The king himself celebrated the offices of religion. He preached with unction, and we may be sure that his courtiers listened with at least an outward semblance of devotion. From the too-faithful portraits of himself which he has bequeathed to us we can still picture to ourselves the heretic king in the pulpit, with his tall, lanky figure, his bandy legs, his pot-belly, his long, lean, haggard face aglow with the fever of religious fanaticism. Yet "the doctrine," as he loved to call it, which he proclaimed to his hearers was apparently no stern message of renunciation in this world, of terrors in the world to

come. The thoughts of death, of judgment, and of a
life beyond the grave, which weighed like a nightmare
on the minds of the Egyptians, seem to have been
banished for a time. Even the name of Osiris, the
awful judge of the dead, is not once mentioned in the
graves at Tell-el-Amarna. All this lasted only during the
life of the reformer. His death was followed by a violent
reaction. The old gods were reinstated in their rank and
privileges : their names and images were restored, and new
temples were built. But all the shrines and palaces reared
by the late king were thrown down : even the sculptures
that referred to him and to his god in rock-tombs and on
the sides of hills were erased or filled up with stucco : his
name appears on no later monument, and was carefully
omitted from all official lists. The new capital was
abandoned, never to be inhabited again. Its plan can
still be traced in the sands of the desert.

Failure
of the
attempt.

This attempt of King Amenophis IV. is only an extreme example of a tendency which appears to have
affected the religion of Egypt as far back as we can
trace it. Therefore, to come back to our point, in attempting to discover the original character of any Egyptian god,
no weight can be given to the identification of him with
other gods, least of all with the sun-god Ra. Far from
helping to follow up the trail, these identifications only cross
and confuse it. The best evidence for the original character
of the Egyptian gods is to be found in their ritual and
myths, so far as these are known, and in the manner in
which they are portrayed on the monuments. It is mainly
on evidence drawn from these sources that I rest my
interpretation of Osiris.

Identifica-
tion with
the sun is
no evidence
of the
original
character
of an
Egyptian
god.

The ground upon which some modern writers seem chiefly
to rely for the identification of Osiris with the sun is that
the story of his death fits better with the solar phenomena
than with any other in nature. It may readily be admitted
that the daily appearance and disappearance of the sun
might very naturally be expressed by a myth of his death
and resurrection ; and writers who regard Osiris as the sun
are careful to indicate that it is the diurnal, and not the
annual, course of the sun to which they understand the

The solar
theory of
Osiris does
not explain
his death
and resur-
rection.

myth to apply.   Thus Renouf, who identified Osiris with
the sun, admitted that the Egyptian sun could not with any
show of reason be described as dead in winter.[1]   But if his
daily death was the theme of the legend, why was it celebrated
by an annual ceremony ?   This fact alone seems fatal to the
interpretation of the myth as descriptive of sunset and sunrise.   Again, though the sun may be said to die daily, in
what sense can he be said to be torn in pieces ? [2]

The death and resurrection of Osiris are more naturally explained by the annual decay and growth of vegetation.

In the course of our inquiry it has, I trust, been made
clear that there is another natural phenomenon to which the
conception of death and resurrection is as applicable as to
sunset and sunrise, and which, as a matter of fact, has been
so conceived and represented in folk-custom.   That phenomenon is the annual growth and decay of vegetation.   A
strong reason for interpreting the death of Osiris as the
decay of vegetation rather than as the sunset is to be found
in the general, though not unanimous, voice of antiquity,
which classed together the worship and myths of Osiris,
Adonis, Attis, Dionysus, and Demeter, as religions of
essentially the same type.[3]   The consensus of ancient

[1] P. Le Page Renouf, *Lectures on the Origin and Growth of Religion* [2] (London, 1884), p. 113.

[2] The late eminent scholar C. P. Tiele, who formerly interpreted Osiris as a sun-god (*History of Egyptian Religion*, pp. 43 *sqq.*), afterwards adopted a view of his nature which approaches more nearly to the one advocated in this book. See his *Geschichte der Religion im Altertum*, i. 35 *sq.*, 123. Professor Ed. Meyer also formerly regarded Osiris as a sun-god ; he now interprets him as a great vegetation god, dwelling in the depths of the earth and causing the plants and trees to spring from it.   The god's symbol, the *ded* pillar (see above, pp. 108 *sq.*), he takes to be a tree-trunk with cross-beams. See Ed. Meyer, *Geschichte des Altertums*, i. p. 67, § 57 (first edition, 1884) ; *id.*, i.[2] 2. pp. 70, 84, 87 (second edition, 1909). Sir Gaston Maspero has also abandoned the theory that Osiris was the sun ; he now supposes that the deity originally personified the Nile. See his *Histoire*

ancienne [4] (Paris, 1886), p. 35 ; and his *Histoire ancienne des Peuples de l'Orient Classique*, i. (Paris, 1895), p. 130. Dr. E. A. Wallis Budge also formerly interpreted Osiris as the Nile (*The Gods of the Egyptians*, i. 122, 123), and this view was held by some ancient writers (Plutarch, *Isis et Osiris*, 32, 34, 36, 38, 39). Compare Miss M. A. Murray, *The Osireion at Abydos* (London, 1904), p. 29.   Dr. Budge now explains Osiris as a deified king. See his *Osiris and the Egyptian Resurrection*, vol. i. pp. xviii, 30 *sq.*, 37, 66 *sq.*, 168, 254, 256, 290, 300, 312, 384.   As to this view see below, pp. 158 *sqq.*

[3] For the identification of Osiris with Dionysus, and of Isis with Demeter, see Herodotus, ii. 42, 49, 59, 144, 156 ; Plutarch, *Isis et Osiris*, 13, 35 ; Diodorus Siculus, i. 13, 25, 96, iv. 1 ; *Orphica*, Hymn 42 ; Eusebius, *Praepar. Evang.* iii. 11. 31 ; Servius on Virgil, *Aen.* xi. 287 ; *id.*, on Virgil, *Georg.* i. 166 ; J. Tzetzes, *Schol. on Lycophron*, 212 ; Διηγήματα, xxii. 2,

opinion on this subject seems too great to be rejected as a mere fancy. So closely did the rites of Osiris resemble those of Adonis at Byblus that some of the people of Byblus themselves maintained that it was Osiris and not Adonis whose death was mourned by them.[1] Such a view could certainly not have been held if the rituals of the two gods had not been so alike as to be almost indistinguishable. Herodotus found the similarity between the rites of Osiris and Dionysus so great, that he thought it impossible the latter could have arisen independently; they must, he supposed, have been recently borrowed, with slight alterations, by the Greeks from the Egyptians.[2] Again, Plutarch, a very keen student of comparative religion, insists upon the detailed resemblance of the rites of Osiris to those of Dionysus.[3] We cannot reject the evidence of such intelligent and trustworthy witnesses on plain matters of fact which fell under their own cognizance. Their explanations of the worships it is indeed possible to reject, for the meaning of religious cults is often open to question; but resemblances of ritual are matters of observation. Therefore, those who explain Osiris as the sun are driven to the alternative of either dismissing as mistaken the testimony of antiquity to the similarity of the rites of Osiris, Adonis, Attis, Dionysus, and Demeter, or of interpreting all these rites as sun-worship. No modern scholar has fairly faced and accepted either side of this alternative. To accept the former would be to affirm

---

in *Mythographi Graeci*, ed. A. Westermann (Brunswick, 1843), p. 368; Nonnus, *Dionys.* iv. 269 *sq.*; Cornutus, *Theologiae Graecae Compendium*, 28; Ausonius, *Epigrammata*, 29 and 30. For the identification of Osiris with Adonis and Attis see Stephanus Byzantius, *s.v.* 'Αμαθοῦς; Damascius, "Vita Isodori," in Photius, *Bibliotheca*, ed. Im. Bekker (Berlin, 1824), p. 343*a*, lines 21 *sq.*; Hippolytus, *Refutatio omnium haeresium*, v. 9. p. 168 ed. Duncker and Schneidewin; *Orphica*, Hymn 42. For the identification of Attis, Adonis, and Dionysus see Socrates, *Historia Ecclesiastica*, iii. 23 (Migne's *Patrologia Graeca*, lxvii. 448); Plutarch, *Quaestiones Conviviales*, iv. 5. 3; Clement of Alexandria, *Protrept.* ii. 19, p. 16 ed. Potter.

[1] Lucian, *De dea Syria*, 7. According to Professor Ed. Meyer, the relations of Egypt to Byblus were very ancient and close; he even suggests that there may have been from early times an Egyptian colony, or at all events an Egyptian military post, in the city. The commercial importance of Byblus arose from its possession of the fine cedar forests on the Lebanon; the timber was exported to Egypt, where it was in great demand. See Ed. Meyer, *Geschichte des Altertums*,[2] i. 2. pp. xix, 391 *sqq.*

[2] Herodotus, ii. 49.

[3] Plutarch, *Isis et Osiris*, 35.

that we know the rites of these deities better than the men
who practised, or at least who witnessed them.   To accept
the latter would involve a wrenching, clipping, mangling, and
distorting of myth and ritual from which even Macrobius
shrank.[1]   On the other hand, the view that the essence of all
these rites was the mimic death and revival of vegetation,
explains them separately and collectively in an easy and
natural way, and harmonizes with the general testimony
borne by the ancients to their substantial similarity.

[1] Osiris, Attis, Adonis, and Dionysus
were all resolved by him into the sun ;
but he spared Demeter (Ceres), whom,
however, he interpreted as the moon.
See the *Saturnalia*, bk. i.

CHAPTER VIII

OSIRIS AND THE MOON

BEFORE we conclude this study of Osiris it will be Osiris was worth while to consider an ancient view of his nature, sometimes interpreted which deserves more attention than it has received in by the modern times. We are told by Plutarch that among the ancients as the moon. philosophers who saw in the gods of Egypt personifications of natural objects and forces, there were some who interpreted Osiris as the moon and his enemy Typhon as the sun, "because the moon, with her humid and generative light, is favourable to the propagation of animals and the growth of plants; while the sun with his fierce fire scorches and burns up all growing things, renders the greater part of the earth uninhabitable by reason of his blaze, and often overpowers the moon herself." [1] Whatever may be thought of the physical qualities here attributed to the moon, the arguments adduced by the ancients to prove the identity of Osiris with that luminary carry with them a weight which has at least not been lightened by the results of modern research. An examination of them and of other evidence pointing in the same direction will, perhaps, help to set the original character of the Egyptian deity in a clearer light. [2]

1. Osiris was said to have lived or reigned twenty-eight years. This might fairly be taken as a mythical expression for a lunar month. [3]

2. His body was reported to have been rent into fourteen pieces. [4] This might be interpreted of the waning moon,

---

[1] Plutarch, *Isis et Osiris*, 41. 384 *sqq.*
[2] On Osiris as a moon-god see E. [3] Plutarch, *Isis et Osiris*, 13, 42.
A. Wallis Budge, *Osiris and the* [4] *Ibid.* 18, 42. The hieroglyphic
Egyptian Resurrection, i. 19-22, 59, texts sometimes speak of fourteen

Evidence
of the
association
of Osiris
with the
moon.

which appears to lose a portion of itself on each of the four-teen days that make up the second half of a lunar month. It is expressly said that his enemy Typhon found the body of Osiris at the full moon ;[1] thus the dismemberment of the god would begin with the waning of the moon.   To primitive man it seems manifest that the waning moon is actually dwindling, and he naturally enough explains its diminution by supposing that the planet is being rent or broken in pieces or eaten away.   The Klamath Indians of Oregon speak of the moon as "the one broken to pieces" with reference to its changing aspect ; they never apply such a term to the sun,[2] whose apparent change of bulk at different seasons of the year is far too insignificant to attract the attention of the savage, or at least to be described by him in such forcible language.   The Dacotas believe that when the moon is full, a great many little mice begin to nibble at one side of it and do not cease till they have eaten it all up, after which a new moon is born and grows to maturity, only to share the fate of its countless predecessors.[3]   A similar belief is held by the Huzuls of the Carpathians, except that they ascribe the destruction of the old moon to wolves instead of to mice.[4]

3. At the new moon of the month Phamenoth, which was the beginning of spring, the Egyptians celebrated what they called "the entry of Osiris into the moon."[5]

4. At the ceremony called "the burial of Osiris" the Egyptians made a crescent-shaped chest "because the moon, when it approaches the sun, assumes the form of a crescent and vanishes."[6]

5. The bull Apis, held to be an image of the soul of Osiris,[7] was born of a cow which was believed to have been

pieces, and sometimes of sixteen, or even eighteen.   But fourteen seems to have been the true number, because the inscriptions of Denderah, which refer to the rites of Osiris, describe the mystic image of the god as composed of fourteen pieces.   See E. A. Wallis Budge, *The Gods of the Egyptians*, ii. 126 *sq.* ; *id.*, *Osiris and the Egyptian Resurrection*, i. 386 *sq.*

[1] Plutarch, *Isis et Osiris*, 8.

[2] A. S. Gatschet, *The Klamath Indians of South-Western Oregon* (Washington, 1890), p. lxxxix.

[3] S. R. Riggs, *Dakota Grammar, Texts, and Ethnography* (Washington, 1893), p. 16.

[4] R. F. Kaindl, *Die Huzulen* (Vienna, 1894), p. 97.

[5] Plutarch, *Isis et Osiris*, 43.

[6] *Ibid.* 43.

[7] *Ibid.* 20, 29.

impregnated, not in the vulgar way by a bull, but by a divine influence emanating from the moon.[1]

6. Once a year, at the full moon, pigs were sacrificed simultaneously to the moon and Osiris.[2]

7. In a hymn supposed to be addressed by Isis to Osiris, it is said that Thoth—

> "*Placeth thy soul in the bark Ma-at,*
> *In that name which is thine, of GOD MOON.*"

And again :—

> "*Thou who comest to us as a child each month,*
> *We do not cease to contemplate thee.*
> *Thine emanation heightens the brilliancy*
> *Of the stars of Orion in the firmament.*" [3]

Here then Osiris is identified with the moon in set terms. If in the same hymn he is said to "illuminate us like Ra" (the sun), that is obviously no reason for identifying him with the sun, but quite the contrary. For though the moon may reasonably be compared to the sun, neither the sun nor anything else can reasonably be compared to itself.

8. In art Osiris is sometimes represented as a human-headed mummy grasping in his hands his characteristic emblems and wearing on his head, instead of the usual crown, a full moon within a crescent.[4]

Now if in one of his aspects Osiris was originally a deity of vegetation, we can easily enough understand why in a later and more philosophic age he should come to be thus identified or confounded with the moon.[5] For as soon as he begins to meditate upon the causes of

The identification of Osiris with the moon appears to be based

---

[1] Plutarch, *Isis et Osiris*, 43 ; *id.*, *Quaest. Conviv.* viii. 1. 3. Compare Herodotus, iii. 28 ; Aelian, *Nat. Anim.* xi. 10 ; Mela, i. 9. 58.

[2] Herodotus, ii. 47 ; Plutarch, *Isis et Osiris*, 8. As to pigs in relation to Osiris, see *Spirits of the Corn and of the Wild*, ii. 24 *sqq.*

[3] P. J. de Horrack, "Lamentations of Isis and Nephthys," *Records of the Past*, ii. (London, N.D.) pp. 121 *sq.* ; H. Brugsch, *Religion und Mythologie der alten Aegypter*, pp. 629 *sq.*; E. A. Wallis Budge, *Osiris and the Egyptian Resurrection*, i. 389. "Apart from the fact that Osiris is actually called

Āsār Āāḥ, i.e. 'Osiris the Moon,' there are so many passages which prove beyond all doubt that at one period at least Osiris was the Moon-god, that it is difficult to understand why Diodorus stated that Osiris was the sun and Isis the moon" (E. A. Wallis Budge, *op. cit.* i. 21).

[4] E. A. Wallis Budge, *Osiris and the Egyptian Resurrection*, i. 59.

[5] According to C. P. Tiele (*Geschichte der Religion im Altertum*, i. 79) the conception of Osiris as the moon was late and never became popular. This entirely accords with the view adopted in the text.

on a comparatively late theory that all things grow and decay with the waxing and waning of the moon.

things, the early philosopher is led by certain obvious, though fallacious, appearances to regard the moon as the ultimate cause of the growth of plants. In the first place he associates its apparent growth and decay with the growth and decay of sublunary things, and imagines that in virtue of a secret sympathy the celestial phenomena really produce those terrestrial changes which in point of fact they merely resemble. Thus Pliny says that the moon may fairly be considered the planet of breath, "because it saturates the earth and by its approach fills bodies, while by its departure it empties them. Hence it is," he goes on, "that shell-fish increase with the increase of the moon and that bloodless creatures especially feel breath at that time ; even the blood of men grows and diminishes with the light of the moon, and leaves and herbage also feel the same influence, since the lunar energy penetrates all things."[1] "There is no doubt," writes Macrobius, "that the moon is the author and framer of mortal bodies, so much so that some things expand or shrink as it waxes or wanes."[2] Again, Aulus Gellius puts in the mouth of a friend the remark that "the same things which grow with the waxing, do dwindle with the waning moon," and he quotes from a commentary of Plutarch's on Hesiod a statement that the onion is the only vegetable which violates this great law of nature by sprouting in the wane and withering in the increase of the moon.[3] Scottish Highlanders allege that in the increase of the moon everything has a tendency to grow or stick together ;[4] and they call the second moon of autumn "the ripening moon" (Gealach an abachaidh), because they imagine that crops ripen as much by its light as by day.[5]

Practical rules founded on this lunar theory.

From this supposed influence of the moon on the life of plants and animals, men in ancient and modern times have deduced a whole code of rules for the guidance of the husbandman, the shepherd, and others in the conduct of

[1] Pliny, Nat. Hist. ii. 221.
[2] Macrobius, Comment. in somnium Scipionis, i. 11. 7.
[3] Aulus Gellius, xx. 8. For the opinions of the ancients on this subject see further W. H. Roscher, Über Selene und Verwandtes (Leipsic, 1890), pp. 61 sqq.
[4] John Ramsay of Ochtertyre, Scotland and Scotsmen in the Eighteenth Century, edited by A. Allardyce (Edinburgh and London, 1888), ii. 449.
[5] J. G. Campbell, Witchcraft and Second Sight in the Highlands and Islands of Scotland (Glasgow, 1902), pp. 306 sq.

their affairs.   Thus an ancient writer on agriculture lays it down as a maxim, that whatever is to be sown should be sown while the moon is waxing, and that whatever is to be cut or gathered should be cut or gathered while it is waning.[1] A modern treatise on superstition describes how the superstitious man regulates all his conduct by the moon : " Whatever he would have to grow, he sets about it when she is in her increase ; but for what he would have made less he chooses her wane." [2]   In Germany the phases of the moon are observed by superstitious people at all the more or even less important actions of life, such as tilling the fields, building or changing houses, marriages, hair-cutting, bleeding, cupping, and so forth.   The particular rules vary in different places, but the principle generally followed is that whatever is done to increase anything should be done while the moon is waxing ; whatever is done to diminish anything should be done while the moon is waning.   For example, sowing, planting, and grafting should be done in the first half of the moon, but the felling of timber and mowing should be done in the second half.[3]   In various parts of Europe it is believed that plants, nails, hair, and corns, cut while the moon is on the increase, will grow again fast, but that if cut while it is on the decrease they will grow slowly or waste

Supposed influence of the phases of the moon on the operations of husbandry

---

[1] Palladius, *De re rustica*, i. 34. 8. Compare *id.* i. 6. 12 ; Pliny, *Nat. Hist.* xviii. 321, *"omnia quae caeduntur, carpuntur, tondentur innocentius decrescente luna quam crescente fiunt"* ; *Geoponica*, i. 6. 8, τινὲς δοκιμάζουσι μηδὲν φθινούσης τῆς σελήνης ἀλλὰ αὐξανομένης φυτεύειν.

[2] J. Brand, *Popular Antiquities of Great Britain* (London, 1882–1883), iii. 144, quoting Werenfels, *Dissertation upon Superstition* (London, 1748), p. 6.

[3] A. Wuttke, *Der deutsche Volksaberglaube*[2] (Berlin, 1869), § 65, pp. 57 sq. Compare J. Grimm, *Deutsche Mythologie*[4] (Berlin, 1875–1878), ii. 595 ; Montanus, *Die deutsche Volksfeste, Volksbräuche und deutscher Volksglaube* (Iserlohn, N.D.), p. 128 ; M. Prätorius, *Deliciae Prussicae* (Berlin, 1871), p. 18 ; O. Schell, "Einige

Bemerkungen über den Mond im heutigen Glauben des bergischen Volkes," *Am Ur-quell*, v. (1894) p. 173.   The rule that the grafting of trees should be done at the waxing of the moon is laid down by Pliny (*Nat. Hist.* xvii. 108). At Deutsch-Zepling in Transylvania, by an inversion of the usual custom, seed is generally sown at the waning of the moon (A. Heinrich, *Agrarische Sitten und Gebräuche unter den Sachsen Siebenbürgens*, Hermannstadt, 1880, p. 7).   Some French peasants also prefer to sow in the wane (F. Chapiseau, *Folk-lore de la Beauce et du Perche*, Paris, 1902, i. 291).   In the Abruzzi also sowing and grafting are commonly done when the moon is on the wane ; timber that is to be durable must be cut in January during the moon's decrease (G. Finamore, *Credenze, Usi e Costumi Abruzzesi*, Palermo, 1890, p. 43).

away.[1] Hence persons who wish their hair to grow thick and long should cut it in the first half of the moon.[2] On the same principle sheep are shorn when the moon is waxing, because it is supposed that the wool will then be longest and most enduring.[3] Some negroes of the Gaboon think that taro and other vegetables never thrive if they are planted after full moon, but that they grow fast and strong if they are planted in the first quarter.[4] The Highlanders of Scotland used to expect better crops of grain by sowing their seed in the moon's increase.[5] On the other hand they thought that garden vegetables, such as onions and kail, run to seed if they are sown in the increase, but that they grow to pot-herbs if they are sown in the wane.[6] So Thomas Tusser advised the peasant to sow peas and beans in the wane of the moon "that they with the planet may rest and arise."[7] The Zulus welcome

---

[1] P. Sébillot, *Traditions et Superstitions de la Haute - Bretagne* (Paris, 1882), ii. 355; L. F. Sauvé, *Folk-lore des Hautes-Vosges* (Paris, 1889), p. 5; J. Brand, *Popular Antiquities of Great Britain*, iii. 150; Holzmayer, "Osiliana," *Verhandlungen der gelehrten Estnichen Gesellschaft zu Dorpat*, vii. (1872) p. 47.

[2] The rule is mentioned by Varro, *Rerum Rusticarum*, i. 37 (where we should probably read "*ne decrescente tondens calvos fiam*," and refer *istaec* to the former member of the preceding sentence); A. Wuttke, *l.c.*; Montanus, *op. cit.* p. 128; P. Sébillot, *l.c.*; E. Meier, *Deutsche Sagen, Sitten und Gebräuche aus Schwaben* (Stuttgart, 1852), p. 511, § 421; W. J. A. von Tettau und J. D. H. Temme, *Die Volkssagen Ostpreussens, Litthauens und Westpreussens* (Berlin, 1837), p. 283; A. Kuhn, *Märkische Sagen und Märchen* (Berlin, 1843), p. 386, § 92; L. Schandein, in *Bavaria, Landes- und Volkskunde des Königreichs Bayern* (Munich, 1860–1867), iv. 2, p. 402; F. S. Krauss, *Volksglaube und religiöser Brauch der Südslaven* (Münster, i. W. 1890), p. 15; E. Krause, "Abergläubische Kuren und sonstiger Aberglaube in Berlin," *Zeitschrift für Ethnologie*, xv. (1883) p. 91; R.

Wuttke, *Sächsische Volkskunde*[2] (Dresden, 1901), p. 369; C. S. Burne and G. F. Jackson, *Shropshire Folk-lore* (London, 1883), p. 259. The reason assigned in the text was probably the original one in all cases, though it is not always the one alleged now.

[3] F. S. Krauss, *op. cit.* p. 16; Montanus, *l.c.*; Varro, *Rerum Rusticarum*, i. 37 (see above, note[2]). However, the opposite rule is observed in the Upper Vosges, where it is thought that if the sheep are shorn at the new moon the quantity of wool will be much less than if they were shorn in the waning of the moon (L. F. Sauvé, *Folk-lore des Hautes-Vosges*, p. 5). In the Bocage of Normandy, also, wool is clipped during the waning of the moon; otherwise moths would get into it (J. Lecœur, *Esquisses du Bocage Normand*, Condé-sur-Noireau, 1883–1887, ii. 12).

[4] Father Lejeune, "Dans la forêt," *Missions Catholiques*, xxvii. (1895) p. 272.

[5] S. Johnson, *Journey to the Western Islands of Scotland* (Baltimore, 1810), p. 183.

[6] J. G. Campbell, *Witchcraft and Second Sight in the Highlands and Islands of Scotland*, p. 306.

[7] Thomas Tusser, *Five Hundred Points of Good Husbandry*, New

the first appearance of the new moon with beating of drums and other demonstrations of joy ; but next day they abstain from all labour, " thinking that if anything is sown on those days they can never reap the benefit thereof." [1]   But in this matter of sowing and planting a refined distinction is sometimes drawn by French, German, and Esthonian peasants ; plants which bear fruit above ground are sown by them when the moon is waxing, but plants which are cultivated for the sake of their roots, such as potatoes and turnips, are sown when the moon is waning.[2]   The reason for this distinction seems to be a vague idea that the waxing moon is coming up and the waning moon going down, and that accordingly fruits which grow upwards should be sown in the former period, and fruits which grow downwards in the latter.   Before beginning to plant their cacao the Pipiles of Central America exposed the finest seeds for four nights to the moonlight,[3] but whether they did so at the waxing or waning of the moon is not said.   Even pots, it would seem, are not exempt from this great law of nature.   In Uganda " potters waited for the new moon to appear before baking their pots ; when it was some days old, they prepared their fires and baked the vessels.   No potter would bake pots when the moon was past the full, for he believed that they would be a failure, and would be sure to crack or break in the burning, if he did so, and that his labour accordingly would go for nothing." [4]

Again, the waning of the moon has been commonly recommended both in ancient and modern times as the proper time for felling trees,[5] apparently because it was

The phases of the moon in relation

Edition (London, 1812), p. 107 (under February).

[1] Fairweather, in W. F. Owen's *Narrative of Voyages to explore the Shores of Africa, Arabia, and Madagascar* (London, 1833), ii. 396 *sq.*

[2] A. Wuttke, *Der deutsche Volksaberglaube*,[3] § 65, p. 58; J. Lecœur, *loc. cit.*; E. Meier, *Deutsche Sagen, Sitten und Gebräuche aus Schwaben*, p. 511, § 422 ; Th. Siebs, " Das Saterland," *Zeitschrift für Volkskunde*, iii. (1893) p. 278 ; Holzmayer, *op. cit.* p. 47.

[3] H. H. Bancroft, *Native Races of*

the *Pacific States* (London, 1875–1876), ii. 719 *sq.*

[4] Rev. J. Roscoe, *The Baganda* (London, 1911), p. 402.

[5] Cato, *De agri cultura*, 37. 4 ; Varro, *Rerum Rusticarum*, i. 37 ; Pliny, *Nat. Hist.* xvi. 190 ; Palladius, *De re rustica*, ii. 22, xii. 15 ; Plutarch, *Quaest. Conviv.* iii. 10. 3 ; Macrobius, *Saturn.* vii. 16 ; A. Wuttke, *l.c.* : *Bavaria, Landes- und Volkskunde des Königreichs Bayern*, iv. 2, p. 402 ; W. Kolbe, *Hessische Volks-Sitten und Gebräuche* [2] (Marburg, 1888), p. 58 ;

to the
felling of
timber

thought fit and natural that the operation of cutting down should be performed on earth at the time when the lunar orb was, so to say, being cut down in the sky. In France before the Revolution the forestry laws enjoined that trees should only be felled after the moon had passed the full; and in French bills announcing the sale of timber you may still read a notice that the wood was cut in the waning of the moon.[1] So among the Shans of Burma, when a house is to be built, it is a rule that "a lucky day should be chosen to commence the cutting of the bamboos. The day must not only be a fortunate one for the builder, but it must also be in the second half of the month, when the moon is waning. Shans believe that if bamboos are cut during the first half of the month, when the moon is waxing, they do not last well, as boring insects attack them and they will soon become rotten. This belief is prevalent all over the East."[2] A like belief obtains in various parts of Mexico. No Mexican will cut timber while the moon is increasing; they say it must be cut while the moon is waning or the wood will certainly rot.[3] In Colombia, South America, people think that corn should only be sown and timber felled when the moon is on the wane. They say that the waxing moon draws the sap up through the trunk and branches, whereas the sap flows down and leaves the wood dry during the wane of the moon.[4] But sometimes the opposite rule is

L. F. Sauvé, *Folk-lore des Hautes-Vosges*, p. 5; F. Chapiseau, *Folk-lore de la Beauce et du Perche*, i. 291 *sq.*; M. Martin, "Description of the Western Islands of Scotland," in J. Pinkerton's *Voyages and Travels*, iii. 630; J. G. Campbell, *Witchcraft and Second Sight in the Highlands and Islands of Scotland*, p. 306; G. Amalfi, *Tradizioni ed Usi nella peninsola Sorrentina* (Palermo, 1890), p. 87; K. von den Steinen, *Unter den Naturvölkern Zentral-Brasiliens* (Berlin, 1894), p. 559. Compare F. de Castelnau, *Expédition dans les parties centrales de l'Amérique du Sud* (Paris, 1851–1852), iii. 438. Pliny, while he says that the period from the twentieth to the thirtieth day of the lunar month was the season generally

recommended, adds that the best time of all, according to universal opinion, was the interlunar day, between the old and the new moon, when the planet is invisible through being in conjunction with the sun.

[1] J. Lecœur, *Esquisses du Bocage Normand*, ii. 11 *sq.*

[2] Mrs. Leslie Milne, *Shans at Home* (London, 1910), p. 100.

[3] Letter of Mr. A. S. F. Marshall, dated Hacienda "La Maronna," Cd. Porfirio Diaz, Coah., Mexico, 2nd October 1908. The writer gives instances confirmatory of this belief. I have to thank Professor A. C. Seward of Cambridge for kindly showing me this letter.

[4] Letter of Mr. Francis S. Schloss to me, dated 58 New Cavendish

adopted, and equally forcible arguments are urged in its defence. Thus, when the Wabondei of Eastern Africa are about to build a house, they take care to cut the posts for it when the moon is on the increase ; for they say that posts cut when the moon is wasting away would soon rot, whereas posts cut while the moon is waxing are very durable.[1] The same rule is observed for the same reason in some parts of Germany.[2]

But the partisans of the ordinarily received opinion have sometimes supported it by another reason, which introduces us to the second of those fallacious appearances by which men have been led to regard the moon as the cause of growth in plants. From observing rightly that dew falls most thickly on cloudless nights, they inferred wrongly that it was caused by the moon, a theory which the poet Alcman expressed in mythical form by saying that dew was a daughter of Zeus and the moon.[3] Hence the ancients concluded that the moon is the great source of moisture, as the sun is the great source of heat.[4] And as the humid power of the moon was assumed to be greater when the planet was waxing than when it was waning, they thought that timber cut during the increase of the luminary would be saturated with moisture, whereas timber cut in the wane would be comparatively dry. Hence we are told that in antiquity carpenters would reject timber felled when the moon was growing or full, because they believed that such timber teemed with sap ;[5] and in the Vosges at the present day people allege that wood cut at the new moon does not dry.[6] We have seen that the same reason is assigned for the same practice in Colombia.[7] In the Hebrides peasants

The moon regarded as the source of moisture.

Street, W., 12th May 1912. Mr. Schloss adds that "as a matter of practical observation, timber, etc., should only be felled when the moon is waning. This has been stated to me not only by natives, but also by English mining engineers of high repute, who have done work in Colombia."

[1] O. Baumann, *Usambara und seine Nachbargebiete* (Berlin, 1891), p. 125.

[2] Montanus, *Die deutsche Volksfeste, Volksbräuche und deutscher Volksglaube*, p. 128.

[3] Plutarch, *Quaest. Conviv.* iii. 10. 3 ; Macrobius, *Saturn.* vii. 16. See further, W. H. Roscher, *Über Selene und Verwandtes* (Leipsic, 1890), pp. 49 *sqq.*

[4] Plutarch and Macrobius, *ll.cc.* ; Pliny, *Nat. Hist.* ii. 223, xx. 1 ; Aristotle, *Problemata*, xxiv. 14, p. 937 B, 3 *sq.* ed. I. Bekker (Berlin).

[5] Macrobius and Plutarch, *ll.cc.*

[6] L. F. Sauvé, *Folk-lore des Hautes-Vosges*, p. 5.

[7] Above, p. 136.

give the same reason for cutting their peats when the moon is on the wane; "for they observe that if they are cut in the increase, they continue still moist and never burn clear, nor are they without smoke, but the contrary is daily observed of peats cut in the decrease."[1]

Thus misled by a double fallacy primitive philosophy comes to view the moon as the great cause of vegetable growth, first, because the planet seems itself to grow, and second, because it is supposed to be the source of dew and moisture. It is no wonder, therefore, that agricultural peoples should adore the planet which they believe to influence so profoundly the crops on which they depend for subsistence. Accordingly we find that in the hotter regions of America, where maize is cultivated and manioc is the staple food, the moon was recognized as the principal object of worship, and plantations of manioc were assigned to it as a return for the service it rendered in the production of the crops. The worship of the moon in preference to the sun was general among the Caribs, and, perhaps, also among most of the other Indian tribes who cultivated maize in the tropical forests to the east of the Andes; and the same thing has been observed, under the same physical conditions, among the aborigines of the hottest region of Peru, the northern valleys of Yuncapata. Here the Indians of Pacasmayu and the neighbouring valleys revered the moon as their principal divinity. The "house of the moon" at Pacasmayu was the chief temple of the district; and the same sacrifices of maize-flour, of wine, and of children which were offered by the mountaineers of the Andes to the Sun-god, were offered by the lowlanders to the Moon-god in order that he might cause their crops to thrive.[2]   In ancient

---

[1] M. Martin, "Description of the Western Islands of Scotland," in J. Pinkerton's *Voyages and Travels*, iii. 630.

[2] E. J. Payne, *History of the New World called America*, i. (Oxford, 1892) p. 495. In his remarks on the origin of moon-worship this learned and philosophical historian has indicated (*op. cit.* i. 493 *sqq.*) the true causes which lead primitive man to trace the growth of plants to the influence of the moon. Compare Sir E. B. Tylor, *Primitive Culture*[2] (London, 1873), i. 130. Payne suggests that the custom of naming the months after the principal natural products that ripen in them may have contributed to the same result. The custom is certainly very common among savages, as I hope to show elsewhere, but whether it has contributed to foster the fallacy in question seems doubtful.

The Indians of Brazil are said to

Babylonia, where the population was essentially agricultural, the moon-god took precedence of the sun-god and was indeed reckoned his father.[1]

Hence it would be no matter for surprise if, after worshipping the crops which furnished them with the means of subsistence, the ancient Egyptians should in later times have identified the spirit of the corn with the moon, which a false philosophy had taught them to regard as the ultimate cause of the growth of vegetation. In this way we can understand why in their most recent forms the myth and ritual of Osiris, the old god of trees and corn, should bear many traces of efforts made to bring them into a superficial conformity with the new doctrine of his lunar affinity.

Thus Osiris, the old corn-god, was afterwards identified with the moon.

---

pay more attention to the moon than to the sun, regarding it as a source both of good and ill. See J. B. von Spix und C. F. von Martius, *Reise in Brasilien* (Munich, 1823–1831), i. 379. The natives of Mori, a district of Central Celebes, believe that the rice-spirit Omonga lives in the moon and eats up the rice in the granary if he is not treated with due respect. See A. C. Kruijt, "Eenige ethnografische aanteekeningen omtrent de Toboengkoe en de Tomori," *Mededeelingen van wege het Nederlandsche Zendelinggenootschap,* xliv. (1900) p. 231.

[1] E. A. Budge, *Nebuchadnezzar, King of Babylon, on recently-discovered inscriptions of this King,* pp. 5 *sq.* ; A. H. Sayce, *Religion of the Ancient Babylonians,* p. 155 ; M. Jastrow, *Religion of Babylonia and Assyria,* pp. 68 *sq.,* 75 *sq.* ; L. W. King, *Babylonian Religion and Mythology* (London, 1899), pp. 17 *sq.* The Ahts of Vancouver Island, a tribe of fishers and hunters, view the moon as the husband of the sun and as a more powerful deity than her (G. M. Sproat, *Scenes and Studies of Savage Life,* London, 1868, p. 206).

CHAPTER IX

THE DOCTRINE OF LUNAR SYMPATHY

The
doctrine
of lunar
sympathy.

IN the preceding chapter some evidence was adduced of the sympathetic influence which the waxing or waning moon is popularly supposed to exert on growth, especially on the growth of vegetation. But the doctrine of lunar sympathy does not stop there; it is applied also to the affairs of man, and various customs and rules have been deduced from it which aim at the amelioration and even the indefinite extension of human life. To illustrate this application of the popular theory at length would be out of place here, but a few cases may be mentioned by way of specimen.

Theory
that all
things wax
or wane
with the
moon.

The natural fact on which all the customs in question seem to rest is the apparent monthly increase and decrease of the moon. From this observation men have inferred that all things simultaneously wax or wane in sympathy with it.[1] Thus the Mentras or Mantras of the Malay Peninsula have a tradition that in the beginning men did not die but grew thin with the waning of the moon, and waxed fat as she neared the full.[2] Of the Scottish Highlanders we are told that "the moon in her increase, full growth, and in her wane are with them the emblems of a rising, flourishing, and declining fortune. At the last period of her revolution they carefully avoid to engage in any business of importance; but the first and middle they seize with avidity, presaging the most auspicious issue to their undertakings."[3] Similarly

---

[1] This principle is clearly recognized and well illustrated by J. Grimm (*Deutsche Mythologie*,[4] ii. 594-596).

[2] D. F. A. Hervey, "The Mentra Traditions," *Journal of the Straits Branch of the Royal Asiatic Society*, No. 10 (Singapore, 1883), p. 190; W. W. Skeat and C. O. Blagden, *Pagan Races of the Malay Peninsula* (London, 1906), ii. 337.

[3] Rev. J. Grant (parish minister of Kirkmichael), in Sir John Sinclair's

in some parts of Germany it is commonly believed that whatever is undertaken when the moon is on the increase succeeds well, and that the full moon brings everything to perfection ; whereas business undertaken in the wane of the moon is doomed to failure.[1]   This German belief has come down, as we might have anticipated, from barbaric times ; for Tacitus tells us that the Germans considered the new or the full moon the most auspicious time for business ;[2] and Caesar informs us that the Germans despaired of victory if they joined battle before the new moon.[3]   The Spartans seem to have been of the same opinion, for it was a rule with them never to march out to war except when the moon was full.   The rule prevented them from sending troops in time to fight the Persians at Marathon,[4] and but for Athenian valour this paltry superstition might have turned the scale of battle and decided the destiny of Greece, if not of Europe, for centuries.   The Athenians themselves paid dear for a similar scruple : an eclipse of the moon cost them the loss of a gallant fleet and army before Syracuse, and practically sealed the fate of Athens, for she never recovered from the blow.[5]   So heavy is the sacrifice which superstition demands of its votaries.   In this respect the Greeks were on a level with the negroes of the Sudan, among whom, if a march has been decided upon during the last quarter of the moon, the departure is always deferred until the first day of the new moon.   No chief would dare to undertake an expedition and lead out his warriors before the appearance of the crescent.   Merchants and private persons observe the same rule on their journeys.[6]   In like manner the Mandingoes of Senegambia pay great attention to the changes of the moon, and think it very unlucky to begin a journey or any other work of consequence in the last quarter.[7]

It is especially the appearance of the new moon, with

Statistical Account of Scotland (Edinburgh, 1791–1799), xii. 457.

[1] A. Kuhn und W. Schwartz, *Norddeutsche Sagen, Märchen und Gebräuche* (Leipsic, 1848), p. 457, § 419.

[2] Tacitus, *Germania*, 11.

[3] Caesar, *De bello Gallico*, i. 50.

[4] Herodotus, vi. 106 ; Lucian, *De astrologia*, 25 ; Pausanias, i. 28. 4.

[5] Thucydides, vii. 50.

[6] Le capitaine Binger, *Du Niger au Golfe de Guinée* (Paris, 1892), ii. 116.

[7] Mungo Park, *Travels in the Interior Districts of Africa*[5] (London, 1807), pp. 406 *sq.*

The
ceremonies
observed at
new moon
are often
magical
rather than
religious,
being
intended
to renew
sympatheti-
cally the
life of man.

its promise of growth and increase, which is greeted with
ceremonies intended to renew and invigorate, by means of
sympathetic magic, the life of man.   Observers, ignorant of
savage superstition, have commonly misinterpreted such
customs as worship or adoration paid to the moon.   In
point of fact the ceremonies of new moon are probably in
many cases rather magical than religious.   The Indians of
the Ucayali River in Peru hail the appearance of the new
moon with great joy.   They make long speeches to her,
accompanied with vehement gesticulations, imploring her
protection and begging that she will be so good as to
invigorate their bodies.[1]   On the day when the new moon
first appeared, it was a custom with the Indians of San Juan
Capistrano, in California, to call together all the young men
for the purpose of its celebration.   *"Correr la luna !"* shouted
one of the old men, " Come, my boys, the moon ! the moon !"
Immediately the young men began to run about in a
disorderly fashion as if they were distracted, while the old
men danced in a circle, saying, " As the moon dieth, and
cometh to life again, so we also having to die will again
live." [2]   An old traveller tells us that at the appearance of
every new moon the negroes of the Congo clapped their
hands and cried out, sometimes falling on their knees, " So
may I renew my life as thou art renewed."   But if the sky
happened to be clouded, they did nothing, alleging that the
planet had lost its virtue.[3]   A somewhat similar custom
prevails among the Ovambo of South-Western Africa.   On
the first moonlight night of the new moon, young and old,
their bodies smeared with white earth, perhaps in imitation
of the planet's silvery light, dance to the moon and address
to it wishes which they feel sure will be granted.[4]   We may
conjecture that among these wishes is a prayer for a renewal
of life.   When a Masai sees the new moon he throws a
twig or stone at it with his left hand, and says, " Give me

[1] W. Smythe and F. Lowe, *Narrative
of a Journey from Lima to Para*
(London, 1836), p. 230.
[2] Father G. Boscana, " Chinigchinich," in *Life in California, by an
American* [A. Robinson] (New York,
1846), pp. 298 *sq.*

[3] Merolla, "Voyage to Congo," in
J. Pinkerton's *Voyages and Travels*,
xvi. 273.

[4] H.   Schinz,   *Deutsch - Südwest-
Afrika* (Oldenburg and Leipsic, N.D.),
p. 319.

long life," or "Give me strength"; and when a pregnant woman sees the new moon she milks some milk into a small gourd, which she covers with green grass. Then she pours the milk away in the direction of the moon and says, "Moon, give me my child safely."[1] Among the Wagogo of German East Africa, at sight of the new moon some people break a stick in pieces, spit on the pieces, and throw them towards the moon, saying, "Let all illness go to the west, where the sun sets."[2] Among the Boloki of the Upper Congo there is much shouting and gesticulation on the appearance of a new moon. Those who have enjoyed good health pray that it may be continued, and those who have been sick ascribe their illness to the coming of the luminary and beg her to take away bad health and give them good health instead.[3] The Esthonians think that all the misfortunes which might befall a man in the course of a month may be forestalled and shifted to the moon, if a man will only say to the new moon, "Good morrow, new moon. I must grow young, you must grow old. My eyes must grow bright, yours must grow dark. I must grow light as a bird, you must grow heavy as iron."[4] On the fifteenth day of the moon, that is, at the time when the luminary has begun to wane, the Coreans take round pieces of paper, either red or white, which represent the moon, and having fixed them perpendicularly on split sticks they place them on the tops of the houses. Then persons who have been forewarned by fortune-tellers of impending evil pray to the moon to remove it from them.[5]

[1] A. C. Hollis, *The Masai* (Oxford, 1905), p. 274.

[2] H. Cole, "Notes on the Wagogo of German East Africa," *Journal of the Anthropological Institute*, xxxii. (1902) p. 330.

[3] John H. Weeks, *Among Congo Cannibals* (London, 1913), p. 142.

[4] J. G. Kohl, *Die deutsch-russischen Ostseeprovinzen* (Dresden and Leipsic, 1841), ii. 279. Compare Boecler-Kreutzwald, *Der Ehsten abergläubische Gebräuche, Weisen und Gewohnheiten* (St. Petersburg, 1854), pp. 142 *sq.*; J. Grimm, *Deutsche Mythologie*,[4] ii. 595, note[1]. The power of regenera-

tion ascribed to the moon in these customs is sometimes attributed to the sun. Thus it is said that the Chiriguanos Indians of South - Eastern Bolivia often address the sun as follows: "Thou art born and disappearest every day, only to revive always young. Cause that it may be so with me." See A. Thouar, *Explorations dans l'Amérique du Sud* (Paris, 1891), p. 50.

[5] W. Woodville Rockhill, "Notes on some of the Laws, Customs, and Superstitions of Korea," *The American Anthropologist*, iv. (Washington, 1891), p. 185.

In India people attempt to absorb the vital influence of the moon by drinking water in which the luminary is reflected. Thus the Mohammedans of Oude fill a silver basin with water and hold it so that the orb of the full moon is mirrored in it. The person to be benefited must look steadfastly at the moon in the basin, then shut his eyes and drink the water at one gulp. Doctors recommend the draught as a remedy for nervous disorders and palpitation of the heart. Somewhat similar customs prevail among the Hindoos of Northern India. At the full moon of the month of Kuar (September-October) people lay out food on the house-tops, and when it has absorbed the rays of the moon they distribute it among their relations, who are supposed to lengthen their life by eating of the food which has thus been saturated with moonshine. Patients are often made to look at the moon reflected in melted butter, oil, or milk as a cure for leprosy and the like diseases.[1]

Naturally enough the genial influence of moonshine is often supposed to be particularly beneficial to children; for will not the waxing moon help them to wax in strength and stature? Hence in the island of Kiriwina, one of the Trobriands Group to the east of New Guinea, a mother always lifts up or presents her child to the first full moon after its birth in order that it may grow fast and talk soon.[2] So among the Baganda of Central Africa it was customary for each mother to take her child out at the first new moon after its birth, and to point out the moon to the infant; this was thought to make the child grow healthy and strong.[3] Among the Thonga of South Africa the presentation of the baby to the moon does not take place until the mother has resumed her monthly periods, which usually happens in the third month after the birth. When the new moon appears, the mother takes a torch or a burning brand from the fire and goes to the ash-heap behind the hut. She is followed by the grandmother carrying the child. At the ash-heap the mother throws the burning stick towards the moon, while the grandmother tosses the

[1] W. Crooke, *Popular Religion and Folk-lore of Northern India* (Westminster, 1896), i. 14 *sq.*

[2] George Brown, D.D., *Melanesians* and *Polynesians* (London, 1910), p. 37.

[3] Rev. J. Roscoe, *The Baganda* (London, 1911), p. 58.

baby into the air, saying, "This is your moon!" The child squalls and rolls over on the ash-heap. Then the mother snatches up the infant and nurses it; so they go home.[1]

The Guarayos Indians, who inhabit the gloomy tropical forests of Eastern Bolivia, lift up their children in the air at new moon in order that they may grow.[2] Among the Apinagos Indians, on the Tocantins River in Brazil, the French traveller Castelnau witnessed a remarkable dance by moonlight. The Indians danced in two long ranks which faced each other, the women on one side, the men on the other. Between the two ranks of dancers blazed a great fire. The men were painted in brilliant colours, and for the most part wore white or red skull-caps made of maize-flour and resin. Their dancing was very monotonous and consisted of a jerky movement of the body, while the dancer advanced first one leg and then the other. This dance they accompanied with a melancholy song, striking the ground with their weapons. Opposite them the women, naked and unpainted, stood in a single rank, their bodies bent slightly forward, their knees pressed together, their arms swinging in measured time, now forward, now backward, so as to join hands. A remarkable figure in the dance was a personage painted scarlet all over, who held in his hand a rattle composed of a gourd full of pebbles. From time to time he leaped across the great fire which burned between the men and the women. Then he would run rapidly in front of the women, stopping now and then before one or other and performing a series of strange gambols, while he shook his rattle violently. Sometimes he would sink with one knee to the ground, and then suddenly throw himself backward. Altogether the agility and endurance which he displayed were remarkable. This dance lasted for hours. When a woman was tired out she withdrew, and her place was taken by another; but the same men danced the monotonous dance all night. Towards midnight the moon attained the zenith and flooded the scene with her bright rays. A change

Infants presented to the moon by the Guarayos Indians of Bolivia and the Apinagos Indians of Brazil.

---

[1] Henri A. Junod, *The Life of a South African Tribe* (Neuchatel, 1912–1913), i. 51.

[2] A. d'Orbigny, *Voyage dans l'Amérique Méridionale*, iii. 1ʳᵉ Partie (Paris and Strasburg, 1844), p. 24.

now took place in the dance. A long line of men and women advanced to the fire between the ranks of the dancers. Each of them held one end of a hammock in which lay a new-born infant, whose squalls could be heard. These babes were now to be presented by their parents to the moon. On reaching the end of the line each couple swung the hammock, accompanying the movement by a chant, which all the Indians sang in chorus. The song seemed to consist of three words, repeated over and over again. Soon a shrill voice was heard, and a hideous old hag, like a skeleton, appeared with her arms raised above her head. She went round and round the assembly several times, then disappeared in silence. While she was present, the scarlet dancer with the rattle bounded about more furiously than ever, stopping only for a moment while he passed in front of the line of women. His body was contracted and bent towards them, and described an undulatory movement like that of a worm writhing. He shook his rattle violently, as if he would fain kindle in the women the fire which burned in himself. Then rising abruptly he would resume his wild career. During this time the loud voice of an orator was heard from the village repeating a curious name without cessation. Then the speaker approached slowly, carrying on his back some gorgeous bunches of brilliant feathers and under his arm a stone axe. Behind him walked a young woman bearing an infant in a loose girdle at her waist ; the child was wrapped in a mat, which protected it against the chill night air. The couple paced slowly for a minute or two, and then vanished without speaking a word. At the same moment the curious name which the orator had shouted was taken up by the whole assembly and repeated by them again and again. This scene in its turn lasted a long time, but ceased suddenly with the setting of the moon. The French traveller who witnessed it fell asleep, and when he awoke all was calm once more : there was nothing to recall the infernal dances of the night.[1]

In explanation of these dances Castelnau merely observes

[1] F. de Castelnau, *Expédition dans les parties centrales de l'Amérique du Sud* (Paris, 1850–1851), ii. 31-34.

that the Apinagos, like many other South American Indians, The presentation of infants to the moon is probably intended to make them grow. pay a superstitious respect to the moon.   We may suppose that the ceremonious presentation of the infants to the moon was intended to ensure their life and growth.   The names solemnly chanted by the whole assembly were probably those which the parents publicly bestowed on their children. As to the scarlet dancer who leaped across the fire, we may conjecture that he personated the moon, and that his strange antics in front of the women were designed to impart to them the fertilizing virtue of the luminary, and perhaps to facilitate their delivery.

Among the Baganda of Central Africa there is general Baganda ceremonies at new moon. rejoicing when the new moon appears, and no work is done for seven days.   When the crescent is first visible at evening, mothers take out their babies and hold them at arms' length, saying, " I want my child to keep in health till the moon wanes."   At the same time a ceremony is performed which may be intended to ensure the king's life and health throughout the ensuing month.   It is a custom with the Baganda to preserve the king's navel-string with great care during his life.   The precious object is called the " Twin " of the king, as if it were his double ; and the ghost of the royal afterbirth is believed to be attached to it.   Enclosed in a pot, which is wrapt in bark cloths, the navel-string is kept in a temple specially built for it near the king's enclosure, and a great minister of state acts as its guardian and priest.   Every new moon, at evening, he carries it in state, wrapped in bark cloths, to the king, who takes it into his hands, examines it, and returns it to the minister.   The keeper of the navel-string then goes back with it to the house and sets it in the doorway, where it remains all night.   Next morning it is taken from its wrappings and again placed in the doorway until the evening, when it is once more swathed in bark cloths and restored to its usual place.[1]   Apparently the navel-string is conceived as a vital portion, a sort of external soul, of the

[1] J. Roscoe, " Further Notes on the Manners and Customs of the Baganda." *Journal of the Anthropological Institute*, xxxii. (1902) pp. 63, 76 ; *id.*, *The Baganda* (London, 1911) pp. 235 *sq.*

In the former passage the part of the king's person which is treated with this ceremony is said to be the placenta, not the navel-string.

king ; and the attentions bestowed on it at the new moon may be supposed to refresh and invigorate it, thereby refreshing and invigorating the king's life.

Baleful influence supposed to be exercised by the moon on children.

The Armenians appear to think that the moon exercises a baleful influence on little children. To avert that influence a mother will show the moon to her child and say, " Thine uncle, thine uncle." For the same purpose the father and mother will mount to the roof of the house at new moon on a Wednesday or Friday. The father then puts the child on a shovel and gives it to the mother, saying, " If it is thine, take it to thee. But if it is mine, rear it and give it to me back." The mother then takes the child and the shovel, and returns them to the father in like manner.[1] A similar opinion as to the noxious influence of moonshine on children was apparently held by the ancient Greeks ; for Greek nurses took great care never to show their infants to the moon.[2] Some Brazilian Indians in like manner guard babies against the moon, believing that it would make them ill. Immediately after delivery mothers will hide themselves and their infants in the thickest parts of the forest in order that the moonlight may not fall on them.[3] It would be easy to understand why the waning moon should be deemed injurious to children ; they might be supposed to peak and pine with its dwindling light. Thus in Angus it is thought that if a child be weaned during the waning of the moon, it will decay all the time that the moon continues to wane.[4] But it is less easy to see why the same deleterious influence on children should be ascribed to moonlight in general.

Use of the moon to increase money or decrease sickness.

There are many other ways in which people have sought to turn lunar sympathy to practical account. Clearly the increase of the moon is the time to increase your goods, and the decrease of the moon is the time to diminish your ills. Acting on this imaginary law of nature many persons in Europe show their money to the new moon or turn it in

---

[1] M. Abeghian, *Der armenische Volksglaube* (Leipsic, 1899), p. 49.

[2] Plutarch, *Quaestiones Conviviales*, iv. 10. 3. 7.

[3] J. B. von Spix und C. F. Ph. von Martius, *Reise in Brasilien* (Munich, 1823–1831), i. 381, iii. 1186.

[4] J. Jamieson, *Dictionary of the Scottish Language*, New Edition edited by J. Longmuir and D. Donaldson (Paisley, 1879–1882), iii. 300 (*s.v.* " Mone ").

their pockets at that season, in the belief that the money will grow with the growth of the planet; sometimes, by way of additional precaution, they spit on the coin at the same time.[1] "Both Christians and Moslems in Syria turn their silver money in their pockets at the new moon for luck; and two persons meeting under the new moon will each take out a silver coin and embrace, saying, 'May you begin and end; and may it be a good month to us.'"[2] Conversely the waning of the moon is the most natural time to get rid of bodily ailments. In Brittany they think that warts vary with the phases of the moon, growing as it waxes and vanishing away as it wanes.[3] Accordingly, they say in Germany that if you would rid yourself of warts you should treat them when the moon is on the decrease.[4] And a German cure for toothache, earache, headache, and so forth, is to look towards the waning moon and say, "As the moon decreases, so may my pains decrease also."[5] However, some Germans reverse the rule. They say, for example, that if you are afflicted with a wen, you should face the waxing moon, lay your finger on the wen, and say thrice, "What I see waxes; what I touch, let it vanish away." After each of these two sentences you should cross yourself thrice. Then go home without speaking to any one, and repeat three paternosters behind the kitchen door.[6] The Huzuls of the Carpathians recommend a somewhat similar, and no doubt equally efficacious, cure for waterbrash. They say that at new moon the patient should run thrice round the house and then say to the moon, "Moon, moon, where wast thou?" "Behind the mountain." "What hast thou eaten there?" "Horse flesh." "Why hast thou brought me nothing?" "Because I forgot." "May the waterbrash

[1] F. Panzer, *Beitrag zur deutschen Mythologie* (Munich, 1848–1855), ii. 260; P. Drechsler, *Sitte, Brauch und Volksglaube in Schlesien*, ii. (Leipsic, 1906) p. 131; W. Henderson, *Folk-lore of the Northern Counties of England* (London, 1879), p. 114; C. S. Burne and G. F. Jackson, *Shropshire Folk-lore* (London, 1883), p. 257; W. Gregor, *Folk-lore of the North-East of Scotland* (London, 1881), p. 151.

[2] C. R. Conder, *Heth and Moab* (London, 1883), p. 286.

[3] P. Sébillot, *Traditions et Superstitions de la Haute-Bretagne* (Paris, 1882), ii. 355.

[4] A. Kuhn, *Märkische Sagen und Märchen* (Berlin, 1843), p. 387, § 93.

[5] *Die gestriegelte Rockenphilosophie* (Chemnitz, 1759), p. 447.

[6] F. Panzer, *Beitrag zur deutschen Mythologie*, ii. 302. Compare J. Grimm, *Deutsche Mythologie*,[4] ii. 596.

forget to burn me!"[1]   Thus a curative virtue appears to be attributed by some people to the waning and by others to the waxing moon.   There is perhaps just as much, or as little, to be said for the one attribution as for the other.

[1] R. F. Kaindl, "Zauberglaube bei den Huzulen," *Globus*, lxxvi. (1899) p. 256.

CHAPTER X

THE KING AS OSIRIS

IN the foregoing discussion we found reason to believe that the Semitic Adonis and the Phrygian Attis were at one time personated in the flesh by kings, princes, or priests who played the part of the god for a time and then either died a violent death in the divine character or had to redeem their life in one way or another, whether by performing a make-believe sacrifice at some expense of pain and danger to themselves, or by delegating the duty to a substitute.[1] Further, we conjectured that in Egypt the part of Osiris may have been played by the king himself.[2] It remains to adduce some positive evidence of this personation.

A great festival called the Sed was celebrated by the Egyptians with much solemnity at intervals of thirty years. Various portions of the ritual are represented on the ancient monuments of Hieraconpolis and Abydos and in the oldest decorated temple of Egypt known to us, that of Usirniri at Busiris, which dates from the fifth dynasty. It appears that the ceremonies were as old as the Egyptian civilization, and that they continued to be observed till the end of the Roman period.[3] The reason for holding them at intervals of thirty

---

[1] See above, vol. i. pp. 16 sq., 48 sqq., 110, 114, 170 sq., 172 sqq., 176 sqq., 179 sqq., 285 sqq., 288 sqq.

[2] See above, pp. 97 sq., 101 sq.

[3] A. Moret, *Du caractère religieux de la royauté Pharaonique* (Paris, 1902), pp. 235-238. The festival is discussed at length by M. Moret (*op. cit.* pp. 235-273). See further R. Lepsius, *Die Chronologie der Aegypter*, i. 161-165; Miss M. A. Murray, *The Osireion*

at Abydos, pp. 32-34; W. M. Flinders Petrie, *Researches in Sinai* (London, 1906), pp. 176-185. In interpreting the festival I follow Professor Flinders Petrie. That the festival occurred, theoretically at least, at intervals of thirty years, appears to be unquestionable; for in the Greek text of the Rosetta Stone Ptolemy V. is called "lord of periods of thirty years," and though the corresponding part of the hieroglyphic

years is uncertain, but we can hardly doubt that the period
was determined by astronomical considerations.   According
to one view, it was based on the observation of Saturn's
period of revolution round the sun, which is, roughly speaking,
thirty years, or, more exactly, twenty-nine years and one
hundred and seventy-four days.[1]   According to another
view, the thirty years' period had reference to Sirius, the
star of Isis.   We have seen that on account of the vague
character of the old Egyptian year the heliacal rising of
Sirius shifted its place gradually through every month of
the calendar.[2]   In one hundred and twenty years the star
thus passed through one whole month of thirty days.   To
speak more precisely, it rose on the first of the month during
the first four years of the period : it rose on the second of
the month in the second four years, on the third of the
month in the third four years ; and so on successively, till in the last four years of the hundred and
twenty years it rose on the last day of the month.   As the
Egyptians watched the annual summer rising of the star with
attention and associated it with the most popular of their
goddesses, it would be natural that its passage from one
month to another, at intervals of one hundred and twenty
years, should be the occasion of a great festival, and that
the long period of one hundred and twenty years should be
divided into four minor periods of thirty years respectively,
each celebrated by a minor festival.[3]   If this theory of the
Sed festivals is correct, we should expect to find that every
fourth celebration was distinguished from the rest by a
higher degree of solemnity, since it marked the completion
of a twelfth part of the star's journey through the twelve

text is lost, the demotic version of the
words is "master of the years of the
Sed festival."   See R. Lepsius, *op.
cit.* pp. 161 *sq.* ; W. Dittenberger,
Orientis Graeci Inscriptiones Selectae,
No. 90, line 2 (vol. i. p. 142); A.
Moret, *op. cit.* 260. However, the
kings appear to have sometimes celebrated the festival at much shorter
intervals, so that the dates of its recurrence cannot safely be used for
chronological purposes.   See Ed.
Meyer, *Nachträge zur ägyptischen*

Chronologie (Berlin, 1908), pp. 43 *sq.*
(*Abhandlungen der königl. Akademie
der Wissenschaften vom Jahre 1907*) ;
id., Geschichte des Altertums,[2] i. 2.
pp. xix. 130.

[1] This was Letronne's theory (R.
Lepsius, *op. cit.* p. 163).

[2] See above, pp. 24 *sqq.,* 34 *sqq.*

[3] This was in substance the theory
of Biot (R. Lepsius, *l.c.*), and it is the
view of Professor W. M. Flinders Petrie
(*Researches in Sinai,* pp. 176 *sqq.*).

months.   Now it appears that in point of fact every fourth
Sed festival was marked off from its fellows by the adjective
tep or "chief," and that these "chief" celebrations fell as a
rule in the years when Sirius rose on the first of the month.[1]
These facts confirm the view that the Sed festival was closely
connected with the star Sirius, and through it with Isis.

However, we are here concerned rather with the meaning   Intention
and the rites of the festival than with the reasons for holding   of the Sed
it once every thirty years.   The intention of the festival   festival to
seems to have been to procure for the king a new lease of   renew the
life, a renovation of his divine energies, a rejuvenescence.   king's life.
In the inscriptions of Abydos we read, after an account of
the rites, the following address to the king: " Thou dost
recommence thy renewal, thou art granted to flourish again
like the infant god Moon, thou dost grow young again, and
that from season to season, like Nun at the beginning of
time, thou art born again in renewing the Sed festivals.
All life comes to thy nostril, and thou art king of the whole
earth for ever."[2]   In short, on these occasions it appears to
have been supposed that the king was in a manner born
again.

But how was the new birth effected?   Apparently the   The king
essence of the rites consisted in identifying the king with   identified
Osiris; for just as Osiris had died and risen again from the   with the
dead, so the king might be thought to die and to live again   dead Osiris
with the god whom he personated.   The ceremony would   at the Sed
thus be for the king a death as well as a rebirth.   Accord-   festival.
ingly in pictures of the Sed festival on the monuments we
see the king posing as the dead Osiris.   He sits in a shrine
like a god, holding in his hands the crook and flail of
Osiris: he is wrapped in tight bandages like the mummified
Osiris; indeed, there is nothing but his name to prove that
he is not Osiris himself.   This enthronement of the king in
the attitude of the dead god seems to have been the principal
event of the festival.[3]   Further, the queen and the king's
daughters figured prominently in the ceremonies.[4]   A

[1] W. M. Flinders Petrie, *Researches
in Sinai*, p. 180.
[2] A. Moret, *Du caractère religieux
de la royauté Pharaonique*, pp. 255 *sq.*
[3] W. M. Flinders Petrie, *Researches*

in Sinai, p. 181.
[4] A. Moret, *op. cit.* p. 240; Miss
M. A. Murray, *The Osireion at Abydos*,
pp. 33 *sq.*, with the slip inserted at p.
33; W. Flinders Petrie, *op. cit.* p. 184.

discharge of arrows formed part of the rites ; [1] and in some sculptures at Carnac the queen is portrayed shooting arrows towards the four quarters of the world, while the king does the same with rings.[2] The oldest illustration of the festival is on the mace of Narmer, which is believed to date from 5500 B.C. Here we see the king seated as Osiris in a shrine at the top of nine steps. Beside the shrine stand fan-bearers, and in front of it is a figure in a palanquin, which, according to an inscription in another representation of the scene, appears to be the royal child. An enclosure of curtains hung on poles surrounds the dancing-ground, where three men are performing a sacred dance. A procession of standards is depicted beside the enclosure ; it is headed by the standard of the jackal-god Up-uat, the " opener of ways " for the dead.[3] Similarly on a seal of King Zer, or rather Khent, one of the early kings of the first dynasty, the monarch appears as Osiris with the standard of the jackal-god before him. In front of him, too, is the ostrich feather on which " the dead king was supposed to ascend into heaven. Here, then, the king, identified with Osiris, king of the dead, has before him the jackal-god, who leads the dead, and the ostrich feather, which symbolizes his reception into the sky." [4] There are even grounds for thinking that in order to complete the mimic death of the king at the Sed festival an effigy of him, clad in the costume of Osiris, was solemnly buried in a cenotaph.[5]

Professor Flinders Petrie's explanation of the Sed festival.

According to Professor Flinders Petrie, " the conclusion may be drawn thus. In the savage age of prehistoric times, the Egyptians, like many other African and Indian peoples, killed their priest-king at stated intervals, in order that the ruler should, with unimpaired life and health, be enabled to maintain the kingdom in its highest condition. The royal daughters were present in order that they might be married to his successor. The jackal-god went before

---

[1] A. Moret, *op. cit.* p. 242.

[2] Miss M. A. Murray, *op. cit.*, slip inserted at p. 33.

[3] W. M. Flinders Petrie, *Researches in Sinai*, p. 183.

[4] W. M. Flinders Petrie, *l.c.* As to the king's name (Khent instead of Zer)

see above, p. 20, note [1].

[5] J. Capart, " Bulletin critique des religions de l'Égypte," *Revue de l'Histoire des Religions*, liii. (1906) pp. 332-334. I have to thank Professor W. M. Flinders Petrie for calling my attention to this passage.

him, to open the way to the unseen world ; and the ostrich
feather received and bore away the king's soul in the breeze
that blew it out of sight.   This was the celebration of the
'end,' the *sed* feast.   The king thus became the dead king,
patron of all those who had died in his reign, who were his
subjects here and hereafter.   He was thus one with Osiris,
the king of the dead.   This fierce custom became changed,
as in other lands, by appointing a deputy king to die in his
stead ; which idea survived in the Coptic Abu Nerūs, with
his tall crown of Upper Egypt, false beard, and sceptre.
After the death of the deputy, the real king renewed his
life and reign.   Henceforward this became the greatest of
the royal festivals, the apotheosis of the king during his life,
after which he became Osiris upon earth and the patron of
the dead in the underworld." [1]

A similar theory of the Sed festival is maintained by
another eminent Egyptologist, M. Alexandre Moret.   He
says : " In most of the temples of Egypt, of all periods,
pictures set forth for us the principal scenes of a solemn
festival called festival of the tail the Sed festival.   It consisted essentially in a representation of the ritual death of the
king followed by his rebirth.   In this case the king is identified with Osiris, the god who in historical times is the hero
of the sacred drama of humanity, he who guides us through
the three stages of life, death, and rebirth in the other world.
Hence, clad in the funeral costume of Osiris, with the tight-
fitting garment clinging to him like a shroud, Pharaoh is conducted to the tomb ; and from it he returns rejuvenated and
reborn like Osiris emerging from the dead.   How was this
fiction carried out? how was this miracle performed?   By
the sacrifice of human or animal victims.   On behalf of the
king a priest lay down in the skin of the animal victim : he
assumed the posture characteristic of an embryo in its
mother's womb : when he came forth from the skin he was
deemed to be reborn ; and Pharaoh, for whom this rite was
celebrated, was himself reborn, or to adopt the Egyptian ex-

Alexandre Moret's theory that at the Sed festivals the king was supposed to die and to be born again.

---

[1] W. M. Flinders Petrie, *Researches in Sinai*, p. 185.   As to the Coptic mock-king see C. B. Klunzinger, *Bilder aus Oberägypten, der Wüste und dem Rothen Meere* (Stuttgart, 1877), pp.   180 *sq.* ; *The Dying God*, pp. 151 *sq.* For examples of human sacrifices offered to prolong the lives of kings see below, vol. ii. pp. 219 *sqq.*

pression, 'he renewed his births.' And in testimony of the due performance of the rites the king girt his loins with the tail, a compendious representative of the skin of the sacrificed beast, whence the name of ' the festival of the tail.'

" How are we to explain the rule that at a certain point of his reign every Pharaoh must undergo this ritual death followed by fictitious rebirth? Is it simply a renewal of the initiation into the Osirian mysteries? or does the festival present some more special features? The ill-defined part played by the royal children in these rites seems to me to indicate that the Sed festival represents other episodes which refer to the transmission of the regal office. At the dawn of civilization in Egypt the people were perhaps familiar with the alternative either of putting their king to death in his full vigour in order that his power should be transmitted intact to his successor, or of attempting to rejuvenate him and to ' renew his life.' The latter measure was an invention of the Pharaohs. How could it be carried out more effectively than by identifying themselves with Osiris, by applying to themselves the process of resurrection, the funeral rites by which Isis, according to the priests, had magically saved her husband from death? Perhaps the fictitious death of the king may be regarded as a mitigation of the primitive murder of the divine king, a transition from a barbarous reality to symbolism." [1]

[1] A. Moret, *Mystères Égyptiens* (Paris, 1913), pp. 187-190. For a detailed account of the Egyptian evidence, monumental and inscriptional, on which M. Moret bases his view of the king's rebirth by deputy from the hide of a sacrificed animal, see pp. 16 *sqq.*, 72 *sqq.* of the same work. Compare his article, " Du sacrifice en Égypte," *Revue de l'Histoire des Religions*, lvii. (1908) pp. 93 *sqq.* In support of the view that the king of Egypt was deemed to be born again at the Sed festival it has been pointed out that on these solemn occasions, as we learn from the monuments, there was carried before the king on a pole an object shaped like a placenta, a part of the human body which many savage or barbarous peoples regard as the twin brother or sister of the new-born child. See C. G. Seligmann and Margaret A. Murray, " Note upon an early Egyptian standard," *Man*, xi. (1911) pp. 165-171. The object which these writers take to represent a human placenta is interpreted by M. Alexandre Moret as the likeness of a human embryo. As to the belief that the afterbirth is a twin brother or sister of the infant, see above, vol. i. p. 93, and below, pp. 169 *sq.*; *The Magic Art and the Evolution of Kings*, i. 82 *sqq.*

Professor J. H. Breasted thinks that the Sed festival is probably " the oldest religious feast of which any trace has been preserved in Egypt " ; he admits that on these occasions " the king assumed the costume and insignia of

Whether this interpretation of the Sed festival be accepted in all its details or not, one thing seems quite certain: on these solemn occasions the god Osiris was personated by the king of Egypt himself. That is the point with which we are here chiefly concerned.

Osiris personated by the king of Egypt.

Osiris, and undoubtedly impersonated him," and further that "one of the ceremonies of this feast symbolized the resurrection of Osiris"; but he considers that the significance of the festival is as yet obscure. See J. H. Breasted, *Development of Religion and Thought in Ancient Egypt* (London, 1912), p. 39.

CHAPTER XI

THE ORIGIN OF OSIRIS

How did the conception of Osiris as a god of vegetation and of the dead originate?

THUS far we have discussed the character of Osiris as he is presented to us in the art and literature of Egypt and in the testimonies of Greek writers ; and we have found that judged by these indications he was in the main a god of vegetation and of the dead. But we have still to ask, how did the conception of such a composite deity originate? Did it arise simply through observation of the great annual fluctuations of the seasons and a desire to explain them? Was it a result of brooding over the mystery of external nature? Was it the attempt of a rude philosophy to lift the veil and explore the hidden springs that set the vast machine in motion? That man at a very early stage of his long history meditated on these things and evolved certain crude theories which partially satisfied his craving after knowledge is certain ; from such meditations of Babylonian and Phrygian sages appear to have sprung the pathetic figures of Adonis and Attis ; and from such meditations of Egyptian sages may have sprung the tragic figure of Osiris.

While Adonis and Attis were subordinate figures in their respective pantheons, Osiris was the greatest and most popular god of Egypt.

Yet a broad distinction seems to sever the myth and worship of Osiris from the kindred myths and worships of Adonis and Attis. For while Adonis and Attis were minor divinities in the religion of Western Asia, completely overshadowed by the greater deities of their respective pantheons, the solemn figure of Osiris towered in solitary grandeur over all the welter of Egyptian gods, like a pyramid of his native land lit up by the last rays of the setting sun when all below it is in shadow. And whereas legend generally represented Adonis and Attis as simple swains, mere herdsmen

158

or hunters whom the fatal love of a goddess had elevated above their homely sphere into a brief and melancholy preeminence, Osiris uniformly appears in tradition as a great and beneficent king. In life he ruled over his people, beloved and revered for the benefits he conferred on them and on the world; in death he reigned in their hearts and memories as lord of the dead, the awful judge at whose bar every man must one day stand to give an account of the deeds done in the body and to receive the final award. In the faith of the Egyptians the cruel death and blessed resurrection of Osiris occupied the same place as the death and resurrection of Christ hold in the faith of Christians. As Osiris died and rose again from the dead, so they hoped through him and in his dear name to wake triumphant from the sleep of death to a blissful eternity. That was their sheet-anchor in life's stormy sea; that was the hope which supported and consoled millions of Egyptian men and women for a period of time far longer than that during which Christianity has now existed on earth. In the long history of religion no two divine figures resemble each other more closely in the fervour of personal devotion which they have kindled and in the high hopes which they have inspired than Osiris and Christ. The sad figure of Buddha indeed has been as deeply loved and revered by countless millions; but he had no glad tidings of immortality for men, nothing but the promise of a final release from the burden of mortality.

And if Osiris and Christ have been the centres of the like enthusiastic devotion, may not the secret of their influence have been similar? If Christ lived the life and died the death of a man on earth, may not Osiris have done so likewise? The immense and enduring popularity of his worship speaks in favour of the supposition; for all the other great religious or semi-religious systems which have won for themselves a permanent place in the affections of mankind, have been founded by individual great men, who by their personal life and example exerted a power of attraction such as no cold abstractions, no pale products of the collective wisdom or folly could ever exert on the minds and hearts of humanity. Thus it was with Buddhism, with

The personal devotion of the Egyptians to Osiris suggests that he may have been a real man; for all the permanent religious or semi-religious systems of the world have been founded by

individual
great men. Confucianism, with Christianity, and with Mohammedanism ; and thus it may well have been with the religion of Osiris. Certainly we shall do less violence to the evidence if we accept the unanimous tradition of ancient Egypt on this point than if we resolve the figure of Osiris into a myth pure and simple. And when we consider that from the earliest to the latest times Egyptian kings were worshipped as gods both in life and in death, there appears to be nothing extravagant or improbable in the view that one of them by his personal qualities excited a larger measure of devotion than usual during his life and was remembered with fonder affection and deeper reverence after his death ; till in time his beloved memory, dimmed, transfigured, and encircled with a halo of glory by the mists of time, grew into the dominant religion of his people. At least this theory is reasonable enough to deserve a serious consideration. If we accept it, we may suppose that the mythical elements, which legend undoubtedly ascribed to Osiris, were later accretions which gathered about his memory like ivy about a ruin. There is no improbability in such a supposition ; on the contrary, all analogy is in its favour, for nothing is more certain than that myths grow like weeds round the great historical figures of the past.

The historical reality of Osiris as an old king of Egypt can be supported by modern African analogies. In recent years the historical reality of Osiris as a king who once lived and reigned in Egypt has been maintained by more than one learned scholar ;[1] and without venturing to pronounce a decided opinion on so obscure and difficult a question, I think it worth while, following the example of Dr. Wallis Budge, to indicate certain modern African analogies which tend to confirm the view that beneath the mythical wrappings of Osiris there lay the mummy of a dead man. At all events the analogies which I shall cite suffice to prove that the custom of worshipping dead kings has not been confined to Egypt, but has been apparently widespread throughout Africa, though the evidence now at our disposal only enables us to detect the observance of the

[1] It is maintained by the discoverer of the tomb of Osiris at Abydos, Monsieur E. Amélineau, in his work *Le Tombeau d'Osiris* (Paris, 1899) and by Dr. E. A. Wallis Budge in his elaborate treatise *Osiris and the Egyptian Resurrection*, in which the author pays much attention to analogies drawn from the religion and customs of modern African tribes.

custom at a few points of the great continent. But even if the resemblance in this respect between ancient Egypt and modern Africa should be regarded as established, it would not justify us in inferring an ethnical affinity between the fair or ruddy Egyptians and the black aboriginal races, who occupy almost the whole of Africa except a comparatively narrow fringe on the northern sea-board. Scholars are still divided on the question of the original home and racial relationship of the ancient Egyptians. It has been held on the one hand that they belong to an indigenous white race which has been always in possession of the Mediterranean coasts of Africa ; and on the other hand it has been supposed that they are akin to the Semites in blood as well as in language, and that they entered Africa from the East, whether by gradual infiltration or on a sudden wave of conquest like the Arabs in the decline of the Roman empire.[1] On either view a great gulf divided them from the swarthy natives of the Sudan, with whom they were always in contact on their southern border ; and though a certain admixture may have taken place through marriage between the two races, it seems unsafe to assume that the religious and political resemblances which can be traced between them are based on any closer relationship than the general similarity in structure and functions of the human mind.

In a former part of this work we saw that the Shilluks, a pastoral and partially agricultural people of the White Nile, worship the spirits of their dead kings.[2] The graves of the deceased monarchs form indeed the national or tribal

The spirits of dead kings worshipped by the Shilluks

---

[1] G. Maspero, *Histoire ancienne des Peuples de l'Orient Classique*, i. 43 *sqq.* ; J. H. Breasted, *History of the Ancient Egyptians*, pp. 29 *sq.* ; Ed. Meyer, *Geschichte des Altertums*,[2] i. 2. pp. 41 *sqq.* The affinity of the Egyptian language to the Semitic family of speech seems now to be admitted even by historians who maintain the African origin of the Egyptians.

[2] *The Dying God,* pp. 17 *sqq.* The information there given was kindly supplied by Dr. C. G. Seligmann, who has since published it with fuller details. See C. G. Seligmann, *The Cult of Nyakang and the Divine Kings of the Shilluk* (Khartoum, 1911), pp. 216-232 (reprint from *Fourth Report of the Wellcome Tropical Research Laboratories, Gordon Memorial College, Khartoum*) ; W. Hofmayr, "Religion der Schilluk," *Anthropos*, vi. (1911) pp. 120-131 ; Diedrich Westermann, *The Shilluk People, their Language and Folklore* (Berlin, preface dated 1912), pp. xxxix. *sqq.* In what follows I have drawn on all these authorities.

of the
White
Nile.

temples ; and as each king is interred at the village where
he was born and where his afterbirth is buried, these grave-
shrines are scattered over the country. Each of them
usually comprises a small group of round huts, resembling
the common houses of the people, the whole being enclosed
by a fence ; one of the huts is built over the grave, the
others are occupied by the guardians of the shrine, who at
first are generally the widows or old men-servants of the
deceased king. When these women or retainers die, they
are succeeded in office by their descendants, for the tombs
are maintained in perpetuity, so that the number of

Sacrifices
to the
dead kings.

temples and of gods is always on the increase. Cattle are
dedicated to these royal shrines and animals sacrificed at
them. For example, when the millet crop threatens to fail
or a murrain breaks out among the beasts, one of the dead
kings will appear to somebody in a dream and demand a
sacrifice. The dream is reported to the king, and he
immediately orders a bullock and a cow to be sent to the
grave of the dead king who appeared in a vision of the
night to the sleeper. This is done ; the bullock is killed and
the cow added to the sacred herd of the shrine. It is
customary, also, though not necessary, at harvest to offer
some of the new millet at the temple-tombs of the kings ;
and sick people send animals to be sacrificed there on their
behalf. Special regard is paid to trees that grow near
the graves of the kings ; and the spirits of the departed
monarchs are believed to appear from time to time in the
form of certain animals. One of them, for example, always
takes the shape of a certain insect, which seems to be the
larva of the *Mantidae*. When a Shilluk finds one of these
insects, he will take it up in his hands and deposit it reverentially at the shrine. Other kings manifest themselves as a
certain species of white birds; others assume the form of
giraffes. When one of these long-legged and long-necked
creatures comes stalking up fearlessly to a village where
there is a king's grave, the people know that the king's soul
is in the animal, and the attendants at the royal tomb testify
their joy at the appearance of their master by sacrificing a
sheep or even a bullock.

But of all the dead kings none is revered so deeply or

occupies so large a place in the minds of the people as Nyakang, the traditional founder of the dynasty and the ancestor of all the kings who have reigned after him to the present day. Of these kings the Shilluks have preserved the memory and the genealogy; twenty-six seem to have sat on the throne since Nyakang, but the period of time covered by their reigns is much shorter than it would have been under conditions such as now prevail in Europe; for down to the time when their country came under British rule it was the regular custom of the Shilluks to put their kings to death as soon as they showed serious symptoms of bodily or mental decay. The custom was based on " the conviction that the king must not be allowed to become ill or senile, lest with his diminishing vigour the cattle should sicken and fail to bear their increase, the crops should rot in the fields, and man, stricken with disease, should die in ever-increasing numbers." [1] It is said that Nyakang, like Romulus, disappeared in a great storm, which scattered all the people about him; in their absence the king took a cloth, tied it tightly round his neck, and strangled himself. According to one account, that is the death which all his successors on the throne have died; [2] but while tradition appears to be unanimous as to the custom of regicide, it varies as to the precise mode in which the kings were relieved of their office and of life. But still the people are convinced that Nyakang did not really die but only vanished mysteriously away like the wind. When a missionary asked the Shilluks as to the manner of Nyakang's death, they were filled with amazement at his ignorance and stoutly maintained that he never died, for were he to die all the Shilluks would die also. [3] The graves of this deified king are shown in various parts of the country.

From time to time the spirit of Nyakang manifests itself to his people in the form of an animal. Any creature of regal port or surpassing beauty may serve as his temporary incarnation. Such among wild animals are lions, crocodiles, little yellow snakes that crawl about men's houses, the finest sorts of antelopes, flamingoes with their rose-pink and scarlet

Worship of Nyakang, the first of the Shilluk kings.

The spirit of Nyakang supposed to manifest itself in certain animals.

[1] C. G. Seligmann, *The Cult of Nyakang*, p. 221.
[2] D. Westermann, *The Shilluk People*, p. xlii.
[3] D. Westermann, *l.c.*

plumage, and butterflies of all sorts with their brilliant and varied hues. An unusually fine head of cattle is also recognized as the abode of the great king's soul ; for example he once appeared in the shape of a white bull, whereupon the living king commanded special sacrifices to be offered in honour of his deified predecessor. When a bird in which the royal spirit is known to be lodged lights on a tree, that tree becomes sacred to Nyakang ; beads and cloths are hung on its boughs, sacrifices and prayers are offered below it. Once when the Turks unknowingly felled such a tree, fear and horror fell on the Shilluks who beheld the sacrilege. They filled the air with lamentations and killed an ox to appease their insulted ancestor.[1] Particular regard is also paid to trees that grow near the graves of Nyakang, though they are not regularly worshipped.[2] In one place two gigantic baobab trees are pointed out as marking the spot where Nyakang once stood, and sacrifices are now offered under their spreading shade.[3]

The deified Nyakang seems to have been a real man. There seems to be no doubt that in spite of the mythical elements which have gathered round his memory, Nyakang was a real man, who led the Shilluks to their present home on the Nile either from the west or from the south ; for on this point tradition varies. "The first and most important ancestor, who is everywhere revered, is Nyakang, the first Shilluk king. He always receives the honourable titles of Father (*uò*), Ancestor (*qua*), King (*red*) or Kings (*ror*), Ancestors, and Great Man Above (*čal duong mal*) to distinguish him from the other great men on earth. Nyakang, as we know, was an historical personage ; he led the Shilluks to the land which they now occupy ; he helped them to victory, made them great and warlike, regulated marriage and law, distributed the country among them, divided it into districts, and in order to increase the dependence of the people on him and to show them his power, became their greatest benefactor by giving himself out as the bestower of rain."[4] Yet Nyakang is now universally revered by the people as a demi-god ; indeed for all practical pur-

---

[1] W. Hofmayr, "Religion der Schilluk," *Anthropos*, vi. (1911) pp. 123 *sq.*; C. G. Seligmann, *op. cit.* p. 230; D. Westermann, *op. cit.* p. xliii.

[2] C. G. Seligmann, *op. cit.* pp. 229 *sq.*

[3] W. Hofmayr, *op. cit.* p. 125.

[4] W. Hofmayr, *op. cit.* p. 123. This writer spells the name of the deified king as Nykang. I have adopted Dr. Seligmann's spelling.

poses his worship quite eclipses that of the supreme god Juok, the creator, who, having ordered the world, committed it to the care of ancestral spirits and demons, and now, dwelling aloft, concerns himself no further with human affairs. Hence men pay little heed to their creator and seldom take his name into their lips except in a few conventional forms of salutation at meeting and parting like our " Good-bye." Far otherwise is it with Nyakang. He " is the ancestor of the Shilluk nation and the founder of the Shilluk dynasty. He is worshipped, sacrifices and prayers are offered to him ; he may be said to be lifted to the rank of a demi-god, though they never forget that he has been a real man. He is expressly designated as ' little ' in comparison with God." Yet " in the political, religious and personal life Nyakang takes a far more important place than Juok. Nyakang is the national hero, of whom each Shilluk feels proud, who is praised in innumerable popular songs and sayings ; he is not only a superior being, but also a man. He is the sublime model for every true Shilluk ; everything they value most in their national and private life has its origin in him : their kingdom and their fighting as well as cattle-breeding and farming. While Nyakang is their good father, who only does them good, Juok is the great, uncontrollable power, which is to be propitiated, in order to avoid his inflictions of evil." [1] Indeed " the whole working religion of the Shilluk is a cult of Nyakang, the semi-divine ancestor of their kings, in each of whom his spirit is immanent." [2] The transmission of the divine or semi-divine spirit of Nyakang to the reigning monarch appears to take place at the king's installation and to be effected by means of a rude wooden effigy of Nyakang, in which the spirit of that deified man is perhaps supposed to be immanent. But however the spiritual transmission may be carried out, " the fundamental idea of the cult of the Shilluk divine kings is the immanence in each of the spirit of Nyakang." [3] Thus the Shilluk kings are encircled with a

[1] Diederich Westermann, *The Shilluk People, their Language and Folklore* (Berlin, preface dated 1912), pp. xlii, xliii. Mr. Westermann gives the names of the demi-god and the god as Nyikang and Jwok respectively. For the sake of uniformity I have altered them to Nyakang and Juok, the forms adopted by Dr. C. G. Seligmann.

[2] C. G. Seligmann, *The Cult of Nyakang and the Divine Kings of the Shilluk* (Khartoum, 1911), p. 220.

[3] C. G. Seligmann, *op. cit.* p. 231.

certain halo of divinity because they are thought to be animated by the divine spirit of their ancestor, the founder of the dynasty.

The belief in the former humanity of Nyakang is confirmed by the analogy of his worship to that of the dead Shilluk kings.

The universal belief of the Shilluks in the former humanity of Nyakang is strongly confirmed by the exact parallelism which prevails between his worship and that of the dead kings his successors. Like them he is worshipped at his tomb; but unlike them he has not one tomb only, but ten scattered over the country. Each of these tombs is called "the grave of Nyakang," though the people well know that nobody is buried there. Like the grave-shrines of the other kings, those of Nyakang consist of a small group of circular huts of the ordinary pattern enclosed by a fence. Only children under puberty and the few old people whose duty it is to take care of the shrines may enter these sacred enclosures. The rites performed at them resemble those observed at the shrines of the kings. Two great ceremonies are annually performed at the shrines of Nyakang: one is observed before the beginning of the rainy season in order to ensure a due supply of rain; the other is a thanksgiving at harvest, when porridge made from the new grain is poured out on the threshold of Nyakang's hut and smeared on the outer walls of the building. Even before the millet is reaped the people cut some of the ripening ears and thrust them into the thatch of the sacred hut. Thus it would seem that the Shilluks believe themselves to be dependent on the favour of Nyakang for the rain and the crops. "As the giver of rain, Nyakang is the first and greatest benefactor of the people. In that country rain is everything, without rain there is nothing. The Shilluk does not trouble his head about artificial irrigation, he waits for the rain. If the rain falls, then the millet grows, the cows thrive, man has food and can dance and marry; for that is the ideal of the Shilluks."[1] Sick people also bring or send sheep as an offering to the nearest shrine of Nyakang in order that they may be healed of their sickness. The attendants of the

---

[1] W. Hofmayr, *op. cit.* p. 125. "It must be remembered that the due growth of the crops, *i.e.* of the most important part of the vegetable world, depends on the well-being of the divine king" (C. G. Seligmann, *op. cit.* p. 229).

sanctuary slaughter the animal, consume its flesh, and give the sufferer the benefit of their prayers.[1]

The example of Nyakang seems to show that under favourable circumstances the worship of a dead king may develop into the dominant religion of a people. There is, therefore, no intrinsic improbability in the view that in ancient Egypt the religion of Osiris originated in that way. Certainly some curious resemblances can be traced between the dead Nyakang and the dead Osiris. Both died violent and mysterious deaths : the graves of both were pointed out in many parts of the country : both were deemed the great sources of fertility for the whole land : and both were associated with certain sacred trees and animals, particularly with bulls. And just as Egyptian kings identified themselves both in life and in death with their deified predecessor Osiris, so Shilluk kings are still believed to be animated by the spirit of their deified predecessor Nyakang and to share his divinity.

Comparison of Nyakang with Osiris.

Another African people who regularly worship, or rather used to worship, the spirits of their dead kings are the Baganda. Their country Uganda lies at the very source of the Nile, where the great river issues from Lake Victoria Nyanza. Among them the ghosts of dead kings were placed on an equality with the gods and received the same honour and worship ; they foretold events which concerned the State, and they advised the living king, warning him when war was likely to break out. The king consulted them periodically, visiting first one and then another of the temples in which the mortal remains of his predecessors were preserved with religious care. But the temple (*malolo*) of a king contained only his lower jawbone and his navel-string (*mulongo*) ; his body was buried elsewhere.[2] For curiously enough the Baganda believed that the part of the body to which the ghost of a dead man adheres above all others is the lower jawbone ; wherever that portion of his person may be carried, the ghost, in the opinion of these people, will follow it, even to the ends of the earth, and will be perfectly content to remain with it so long as the jawbone is

The spirits of dead kings worshipped by the Baganda of Central Africa.

[1] C. G. Seligmann, *op. cit.* p. 227.

[2] Rev. J. Roscoe, *The Baganda* (London, 1911), p. 283.

honoured.[1] Hence the jawbones of all the kings of Uganda from the earliest times to the present day have been preserved with the utmost care, each of them being deposited, along with the stump of the monarch's navel-string, in a temple specially dedicated to the worship of the king's ghost; for it is believed that the ghosts of the deceased monarchs would quarrel if they shared the same temple, the question of precedence being one which it would be very difficult for them to adjust to their mutual satisfaction.[2] All the temples of the dead kings stand in the district called Busiro, which means the place of the graves, because the tombs as well as the temples of the departed potentates are situated within its boundaries. The supervision of the temples and of the estates attached to them was a duty incumbent on the *Mugema* or earl of Busiro, one of the few hereditary chiefs in the country. His principal office was that of Prime Minister (*Katikiro*) to the dead kings.[3]

Tombs of the dead kings of Uganda.

When a king dies, his body is sent to Busiro and there embalmed. Then it is laid to rest in a large round house, which has been built for its reception on the top of a hill. This is the king's tomb. It is a conical structure supported by a central post, with a thatched roof reaching down to the ground. Round the hut a high strong fence of reeds is erected, and an outer fence encircles the whole at some distance lower down the hill. Here the body is placed on a bedstead; the sepulchral chamber is filled with bark cloths till it can hold no more, the mainpost is cut down, and the door of the tomb closed, so that no one can enter it again. When that was done, the wives of the late king used to be brought, with their arms pinioned, and placed at intervals round the outer wall of the tomb, where they were clubbed to death. Hundreds of men were also killed in the space between the two fences, that their ghosts might wait on the ghost of the dead king in the other world. None of their bodies were buried; they were left to rot where they fell. Then the gates in the fences were closed; and three chiefs

---

[1] Rev. J. Roscoe, *op. cit.* pp. 113, 282.

[2] Rev. J. Roscoe, *op. cit.* pp. 110, 282, 285.

[3] Rev. J. Roscoe, *op. cit.* pp. 104, 252 *sq.*; L. F. Cunningham, *Uganda and its People* (London, 1905), p. 226).

with their men guarded the dead bodies from the wild
beasts and the vultures. But the hut in which the king's
body reposed was never repaired ; it was allowed to moulder
and fall into decay.[1]

Five months later the jawbone of the royal corpse was
removed in order to be fashioned into an effigy or representative of the dead king. For this purpose three chiefs
entered the tomb, not through the door, but by cutting a hole
through the wall, and having severed the head from the
body they brought it out, carefully filling up the hole in the
wall behind them, replacing the thatch, and securing the
gates in the fence. When the jawbone had been removed
by a chief of the Civet clan, the skull was sent back to Busiro
and buried with honour near the mouldering tomb. In
contrast to the neglect of the tomb where the royal body
lay, the place where the skull was buried was kept in good
repair and guarded by some of the old princesses and
widows. As for the jawbone, it was put in an ant-hill and
left there till the ants had eaten away all the flesh. Then,
after it had been washed in beer and milk, it was decorated
with cowry-shells and placed in a wooden vessel ; this vessel
was next wrapt in bark cloths till it assumed a conical
shape, about two and a half feet high by a foot and a half
broad at the base. This conical packet, decorated on the
outside with beads, was treated as an image of the deceased
king or rather as if it were the king himself in life, for it
was called simply " The King." Beside it was placed the
stump of the king's navel-string, similarly wrapt in bark
cloths and decorated, though not made up into a conical
shape.[2] The reason for preserving both the jawbone and
the navel-string was that the ghost of the king was supposed to attach itself to his jawbone, and the ghost of his
double to his navel-string. For in the belief of the Baganda
every person has a double, namely, the afterbirth or placenta,
which is born immediately after him and is regarded by the

Ghosts of the dead kings of Uganda supposed to adhere to their lower jaw-bones and their navel-strings, which are accordingly preserved in temples dedicated to the worship of the kings.

[1] Rev. J. Roscoe, *The Baganda*,
pp. 104-107, *id.*, "Notes on the
Manners and Customs of the Baganda,"
*Journal of the Anthropological Insti-
tute*, xxxi. (1901) p. 129 ; *id.*,
" Further Notes on the Manners and
Customs of the Baganda," *ibid.*, xxxii.
(1902) pp. 44 *sq.* Compare L. F.
Cunningham, *Uganda and its People*
(London, 1905), pp. 224, 226.

[2] Rev. J. Roscoe, *The Baganda*,
pp. 109 *sq.*

people as a second child. Now that double has a ghost of
its own, which adheres to the navel-string; and if the
person is to remain healthy, it is essential that the ghost of
his double should be carefully preserved. Hence every
Baganda man and woman keeps his or her navel-string
wrapt up in bark cloth as a treasure of great price on which
his health and prosperity are dependent; the precious little
bundle is called his Twin (*mulongo*), because it contains the
ghost of his double, the afterbirth. If that is deemed
necessary for everybody, much more is it deemed essential
for the welfare of the king; hence during his life the stump
of his navel-string is kept, as we saw,[1] by one of the
principal ministers of state and is inspected by the king
himself every month. And when his majesty has departed
this life, the unity of his spirit imperatively demands that
his own ghost and the ghost of his double should be kept
together in the same place; that is why the jawbone and
the navel-string of every dead king are carefully preserved
in the same temple, because the two ghosts adhere respectively to these two parts of his person, and it would be
unreasonable and indeed cruel to divide them.[2]

The temples of the dead kings of Uganda.

The two ghosts having been thus safely lodged in the
two precious parcels, the next thing was to install them in
the temple, where they were to enter on their career of
beneficent activity. A site having been chosen, the whole
country supplied the labour necessary for building the
temple; and ministers were appointed to wait upon the
dead king. The officers of state who had held important
posts during his life retained their titles and continued to
discharge their duties towards their old master in death.
Accordingly houses were built for them near the temple.
The dowager queen also took up her residence at the
entrance to the temple enclosure, and became its principal
guardian. Many also of the king's widows of lower rank
were drafted off to live inside the enclosure and keep
watch over it. When the queen or any of these widows
died, her place was supplied by another princess or a

[1] Above, p. 147.

[2] Rev. J. Roscoe, "Kibuka, the

War God of the Baganda," *Man*, vii.
(1907) pp. 164 *sq.*; *id.*, *The Baganda*,
pp. 235 *sq.*

woman of the same clan ; for the temple was maintained in perpetuity.   However, when the reigning king died, the temple of his predecessor lost much of its importance, though it was still kept up in a less magnificent style ; indeed no temple of a dead king was allowed to disappear altogether.[1]   Of all the attendants at the temple the most important probably was the prophet or medium (*mandwa*), whose business it was from time to time to be inspired by the ghost of the deceased monarch and to give oracles in his name.   To this holy office he dedicated himself by drinking a draught of beer and a draught of milk out of the dead king's skull.[2]

The temple consecrated to the worship of a king regularly stood on a hill.   The site was generally chosen by the king in his life, but sometimes his choice was set aside by his successor, who gave orders to build the temple in another place.[3]   The structure was a large conical or bee-hive-shaped hut of the ordinary pattern, divided internally into two chambers, an outer and an inner.   Any person might enter the outer chamber, but the inner was sacred and no profane person might set foot in it ; for there the holy relics of the dead king, his jawbone and his navel-string, were kept for safety in a cell dug in the floor, and there, in close attendance on them, the king's ghost was believed to dwell.   In front of the partition which screened this Holy of Holies from the gaze of the multitude there stood a throne, covered with lion and leopard skins and fenced off from the rest of the sacred edifice by a glittering rail of brass spears, shields, and knives. A forest of poles, supporting the roof, formed a series of aisles in perfect line, and at the end of the central nave appeared, like the altar of a Christian church, the throne in all its glory.   When the king's ghost held a reception, the holy relics, the jawbone and the navel-string, each in its decorated wrappings, were brought forth and set on the throne ; and every person who entered the temple bowed to the ground

Oracles given by the dead kings of Uganda by the mouth of an inspired prophet.

---

[1] Rev. J. Roscoe, *The Baganda,* pp. 110-112, 283 *sq.*

[2] Rev. J. Roscoe, "Notes on the Manners and Customs of the Baganda," *Journal of the Anthropological Institute,* xxxi. (1901) pp. 129 *sq.*; *id.,*

"Further Notes on the Manners and Customs of the Baganda," *ibid.,* xxxii. (1902) p. 45.

[3] Rev. J. Roscoe, *The Baganda,* p. 283.

and greeted the jawbone in an awestruck voice, for he regarded it as the king in person. Solemn music played during the reception, the drums rolling and the women chanting, while they clapped their hands to the rhythm of the songs. Sometimes the dead king spoke to the congregation by the voice of his prophet. That was a great event. When the oracle was about to be given to the expectant throng, the prophet stepped up to the throne, and addressing the spirit informed him of the business in hand. Then he smoked one or two pipes, and the fumes bringing on the prophetic fit, he began to rave and to speak in the very voice and with the characteristic turns of speech of the departed monarch, for the king's spirit was now in him. This message from the world beyond the grave was naturally received with rapt attention. Gradually the fit of inspiration passed : the voice of the prophet resumed its natural tones : the spirit had departed from him and returned to its abode in the inner room. Such a solemn audience used to be announced beforehand by the beating of the drums in the early morning, and the worshippers brought with them to the temple offerings of food for the dead king, as if he were still alive.[1]

Visit paid by the living king to the temple of his dead father.

But the greatest day of all was when the reigning king visited the temple of his father. This he did as a rule only once during his reign. Nor did the people approve of the visits being repeated, for each visit was the signal for the death of many. Yet, attracted by a painful curiosity, crowds assembled, followed the monarch to the temple, and thronged to see the great ceremony of the meeting between the king and the ghost of his royal father. The sacred relics were displayed : an old man explained them to the monarch and placed them in his hands : the prophet, inspired by the dead king's spirit, revealed to the living king his destiny. The interview over, the king was carried back to his house. It was on the return journey that he always gave, suddenly and without warning, the signal of death. Obedient to his

[1] Rev. J. Roscoe, "Notes on the Manners and Customs of the Baganda," *Journal of the Anthropological Institute,* xxxi. (1901) p. 130 ; *id.,* "Further Notes on the Manners and Customs of the Baganda," *ibid.,* xxxii. (1902) p. 46 ; *id., The Baganda,* pp. 283-285.

orders the guards rushed upon the crowd, captured hundreds of spectators, pinioned them, marched them back to the temple, and slaughtered them within the precincts, that their ghosts might wait on the ghost of the dead king.[1] But though the king rarely visited his father's ghost at the temple, he had a private chapel for the ghost within the vast enclosure of the royal residence ; and here he often paid his devotions to the august spirit, of whom he stood greatly in awe. He took his wives with him to sing the departed monarch's praise, and he constantly made offerings at the shrine. Thither, too, would come the prophet to suck words of wisdom from the venerable ghost and to impart them to the king, who thus walked in the counsel of his glorified father.[2]

In Kiziba, a district of Central Africa on the western side of Lake Victoria Nyanza, the souls of dead kings become ruling spirits ; temples are built in their honour and priests appointed to serve them. The people are composed of two different races, the Bairu, who are aboriginals, and the Bahima, who are immigrants from the north. The royal family belongs to the Bahima stock. In his lifetime the king's person is sacred ; and all his actions, property, and so forth are described by special terms appropriated to that purpose. The people are divided into totemic clans : the totems (*muziro*) are mostly animals or parts of animals : no man may kill or eat his totem animal, nor marry a woman who has the same totem as himself. The royal family seems to have serpents for their totem ; after death the king's soul lives in a serpent, while his body is buried in the hut where he died. The people revere a supreme god named Rugaba, who is believed to have created man and cattle ; but they know little about him, and though they

---

[1] Rev. J. Roscoe, *The Baganda*, pp. 112, 284.

[2] Rev. J. Roscoe, *The Baganda*, p. 112. It may be worth while to quote an early notice of the worship of the Kings of Uganda. See C. T. Wilson and R. W. Felkin, *Uganda and the Egyptian Soudan* (London, 1882), i. 208 : "The former kings of the country appear also to be regarded as demi-gods, and their graves are kept with religious care, and houses are erected over them, which are under the constant supervision of one of the principal chiefs of the country, and where human sacrifices are also occasionally offered." The graves here spoken of are no doubt the temples in which the jawbones and navel-strings of the dead kings are kept and worshipped.

occasionally pray to him, particularly in the case of a difficult birth, he has no priests and receives no sacrifices. The business of the priests is to act as intermediaries, not between God and man, but between men and the spirits. The spirits are believed to have been formerly kings of the world. The highest of them is a certain Wamara, who rules over the souls of the dead, and who would seem to have been a great king in his life. Temples are built for him ; they are like the houses of men, but only half as large. A perpetual holy fire is kept up in each temple, and the priest passes the night in it. He receives white sheep or goats as victims, and generally acts also as a diviner or physician. When a man is very ill, he thinks that Wamara, the lord of the spirits of the dead, is summoning him to the far country ; so he sends a sacrifice to Wamara's priest, who prays to the spirit to let the sick man live yet a while.[1] This great spirit of an ancient king, who now rules over the dead, resembles the Egyptian Osiris.

The worship of ancestral spirits among the Bantu tribes of Northern Rhodesia.

The Bantu tribes who inhabit the great tableland of Northern Rhodesia revere a supreme being whom they call Leza, but their ideas about him are hazy. Thunder, lightning, earthquakes, rain, and other natural phenomena are grouped together under his name as manifestations of his power. Among the more progressive tribes, such as the Awemba and the Wabisa, the great god is thought to take some interest in human affairs ; and though they do not pray to him, they nevertheless invoke him by his names of praise, which set forth his attributes as the protector and judge of mankind. It is he, too, who receives the souls of the departed. " Yet, as far as the dominant Wemba tribe is concerned, the cult of Leza is outside their ordinary religion. There is no direct access to him by prayer or by sacrifices, which are made to Mulenga and the other great

---

[1] Hermann Rehse, *Kiziba, Land und Leute* (Stuttgart, 1910), pp. 4-7, 106 *sqq.*, 121, 125 *sqq.*, 130. Among the totems of the people are the long-tailed monkey (*Cercopithecus*), a small species of antelope, the locust, the hippopotamus, the buffalo, the otter, dappled cows, and the hearts of all animals. The members of the clan which is charged with the duty of burying the king's body have for their totem the remains of a goat that has been killed by a leopard. See H. Rehse, *op. cit.* pp. 5 *sq.*

tribal and ancestral spirits instead.   For upon such animism is founded the whole fabric of Wemba religion."[1]   The ancestral spirits whom the Awemba and all other tribes of this region worship may be divided into two main classes. First come the spirits of departed chiefs, who are publicly worshipped by the whole tribe ; and second come the spirits of near relations who are worshipped privately by each head of a family.[2] "Among the Awemba there is no special shrine for these purely family spirits, who are worshipped inside the hut, and to whom family sacrifice of a sheep, a goat, or a fowl is made, the spirit receiving the blood spilt on the ground, while all the members of the family partake of the flesh together. For a religious Wemba man the cult of the spirit of his nearest relations (of his grandparents, or of his deceased father, mother, elder brother, or maternal uncle) is considered quite sufficient.   Out of these spirit relatives a man will worship one whom he considers as his special familiar, for various reasons.   For instance, the diviner may have told him that his last illness was caused because he had not respected the spirit of his uncle ; accordingly he will be careful in future to adopt his uncle as his tutelary spirit.   As a mark of such respect he may devote a cow or a goat to one of the spirits of his ancestors.   Holding the fowl, for instance, in his hands, he will dedicate it, asking the spirit to come and abide in it, upon which the fowl is let go, and is afterwards called by the name of the spirit.   If the necessities, however, of the larder demand that it should be killed, another animal is taken, and the spirit is asked to accept it as a substitute ! Before beginning any special task, such as hoeing a new garden, or going on a journey, Wemba men invoke their tutelary spirits to be with them and to assist their efforts, in short ejaculatory prayers usually couched in a set formula. Among many of the tribes in the North Luangwa district longer formal prayers are still made to all the deceased ancestors of the clan at the time of harvest, asking them to protect the crops and to drive away illnesses and evil spirits from

[1] C. Gouldsbury and H. Sheane, *The Great Plateau of Northern Rhodesia* (London, 1911), pp. 80 *sq.*

[2] C. Gouldsbury and H. Sheane, *The Great Plateau of Northern Rhodesia*, pp. 82 *sq.*

the family, which honours them with libations of beer and offerings of the first-fruits." [1]

The worship of ancestral spirits is apparently the main practical religion of all the Bantu tribes.

Thus among these tribes, who all belong to the great Bantu family, the public worship which a whole tribe pays to the souls of its dead chiefs is probably nothing but an extension of the private worship which every family pays privately to the souls of its dead members. And just as the members of his family whom a man worships privately are not mythical beings conjured up by imagination out of a distant past, but were once real men like himself whom he knew in life, it may be his father, or uncle, or elder brother, so we may be sure that in like manner the dead chiefs revered by the whole tribe are not creations of the mythical fancy, but were once real men of flesh and blood, who ruled over the tribe, and whose memory has been more or less faithfully preserved by tradition. In this respect the tribes of Northern Rhodesia are typical of all the tribes of that great Bantu family which occupies nearly the whole southern half of Africa, from the great equatorial lakes to the Cape of Good Hope. The main practical religion of all these numerous and widespread peoples appears to be the worship of their ancestors.

The worship of ancestral spirits among the Bantu tribes of South Africa.

To adduce in full the evidence which points to this conclusion would lead us too far from our present subject; it must suffice to cite a few typical statements of competent authorities which refer to different tribes of the Bantu stock. Speaking with special reference to the tribes of South-Eastern Africa, the Rev. James Macdonald tells us that "the religion of the Bantu, which they not only profess but really regulate their conduct by, is based on the belief that the spirits of their ancestors interfere constantly in their affairs. Every man worships his own ancestors and offers sacrifices to avert their wrath. The clan worships the spirits of the ancestors of its chiefs, and the tribe worships the spirits of the ancestors of the paramount chief." [2] "The religion of the Bantu was based upon the supposition of the

---

[1] C. Gouldsbury and H. Sheane, *op. cit.* pp. 84 *sq.*

[2] Rev. James Macdonald, "Manners, Customs, Superstitions, and Religions of South African Tribes," *Journal of the Anthropological Institute*, xix. (1890) p. 286. Compare *id.*, *Light in Africa* (London, 1890), p. 191.

existence of spirits that could interfere with the affairs of this world.   These spirits were those of their ancestors and their deceased chiefs, the greatest of whom had control over lightning.   When the spirits became offended or hungry they sent a plague or disaster until sacrifices were offered and their wrath or hunger was appeased.   The head of a family of commoners on such an occasion killed an animal, and all ate of the meat, as the hungry ghost was supposed to be satisfied with the smell."[1]   For example, in the year 1891 the son of a chief of the Pondomisi tribe was arrested for an assault and sent for trial before a colonial court.   It chanced to be a season of intense heat and severe drought, and the Pondomisi tribe attributed these calamities to the wrath of a dead chief named Gwanya, very famous in his lifetime, whose body, fastened to a log, had been buried under a heap of stones in a deep pool of the Lina river. This redoubtable chieftain was the seventh ancestor in the direct line of the man who had committed the assault ; and he warmly resented the indignity which the whites had done to a noble scion of his house by consigning him to durance vile.   To appease the natural .indignation of the ghost, the tribesmen killed cattle on the banks of the pool which contained his grave, and threw the flesh into the water along with new dishes full of beer.   The prisoner, however, was convicted of the assault and sentenced by the ruthless magistrate, who was no respecter of ghosts, to pay a fine. But the tribe clubbed together and paid the fine for him ; and a few days later rain fell in plenty.   The mollified ghost had opened the celestial sluices.[2]

Another writer, describing the religion of the South

---

[1] G. McCall Theal, *Records of South-Eastern Africa*, vii. (1901) pp. 399 *sq.*   With regard to the ghost who controls lightning see Mr. Warner's notes in Col. Maclean's *Compendium of Kafir Laws and Customs* (Cape Town, 1866), pp. 82 *sq.* : " The Kafirs have strange notions respecting the lightning.   They consider that it is governed by the *umshologu*, or ghost, of the greatest and most renowned of their departed chiefs ; and who is emphatically styled the *inkosi* ; but they are not at all clear as to which of their ancestors is intended by this designation.   Hence they allow of no lamentation being made for a person killed by lightning ; as they say that it would be a sign of disloyalty to lament for one whom the *inkosi* had sent for, and whose services he consequently needed ; and it would cause him to punish them, by making the lightning again to descend and do them another injury."

[2] G. McCall Theal, *op. cit.* vii. 400.

Sacrifices
to the dead
among
the Bantu
tribes of
South
Africa.

African Bantus, tells us that " the ancestral spirits love the
very things they loved before they passed through the flesh ;
they cherish the same desires and have the same antipathies.
The living cannot add to the number of the wives of ancestral
spirits ; but they can kill cattle in their honour and keep
their praise and memory alive on earth.   Above all things,
they can give them beef and beer.   And if the living do
not give them sufficient of these things the spirits are supposed
to give the people a bad time : they send drought, and sickness, and famine, until people kill cattle in their honour.
When men are alive they love to be praised and flattered,
fed and attended to ; after death they want the very same
things, for death does not change personality. . . . In
time of drought, or sickness, or great trouble, there would
be great searchings of heart as to which ancestor had been
neglected, for the trouble would be supposed to be caused
by the neglected ancestor.   Most of the people would get
the subject on their nerves (at least, as far as a Kafir could
get anything on the leather strings which do duty for nerves),
and some one would be sure to have a vivid dream in which
an ancestor would complain that the people had not praised
him half enough of late.   So an ox would be killed, either
by the head-man of the kraal or by a diviner.   Then the
man would say over the ox as it was being killed, ' Cry out,
ox of So-and-So ; listen to us, So-and-So ; this is your ox ;
we praise you by all your laud-giving names, and tell of all
your deeds ; do not be angry with us any more ; do you not
see that this is your ox ?   Do not accuse us of neglecting
you ; when, forsooth, have we ceased to praise you and offer
you meat and beer ?   Take note, then, that here is another
ox we are offering to you.'   When the ox is dead some of
the meat is mixed with herbs and medicines and placed in
a hut with a bowlful of blood.   This meat is placed in the
part of the hut where the man loved to sit while he was
alive, and some one is told off to guard the sacrifice.   The
meat is left for a night, or longer, and the spirits are
supposed to come and enjoy the smell, or drink the serum
which oozes from the meat, and to inhale the smell of the
beer.   The priest or diviner will then sprinkle the people
and the huts with medicine made from the contents of the

stomach of the ox. He places a little on a sherd ; when this is dry he burns it and calls on the spirits to smell the incense. After the meat has been left for a certain time it is taken out and cooked, and eaten by the men near the cattle kraal in public. . . . If the trouble does not vanish after this ceremony the people get angry and say to the spirits, ' When have we ceased to kill cattle for you, and when have we ever refused to praise you by your praise-names ? Why, then, do you treat us so shabbily ? If you do not behave better we shall utterly forget your names, and then what will you do when there is no one to praise you ? You will have to go and live on grasshoppers. If you do not mend your ways we shall forget you. What use is it that we kill oxen for you and praise you ? You do not give us rain or crops, or cause our cattle to bear well ; you show no gratitude in return for all we do for you. We shall utterly disown you. We shall tell the people that, as for us, we have no ancestral spirits, and this will be to your shame. We are disgusted with you.' "[1] Thus the sweet savour of beef and beer does not suffice to content Caffre ghosts ; they share the love of praise and flattery with many gods of higher rank.

Among the Basutos, an important Bantu people of South Africa, "each family is supposed to be under the direct influence and protection of its ancestors ; but the tribe, taken as a whole, acknowledges for its national gods the ancestors of the reigning sovereign. Thus, the Basutos address their prayers to Monaheng and Motlumi, from whom their chiefs are descended. The Baharutsis and the Barolongs invoke Tobege and his wife Mampa. Mampa makes known the will of her husband, announcing each of her revelations by these words, ' *O re! O re!*' 'He has said ! he has said ! ' They make a distinction between the ancient and modern divinities. The latter are considered inferior in power, but more accessible ; hence this formula, which is often used : ' New gods ! entreat the ancient gods for us ! ' In all countries spirits are more the objects of fear than of love. A deep feeling of terror generally accompanies the idea that the dead dispose of the lot of the living.

Worship of the dead among the Basutos.

[1] Dudley Kidd, *The Essential Kafir* (London, 1904), pp. 88-91.

The ancients spoke much of incensed shades. If they sacrificed to the manes, it was generally in order to appease them. These ideas perfectly correspond to those of the Basutos. They conjure rather than pray ; although they seek to gain favours, they think more of averting chastisement. Their predominating idea as to their ancestors is, that they are continually endeavouring to draw them to themselves. Every disease is attributed to them ; thus medicine among these people is almost entirely a religious affair. The first thing is to discover, by means of the *litaola* (divining bones), under the influence of what *molimo* the patient is supposed to be. Is it an ancestor on the father's side or the mother's? According as fate decides, the paternal or maternal uncle will offer the purifying sacrifice, but rarely the father or brother. This sacrifice alone can render efficacious the medicines prescribed by the *ngaka* (doctor). . . . As soon as a person is dead he takes his place among the family gods. His remains are deposited in the cattle-pen. An ox is immolated over his grave : this is the first oblation made to the new divinity, and at the same time an act of intercession in his favour, serving to ensure his happy reception in the subterranean regions. All those present aid in sprinkling the grave, and repeat the following prayer : ' Repose in peace with the gods ; give us tranquil nights.' " [1]

Worship of the dead among the Thonga. Similarly among the Thonga, another Bantu tribe of South Africa, " any man, who has departed this earthly life, becomes a *shikwembu*, a god " ; [2] " when an old decrepit man or woman dies, he at once becomes a god : he has entered the domain of infinity." [3] In this tribe " the spirits of the ancestors are the main objects of religious worship. They form the principal category of spirits." [4] " On the one hand, the ancestor-gods are truly gods, endowed with the attributes of divinity ; whilst, on the other, they seem to be nothing but mere human beings, exactly on the same level as their worshippers." [5] There are two great classes

[1] Rev. E. Casalis, *The Basutos* (London, 1861), pp. 248-250.
[2] Henri A. Junod, *The Life of a South African Tribe* (Neuchâtel, 1912–

1913), ii. 347.
[3] H. A. Junod, *op. cit.* ii. 385.
[4] H. A. Junod, *op. cit.* ii. 344.
[5] H. A. Junod, *op. cit.* ii. 385.

of these ancestor-gods, to wit, "those of the family, and those of the country, the latter being those of the reigning family. They do not differ as regards their nature. In national calamities those of the country are invoked, whilst, for purely family matters, those of the family are called upon. Moreover, each family has two sets of gods, those on the father's side and those on the mother's, those of *kweru* and those of *bakokwana*. They are equal in dignity. Both can be invoked, and the divinatory bones are always asked to which the offering must be made. It seems, however, as if the gods on the mother's side were more tender-hearted and more popular than those on the father's. The reason for this is, perhaps, that relations are easier with the family of the mother than with that of the father. It is also just possible that it is a relic of the matriarchal period, when the ancestors of the mother only were known, and consequently invoked. At any rate, the part played by *batukulu* [uterine] nephews in the offerings shows that they are the true representatives of the gods, not of those of their father, but of their mother." [1] Among the Thonga "the belief in the continuation of life after death is universal, being at the base of the ancestrolatry, which is the religion of the tribe." [2] "How real is the ancestrolatry, the religion of the Thonga, of, in fact, all the South African Bantus ! How frequent and manifold are its manifestations ! This is the first, and the most perceptible set of their religious intuitions, and any European, who has stayed in their villages, learnt their language, and tried to understand their customs, has had the opportunity of familiarizing himself with this religion." [3]

Among the Basutos and Bechuanas, who also belong to the great Bantu family, the sacrificial ritual is not highly developed. "Only in great misfortunes which affect the whole people or the royal family, a black ox is slaughtered ; for in such cases they always think that the angry spirits of the departed are the cause of all the suffering. '*Re amogioa ki badimo*,' say the people, 'the spirits are robbing us.' The ox is led to the chief's grave ; there they

Sacrifices to dead chiefs among the Basutos and Bechuanas.

[1] H. A. Junod, *op. cit.* ii. 348 *sq.*   [2] H. A. Junod, *op. cit.* ii. 341.
[3] H. A. Junod, *op. cit.* ii. 346.

pray, ' Lord, we are come to call upon thee, we who are thy children ; make not our hearts troubled ; take not, Lord, that which is ours.' The old chief is honoured and praised in songs, he is invoked by all his praise-names, the ox is killed and its flesh eaten, but the blood and the contents of the stomach are poured on the grave, and there the bones of the sacrificed animal are also deposited." [1]

Worship of the dead among the Zulus.

The Zulus, another great Bantu tribe of South Africa, believe in the existence of a being whom they call Unkul-unkulu, which means " the Old-Old-one, the most ancient man." They say that " it is he who was the first man ; he broke off in the beginning. We do not know his wife ; and the ancients do not tell us that he had a wife." [2] This Old-Old-one or Great-Great-one " is represented as having made all things—men, cattle, water, fire, the mountains, and whatever else is seen. He is also said to have appointed their names. Creation was effected by splitting a reed, when the first man and other things issued from the cleft." [3] Further, the Zulus and other Caffre tribes of Natal " believe that, when a person dies, his *i-hloze* or *isi-tute* survives. These words are translated 'spirit,' and there seems no objection to the rendering. They refer to something mani-festly distinguished from the body, and the nature of which the prophets endeavour to explain by saying that it is identical with the shadow. The residence of the *ama-hloze*, or spirits, seems to be beneath ; the practice of breaking a man's assagais, before they are buried with him, shows that he is believed to return to earth through the grave ; while it appears to be generally thought that, if the earth were removed from the grave, the ghost would return and frighten his descendants. When spirits have entered the future state, they are believed to possess great power ; prosperity is ascribed to their favour, and misfortune to their anger ; they are elevated in fact to the rank of deities, and (except where the Great-Great is worshipped concurrently with them) they are the only objects of a Kafir's adoration. Their attention

[1] A. Merensky, *Beiträge zur Kennt-nis Süd-Afrikas* (Berlin, 1875), p. 130.
[2] Rev. H. Callaway, *The Religious System of the Amazulu*, i. (Natal, Springvale, etc., 1868) pp. 1 *sq.*
[3] Rev. Joseph Shooter, *The Kafirs of Natal and the Zulu Country* (London, 1857), p. 159.

(or providence) is limited to their own relatives—a father caring for the family, and a chief for the tribe, which they respectively left behind them.   They are believed to occupy the same relative position as they did in the body, the departed spirit of a chief being sometimes invoked to compel a man's ancestors to bless him." [1]

"To these shades of the dead, especially to the ghosts of their great men, as Jama, Senzangakona, and Chaka, their former kings, they look for help, and offer sacrifices ; that is, slaughter cattle to them, and offer a sort of prayer, in time of danger and distress. . . . When they are sick, they slaughter cattle to the shades, and say, 'Father, look on me, that this disease may cease from me.   Let me have health on the earth, and live a long time.'   They carry the meat into the house, and shut it up there, saying, 'Let the paternal shades eat, so shall they know that the offering was made for them, and grant us great wealth, so that both we and our children may prosper.'   In the cattle-fold they talk a long time, praising the ghosts ; they take the contents of the stomach, and strew it upon all the fold.   Again they take it, and strew it within the houses, saying, 'Hail, friend ! Thou of such a place, grant us a blessing, beholding what we have done.   You see this distress ; may you remove it, since we have given you our animal.   We know not what more you want, whether you still require anything more or not.'   They say, 'May you grant us grain, that it may be abundant, that we may eat, of course, and not be in need of anything, since now we have given you what you want.'   They say, 'Yes, for a long time have you preserved me in all my going. Behold, you see, I have just come to have a kraal.   This kraal was built by yourself, father ; and now why do you consent to diminish your own kraal?   Build on us as you have begun, let it be large, that your offspring, still here above, may increase, increasing in knowledge of you, whence cometh great power.'   Sometimes they make beer for the ghosts, and leave a little in the pot, saying, 'It will be eaten by the ghosts that they may grant an abundant harvest again, that we may not have a famine.'   If one is on the point of being injured by anything, he says, 'I was pre-

Sacrifices and prayers to the dead among the Zulus.

[1] Rev. J. Shooter, *op. cit.* p. 161.

served by our divinity, which was still watching over me.'
Perhaps he slaughters a goat in honour of the same, and
puts the gall on his head ; and when the goat cries out for
pain of being killed, he says, ' Yes, then, there is your animal,
let it cry, that ye may hear, ye our gods who have preserved
me ; I myself am desirous of living on thus a long time here
on the earth ; why then do you call me to account, since I
think I am all right in respect to you ?   And while I live, I
put my trust in you, our paternal and maternal gods.' " [1]

A native
Zulu
account
of the
worship of
the dead.
" Black people," say the Zulus, " do not worship all
Amatongo indifferently, that is, all the dead of their tribe.
Speaking generally, the head of each house is worshipped
by the children of that house ; for they do not know the
ancients who are dead, nor their laud-giving names, nor their
names.   But their father whom they knew is the head by
whom they begin and end in their prayer, for they know
him best, and his love for his children ; they remember his
kindness to them whilst he was living ; they compare his
treatment of them whilst he was living, support themselves
by it, and say, ' He will still treat us in the same way now
he is dead.   We do not know why he should regard others
besides us ; he will regard us only.'   So it is then although
they worship the many Amatongo of their tribe, making a
great fence around them for their protection ; yet their father
is far before all others when they worship the Amatongo.
Their father is a great treasure to them even when he is
dead.   And those of his children who are already grown up
know him thoroughly, his gentleness, and his bravery.   And
if there is illness in the village, the eldest son lauds him
with the laud-giving names which he gained when fighting
with the enemy, and at the same time lauds all the other
Amatongo ; the son reproves the father, saying, ' We for our
parts may just die.   Who are you looking after ?   Let us
die all of us, that we may see into whose house you will
enter.[2]   You will eat grasshoppers ; you will no longer be

---

[1] Rev. Lewis Grout, *Zulu-land, or
Life among the Zulu-Kafirs* (Phila-
delphia, N.D.), pp. 137, 143-145.
[2] " That is, they suggest to the
Itongo [ancestral spirit, singular of
Amatongo], by whose ill-will or want

of care they are afflicted, that if they
should all die in consequence, and thus
his worshippers come to an end, he
would have none to worship him ; and
therefore for his own sake, as well as
for theirs, he had better preserve his

invited to go anywhere, if you destroy your own village.' After that, because they have worshipped him, they take courage saying, ' He has heard ; he will come and treat our diseases, and they will cease.' Such then is the faith which children have in the Itongo [ancestral spirit] which is their father. And if there is a chief wife of a village, who has given birth to children, and if her husband is not dead, her Itongo is much reverenced by her husband and all the children. And that chief wife becomes an Itongo which takes great care of the village. But it is the father especially that is the head of the village."[1] Thus among the Zulus it is the spirits of those who have just died, especially the spirits of fathers and mothers, who are most revered and worshipped. The spirits of the more remote dead are forgotten.

When the missionaries inquired into the religious ideas of the Herero, a Bantu tribe of German South-West Africa, they heard much of a certain Mukuru, whom at first they took to be the great god of heaven and earth. Accordingly they adopted Mukuru as the native name for the Christian God, and set out on their mission to preach the glad tidings of Mukuru and his divine Son to the poor benighted heathen. But their first experiences were disconcerting. Again and again when they arrived in a village and announced their intention to the chief, they were brought up very short by that great man, who told them with an air of astonishment that he himself was Mukuru. For example, Messrs. Büttner and Irle paid a visit to an old chief named Tjenda and remonstrated with him on the impropriety of which he had been guilty in giving a baptized girl in marriage to a native gentleman whose domestic arrangements were framed on the polygamous patriarchal pattern. "Mukuru will punish you for that," said Mr. Büttner. "What?" roared the chief. "Who's Mukuru? Why, I am Mukuru in my own tribe," and he

The worship of the dead among the Herero of German South-West Africa.

---

people, that there may be a village for him to enter, and meat of the sacrifices for him to eat."

[1] Rev. Henry Callaway, *The Religious System of the Amazulu*, Part ii.,

Amatongo or Ancestor Worship as existing among the Amazulu, in their own words, with a translation into English (Natal, Springvale, etc., 1869), pp. 144-146.

bundled the two missionaries out of the village. A repetition of these painful incidents at last impressed on the minds of the missionaries the conviction that Mukuru was not God at all but merely the head of a family, an ancestor, whether alive or dead.[1] They ascertained at the same time that the Herero recognize a good god who dwells in heaven and bears the name of Ndjambi Karunga. But they do not worship him nor bring him offerings, because he is so kind that he hurts nobody, and therefore they need not fear him. " Rather they share the opinion of the other Bantu tribes that Ndjambi, the good Creator, has withdrawn to heaven and left the government on earth to the demons." [2] " It is true that the Herero are acquainted with punishment for what is bad. But that punishment they ascribe to Mukuru or their ancestors. It is their ancestors (*Ovakuru*[3]) whom they must fear ; it is they who are angry and can bring danger and misfortune on a man. So it is intelligible that the whole of their worship turns, not on Ndjambi Karunga, but on their ancestors. It is in order to win and keep their favour, to avert their displeasure and wrath, in short to propitiate them, that the Herero bring their many offerings ; they do so not out of gratitude, but out of fear, not out of love, but out of terror. Their religion is a worship of ancestors with here and there touches of fetishism." [4] " Thus among the Herero, as among all Bantu tribes, there exists a religious dualism : they know the highest, the true God, but they worship their ancestors." [5] And among the worshipful

Ancestral spirits (Ovakuru) worshipped by the Herero.

---

[1] Missionar J. Irle, *Die Herero, ein Beitrag zur Landes- Volks- und Missionskunde* (Gütersloh, 1906), pp. 72 *sq.*

[2] J. Irle, *op. cit.* p. 73.

[3] *Ovakuru,* the plural form of *Mukuru.*

[4] J. Irle, *op. cit.* p. 74.

[5] J. Irle, *op. cit.* p. 75. The writer tells us (*l.c.*) that the Herero name for the good celestial God, whom they acknowledge but do not worship, is common, in different forms, to almost all the Bantu tribes. Among the Ovambo it is Kalunga ; among tribes of Loango, the Congo, Angola and Benguela it is Zambi, Njambi, Ambi, Njame, Onjame, Ngambe, Nsambi ; in the Cameroons it is Nzambi, etc. Compare John H. Weeks, *Among Congo Cannibals* (London, 1913), pp. 246 *sq.* : "We have found a vague knowledge of a Supreme Being, and a belief in Him, very general among those tribes on the Congo with which we have come into contact. . . . On the Lower Congo He is called *Nzambi,* or by His fuller title *Nzambi a mpungu* ; no satisfactory root word has yet been found for *Nzambi,* but for *mpungu* there are sayings and proverbs that clearly indicate its meaning as, most of all, supreme, highest, and *Nzambi a mpungu* as the Being most High,

ancestors "the old dead chiefs of every tribe take the first place. The son of a great dead chief and the whole tribe worship that old father as their god. But the remote ancestors of that chief they do not worship, indeed they hardly know them by name and can no longer point to their graves." [1] Thus with the Herero, as with the Zulus, it is the recent and well-remembered dead who are chiefly or exclusively worshipped; as the souls of the departed recede

---

or Supreme. On the Upper Congo among the Bobangi folk the word used for the Supreme Being is *Nyambe*; among the Lulanga people, *Nzakomba*; among the Boloki, *Njambe*; among the Bopoto people it is *Libanza*. . . . It is interesting to note that the most common name for the Supreme Being on the Congo is also known, in one form or another, over an extensive area of Africa reaching from 6° north of the Equator away to extreme South Africa; as, for example, among the Ashanti it is *Onyame*, at Gaboon it is *Anyambie*, and two thousand miles away among the Barotse folk it is *Niambe*. These are the names that stand for a Being who is endowed with strength, wealth, and wisdom by the natives; and He is also regarded and spoken of by them as the principal Creator of the world, and the Maker of all things. . . . But the Supreme Being is believed by the natives to have withdrawn Himself to a great distance after performing His creative works; that He has now little or no concern in mundane affairs; and apparently no power over spirits and no control over the lives of men, either to protect them from malignant spirits or to help them by averting danger. They also consider the Supreme Being (*Nzambi*) as being so good and kind that there is no need to appease Him by rites, ceremonies or sacrifices. Hence they never pray to this Supreme One, they never worship Him, or think of Him as being interested in the doings of the world and its peoples."

[1] J. Irle, *op. cit.* p. 77. Mr. Irle's account of the religion of the Herero or Ovaherero is fully borne out by the testimony of earlier missionaries among the tribe. See Rev. G. Viehe, "Some Customs of the Ovaherero" (*South African*) *Folk-lore Journal*, i. (Cape Town, 1879) pp. 64 *sq.*: "The religious customs and ceremonies of the Ovaherero are all rooted in the presumption that the deceased continue to live, and that they have a great influence on earth, and exercise power over the life and death of man. This influence and power is ascribed especially to those who have been great men, and who become *Ovakuru* after death. The numerous religious customs and ceremonies are a worshipping of the ancestors." Further, Mr. Viehe reports that "the Ovaherero have a slight idea of another being (Supreme being?) which differs greatly from the *Ovakuru*, is superior to them, and is supposed never to have been a human being. It is called *Karunga*. . . . *Karunga* does only good; whilst the influence of the *Ovakuru* is more feared than wished for; and, therefore, it is not thought necessary to bring sacrifices to *Karunga* to guard against his influence." He is situated so high, and is so superior to men "that he takes little special notice of them; and so the Ovaherero, on their part, also trouble themselves little about this superior being" (*op. cit.* p. 67 note *). Similar evidence is given by another missionary as to the belief of the Herero in a superior god Karunga and their fear and worship of ancestral spirits. See the Rev. H. Beiderbecke, "Some Religious Ideas and Customs of the Ovaherero" (*South African*) *Folk-lore Journal*, ii. (Cape Town, 1880) pp. 88 *sqq.*

further and further into the past their memory perishes, and the nimbus of supernatural glory which encircled it for a time fades gradually away.

The worship of the dead among the Ovambo.

The religion of the Ovambo, another Bantu tribe of German South-West Africa, is similar. They also recognize a great being named Kalunga, who created the world and man, but they neither fear nor worship him. A far greater part is played in the religion of the Ovambo by their belief in spirits, and amongst the worshipful spirits a conspicuous place is assigned to the souls of the dead. Every man leaves behind him at death a spirit, which continues to exist on earth and can influence the living ; for example, it may enter into their bodies and thereby cause all sorts of sickness. However, the souls of ordinary dead men can exert their influence only on members of their own families ; the souls of dead chiefs, on the other hand, have power over the rain, which they can either give or withhold. To these powerful spirits a portion of the new corn is offered at harvest as a thank - offering for their forbearance in not visiting the people with sickness, and above all for their bounty in sending down the fertilizing showers on the crops. The souls of dead magicians are particularly dreaded ; and to prevent the multiplication of these dangerous spirits it is customary to dismember their bodies, severing the arms and legs from the trunk and cutting the tongue out of the mouth. If these precautions are taken immediately after death, the soul of the dead man cannot become a dangerous ghost ; the mutilation of his body has practically disarmed his spirit.[1]

The worship of the dead among the Wahehe of German East Africa.

The Wahehe, a Bantu tribe of German East Africa, believe in a great invisible spirit named Nguruhi, who created the world and rules both human destiny and the elements. He it is who makes the rain to fall, the sun to shine, the wind to blow, the thunder to roll, and the crops to grow. "This god is accordingly conceived as all-powerful, yet with the limitation that he only exercises a general power of direction over the world, especially human fate, while the *masoka*, the spirits of the dead, wield a per-

[1] Hermann Tönjes, *Ovamboland, Land, Leute, Mission* (Berlin, 1911), pp. 193-197.

manent and very considerable influence on the course of particular events. Nguruhi is lord also of all the spirits of the dead (*masoka*), but his relation to them has not been further thought out. With this Supreme Being the people hold no intercourse by means of prayer, sacrifice, or in any other way. He stands remote from the religious life of the Wahehe and really serves only as an explanation of all those things and events which are otherwise inexplicable. All religious intercourse, all worship centres alone on the spirits of the dead. Hence if we speak of a religion of the Wahehe, it must be described as a pure worship of ancestors." [1]   The human soul quits the body at death and at once becomes an ancestral spirit (*m'soka*), invisible and endowed with complete liberty of motion. Even the youngest children have souls which rank among the ancestral spirits at death. Hence the great multitude of the dead comprises spirits of all ages, from the infant one day old to the grey-haired patriarch. They are good or bad according as they were good or bad in life, and their social position also is unchanged. He who was powerful in life is powerful also in death ; he who was a nobody among men is a nobody also among the spirits. Hence the ghost of a great man can do more for the living than the ghost of a common man ; and the ghost of a man can do more than the ghost of a woman. Yet even the meanest ghost has power over the greatest living man, who can only defend himself by appealing for help to stronger ancestral spirits. Thus while the Supreme Being exercises a general superintendence over affairs, the real administration is in the hands of the ancestral spirits. While he, for example, regulates the weather as a whole, it is the ghosts who cause each particular shower to fall or the sun to break out in glory from the clouds. If he sends, plagues on the whole people or stays the ravages of disease, it is the ghosts who make each individual sick or sound. These powerful spirits exert themselves especially to help their descendants, though they

---

[1] E. Nigmann, *Die Wahehe* (Berlin, 1908), pp. 22 *sq.* The writer does not describe the Wahehe as a Bantu tribe, but from the characteristic prefixes which they employ to designate the tribe, individual tribesmen, the country, and so forth (*op. cit.* p. 124) we may infer that the people belong to the Bantu stock.

do not hesitate to plague their own kith and kin if they think themselves neglected. They flit freely through the air and perch on trees, mountains, and so forth, but they lodge by preference at their graves, and you are always sure of finding them there, if you wish to consult them.[1] That is why in the country of the Wahehe the only places of sacrifice are the graves; temples and altars are unknown.[2] However, it is only the bodies of considerable persons that are buried; the corpses of common folk are simply thrown away in the bush;[3] so that the number of graves and consequently of sacrificial places is strictly limited. The spirits of the dead appear to the living most commonly in dreams to give them information or warning, but oftener to chide and torment them. So the sleeper wakes in a fright and consults a diviner, who directs him what he must do in order to appease the angry ghost. Following the directions of his spiritual adviser the man sacrifices an ox, or it may be only a sheep or a fowl, at the tomb of one of his ancestors, prays to the ghost, and having scattered a few morsels of the victim's flesh on the grave, and spat a mouthful of beer upon it, retires with his family to feast on the remainder of the carcase. Such sacrifices to the dead are offered on occasion of sickness, the lack of male heirs, a threatened war, an intended journey, in short, before any important undertaking of which the issue is doubtful; and they are accompanied by prayers for health, victory, good harvests, and so forth.[4]

The worship of the dead among the Bahima of Ankole, in Central Africa.

Once more, the Bahima, a Bantu people of Ankole, in Central Africa, believe in a supreme god Lugaba, who dwells in the sky and created man and beast; but "this supreme being is not worshipped nor are offerings made to him; he has no sacred place. Although they talk freely about him, and acknowledge him to be their great benefactor, they accept all his gifts as a matter of course, and make him no offering in return. . . . One must not, therefore, conclude that the Bahima are an irreligious people; like most of the Bantu tribes their religion consists chiefly in dealing with ghosts of departed relatives, and in standing well with them;

---

[1] E. Nigmann, *Die Wahehe*, pp. 23 sq.

[2] E. Nigmann, *op. cit.* p. 35.

[3] E. Nigmann, *op. cit.* p. 39.

[4] E. Nigmann, *op. cit.* pp. 24 *sqq.*, 35 *sqq.*

from the king to the humblest peasant the ghosts call for daily consideration and constant offerings, whilst the deities are only sought in case of great trials or national calamities." [1]

To return, now, to the worship of dead chiefs or kings among the Bantu tribes of Northern Rhodesia. The spirits of dead chiefs had priestesses to wait upon them, who were called the "wives of the departed." These were elderly women who led a celibate life and swept the huts dedicated to the ghosts of the chiefs. The aid of these dead potentates was invoked in time of war and in seasons of drought, and special offerings were brought to their shrines at harvest.[2] Among the Awemba, who form the aristocracy of the country,[3] when a diviner announced that a drought was caused by the spirits of dead chiefs or kings buried at Mwaruli, a bull would be sent to be sacrificed to the souls of the deceased rulers ; or if the drought was severe, a human victim would be despatched, and the high priest would keep him caged in a stoutly woven fish-basket, until the preparations for the sacrifice were complete.[4] Among the Yombe no one might eat of the first-fruits of the crops until the living chief had sacrificed a bull before the tomb of his grandfather, and had deposited pots of fresh beer and porridge, made from the first-fruits, in front of the shrine. The ground about the tomb was then carefully weeded, and the blood of the sacrificial victim sprinkled on the freshly turned up soil and on the rafters of the little hut. After thanking the ghost of his grandfather for the harvest, and begging him to partake of the first-fruits, the chief and his train withdrew to feast on the carcase and the fresh porridge and beer at the village.[5] When the head chief or king of the Awemba had resolved

The worship of dead chiefs or kings among the Bantu tribes of Northern Rhodesia.

[1] Rev. J. Roscoe, "The Bahima, a Cow Tribe of Enkole," *Journal of the Royal Anthropological Institute*, xxxvii. (1907) pp. 108 *sq.* The supreme god Lugaba is no doubt the same with the supreme god Rugaba worshipped by the Bahimas in Kiziba. See above, p. 173. With regard to the religion of the Baganda the same authority tells us that "the last, and possibly the most venerated, class of religious objects were the ghosts of departed relatives. The power of ghosts for good or evil was incalculable" (*The Baganda*, p. 273).

[2] C. Gouldsbury and H. Sheane, *The Great Plateau of Northern Rhodesia*, p. 83.

[3] C. Gouldsbury and H. Sheane, *op. cit.* p. 11.

[4] C. Gouldsbury and H. Sheane, *op. cit.* p. 292.

[5] C. Gouldsbury and H. Sheane, *op. cit.* pp. 294 *sq.*

to make war on a distant enemy, he and the older men of the tribe would pray daily for victory to the spirits of the dead kings, his predecessors. The day before the army was to set forth, the great war-drum boomed out and the warriors flocked together from the outlying districts under their respective captains. In the dusk of the evening the king and the elderly women, who passed for the wives of the dead kings and tended their shrines at the capital, went and prayed at these shrines that the souls of the departed monarchs would keep the war-path free from foes and lead the king in a straight course to the enemy's stockade. These solemn prayers the king led in person, and the women beat their bare breasts as they joined in the earnest appeal. Next morning the whole army was marshalled in front of the ghost-huts of the dead kings: the living king danced a war-dance before his ancestors, while his chief wife sprinkled him with holy flour; and all prostrated themselves in supplication before the shrines.[1]

Among these tribes the spirits of dead chiefs or kings are thought sometimes to take bodily possession of men and women or to be incarnate in animals.

Among these tribes of Northern Rhodesia the spirits of dead chiefs or kings sometimes take possession of the bodies of live men or women and prophesy through their mouths. When the spirit of a dead chief comes over a man, he begins to roar like a lion, whereupon the women gather together and beat the drums, shouting that the chief has come to visit the village. The man thus temporarily inspired will prophesy of future wars or impending attacks by lions. While the inspiration lasts, he may eat nothing cooked by fire, but only unfermented dough. However, the spirit of a departed chief takes possession of women oftener than of men. "These women assert that they are possessed by the soul of some dead chief, and when they feel the divine afflatus, whiten their faces to attract attention, and anoint themselves with flour, which has a religious and sanctifying potency. One of their number beats a drum, and the others dance, singing at the same time a weird song, with curious intervals. Finally, when they have arrived at the requisite pitch of religious exaltation, the possessed woman falls to the ground, and bursts forth

---

[1] J. H. West Sheane, "Wemba Warpaths," *Journal of the African Society*, No. xli. (October, 1911) pp. 25 *sq.*

into a low and almost inarticulate chant, which has a most uncanny effect. All are silent at once, and the *bashing'anga* (medicine-men) gather round to interpret the voice of the spirit." [1] Sometimes the spirits of departed chiefs are reincarnated in animals, which are then revered as the abodes of the dead rulers. Thus the paramount chief of the Amambwe is incarnated after death in the form of a young lion, while Bisa and Wiwa chiefs come back in the shape of pythons. In one of the rest-houses near Fife a tame python waxed fat on the offerings of fowls and sour beer which the Winamwanga presented to it in the fond belief that it housed the spirit of one of their dead chiefs. One day unfortunately for himself the reptile deity ventured to dispute the possession of the rest-house with a German cattle-dealer who was passing by ; a discharge of shot settled the dispute in favour of the cattle-dealer, and the worshippers of the deity beheld him no more.[2]

Another Bantu people who worship the spirits of their dead kings are the Barotse or Marotse of the Upper Zambesi. The Barotse believe in a supreme god, the creator of all things, whom they call Niambe. He lives in the sun, and by his marriage with the moon begat the world, the animals, and last of all men. But the cunning and ferocity of his creature man terrified the beneficent creator, so that he fled from earth and escaped up the thread of a spider's web to heaven. There he still retains a certain power to interfere in human affairs, and that is why men sometimes pray and sacrifice to him. For example, the worshipper salutes the rising sun and offers him a vessel of water, no doubt to quench the thirst of the deity on his hot journey across the sky. Again, when a long drought has prevailed, a black ox is sacrificed to Niambe " as a symbol of the clouds big with the longed-for rain." And before they sow the fields, the women pile the seeds and their digging hoes in a heap, and pray to the god that he would render their labour fruitful.[3]

Belief of the Barotse in a supreme god Niambe.

---

[1] C. Gouldsbury and H. Sheane, *The Great Plateau of Northern Nigeria,* p. 83.

[2] C. Gouldsbury and H. Sheane, *op. cit.* p. 84.

[3] Eugène Béguin, *Les Ma-rotsé* (Lausanne and Fontaines, 1903), pp. 118 *sq.*

Yet while they acknowledge the divine supremacy of Niambe, the Barotse address their prayers most frequently to the inferior deities, the *ditino*, who are the deified kings of the country. The tombs of the departed monarchs may be seen near the villages which they inhabited in life. Each tomb stands in a grove of beautiful trees and is encircled by a tall palisade of pointed stakes, covered with fine mats, like the palisade which surrounds the royal residence of a living king. Such an enclosure is sacred ; the people are forbidden to enter it lest they should disturb the ghost of him who sleeps below. But the inhabitants of the nearest village are charged with the duty of keeping the tomb and the enclosure in good order, repairing the palisade, and replacing the mats when they are worn out. Once a month, at the new moon, the women sweep not only the grave and the enclosure but the whole village. The guardian of the tomb is at the same time a priest ; he acts as intermediary between the god and the people who come to pray to the deity. He bears the title of Ngomboti ; he alone has the right to enter the sacred enclosure ; the profane multitude must stand at a respectful distance. Even the king himself, when he comes to consult one of his ancestors, is forbidden to set foot on the holy ground. In presence of the god, or, as they call him, the Master of the Tomb, the monarch must bear himself like a slave in the presence of his lord. He kneels down near the entrance, claps his hands, and gives the royal salute ; and from within the enclosure the priest solemnly returns the salute, just as the king himself, when he holds his court, returns the salute of his subjects. Then the suppliant, whether king or commoner, makes his petition to the deity and deposits his offering ; for no man may pray to the god with empty hands. Inside the enclosure, close to the entrance, is a hole which is supposed to serve as a channel of communication with the spirit of the deified king. In it the offerings are placed. Often they consist of milk which is poured into the hole ; and the faster it drains away, the more favourably inclined is the god thought to be to the petitioner. More solid offerings, such as flesh, clothes, and glass beads, become the property of the priest after they have been allowed to lie for a decent time beside the sacred

aperture of the tomb. The spirits of dead kings are thus
consulted on matters of public concern as well as by private
individuals touching their own affairs. If a war is to be
waged, if a plague is raging among the people or a murrain
among the cattle, if the land is parched with drought, in
short, if any danger threatens or any calamity has afflicted
the country, recourse is had to these local gods, dwelling
each in his shady grove, not far from the abodes of the
living. They are near, but the great god in heaven is far
away. What wonder, therefore, that their help is often
sought while he is neglected ? They are national heroes as
well as gods ; their history is remembered ; men tell of the
doughty deeds they did in their lifetime ; why should they
not be able to succour their votaries now that they have put
on immortality ? All over the country these temple-tombs
may be seen. They serve as historical monuments to recall
to the people the names of their former kings and the annals
of their country. One of the most popular of the royal
shrines is near Senanga at the southern end of the great
plain of the Barotse. Voyagers who go down the Zambesi
do not fail to pay their devotions at the shrine, that the god
of the place may make their voyage to prosper and may
guard the frail canoe from shipwreck in the rush and roar
of the rapids ; and when they return in safety they repair
again to the sacred spot to deposit a thank-offering for the
protection of the deity.[1]

The foregoing examples suffice to prove that the worship
of dead chiefs and kings has been an important, perhaps we
may even say, the most important element in the religion
of many African tribes. Regarded from the native point
of view nothing could be more natural. The king rules
over his people in life ; and since all these tribes entertain
a firm and unquestioning belief not only in the existence
but in the power of the spirits of the dead, they necessarily
conclude that of all the departed spirits none can be so
potent for good or evil, none therefore need to be propitiated so earnestly by prayer and sacrifice, as the souls of
dead kings. Thus while every family worships privately the

Thus the worship of dead kings has been an important element in the religion of many African tribes.

[1] Eugène Béguin, *Les Ba-rotsé*, pp. 120-123. Compare *Totemism and Exogamy*, iv. 306 *sq.*

spirits of its own ancestors, the whole tribe worships publicly the spirits of its departed monarchs, paying to each of these invisible potentates, whose reality they never dream of doubting, a homage of precisely the same sort as that which they render to his living successor on the throne. Such a religion of the dead is by no means incompatible with the recognition of higher spiritual powers who may have an origin quite independent of the worship of ancestors. We have seen in point of fact that many tribes, whose practical religion is concentrated chiefly on their dead, nevertheless acknowledge the existence of a supreme god, the creator of man and of all things, whom they do not regard as a glorified ghost. The Baganda, the most progressive and advanced of all the Bantu tribes, had a whole pantheon of gods whom they sharply distinguished from the worshipful spirits of their forefathers.

Perhaps some African gods, who are now distinguished from ghosts, were once dead men.

Yet in spite of this distinction we may suspect that in many cases the seeming line of division between gods and worshipful ghosts is deceptive ; and that the magic touch of time, which distorts and magnifies the past, especially among peoples who see it only through the haze of oral tradition, has glorified and transfigured many a dead man into a deity. This at all events seems to have been the history of some of the Baganda gods. On this subject our best authority says that " the principal gods appear to have been at one time human beings, noted for their skill and bravery, who were afterwards deified by the people and invested with supernatural powers." [1] " Mukasa held the highest rank among the gods of Uganda. He was a benign god ; he never asked for the life of any human being, but animals were sacrificed to him at the yearly festivals, and also at other times when the king, or a leading chief, wished to consult him. He had nothing to do with war, but sought to heal the bodies and minds of men. He was the god of plenty ; he gave the people an increase of food, cattle, and children. From the legends still current it seems to be almost certain that he was a human being who, because of his benevolence, came to be regarded as a god. . . . The legends about Mukasa are of great interest ; they show how the human element

[1] Rev. J. Roscoe, *The Baganda* (London, 1911), p. 271.

has been lost in the divine, how the natural has been effaced by the supernatural, until, in the minds of the common people, only the supernatural remains." [1]

If we cannot prove that the great god Mukasa himself was once a man, we have very tangible evidence that his brother the war-god Kibuka was so. For like the dead kings of Uganda, Kibuka was worshipped in a great conical hut resembling the huts which living people inhabit : like them, his spirit was supposed to enter from time to time into the body of his priest and to give oracles through him ; and like them he was represented in his temple by his personal relics, his jawbone and his navel-string, which were rescued from the ruins of his temple and now rest in the Ethnological Museum at Cambridge. In face of this complete parallelism between the god and the kings whose personal existence is not open to question, it seems difficult to doubt that Kibuka was once like them a real man, and that he spoke with the jawbone and made bodily use of the other corporeal organs which were preserved in his temple. [2]

The human remains of Kibuka, the war-god of the Baganda.

These analogies lend some support to the theory that in ancient Egypt, where the kings were worshipped by their people both in life and death, Osiris may have been originally nothing but one of these deified monarchs whose worship gradually eclipsed that of all the rest and ended by rivalling or even surpassing that of the great sun-god himself. We have seen that at Abydos, one of the principal centres of his worship, the tomb of Osiris was identified with the tomb of King Khent, one of the earliest monarchs of the first Egyptian dynasty, and that in this tomb were found a woman's richly jewelled arm and a human skull lacking the lower jawbone, which may well be the head of the king himself and the arm of his queen. The carved monument of Osiris which was found in the sepulchral chamber appears indeed to be a

Thus it is possible that Osiris and Isis may have been a real king and queen of Egypt, perhaps identical with King Khent and his queen.

---

[1] Rev. J. Roscoe, *op. cit.* pp. 290, 291. In the worship of Mukasa "the principal ceremony was the annual festival, when the king sent his presents to the god, to secure a blessing on the crops and on the people for the year" (J. Roscoe, *op. cit.* p. 298).

[2] Rev. J. Roscoe, "Kibuka, the War God of the Baganda," *Man*, vii.

1907) pp. 161-166 ; *id., The Baganda*, pp. 301-308. Among the personal relics of Kibuka kept in his temple were his genital organs ; these also were rescued when the Mohammedans burned down his temple in the civil wars of 1887–1890. They are now with the rest of the god's, or rather the man's, remains at Cambridge.

work of late Egyptian art, but it may have replaced an earlier sarcophagus. Certainly we may reasonably suppose that the identification of the tomb of Osiris with the tomb of King Khent was very ancient; for though the priests may have renewed the sculptured effigy of the dead god, they would hardly dare to shift the site of the Holy Sepulchre.[1] Now the sepulchre is distant about a mile and a half from the temple in which Osiris was worshipped as a god. There is thus a curious coincidence, if there is nothing more, between the worship of Osiris and the worship of the dead kings of Uganda. As a dead king of Uganda was worshipped in a temple, while his headless body reposed at some distance in a royal tomb, and his head, without the lower jawbone, was buried by itself near the grave, so Osiris was worshipped in a temple not far from the royal tomb which tradition identified with his grave. Perhaps after all tradition was right. It is possible, though it would be very rash to affirm, that Osiris was no other than the historical King Khent of the first dynasty;[2] that the skull found in the tomb is the skull of Osiris himself; and that while it reposed in the grave the missing jawbone was preserved, like the jawbone of a dead king of Uganda, as a holy and perhaps

[1] This consideration is rightly urged by H. Schäfer as a strong argument in favour of the antiquity of the tradition which associated the grave of Osiris with the grave of King Khent. See H. Schäfer, *Die Mysterien des Osiris in Abydos* (Leipsic, 1904), pp. 28 *sq.*

[2] One of the commonest and oldest titles of Osiris was Chent (Khent)-Ament or Chenti (Khenti)-Amenti, as the name is also written. It means "Chief of those who are in the West" and refers to the Egyptian belief that the souls of the dead go westward. See R. V. Lanzone, *Dizionario di Mitologia Egizia*, p. 727; H. Brugsch, *Religion und Mythologie der alten Aegypter*, p. 617; A. Erman, *Die ägyptische Religion*,[2] pp. 23, 103 *sq.*; J. H. Breasted, *Development of Religion and Thought in Ancient Egypt*, pp. 38, 143 (who spells the name Khenti-Amentiu); E. A. Wallis Budge, *Osiris and the Egyptian Resurrection*, i. 31 *sq.*, 67. "Khenti-Amenti was one of the oldest gods of Abydos, and was certainly connected with the dead, being probably the ancient local god of the dead of Abydos and its neigbourhood. Now, in the Pyramid Texts, which were written under the VIth dynasty, there are several mentions of Khenti-Amenti, and in a large number of instances the name is preceded by that of Osiris. It is quite clear, therefore, that the chief attributes of the one god must have resembled those of the other, and that Osiris Khenti-Amenti was assumed to have absorbed the powers of Khenti-Amenti. In the representations of the two gods which are found at Abydos there is usually no difference, at least not under the XVIIIth and XIXth dynasties" (E. A. Wallis Budge, *op. cit.* i. 31). However, it would be unsafe to infer that the resemblance between the name of the god and the name of the king is more than accidental.

oracular relic in the neighbouring temple.   If that were so, we should be almost driven to conclude that the bejewelled woman's arm found in the tomb of Osiris is the arm of Isis.

In support of the conclusion that the myth and religion of Osiris grew up round the revered memory of a dead man we may quote the words in which the historian of European morals describes the necessity under which the popular imagination labours of embodying its cherished ideals in living persons.   He is referring to the dawn of the age of chivalry, when in the morning twilight the heroic figure of Charlemagne rose like a bright star above the political horizon, to be thenceforth encircled by a halo of romance like the nimbus that shone round the head of Osiris.   " In order that the tendencies I have described should acquire their full force, it was necessary that they should be repre- sented or illustrated in some great personage, who, by the splendour and the beauty of his career, could fascinate the imaginations of men.   It is much easier to govern great masses of men through their imagination than through their reason.   Moral principles rarely act powerfully upon the world, except by way of example or ideals.   When the course of events has been to glorify the ascetic or mon- archical or military spirit, a great saint, or sovereign, or soldier will arise, who will concentrate in one dazzling focus the blind tendencies of his time, kindle the enthusiasm and fascinate the imagination of the people.   But for the pre- vailing tendency, the great man would not have arisen, or would not have exercised his great influence.   But for the great man, whose career appealed vividly to the imagina- tion, the prevailing tendency would never have acquired its full intensity." [1]

Whether the parallel thus suggested between Charle- magne, the mediaeval ideal of a Christian knight, and Osiris, the ancient Egyptian ideal of a just and beneficent monarch, holds good or not, it is now impossible to determine.   For while Charlemagne stands near enough to allow us clearly to discern his historical reality, Osiris is so remote that we can no longer discriminate with any certitude between the

Suggested parallel between Osiris and Charle- magne.

The question of the historical reality of Osiris left open.

[1] W. E. H. Lecky, *History of European Morals from Augustus to* *Charlemagne*, Third Edition (London, 1877), ii. 271.

elements of history and fable which appear to have blended in his traditional character. I am content to indicate bare possibilities: dogmatism on such points would be in the highest degree rash and unbecoming. Whether Osiris and Isis were from first to last purely imaginary beings, the ideal creations of a primitive philosophy, or whether they were originally a real man and woman about whom after death the myth-making fancy wove its gossamer rainbow-tinted web, is a question to which I am not bold enough to give a decided answer.

CHAPTER XII

MOTHER-KIN AND MOTHER GODDESSES

§ 1. *Dying Gods and Mourning Goddesses*

WE have now concluded our inquiry into the nature and worship of the three Oriental deities Adonis, Attis, and Osiris. The substantial similarity of their mythical character justifies us in treating of them together. All three apparently embodied the powers of fertility in general and of vegetation in particular. All three were believed to have died and risen again from the dead ; and the divine death and resurrection of all three were dramatically represented at annual festivals, which their worshippers celebrated with alternate transports of sorrow and joy, of weeping and exultation. The natural phenomena thus mythically conceived and mythically represented were the great changes of the seasons, especially the most striking and impressive of all, the decay and revival of vegetation ; and the intention of the sacred dramas was to refresh and strengthen, by sympathetic magic, the failing energies of nature, in order that the trees should bear fruit, that the corn should ripen, that men and animals should reproduce their kinds.

But the three gods did not stand by themselves. The mythical personification of nature, of which all three were in at least one aspect the products, required that each of them should be coupled with a goddess, and in each case it appears that originally the goddess was a more powerful and important personage than the god. At all events it is always the god rather than the goddess who comes to a sad end, and whose death is annually mourned. Thus, whereas Osiris was slain by Typhon, his divine spouse Isis survived

Essential similarity of Adonis, Attis, and Osiris.

The superiority of the goddesses associated with Adonis, Attis, and Osiris points to a system of mother-kin.

201

and brought him to life again.   This feature of the myth
seems to indicate that in the beginning Isis was, what
Astarte and Cybele always continued to be, the stronger
divinity of the pair.   Now the superiority thus assigned to
the goddess over the god is most naturally explained as the
result of a social system in which maternity counted for
more than paternity, descent being traced and property
handed down through women rather than through men.   At
all events this explanation cannot be deemed intrinsically
improbable if we can show that the supposed cause has produced the very same effect among existing peoples, about
whose institutions we possess accurate information.   This I
will now endeavour to do.

§ 2. *Influence of Mother-Kin on Religion*

Mother-kin
and father-
kin.

The social system which traces descent and transmits
property through the mother alone may be called mother-
kin, while the converse system which traces descent and
transmits property through the father alone may be called
father-kin.[1]   A good example of the influence which mother-
kin may exert on religion is furnished by the Khasis of Assam,
whose customs and beliefs have lately been carefully recorded
by a British officer specially charged with the study of the
native races of the province.[2]   Like the ancient Egyptians
and the Semites of Syria and Mesopotamia, the Khasis live
in settled villages and maintain themselves chiefly by the
cultivation of the ground ; yet "their social organization
presents one of the most perfect examples still surviving of
matriarchal institutions, carried out with a logic and thorough-
ness which, to those accustomed to regard the status and
authority of the father as the foundation of society, are
exceedingly remarkable.   Not only is the mother the head
and source, and only bond of union, of the family : in the
most primitive part of the hills, the Synteng country, she
is the only owner of real property, and through her alone is

The
Khasis of
Assam
have
mother-
kin, and
among
them
goddesses
predomin-
ate over
gods and
priestesses
over
priests.

---

[1] I have adopted the terms "mother-
kin" and "father-kin" as less ambiguous than the terms "mother-right"
and "father-right," which I formerly
employed in the same sense.

[2] *The Khasis*, by Major P. R. T.
Gurdon, I.A., Deputy Commissioner
Eastern Bengal and Assam Commission,
and Superintendent of Ethnography in
Assam (London, 1907).

inheritance transmitted.[1] The father has no kinship with
his children, who belong to their mother's clan ; what he
earns goes to his own matriarchal stock, and at his death
his bones are deposited in the cromlech of his mother's kin.
In Jowai he neither lives nor eats in his wife's house, but
visits it only after dark. In the veneration of ancestors,
which is the foundation of the tribal piety, the primal
ancestress (*Ka Iāwbei*) and her brother are the only persons
regarded. The flat memorial stones set up to perpetuate
the memory of the dead are called after the woman who
represents the clan (*māw kynthei*), and the standing stones
ranged behind them are dedicated to the male kinsmen on
the mother's side. In harmony with this scheme of ancestor
worship, the other spirits to whom propitiation is offered are
mainly female, though here male personages also figure.
The powers of sickness and death are all female, and these
are those most frequently worshipped. The two protectors
of the household are goddesses, though with them is also
revered the first father of the clan, *U Thāwlang.* Priestesses assist at all sacrifices, and the male officiants are
only their deputies ; in one important state, Khyrim, the
High Priestess and actual head of the State is a woman,
who combines in her person sacerdotal and regal functions." [2] Thus amongst the Khasis of the present day the

---

[1] " The Khasi saying is, ' *long jaid
na ka kynthei*' (from the woman sprang
the clan). The Khasis, when reckoning descent, count from the mother
only ; they speak of a family of brothers
and sisters, who are the great grandchildren of one great grandmother, as
shi kpoh, which, being literally translated, is one womb, *i.e.* the issue of
one womb. The man is nobody "
(P. R. T. Gurdon, *The Khasis*, p. 82).
" All land acquired by inheritance must
follow the Khasi law of entail, by which
property descends from the mother to
the youngest daughter, and again from
the latter to her youngest daughter.
Ancestral landed property must therefore be always owned by women. The
male members of the family may cultivate such lands, but they must carry
all the produce to the house of their
mother, who will divide it amongst the

members of the family " (*op. cit.* p. 88).
" The rule amongst the Khasis is that
the youngest daughter 'holds' the
religion, ' *ka bat ka niam.*' Her house
is called, ' *ka iing seng,*' and it is here
that the members of the family assemble
to witness her performance of the family
ceremonies. Hers is, therefore, the
largest share of the family property,
because it is she whose duty it is to
perform the family ceremonies, and
propitiate the family ancestors " (*op.
cit.* p. 83).

[2] Sir C. J. Lyall, in his Introduction
to *The Khasis*, by Major P. R. T.
Gurdon, pp. xxiii. *sq.* Sir C. J. Lyall
himself lived for many years among
the Khasis and studied their customs.
For the details of the evidence on which
his summary is based see especially pp.
63 *sqq.*, 68 *sq.*, 76, 82 *sqq.*, 88, 106
sqq., 109 *sqq.*, 112 *sq.*, 121, 150, of

superiority of the goddess to the god, and especially of the revered ancestress to the revered ancestor, is based directly on the social system which traces descent and transmits property through women only.   It is not unreasonable therefore to suppose that in Western Asia the superiority of the Mother Goddess to the Father God originated in the same archaic system of mother-kin.

Again, the Pelew Islanders have mother-kin, and the deities of their clans are all goddesses.

Another instance of the same cause producing the same effect may be drawn from the institutions of the Pelew Islanders, which have been described by an accurate observer long resident in the islands.   These people, who form a branch of the Micronesian stock, are divided into a series of exogamous families or clans with descent in the female line,[1] so that, as usually happens under such a system, a man's heirs are not his own children but the children of his sister or of his maternal aunt.[2]   Every family or clan traces its descent from a woman, the common mother of the whole kin,[3] and accordingly the members of the clan worship a goddess, not a god.[4]   These families or clans, with female descent and a worship of goddesses rather than of gods, are grouped together in villages, each village comprising

---

Major Gurdon's book.   As to the Khasi priestesses, see above, vol. i. p. 46.

[1] J. Kubary, *Die socialen Einrichtungen der Pelauer* (Berlin, 1885), pp. 35 *sq.*   The writer calls one of these kins indifferently a *Familie* or a *Stamm*.

[2] J. S. Kubary, "Die Todtenbestattung auf den Pelau-Inseln," *Original-Mittheilungen aus der ethnologischen Abtheilung der königlichen Museen zu Berlin*, i. (Berlin, 1885) p. 7.

[3] J. Kubary, *Die socialen Einrichtungen der Pelauer*, p. 40.

[4] J. Kubary, "Die Religion der Pelauer," in A. Bastian's *Allerlei aus Volks- und Menschenkunde* (Berlin, 1888), i. 20-22.   The writer says that the family or clan gods of the Pelew Islanders are too many to be enumerated, but he gives as a specimen a list of the family deities of one particular district (Ngarupesang).   Having done so he observes that they are all goddesses, and he adds that "this is explained by the importance of the woman for the clan.   The deity of the mother is inherited, that of the father is not" (*op. cit.* p. 22).   As he says nothing to indicate that the family deities of this particular district are exceptional, we may infer, as I have done, that the deities of all the families or clans are goddesses.   Yet a few pages previously (pp. 16 *sq.*) he tells us that a village which contains twenty families will have at least forty deities, if not more, "for some houses may have two *kalids* [deities], and every house has also a goddess."   This seems to imply that the families or clans have gods as well as goddesses.   The seeming discrepancy is perhaps to be explained by another statement of the writer that "in the family only the *kalids* [deities] of the women count" ("*sich geltend machen*," J. Kubary, *Die socialen Einrichtungen der Pelauer*, p. 38).

about a score of clans and forming with its lands a petty independent state.[1] Every such village-state has its special deity or deities, generally a god and a goddess. But these political deities of the villages are said to be directly derived from the domestic deities of the families or clans,[2] from which it seems to follow that among these people gods are historically later than goddesses and have been developed out of them.[3] The late origin of the gods as compared with the goddesses is further indicated by the nature of their names.[4]

This preference for goddesses over gods in the clans of the Pelew Islanders has been explained, no doubt rightly, by the high importance of women in the social system of the people.[5] For the existence of the clan depends entirely on the life of the women, not at all upon the life of the men. If the women survive, it is no matter though every man of the clan should perish ; for the women will, as usual, marry men of another clan, and their offspring will inherit their mother's clan, thereby prolonging its existence. Whereas if the women of the clan all die out, the clan necessarily becomes extinct, even though every man of it should survive ; for the men must, as usual, marry women of another clan, and their offspring will inherit their mothers' clan, not the clan of their fathers, which accordingly, with the death of the fathers, is wiped out from the community. Hence in these islands women bear the titles of *Adhalál a pelú*, ' Mothers of the Land," and *Adhalál a blay*, " Mothers of the Clan," and they are said to enjoy complete equality with the men in every respect.[6] Indeed, in one passage our principal authority speaks of "the predominance of feminine influence in the social condition of the people," and asserts without qualification that the women are politically and

This pre- ference for goddesses is to be explained by the importance of women in the social system of the Pelew Islanders.

---

[1] J. Kubary, *Die socialen Einrich- tungen der Pelauer*, pp. 33 *sq.*, 63 ; *id.*, " Die Religion der Pelauer," in A. Bastian's *Allerlei aus Volks- und Men- schenkunde*, i. 16.

[2] J. Kubary, " Die Religion der Pelauer," in A. Bastian's *Allerlei aus Volks- und Menschenkunde*, i. 15-17, 22, 25-27.

[3] From the passages cited in the preceding note it appears that this was Kubary's opinion, though he has not stated it explicitly.

[4] J. Kubary, "Die Religion der Pelauer," in A. Bastian's *Allerlei aus Volks- und Menschenkunde*, i. 28 *sq.*

[5] J. Kubary, *Die socialen Einrich- tungen der Pelauer*, p. 38. See also above, p. 204, note [4].

[6] J. Kubary, *l.c.*

socially superior to the men.[1]   The eldest women of the clan
exercise, he tells us, the most decisive influence on the conduct of its affairs, and the headman does nothing without
full consultation with them, a consultation which in the great
houses extends to affairs of state and foreign politics.[2]   Nay,
these elder women are even esteemed and treated as equal
to the deities in their lifetime.[3]

The high
position of
women in
the Pelew
Islands has
also an
industrial
basis ; for
they alone
cultivate
the taro,
the staple
food of
the people.

But the high position which women thus take in Pelew
society is not a result of mother-kin only.   It has an industrial as well as a kinship basis.   For the Pelew Islanders
subsist mainly on the produce of their taro fields, and the
cultivation of this, their staple food, is the business of the
women alone.   " This cardinal branch of Pelew agriculture,
which is of paramount importance for the subsistence of the
people, is left entirely in the hands of the women.   This
fact may have contributed materially to the predominance
of female influence in the social condition of the people.
The women do not merely bestow life on the people, they
also do that which is most essential for the preservation of
life, and therefore they are called *Adhalál a pelú*, the
'Mothers of the Land,' and are politically and socially
superior to men.   Only their offspring enjoy the privilege of
membership of the state (the children of the men are, strictly
speaking, strangers destitute of rights), and the oldest women
of the families are esteemed and treated as equal to deities
even in their lifetime, and they exercise a decisive influence
on the conduct of affairs of state.   No chief would venture
to come to a decision without first consulting with the
Adhalál a blay, the 'Mothers of the Family.'   From this
point of view it is impossible to regard the assignment
of the taro cultivation to women as a consequence of
their subordinate position in society : the women themselves
do not so regard it.   The richest woman of the village looks
with pride on her taro patch, and although she has female
followers enough to allow her merely to superintend the
work without taking part in it, she nevertheless prefers to
lay aside her fine apron and to betake herself to the deep

---

[1] See the statement of Kubary
quoted in the next paragraph.

[2] J. Kubary, *Die socialen Einrich-*

tungen der Pelauer, p. 39.

[3] See the statement of Kubary quoted
in the next paragraph.

mire, clad in a small apron that hardly hides her nakedness, with a little mat on her back to protect her from the burning heat of the sun, and with a shade of banana leaves for her eyes. There, dripping with sweat in the burning sun and coated with mud to the hips and over the elbows, she toils to set the younger women a good example. Moreover, as in every other occupation, the *kaliths*, the gods, must also be invoked, and who could be better fitted for the discharge of so important a duty than the Mother of the House?"[1] It seems clear that in any agricultural people who, like the Pelew Islanders, retain mother-kin and depute the labours of husbandry to women, the conception of a great Mother Goddess, the divine source of all fertility, might easily originate. Perhaps the same social and industrial conditions may have combined to develop the great Mother Goddesses of Western Asia and Egypt.

But in the Pelew Islands women have yet another road to power. For some of them are reputed to be the wives of gods, and act as their oracular mouthpieces. Such prophetesses are called *Amlaheys*, and no surprise is felt when one of them is brought to bed. Her child passes for the offspring of the god, her divine husband, and goes about with his hair hanging loose in token of his superhuman parentage. It is thought that no mortal man would dare to intrigue with one of these human wives of a god, since the jealous deity would surely visit the rash culprit with deadly sickness and a lingering decline.[2] But in these islands men as well as women are often possessed by a deity and speak in his name. Under his inspiration they mimic, often with great histrionic skill, the particular appearance and manner which are believed to be characteristic of the indwelling divinity. These inspired men (*Korongs*) usually enjoy great consideration and exert a powerful influence over the whole community. They always acquire wealth in the exercise of their profession. When they are not themselves chiefs, they are treated as chiefs or even preferred to them. In not a few places the deity whom

Both men and women in the Pelew Islands attain to power by posing as the inspired mouthpieces of the gods.

[1] J. S. Kubary, *Ethnographische Beiträge zur Kenntniss des Karolinen Archipels* (Leyden, 1895), p. 159. On the importance of the taro or sweet potato as the staple food of the people, see *ib.* pp. 156 *sq.*

[2] J. Kubary, "Die Religion der Pelauer," in A. Bastian's *Allerlei aus Volks- und Menschenkunde*, i. 34.

they personate is also the political head of the land ; and in that case his inspired priest, however humble his origin, ranks as a spiritual king and rules over all the chiefs. Indeed we are told that, with the physical and intellectual decay of the race, the power of the priests is more and more in the ascendant and threatens, if unchecked, to develop before long into an absolute theocracy which will swallow up every other form of government.[1]

Parallel between the Pelew Islands of to-day and the religious and social state of Western Asia and Egypt in antiquity.

Thus the present, or at least the recent, state of society and religion in the Pelew Islands presents some interesting parallels to the social and religious condition of Western Asia and Egypt in early days, if the conclusions reached in this work are correct.   In both regions we see a society based on mother-kin developing a religion in which goddesses of the clan originally occupied the foremost place, though in later times, as the clans coalesced into states, the old goddesses have been rivalled and to some extent supplanted by the new male gods of the enlarged pantheon. But in the religion of the Pelew Islanders, as in that of the Khasis and the ancient Egyptians, the balance of power has never wholly shifted from the female to the male line, because society has never passed from mother-kin to father-kin.   And in the Pelew Islands as in the ancient East we see the tide of political power running strongly in the direction of theocracy, the people resigning the conduct of affairs into the hands of men who claimed to rule them in the name of the gods.   In the Pelew Islands such men might have developed into divine kings like those of Babylon and Egypt, if the natural course of evolution had not been cut short by the intervention of Europe.[2]

The evidence of the Khasis and the Pelew Islanders, two peoples very remote and very different from each other, suffices to prove that the influence which mother-kin may exert on religion is real and deep.   But in order

---

[1] J. Kubary, "Die Religion der Pelauer," in A. Bastian's *Allerlei aus Volks- und Menschenkunde*, i. 30-35. The author wrote thus in the year 1883, and his account of the Pelew religion was published in 1888. Compare his work *Die socialen Einrich-* *tungen der Pelauer*, p. 81.   Great changes have probably taken place in the islands since Kubary wrote.

[2] For some other parallels between the state of society and religion in these two regions, see Note IV. at the end of the volume.

to dissipate misapprehensions, which appear to be rife on this subject, it may be well to remind or inform the reader that the ancient and widespread custom of tracing descent and inheriting property through the mother alone does not by any means imply that the government of the tribes which observe the custom is in the hands of women ; in short, it should always be borne in mind that mother-kin does not mean mother-rule. On the contrary, the practice of mother-kin prevails most extensively amongst the lowest savages, with whom woman, instead of being the ruler of man, is always his drudge and often little better than his slave. Indeed, so far is the system from implying any social superiority of women that it probably took its rise from what we should regard as their deepest degradation, to wit, from a state of society in which the relations of the sexes were so loose and vague that children could not be fathered on any particular man.[1]

Mother-kin does not imply that the government is in the hands of women.

When we pass from the purely savage state to that higher plane of culture in which the accumulation of property, and especially of landed property, has become a powerful instrument of social and political influence, we naturally find that wherever the ancient preference for the female line of descent has been retained, it tends to increase the importance and enhance the dignity of woman ; and her aggrandizement is most marked in princely families, where she either herself holds royal authority as well as private property, or at least transmits them both to her consort or her children. But this social advance of women has never been carried so far as to place men as a whole in a position of political subordination to them. Even where the system of mother-kin in regard to descent and property has prevailed most fully, the actual government has generally, if not invariably, remained in the hands of men. Exceptions have no doubt occurred ; women have occasionally arisen

The inheritance of property, especially of landed property, through the mother certainly tends to raise the social importance of women, but this tendency is never carried so far as to subordinate men politically to women.

---

[1] Compare E. Stephan und F. Graebner, *Neu-Mecklenburg* (Berlin, 1907), p. 107 note [1] : "It is necessary always to repeat emphatically that the terms father-right and mother-right indicate simply and solely the group-membership of the individual and the systems of relationship which that membership implies, but that they have nothing at all to do with the higher or lower position of women. Rather the opposite might be affirmed, namely, that woman is generally more highly esteemed in places where father-right prevails than in places where mother-right is the rule."

who by sheer force of character have swayed for a time the destinies of their people. But such exceptions are rare and their effects transitory ; they do not affect the truth of the general rule that human society has been governed in the past and, human nature remaining the same, is likely to be governed in the future, mainly by masculine force and masculine intelligence.

To this rule the Khasis, with their elaborate system of mother - kin, form no exception. For among them, while landed property is both transmitted through women and held by women alone, political power is transmitted indeed through women, but is held by men ; in other words, the Khasi tribes are, with a single exception, governed by kings, not by queens. And even in the one tribe, which is nominally ruled by women, the real power is delegated by the reigning queen or High Priestess to her son, her nephew, or a more distant male relation. In all the other tribes the kingship may be held by a woman only on the failure of all male heirs in the female line.[1] So far is mother-kin from implying mother-rule. A Khasi king inherits power in right of his mother, but he exercises it in his own. Similarly the Pelew Islanders, in spite of their system of mother-kin, are governed by chiefs, not by chieftainesses. It is true that there are chieftainesses, and that they indirectly exercise much influence ; but their direct authority is limited to the affairs of women, especially to the administration of the women's clubs or associations, which

[1] Major P. R. T. Gurdon, *The Khasis*, pp. 66-71. The rule of succession is as follows. A *Siem*, or king, "is succeeded by the eldest of his uterine brothers ; failing such brothers, by the eldest of his sisters' sons ; failing such nephews, by the eldest of the sons of his sisters' daughters; failing such grand-nephews, by the eldest of the sons of his mother's sisters ; and, failing such first cousins, by the eldest of his male cousins on the female side, other than first cousins, those nearest in degree of relationship having prior claim. If there were no heirs male, as above, he would be succeeded by the eldest of his uterine sisters ; in the absence of such sisters, by the eldest of his sisters' daughters ; failing such nieces, by the eldest of the daughters of his sisters' daughters ; failing such grand-nieces, by the eldest of the daughters of his mother's sisters; and failing such first cousins, by the eldest of his female cousins on the female side, other than first cousins, those nearest in degree of relationship having prior claim. A female *Siem* would be succeeded by her eldest son, and so on " (*op. cit.* p. 71). The rule illustrates the logical precision with which the system of mother-kin is carried out by these people even when the intention is actually to exclude women from power.

answer to the clubs or associations of the men.[1] And to take another example, the Melanesians, like the Khasis and the Pelew Islanders, have the system of mother-kin, being similarly divided into exogamous clans with descent in the female line ; " but it must be understood that the mother is in no way the head of the family. The house of the family is the father's, the garden is his, the rule and government are his." [2]

We may safely assume that the practice has been the same among all the many peoples who have retained the ancient system of mother-kin under a monarchical constitution. In Africa, for example, the chieftainship or kingship often descends in the female line, but it is men, not women, who inherit it.[3] The theory of a gynaecocracy is in truth a dream of visionaries and pedants. And equally chimerical is the idea that the predominance of goddesses under a system of mother-kin like that of the Khasis is a creation of the female mind. If women ever created gods, they would be more likely to give them masculine than feminine features. In point of fact the great religious ideals which have permanently impressed themselves on the world seem always to have been a product of the male imagination. Men make gods and women worship them. The combination of ancestor-worship with mother-kin furnishes a simple and sufficient explanation of the superiority of goddesses over gods in a state of society where these conditions prevail. Men naturally assign the first place in their devotions to the ancestress from whom they trace their descent. We need not resort to a fantastic hypothesis of the preponderance of the feminine fancy in order to account for the facts.

The theory that under a system of mother-kin the women rule the men and set up goddesses for them to

The theory of a gynaecocracy and of the predominance of the female imagination in religion is an idle dream

---

[1] J. Kubary, *Die socialen Einrichtungen der Pelauer*, pp. 35, 39 *sq.*, 73-83. See also above, pp. 204 *sq.*

[2] R. H. Codrington, *The Melanesians* (Oxford, 1891), p. 34.

[3] See A. H. Post, *Afrikanische Jurisprudenz* (Oldenburg and Leipsic, 1887), i. 140 *sq.* Captain W. Gill reports that the Su-Mu, a Man-Tzŭ tribe in Southern China numbering

some three and a half millions, is always ruled by a queen (*The River of Golden Sand*, London, 1880, i. 365). But Capt. Gill was not nearer to the tribe than a six days' journey ; and even if his report is correct we may suppose that the real power is exercised by men, just as it is in the solitary Khasi tribe which is nominally governed by a woman.

But mother-kin is a solid fact, which can hardly have failed to modify the religion of the peoples who practise it.

worship is indeed so improbable in itself, and so contrary to experience, that it scarcely deserves the serious attention which it appears to have received.[1]   But when we have brushed aside these cobwebs, as we must do, we are still left face to face with the solid fact of the wide prevalence of mother-kin, that is, of a social system which traces descent and transmits property through women and not through men.   That a social system so widely spread and so deeply rooted should have affected the religion of the peoples who practise it, may reasonably be inferred, especially when we remember that in primitive communities the social relations of the gods commonly reflect the social relations of their worshippers.   How the system of mother-kin may mould religious ideas and customs, creating goddesses and assigning at least a nominal superiority to priestesses over priests, is shown with perfect lucidity by the example of the Khasis, and hardly less clearly by the example of the Pelew Islanders. It cannot therefore be rash to hold that what the system has certainly done for these peoples, it may well have done for many more.   But unfortunately through lack of documentary evidence we are seldom able to trace its influence so clearly.

§ 3. *Mother-Kin and Mother Goddesses in the Ancient East*

Mother-kin and mother-goddesses in Western Asia.

While the combination of mother-kin in society with a preference for goddesses in religion is to be found as a matter of fact among the Khasis and Pelew Islanders of to-day, the former prevalence of mother-kin in the lands where the great goddesses Astarte and Cybele were worshipped is a matter of inference only.   In later times father-kin had certainly displaced mother-kin among the Semitic worshippers of Astarte, and probably the same change had taken place among the Phrygian worshippers of Cybele.   Yet the older

[1] The theory, or at all events the latter part of it, has been carefully examined by Dr. L. R. Farnell; and if, as I apprehend, he rejects it, I agree with him.   See his article "Sociological Hypotheses concerning the position of Women in Ancient Religion," *Archiv für Religionswissen-* *schaft*, vii. (1904) pp. 70-94; his *Cults of the Greek States* (Oxford, 1896–1909), iii. 109 *sqq.*; and *The Hibbert Journal*, April 1907, p. 690.   But I differ from him, it seems, in thinking that mother-kin is favourable to the growth of mother goddesses.

custom lingered in Lycia down to the historical period;[1] and we may conjecture that in former times it was widely spread through Asia Minor. The secluded situation and rugged mountains of Lycia favoured the survival of a native language and of native institutions long after these had disappeared from the wide plains and fertile valleys which lay on the highroads of war and commerce. Lycia was to Asia Minor what the highlands of Wales and of Scotland have been to Britain, the last entrenchments where the old race stood at bay. And even among the Semites of antiquity, though father-kin finally prevailed in matters of descent and property, traces of an older system of mother-kin, with its looser sexual relations, appear to have long survived in the sphere of religion. At all events one of the most learned and acute of Semitic scholars adduced what he regarded as evidence sufficient to prove "that in old Arabian religion gods and goddesses often occurred in pairs, the goddess being the greater, so that the god cannot be her Baal, that the goddess is often a mother without being a wife, and the god her son, and that the progress of things was towards changing goddesses into gods or lowering them beneath the male deity."[2]

In Egypt the archaic system of mother-kin, with its preference for women over men in matters of property and inheritance, lasted down to Roman times, and it was tradi- *Mother-kin in ancient Egypt.*

---

[1] The Lycians traced their descent through women, not through men; and among them it was the daughters, not the sons, who inherited the family property. See Herodotus, i. 174; Nicolaus Damascenus, in Stobaeus, *Florilegium*, xliv. 41 (*Fragmenta Historicorum Graecorum*, ed. C. Müller, iii. 461); Plutarch, *De mulierum virtutibus*, 9. An ancient historian even asserts that the Lycians were ruled by women (ἐκ παλαιοῦ γυναικοκρατοῦνται, Heraclides Ponticus, Frag. 15, in *Fragmenta Historicorum Graecorum*, ed. C. Müller, ii. 217). Inscriptions found at Dalisandos, in Isauria, seem to prove that it was not unusual there to trace descent through the mother even in the third or the fourth century after Christ. See Sir W. M. Ramsay, "The Permanence of Religion at Holy Places in the East," *The Expositor*, November 1906, p. 475. Dr. L. Messerschmidt seems to think that the Lycians were Hittites (*The Hittites*, p. 20). Scholars are not agreed as to the family of speech to which the Lycian language belongs. Some think that it was an Indo-European tongue; but this view is now abandoned by Professor Ed. Meyer (*Geschichte des Altertums*,[2] i. 2. p. 626).

[2] W. Robertson Smith, *Kinship and Marriage in Early Arabia*[2] (London, 1903), p. 306. The hypothesis of the former existence of mother-kin among the Semites is rejected by Professor Ed. Meyer (*Geschichte des Altertums*,[2] i. 2, p. 360) and W. W. Graf Baudissin (*Adonis und Esmun*, pp. 46 *sq.*).

tionally based on the example of Isis, who had avenged her husband's murder and had continued to reign after his decease, conferring benefits on mankind. "For these reasons," says Diodorus Siculus, "it was appointed that the queen should enjoy greater power and honour than the king, and that among private people the wife should rule over her husband, in the marriage contract the husband agreeing to obey his wife in all things."[1] A corollary of the superior position thus conceded to women in Egypt was that the obligation of maintaining parents in their old age rested on the daughters, not on the sons, of the family.[2]

Marriages of brothers with sisters in ancient Egypt.

The same legal superiority of women over men accounts for the most remarkable feature in the social system of the ancient Egyptians, to wit, the marriage of full brothers with full sisters. That marriage, which to us seems strange and unnatural, was by no means a whim of the reigning Ptolemies; on the contrary, these Macedonian conquerors appear, with characteristic prudence, to have borrowed the custom from their Egyptian predecessors for the express purpose of conciliating native prejudice. In the eyes of the Egyptians "marriage between brother and sister was the best of marriages, and it acquired an ineffable degree of sanctity when the brother and sister who contracted it were themselves born of a brother and sister, who had in their turn also sprung from a union of the same sort."[3] Nor did the principle apply only to gods and kings. The common people acted on it in their daily life. They regarded marriages between brothers and sisters as the most natural and reasonable of all.[4] The evidence of legal documents,

[1] Diodorus Siculus, i. 27. 1 *sq.* In spite of this express testimony to the existence of a true gynaecocracy in ancient Egypt, I am of opinion that the alleged superiority of the queen to the king and of the wife to her husband must have been to a great extent only nominal. Certainly we know that it was the king and not the queen who really governed the country; and we can hardly doubt that in like manner it was for the most part the husband and not the wife who really ruled the house, though unquestionably in regard to property the law seems to have granted important rights to women which it denied to men. On the position of women in ancient Egypt see especially the able article of Miss Rachel Evelyn White (Mrs. Wedd), "Women in Ptolemaic Egypt," *Journal of Hellenic Studies*, xviii. (1898) pp. 238-256.

[2] Herodotus, ii. 35.

[3] Sir Gaston Maspero, quoted by Miss R. E. White, *op. cit.* p. 244.

[4] J. Nietzold, *Die Ehe in Ägypten zur ptolemäisch-römischen Zeit* (Leipzic, 1903), p. 12.

including marriage contracts, tends to prove that such unions were the rule, not the exception, in ancient Egypt, and that they continued to form the majority of marriages long after the Romans had obtained a firm footing in the country. As we cannot suppose that Roman influence was used to promote a custom which must have been abhorrent to Roman instincts, we may safely assume that the proportion of brother and sister marriages in Egypt had been still greater in the days when the country was free.[1]

It would doubtless be a mistake to treat these marriages as a relic of savagery, as a survival of a tribal communism which knew no bar to the intercourse of the sexes. For such a theory would not explain why union with a sister was not only allowed, but preferred to all others. The true motive of that preference was most probably the wish of brothers to obtain for their own use the family property, which belonged of right to their sisters, and which otherwise they would have seen in the enjoyment of strangers, the husbands of their sisters. This is the system which in Ceylon is known as *beena* marriage. Under it the daughter, not the son, is the heir. She stays at home, and her husband comes and lives with her in the house ; but her brother goes away and dwells in his wife's home, inheriting nothing from his parents.[2] Such a system could not fail in time to prove irksome. Men would be loth to quit the old home, resign the ancestral property to a stranger, and go out to seek their fortune empty-handed in the world. The remedy was obvious. A man had nothing to do but to marry his sister himself instead of handing her over to another. Having done so he stayed at home and enjoyed the family estate in virtue of his marriage with the heiress. This simple and perfectly effective expedient for keeping the property in the

Such marriages were based on a wish to keep the property in the family.

---

[1] A. Erman, *Ägyten und ägyptisches Leben im Altertum*, pp. 221 *sq.*; U. Wilcken, "Arsinoitische Steuerprofessionen aus dem Jahre 189 n. Chr.," *Sitzungsberichte der könig. Preuss. Akademie der Wissenschaften zu Berlin*, 1883, p. 903 ; J. Nietzold, *Die Ehe in Ägypten zur ptolemäisch-römischen Zeit*, pp. 12-14.

[2] J. F. McLennan, *Studies in Ancient History* (London, 1886), pp. 101 *sqq.* Among the Kocchs of North-Eastern India "the property of the husband is made over to the wife ; when she dies it goes to her daughters, and when he marries he lives with his wife's mother" (R. G. Latham, *Descriptive Ethnology*, London, 1859, i. 96).

family most probably explains the custom of brother and sister marriage in Egypt.[1]

Thus the union of Osiris with his sister Isis was not a freak of the story-teller's fancy : it reflected a social custom which was itself based on practical considerations of the most solid kind. When we reflect that this practice of mother-kin as opposed to father-kin survived down to the latest times of antiquity, not in an obscure and barbarous tribe, but in a nation whose immemorial civilization was its glory and the wonder of the world, we may without being extravagant suppose that a similar practice formerly prevailed in Syria and Phrygia, and that it accounts for the superiority of the goddess over the god in the divine partnerships of Adonis and Astarte, of Attis and Cybele. But the ancient system both of society and of religion had undergone far more change in these countries than in Egypt, where to the last the main outlines of the old structure could be traced in the national institutions to which the Egyptians clung with a passionate, a fanatical devotion. Mother-kin, the divinity of kings and queens, a sense of the original connexion of the gods with nature— these things outlived the Persian, the Macedonian, the Roman conquest, and only perished under the more powerful solvent

of Christianity. But the old order did not vanish at once with the official establishment of the new religion. In the age of Constantine the Greeks of Egypt still attributed the rise of the Nile to Serapis, the later form of Osiris, alleging

---

[1] This is in substance the explanation which Miss Rachel Evelyn White (Mrs. Wedd) gives of the Egyptian custom. See her paper, "Women in Ptolemaic Egypt," *Journal of Hellenic Studies*, xviii. (1898) p. 265. Similarly Mr. J. Nietzold observes that "economical considerations, especially in the case of great landowners, may often have been the occasion of marriages with sisters, the intention being in this way to avoid a division of the property" (*Die Ehe in Ägypten*, p. 13). The same explanation of the custom has been given by Prof. W. Ridgeway. See his "Supplices of Aeschylus," in *Praelections delivered before the Senate* of *the University of Cambridge* (Cambridge, 1906), pp. 154 *sq.* I understand from Professor W. M. Flinders Petrie that the theory has been a commonplace with Egyptologists for many years. McLennan explained the marriage of brothers and sisters in royal families as an expedient for shifting the succession from the female to the male line ; but he did not extend the theory so as to explain similar marriages among common people in Egypt, perhaps because he was not aware of the facts. See J. F. McLennan, *The Patriarchal Theory*, edited and completed by D. McLennan (London, 1885), p. 95.

that the inundation¯could not take place if the standard
cubit, which was used to measure it, were not deposited
according to custom in the temple of the god. The emperor
ordered the cubit to be transferred to a church ; and next
year, to the general surprise, the river rose just as usual.[1]
Even at a later time Athanasius himself had to confess with
sorrow and indignation that under his own eyes the Egyptians
still annually mourned the death of Osiris.[2] The end came
with the destruction of the great Serapeum at Alexandria,
the last stronghold of the heathen in Egypt. It perished in
a furious and bloody sedition, in which Christians and pagans
seem to have vied with each other in mutual atrocities.
After its fall the temples were levelled with the ground or
converted into churches, and the images of the old gods
went to the melting-pot to be converted into base uses for
the rabble of Alexandria.[3]

The singular tenacity with which the Egyptian people *Egyptian*
maintained their traditional beliefs and customs for thousands *conserva-*
of years sprang no doubt from the stubborn conservatism *tism partly*
of the national character. Yet that conservatism was itself *natural*
in great measure an effect of geographical and climatic *and habits*
conditions and of the ways of life which they favoured. *of life.*
Surrounded on every side by deserts or almost harbourless
seas, the Egyptians occupied a position of great natural
strength which for long ages together protected them from
invasion and allowed their native habits to set and harden,
undisturbed by the subversive influence of foreign conquest.
The wonderful regularity of nature in Egypt also conduced
to a corresponding stability in the minds of the people.
Year in, year out, the immutable succession of the seasons
brought with it the same unvarying round of agricultural
toil. What the fathers had done, the sons did in the
same manner at the same season, and so it went on from

---

[1] Socrates, *Historia Ecclesiastica*, i.
18 (Migne's *Patrologia Graeca*, lxvii.
121). The learned Valesius, in his
note on this passage, informs us that
the cubit was again transferred by the
Emperor Julian to the Serapeum, where
it was left in peace till the destruction
of that temple.

[2] Athanasius, *Oratio contra Gentes*,

10 (Migne's *Patrologia Graeca*, **xxv.**
24).

[3] Socrates, *Historia Ecclesiastica*, v.
16 *sq.* (Migne's *Patrologia Graeca*,
lxvii. 604 *sq.*) ; Sozomenus, *Historia
Ecclesiastica*, vii. 15 (Migne's *Patrologia Graeca*, lxvii. 1152 *sq.*). These
events took place under the Emperor
Theodosius in the year 391 A.D.

generation to generation. This monotonous routine is common indeed to all purely agricultural communities, and everywhere tends to beget in the husbandman a settled phlegmatic habit of mind very different from the mobility, the alertness, the pliability of character which the hazards and uncertainties of commerce and the sea foster in the merchant and the sailor. The saturnine temperament of the farmer is as naturally averse to change as the more mercurial spirit of the trader and the seaman is predisposed to it. But the stereotyping of ideas and of customs was carried further in Egypt than in most lands devoted to husbandry by reason of the greater uniformity of the Egyptian seasons and the more complete isolation of the country.

The old type of Osiris better preserved than those of Adonis and Attis.

The general effect of these causes was to create a type of national character which presented many points of resemblance to that of the Chinese. In both we see the same inflexible strength of will, the same astonishing industry, the same strange blend of humanity and savagery, the same obstinate adherence to tradition, the same pride of race and of ancient civilization, the same contempt for foreigners as for upstarts and barbarians, the same patient outward submission to an alien rule combined with an unshakeable inward devotion to native ideals. It was this conservative temper of the people, bred in great measure of the physical nature of their land, which, so to say, embalmed the memory of Osiris long after the corresponding figures of Adonis and Attis had suffered decay. For while Egypt enjoyed profound repose, the tides of war and conquest, of traffic and commerce, had for centuries rolled over Western Asia, the native home of Adonis and Attis ; and if the shock of nationalities in this great meeting-ground of East and West was favourable to the rise of new faiths and new moralities, it was in the same measure unfavourable to the preservation of the old.

NOTES

I

MOLOCH THE KING

I CANNOT leave the evidence for the sacred character of Jewish kings [1] without mentioning a suggestion which was made to me by my friend and teacher the Rev. Professor R. H. Kennett. He thinks that Moloch, to whom first-born children were burnt by their parents in the valley of Hinnom, outside the walls of Jerusalem,[2] may have been originally the human king regarded as an incarnate deity. Certainly the name of Moloch, or rather Molech (for so it is always written in the Massoretic text [3]), is merely a slightly dis-

[1] See above, vol. i. pp. 17 *sqq.*

[2] *The Dying God*, pp. 168 *sqq.* ; G. F. Moore, in *Encyclopaedia Biblica*, *s.v.* "Molech." The phrase translated "make pass through the fire to Molech" (2 Kings xxiii. 10) means properly, Professor Kennett tells me, "make to pass over by means of fire to Molech," where the verb has the sense of "make over to," "dedicate," "devote," as appears from its use in Exodus xiii. 12 ("set apart," English Version) and Ezekiel xx. 26. That the children were not made simply to pass through the fire, but were burned in it, is shown by a comparison of 2 Kings xvi. 3, xxiii. 10, Jeremiah xxxii. 35, with 2 Chronicles xxviii. 3, Jeremiah vii. 31, xix. 5. As to the use of the verb הֶעֱבִיר in the sense of "dedicate," "devote," see G. F. Moore, *s.v.* "Molech," *Encyclopaedia Biblica*, iii. 3184; F. Brown, S. R. Driver, and C. A. Briggs, *Hebrew and English Lexicon of the Old Testament* (Oxford, 1906), p. 718. "The testimony of both the prophets and the laws is abundant and unambiguous that the victims were slain and burnt as a holocaust" (G. F. Moore, in *Encyclopaedia Biblica*, iii. 3184). Similarly Principal J. Skinner translates the phrase in 2 Kings xvi. 3 by "dedicated his son by fire," and remarks that the expression, "whatever its primary sense may be, undoubtedly denoted actual burning" (commentary on Kings in *The Century Bible*). The practice would seem to have been very ancient at Jerusalem, for tradition placed the attempted burnt-sacrifice of Isaac by his father Abraham on Mount Moriah, which was no other than Mount Zion, the site of the king's palace and of the temple of Jehovah. See Genesis xxii. 1-18; 2 Chronicles iii. 1; J. Benzinger, *Hebräische Archäologie* (Freiburg i. Baden and Leipsic, 1894), pp. 45, 233; T. K. Cheyne, *s.v.* "Moriah," *Encyclopaedia Biblica*, iii. 3200 *sq.*

[3] Leviticus xviii. 21, xx. 2-5; 1 Kings xi. 7; 2 Kings xxiii. 10; Jeremiah xxxii. 35.

Moloch perhaps the human king regarded as an incarnate deity.

guised form of *melech*, the ordinary Hebrew word for "king," the scribes having apparently given the dreadful word the vowels of bosheth, "shameful thing."[1] But it seems clear that in historical times the Jews who offered these sacrifices identified Molech, not with the human king, but with Jehovah, though the prophets protested against the custom as an outrage on the divine majesty.[2]

The sacrifices to Moloch may have been intended to prolong the king's life. Vicarious sacrifices for a king or queen in Sweden, Persia, and Madagascar.

If, however, these sacrifices were originally offered to or in behalf of the human king, it is possible that they were intended to prolong his life and strengthen his hands for the performance of those magical functions which he was expected to discharge for the good of his people. The old kings of Sweden answered with their heads for the fertility of the ground,[3] and we read that one of them, Aun or On by name, sacrificed nine of his sons to Odin at Upsala in order that his own life might be spared. After the sacrifice of his second son he received from the god an oracle that he should live as long as he gave him one of his sons every tenth year. When he had thus sacrificed seven sons, the ruthless father still lived, but was so feeble that he could no longer walk and had to be carried in a chair. Then he offered up his eighth son and lived ten years more, bedridden. After that he sacrificed his ninth son, and lived ten years more, drinking out of a horn like a weaned child. He now wished to sacrifice his last remaining son to Odin, but the Swedes would not let him, so he died and was buried in a mound at Upsala.[4] In this Swedish tradition the king's children seem to have been looked upon as substitutes offered to the god in place of their father, and apparently this was also the current explanation of the slaughter of the first-born in the later times of Israel.[5] On that view the sacrifices were vicarious, and therefore purely religious, being intended to propitiate a stern and exacting deity. Similarly we read that when Amestris, wife of Xerxes, was grown old, she sacrificed on her behalf twice seven noble children to the

---

[1] W. Robertson Smith, *The Religion of the Semites*,[2] p. 372, note [1].

[2] "It is plain, from various passages of the prophets, that the sacrifices of children among the Jews before the captivity, which are commonly known as sacrifices to Moloch, were regarded by the worshippers as oblations to Jehovah, under the title of king" (W. Robertson Smith, *Religion of the Semites*,[2] p. 372, referring to Jeremiah vii. 31, xix. 5, xxxii. 35; Ezekiel xxiii. 39; Micah vi. 7). The same view is taken by Prof. G. F. Moore, in *Encyclopaedia Biblica*, *s.v.* "Molech," vol. iii. 3187 *sq.*

[3] *The Magic Art and the Evolution of Kings*, i. 366 *sq.*

[4] "Ynglinga Saga," 29, in *The Heimskringla or Chronicle of the Kings of Norway*, translated by S. Laing (London, 1844), i. 239 *sq.*; H. M. Chadwick, *The Cult of Othin* (London, 1899), pp. 4, 27; *The Dying God*, pp. 160 *sq.* Similarly in Peru, when a person of note was sick, he would sometimes sacrifice his son to the idol in order that his own life might be spared. See A. de Herrera, *The General History of the Vast Continent and Islands of America*, translated by Capt. J. Stevens (London, 1725-1726), iv. 347 *sq.*

[5] Micah vi. 6-8.

earth god by burying them alive.[1]   If the story is true—and it rests on the authority of Herodotus, a nearly contemporary witness—we may surmise that the aged queen acted thus with an eye to the future rather than to the past; she hoped that the grim god of the nether-world would accept the young victims in her stead, and let her live for many years.   The same idea of vicarious suffering comes out in a tradition told of a certain Hova king of Madagascar, who bore the sonorous name of Andriamasinavalona.   When he had grown sickly and feeble, the oracle was consulted as to the best way of restoring him to health.   "The following result was the consequence of the directions of the oracle.   A speech was first delivered to the people, offering great honours and rewards to the family of any individual who would freely offer himself to be sacrificed, in order to the king's recovery.   The people shuddered at the idea, and ran away in different directions.   One man, however, presented himself for the purpose, and his offer was accepted.   The sacrificer girded up his loins, sharpened his knife, and bound the victim.   After which, he was laid down with his head towards the east, upon a mat spread for the purpose, according to the custom with animals on such occasions, when the priest appeared, to proceed with all solemnity in slaughtering the victim by cutting his throat.   A quantity of red liquid, however, which had been prepared from a native dye, was spilled in the ceremony; and, to the amazement of those who looked on, blood seemed to be flowing all around.   The man, as might be supposed, was unhurt; but the king rewarded him and his descendants with the perpetual privilege of exemption from capital punishment for any violation of the laws.   The descendants of the man to this day form a particular class, called *Tay maty manota*, which may be translated, 'Not dead, though transgressing.' Instances frequently occur, of individuals of this class appropriating bullocks, rice, and other things belonging to the sovereign, as if they were their own, and escaping merely with a reprimand, while a common person would have to suffer death, or be reduced to slavery." [2]

Sometimes, however, the practices intended to prolong the king's life seem to rest on a theory of nutrition rather than of substitution; in other words, the life of the victims, instead of being offered vicariously to a god, is apparently supposed to pass directly into the body of the sacrificer, thus refreshing his failing strength and prolonging his existence.   So regarded, the custom is magical rather than religious in character, since the desired effect is thought to follow directly without the intervention of a deity.   At all events, it can be shown that sacrifices of this sort have been offered to prolong the life of kings in other parts of the world.   Thus in regard to

Other sacrifices for prolonging the king's life appear to be magical rather than religious.

[1] Herodotus, vii. 114; Plutarch, *De superstitione*, 13.

[2] W. Ellis, *History of Madagascar* (London, N.D.), i. 344 *sq.*

Custom in
the Niger
delta.
some of the negroes who inhabit the delta of the Niger we read that : " A custom which formerly was practised by the Ibani, and is still prevalent among all the interior tribes, consists in prolonging the life of a king or ancestral representative by the daily, or possibly weekly, sacrifice of a chicken and egg. Every morning, as soon as the patriarch has risen from his bed, the sacrificial articles are procured either by his mother, head wife, or eldest daughter, and given to the priest, who receives them on the open space in front of the house. When this has been reported to the patriarch, he comes outside and, sitting down, joins in the ceremony. Taking the chicken in his hand, the priest first of all touches the patriarch's face with it, and afterwards passes it over the whole of his body. He then cuts its throat and allows the blood to drop on the ground. Mixing the blood and the earth into a paste, he rubs it on the old man's forehead and breast, and this is not to be washed off under any circumstances until the evening. The chicken and the egg, also a piece of white cloth, are now tied on to a stick, which, if a stream is in the near vicinity, is planted in the ground at the waterside. During the carriage of these articles to the place in question, all the wives and many members of the household accompany the priest, invoking the deity as they go to prolong their father's life. This is done in the firm conviction that through the sacrifice of each chicken his life will be accordingly prolonged." [1]

The ceremony thus described is, like so many other rites, a combination of magic and religion ; for whereas the prayers to the god are religious, the passing of the victim over the king's body and the smearing of him with its blood are magical, being plainly intended to convey to him directly, without the mediation of any deity, the life of the fowl. In the following instances the practices for prolonging the king's life seem to be purely magical. Among the Zulus, at one of the annual feasts of first-fruits, a bull is killed by a particular regiment. In slaughtering the beast they may not use spears or sticks, but must break its neck or choke it with their bare hands. " It is then burned, and the strength of the bull is supposed to enter into the king, thereby prolonging his life." [2] Again, in an early Portuguese historian we read of a Caffre king of East Africa that " it is related of this Monomotapa that he has a house where he commands bodies of men who have died at the hands of the law to be hung up, and where thus hanging all the humidity

Customs
observed
by the
Zulus and
Caffres to
prolong the
king's life.

---

[1] Major A. G. Leonard, *The Lower Niger and its Tribes* (London, 1906), p. 457.

[2] D. Leslie, *Among the Zulus and Amatongas* [2] (Edinburgh, 1875), p. 91. This sacrifice may be the one described by J. Shooter, *The Kafirs of Natal* (London, 1857), p. 26. The reason for not stabbing the animal is perhaps a wish not to lose any of the blood, but to convey its life intact to the king. The same reason would explain the same rule which the Baganda observed in killing a human victim for the same purpose (see below, p. 224).

of their bodies falls into vases placed underneath, and when all has dropped from them and they shrink and dry up he commands them to be taken down and buried, and with the fat and moisture in the vases they say he makes ointments with which he anoints himself in order to enjoy long life—which is his belief—and also to be proof against receiving harm from sorcerers." [1]

The Baganda of Central Africa used to kill men on various occasions for the purpose of prolonging the king's life; in all cases it would seem to be thought that the life of the murdered man was in some mysterious fashion transferred to the king, so that the monarch received thereby a fresh accession of vital energy. For example, whenever a particular royal drum had a new skin put on it, not only was a cow killed to furnish the skin and its blood run into the drum, but a man was beheaded and the spouting blood from the severed neck was allowed to gush into the drum, "so that, when the drum was beaten, it was supposed to add fresh life and vigour to the king from the life of the slain man." [2] Again, at the coronation of a new king, a royal chamberlain was chosen to take charge of the king's inner court and to guard his wives. From the royal presence the chamberlain was conducted, along with eight captives, to one of the human shambles; there he was blindfolded while seven of the men were clubbed to death, only the dull thud and crashing sound telling him of what was taking place. But when the seven had been thus despatched, the bandages were removed from the chamberlain's eyes and he witnessed the death of the eighth. As each man was killed, his belly was ripped open and his bowels pulled out and hung round the chamberlain's neck. These deaths were said to add to the King's vigour and to make the chamberlain strong and faithful. [3] Nor were these the only human sacrifices offered at a king's coronation for the purpose of strengthening the new monarch. When the king had reigned two or three months, he was expected to hunt first a leopard and then a bushbuck. On the night after the hunt of the bushbuck, one of the ministers of State caught a man and brought him before the king in the dark; the king speared him slightly, then the man was strangled and the body thrown into a papyrus swamp, that it might never be found again. Another ceremony performed about this time to confirm the king in his kingdom was to catch a man, bind him, and bring him before the king, who wounded him slightly with a spear. Then the man was put to death. These men were killed to invigorate the king. [4]

Marginal notes:
Customs observed by the Baganda to prolong the king's life.

Human victims killed in order to invigorate the king.

---

[1] J. Dos Santos, *Eastern Ethiopia*, bk. ii. chap. 16 (G. M'Call Theal's *Records of South-Eastern Africa*, vii. 289).

[2] Rev. J. Roscoe, *The Baganda* (London, 1911), pp. 27 *sq.*

[3] Rev. J. Roscoe, *The Baganda*, p. 200.

[4] Rev. J. Roscoe, *The Baganda*, pp. 209 *sq.*

Chief's son killed to provide the king with anklets.

When a king of Uganda had reigned some time, apparently several years, a ceremony was performed for the sake of prolonging his life. For this purpose the king paid a visit—a fatal visit—to a chief of the Lung-fish clan, who bore the title of Nankere and resided in the district of Busiro, where the tombs and temples of the kings were situated. When the time for the ceremony had been appointed, the chief chose one of his own sons, who was to die that the king might live. If the chief had no son, a near relation was compelled to serve as a substitute. The hapless youth was fed and clothed and treated in all respects like a prince, and taken to live in a particular house near the place where the king was to lodge for the ceremony. When the destined victim had been feasted and guarded for a month, the king set out on his progress from the capital. On the way he stopped at the temple of the great god Mukasa; there he changed his garments, leaving behind him in the temple those which he had been wearing. Also he left behind him all his anklets, and did not put on any fresh ones, for he was shortly to receive new anklets of a remarkable kind. When the king arrived at his destination, the chief met him, and the two exchanged a gourd of beer. At this interview the king's mother was present to see her son for the last time; for from that moment the two were never allowed to look upon each other again. The chief addressed the king's mother informing her of this final separation; then turning to the king he said, " You are now of age; go and live longer than your forefathers." Then the chief's son was introduced. The chief took him by the hand and presented him to the king, who passed him on to the body-guard; they led him outside and killed him by beating him with their clenched fists. The muscles from the back of the body of the murdered youth were removed and made into two anklets for the king, and a strip of skin cut from the corpse was made into a whip, which was kept in the royal enclosure for special feasts. The dead body was thrown on waste land and guarded against wild beasts, but not buried.[1]

The king's game.

When that ceremony was over, the king departed to go to another chief in Busiro; but on the way thither he stopped at a place called Baka and sat down under a great tree to play a game of spinning fruit-stones. It is a children's game, but it was no child's play to the man who ran to fetch the fruit-stones for the king to play with; for he was caught and speared to death on the spot for the purpose of prolonging the king's life. After the game had been played the king with his train passed on and lodged with a certain princess till the anklets made from the muscles of the chief's murdered son were ready for him to wear;

[1] Rev. J. Roscoe, *The Baganda*, pp. 210 *sq.*

it was the princess who had to superintend the making of these royal ornaments.[1]

When all these ceremonies were over, the king made a great feast.   At this feast a priest went about carrying under his mantle the whip that had been made from the skin of the murdered young man.   As he passed through the crowd of merrymakers, he would flick a man here and there with the whip, and it was believed that the man on whom the lash lighted would be childless and might die, unless he made an offering of either nine or ninety cowrie shells to the priest who had struck him.   Naturally he hastened to procure the shells and take them to the striker, who, on receiving them, struck the man on the shoulder with his hand, thus restoring to him the generative powers of which the blow of the whip had deprived him.   At the end of the feast the drummers removed all the drums but one, which they left as if they had forgotten it.   Somebody in the crowd would notice the apparent oversight and run after the drummers with the drum, saying, " You have left one behind."   The thanks he received was that he was caught and killed and the bones of his upper arm made into drumsticks for that particular drum.   The drum was never afterwards brought out during the whole of the king's reign, but was kept covered up till the time came to bring it out on the corresponding feast of his successor.   Yet from time to time the priest, who had flicked the revellers with the whip of human skin, would dress himself up in a mantle of cow-hide from neck to foot, and concealing the drumstick of human bones under his robe would go into the king's presence, and suddenly whipping out the bones from his bosom would brandish them in the king's face.   Then he would as suddenly hide them again, but only to repeat the manoeuvre.   After that he retired and restored the bones to their usual place.   They were decorated with cowrie shells and little bells, which jingled as he shook them at the king.[2]

The precise meaning of these latter ceremonies is obscure ; but we may suppose that just as the human blood poured into a drum was thought to pass into the king's veins in the booming notes of the drum, so the clicking of the human bones and the jingling of their bells were supposed to infuse into the royal person the vigour of the murdered man.   The purpose of flicking commoners with the whip made of human skin is even more obscure ; but we may conjecture that the life or virility of every man struck with the whip was supposed to be transmitted in some way to the king, who thus recruited his vital, and especially his reproductive, energies at this solemn feast.   If I am right in my interpretation, all these Baganda

The whip of human skin.

Modes in which the strength of the human victims was thought to pass into the king.

<hr>

[1] Rev. J. Roscoe, *The Baganda,* pp. 211 *sq.*   I have abridged the

account of the ceremonies.
[2] Rev. J. Roscoe, *op. cit.* pp. 213 *sq.*

modes of strengthening the king and prolonging his life belonged to the nutritive rather than to the vicarious type of sacrifice, from which it will follow that they were magical rather than religious in character.

The same thing may perhaps be said of the wholesale massacres which used to be perpetrated when a king of Uganda was ill. At these times the priests informed the royal patient that persons marked by a certain physical peculiarity, such as a cast of the eye, a particular gait, or a distinctive colouring, must be put to death. Accordingly the king sent out his catchpoles, who waylaid such persons in the roads and dragged them to the royal enclosure, where they were kept until the tale of victims prescribed by the priest was complete. Before they were led away to one of the eight places of execution, which were regularly appointed for this purpose in different parts of the kingdom, the victims had to drink medicated beer with the king out of a special pot, in order that he might have power over their ghosts, lest they should afterwards come back to torment him. They were killed, sometimes by being speared to death, sometimes by being hacked to pieces, sometimes by being burned alive. Contrary to the usual custom of the Baganda, the bodies, or what remained of the bodies, of these unfortunates were always left unburied on the place of execution.[1] In what way precisely the sick king was supposed to benefit by these massacres of his subjects does not appear, but we may surmise that somehow the victims were believed to give their lives for him or to him.

Thus it is possible that in Israel also the sacrifices of children to Moloch were in like manner intended to prolong the life of the human king (*melech*) either by serving as substitutes for him or by recruiting his failing energies with their vigorous young life. But it is equally possible, and perhaps more probable, that the sacrifice of the first-born children was only a particular application of the ancient law which devoted to the deity the first-born of every womb, whether of cattle or of human beings.[2]

[1] From information furnished by my friend the Rev. J. Roscoe. Compare his book, *The Baganda*, pp. 331 *sqq.*

[2] See *The Dying God*, pp. 166 *sqq.*

II

THE WIDOWED FLAMEN

§ 1. *The Pollution of Death*

A DIFFERENT explanation of the rule which obliged the Flamen Dialis to resign the priesthood on the death of his wife[1] has been suggested by my friend Dr. L. R. Farnell. He supposes that such a bereavement would render the Flamen ceremonially impure, and therefore unfit to hold office.[2] It is true that the ceremonial pollution caused by death commonly disqualifies a man for the discharge of sacred functions, but as a rule the disqualification is only temporary and can be removed by seclusion and the observance of purificatory rites, the length of the seclusion and the nature of the purification varying with the degree of relationship in which the living stand to the dead. Thus, for example, if one of the sacred eunuchs at Hierapolis-Bambyce saw the dead body of a stranger, he was unclean for that day and might not enter the sanctuary of the goddess ; but next day after purifying himself he was free to enter. But if the corpse happened to be that of a relation he was unclean for thirty days and had to shave his head before he might set foot within the holy precinct.[3] Again, in the Greek island of Ceos persons who had offered the annual sacrifices to their departed friends were unclean for two days afterwards and might not enter a sanctuary ; they had to purify themselves with water.[4] Similarly no one might go into the shrine of Men Tyrannus for ten days after being in contact with the dead.[5] Once more, at Stratonicea in Caria a chorus of thirty noble boys, clad in white and holding branches in their hands, used to sing a hymn daily in honour of Zeus and Hecate ; but if one of them were sick or had suffered a domestic bereavement, he was for the time being excused, not permanently excluded, from the

Theory that the resignation of the widowed Flamen Dialis was caused by the pollution of death.

---

[1] See above, vol. i. p. 45.

[2] *The Hibbert Journal*, April 1907, p. 689.

[3] Lucian, *De dea Syria*, 53.

[4] G. Dittenberger, *Sylloge Inscriptionum Graecarum*,[2] vol. ii. pp. 725 *sqq.*, Nos. 877, 878.

[5] G. Dittenberger, *op. cit.* vol. ii. pp. 429 *sq.*, No. 633.

227

performance of his sacred duties.[1] On the analogy of these and similar cases we should expect to find the widowed Flamen temporarily debarred from the exercise of his office, not permanently relieved of it.

Apparent parallel among the Todas.

However, in support of Dr. Farnell's view I would cite an Indian parallel which was pointed out to me by Dr. W. H. R. Rivers.   Among the Todas of the Neilgherry Hills in Southern India the priestly dairyman (*palol*) is a sacred personage, and his life, like that of the Flamen Dialis, is hedged in by many taboos.   Now when a death occurs in his clan, the dairyman may not attend any of the funeral ceremonies unless he gives up office, but he may be re-elected after the second funeral ceremonies have been completed, In the interval his place must be taken by a man of another clan. Some eighteen or nineteen years ago a man named Karkievan resigned the office of dairyman when his wife died, but two years later he was re-elected and has held office ever since.   There have meantime been many deaths in his clan, but he has not attended a funeral, and has not therefore had to resign his post again. Apparently in old times a more stringent rule prevailed, and the dairyman was obliged to vacate office whenever a death occurred in his clan.   For, according to tradition, the clan of Keadrol was divided into its two existing divisions for the express purpose of ensuring that there might still be men to undertake the office of dairyman when a death occurred in the clan, the men of the one division taking office whenever there was a death in the other.[2]

At first sight this case may seem exactly parallel to the case of the Flamen Dialis and the Flaminica on Dr. Farnell's theory ; for here there can be no doubt whatever that it is the pollution of death which disqualifies the sacred dairyman from holding office, since, if he only avoids that pollution by not attending the funeral, he is allowed at the present day to retain his post.   On this analogy we might suppose that it was not so much the death of his wife as the attendance at her funeral which compelled the Flamen Dialis to resign, especially as we know that he was expressly forbidden to touch a dead body or to enter the place where corpses were burned.[3]

But on inspection the analogy breaks down.

But a closer inspection of the facts proves that the analogy breaks down at some important points.   For though the Flamen Dialis was forbidden to touch a dead body or to enter a place where corpses were burned, he was permitted to attend a funeral ;[4] so that there could hardly be any objection to his attending the funeral of

---

[1] *Corpus Inscriptionum Graecarum*, ed. Aug. Boeckh, etc. (Berlin, 1828–1877), vol. ii. pp. 481 *sqq.*, No. 2715, οὔσης ἐξουσίας το[ῖς παισίν, ἐά]ν τινες αὐτῶν μὴ ὦσιν ὑγιεῖς ἢ πένθει οἰκείῳ κατέχωνται, where I understand ἐξουσία

to mean " leave of absence."
[2] W. H. R. Rivers, *The Todas* (London, 1906), pp. 99 *sq.*
[3] Aulus Gellius, x. 15. 24.
[4] Aulus Gellius, *l.c.* : "*funus tamen exequi non est religio.*"

his wife. This permission clearly tells against the view that it was the mere pollution of death which obliged him to resign office when his wife died. Further, and this is a point of fundamental difference between the two cases, whereas the Flamen Dialis was bound to be married, and married too by a rite of special solemnity,[1] there is no such obligation on the sacred dairyman of the Todas ; indeed, if he is married, he is bound to live apart from his wife during his term of office.[2] Surely the obligation laid on the Flamen Dialis to be married of itself implies that with the death of his wife he necessarily ceased to hold office : there is no need to search for another reason in the pollution of death which, as I have just shown, does not seem to square with the permission granted to the Flamen to attend a funeral. That this is indeed the true explanation of the rule in question is strongly suggested by the further and apparently parallel rule which forbade the Flamen to divorce his wife ; nothing but death might part them.[3] Now the rule which enjoined that a Flamen must be married, and the rule which forbade him to divorce his wife, have obviously nothing to do with the pollution of death, yet they can hardly be separated from the other rule that with the death of his wife he vacated office. All three rules are explained in the most natural way on the hypothesis which I have adopted, namely, that this married priest and priestess had to perform in common certain rites which the husband could not perform without his wife. The same obvious solution of the problem was suggested long ago by Plutarch, who, after asking why the Flamen Dialis had to lay down office on the death of his wife, says, amongst other things, that " perhaps it is because she performs sacred rites along with him (for many of the rites may not be performed without the presence of a married woman), and to marry another wife immedi-

---

[1] Gaius, *Instit.* i. 112, " *quod jus etiam nostris temporibus in usu est : nam flamines majores, id est Diales, Martiales, Quirinales, item reges sacrorum, nisi* (qui) *ex farreatis nati* sunt *non leguntur : ac ne ipsi quidem sine confarreatione sacerdotium habere possunt* " ; Servius on Virgil, *Aen.* iv. 103, " *quae res ad farreatas nuptias pertinet, quibus flaminem et flaminicam jure pontificio in matrimonium necesse est convenire.* " For a fuller description of the rite see Servius, on Virgil, *Aen.* iv. 374. From the testimony of Gaius it appears that not only the Flamen Dialis but all the other principal Flamens were bound to be married. However, the text of Gaius in this passage is somewhat uncertain. I have quoted it from P. E. Huschke's third

edition (Leipsic, 1878).

[2] W. H. R. Rivers, *The Todas,* p. 99. According to an old account, there was an important exception to the rule, but Dr. Rivers was not able to verify it ; he understood that during the tenure of his office the dairyman is really celibate.

[3] Aulus Gellius, x. 15. 23, " *Matrimonium flaminis nisi morte dirimi jus non est* " ; Festus, p. 89, ed. C. O. Müller, *s.v.* " Flammeo " ; Plutarch, *Quaestiones Romanae,* 50. Plutarch mentions as an illegal exception that in his own time the Emperor Domitian allowed a Flamen to divorce his wife, but the ceremony of the divorce was attended by " many awful, strange, and gloomy rites " performed by the priests.

ately on the death of the first would hardly be possible or decent." [1]
This simple explanation of the rule seems quite sufficient, and it
would clearly hold good whether I am right or wrong in further supposing that the human husband and wife in this case represented a
divine husband and wife, a god and goddess, to wit Jupiter and
Juno, or rather Dianus (Janus) and Diana; [2] and that supposition
in its turn might still hold good even if I were wrong in further conjecturing that of this divine pair the goddess (Juno or rather Diana)
was originally the more important partner.

Customs of the Kota and Jewish priests.

However it is to be explained, the Roman rule which forbade the
Flamen Dialis to be a widower has its parallel among the Kotas, a
tribe who, like the Todas, inhabit the Neilgherry Hills of Southern
India.　For the higher Kota priests are not allowed to be
widowers; if a priest's wife dies while he is in office, his appoint-
ment lapses.　At the same time priests "should avoid pollution,
and may not attend a Toda or Badaga funeral, or approach the
seclusion hut set apart for Kota women." [3]　Jewish priests were
specially permitted to contract the pollution of death for near relations, among whom father, mother, son, daughter, and unmarried
sister are particularly enumerated; but they were forbidden to contract the pollution for strangers.　However, among the relations for
whom a priest might thus defile himself a wife is not mentioned. [4]

§ 2. *The Marriage of the Roman Gods*

The theory that the Roman gods were celibate is contradicted by Varro and Seneca.

The theory that the Flamen Dialis and his wife personated a
divine couple, whether Jupiter and Juno or Dianus (Janus) and
Diana, supposes a married relation between the god and goddess,
and so far it would certainly be untenable if Dr. Farnell were right
in assuming, on the authority of Mr. W. Warde Fowler, that the
Roman gods were celibate. [5]　On that subject, however, Varro, the

[1] Plutarch, *Quaestiones Romanae*, 50.
That the wives of Roman priests aided
their husbands in the performance of
sacred rites is mentioned by Dionysius
of Halicarnassus, who attributes the
institution of these joint priesthoods
to Romulus (*Antiquit. Rom.* ii. 22).

[2] The epithet Dialis, which was
applied to the Flaminica as well as to
the Flamen (Aulus Gellius, x. 15. 26;
Servius, on Virgil, *Aen.* iv. 137),
would of itself prove that husband and
wife served the same god or pair of
gods; and while the word was doubt-
fully derived by Varro from Jove (*De
lingua Latina*, v. 84), we are expressly
told that the Flamen was the priest
and the Flaminica the priestess of that

god (Plutarch, *Quaest. Rom.* 109;
Festus, p. 92, ed. C. O. Müller, *s.v.*
"Flammeo"). There is therefore
every reason to accept the statement of
Plutarch (*Quaest. Rom.* 86) that the
Flaminica was reputed to be sacred to
Juno, the divine partner of Jupiter, in
spite of the objections raised by Mr. W.
Warde Fowler ("Was the Flaminica
Dialis priestess of Juno?" *Classical
Review*, ix. (1895) pp. 474 *sqq.*).

[3] E. Thurston, *Castes and Tribes
of Southern India* (Madras, 1909), iv.
10.

[4] Leviticus, xxi. 1-3; Ezekiel, xliv.
25.

[5] *The Hibbert Journal*, iv. (1906)
p. 932.

most learned of Roman antiquaries, was of a contrary opinion. He not only spoke particularly of Juno as the wife of Jupiter,[1] but he also affirmed generally, in the most unambiguous language, that the old Roman gods were married, and in saying so he referred not to the religion of his own day, which had been modified by Greek influence, but to the religion of the ancient Romans, his ancestors.[2] Seneca ridiculed the marriage of the Roman gods, citing as examples the marriages of Mars and Bellona, of Vulcan and Venus, of Neptune and Salacia, and adding sarcastically that some of the goddesses were spinsters or widows, such as Populonia, Fulgora, and Rumina, whose faded charms or unamiable character had failed to attract a suitor.[3]

Again, the learned Servius, whose commentary on Virgil is a gold mine of Roman religious lore, informs us that the pontiffs celebrated the marriage of the infernal deity Orcus with very great solemnity;[4] and for this statement he would seem to have had the authority of the pontifical books themselves, for he refers to them in the same connexion only a few lines before. As it is in the highest degree unlikely that the pontiffs would solemnize any foreign rites, we may safely assume that the marriage of Orcus was not borrowed from Greek mythology, but was a genuine old Roman ceremony, and this is all the more probable because Servius, our authority for the custom, has recorded some curious and obviously ancient taboos which were observed at the marriage and in the ritual of Ceres, the goddess who seems to have been joined in wedlock to Orcus. One of these taboos forbade the use of wine, the other forbade persons to name their father or daughter.[5]

The marriage of Orcus.

---

[1] Varro, *De lingua Latina*, v. 67, "*Quod Jovis Juno conjux et is caelum.*"

[2] Augustine, *De civitate Dei*, iv. 32, "*Dicit etiam [scil. Varro] de generationibus deorum magis ad poetas quam ad physicos fuisse populos inclinatos, et ideo et sexum et generationes deorum majores suos, id est veteres credidisse Romanos et eorum constituisse conjugia.*"

[3] Seneca, quoted by Augustine, *De civitate Dei*, vi. 10, "*Quid quod et matrimonia, inquit, deorum jungimus, et ne pie quidem, fratrum ac sororum ? Bellonam Marti conlocamus, Vulcano Venerem, Neptuno Salaciam. Quosdam tamen caelibes relinquimus, quasi condicio defecerit, praesertim cum quaedam viduae sint, ut Populonia vel Fulgora et diva Rumina ; quibus non miror petitorem defuisse.*" In this passage the marriage of Venus to Vulcan is probably Greek ; all the rest is pure Roman.

[4] Servius, on Virgil, *Georg.* i. 344, "*Aliud est sacrum, aliud nuptias Cereri celebrare, in quibus re vera vinum adhiberi nefas fuerat, quae Orci nuptiae dicebantur, quas praesentia sua pontifices ingenti solemnitate celebrabant.*"

[5] Servius, on Virgil, *Georg.* i. 344, and on *Aen.* iv. 58. As to the prohibition of wine, compare Macrobius, *Saturn.* iii. 11. There seems to be no doubt that Orcus was a genuine old Italian god of death and the dead. See the evidence collected by R. Peter, *s.v.* "Orcus," in W. H. Roscher's *Lexikon der griech. und röm. Mythologie*, iii. 940 *sqq.*, who says that "Orcus was obviously one of those old Roman gods who occupied the thoughts of the people in the most lively manner." On the other hand, Prof. G. Wissowa supposes that Orcus is merely a borrowed form of the Greek Horkos (*Religion und Kultus der Römer*,[2] p. 310). But Horkos

Further, the learned Roman antiquary Aulus Gellius quotes from " the books of the priests of the Roman people " (the highest possible authority on the subject) and from " many ancient speeches " a list of old Roman deities, in which there seem to be at least five pairs of males and females.[1] More than that he proves conclusively by quotations from Plautus, the annalist Cn. Gellius, and Licinius Imbrex that these old writers certainly regarded one at least of the pairs (Mars and Nerio) as husband and wife ;[2] and we have good ancient evidence for viewing in the same light three others of the pairs. Thus the old annalist and antiquarian L. Cincius Alimentus, who fought against Hannibal and was captured by him, affirmed in his work on the Roman calendar that Maia was the wife of Vulcan ;[3] and as there was a Flamen of Vulcan, who sacrificed to Maia on May Day,[4] it is reasonable to suppose that he was assisted in the ceremony by a Flaminica, his wife, just as on my hypothesis the Flamen Dialis was assisted by his wife the Flaminica. Another old Roman historian, L. Calpurnius Piso, who wrote in the second century B.C., said that the name of Vulcan's wife was not Maia but

---

was not a god of death and the dead ; he was simply a personified oath (ὅρκος ; see Hesiod, *Works and Days*, 804 Ὅρκον γεινόμενον, τὸν Ἔρις τέκε πῆμ' ἐπιόρκοις), an abstract idea which makes no figure in Greek mythology and religion. That such a rare and thin Greek abstraction should through a gross misunderstanding be transformed into a highly popular Roman god of death, who not only passed muster with the people but was admitted by the pontiffs themselves to the national pantheon and honoured by them with a solemn ritual, is in the last degree improbable.

[1] Aulus Gellius, xiii. 23 (22), 1 *sq.*, " *Conprecationes deum inmortalium, quae ritu Romano fiunt, expositae sunt in libris sacerdotum populi Romani et in plerisque antiquis orationibus. In his scribtum est: Luam Saturni, Salaciam Neptuni, Horam Quirini, Virites Quirini, Maiam Volcani, Heriem Junonis, Moles Martis Nerienemque Martis.*" As to this list see Mr. W. Warde Fowler, *Roman Festivals of the Period of the Republic* (London, 1899), pp. 60-62 ; *id., The Religious Experience of the Roman People* (London, 1911), pp. 150 *sqq.*, 481 *sqq.* He holds (p. 485) that the feminine names Salacia, etc., do not

designate goddesses, the wives of the gods, but that they " indicate functions or attributes of the male deity to whom they are attached."

[2] Aulus Gellius, xiii. 23 (22), 11-16.

[3] Macrobius, *Saturn.* i. 12. 18, " *Cingius mensem* [*Maium*] *nominatum putat a Maia, quam Vulcani dicit uxorem, argumentoque utitur quod flamen Vulcanalis Kalendis Maiis huic deae rem divinam facit: sed Piso uxorem Vulcani Majestam, non Maiam, dicit vocari.*" The work of Cincius (Cingius) is mentioned by Macrobius in the same chapter (§ 12, " *Cingius in eo libro quem de fastis reliquit*"). As to the life and writings of this old annalist and antiquary see M. Schanz, *Geschichte der römischen Litteratur,*[2] i. (Munich, 1898), p. 128 ; G. Wissowa, Münzer, and Cichorius, *s.v.* " Cincius," in Pauly-Wissowa's *Realencyclopädie der classischen Altertumswissenschaft,* iii. 2555 *sqq.* All these writers distinguish the old annalist from the antiquary, whom they take to have been a later writer of the same name. But the distinction appears to be purely arbitrary and destitute of any ancient authority.

[4] Macrobius, *Saturn.* i. 12. 18 See the preceding note.

Majestas.[1] In saying so he may have intended to correct what he believed to be a mistake of his predecessor L. Cincius. Again, that Salacia was the wife of Neptune is perhaps implied by Varro,[2] and is positively affirmed by Seneca, Augustine, and Servius.[3] Again, Ennius appears to have regarded Hora as the wife of Quirinus, for in the first book of his Annals he declared his devotion to that divine pair.[4] In fact, of the five pairs of male and female deities cited by Aulus Gellius from the priestly books and ancient speeches the only one as to which we have not independent evidence that it consisted of a husband and wife is Saturn and Lua ; and in regard to Lua we know that she was spoken of as a mother,[5] which renders it not improbable that she was also a wife. However, according to some very respectable authorities the wife of Saturn was not Lua, but Ops,[6] so that we have two independent lines of proof that Saturn was supposed to be married.

Lastly, the epithets " father " and " mother " which the Romans bestowed on many of their deities [7] are most naturally understood

---

[1] Macrobius, *Saturn.* i. 12. 18. See the passage cited above, p. 232, note[3].

[2] Varro, *De lingua Latina*, v. 72, " *Salacia Neptuni a salo.*" This was probably one of the cases which Varro had in his mind when he stated that the ancient Roman gods were married.

[3] Augustine, *De civitate Dei*, vii. 22, "*Jam utique habebat Salaciam Neptunus uxorem*"; Servius, on Virgil, *Aen.* x. 76, "*Sane hanc Veniliam quidam Salaciam accipiunt, Neptuni uxorem.*" As for Seneca's evidence see above, p. 231, note[3].

[4] Nonius Marcellus, *De compendiosa doctrina*, p. 125, ed. L. Quicherat (Paris, 1872), "*Hora juventutis dea. Ennius Annali[um] lib. i. [Teque,] Quirine pater, veneror, Horamque Quirini.*"

[5] Livy, viii. 1. 6, xlv. 33. 2.

[6] Festus, p. 186, ed. C. O. Müller, "*Opima spolia dicuntur originem quidem trahentia ab Ope Saturni uxore*"; *id.*, p. 187, "*Opis dicta est conjux Saturni*"; Macrobius, *Saturnal.* i. 10. 19, "*Hanc autem deam Opem Saturni conjugem crediderunt, et ideo hoc mense Saturnalia itemque Opalia celebrari, quod Saturnus ejusque uxor tam frugum quam fructuum repertores esse creduntur.*" Varro couples Saturn and Ops together (*De lingua Latina*, v. 57, "*Principes in Latio Saturnus et Ops*"; compare *id.*, v. 64), but

without expressly affirming them to be husband and wife. Professor G. Wissowa, however, argues that the male partner (he would not say husband) of Ops was not Saturn but Consus. See G. Wissowa, "*De feriis anni Romanorum vetustissimi observationes selectae,*" reprinted in his *Gesammelte Abhandlungen zur römischen Religions-und Stadtgeschichte* (Munich, 1904), pp. 156 *sqq.* His view is accepted by Mr. W. Warde Fowler (*Roman Festivals of the Period of the Republic*, p. 212 ; *The Religious Experience of the Roman People*, p. 482).

[7] Lactantius, *Divin. Instit.* iv. 3, "*Itaque et Jupiter a precantibus pater vocatur, et Saturnus, et Janus, et Liber, et ceteri deinceps, quod Lucilius in deorum consilio irridet :*

  Ut nemo sit nostrum, quin aut   pater optimus divum
  Ut Neptunus pater, Liber, Satur-   nus pater, Mars,
  Janus, Quirinus pater nomen   dicatur ad unum."

Compare Aulus Gellius, v. 12. 5; Servius, on Virgil, *Georg.* ii. 4. Roman goddesses who received the title of Mother were Vesta, Earth, Ops, Matuta, and Lua. As to Mother Vesta see *The Magic Art and the Evolution of Kings*, ii. 229 ; as to Mother Earth see H. Dessau, *Inscriptiones*

Paternity and maternity of Roman deities.

to imply paternity and maternity; and if the implication is admitted, the inference appears to be inevitable that these divine beings were supposed to exercise sexual functions, whether in lawful marriage or in unlawful concubinage. As to Jupiter in particular his paternity is positively attested by Latin inscriptions, one of them very old, which describe Fortuna Primigenia, the great goddess of Praeneste, as his daughter.[1] Again, the rustic deity Faunus, one of the oldest and most popular gods of Italy,[2] was represented by tradition in the character of a husband and a father; one of the epithets applied to him expressed in a coarse way his generative powers.[3] Fauna or the Good Goddess (*Bona Dea*), another of the oldest native Italian deities, was variously called his wife or his daughter, and he is said to have assumed the form of a snake in order to cohabit with her.[4] Again, the most famous of all Roman myths represented the founder

---

Latinae Selectae, Nos. 3950-3955, 3960; as to Mother Ops see Varro, *De lingua Latina*, v. 64; as to Mother Matuta see L. Preller, *Römische Mythologie*,[3] i. 322 *sqq.*; G. Wissowa, *Religion und Kultus der Römer*,[2] pp. 110 *sqq.*; *id.*, *s.v.* "Mater Matuta," in W. H. Roscher's *Lexikon der griech. und röm. Mythologie*, ii. 2462 *sqq.* I cite these passages only to prove that the Romans commonly applied the titles "father" and "mother" to their deities. The inference that these titles implied paternity or maternity is my own, but in the text I have given some reasons for thinking that the Romans themselves accepted the implication. Mr. W. Warde Fowler, on the other hand, prefers to suppose that the titles were employed in a merely figurative sense to "imply the dependence of the human citizen upon his divine protector"; but he admits that what exactly the Romans understood by *pater* and *mater* applied to deities is not easy to determine (*The Religious Experience of the Roman People*, pp. 155-157). He makes at the same time the important observation that the Romans never, so far as he is aware, applied the terms Father and Mother to foreign gods, but "always to *di indigetes*, those on whom the original Roman stock looked as their fellow-citizens and guardians." The limitation is significant and seems more naturally explicable on my hypothesis

than on that of my learned friend.

[1] See *Corpus Inscriptionum Latinarum*, xiv. Nos. 2862, 2863; H. Dessau, *Inscriptiones Latinae Selectae*, Nos. 3684, 3685; R. Peter, *s.v.* "Fortuna," in W. H. Roscher's *Lexikon der griechischen und römischen Mythologie*, i. 1542; G. Wissowa, *Religion und Kultus der Römer*,[2] p. 259. I have to thank my learned and candid friend Mr. W. Warde Fowler for referring me to this good evidence of Jupiter's paternal character.

[2] L. Preller, *Römische Mythologie*[3] (Berlin, 1881-1883), i. 379.

[3] The epithet *Inuus* applied to Faunus was so understood by the ancients, and this suffices to prove the conception they had of the god's virility, whether the etymology was right or wrong. See Servius, on Virgil, *Aen.* vi. 775, "*Dicitur autem Inuus ab ineundo passim cum omnibus animalibus.*" As to the title see G. Wissowa, *Religion und Kultus der Römer*,[2] p. 211, who, however, rejects the ancient etymology and the identification of Inuus with Faunus.

[4] Macrobius, *Saturn.* i. 12. 21-24; Lactantius, *Divin. Instit.* i. 22; Servius, on Virgil, *Aen.* viii. 314; Plutarch, *Caesar*, 9; *id.*, *Quaest. Roman.* 20. According to Varro, the goddess was the daughter of Faunus (Macrobius, *Saturn.* i. 12. 27); according to Sextus Clodius she was his wife (Lactantius, *l.c.*; compare Arnobius, *Adversus nationes*, v. 18).

of Rome himself, Romulus and his twin brother Remus, as begotten by the god Mars on a Vestal Virgin ;[1] and every Roman who accepted the tradition thereby acknowledged the fatherhood of the god in the physical, not in a figurative, sense of the word. If the story of the birth of Romulus and Remus should be dismissed as a late product of the mythical fancy working under Greek influence, the same objection can hardly be urged against the story of the birth of another Roman king, Servius Tullius, who is said to have been a son of the fire-god and a slave woman ; his mother conceived him beside the royal hearth, where she was impregnated by a flame that shot out from the fire in the shape of the male organ of generation.[2] It would scarcely be possible to express the physical fatherhood of the fire-god in more unambiguous terms. Now a precisely similar story was told of the birth of Romulus himself ;[3] and we may suspect that this was an older form of the story than the legend which fathered the twins on Mars. Similarly, Caeculus, the founder of Praeneste, passed for a son of the fire-god Vulcan. It was said that his mother was impregnated by a spark which leaped from the fire and struck her as she sat by the hearth. In later life, when Caeculus boasted of his divine parentage to a crowd, and they refused to believe him, he prayed to his father to give the unbelievers a sign, and straightway a lambent flame surrounded the whole multitude. The proof was conclusive, and henceforth Caeculus passed for a true son of the fire-god.[4] Such tales of kings or heroes begotten by the fire-god on mortal women appear to be genuine old Italian myths, which may well go back far beyond the foundation of Rome to the common fountain of Aryan mythology ; for the marriage customs observed by various branches of the Aryan family point clearly to a belief in the power of fire to impregnate women.[5]

On the whole, if we follow the authority of the ancients themselves, we seem bound to conclude that the Roman gods, like those of many other early peoples, were believed to be married and to beget children. It is true that, compared with the full-blooded gods of Greece, the deities of Rome appear to us shadowy creatures, pale abstractions garbed in little that can vie with the gorgeous pall of myth and story which Grecian fancy threw around its divine creations. Yet the few specimens of Roman mythology which have survived the wreck of antiquity [6]

We must conclude that the Roman gods were thought to be married and to beget children.

---

[1] Livy, i. 4. 2 ; Plutarch, *Romulus*, 4 ; Dionysius Halicarnasensis, *Antiquit. Roman.* i. 77.

[2] See *The Magic Art and the Evolution of Kings*, ii. 195 *sq.*

[3] Plutarch, *Romulus*, 2. Plutarch's authority was Promathion in his history of Italy. See *The Magic Art and the Evolution of Kings*, ii. 196.

[4] Servius, on Virgil, *Aen.* vii. 678.

[5] *The Magic Art and the Evolution of Kings*, ii. 230 *sq.*

[6] Such, for example, as the loves of Vertumnus for Pomona (Ovid, *Metam.* xiv. 623 *sqq.*), of Jupiter for Juturna (Ovid, *Fasti*, ii. 585 *sqq.*), and of Janus for Carna (Ovid, *Fasti*, vi. 101 *sqq.*) and for Camasene (Servius, on

justify us in believing that they are but fragments of far more copious traditions which have perished. At all events the comparative aridity and barrenness of the Roman religious imagination is no reason for setting aside the positive testimony of learned Roman writers as to a point of fundamental importance in their own religion about which they could hardly be mistaken. It should never be forgotten that on this subject the ancients had access to many sources of information which are no longer open to us, and for a modern scholar to reject their evidence in favour of a personal impression derived from a necessarily imperfect knowledge of the facts seems scarcely consistent with sound principles of history and criticism.[1]

§ 3. Children of Living Parents in Ritual

Rule of Greek and Roman ritual that certain offices could only be held by boys whose parents were both alive.

But Dr. Farnell adduces another argument in support of his view that it was the pollution of death which obliged the widowed Flamen Dialis to resign the priesthood. He points to what he considers the analogy of the rule of Greek ritual which required that certain sacred offices should be discharged only by a boy whose parents were both alive.[2] This rule he would explain in like manner by supposing that the death of one or both of his parents would render a boy ceremonially impure and therefore unfit to perform religious functions. Dr. Farnell might have apparently strengthened his case by observing that the Flamen Dialis and the Flaminica Dialis were themselves assisted in their office, the one by a boy, the other by a girl, both of whose parents must be alive.[3] At first sight this fits in

---

Virgil, *Aen.* viii. 330). The water-nymph Juturna beloved by Jupiter is said to have been the daughter of the river Vulturnus, the wife of Janus, and the mother of Fontus (Arnobius, *Adversus nationes*, iii. 29). Janus in particular would seem to have been the theme of many myths, and his claim to be a genuine Italian god has never been disputed.

[1] The marriage of the Roman gods has been denied by E. Aust (*Die Religion der Römer*, Münster i. W. 1899, pp. 19 *sq.*) and Professor G. Wissowa (*Religion und Kultus der Römer*,[2] pp. 26 *sq.*), as well as by Mr. W. Warde Fowler. On the other hand, the evidence for it has been clearly and concisely stated by L. Preller, *Römische Mythologie*,[3] i. 55-57. It is with sincere diffidence that I venture to differ on a point of Roman religion from the eminent scholars I have named. But without for a moment

pitting my superficial acquaintance with Roman religion against their deep learning, I cannot but think that the single positive testimony of Varro on a matter about which he could scarcely be ignorant ought to outweigh the opinion of any modern scholar, however learned and able.

[2] *The Hibbert Journal*, April 1907, p. 689. Such a boy was called a παῖς ἀμφιθαλής, "a boy blooming on both sides," the metaphor being drawn from a tree which sends out branches on both sides. See Plato, *Laws*, xi. 8, p. 927 D; Julius Pollux, iii. 25; Hesychius and Suidas, *s.v.* ἀμφιθαλής.

[3] Festus, p. 93, ed. C. O. Müller, *s.vv.* "Flaminius" and "Flaminia." That certain Roman rites had to be performed by the children of living parents is mentioned in general terms by Dionysius of Halicarnassus (*Antiquit. Rom.* ii. 22).

perfectly with his theory: the Flamen, the Flaminica, and their youthful ministers were all rendered incapable of performing their sacred duties by the taint or corruption of death.

But a closer scrutiny of the argument reveals a flaw. It proves too much. For observe that in these Greek and Roman offices held by boys and girls the disqualification caused by the death of a parent is necessarily lifelong, since the bereavement is irreparable. Accordingly, if Dr. Farnell's theory is right, the ceremonial pollution which is the cause of the disqualification must also be lifelong; in other words, every orphan is ceremonially unclean for life and thereby excluded for ever from the discharge of sacred duties. So sweeping a rule would at a stroke exclude a large, if not the larger, part of the population of any country from the offices of religion, and lay them permanently under all those burdensome restrictions which the pollution of death entails among many nations; for obviously a large, if not the larger, part of the population of any country at any time has lost one or both of its parents by death. No people, so far as I know, has ever carried the theory of the ceremonial pollution of death to this extremity in practice. And even if it were supposed that the taint wore off or evaporated with time from common folk so as to let them go about their common duties in everyday life, would it not still cleave to priests? If it incapacitated the Flamen's minister, would it not incapacitate the Flamen himself? In other words, would not the Flamen Dialis be obliged to vacate office on the death of his father or mother? There is no hint in ancient writers that he had to do so. And while it is generally unsafe to argue from the silence of our authorities, I think that we may do so in this case without being rash; for Plutarch not only mentions but discusses the rule which obliged the Flamen Dialis to resign office on the death of his wife,[1] and if he had known of a parallel rule which compelled him to retire on the death of a parent, he would surely have mentioned it. But if the ceremonial pollution which would certainly be caused by the death of a parent did not compel the Flamen Dialis to vacate office, we may safely conclude that neither did the similar pollution caused by the death of his wife. Thus the argument adduced by Dr. Farnell in favour of his view proves on analysis to tell strongly against it.

But if the rule which excluded orphans from certain sacred offices cannot with any probability be explained on the theory of their ceremonial pollution, it may be worth while to inquire whether another and better explanation of the rule cannot be found. For that purpose I shall collect all the cases of it known to me. The collection is doubtless far from complete: I only offer it as a starting-point for research.

Marginal notes:
But the rule which excludes orphans from certain sacred offices cannot be based on a theory that they are ceremonially unclean through the death of their parents.

Examples of the exclusion of orphans from sacred offices.

[1] Plutarch, *Quaestiones Romanae*, 50.

Boys and
girls of
living
parents
employed
in Greek
rites at the
vintage,
harvest-
home, and
sowing.

At the time of the vintage, which in Greece falls in October, Athenian boys chosen from every tribe assembled at the sanctuary of Dionysus, the god of the vine. There, branches of vines laden with ripe grapes were given to them, and holding them in their hands they raced to the sanctuary of Athena Sciras. The winner received and drained a cup containing a mixture of olive-oil, wine, honey, cheese, and barley-groats. It was necessary that both the parents of each of these boy-runners should be alive.[1] At the same festival, and perhaps on the same day, an Athenian boy, whose parents must both be alive, carried in procession a branch of olive wreathed with white and purple wool and decked with fruits of many kinds, while a chorus sang that the branch bore figs, fat loaves, honey, oil, and wine. Thus they went in procession to a temple of Apollo, at the door of which the boy deposited the holy bough. The ceremony is said to have been instituted by the Athenians in obedience to an oracle for the purpose of supplicating the help of the god in a season of dearth.[2] Similar boughs similarly laden with fruits and loaves were hung up on the doors of every Athenian house and allowed to remain there a year, at the end of which they were replaced by fresh ones. While the branch was being fastened to the door, a boy whose parents were both alive recited the same verses about the branch bearing figs, fat loaves, honey, oil, and wine. This custom also is said to have been instituted for the sake of putting an end to a dearth.[3] The people of Magnesia on the Maeander vowed a bull every year to Zeus, the Saviour of the City, in the month of Cronion, at the beginning of sowing, and after maintaining the animal at the public expense throughout the winter they sacrificed it, apparently at harvest-time, in the following summer. Nine boys and nine girls, whose fathers and mothers were all living, took part in the religious services of the consecration and the sacrifice of the bull. At the consecration public prayers were offered for the safety of the city and the land, for the safety of the citizens and their wives and children, for the safety of all that dwelt in the city and the land, for peace and wealth and abundance of corn and all other fruits, and for the cattle. A herald led the prayers, and the priest and priestess, the boys and girls, the high officers and magistrates, all

---

[1] Proclus, in Photius, *Bibliotheca*, p. 322 A, ed. I. Bekker (Berlin, 1824); Athenaeus, xi. 92, pp. 495 *sq.*; Scholiast on Nicander, *Alexipharmaca*, 109. Only the last of these writers mentions that the boys had to be ἀμφιθαλεῖς. As to this and the following custom see A. Mommsen, *Feste der Stadt Athen im Altertum* (Leipsic, 1898), pp. 278 *sqq.*; W. Mannhardt, *Antike Wald-und Feldkulte*, pp. 214 *sqq.*

[2] Eustathius, on Homer, *Iliad*, xxii. 495, p. 1283; *Etymologicum Magnum*, p. 303. 18 *sqq.*, *s.v.* Εἰρεσιώνη; Plutarch, *Theseus*, 22. According to a scholiast on Aristophanes (*Plutus*, 1054) the branch might be either of olive or laurel.

[3] Scholiast on Aristophanes, *Plutus*, 1054.

joined in these solemn petitions for the welfare of their country.[1] Among the Karo-Bataks of Central Sumatra the threshing of the rice is the occasion of various ceremonies, and in these a prominent part is played by a girl, whose father and mother must be both alive. Her special duty is to take care of the sheaf of rice in which the soul of the rice is believed to reside. This sheaf usually consists of the first rice cut and bound in the field; it is treated exactly like a person.[2]

The rites thus far described, in which boys and girls of living parents took part, were clearly ceremonies intended specially to ensure the fertility of the soil. This is indicated not merely by the nature of the rites and of the prayers or verses which accompanied them, but also by the seasons at which they were observed; for these were the vintage, the harvest-home, and the beginning of sowing. We may therefore compare a custom practised by the Roman Brethren of the Ploughed Fields (*Fratres Arvales*), a college of priests whose business it was to perform the rites deemed necessary for the growth of the corn. As a badge of office they wore wreaths of corn-ears, and paid their devotions to an antique goddess of fertility, the Dea Dia. Her home was in a grove of ancient evergreen oaks and laurels out in the Campagna, five miles from Rome. Hither every year in the month of May, when the fields were ripe or ripening to the sickle, reaped ears of the new corn were brought and hallowed by the Brethren with quaint rites, that a blessing might rest on the coming harvest. The first or preliminary consecration of the ears, however, took place, not in the grove, but in the house of the Master of the Brethren at Rome. Here the Brethren were waited upon by four free-born boys, the children of living fathers and mothers. While the Brethren reclined on couches, the boys were allowed to sit on chairs and partake of the feast, and when it was over they carried the rest of the now hallowed corn and laid it on the altar.[3]

Boys of living parents employed in the rites of the Arval Brothers.

[1] O. Kern, *Die Inschriften von Magnesia am Maeander* (Berlin, 1900), No. 98; G. Dittenberger, *Sylloge Inscriptionum Graecarum*,[2] vol. ii. pp. 246 *sqq*., No. 553. This inscription has been well expounded by Prof. M. P. Nilsson (*Griechische Feste*, Leipsic, 1906, pp. 23-27). I follow him and Dittenberger in regarding the month of Artemision, when the bull was sacrificed, as the harvest month corresponding to the Attic Thargelion.

[2] J. H. Neumann, "Iets over den landbouw bij de Karo-Bataks," *Mededeelingen van wege het Nederlandsche Zendelinggenootschap*, xlvi. (1902) p. 381.

[3] G. Henzen, *Acta Fratrum Arvalium* (Berlin, 1874), pp. vi. *sq*., cix cx. cxix. cliii. clix. clxxxvii. 12, 13, 15. As to the evergreen oaks and laurels of the grove, see *ib*., pp. 137, 138; as to the wreaths of corn-ears, see *ib*., pp. 26, 28; Aulus Gellius, vii. 7. 8. That the rites performed by the Arval Brothers were intended to make the fields bear corn is expressly stated by Varro (*De lingua Latina*, v. 85, "*Fratres Arvales dicti sunt, qui sacra publica faciunt propterea ut fruges ferant arva*"). On the Arval Brothers and their rites see also L. Preller, *Römische Mythologie*,[3] ii. 29 *sqq*.; J. Marquardt,

In fertility
rites the
employ-
ment of
such
children is
intelligible
on the
principle
of sym-
pathetic
magic.
Sons of
living
parents
employed
to cut the
olive-
wreath
at Olympia
and the
laurel-
wreath at
Tempe.

In these and all other rites intended to ensure the fertility of the ground, of cattle, or of human beings, the employment of children of living parents seems to be intelligible on the principle of sympathetic magic; for such children might be deemed fuller of life than orphans, either because they "flourished on both sides," as the Greeks put it, or because the very survival of their parents might be taken as a proof that the stock of which the children came was vigorous and therefore able to impart of its superabundant energy to others.

But the rites in which the children of living parents are required to officiate do not always aim at promoting the growth of the crops. At Olympia the olive-branches which formed the victors' crowns had to be cut from a sacred tree with a golden sickle by a lad whose father and mother must be both alive.[1] The tree was a wild olive growing within the holy precinct, at the west end of the temple of Zeus. It bore the name of the Olive of the Fair Crown, and near it was an altar to the Nymphs of the Fair Crowns.[2] At Delphi every eighth year a sacred drama or miracle-play was acted which drew crowds of spectators from all parts of Greece. It set forth the slaying of the Dragon by Apollo. The principal part was sustained by a lad, the son of living parents, who seems to have personated the god himself. In an open space the likeness of a lordly palace, erected for the occasion, represented the Dragon's den. It was attacked and burned by the lad, aided by women who carried blazing torches. When the Dragon had received his deadly wound, the lad, still acting the part of the god, fled far away to be purged of the guilt of blood in the beautiful Vale of Tempe, where the Peneus flows in a deep wooded gorge between the snowy peaks of Olympus and Ossa, its smooth and silent tide shadowed by overhanging trees and tall white cliffs. In places these great crags rise abruptly from the stream and approach each other so near that only a narrow strip of sky is visible overhead; but where they recede a little, the meadows at their foot are verdant with evergreen shrubs, among which Apollo's own laurel may still be seen. In antiquity the god himself, stained with the Dragon's blood, is said to have come, a haggard footsore wayfarer, to this wild secluded glen and there plucked branches from one of the laurels that grew in its green thickets beside the rippling river. Some of them he used to twine a wreath for his brows, one of them he carried in his hand, doubtless in order that, guarded by the sacred plant, he might escape the hobgoblins which

---

Römische Staatsverwaltung, iii.[2] (Leipsic, 1885) pp. 447-462 ; G. Wissowa, *Religion und Kultus der Römer*,[2] pp. 561 *sqq.* ; J. B. Carter, *s.v.* "Arval Brothers," in J. Hastings's *Encyclo-*

paedia of Religion and Ethics, ii. (Edinburgh, 1909) pp. 7 *sqq.*

[1] Scholiast on Pindar, *Olymp.* iii. 60.

[2] Pausanias, v. 15. 3.

dogged his steps. So the boy, his human representative, did the same, and brought back to Delphi wreaths of laurel from the same tree to be awarded to the victors in the Pythian games. Hence the whole festival of the Slaying of the Dragon at Delphi went by the name of the Festival of Crowning.[1] From this it appears that at Delphi as well as at Olympia the boughs which were used to crown the victors had to be cut from a sacred tree by a boy whose parents must be both alive.

At Thebes a festival called the Laurel-bearing was held once in every eight years, when branches of laurel were carried in procession to the temple of Apollo. The principal part in the procession was taken by a boy who held a laurel bough and bore the title of the Laurel-bearer : he seems to have personated the god himself. His hair hung down on his shoulders, and he wore a golden crown, a bright-coloured robe, and shoes of a special shape : both his parents must be alive.[2] We may suppose that the golden crown which he wore was fashioned in the shape of laurel leaves and replaced a wreath of real laurel. Thus the boy with the laurel wreath on his head and the laurel bough in his hand would resemble the traditional equipment of Apollo when he purified himself for the slaughter of the dragon. We may conjecture that at Thebes the Laurel-bearer originally personated not Apollo but the local hero Cadmus, who slew the dragon and had like Apollo to purify himself for the slaughter. The conjecture is confirmed by vase-paintings which represent Cadmus crowned with laurel preparing to attack the dragon or actually in combat with the monster, while goddesses bend over him holding out wreaths of laurel as the meed of victory.[3] On this hypothesis the octennial Delphic Festival of Crowning and the octennial Theban Festival of Laurel-bearing were closely akin : in both the prominent part played by the laurel was purificatory or expiatory.[4] Thus at Olympia, Delphi, and Thebes a boy whose

Sons of living parents acted as Laurel-bearers at Thebes.

[1] Plutarch, *Quaestiones Graecae*, 12; *id.*, *De defectu oraculorum*, 15; Aelian, *Varia Historia*, iii. 1 ; Strabo, ix. 3. 12, p. 422. In a note on Pausanias (ii. 7. 7, vol. iii. pp. 53 *sqq.*) I have described the festival more fully and adduced savage parallels. As to the Vale of Tempe see W. M. Leake, *Travels in Northern Greece* (London, 1835), iii. 390 *sqq.* The rhetoric of Livy (xliv. 6. 8) has lashed the smooth and silent current of the Peneus into a roaring torrent.

[2] Proclus, in Photius, *Bibliotheca*, ed. I. Bekker, p. 321.

[3] O. Crusius, *s.v.* "Kadmos," in W. H. Roscher's *Lexikon der griech. und röm. Mythologie*, ii. 830, 838, 839.

On an Etruscan mirror the scene of Cadmus's combat with the dragon is surrounded with a wreath of laurel (O. Crusius, *op. cit.* ii. 862). My learned friend Mr. A. B. Cook was the first to call attention to these vase-paintings in confirmation of my view that the Festival of the Laurel-bearing celebrated the destruction of the dragon by Cadmus. See A. B. Cook, "The European Sky-God," *Folk-lore*, xv. (1904) p. 411, note [224]; and my note on Pausanias, ix. 10. 4 (vol. v. pp. 41 *sqq.*).

[4] I have examined both festivals more closely in a former part of this work (*The Dying God*, pp. 78 *sqq.*), and have shown grounds for holding

parents were both alive was entrusted with the duty of cutting or wearing a sacred wreath at a great festival which recurred at intervals of several years.[1]

If wreaths were originally amulets, we could understand why children of living parents were chosen to cut and wear them.

Why a boy of living parents should be chosen for such an office is not at first sight clear ; the reason might be more obvious if we understood the ideas in which the custom of wearing wreaths and crowns had its origin. Probably in many cases wreaths and crowns were amulets before they were ornaments ; in other words, their first intention may have been not so much to adorn the head as to protect it from harm by surrounding it with a plant, a metal, or any other thing which was supposed to possess the magical virtue of banning baleful influences. Thus the Arabs of Moab will put a circlet of copper on the head of a man who is suffering from headache, for they believe that this will banish the pain ; and if the pain is in an arm or a leg, they will treat the ailing limb in like manner. They think that red beads hung before the eyes of children who are afflicted with ophthalmia will rid them of the malady, and that a red ribbon tied to the foot will prevent it from stumbling on a stony path.[2] Again, the Melanesians of the Gazelle Peninsula in New Britain often deck their dusky bodies with

---

that the old octennial cycle in Greece, based on an attempt to harmonize solar and lunar time, gave rise to an octennial festival at which the mythical marriage of the sun and moon was celebrated by the dramatic marriage of human actors, who appear sometimes to have been the king and queen. In the Laurel-bearing at Thebes a clear reference to the astronomical character of the festival is contained in the emblems of the sun, moon, stars, and days of the year which were carried in procession (Proclus, *l.c.*) ; and another reference to it may be detected in the legendary marriage of Cadmus and Harmonia. Dr. L. R. Farnell supposes that the festival of the Laurel-bearing " belongs to the maypole processions, universal in the peasant-religion of Europe, of which the object is to quicken the vitalizing powers of the year in the middle of spring or at the beginning of summer " (*The Cults of the Greek States*, iv. 285). But this explanation appears to be in-consistent with the octennial period of the festival.

[1] We may conjecture that the Olympic, like the Delphic and the Theban, festival was at first octennial, though in historical times it was

quadrennial. Certainly it seems to have been based on an octennial cycle. See the Scholiast on Pindar, *Olymp.* iii. 35 (20) ; Aug. Boeckh on Pindar, *Explicationes* (Leipsic, 1821), p. 138 ; L. Ideler, *Handbuch der mathematischen und technischen Chronologie*, i. 366 *sq.* ; G. F. Unger, " Zeitrechnung der Griechen und Römer," in Iwan Müller's *Handbuch der klassischen Altertums-wissenschaft*, i. (Nördlingen, 1886) pp. 605 *sq.* ; K. O. Müller, *Die Dorier*[2] (Breslau, 1844), ii. 483. The Pythian games, which appear to have been at first identical with the Delphic Festival of Crowning, were held originally at intervals of eight instead of four years. See the Scholiast on Pindar, *Pyth.* Argum. p. 298, ed. A. Boeckh (Leipsic, 1819) ; Censorinus, *De die natali*, xviii. 6 ; compare Eustathius on Homer, *Od.* iii. 267, p. 1466. 29. As to the original identity of the Pythian games and the Festival of Crowning see Th. Schreiber, *Apollon Pythoktonos* (Leipsic, 1879), pp. 37 *sq.* ; A. B. Cook, " The European Sky-God," *Folk-lore*, xv. (1904) pp. 404 *sq.*

[2] Antonin Jaussen, *Coutumes des Arabes au pays de Moab* (Paris, 1908), p. 382.

flowers, leaves, and scented herbs not only at festivals but on other occasions which to the European might seem inappropriate for such gay ornaments. But in truth the bright blossoms and verdant foliage are not intended to decorate the wearer but to endow him with certain magical virtues, which are supposed to inhere in the flowers and leaves. Thus one man may be seen strutting about with a wreath of greenery which passes round his neck and droops over his shoulders, back, and breast. He is not a mere dandy, but a lover who hopes that the wreath will work as a charm on a woman's heart. Again, another may be observed with a bunch of the red dracaena leaves knotted round his neck and the long stalk hanging down his back. He is a soldier, and these leaves are supposed to make him invulnerable. But if the lover should fail to win the affections of his swarthy mistress, if the warrior should be wounded in battle, it never occurs to either of them to question the magical virtue of the charm; they ascribe the failure either to the more potent charm of another magician or to some oversight on their own part.[1] On the theory that wreaths and garlands serve as amulets to protect the wearer against the powers of evil we can understand not only why in antiquity sacred persons such as priests and kings wore crowns, but also why dead bodies, sacrificial victims, and in certain circumstances even inanimate objects such as the implements of sacrifice, the doors of houses, and so forth, were decorated or rather guarded by wreaths.[2] Further, on this hypothesis we may perhaps perceive why children of living parents were specially chosen to cut or wear sacred wreaths. Since such children were apparently supposed to be endowed with a more than common share of vital energy, they might be deemed peculiarly fitted to make or wear amulets which were designed to protect the wearer from injury and death: the current of life which circulated in their own veins overflowed, as it were, and reinforced the magic virtue of the wreath. For the same reason such children would naturally be chosen to personate gods, as they seemingly were at Delphi and Thebes.

At Ephesus, if we may trust the evidence of the Greek romance-writer, Heliodorus, a boy and girl of living parents used to hold for a year the priesthood of Apollo and Artemis respectively. When their

Children of living parents acting as

---

[1] R. Parkinson, *Dreissig Jahre in der Südsee* (Stuttgart, 1907), pp. 150-152.

[2] On the use of crowns and wreaths in classical antiquity see W. Smith's *Dictionary of Greek and Roman Antiquities*,[3] i. 545 *sqq.*, *s.v.* "Corona"; E. Saglio, *s.v.* "Corona," in Ch. Daremberg et E. Saglio's *Dictionnaire des Antiquités Grecques et Romaines*, iii. 1520 *sqq.* In time of mourning the

ancients laid aside crowns (Athenaeus, xv. 16, p. 675 A); and so did the king at Athens when he tried a homicide (Aristotle, *Constitution of Athens*, 57). I mention these cases because they seem to conflict with the theory in the text, in accordance with which crowns might be regarded as amulets to protect the wearer against ghosts and the pollution of blood.

priest and priestess of Apollo and Artemis.

period of office was nearly expired, they led a sacred embassy to Delos, the birthplace of the divine brother and sister, where they superintended the musical and athletic contests and laid down the priesthood.[1]　At Rome no girl might be chosen a Vestal Virgin unless both her father and mother were living;[2] yet there is no evidence or probability that a Vestal vacated office on the death of a parent; indeed she generally held office for life.[3]　This alone may suffice to prove that the custom of entrusting certain sacred duties to children of living parents was not based on any notion that orphans as such were ceremonially unclean.　Again, the dancing priests of Mars, the Salii, must be sons of living parents;[4] but as in the case of the Vestals this condition probably only applied at the date of their election, for they seem like the Vestals to have held office for life.　At all events we read of a lively old gentleman who still skipped and capered about as a dancing priest with an agility which threw the efforts of his younger colleagues into the shade.[5] Again, at the public games in Rome boys of living parents had to escort the images of the gods in their sacred cars, and it was a dire omen if one of them relaxed his hold on the holy cart or let a strap slip from his fingers.[6]　And when the stout Roman heart was shaken by the appalling news that somebody had been struck by lightning, that the sky had somewhere been suddenly overcast, or that a she-mule had been safely delivered of a colt, boys and girls whose fathers and mothers were still alive used to be sought out and employed to help in expiating the terrific prodigy.[7]　Again, when the Capitol had been sacked and burned by the disorderly troops of Vitellius, solemn preparations were made to rebuild it.　The whole area was enclosed by a cordon of fillets and wreaths.　Then soldiers chosen for their auspicious names entered within the barriers holding branches of lucky trees in their hands; and afterwards the Vestal Virgins, aided by boys and girls of living parents, washed the foundations with water drawn from springs and rivers.[8]　In this ceremony the choice of such children seems to be based on the same idea as the choice of such water; for as running water is deemed to

At Rome the Vestals and the Salii must be the children of parents who were alive at the date of the election.

Children of living parents employed in expiatory rites at Rome.

---

[1] Heliodorus, *Acthiopica*, i. 22.

[2] Aulus Gellius, i. 12. 2.

[3] Dionysius Halicarnasensis, *Antiquit. Rom.* ii. 67; Plutarch, *Numa*, 10.　We read of a Vestal who held office for fifty-seven years (Tacitus, *Annals*, ii. 86).　It is unlikely that the parents of this venerable lady were both alive at the date of her decease.

[4] Dionysius Halicarnasensis, *Antiquit. Rom.* ii. 71.

[5] Macrobius, *Sat.* iii. 14. 14.　That the rule as to their parents being both alive applied to the Vestals and Salii

only at the time of their entrance on office is recognized by Marquardt (*Römische Staatsverwaltung*, iii.[2] 228, note[1]).

[6] Cicero, *De haruspicum responso*, 11.

[7] Livy, xxxvii. 3; Macrobius, *Saturn.* i. 6. 13 *sq.*; Vopiscus, *Aurelianus*, 19 (where the words "*patrimis matrimisque pueris carmen indicite*" are omitted from the text by H. Peter).

[8] Tacitus, *Histor.* iv. 53.　For the sack and conflagration of the Capitol see *id.* iii. 71-75.

be especially alive,[1] so the vital current might be thought to flow without interruption in the children of living parents but to stagnate in orphans. Hence the children of living parents rather than orphans would naturally be chosen to pour the living water over the foundations, and so to lend something of their own vitality or endurance to a building that was designed to last for ever.

On the same principle we can easily understand why the children of living parents should be especially chosen to perform certain offices at marriage. The motive of such a choice may be a wish to ensure by sympathetic magic the life of the newly wedded pair and of their offspring. Thus at Roman marriages the bride was escorted to her new home by three boys whose parents were all living. Two of the boys held her, and the third carried a torch of buckthorn or hawthorn in front of her,[2] probably for the purpose of averting the powers of evil; for buckthorn or hawthorn was credited with this magical virtue.[3] At marriages in ancient Athens a boy whose parents were both living used to wear a wreath of thorns and acorns and to carry about a winnowing-fan full of loaves, crying, "I have escaped the bad, I have found the better."[4] In modern Greece on the Sunday before a marriage the bridegroom sends to the bride the wedding cake by the hands of a boy, both of whose parents must be living. The messenger takes great care not to stumble or to injure the cake, for to do either would be a very bad omen. He may not enter the bride's house till she has taken the cake from him. For this purpose he lays it down on the threshold of the door, and then both of them, the boy and the bride, rush at it and try to seize the greater part of the cake. And when cattle are being slaughtered for the marriage festivities, the first beast killed for the bride's house must be killed by a youth whose parents are both alive. Further, a son of living parents must solemnly fetch the water with which the bridegroom's head is ceremonially washed by women before marriage. And on the day after the marriage bride and bridegroom go in procession to the well or spring from which they are henceforth to fetch their water. The bride greets the spring, drinks of the water from the hollow of her hand, and throws money and food into it. Then follows a dance, accompanied by a song, round about the spring. Lastly, a lad whose parents are both living draws water from the spring in a special vessel and carries it to the house of the bridal pair without speaking a word: this "unspoken water," as it is called, is regarded

Children of living parents employed at marriage ceremonies in Greece, Italy, Albania, Bulgaria, and Africa.

---

[1] Flowing water in Hebrew is called "living water" (מַיִם חַיִּים).

[2] Festus, *De verborum significatione*, ed. C. O. Müller (Leipsic, 1839), pp. 244, 245, *s.v.* "Patrimi et matrimi pueri.".

[3] Ovid, *Fasti*, vi. 129 *sq.*, 165-168.

[4] Zenobius, *Proverb.* iii. 98; Plutarch, *Proverb.* i. 16; Apostolius, *Proverb.* viii. 16 (*Paroemiographi Graeci*, ed. Leutsch et Schneidewin, i. 82, 323 *sq.*, ii. 429); Eustathius, on Homer, *Od.* xii. 357, p. 1726; Photius, *Lexicon, s.v.* ἔφυγον κακόν.

as peculiarly holy and wholesome. When the young couple return from the spring, they fill their mouths with the "unspoken water" and try to spirt it on each other inside the door of the house.[1] In Albania, when women are baking cakes for a wedding, the first to put hand to the dough must be a maiden whose parents are both alive and who has brothers, the more the better; for only such a girl is deemed lucky. And when the bride has dismounted from her horse at the bridegroom's door, a small boy whose parents are both alive (for only such a boy is thought to bring luck) is passed thrice backwards and forwards under the horse's belly, as if he would girdle the beast.[2] Among the South Slavs of Bulgaria a little child whose father and mother are both alive helps to bake the two bridal cakes, pouring water and salt on the meal and stirring the mixture with a spurtle of a special shape; then a girl lifts the child in her arms, and the little one touches the roof-beam thrice with the spurtle, saying, "Boys and girls." And when the bride's hair is to be dressed for the wedding day, the work of combing and plaiting it must be begun by a child of living parents.[3] Among the Eesa and Gadabursi, two Somali tribes, on the morning after a marriage "the bride's female relations bring presents of milk, and are accompanied by a young male child whose parents are living. The child drinks some of the milk before any one else tastes it; and after him the bridegroom, if his parents are living; but if one or both of his parents are dead, and those of the bride living, she drinks after the child. By doing this they believe that if the newly-married woman bears a child the father will be alive at the time."[4] A slightly different application of the same principle appears in the old Hindoo rule that when a bride reached the house of her husband, she should be made to descend from the chariot by women of good character whose husbands and sons were living, and that afterwards these women should seat the bride on a bull's hide, while her husband recited the verse, "Here ye cows, bring forth calves."[5] Here the ceremony of seating the young wife on a bull's hide seems plainly intended to make her fruitful through the generative virtue of the bull; while the attendance of women, whose husbands and sons are living, is no doubt a device for ensuring, by sympathetic magic, the life both of the bride's husband and of her future off-spring.

[1] C. Wachsmuth, *Das alte Griechenland im neuen* (Bonn, 1864), pp. 83-85, 86, 87, 100 *sq.*

[2] J. G. von Hahn, *Albanesische Studien* (Jena, 1854), i. 144, 146.

[3] F. S. Krauss, *Sitte und Brauch der Süd-Slaven* (Vienna, 1885), pp. 438, 441.

[4] Captain J. S. King, "Notes on the Folk-lore and some Social Customs of the Western Somali Tribes," *The Folk-lore Journal*, vi. (1888) p. 124. Compare Ph. Paulitschke, *Ethnographie Nordost-Afrikas, die materielle Cultur der Danâkil, Galla und Somâl* (Berlin, 1893), p. 200.

[5] *The Grihya-Sûtras*, translated by H. Oldenberg, Part ii. (Oxford, 1892) p. 50 (*The Sacred Books of the East*, vol. xxx.).

In the Somali custom just described the part played by the child of living parents is unambiguous and helps to throw light on the obscurer cases which precede. Such a child is clearly supposed to impart the virtue of longevity to the milk of which it partakes, and so to transmit it to the newly married pair who afterwards drink of the milk. Similarly, we may suppose that in all marriage rites at least, if not in religious rites generally, the employment of children of living parents is intended to diffuse by sympathy the blessings of life and longevity among all who participate in the ceremonies. This intention seems to underlie the use which the Malagasy make of the children of living parents in ritual. Thus, when a child is a week old, it is dressed up in the finest clothes that can be got, and is then carried out of the house by some person whose parents are both still living; afterwards it is brought back to the mother. In the act of being carried out and in, the infant must be twice carefully lifted over the fire, which is placed near the door. If the child is a boy, the axe, knife, and spear of the family, together with any building tools that may be in the house, are taken out of it at the same time. "The implements are perhaps used chiefly as emblems of the occupations in which it is expected the infant will engage when it arrives at maturer years; and the whole may be regarded as expressing the hopes cherished of his activity, wealth, and enjoyments."[1] On such an occasion the service of a person whose parents are both alive seems naturally calculated to promote the longevity of the infant. For a like reason, probably, the holy water used at the Malagasy ceremony of circumcision is drawn from a pool by a person whose parents are both still living.[2] The same idea may explain a funeral custom observed by the Sihanaka of Madagascar. After a burial the family of the deceased, with their near relatives and dependents, meet in the house from which the corpse was lately removed "to drink rum and to undergo a purifying and preserving baptism called *fàfy rànom-bôahàngy*. Leaves of the lemon or lime tree, and the stalks of two kinds of grass, are gathered and placed in a vessel with water. A person, both of whose parents are living, is chosen to perform the rite, and this 'holy water' is then sprinkled upon the walls of the house and upon all assembled within them, and finally around the house outside."[3] Here a person whose parents are both living appears to be credited with a more than common share of life and longevity; from which it naturally follows that he is better fitted than any one else to perform a ceremony intended to avert the danger of death from the household.

The notion that a child of living parents is endowed with a

Marginal notes: Children of living parents apparently supposed to impart life and longevity.

Child of living parents employed in funeral rites.

[1] Rev. William Ellis, *History of Madagascar* (London, N.D.), i. 151 *sq.*
[2] Rev. W. Ellis, *op. cit.* i. 180.
[3] J. Pearse, "Customs connected with Death and Burial among the Sihanaka," *The Antananarivo Annual and Madagascar Magazine*, vol. ii. (a reprint of the second four numbers, 1881–1884) (Antananarivo, 1896) p. 152.

The use
of children
of living
parents in
ritual may
be ex-
plained by
a notion
that they
are fuller
of life and
therefore
luckier
than
orphans.

higher degree of vitality than an orphan probably explains all the cases of the employment of such a child in ritual, whether the particular rite is designed to ensure the fertility of the ground or the fruitfulness of women, or to avert the danger of death and other calamities. Yet it might be a mistake to suppose that this notion is always clearly apprehended by the persons who practise the customs. In their minds the definite conception of super-abundant and overflowing vitality may easily dissolve into a vague idea that the child of living parents is luckier than other folk. No more than this seems to be at the bottom of the Masai rule that when the warriors wish to select a chief, they must choose "a man whose parents are still living, who owns cattle and has never killed anybody, whose parents are not blind, and who himself has not a discoloured eye."[1] And nothing more is needed to explain the ancient Greek custom which assigned the duty of drawing lots from an urn to a boy under puberty whose father and mother were both in life.[2] At Athens it would appear that registers of these boys were kept, perhaps in order that the lads might discharge, as occasion arose, those offices of religion which required the service of such auspicious youths.[3] The atrocious tyrant Heliogabalus, one of the worst monsters who ever disgraced the human form, caused search to be made throughout Italy for noble and handsome boys whose parents were both alive, and he sacrificed them to his barbarous gods, torturing them first and grabbling among their entrails afterwards for omens. He seems to have thought that such victims would be peculiarly acceptable to the Syrian deities whom he worshipped; so he encouraged the torturers and butchers at their work, and thanked the gods for enabling him to ferret out "their friends."[4]

[1] A. C. Hollis, *The Masai* (Oxford, 1905), p. 299.

[2] Lucian, *Hermotimus*, 57.

[3] A fragmentary list of these youths is preserved in an Athenian inscription of the year 91 or 90 B.C. See Ch. Michel, *Recueil d'Inscriptions Grecques*, Supplément, i. (Paris, 1912) p. 104, No. 1544.

[4] Aelius Lampridius, *Antoninus Heliogabalus*, viii. 1 *sq*. The historian thinks that the monster chose these victims merely for the pleasure of rending the hearts of both the parents.

III

A CHARM TO PROTECT A TOWN

THE tradition that a Lydian king tried to make the citadel of Sardes impregnable by carrying round it a lion [1] may perhaps be illustrated by a South African custom. When the Bechuanas are about to found a new town, they observe an elaborate ritual. They choose a bull from the herd, sew up its eyelids with sinew, and then allow the blinded animal to wander at will for four days. On the fifth day they track it down and sacrifice it at sunset on the spot where it happens to be standing. The carcase is then roasted whole and divided among the people. Ritual requires that every particle of the flesh should be consumed on the spot. When the sacrificial meal is over, the medicine-men take the hide and mark it with appropriate medicines, the composition of which is a professional secret. Then with one long spiral cut they convert the whole hide into a single thong. Having done so they cut up the thong into lengths of about two feet and despatch messengers in all directions to peg down one of those strips in each of the paths leading to the new town. "After this," it is said, "if a foreigner approaches the new town to destroy it with his charms, he will find that the town has prepared itself for his coming." [2] Thus it would seem that the pastoral Bechuanas attempt to place a new town under the protection of one of their sacred cattle [3] by distributing pieces of its hide at all points where an enemy could approach it, just as the Lydian king thought to place the citadel of his capital under the protection of the lion-god by carrying the animal round the boundaries.

Further, the Bechuana custom may throw light on a widespread legend which relates how a wily settler in a new country bought from the natives as much land as could be covered with a hide, and how he then proceeded to cut the hide into thongs and to claim as much land as could be enclosed by the thongs. It was thus,

Margin note: The Bechuanas use the hide of a sacrificial ox at founding a new town.

Margin note: The custom may explain the legend of the foundation of Carthage and similar tales.

[1] See above, vol. i. p. 184.
[2] Rev. W. C. Willoughby, "Notes on the Totemism of the Becwana," *Journal of the Anthropological Institute,* xxxv. (1905) pp. 303 *sq.*

[3] For more evidence of the sanctity of cattle among the Bechuanas see the Rev. W. C. Willoughby, *op. cit.* pp. 301 *sqq.*

according to the Hottentots, that the first European settlers obtained a footing in South Africa.[1]   But the most familiar example of such stories is the tradition that Dido procured the site of Carthage in this fashion, and that the place hence received the name of Byrsa or "hide."[2]   Similar tales occur in the legendary history of Saxons and Danes,[3] and they meet us in India, Siberia, Burma, Cambodia, Java, and Bali.[4]   The wide diffusion of such stories confirms the conjecture of Jacob Grimm that in them we have a reminiscence of a mode of land measurement which was once actually in use, and of which the designation is still retained in the English *hide*.[5] The Bechuana custom suggests that the mode of measuring by a hide may have originated in a practice of encompassing a piece of land with thongs cut from the hide of a sacrificial victim in order to place the ground under the guardianship of the sacred animal.

The ox whose hide is used is blinded in order that the new town may be invisible to its enemies.   But why do the Bechuanas sew up the eyelids of the bull which is to be used for this purpose?   The answer appears to be given by the ceremonies which the same people observe when they are going out to war.   On that occasion a woman rushes up to the army with her eyes shut and shakes a winnowing-fan, while she cries out, " The army is not seen !   The army is not seen ! "   And a medicine-man at the same time sprinkles medicine over the spears, crying out in like manner, " The army is not seen !   The army is not seen ! " After that they seize a bull, sew up its eyelids with a hair of its tail, and drive it for some distance along the road which the army is to take.   When it has preceded the army a little way, the bull is sacrificed, roasted whole, and eaten by the warriors.   All the flesh must be consumed on the spot.   Such parts as cannot be eaten are burnt with fire.   Only the contents of the stomach are carefully preserved

[1] T. Arbousset et F. Daumas, *Voyage d'Exploration au Nord-est de la Colonie du Cap de Bonne-Espérance* (Paris, 1842), p. 49.

[2] Virgil, *Aen.* i. 367 *sq.*, with the commentary of Servius ; Justin, xviii. 5. 9.   Thongs cut from the hide of the ox sacrificed to the four-handed Apollo were given as prizes.   See Hesychius, *s.v. κυνακλας* ; compare *id.*, *πυρϣλοφοι.* Whether the Greek custom was related to those discussed in the text seems doubtful.   I have to thank my colleague and friend Professor R. C. Bosanquet for calling my attention to these passages of Hesychius.

[3] Saxo Grammaticus, *Historia Danica*, ix. vol. i. pp. 462 *sq.* ed. P. E. Müller (Copenhagen, 1839–1858) (where the hide employed is that of a horse) ; J. Grimm, *Deutsche Rechtsalterthümer*[3] (Göttingen, 1881), pp. 90 *sq.*

Compare R. Köhler, " Sage von Landerwerbung durch zerschnittene Häute," *Orient und Occident*, iii. 185-187.

[4] Lieutenant-Colonel James Tod, *Annals and Antiquities of Rajast'han*, ii. (London, 1832) p. 235 ; W. Radloff, *Proben der Volkslitteratur der türkischen Stämme Süd-Sibiriens*, iv. (St. Petersburg, 1872) p. 179 ; A. Bastian, *Die Voelker des oestlichen Asien* (Leipzig, Jena, 1866–1871), i. 25, iv. 367 *sq.* ; T. Stamford Raffles, *History of Java* (London, 1817), ii. 153 *sq.* ; R. van Eck, " Schetsen van het eiland Bali," *Tijdschrift voor Nederlandsch-Indië*, Feb. 1880, p. 117.   The substance of all these stories, except the first, was given by me in a note on " Hide-measured Lands," *The Classical Review*, ii. (1888) p. 322.

[5] J. Grimm, *Deutsche Rechtsalterthümer*, pp. 538 *sq.*

as a charm which is to lead the warriors to victory. Chosen men carry the precious guts in front of the army, and it is deemed most important that no one should precede them. When they stop, the army stops, and it will not resume the march till it sees that the men with the bull's guts have gone forward.[1] The meaning of these ceremonies is explained by the cries of the woman and the priest, "The army is not seen! The army is not seen!" Clearly it is desirable that the army should not be perceived by the enemies until it is upon them. Accordingly on the principles of homoeopathic magic the Bechuanas apparently imagine that they can make themselves invisible by eating of the flesh of a blind bull, blindness and invisibility being to their simple minds the same thing. For the same reason the bowels of the blind ox are carried in front of the army to hide its advance from hostile eyes. In like manner the custom of sacrificing and eating a blind ox on the place where a new town is to be built may be intended to render the town invisible to enemies. At all events the Bawenda, a South African people who belong to the same Bantu stock as the Bechuanas, take great pains to conceal their kraals from passers-by. The kraals are built in the forest or bush, and the long winding footpaths which lead to them are often kept open only by the support of a single pole here and there. Indeed the paths are so low and narrow that it is very difficult to bring a horse into such a village. In time of war the poles are removed and the thorny creepers fall down, forming a natural screen or bulwark which the enemy can neither penetrate nor destroy by fire. The kraals are also surrounded by walls of undressed stones with a filling of soil; and to hide them still better from the view of the enemy the tops of the walls are sown with Indian corn or planted with tobacco. Hence travellers passing through the country seldom come across a Bawenda kraal. To see where the Bawenda dwell you must climb to the tops of mountains and look down on the roofs of their round huts peeping out of the surrounding green like clusters of mushrooms in the woods.[2] The object which the Bawenda attain by these perfectly rational means, the Bechuanas seek to compass by the sacrifice and consumption of a blind bull.

This explanation of the use of a blinded ox in sacrifice is confirmed by the reasons alleged by a Caffre for the observance of a somewhat similar custom in purificatory ceremonies after a battle. On these occasions the Bechuanas and other Caffre tribes of South Africa kill a black ox and cut out the tip of its tongue, an eye, a piece of the ham-string, and a piece of the principal sinew of the

This explanation of the use of a blinded ox is confirmed by a Caffre custom.

---

[1] Rev. W. C. Willoughby, "Notes on the Totemism of the Becwana," *Journal of the Anthropological Institute*, xxxv. (1905) p. 304.

[2] Rev. E. Gottschling, "The Bawenda, a Sketch of their History and Customs," *Journal of the Anthropological Institute*, xxxv. (1905) pp. 368 *sq.*

shoulder. These parts are fried with certain herbs and rubbed into the joints of the warriors. By cutting out the tongue of the ox they think to prevent the enemy from wagging his tongue against them ; by severing the sinews of the ox they hope to cause the enemy's sinews to fail him in the battle ; and by removing the eye of the ox they imagine that they prevent the enemy from casting a covetous eye on their cattle.[1]

[1] T. Arbousset et F. Daumas, *Relation d'un Voyage d'Exploration*, pp. 561-565.

IV

SOME CUSTOMS OF THE PELEW ISLANDERS

WE have seen that the state of society and religion among the Pelew Islanders in modern times presents several points of similarity to the condition of the peoples about the Eastern Mediterranean in antiquity.[1] Here I propose briefly to call attention to certain other customs of the Pelew Islanders which may serve to illustrate some of the institutions discussed in this volume.

§ 1. *Priests dressed as Women*

In the Pelew Islands it often happens that a goddess chooses a man, not a woman, for her minister and inspired mouthpiece. When that is so, the favoured man is thenceforth regarded and treated as a woman. He wears female attire, he carries a piece of gold on his neck, he labours like a woman in the taro fields, and he plays his new part so well that he earns the hearty contempt of his fellows.[2] The pretended change of sex under the inspiration of a female spirit perhaps explains a custom widely spread among savages, in accordance with which some men dress as women and act as women through life. These unsexed creatures often, perhaps generally, profess the arts of sorcery and healing, they communicate with spirits, and are regarded sometimes with awe and sometimes with contempt, as beings of a higher or lower order than common folk. Often they are dedicated and trained to their vocation from childhood. Effeminate sorcerers or priests of this sort are found among the Sea Dyaks of Borneo,[3] the Bugis of South

In the Pelew Islands a man who is inspired by a goddess wears female attire and is treated as a woman. This pretended change of sex under the inspiration of a female spirit may explain a

[1] Above, pp. 204 *sqq.*

[2] J. Kubary, "Die Religion der Pelauer," in A. Bastian's *Allerlei aus Volks- und Menschenkunde* (Berlin, 1888), i. 35.

[3] C. A. L. M. Schwaner, *Borneo* (Amsterdam, 1853), i. 186; M. T. H. Perelaer, *Ethnographische Beschrijving der Dajaks* (Zalt-Bommel, 1870), pp.

32-35; Captain Rodney Mundy, *Narrative of Events in Borneo and Celebes from the Journals of James Brooke, Esq., Rajah of Sarawak* (London, 1848), ii. 65 *sq.*; Charles Brooke, *Ten Years in Sarawak* (London, 1866), ii. 280; H. Low, *Sarawak* (London, 1848), pp. 174-177; The Bishop of Labuan, "On the Wild

widespread custom whereby men dress and live like women.

Celebes,[1] the Patagonians of South America,[2] and the Aleutians and many Indian tribes of North America.[3] In the island of Rambree, off the coast of Aracan, a set of vagabond "conjurors," who dressed and lived as women, used to dance round a tall pole, invoking the aid of their favourite idol on the occasion of any calamity.[4] Male members of the Vallabha sect in India often seek to win the favour of the god Krishna, whom they specially revere, by wearing their hair long and assimilating themselves to women; even their spiritual chiefs, the so-called Maharajas, sometimes simulate the appearance of women when they lead the worship of their followers.[5] In Madagascar we hear of effeminate men who wore female attire and acted as women, thinking thereby to do God service.[6] In the kingdom of Congo there was a sacrificial priest who commonly dressed as a woman and

Tribes of the North-West Coast of Borneo," *Transactions of the Ethnological Society of London*, N.S. ii. (1863) pp. 31 *sq.*; Spenser St. John, *Life in the Forests of the Far East*[2] (London, 1863), i. 73. In Sarawak these men are called *manangs*, in Dutch Borneo they are called *bazirs* or *bassirs*.

[1] Captain R. Mundy, *op. cit.* i. 82 *sq.*; B. F. Matthes, *Over de Bissoes of heidensche Priesters en Priesteressen der Boeginezen* (Amsterdam, 1872), pp. 1 *sq.*

[2] Th. Falkner, *Description of Patagonia* (Hereford, 1774), p. 117; J. Hutchnson, "The Tehuelche Indians of Patagonia," *Transactions of the Ethnological Society of London*, N.S. vii. (1869) p. 323. Among the Guaycurus of Southern Brazil there is a class of men who dress as women and do only women's work, such as spinning, weaving, and making pottery. But so far as I know, they are not said to be sorcerers or priests. See C. F. Ph. v. Martius, *Zur Ethnographie Amerikas zumal Brasiliens* (Leipsic, 1867), pp. 74 *sq.*

[3] G. H. von Langsdorff, *Reise um die Welt* (Frankfort, 1812), ii. 43; H. J. Holmberg, "Über die Völker des Russischen Amerika," *Acta Societatis Scientiarum Fennicae*, iv. (Helsingfors, 1856) pp. 400 *sq.*; W. H. Dall, *Alaska* (London, 1870), pp. 402 *sq.*; Ross Cox, *The Columbia River*[2] (London, 1832), i. 327 *sqq.*; Father G. Boscana, "Chinigchinich," in [A. Robinson's] *Life in California* (New York, 1846),

pp. 283 *sq.*; S. Powers, *Tribes of California* (Washington, 1877), pp. 132 *sq.*; H. H. Bancroft, *Native Races of the Pacific States* (London, 1875–1876), i. 82, 92, 415, 585, 774; Hontan, *Mémoires de l'Amérique Septentrionale* (Amsterdam, 1705), p. 144; J. F. Lafitau, *Mœurs des Sauvages Amériquains* (Paris, 1724), i. 52-54; Charlevoix, *Histoire de la Nouvelle France* (Paris, 1744), vi. 4 *sq.*; W. H. Keating, *Expedition to the Source of St. Peter's River* (London, 1825), i. 227 *sq.*, 436; George Catlin, *North American Indians*[4] (London, 1844), ii. 214 *sq.*; Maximilian Prinz zu Wied, *Reise in das innere Nord - America* (Coblentz, 1839–1841), ii. 132 *sq.*; D. G. Brinton, *The Lenâpé and their Legends* (Philadelphia, 1885), pp. 109 *sq.*; J. G. Müller, *Geschichte der amerikanischen Urreligionen*[2] (Bâle, 167), pp. 44 *sq.*, 418. Among the tribes which permitted the custom were the Illinois, Mandans, Dacotas (Sioux), Sauks, and Foxes, to the east of the Rocky Mountains, the Yukis, Pomos, and Pitt River Indians of California, and the Koniags of Alaska.

[4] Lieut. W. Foley, "Journal of a Tour through the Island of Rambree," *Journal of the Asiatic Society of Bengal*, iv. (Calcutta, 1835) p. 199.

[5] Monier Williams, *Religious Life and Thought in India* (London, 1883), p. 136. Compare J. A. Dubois, *Mœurs, Institutions, et Cérémonies des Peuples de l'Inde* (Paris, 1825), i. 439.

[6] O. Dapper, *Description de l Afrique* (Amsterdam, 1686), p. 467.

gloried in the title of the Grandmother. The post of Grandmother must have been much coveted, for the incumbent might not be put to death, whatever crimes or rascalities he committed; and to do him justice he appears commonly to have taken full advantage of this benefit of clergy. When he died, his fortunate successor dissected the body of the deceased Grandmother, extracting his heart and other vital organs, and amputating his fingers and toes, which he kept as priceless relics, and sold as sovereign remedies for all the ills that flesh is heir to.[1]

We may conjecture that in many of these cases the call to this strange form of the religious life came in the shape of a dream or vision, in which the dreamer or visionary imagined himself to be a woman or to be possessed by a female spirit; for with many savage races the disordered fancies of sleep or ecstasy are accepted as oracular admonitions which it would be perilous to disregard. At all events we are told that a dream or a revelation of some sort was the reason which in North America these men-women commonly alleged for the life they led; it had been thus brought home to them, they said, that their medicine or their salvation lay in living as women, and when once they had got this notion into their head nothing could drive it out again. Many an Indian father attempted by persuasion, by bribes, by violence, to deter his son from obeying the mysterious call, but all to no purpose.[2] Among the Sauks, an Indian tribe of North America, these effeminate beings were always despised, but sometimes they were pitied " as labouring under an unfortunate destiny which they cannot avoid, being supposed to be impelled to this course by a vision from the female spirit that resides in the moon."[3] Similarly the Omahas, another

Such transformations seem to have been often carried out in obedience to intimations received in dreams or in ecstasy.

---

[1] J. B. Labat, *Relation historique de l'Éthiopie Occidentale* (Paris, 1732), ii. 195-199. Wherever men regularly dress as women, we may suspect that a superstitious motive underlies the custom even though our authorities do not mention it. The custom is thus reported among the Italmenes of Kamtschatka (G. W. Steller, *Beschreibung von dem Lande Kamtschatka*, Frankfort and Leipsic, 1774, pp. 350 *sq.*), the Lhoosais of South - Eastern India (Capt. T. H. Lewin, *Wild Races of South-Eastern India*, London, 1870, p. 255), and the Nogay or Mongutay of the Caucasus (J. Reinegg, *Beschreibung des Kaukasus*, St. Petersburg, Gotha, and Hildesheim, 1796-1797, i. 270). Among the Lhoosais or Lushais not only do men sometimes dress like women and consort and work with them (T. H. Lewin,

l.c.), but, on the other hand, women sometimes dress and live like men, adopting masculine habits in all respects. When one of these unsexed women was asked her reasons for adopting a masculine mode of life, she at first denied that she was a woman, but finally confessed "that her *khua-vang* was not good, and so she became a man." See the extract from the *Pioneer Mail* of May 1890, quoted in *The Indian Antiquary*, xxxii. (1903) p. 413. The permanent transformation of women into men seems to be much rarer than the converse change of men into women.

[2] Maximilian Prinz zu Wied, *Reise in das innere Nord-America*, ii. 133.

[3] W. H. Keating, *Expedition to the Source of St. Peter's River*, i. 227 *sq.*

Indian tribe of North America, " believe that the unfortunate beings, called *Min-qu-ga*, are mysterious or sacred because they have been affected by the Moon Being. When a young Omaha fasted for the first time on reaching puberty, it was thought that the Moon Being appeared to him, holding in one hand a bow and arrows and in the other a pack strap, such as the Indian women use. When the youth tried to grasp the bow and arrows the Moon Being crossed his hands very quickly, and if the youth was not very careful he seized the pack strap instead of the bow and arrows, thereby fixing his lot in after life. In such a case he could not help acting the woman, speaking, dressing, and working just as Indian women used to do." [1] Among the Ibans or Sea Dyaks of Borneo the highest class of sorcerers or medicine-men (*manangs*) are those who are believed to have been transformed into women. Such a man is therefore called a " changed medicine-man " (*manang bali*) on account of his supposed change of sex. The call to transform himself into a woman is said to come as a supernatural command thrice repeated in dreams ; to disregard the command would mean death. Accordingly he makes a feast, sacrifices a pig or two to avert evil consequences from the tribe, and then assumes the garb of a woman. Thenceforth he is treated as a woman and occupies himself in feminine pursuits. His chief aim is to copy female manners and habits as accurately as possible. He is employed for the same purposes as an ordinary medicine-man and his methods are similar, but he is paid much higher fees and is often called in when others have been unable to effect a cure. [2] Similarly among the Chukchees of North-Eastern Asia there are shamans or medicine-men who assimilate themselves as far as possible to women, and who are believed to be called to this vocation by spirits in a dream. The call usually comes at the critical age of early youth when the shamanistic inspiration, as it is called, first manifests itself. But the call is much dreaded by the youthful adepts, and some of them prefer death to obedience. There are, however, various stages or degrees of transformation. In the first stage the man apes a woman only in the manner of braiding and arranging the hair of his head. In the second he dons female attire ; in the third stage he adopts as far as possible the life and characteristics of the female sex. A young man who is undergoing this final transformation abandons all masculine occupations and manners. He throws away the rifle and the lance, the lasso of the reindeer herdsman, and the harpoon of the seal-hunter, and betakes himself to the needle and the skin-scraper instead. He learns the use of them quickly,

Marginal notes:
Transformed medicine-men among the Sea Dyaks.

Transformed medicine-men among the Chukchees.

---

[1] Rev. J. Owen Dorsey, "A Study of Siouan Cults," *Eleventh Annual Report of the Bureau of Ethnology* (Washington, 1894), p. 378.

[2] E. H. Gomes, *Seventeen Years among the Sea Dyaks of Borneo* (London, 1911), p. 179 ; Ch. Hose and W. McDougall, *The Pagan Tribes of Borneo* (London, 1912), ii. 116.

because the spirits are helping him all the time. Even his pronunciation changes from the male to the female mode. At the same time his body alters, if not in outward appearance, at least in its faculties and forces. He loses masculine strength, fleetness of foot, endurance in wrestling, and falls into the debility and helplessness of a woman. Even his mental character undergoes a change. His old brute courage and fighting spirit are gone ; he grows shy and bashful before strangers, fond of small talk and of dandling little children. In short he becomes a woman with the appearance of a man, and as a woman he is often taken to wife by another man, with whom he leads a regular married life. Extraordinary powers are attributed to such transformed shamaṇs. They are supposed to enjoy the special protection of spirits who play the part of supernatural husbands to them. Hence they are much dreaded even by their colleagues in the profession who remain mere men ; hence, too, they excel in all branches of magic, including ventriloquism.[1] Among the Teso of Central Africa medicine-men often dress as women and wear feminine ornaments, such as heavy chains of beads and shells round their heads and necks.[2]

And just as a man inspired by a goddess may adopt female attire, so conversely a woman inspired by a god may adopt male costume. In Uganda the great god Mukasa, the deity of the Victoria Nyanza Lake and of abundance, imparted his oracles through a woman, who in ordinary life dressed like the rest of her sex in a bark cloth wrapped round the body and fastened with a girdle, so as to leave the arms and shoulders bare ; but when she prophesied under the inspiration of the god, she wore two bark cloths knotted in masculine style over her shoulders and crossing each other on her breast and back.[3] When once the god had chosen her, she retained office for life ; she might not marry or converse with any man except one particular priest, who was always present when she was possessed by the deity.[4]

Women inspired by a god dress as men.

Perhaps this assumed change of sex under the inspiration of a goddess may give the key to the legends of the effeminate Sardanapalus and the effeminate Hercules,[5] as well as to the practice of the effeminate priests of Cybele and the Syrian goddess. In all

The theory of inspiration by a female spirit

---

[1] Waldemar Bogoras, *The Chukchee* (Leyden and New York, 1904-1909), pp. 448-453 (*The Jesup North Pacific Expedition*, vol. vii. ; *Memoir of the American Museum of Natural History*).

[2] Rev. A. L. Kitching, *On the Backwaters of the Nile* (London, 1912), p. 239, with the plate.

[3] For this information I have to thank my friend the Rev. J. Roscoe. He tells me that according to tradition Mukasa used to give his oracles by the mouth of a man, not of a woman. To wear two bark cloths, one on each shoulder, is a privilege of royalty and of priests. The ordinary man wears a single bark cloth knotted on one shoulder only. With the single exception mentioned in the text, women in Uganda never wear bark cloths fastened over the shoulders.

[4] Rev. J. Roscoe, *The Baganda* (London, 1911), p. 297.

[5] *The Scapegoat*, pp. 387 *sqq.*

perhaps
explains
the legends
of the
effeminate
Sardan-
apalus
and the
effeminate
Hercules,
both of
whom may
have been
thought
to be
possessed
by the
great
Asiatic
goddess
Astarte
or her
equivalent.

such cases the pretended transformation of a man into a woman would be intelligible if we supposed that the womanish priest or king thought himself animated by a female spirit, whose sex, accordingly, he felt bound to imitate. Certainly the eunuch priests of Cybele seem to have bereft themselves of their manhood under the supposed inspiration of the Great Goddess.[1] The priest of Hercules at Antimachia, in Cos, who dressed as a woman when he offered sacrifice, is said to have done so in imitation of Hercules who disguised himself as a woman to escape the pursuit of his enemies.[2] So the Lydian Hercules wore female attire when he served for three years as the purchased slave of the imperious Omphale, Queen of Lydia.[3] If we suppose that Queen Omphale, like Queen Semiramis, was nothing but the great Asiatic goddess,[4] or one of her Avatars, it becomes probable that the story of the womanish Hercules of Lydia preserves a reminiscence of a line or college of effeminate priests who, like the eunuch priests of the Syrian goddess, dressed as women in imitation of their goddess and were supposed to be inspired by her. The probability is increased by the practice of the priests of Hercules at Antimachia, in Cos, who, as we have just seen, actually wore female attire when they were engaged in their sacred duties. Similarly at the vernal mysteries of Hercules in Rome the men were draped in the garments of women;[5] and in some of the rites and processions of Dionysus also men wore female attire.[6] In

[1] Catullus, lxiii. This is in substance the explanation of the custom given by Dr. L. R. Farnell, who observes that "the mad worshipper endeavoured thus against nature to assimilate himself more closely to his goddess" ("Sociological hypotheses concerning the position of women in ancient religion," *Archiv für Religionswissenschaft*, vii. (1904) p. 93). The theory is not necessarily inconsistent with my conjecture as to the magical use made of the severed parts. See above, vol. i. pp. 268 *sq.*

[2] Plutarch, *Quaestiones Graecae*, 58.

[3] Apollodorus, *Bibliotheca*, ii. 6. 2 *sq.*; Athenaeus, xii. 11, pp. 515 F–516 B; Diodorus Siculus, iv. 31; Joannes Lydus, *De magistratibus*, iii. 64; Lucian, *Dialogi deorum*, xiii. 2; Ovid, *Heroides*, ix. 55 *sqq.*; Statius, *Theb.* x. 646-649.

[4] On Semiramis in this character see above, vol. i. pp. 176 *sq.*; *The Scapegoat*, pp. 369 *sqq.*

[5] Joannes Lydus, *De mensibus*, iv. 46, p. 81, ed. I. Bekker (Bonn, 1837).

Yet at Rome, by an apparent contradiction, women might not be present at a sacrifice offered to Hercules (Propertius, v. 9. 67-70; see further above, vol. i. p. 113, note [1]), and at Gades women might not enter the temple of Melcarth, the Tyrian Hercules (Silius Italicus, iii. 22). There was a Greek proverb, "A woman does not go to a temple of Hercules" (Macarius, *Cent.* iii. 11; *Paroemiographi Graeci*, ed. Leutsch et Schneidewin, i. 392, ii. 154). Roman women did not swear by Hercules (Aulus Gellius, xi. 6).

[6] Lucian, *Calumniae non temere credendum*, 16; Hesychius and Suidas, *s.v.* Ἰθύφαλλοι. At the Athenian vintage festival of the Oschophoria a chorus of singers was led in procession by two young men dressed exactly like girls; they carried branches of vines laden with ripe clusters. The procession was said to be in honour of Dionysus and Athena or Ariadne. See Proclus, quoted by Photius, *Bibliotheca*, p. 322a, ed. I. Bekker (Berlin, 1824); Plutarch, *Theseus*, 23.

legend and art there are clear traces of an effeminate Dionysus, who perhaps figured in a strange ceremony for the artificial fertilization of the fig.[1] Among the Nahanarvals, an ancient German tribe, a priest garbed as a woman presided over a sacred grove.[2] These and similar practices[3] need not necessarily have any connexion with the social system of mother-kin. Wherever a goddess is revered and the theory of inspiration is held, a man may be thought to be possessed by a female spirit, whether society be organized on mother-kin or on father-kin. Still the chances of such a transformation of sex will be greater under mother-kin than under father-kin if, as we have found reason to believe, a system of mother-kin is more favourable to the development and multiplication of goddesses than of gods. It is therefore, perhaps, no mere accident that we meet with these effeminate priests in regions like the Pelew Islands and Western Asia, where the system of mother-kin either actually prevails or has at least left traces of it behind in tradition and custom. Such traces, for example, are to be found in Lydia and Cos,[4] in both of which the effeminate Hercules had his home.

[1] Clement of Alexandria, *Protrept.* ii. 34, pp. 29 *sq.*, ed. Potter ; Arnobius, *Adversus Nationes*, v. 28; *Mythographi Graeci*, ed. A. Westermann (Brunswick, 1843), p. 368 ; J. Tzetzes, *Scholia on Lycophron*, 212. As to the special association of the fig with Dionysus, see Athenaeus, iii. 14, p. 78. As to the artificial fertilization of the fig, see *The Magic Art and the Evolution of Kings*, ii. 314 *sq.* On the type of the effeminate Dionysus in art see E. Thraemer, *s.v.* "Dionysos," in W. H. Roscher's *Lexikon der griech. und röm. Mythologie*, i. 1135 *sqq.*

[2] Tacitus, *Germania*, 43. Perhaps, as Professor Chadwick thinks, this priest may have succeeded to a priestess when the change from mother-kin to father-kin took place. See H. M. Chadwick, *The Origin of the English Nation* (Cambridge, 1907), p. 339.

[3] In Cyprus there was a bearded and masculine image of Venus (probably Astarte) in female attire : according to Philochorus, the deity thus represented was the moon, and sacrifices were offered to him or her by men clad as women, and by women clad as men. See Macrobius, *Saturn.* iii. 7. 2 *sq.*; Servius on Virgil, *Aen.* ii. 632. A similar exchange of garments took place between Argive men and women at the festival of the Hybristica, which fell in the month of Hermes, either at the new moon or on the fourth of the month. See Plutarch, *De mulierum virtutibus*, 4 ; Polyaenus, viii. 33. On the thirteenth of January flute-players paraded the streets of Rome in the garb of women (Plutarch, *Quaestiones Romanae*, 55).

[4] For traces of mother-kin in Lydia see *The Magic Art and the Evolution of Kings*, ii. 281 *sq.* With regard to Cos we know from inscriptions that at Halasarna all who shared in the sacred rites of Apollo and Hercules had to register the names of their father, their mother, and of their mother's father ; from which it appears that maternal descent was counted more important than paternal descent. See H. Collitz und F. Bechtel, *Sammlung der griechischen Dialekt-Inschriften*, iii. 1 (Göttingen, 1899), pp. 382-393, Nos. 3705, 3706; G. Dittenberger, *Sylloge Inscriptionum Graecarum*,[2] vol. ii. pp. 396 *sqq.*, No. 614 ; Ch. Michel, *Recueil d'Inscriptions Grecques*, pp. 796 *sq.*, No. 1003 ; J. Toepffer, *Attische Genealogie* (Berlin, 1889), pp. 192 *sq.* On traces of mother-kin in the legend and ritual of Hercules see A. B. Cook, "Who was the wife of Hercules?" *The Classical Review*, xx. (1906) pp. 376 *sq.* Mr. Cook conjectures that a Sacred Marriage of

But the exchange of costume between men and women has probably been practised also from other motives, for example, from a wish to avert the Evil Eye. This motive seems to explain the interchange of male and female costume between bride and bridegroom at marriage.

But the religious or superstitious interchange of dress between men and women is an obscure and complex problem, and it is unlikely that any single solution would apply to all the cases. Probably the custom has been practised from many different motives. For example, the practice of dressing boys as girls has certainly been sometimes adopted to avert the Evil Eye;[1] and it is possible that the custom of changing garments at marriage, the bridegroom disguising himself as a woman, or the bride disguising herself as a man, may have been resorted to for the same purpose. Thus in Cos, where the priest of Hercules wore female attire, the bridegroom was in like manner dressed as a woman when he received his bride.[2] Spartan brides had their hair shaved, and were clad in men's clothes and booted on their wedding night.[3] Argive brides wore false beards when they slept with their husbands for the first time.[4] In Southern Celebes a bridegroom at a certain point of the long and elaborate marriage ceremonies puts on the garments which his bride has just put off.[5] Among the Jews of Egypt in the Middle Ages the bride led the wedding dance with a helmet on her head and a sword in her hand, while the bridegroom adorned himself as a woman and put on female attire.[6] At a Brahman marriage in Southern India " the bride is dressed up as a boy, and another girl is dressed up to represent the bride. They are taken in procession through the street, and, on returning, the pseudo-bridegroom is made to speak to the real bridegroom in somewhat insolent tones, and some mock play is indulged in. The real bridegroom is addressed as if he was the syce (groom) or gumasta (clerk) of the pseudo-bridegroom, and is sometimes treated as a thief, and judgment passed on him by the latter."[7] Among the Bharias

---

Hercules and Hera was celebrated in Cos. We know in fact from a Coan inscription that a bed was made and a marriage celebrated beside the image of Hercules, and it seems probable that the rite was that of a Sacred Marriage, though some scholars interpret it merely of an ordinary human wedding. See G. Dittenberger, *Sylloge Inscriptionum Graecarum*,[2] vol. ii. pp. 577 *sqq.*, No. 734; R. Dareste, B. Haussoulier, Th. Reinach, *Recueil d'Inscriptions Juridiques Grecques*, Deuxième Série (Paris, 1898), No. xxiv. B, pp. 94 *sqq.*; Fr. Back, *De Graecorum caerimoniis in quibus homines deorum vice fungebantur* (Berlin, 1883), pp. 14-24.

[1] *Panjab Notes and Queries*, i. (1884) §§ 219, 869, 1007, 1029; *id.* ii. (1885) §§ 344, 561, 570; *Journal of the Anthropological Society of Bombay*, i. (1886) p. 123; *North Indian Notes and Queries*, iii. (1893) § 99. Compare my notes, "The Youth of Achilles," *The Classical Review*, vii. (1893) pp. 292 *sq.*; and on Pausanias, i. 22. 6 (vol. ii. p. 266).

[2] Plutarch, *Quaestiones Graecae*, 58.

[3] Plutarch, *Lycurgus*, 15.

[4] Plutarch, *De mulierum virtutibus*, 4.

[5] B. F. Matthes, *Bijdragen tot de Ethnologie van Zuid - Celebes* (The Hague, 1875), p. 35. The marriage ceremonies here described are especially those of princes.

[6] Sepp, *Altbayerischer Sagenschatz* (Munich, 1876), p. 232, referring to Maimonides.

[7] E. Thurston, *Ethnographic Notes in Southern India* (Madras, 1906), p. 3.

of the Central Provinces of India "the bridegroom puts on women's ornaments and carries with him an iron nut-cutter or dagger to keep off evil spirits."[1] Similarly among the Khangars, a low Hindustani caste of the same region, "the bridegroom is dressed in a yellow gown and overcloth, with trousers of red chintz, red shoes, and a marriage crown of date-palm leaves. He has the silver ornaments usually worn by women on his neck, as the *khang-wāri* or silver ring and the *hamel* or necklace of rupees. In order to avert the evil eye he carries a dagger or nut-cracker, and a smudge of lampblack is made on his forehead to disfigure him and thus avert the evil eye, which, it is thought, would otherwise be too probably attracted by his exquisitely beautiful appearance in his wedding garments."[2] These examples render it highly probable that, like the dagger or nut-cracker which he holds in his hand, the woman's ornaments which he wears are intended to protect the bridegroom against demons or the evil eye at this critical moment of his life, the protection apparently consisting in a disguise which enables him to elude the unwelcome attentions of malignant beings.[3]

A similar explanation probably accounts for the similar exchange of costume between other persons than the bride and bridegroom at marriage. For example, after a Bharia wedding, "the girl's mother gets the dress of the boy's father and puts it on, together with a false beard and moustaches, and dances holding a wooden ladle in one hand and a packet of ashes in the other. Every time she approaches the bridegroom's father on her rounds she spills some of the ashes over him and occasionally gives him a crack on the head with her ladle, these actions being accompanied by bursts of laughter from the party and frenzied playing by the musicians. When the party reach the bridegroom's house on their return, his mother and the other women come out, and burn a little mustard and human hair in a lamp, the unpleasant smell emitted by these articles being considered potent to drive away evil spirits."[4] Again, after a Khangar wedding the father of the bridegroom, dressed in women's clothes, dances with the mother of the bride, while the two throw turmeric mixed with water on each other.[5] Similarly after a

The same explanation may account for the inter-change of male and female costume between other persons at marriage.

The pseudo-bridegroom is apparently the bride in masculine attire.

[1] *Central Provinces, Ethnographic Survey*, iii. *Draft Articles on Forest Tribes* (Allahabad, 1907), p. 31.

[2] *Central Provinces, Ethnographic Survey*, i. *Draft Articles on Hindustani Castes* (Allahabad, 1907), p. 48.

[3] Elsewhere I have conjectured that the wearing of female attire by the bridegroom at marriage may mark a transition from mother-kin to father-kin, the intention of the custom being

to transfer to the father those rights over the children which had previously been enjoyed by the mother alone. See *Totemism* (Edinburgh, 1887), pp. 78 *sq.* ; *Totemism and Exogamy*, i. 73. But I am now disposed to think that the other explanation suggested in the text is the more probable.

[4] *Central Provinces, Ethnographic Survey*, iii. *Draft Articles on Forest Tribes* (Allahabad, 1907), p. 31.

[5] *Central Provinces, Ethnographic Survey*, i. *Draft Articles on Hindu-*

wedding of the Bharbhunjas, another Hindustani caste of the Central Provinces, the bridegroom's father dances before the family in women's clothes which have been supplied by the bride's father.[1] Such disguises and dances may be intended either to protect the disguised dancer himself against the evil eye or perhaps rather to guard the principal personages of the ceremony, the bride and bride-groom, by diverting the attention of demons from them to the guiser.[2] However, when at marriage the bride alone assumes the costume and appearance of the other sex, the motive for the disguise may perhaps be a notion that on the principle of homoeopathic magic she thereby ensures the birth of a male heir. Similarly in Sweden there is a popular superstition that "on the night preceding her nuptials the bride should have a baby-boy to sleep with her, in which case her first-born will be a son";[3] and among the Kabyles, when a bride dismounts from her mule at her husband's house, a young lad leaps into the saddle before she touches the ground, in order that her first child may be a boy.[4]

Women's dress assumed by men for the purpose of deceiving demons and ghosts. Be that as it may, there is no doubt that the assumption of woman's dress is sometimes intended to disguise a man for the purpose of deceiving a demon. Thus among the Boloki or Bangala on the Upper Congo a man was long afflicted with an internal malady. When all other remedies had failed, a witch-doctor in-formed the sufferer that the cause of his trouble was an evil spirit, and that the best thing he could do was to go far away where the devil could not get at him, and to remain there till he had recovered his health. The patient followed the prescription. At dead of night he left his house, taking only two of his wives with him and telling no one of his destination, lest the demon should hear it and follow him. So he went far away from his town, donned a woman's dress, and speaking in a woman's voice he pretended to be other than he was, in order that the devil should not be able to find him at his new address. Strange to say, these sage measures failed to

---

stani Castes (Allahabad, 1907), p. 48.

[1] *Central Provinces, Ethnographic Survey*, vi. *Draft Articles on Hindustani Castes*, Second Series (Allahabad, 1911), p. 50.

[2] Compare W. Crooke, *Popular Religion and Folk-lore of Northern India* (Westminster, 1896), ii. 8, who proposes, with great probability, to explain on a similar principle, the European marriage custom known as the False Bride. For more instances of the interchange of male and female costume at marriage between persons other than the bridegroom see Capt. J. S. King, "Social Customs of the Western

Somali Tribes," *The Folk-lore Journal*, vi. (1888) p. 122; J. P. Farler, "The Usambara Country in East Africa," *Proceedings of the Royal Geographical Society*, N.S. i. (1879) p. 92; Major J. Biddulph, *Tribes of the Hindoo Koosh* (Calcutta, 1880), pp. 78, 80; G. A. Grierson, *Bihar Peasant Life* (Calcutta, 1885), p. 365; A. de Gubernatis, *Usi Nuziali in Italia*[2] (Milan, 1878), p. 190; P. Sébillot, *Coutumes Populaires de la Haute-Bretagne* (Paris, 1886), p. 438.

[3] L. Lloyd, *Peasant Life in Sweden* (London, 1870), p. 85.

[4] J. Liorel, *Kabylie du Jurjura* (Paris, N.D.), p. 406.

effect a cure, and wearying of exile he at last returned home, where he continued to dress and speak as a woman.[1]   Again, the Kuki-Lushai of Assam believe that if a man kills an enemy or a wild beast, the ghost of the dead man or animal will haunt him and drive him mad.   The only way of averting this catastrophe is to dress up as a woman and pretend to be one.   For example, a man who had shot a tiger and was in fear of being haunted by the animal's ghost, dressed himself up in a woman's petticoat and cloth, wore ivory earrings, and wound a mottled cloth round his head like a turban. Then smoking a woman's pipe, carrying a little basket, and spinning a cotton spindle, he paraded the village followed by a crowd roaring and shrieking with laughter, while he preserved the gravity of a judge, for a single smile would have been fatal.   To guard against the possibility of unseasonable mirth, he carried a porcupine in his arms, and if ever, tickled beyond the pitch of endurance, he burst into a guffaw, the crowd said, "It was the porcupine that laughed."   All this was done to mortify the pride of the tiger's ghost by leading him to believe that he had been shot by a woman.[2]

The same dread of attracting the attention of dangerous spirits at critical times perhaps explains the custom observed by some East African tribes of wearing the costume of the opposite sex at circumcision.   Thus, when Masai boys have been circumcised they dress as women, wearing earrings in their ears and long garments that reach to the ground.   They also whiten their swarthy faces with chalk.   This costume they retain till their wounds are healed, whereupon they are shaved and assume the skins and ornaments of warriors.[3]   Among the Nandi, a tribe of British East Africa, before boys are circumcised they receive a visit from young girls, who give them some of their own garments and ornaments.   These the boys put on and wear till the operation of circumcision is over, when they exchange the girls' clothes for the garments of women, which, together with necklaces, are provided for them by their mothers ; and these women's garments the newly circumcised lads must continue to wear for months afterwards.   Girls are also circumcised among the Nandi, and before they submit to the operation they attire themselves in men's garments and carry clubs in their hands.[4]

If such interchange of costume between men and women is

Exchange of costume between the sexes at circumcision.

[1] Rev. J. H. Weeks, *Among Congo Cannibals* (London, 1913), p. 267. Compare *id.*, "Anthropological Notes on the Bangala of the Upper Congo River," *Journal of the Royal Anthropological Institute*, xl. (1910) pp. 370 *sq.*

[2] Lieut. - Colonel J. Shakespear, "The Kuki-Lushai Clans," *Journal of the Royal Anthropological Institute,* xxxix. (1909) pp. 380 *sq.*

[3] A. C. Hollis, *The Masai* (Oxford, 1905), p. 298.

[4] A. C. Hollis, *The Nandi* (Oxford, 1909), pp. 53-58.   Mr. Hollis informs me that among the Akikuyu, another tribe of British East Africa, the custom of boys dressing as girls at or after circumcision is also observed.

Other cases of the interchange of male and female costume.

intended to disguise the wearers against demons, we may compare the practice of the Lycian men, who regularly wore women's dress in mourning;[1] for this might be intended to conceal them from the ghost, just as perhaps for a similar reason some peoples of antiquity used to descend into pits and remain there for several days, shunning the light of the sun, whenever a death had taken place in the family.[2] A similar desire to deceive spirits may perhaps explain a device to which the Loeboes, a primitive tribe of Sumatra, resort when they wish to obtain male or female offspring. If parents have several sons and desire that the next child shall be a girl, they dress the boys as girls, cut their hair after the girlish fashion, and hang necklaces round their necks. On the contrary, when they have many daughters and wish to have a son, they dress the girls up as boys.[3]

Conclusion.

On the whole we conclude that the custom of men dressing as women and of women dressing as men has been practised from a variety of superstitious motives, among which the principal would seem to be the wish to please certain powerful spirits or to deceive others.

§ 2. *Prostitution of Unmarried Girls*

The systematic prostitution of unmarried girls for hire in the Pelew Islands seems to be a form of sexual communism and of group-marriage.

Like many peoples of Western Asia in antiquity, the Pelew Islanders systematically prostitute their unmarried girls for hire. Hence, just as in Lydia and Cyprus of old, the damsels are a source of income to their family, and women wait impatiently for the time when their young daughters will be able to help the household by their earnings. Indeed the mother regularly anticipates the time by depriving the girl of her virginity with her own hands.[4] Hence the theory that the prostitution of unmarried girls is a device to destroy their virginity without risk to their husbands is just as inapplicable to the Pelew Islanders as we have seen it to be to the peoples of Western Asia in antiquity. When a Pelew girl has thus been prepared for her vocation by her mother, she sells her favours to all the men of her village who can pay for them and who do not belong to her own exogamous clan; but she never grants her favours to the same man twice. Accordingly in every village of the Pelew Islands it may be taken as certain that the men and women know each other carnally, except that members of the same clan are debarred from each other by the rule of exogamy.[5] Thus a well-marked form of sexual communism, limited only by the exogamous prohibitions which attach to the clans, prevails among these people. Nor is this communism restricted to the inhabit-

---

[1] Plutarch, *Consolatio ad Apollonium*, 22; Valerius Maximus, ii. 6. 13.

[2] Plutarch, *l.c.*

[3] J. Kreemer, "De Loeboes in Mandailing," *Bijdragen tot de Taal-Land- en Volkenkunde van Neder-landsch-Indië*, lxvi. (1912) p. 317.

[4] J. Kubary, *Die socialen Einrichtungen der Pelauer*, pp. 50 *sq.*

[5] J. Kubary, *op. cit.* p. 51.

ants of the same village, for the girls of each village are regularly sent away to serve as prostitutes (*armengols*) in another village. There they live with the men of one of the many clubs or associations (*kaldebekels*) in the clubhouse (*blay*), attending to the house, consorting freely with the men, and receiving pay for their services. A girl leading this life in the clubhouse of another village is well treated by the men : a wrong done to her is a wrong done to the whole club ; and in her own village her value is increased, not diminished, by the time she thus spends as a prostitute in a neighbouring community. After her period of service is over she may marry either in the village where she has served or in her own. Sometimes many or all of the young women of a village go together to act as prostitutes (*armengols*) in a neighbouring village, and for this they are well paid by the community which receives them. The money so earned is divided among the chiefs of the village to which the damsels belong. Such a joint expedition of the unmarried girls of a village is called a *blolobol*. But the young women never act as *armengols* in any clubhouse of their own village.[1]

Thus, while the Pelew custom of prostituting the unmarried girls to all the men of their own village, but not of their own clan, is a form of sexual communism practised within a local group, the custom of prostituting them to men of other villages is a form of sexual communism practised between members of different local groups ; it is a kind of group-marriage. These customs of the Pelew Islanders therefore support by analogy the hypothesis that among the ancient peoples of Western Asia also the systematic prostitution of unmarried women may have been derived from an earlier period of sexual communism.[2]

A somewhat similar custom prevails in Yap, one of the western group of the Caroline Islands, situated to the north of the Pelew group. In each of the men's clubhouses " are kept three or four unmarried girls or *Mespil*, whose business it is to minister to the pleasures of the men of the particular clan or brotherhood to which the building belongs. As with the Kroomen on the Gold Coast, each man, married or single, takes his turn by rotation in the rites through which each girl must pass before she is deemed ripe for marriage. The natives say it is an ordeal or preliminary trial to fit them for the cares and burden of maternity. She is rarely a girl of the same village, and, of course, must be sprung from a different sept. Whenever she wishes to become a *Langin* or respectable married woman, she may, and is thought none the less of for her frailties as a *Mespil*. . . . But I believe this self-immolation before marriage is confined to the daughters of the inferior chiefs and

The custom supports by analogy the derivation of the similar Asiatic custom from a similar state of society.

Somewhat similar custom observed in Yap, one of the Caroline Islands.

---

[1] J. Kubary, *op. cit.* pp. 51-53, 91-98.
[2] See above, vol. i. pp. 39 *sqq*.

commons. The supply of *Mespil* is generally kept up by the purchase of slave girls from the neighbouring districts."[1] According to another account a *mespil* "must always be stolen, by force or cunning, from a district at some distance from that wherein her captors reside. After she has been fairly, or unfairly, captured and installed in her new home, she loses no shade of respect among her own people; on the contrary, have not her beauty and her worth received the highest proof of her exalted perfection, in the devotion, not of one, but of a whole community of lovers?"[2] However, though the girl is nominally stolen from another district, the matter is almost always arranged privately with the local chief, who consents to wink hard at the theft in consideration of a good round sum of shell money and stone money, which serves "to salve the wounds of a disrupted family and dispel all thoughts of a bloody retaliation. Nevertheless, the whole proceeding is still carried out with the greatest possible secrecy and stealth."[3]

§ 3. *Custom of slaying Chiefs*

In the Pelew Islands the heir to the chieftainship of a clan has a formal right to slay his predecessor.

In the Pelew Islands when the chief of a clan has reigned too long or has made himself unpopular, the heir has a formal right to put him to death, though for reasons which will appear this right is only exercised in some of the principal clans. The practice of regicide, if that word may be extended to the assassination of chiefs, is in these islands a national institution regulated by exact rules, and every high chief must lay his account with it. Indeed so well recognized is the custom that when the heir-apparent, who under the system of mother-kin must be a brother, a nephew, or a cousin on the mother's side, proves himself precocious and energetic, the people say, "The cousin is a grown man. The chief's *tobolbel* is nigh at hand."[4]

The plot of death and its execution.

In such cases the plot of death is commonly so well hushed up that it seldom miscarries. The first care of the conspirators is to discover where the doomed man keeps his money. For this purpose an old woman will sleep for some nights in the house and make inquiries quietly, till like a sleuth-hound she has nosed the hoard. Then the conspirators come, and the candidate for the chieftainship despatches his predecessor either with his own hand or by the hand of a young cousin. Having done the deed he takes possession of the official residence, and applies to the widow

[1] F. W. Christian, *The Caroline Islands* (London, 1899), pp. 290 *sq.* Compare W. H. Furness, *The Island of Stone Money, Uap of the Carolines* (Philadelphia and London, 1910), pp. 46 *sqq.*

[2] W. H. Furness, *op. cit.* pp. 46 *sq.*

[3] W. H. Furness, *op. cit.* pp. 49 *sq.*

[4] J. Kubary, *Die socialen Einrichtungen der Pelauer*, p. 43. The writer does not translate the word *tobolbel*, but the context sufficiently explains its meaning.

of the deceased the form of persuasion technically known as *meleket*. This consists of putting a noose round her neck, and drawing it tighter and tighter till she consents to give up her late husband's money. After that the murderer and his friends have nothing further to do for the present, but to remain quietly in the house and allow events to take their usual course.

Meantime the chiefs assemble in the council-house, and the loud droning notes of the triton-shell, which answers the purpose of a tocsin, summon the whole population to arms. The warriors muster, and surrounding the house where the conspirators are ensconced they shower spears and stones at it, as if to inflict condign punishment on the assassins. But this is a mere blind, a sham, a legal fiction, intended perhaps to throw dust in the eyes of the ghost and make him think that his death is being avenged. In point of fact the warriors take good care to direct their missiles at the roof or walls of the house, for if they threw them at the windows they might perhaps hurt the murderer. After this formality has been satisfactorily performed, the regicide steps out of the house and engages in the genial task of paying the death duties to the various chiefs assembled. When he has observed this indispensable ceremony, the law is satisfied : all constitutional forms have been carried out : the assassin is now the legitimate successor of his victim and reigns in his stead without any further trouble.

But if he has omitted to massacre his predecessor and has allowed him to die a natural death, he suffers for his negligence by being compelled to observe a long series of complicated and irksome formalities before he can make good his succession in the eyes of the law. For in that case the title of chief has to be formally withdrawn from the dead man and conferred on his successor by a curious ceremony, which includes the presentation of a coco-nut and a taro plant to the new chief. Moreover, at first he may not enter the chief's house, but has to be shut up in a tiny hut for thirty or forty days during all the time of mourning, and even when that is over he may not come out till he has received and paid for a human head brought him by the people of a friendly state. After that he still may not go to the sea-shore until more formalities have been fully observed. These comprise a very costly fishing expedition, which is conducted by the inhabitants of another district and lasts for weeks. At the end of it a net full of fish is brought to the chief's house, and the people of the neighbouring communities are summoned by the blast of trumpets. As soon as the stranger fishermen have been publicly paid for their services, a relative of the new chief steps across the net and solemnly splits a coco-nut in two with an old-fashioned knife made of a Tridacna shell, while at the same time he bans all the evils that might befall his kinsman. Then, without looking at the nut, he throws the pieces on the ground, and if they

Marginal notes:

Ceremonies observed before the assassin is recognized as chief in room of his victim.

But the formalities which a chief has to observe at his accession are much more complicated and tedious if he has not murdered his predecessor.

fall so that the two halves lie with the opening upwards, it is an omen that the chief will live long. The pieces of the nut are then tied together and taken to the house of another chief, the friend of the new ruler, and there they are kept in token that the ceremony has been duly performed. Thereupon the fish are divided among the people, the strangers receiving half. This completes the legal ceremonies of accession, and the new chief may now go about freely. But these tedious formalities and others which I pass over are dispensed with when the new chief has proved his title by slaying his predecessor. In that case the procedure is much simplified, but on the other hand the death duties are so very heavy that only rich men can afford to indulge in the luxury of regicide. Hence in the Pelew Islands of to-day, or at least of yesterday, the old-fashioned mode of succession by slaughter is now restricted to a few families of the bluest blood and the longest purses.[1]

The Pelew custom shows how regicide may be regarded as an ordinary incident of constitutional government. If this account of the existing or recent usage of the Pelew Islanders sheds little light on the motives for putting chiefs to death, it well illustrates the business-like precision with which such a custom may be carried out, and the public indifference, if not approval, with which it may be regarded as an ordinary incident of constitutional government. So far, therefore, the Pelew custom bears out the view that a systematic practice of regicide, however strange and revolting it may seem to us, is perfectly compatible with a state of society in which human conduct and human life are estimated by a standard very different from ours. If we would understand the early history of institutions, we must learn to detach ourselves from the prepossessions of our own time and country, and to place ourselves as far as possible at the standpoint of men in distant lands and distant ages.

[1] J. Kubary, *Die socialen Einrichtungen der Pelauer*, pp. 43-45, 75-78.

INDEX

Library of the Mystic Arts
A LIBRARY OF ANCIENT AND MODERN CLASSICS

1. THE STUDY AND PRACTICE OF YOGA by Harvey Day. A practical manual on Yoga postures and exercises which are within the capabilities of any individual. It shows how this ancient science helps to induce clear thinking, control weight and aid in preserving a youthful appearance and physique. Illustrated. $3.75

2. YOGA—The Method of Re-Integration by Alain Danielou: Yoga as defined in the Hindu Scriptures with an appendix of Sanskrit text. Processes by which the subconscious may be controlled are treated at length. These processes can lead to unusual attainments both spiritually and intellectually. Illustrated. $3.75

3. THE ORIGINS OF CHRISTIANITY by F. C. Coneybeare. This absorbing volume takes a bold course away from the traditional and conventional story of Jesus; Paul's decisive role is made clear. $6.00

4. EGYPTIAN MAGIC by Sir Wallis Budge. The Egyptian priest made darkness as well as light his realm; his power was exercised by names, spells, enchantments, amulets, pictures and ceremonies accompanied by potent words to be spoken in a certain manner. Illustrated. $5.00

5. MAGIC AND MYSTERY IN TIBET by Alexandra David-Neel. "Precisely the person to explore Tibet . . . absolutely fearless. Her accounts of Tibetan religious ceremonies and beliefs are the fullest and best we have."—The New Yorker. Illustrated. $6.00

6. THE PARTING OF THE WAY—Lao Tzu and the Taoist Movement by Holmes Welch. There is entertaining exposition on the search for the Isles of the Blest; Chinese Yoga; alchemy; the Dionysian Rites for the Salvation of Souls; sexual orgies; church states defended by Taoist armies; cult of drunkenness. $5.00

7. A PICTORIAL ANTHOLOGY OF WITCHCRAFT, MAGIC AND ALCHEMY by Grillot de Givry. The author garners together 376 pictures "from the most curious, characteristic and rare of those illustrating works on sorcery, magic, astrology, cheiromancy, and alchemy, including works in manuscript and incunabula form. The dates of the selected sources range from the Middle Ages to the eve of the nineteenth century period." Graphic illustration is the author's successful answer to the knotty problems arising when one tries to explain occult concepts. In words and pictures, the author makes clear what the alchemist was searching for, what his various tools looked like, and how they were made and used. He does the same for the other occult practitioners. The author divides the volume into three sections, Book I: Sorcerers, Book II: Magicians, and Book III: Alchemists. Perhaps the rarest illustrations are in the section on Kabbalah in Book II. Printed in a large format (7¼" x 10"), the 376 illustrations have been reproduced by photo-offset on specially-etched plates on unusually fine paper. $10.00

8. DOWN THERE by Joris-Karl Huysmans. DOWN THERE will interest, repel, disgust, fascinate or horrify. This classic of satanism is a horrifying account of Durtal, a hero whose exploits are based on two of the super-villains of all time. One, the Abbé Boullan who founded with his nun-mistress the Society for the Reparation of Souls, which had as its chief activity the obscene and profane medication of ailing nuns. Later as an exorcist his patients were again distressed nuns, his treatment supernatural sexual intercourse with Christ and others, including himself. Huysmans interweaves Boullan's career with that of Marshal Gilles de Rais, arch-satanist companion, mentor and protector of Jeanne d'Arc.

Huysmans himself paid an awful price both physically and mentally for his investigations into occultism and satanism. Though a devout Catholic, he protected himself with bizarre rites against "fluidic fisticuffs" and other eerie sensations which troubled him.

Presented as a novel, this book can also serve as a

reference on satanism. Huysmans made excellent use of the documents on sorcery, alchemy and satanism as well as of conversations he had had with people intimately acquainted with occult practices. $5.00

9. THE SACRED FIRE—The Story of Sex in Religion by B. Z. Goldberg. The sexual symbolism underlying expressions of faith from prehistoric farmers to present-day evangelists is examined in the light of wide anthropological, historical and sociological evidence. Illustrated. $7.50

10. JESUS by Charles Guignebert, late Professor in the History of Christianity at the Sorbonne. He impartially sums up the results of a century and a half of Biblical criticism and the result has the effect of a blockbuster. $7.50

12. WORTH LIVING FOR by Eva Bartok. This is the autobiography of the famous Hungarian film star. It is an eloquent testimonial to the spiritual fulfillment to be found in Subud. The climax of the book is Eva Bartok's meetings with Pak Subuh, the Indonesian founder of Subud. $3.50

13. CONCERNING SUBUD, The Story Of A New Spiritual Force by John G. Bennett. Since 1920 Bennett has been known as a writer and speaker for Gurdjieff's system. Here is the story of Pak Subuh's spiritual ministry since 1923. $3.95

14. THE JEWISH WORLD IN THE TIME OF JESUS by Charles Guignebert. The Old Testament closes hundreds of years before Jesus, the New is written long after his death. What, then, do most of us know about his Jewish world? Nothing! Now here is that world—its Essenes, gnostics, magicians, angels and demons, hermetic books and Messiahs. $6.00

15. THE TRAINING OF THE ZEN BUDDHIST MONK by Daisetz Teitaro Suzuki. The clearest introduction to Zen that one could hope for, by the dean of the interpreters to the Western world. 27 illustrations. $5.00

16. THE SELECTED WRITINGS OF THE MARQUIS DE SADE. Now available, the famed controversial works only researchers could see on the restricted shelves. Selected and translated with an introduction by Leonard de Saint-Yves. $4.95

17. AN ENCYCLOPAEDIA OF OCCULTISM by Lewis Spence. A Compendium of Information on the Occult Sciences, Occult Personalities, Psychic Science, Demonology, Magic, Spiritism, Mysticism and Metaphysics. More than 2500 entries and articles. 488 double-column pages size 8 x 10". Alphabetically arranged with an eleven-page Master Index. Deluxe Edition, bound in buckram and elephant-hide and boxed. $15.00

18. THE PICTORIAL KEY TO THE TAROT by Arthur Edward Waite. Being fragments of a secret tradition under the veil of divination. With 78 plates in full color, illustrating the Greater and Lesser Arcana, from designs by Pamela Colman Smith. $7.50

19. SEVENTY-EIGHT TAROT CARDS IN FULL COLOR. Created by Pamela Colman Smith and Arthur Edward Waite. $5.00

20. POLTERGEISTS by Sir Sacheverell Sitwell. The noisy and prankish ghosts you read about in newspapers are Mr. Sitwell's subject. He leaves little doubt that poltergeists exist and that no purely natural explanation can account for them. The author with his brother Osbert and sister Edith are the most famous writing family in the world today. $5.75

21. COSMIC CONSCIOUSNESS by R. M. Bucke, M.D. One of the great classics of mystical experience, written sixty years ago but still ahead of its time. Neither supernatural nor supranormal, cosmic consciousness is the emergence of a new human faculty which is placing the people of the next epoch as far above us as we are above the simple consciousness of animals. $5.95

22. THE HOLY KABBALAH by Arthur Edward Waite with an Introduction by Kenneth Rexroth. Kabbalah is the occult and secret tradition in Judaism. Its origins go far back into the dim past. Perhaps the most likely guess is that it began in Persia and was brought back to Palestine when Cyrus permitted the Jews to return (fourth century B.C.). It was probably part of the doctrine of the seventy books which constituted a hermeneutic literature open only to the initiate (this we learn from 4 Esdras XIV. 45-6). It has been in men's minds ever since, and it remains alive to this day, both as a mysticism and as a magic, not only among Jews but also among Christians and modern-day students of the occult. A. E. Waite was one of the few persons in modern times, Jew or Gentile, to write a sensible and sound book on Kabbalah. THE HOLY KABBALAH is Waite's greatest work. No other Gentile writer on Kabbalism can be remotely compared to him, and no modern Jewish writers are any better. We have to go back to the great **zaddikim** of Hasidism to find such a thorough Kabbalist and they, alas, present altogether too many problems of their own to be readily assimilated by anyone in the twentieth century. Kenneth Rexroth's Introduction makes clear what the Kabbalah is and what Waite can tell us about it. When we have read the book, we must agree with Rexroth's conclusion: "Kabbalism is the great poem of Judaism, a tree of symbolic jewels showing forth the doctrine of the universe as the vesture of Deity, of the community as the embodiment of Deity, and of love as the acting of God in man." 672 pages, 6⅛" x 9¼".
$10.00

23. THE HAUNTED MIND by Nandor Fodor. From his practice as a psychoanalyst and psychic researcher, Dr. Fodor has selected some 20 cases as the most interesting. They include mediumship, levitation, communication after death. $5.00

24. THE BOOK OF THE DEAD—The Hieroglyphic Transcript of the Papyrus of ANI, the Translation into English and An Introduction by E. A. Wallis Budge, Late Keeper of the Egyptian and Assyrian Antiquities in The British Museum. The Book Of The Dead is the great collection of texts which the ancient Egyptian scribes composed for the benefit of the dead spells and incantations, hymns and litanies, magical formulae and names, words of power and prayers, cut or painted on walls of pyramids and tombs, and painted on coffins and sarcophagi and rolls of papyri. 15 pages of plates. Complete hieroglyphic reproductions with the transcriptions. 736 pages, 6⅛" x 9¼". $12.50

25. THE VAMPIRE: His Kith and Kin by Montague Summers, author of THE HISTORY OF WITCHCRAFT and THE GEOGRAPHY OF WITCHCRAFT. The fascination of this theme has deep roots in human history. "Vampire" comes from a Slavonic word and this belief has had a peculiar intensity among the Slavonic peoples. "The fuller knowledge of these horrors reached western Europe in detail during the Eighteenth Century." $6.00

26. FRAGMENTS OF A FAITH FORGOTTEN — The Gnostics: A Contribution to the Study of the Origins of Christianity by G. R. S. Mead. Until recently, almost all we knew about the Gnostics we were told by the Church Fathers who had burned the Gnostic literature. Gnosticism found in G. R. S. Mead a true and disinterested scholar; he made available to the English-speaking world his translations of Gnostic texts which had survived in Coptic in Ethiopia and in Egypt. FRAGMENTS OF A FAITH FORGOTTEN is an anthology of these Gnostic texts together with Mead's explanations. The Introduction by Kenneth Rexroth is correctly called "A Primer of Gnosticism." 704 pages, 6⅛" x 9¼". $10.00

27. THE SIDDUR: The Traditional Jewish Prayer Book. An entirely new translation by Dr. David de Sola Pool, Rabbi Emeritus of the Spanish and Portuguese Synagogue of New York City. Translation approved by the Rabbinical Council of America. English and Hebrew on facing pages. A deluxe edition, 7¼ x 10¼ inches, approximately 900 pages, three-piece library binding, sturdy, printed slipcase. $17.50

28. CAGLIOSTRO by W. R. H. Trowbridge. Cagliostro figures as one of the great pioneers in every serious account of hypnotism and telepathy, magic and alchemy, precognition and spiritualism, psychic healing and modern mysticism. Yet the simplest facts about his life and his teachings remain bitterly disputed now, two hundred years after he was born. Savant or scoundrel! Here is the true role of this splendid, tragic figure! $6.50

29. AMULETS AND TALISMANS by E. A. Wallis Budge. The original texts with translations and descriptions of a long series of Egyptian, Sumerian, Assyrian, Hebrew, Christian, Gnostic and Muslim Amulets and Talismans and Magical Figures, with chapters on the Evil Eye, the origin of the Amulet, the Pentagon, the Swastika, the Cross (Pagan and Christian), the properties of Stones, Rings, Divination, Numbers, the Kabbalah, Ancient Astrology. 22 pages of plates. 300 illustrations. 592 pages, 6⅛" x 9¼". $10.00

30. SCIENCE AND PSYCHICAL PHENOMENA and APPARITIONS by G. N. M. Tyrrell. These two famous classics of psychical research are now bound together in one volume. They are the best introduction to the subject. $7.50

31. THE BOOK OF CEREMONIAL MAGIC by A. E. Waite. Readers have met the distinguished author before; he wrote THE HOLY KABBALAH and THE PICTORIAL KEY TO THE TAROT. The present book is a complete Grimoire. Part I, the Literature of Ceremonial Magic, provides the key passages from the principal texts of the 14th, 15th and 16th centuries. Part II contains the complete Grimoire, the best source of magical procedure extant. 9 plates and 94 line drawings. 6⅛" x 9¼". $10.00

33. OSIRIS: The Egyptian Religion of Resurrection by E. A. Wallis Budge. Frazer's Golden Bough has made us familiar with a god who dies each year that he and his worshippers may live anew. Attis, Adonis, Osiris are the great examples. Sir Wallis Budge gives us the definitive study of Osiris in depth. Much of it is startling indeed. Egyptian religion in its cruelty, its cannibalism, its bloodthirstiness, its general coloring, is African through and through. Osiris himself is both the father and the slain. It is his son Horus, the living and victorious Savior, who, "when his arm grew strong," triumphs over Osiris' brother and slayer, Set, and Osiris is resurrected as god-man. 896 pages, 6⅛" x 9¼". 14 pages of plates, 212 illustrations, and hundreds of hieroglyphic reproductions and transcriptions. $15.00

34. HUMAN PERSONALITY AND ITS SURVIVAL OF BODILY DEATH by F. W. H. Myers. Foreword by Aldous Huxley. Myers made two outstanding contributions: (1) His theory of telepathy as one of the basic laws of life; (2) his conception of "subliminal," which today we call the unconscious, as the greater portion of human personality. William James wrote: "Frederic Myers will always be remembered in psychology as the pioneer who staked out a vast tract of mental wilderness and planted the flag of genuine science on it." Gardner Murphy says: "Myers is the great central classic of psychical research." Aldous Huxley finds Myers' account of the unconscious more comprehensive and truer to the data of experience than Freud's.

One reason this great book has been neglected is the arrangement of material in the original two-volume HUMAN PERSONALITY. The majority of the illustrative examples were placed in the appendices at the end of each volume. One not only had to sift through a voluminous amount of material, but also had to turn from text to appendix and back again — sometimes **several** times in order to read a single page of text. This new volume of 416 large pages, with its streamlined design, provides the essence of Myers' thought — simpler to get at — yet with its original underpinning still intact. The reader is saved the trouble of turning from text to appendix because in this edition all the case material is incorporated within the text. Except for this editing and re-arranging of the material, the words are still Myers' own; no essential idea of his has been omitted. $10.00

35. THE BROTHERHOOD OF THE ROSY CROSS, by Arthur Edward Waite. The author's account bears very little resemblance to the claims of the Theosophists and latter-day Rosicrucians. To put it more plainly, our author has taken their skins off in the course of establishing the true story. But all this is only to make way for his reverence and love for the real Rosicrucians. The myths and frauds fall away and there emerges the inspiring true history of Rosicrucianism, its original doctrines, their unfolding and changing, what was and what was not its relationship to Freemasonry, a most notable chapter on the great English Rosicrucian Robert Fludd, and a particularly fascinating chapter on the history of the Rosy Cross in Russia.

To be a Rosicrucian meant peril of life and limb in the intolerant societies of the seventeenth and eighteenth centuries. But is it necessary to continue a Secret Tradition in the nineteenth and twentieth centuries? The author thinks it remains necessary. 29 pages of plates. 704 pages, 6⅛" x 9¼". $10.00

36. COLOR PSYCHOLOGY AND COLOR THERAPY, by Faber Birren. Faber Birren makes his living by prescribing color. He prescribes it to government, to education, to the armed forces, to architecture, to industry and commerce. His work has been acknowledged and recommended by the Council on Industrial Health of the American Medical Association. Birren's color code for safety has become internationally accepted in countries as remote from each other as England, Japan, Italy, Argentina, Uruguay. This book gives his prescriptions and how they are arrived at.

$7.50

37. ANCIENT, MEDIEVAL AND MODERN CHRISTIANITY: The Evolution of a Religion, by Charles Guignebert. The late Professor of the History of Christianity at the Sorbonne here applies the theory of evolution to Christianity itself. The author believes that every religion is born, develops, adapts and transforms itself, grows old and dies. Ancient Christianity was a purely Eastern religion. It was followed by, in effect, another religion full of doctrines and things which would have been strange and incomprehensible to the Apostles. Still another religion emerges in modern Roman Catholicism. Guignebert warms these scientific truths, which may be unpleasant to professing Christians, by his fervent belief that the honest study of religion is "the mother of tolerance and religious peace." 640 pages, 6⅛" x 9¼". $7.50

38. THE HOLY GRAIL: The Galahad Quest in the Arthurian Literature by Arthur Edward Waite. All the journeys and adventures of the Knights of the Round Table lead to the Holy Grail. It becomes clear that they are not really journeys on horseback by knights clothed in armor, but journeys of the spirit. The gay ladies prove to be immortal goddesses. Doubly strange is Lancelot, the hero of a great illicit love who, in still another illicit union, fathers Sir Galahad, the Christ-like winner of the quest for the Holy Grail. Triply strange is the Grail itself, for no two accounts agree on its shape, nature, guardians or whereabouts. Yet all this has a plain, if profound, meaning. Its meaning was necessarily hidden in the Middle Ages, otherwise its authors would have been sent to the stake. For beneath its pious surface, the Grail is as subversive as is all true mysticism. A. E. Waite has given back to us, as no other scholar has, the true and full meaning of the quest for the Holy Grail. Giant octavo, 640 pages.

$10.00